Recent Advances in Signal Processing

Recent Advances in Signal Processing

Edited by
Ashraf A. Zaher

Recent Advances in Signal Processing,
Edited by Ashraf A. Zaher

CBS, Edition **2017**

Published by InTech
Janeza Trdine 9, 51000 Rijeka, Croatia

Additional hard copies can be obtained from orders@intechopen.com

Recent Advances in Signal Processing,
Edited by Ashraf A. Zaher
p. cm.
ISBN 978-953-307-002-5

Preface

The signal processing task is a very critical issue in the majority of new technological inventions and challenges in a variety of applications in both science and engineering fields. Classical signal processing techniques have largely worked with mathematical models that are linear, local, stationary, and Gaussian. They have always favored closed-form tractability over real-world accuracy. These constraints were imposed by the lack of powerful computing tools. During the last few decades, signal processing theories, developments, and applications have matured rapidly and now include tools from many areas of mathematics, computer science, physics, and engineering. This was mainly due to the revolutionary advances in the digital technology and the ability to effectively use digital signal processing (DSP) that rely on the use of very large scale integrated technologies and efficient computational methods such as the fast Fourier transform (FFT). This trend is expected to grow exponentially in the future, as more and more emerging technologies are revealed in the fields of digital computing and software development.

It is still an extremely skilled work to properly design, build and implement an effective signal processing tool able to meet the requirements of the increasingly demanding and sophisticated modern applications. This is especially true when it is necessary to deal with real-time applications of huge data rates and computational loads. These applications include image compression and encoding, speech analysis, wireless communication systems, biomedical real-time data analysis, cryptography, steganography, and biometrics, just to name a few. Moreover, the choice between whether to adopt a software or hardware approach, for implementing the application at hand, is considered a bottleneck. Programmable logic devices, e.g. FPGAs provide an optimal compromise, as the hardware configuration can be easily tailored using specific hardware descriptive languages (HDLs).

This book is targeted primarily toward both students and researchers who want to be exposed to a wide variety of signal processing techniques and algorithms. It includes 27 chapters that can be categorized into five different areas depending on the application at hand. These five categories are ordered to address image processing, speech processing, communication systems, time-series analysis, and educational packages respectively. The book has the advantage of providing a collection of applications that are completely independent and self-contained; thus, the interested reader can choose any chapter and skip to another without losing continuity. Each chapter provides a comprehensive survey of the subject area and terminates with a rich list of references to provide an in-depth coverage of the application at hand. Understanding the fundamentals of representing signals and systems in both time, spatial, and frequency domains is a prerequisite to read this book, as it is assumed that the reader is familiar with them. Knowledge of other transform methods, such as the Laplace transform and the Z-transform, along with knowledge of some computational intelligence techniques is an assist. In addition, experience with MATLAB programming (or a similar tool) is useful, but not essential. This book is application-oriented and it mainly addresses the design, implementation, and/or the improvements of existing or new technologies, and also provides some novel algorithms either in software, hardware, or both forms. The reported techniques are based on time-domain analysis, frequency-domain analysis, or a hybrid combination of both.

This book is organized as follows. The first 14 chapters investigate applications in the field of image processing, the next six chapters address applications in speech and audio processing, and the last seven chapters deal with applications in communication systems, real-time data handling, and interactive educational packages, respectively. There is a great deal of overlap between some of the chapters, as they might be sharing the same theory, application, or approach; yet, we chose to organize the chapter into the following five sections:

I. Image Processing:

This section contains 14 chapters that explore different applications in the field of image processing. These applications cover a variety of topics related to segmentation, encoding, restoration, steganography, and denoising. Chapters (1) to (14) are arranged into groups based on the application of interest as explained in the following table:

Chapter(s)	Main topic (application)
1 - 3	Image segmentation and encoding
4 - 6	Medical applications
7 & 8	Data hiding
9 & 10	Image classification
11& 12	Biometric applications
13 & 14	Noise suppression

Chapter (1) proposes a software approach to image stabilization that depends on two consequent steps of global image registration and image fusion. The improved reliability and the reduced size and cost of this approach make it ideal for small mobile devices. Chapter (2) investigates contour retrieval in images via estimating the parameters of rectilinear or circular contours as a source localization problem in high-resolution array processing. It presents a subspace-based line detection algorithm for the estimation of rectilinear contours based on signal generation upon a linear antenna. Chapter (3) proposes a locally adaptive resolution (LAR) codec as a contribution to the field of image compression and encoding. It focuses on a few representative features of the LAR technology and its preliminary associated performances, while discussing their potential applications in different image-related services.

Chapter (4) uses nonlinear locally adaptive transformations to perform image registration with application to MRI brains scan. Both parametric and nonparametric transformations, along with the use of multi-model similarity measures, are used to robustify the results to tissue intensity variations. Chapter (5) describes a semi-automated segmentation method for dynamic contrast-enhanced MRI sequences for renal function assessment. The superiority of the proposed method is demonstrated via testing and comparing it with manual segmentation by radiologists. Chapter (6) uses a hybrid technique of motion estimation and segmentation that are based on variational techniques to improve the performance of cardiac motion application in indicating heart diseases.

Chapter (7) investigates the problem of restricting color information for images to only authorized users. It surveys some of the reported solutions in the literature and proposes an improved technique to hide a 512-color palette in an 8-bit gray level image. Chapter (8) introduces a novel application of the JPEG2000-based information hiding for synchronized and scalable 3D visualization. It also provides a compact, yet detailed, survey of the state of the art techniques in the field of using DWT in image compression and encoding.

Chapter (9) uses a content-based image-retrieval technique to validate the results obtained from defects-detection algorithms, in Ad-hoc features, to find similar images suffering from the same defects in order to classify the questioned image as defected or not. Chapter (10) explores a novel approach for automatic crack detection and classification for the purpose of roads maintenance and estimating pavement surface conditions. This approach relies on image processing and pattern recognition techniques using a framework based on local statistics, computed over non-overlapping image regions.

Chapter (11) proposes a robust image segmentation method to construct a contact-free hand identification system via using infrared illumination and templates that guide the user in order to minimize the projective distortions. This biometric identification system is tested on a real-world database, composed by 102 users and more than 4000 images, resulting in an EER of 3.2%. Chapter (12) analyzes eye movements of subjects when looking freely at dynamic stimuli such as videos. This study uses face detection techniques to prove that faces are very salient in both static and dynamic stimuli.

Chapter (13) reports the use of specialized denoising algorithms that deal with correlated noise in images. Several useful noise estimation techniques are presented that can be used when creating or adapting a white noise denoising algorithm for use with correlated noise.

Chapter (14) presents a novel technique that estimates and eliminates additive noise inherent in images acquired under incoherent illumination. This technique combines the two methods of scatter plot and data masking to preserve the physical content of polarization-encoded images.

II. Speech/Audio Processing:

This section contains six chapters that explore different applications in the field of speech and audio processing. These applications cover a variety of topics related to speech analysis, enhancement of audio quality, and classification of both audio and speech. Chapters (15) to (20) are arranged into groups based on the application of interest as explained in the following table:

Chapter(s)	Main topic (application)
15 & 16	Speech/audio enhancement
17 & 18	Biometric applications
19 & 20	Speech/audio analysis

Chapter (15) proposes an improved iterative Wiener filter (IWF) algorithm based on the time-varying complex auto regression (TV-CAR) speech analysis for enhancing the quality of speech. The performance of the proposed system is compared against the famous linear predictive coding (LPC) method and is shown to be superior. Chapter (16) introduces a robust echo detection algorithm in mobile phones for improving the calls quality. The structure for the echo detector is based on comparison of uplink and downlink pitch periods. This algorithm has the advantage of processing adaptive multi-rate (AMR) coded speech signals without decoding them first and its performance is demonstrated to be satisfactory.

Chapter (17) investigates the problem of voice/speaker recognition. It compares the effectiveness of using a combination of vector quantization (VQ) and different forms for the Mel frequency cepstral coefficients (MFCCs) when using the Gaussian mixture model for modeling the speaker characteristics. Chapter (18) deals with issues, related to processing and mining of specific speech information, which are commonly ignored by the mainstream research in this field. These issues focus on speech with emotional content, effects of drugs and Alcohol, speakers with disabilities, and various kinds of pathological speech.

Chapter (19) uses narrow-band filtering to construct an estimation technique of instantaneous parameters used in sinusoidal modeling. The proposed method utilizes pitch detection and estimation for achieving good analysis of speech signals. Chapter (20) conducts an experimental study on 420 songs from four different languages to perform statistical analysis of the music information that can be used as prior knowledge in formulating constrains for music information extraction systems.

III. Communication Systems:

This section contains three chapters that deal with the transmission of signals through public communication channels. Chapters (21) to (23) discuss the problems of modeling and simulation of multi-input multi-output wireless channels, multi-antenna receivers, and chaos-based cryptography, respectively. Chapter (21) discusses how to construct channel simulators for multi-input multi-output (MIMO) communication systems for testing physical layer algorithms such as channel estimation. It also presents the framework, techniques, and theories in this research area. Chapter (22) presents a new approach to the broadcast channel problem that is based on combining dirty-paper coding (DPC) with zero-forcing (ZF) precoder and optimal beamforming design. This approach can be applied to the case when several antennas coexist at the receiver. It also introduces an application that deals with the cooperation design in wireless sensor networks with intra and intercluster interference. Chapter (23) investigates three important steps when establishing a secure communication system using chaotic signals. Performing fast synchronization, identifying unknown parameters, and generating robust cryptography are analyzed. Different categories of systems are introduced and real-time implementation issues are discussed.

IV. Time-series Processing:

This section contains three chapters that deal with real-time data handling and processing. These data can be expressed as functions of time, sequence of images, or readings from sensors. It provides three different applications. Chapter (24) introduces an application, which is based on the fusion of electronecephalography (EEG) and functional magnetic resonance imaging (fMRI), for the detection of seizure. It proposes a novel constrained spatial independent component analysis (ICA) algorithm that outperforms the existing unconstrained algorithm in terms of estimation error and closeness between the component time course and the seizure EEG signals. Chapter (25) introduces the design and implementation of a real-time measurement system for estimating the air parameters that are vital for effective and reliable flights. The proposed system is installed in the cockpit of the aircraft and uses two embedded PCs and four FPGA signal processing boards. It utilizes laser beams for estimating the air parameters necessary for the safety of the flight. Chapter (26) discusses the performance of the target signal port-starboard discrimination for underwater towed multi-line arrays that have typical applications in military underwater surveillance and seismic exploring

V. Educational Systems:

Chapter (27) introduces an open source software package that can be used as an educational tool for teaching signal processing in a variety of fields including image and audio processing. It provides an interactive environment that is easy to use with GUI and web interface that is XML-based. This package can be used as an alternative to other existing packages including J-DSP, Simulink and SciLab.

November 2009

Ashraf A. Zaher

Contents

Contents

Contents

1

Digital Image Stabilization

Marius Tico
Nokia Research Center
Palo Alto, CA, USA

1. Introduction

The problem of image stabilization dates since the beginning of photography, and it is basically caused by the fact that any known image sensor needs to have the image projected on it during a period of time called integration time. Any motion of the camera during this time causes a shift of the image projected on the sensor resulting in a degradation of the final image, called motion blur.

The ongoing development and miniaturization of consumer devices that have image acquisition capabilities increases the need for robust and efficient image stabilization solutions. The need is driven by two main factors: (i) the difficulty to avoid unwanted camera motion when using a small hand-held device (like a camera phone), and (ii) the need for longer integration times due to the small pixel area resulted from the miniaturization of the image sensors in conjunction with the increase in image resolution. The smaller the pixel area the less photons/second could be captured by the pixel such that a longer integration time is needed for good results.

It is of importance to emphasize that we make a distinction between the terms "digital image stabilization" and "digital video stabilization". The latter is referring to the process of eliminating the effects of unwanted camera motion from video data, see for instance Erturk & Dennis (2000); Tico & Vehviläinen (2005), whereas digital image stabilization is concerned with correcting the effects of unwanted motions that are taking place during the integration time of a single image or video frame.

The existent image stabilization solutions can be divided in two categories based on whether they are aiming to correct or to prevent the motion blur degradation. In the first category are those image stabilization solutions that are aiming for restoring a single image shot captured during the exposure time. This is actually the classical case of image capturing, when the acquired image may be corrupted by motion blur, caused by the motion that have taken place during the exposure time. If the point spread function (PSF) of the motion blur is known then the original image can be restored, up to some level of accuracy (determined by the lost spatial frequencies), by applying an image restoration approach Gonzalez & Woods (1992); Jansson (1997). However, the main difficulty is that in most practical situations the motion blur PSF is not known. Moreover, since the PSF depends of the arbitrary camera motion during the exposure time, its shape is different in any degraded image as exemplified in Fig. 1. Another difficulty comes from the fact that the blur degradation is not spatially invariant over the image area. Thus, moving objects in the scene may result in very different blur models in certain image areas. On the other hand, even less dynamic scenes may contain different blur models in different regions in accordance to the distance between the objects and the camera,

Fig. 1. Different camera motions cause different blur degradations.

i.e., during a camera translation close objects have larger relative motions than distant objects, phenomenon known as "parallax".

In order to cope with the insufficient knowledge about the blur PSF one could adopt a blind de-convolution approach, e.g., Chan & Wong (1998); You & Kaveh (1996). Most of these methods are computationally expensive and they have reliability problems even when dealing with spatially invariant blur. Until now, published research results have been mainly demonstrated on artificial simulations and rarely on real world images, such that their potential use in consumer products seems rather limited for the moment.

Measurements of the camera motion during the exposure time could help in estimating the motion blur PSF and eventually to restore the original image of the scene. Such an approach have been introduced by Ben-Ezra & Nayar (2004), where the authors proposed the use of an extra camera in order to acquire motion information during the exposure time of the principal camera. A different method, based on specially designed high-speed CMOS sensors has been proposed by Liu & Gamal (2003). The method exploits the possibility to independently control the exposure time of each image pixel in a CMOS sensor. Thus, in order to prevent motion blur the integration is stopped selectively in those pixels where motion is detected.

Another way to estimate the PSF has been proposed in Tico et al. (2006); Tico & Vehviläinen (2007a); Yuan et al. (2007), where a second image of the scene is taken with a short exposure. Although noisy, the secondary image is much less affected by motion blur and it can be used as a reference for estimating the motion blur PSF which degraded the principal image.

In order to cope with the unknown motion blur process, designers have adopted solutions able to prevent such blur for happening in the first place. In this category are included all optical image stabilization (OIS) solutions adopted nowadays by many camera manufactures. These solutions are utilizing inertial senors (gyroscopes) in order to measure the camera motion, following then to cancel the effect of this motion by moving either the image sensor Konika Minolta Inc. (2003), or some optical element Canon Inc. (2006) in the opposite direction. The miniaturization of OIS systems did not reach yet the level required for implementation in a small device like a camera phone. In addition, most current OIS solutions cannot cope well with longer exposure times. In part this is because the inertial motion sensors, used to measure the camera motion, are less sensitive to low frequency motions than to medium and high frequency vibrations. Also, as the exposure time increases the mechanism may drift due to accumulated errors, producing motion blurred images (Fig. 2).

An image acquisition solution that can prevent motion blur consists of dividing long exposure times in shorter intervals, following to capture multiple short exposed image frames of

(a) (b) (c)

Fig. 2. Optical image stabilization examples at different shutter speeds. The images have been captured with a hand-held camera using Canon EF-S 17-85mm image stabilized lens. The exposure times used in taking the pictures have been: (a) 1/25sec, (b) 1/8sec, and (c) 1/4sec. The images get increasingly blurred as the shutter speed slows down.

the same scene. Due to their short exposure, the individual frames are corrupted by sensor noises (e.g., photon-shot noise, readout noise) Nakamura (2006) but, on the other hand, they are less affected by motion blur. Consequently, a long exposed and motion blur free picture can be synthesized by registering and fusing the available short exposed image frames (see Tico (2008a;b); Tico & Vehviläinen (2007b)). Using this technique the effect of camera motion is transformed from a motion blur degradation into a misalignment between several image frames. The advantage is that the correction of the misalignment between multiple frames is more robust and computationally less intensive than the correction of a motion blur degraded image.

In this chapter we present the design of such a multi-frame image stabilization solution, addressing the image registration and fusion operations. A global registration approach, described in Section 2, assists the identification of corresponding pixels between images. However the global registration cannot solve for motion within the scene as well as for parallax. Consequently one can expect local misalignments even after the registration step. These will be solved in the fusion process described in Section 3.

2. Image registration

Image registration is essential for ensuring an accurate information fusion between the available images. The existent approaches to image registration could be classified in two categories: feature based, and image based methods, Zitova & Flusser (2003). The feature based methods rely on determining the correct correspondences between different types of visual features extracted from the images. In some applications, the feature based methods are the most effective ones, as long as the images are always containing specific salient features (e.g., minutiae in fingerprint images Tico & Kuosmanen (2003)). On the other hand when the number of detectable feature points is small, or the features are not reliable due to various image degradations, a more robust alternative is to adopt an image based registration approach, that utilizes directly the intensity information in the image pixels, without searching for specific visual features.

In general a parametric model for the two-dimensional mapping function that overlaps an "input" image over a "reference" image is assumed. Let us denote such mapping function by $\mathbf{t}(\mathbf{x};\mathbf{p}) = [t_x(\mathbf{x};\mathbf{p})\ t_y(\mathbf{x};\mathbf{p})]^t$, where $\mathbf{x} = [x\ y]^t$ stands for the coordinates of an image pixel, and $\mathbf{p}$ denotes the parameter vector of the transformation. Denoting the "input" and "reference" images by h and g respectively, the objective of an image based registration approach is to estimate the parameter vector $\mathbf{p}$ that minimizes a cost function (e.g., the sum of square differences) between the transformed input image $h(\mathbf{t}(\mathbf{x};\mathbf{p}))$ and the reference image $g(\mathbf{x})$.

The minimization of the cost function, can be achieved in various ways. A trivial approach would be to adopt an exhaustive search among all feasible solutions by calculating the cost function at all possible values of the parameter vector. Although this method ensures the discovery of the global optimum, it is usually avoided due to its tremendous complexity. To improve the efficiency several alternatives to the exhaustive search technique have been developed by reducing the searching space at the risk of losing the global optimum, e.g., logarithmic search, three-step search, etc, (see Wang et al. (2002)). Another category of image based registration approaches, starting with the work of Lucas & Kanade (1981), and known also as gradient-based approaches, assumes that an approximation to image derivatives can be consistently estimated, such that the minimization of the cost function can be achieved by applying a gradient-descent technique (see also Baker & Matthews (2004); Thevenaz & Unser (1998)). An important efficiency improvement, for Lucas-Kanade algorithm, has been proposed in Baker & Matthews (2004), under the name of "Inverse Compositional Algorithm" (ICA). The improvement results from the fact that the Hessian matrix of the cost function, needed in the optimization process, is not calculated in each iteration, but only once in a pre-computation phase.

In this work we propose an additional improvement to gradient-based methods, that consists of simplifying the repetitive image warping and interpolation operations that are required during the iterative minimization of the cost function. Our presentation starts by introducing an image descriptor in Section 2.1, that is less illumination dependent than the intensity component. Next, we present our registration algorithm in Section 2.2, that is based on matching the proposed image descriptors of the two images instead their intensity components.

2.1 Preprocessing

Most of the registration methods proposed in the literature are based on matching the intensity components of the given images. However, there are also situations when the intensity components do not match. The most common such cases are those in which the two images have been captured under different illumination conditions, or with different exposures.

In order to cope with such cases we propose a simple preprocessing step aiming to extract an illumination invariant descriptor from the intensity component of each image. Denoting by $H(\mathbf{x})$ the intensity value in the pixel $\mathbf{x}$, and with $\text{avg}(H)$ the average of all intensity values in the image, we first calculate $\bar{H}(\mathbf{x}) = H(\mathbf{x})/\text{avg}(H)$, in order to gain more independence from the global scene illumination. Next, based on the gradient of $\bar{H}$ we calculate $H_g(\mathbf{x}) = |\bar{H}_x(\mathbf{x})| + |\bar{H}_y(\mathbf{x})|$ in each pixel, and $\text{med}(H_g)$ as the median value of $H_g(\mathbf{x})$ over the entire image.

Finally, the actual descriptor that we are using in the registration operation is given by the following binary image

$$h(\mathbf{x}) = \begin{cases} 1 & \text{if } H_g(\mathbf{x}) > \text{med}(H_g) \\ 0 & \text{otherwise} \end{cases} \tag{1}$$

2.2 Registration algorithm

In the following we describe an image based registration method that is using a multi-resolution coarse to fine strategy. Typically in such algorithm, at each iteration step one of the images should be warped in accordance to the parameters estimated so far. In our method this warping operation is highly simplified on the expense of increase memory usage.

The levels of the multi-resolution representation are over-sampled, and they are obtained by iteratively smoothing the original image descriptor h, such that to obtain smoother and smoother versions of it. Let $\tilde{h}_\ell$ denotes the smoothed image resulted after ℓ-th low-pass filtering iterations ($\tilde{h}_0 = h$). The smoothed image at next iteration can be calculated by applying one-dimensional filtering along the image rows and columns as follows:

$$\tilde{h}_{\ell+1}(x,y) = \sum_r w_r \sum_c w_c \tilde{h}_\ell \left(x - 2^\ell c, y - 2^\ell r \right), \tag{2}$$

where w_k are the taps of a low-pass filter.

The registration approach takes advantage of the fact that each decomposition level ($\tilde{h}_\ell$) is over-sampled, and hence it can be reconstructed by a subset of its pixels. This property allows to enhance the efficiency of the registration process by using only a subset of the pixels in the registration algorithm. The advantage offered by the availability of over-sampled decomposition level, is that the set of pixels that can be used in the registration is not unique. A broad range of geometrical transformations can be approximated by simply choosing a different set of pixels to describe the sub-sampled image level. In this way, the over-sampled image level is regarded as a "reservoir of pixels" for different warped sub-sampled versions of the image, which are needed at different stages in the registration algorithm.

Let $\mathbf{x}_{n,k} = [x_{n,k}\ y_{n,k}]^t$, for n,k integers, denote the coordinates of the selected pixels into the smoothed image ($\tilde{h}_\ell$). A low-resolution version of the image ($\hat{h}_\ell$) can be obtained by collecting the values of the selected pixels: $\hat{h}_\ell(n,k) = \tilde{h}_\ell(\mathbf{x}_{n,k})$. Moreover, given an invertible geometrical transformation function $\mathbf{t}(\mathbf{x};\mathbf{p})$, the warping version of the low resolution image can be obtained more efficiently by simply selecting another set of pixels from the area of the smoothed image, rather than warping and interpolating the low-resolution image $\hat{h}_\ell$. This is: $\hat{h}'_\ell(n,k) = \tilde{h}_\ell(\mathbf{x}'_{n,k})$, where $\mathbf{x}'_{n,k} = \text{round}\left(\mathbf{t}^{-1}(\mathbf{x}_{n,k};\mathbf{p})\right)$.

The process described above is illustrated in Fig.3, where the images shown on the bottom row represent two low-resolutions warped versions of the original image (shown in the top-left corner). The two low-resolution images are obtained by sampling different pixels from the smoothed image (top-right corner) without interpolation.

The registration method used in our approach is presented in Algorithm 1. The algorithm follows a coarse to fine strategy, starting from a coarse resolution level and improving the parameter estimate with each finer level, as details in the Algorithm 2. The proposed algorithm relies on matching image descriptors (1) derived from each image rather than image intensity components.

Algorithm 2 presents the registration parameter estimation at one resolution level. In this algorithm, the constant N_0, specifies the number of iterations the algorithm is performing

Fig. 3. Low-resolution image warping by re-sampling an over-sampled image decomposition level.

Algorithm 1 Global image registration

Input: the input and reference images plus, if available, an initial guess of the parameter vector $\mathbf{p} = [p_1\ p_2\ \cdots\ p_K]^t$.
Output: the parameter vector that overlaps the input image over the reference image.

1- Calculate the descriptors (1) for input and reference images, denoted here by h and g, respectively.

2- Calculate the decomposition levels of the two image descriptors $\{\tilde{h}_\ell, \tilde{g}_\ell \mid \ell_{min} \leq \ell \leq \ell_{max}\}$.

3- For each level ℓ between ℓ_{max} and ℓ_{min}, do Algorithm 2.

after finding a minima of the error function. This is set in order to reduce the chance of ending in a local minima. As shown in the algorithm the number of iterations is reset to N_0, every time a new minima of the error function is found. The algorithm stops only if no other minima is found in N_0 iterations. In our experiments a value $N_0 = 10$ has been used.

Algorithm 2 Image registration at one level

Input: the ℓ-th decomposition level of the input and reference images $(\tilde{h}_\ell,\ \tilde{g}_\ell)$, plus the parameter vector $\mathbf{p} = [p_1\ p_2\ \cdots\ p_K]^t$ estimated at the previous coarser level.
Output: a new estimate of the parameter vector $\mathbf{p}_{out}$ that overlaps $\tilde{h}_\ell$ over $\tilde{g}_\ell$.
Initialization: set minimum matching error $E_{min} = \infty$, number of iterations $N_{iter} = N_0$

1- Set the initial position of the sampling points $\mathbf{x}_{n,k}$ in the vertex of a rectangular lattice of period $D = 2^\ell$, over the area of the reference image $\tilde{g}_\ell$.

2- Construct the reference image at this level: $\hat{g}(n,k) = \tilde{g}_\ell(\mathbf{x}_{n,k})$.

3- For each parameter p_i of the warping function calculate the image

$$J_i(n,k) = \hat{g}_x(n,k)\frac{\partial t_x(\mathbf{x};\mathbf{0})}{\partial p_i} + \hat{g}_y(n,k)\frac{\partial t_y(\mathbf{x};\mathbf{0})}{\partial p_i}$$

where $\hat{g}_x$, $\hat{g}_y$ denote a discrete approximation of the gradient components of the reference image.

4- Calculate the first order approximation of the $K \times K$ Hessian matrix, whose element (i,j) is given by:

$$\mathbf{H}(i,j) = \sum_{n,k} J_i(n,k)J_j(n,k)$$

5- Calculate a $K \times K$ updating matrix $\mathbf{U}$, as explain in the text.

Iterations: while $N_{iter} > 0$

6- Construct the warped low-resolution input image in accordance to the warping parameters estimated so far: $\hat{h}(n,k) = \tilde{h}_\ell(\text{round}\left(\mathbf{t}^{-1}(\mathbf{x}_{n,k};\mathbf{p})\right))$.

7- Determine the overlapping area between $\hat{h}$ and $\hat{g}$, as the set of pixel indices Ψ such that any pixel position $(n,k) \in \Psi$ is located inside the two images.

8- Calculate the error image $e(n,k) = \hat{h}(n,k) - \hat{g}(n,k)$, for any $(n,k) \in \Psi$.

9- Calculate a smooth version $\tilde{e}$ of the error image by applying a 2×2 constant box filter, and determine total error $E = \sum_{(n,k)\in\Psi} |\tilde{e}(n,k)|$.

10- If $E \geq E_{min}$ then $N_{iter} = N_{iter} - 1$, otherwise update $E_{min} = E$, $N_{iter} = N_0$, and $\mathbf{p}_{out} = \mathbf{p}$.

11- Calculate the $K \times 1$ vector $\mathbf{q}$, with $\mathbf{q}(i) = \sum_{(n,k)\in\Psi} \tilde{e}(n,k)J_i(n,k)$.

12- Update the parameter vector $\mathbf{p} = \mathbf{p} + \mathbf{U}\mathbf{q}$

The parameter update (i.e., line 12 in Algorithm 2) makes use of an updating matrix $\mathbf{U}$ calculated in step 5 of the algorithm. This matrix depends of the functional form of the geometrical transformation assumed between the two images, $\mathbf{t}(\mathbf{x};\mathbf{p})$. For instance, in case of affine transformation

$$\mathbf{t}(\mathbf{x};\mathbf{p}) = \begin{bmatrix} (1-p_3)x + p_4 y + p_1 \\ p_5 x + (1-p_6)y + p_2 \end{bmatrix}, \tag{3}$$

the parameter update matrix is

$$\mathbf{U} = \text{diag}\,(D, D, 1, 1, 1, 1)\,\mathbf{H}^{-1}, \tag{4}$$

whereas in case of a projective transformation

$$\mathbf{t}(\mathbf{x};\mathbf{p}) = \begin{bmatrix} (1-p_3)x + p_4 y + p_1 \\ p_5 x + (1-p_6)y + p_2 \end{bmatrix} / (p_7 x + p_8 y + 1), \tag{5}$$

we have

$$\mathbf{U} = \text{diag}\,(D, D, 1, 1, 1, 1, 1/D, 1/D)\,\mathbf{H}^{-1}. \tag{6}$$

In our implementation of multi-resolution image decomposition (2), we used a symmetric filter w of size 3, whose taps are respectively $w_{-1} = 1/4$, $w_0 = 1/2$, and $w_1 = 1/4$. Also, in order to reduce the storage space the first level of image decomposition (i.e., $\tilde{h}_1$), is subsampled by 2, such that any higher decomposition level is half the size of the original image.

3. Fusion of multiple images

The pixel brightness delivered by an imaging system is related to the exposure time through a non-linear mapping called "radiometric response function", or "camera response function" (CRF). There are a variety of techniques (e.g., Debevec & Malik (1997); Mitsunaga & Nayar (1999)) that can be used for CRF estimation. In our work we assume that the CRF function of the imaging system is known, and based on that we can write down the following relation for the pixel brightness value:

$$I(\mathbf{x}) = \text{CRF}\,(g(\mathbf{x})\Delta t) \tag{7}$$

where $\mathbf{x} = [x\ y]^T$ denotes the spatial position of an image pixel, $I(\mathbf{x})$ is the brightness value delivered by the system, $g(\mathbf{x})$ denotes the irradiance level caused by the light incident on the pixel $\mathbf{x}$ of the imaging sensor, and Δt stands for the exposure time of the image.

Let I_k, for $k \in \{1, \ldots, K\}$ denote the K observed image frames whose exposure times are denoted by Δt_k. A first step in our algorithm is to convert each image to the linear (irradiance) domain based on knowledge about the CRF function, i.e.,

$$g_k(\mathbf{x}) = (1/\Delta t_k)\,\text{CRF}^{-1}\,(I_k(\mathbf{x}))\,,\ \text{for all } k \in \{1, \ldots, K\}. \tag{8}$$

We assume the following model for the K observed irradiance images:

$$g_k(\mathbf{x}) = f_k(\mathbf{x}) + n_k(\mathbf{x}), \tag{9}$$

where where $\mathbf{x} = [x\ y]^T$ denotes the spatial position of an image pixel, g_k is the k-th observed image frame, n_k denotes a zero mean additive noise, and f_k denotes the latent image of the scene at the moment the k-th input frame was captured. We emphasize the fact that the scene may change between the moments when different input frames are captured. Such changes could be caused by unwanted motion of the camera and/or by the motion of different objects in the scene. Consequently, the algorithm can provide a number of K different estimates of the latent scene image each of them corresponding to a different reference moment.

In order to preserve the consistency of the scene, we select one of the input images as reference, following to aim for improving the selected image based on the visual data available in all captured images. In the following, we denote by g_r, ($r \in \{1,\ldots,K\}$) the reference image observation, and hence the objective of the algorithm is to recover an estimate of the latent scene image at moment r, i.e., $f = f_r$.

The restoration process is carried out based on a spatiotemporal block processing. Assuming a division of g_r in non-overlapping blocks of size $B \times B$ pixels, the restored version of each block is obtained as a weighted average of all blocks located in a specific search range, inside all observed images.

Let $\mathbf{X}_\mathbf{x}^B$ denote the sub-set of spatial locations included into a block of $B \times B$ pixels centered in the pixel $\mathbf{x}$, i.e.:

$$\mathbf{X}_\mathbf{x}^B = \left\{\mathbf{y} \in \Omega \mid [-B \;\; -B]^T < 2(\mathbf{y}-\mathbf{x}) \le [B \; B]^T\right\}, \tag{10}$$

where the inequalities are componentwise, and Ω stands for the image support. Also, let $g(\mathbf{X}_\mathbf{x}^B)$ denote the $B^2 \times 1$ column vector comprising the values of all pixels from an image g that are located inside the block $\mathbf{X}_\mathbf{x}^B$.

The restored image is calculated block by block as follows

$$\hat{f}(\mathbf{X}_\mathbf{x}^B) = \frac{1}{Z}\sum_{k=1}^{K}\sum_{\mathbf{y}\in\mathbf{X}_\mathbf{x}^S} w_k(\mathbf{x},\mathbf{y})\, g_k(\mathbf{X}_\mathbf{y}^B), \text{ for all } \mathbf{X}_\mathbf{x}^B, \tag{11}$$

where $Z = \sum_{k=1}^{K}\sum_{\mathbf{y}\in\mathbf{X}_\mathbf{x}^S} w_k(\mathbf{x},\mathbf{y})$, is a normalization value, $\mathbf{X}_\mathbf{x}^S$ denotes the spatial search range of size $S \times S$ centered in $\mathbf{x}$, and $w_k(\mathbf{x},\mathbf{y})$ is a scalar weight value assigned to an input block $\mathbf{X}_\mathbf{y}^B$ from image g_k.

The weight values are emphasizing the input blocks that are more similar with the reference block. Note that, at the limit, by considering only the most similar such block from each input image we obtain the block corresponding to the optical flow between the reference image and that input image, as in Tico & Vehviläinen (2007b). In such a case the weighted average (11) comprises only a small number of contributing blocks for each reference block. If more computational power is available, we can chose the weight values such that to use more blocks for the restoration of each reference block, like for instance in the solution presented in Tico (2008a), where the restoration of each reference block is carried out by considering all visually similar blocks found either inside the reference image or inside any other input image. Although the use of block processing is more efficient for large images, it might create artifacts in detailed image areas. In order to cope with this aspect, the solution presented in Tico (2008a), proposes a mechanism for adapting the block size to the local image content, by using smaller blocks in detail areas and larger blocks in smooth areas of the image. We conclude this section by summarizing the operations of a multi-frame image stabilization solutions in Algorithm 3.

Algorithm 3 Stabilization algorithm

Input: multiple input images of the scene.
Output: one stabilized image of the scene.

1- Select a reference image either in a manual or an automatic manner. Manual selection can be based on preferred scene content at the moment the image frame was captured, whereas automatic selection could be trivial (i.e., selecting the first frame), or image quality based (i.e., selecting the higher quality frame based on a quality criteria). In our work we select the reference image frame as the one that is the least affected by blur. To do this we employ a sharpness measure, that consists of the average energy of the image in the middle frequency band, calculated in the FFT domain.

2- Convert the input images to a linear color space by compensating for camera response function non-linearity.

3- Register the input images with respect to the reference image.

4- Estimate the additive noise variance in each input image. Instead using a global variance value for the entire image, in our experiments we employed a linear model for the noise variance with respect to the intensity level in order to emulate the Poisson process of photon counting in each sensor pixel.

5- Restore each block of the reference image in accordance to (11).

6- Convert the resulted irradiance estimate $\hat{f}(\mathbf{x})$, of the final image, back to the image domain, $\hat{I}(\mathbf{x}) = \text{CRF}(\hat{f}(\mathbf{x})\Delta t)$, based on the desired exposure time Δt. Alternatively, in order to avoid saturation and hence to extend the dynamic range of the captured image, one can employ a tone mapping procedure (e.g., Jiang & Guoping (2004)) for converting the levels of the irradiance image estimate into the limited dynamic range of the display system.

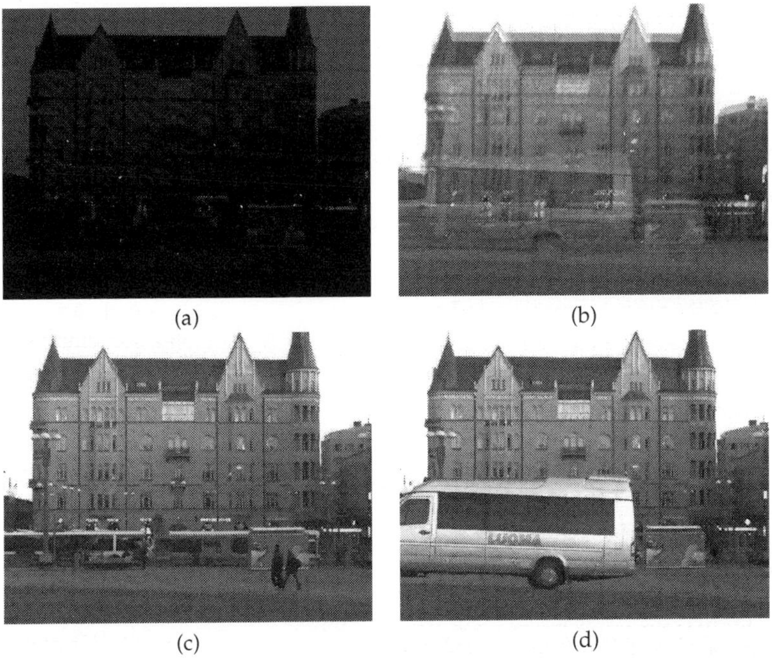

Fig. 4. Real image example: (a) one input image out of four, (b) overlapping all four input images, (c,d) two different results obtained by selecting different reference moments.

(a) (b)

Fig. 5. Fragment from Fig. 4: (a) the digitally gained reference image, (b) the same fragment from the result.

(a) (b)

Fig. 6. Real imaging examples: (a) auto-exposed image taken with a camera phone (exposure time: 1.8 sec), (b) stabilized image by fusing four frames with exposure time of 0.3 sec each.

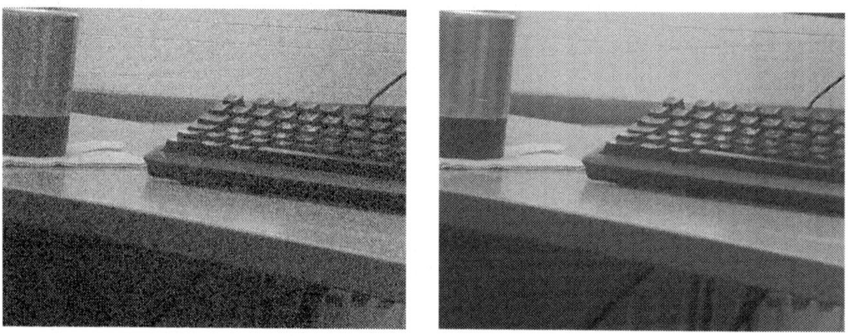

(a) (b)

Fig. 7. Applying the proposed algorithm onto a single input image (a), delivers a noise filtered version (b), of the input image.

4. Examples

A visual example of the presented method is shown in Fig. 4. In total a number of four short exposed image frames (like the one shown in Fig. 4(a)) have been captured. During the time the individual images have been captured the scene was changed due to moving objects, as reveal by Fig. 4 (b). Applying the proposed algorithm we can recover a high quality image at any moment by choosing the reference frame properly, as exemplified by Fig. 4 (c) and (d). The improvement in image quality achieved by combining multiple images is demonstrated by the fragment in Fig. 5 that shows significant reduction in image noise between one input image Fig. 5(a) and the result Fig. 5(b).

Two examples using images captured with a mobile phone camera are shown in Fig. 6 and Fig. 7. In both cases the algorithm was applied onto the Bayer RAW image data before image pipeline operations. A simple linear model for the noise variance with respect to the intensity level was assumed in order to emulate the Poisson process of photon counting in each sensor pixel Nakamura (2006), for each color channel.

Fig. 6(a), shows an image obtained without stabilization using the mobile device set on automatic exposure. Due to unwanted camera motion the resulted image is rather blurry. For comparison, Fig. 6(b), shows the image obtained with our proposed stabilization algorithm by fusing several short exposed images of the same scene. An example when the proposed algorithm is applied onto a single input image is shown in Fig. 7. In this case the algorithm acts as a noise filtering method delivering the image Fig. 7(b), by reducing the noise present in the input image Fig. 7(a).

5. Conclusions and future work

In this chapter we presented a software solution to image stabilization based on fusing the visual information between multiple frames of the same scene. The main components of the algorithm, global image registration and image fusion have been presented in detail along with several visual examples. An efficient coarse to fine image based registration solution is obtained by preserving an over-sampled version of each pyramid level in order to simplify the warping operation in each iteration step. Next the image fusion step matches the visual similar image blocks between the available frames coping thereby with the presence of moving objects in the scene or with the inability of the global registration model to describe the camera motion. The advantages of such a software solution against the popular hardware opto-mechanical image stabilization systems include: (i) the ability to prevent blur caused by moving objects in a dynamic scene, (ii) the ability to deal with longer exposure times and stabilized not only high frequency vibrations but also low frequency camera motion during the integration time, and (iii) the reduced cost and size required for implementation in small mobile devices. The main disadvantage is the need to capture multiple images of the scene. However, nowadays most camera devices provide a "burst" mode that ensures fast capturing of multiple images. Future work would have to address several other applications that can take advantage of the camera "burst" mode by fusing multiple images captured with similar of different exposure and focus parameters.

6. References

Baker, S. & Matthews, I. (2004). Lucas-Kanade 20 Years On: A Unifying Framework, *International Journal of Computer Vision* .

Ben-Ezra, M. & Nayar, S. K. (2004). Motion-Based Motion Deblurring, *IEEE Transactions on Pattern Analysis and Machine Intelligence* **26**(6): 689–698.

Canon Inc. (2006). Shift-Method Optical Image Stabilizer.
URL: *www.canon.com/technology/dv/02.html*

Chan, T. F. & Wong, C.-K. (1998). Total Variation Blind Deconvolution, *IEEE Transactions on Image Processing* **7**(3): 370–375.

Debevec, P. E. & Malik, J. (1997). Recovering High Dynamic Range Radiance Maps from Photographs, *Proc. of International Conference on Computer Graphics and Interactive Techniques (SIGGRAPH)*.

Erturk, S. & Dennis, T. (2000). Image sequence stabilization based on DFT filtering, *IEE Proc. On Vision Image and Signal Processing* **147**(2): 95–102.

Gonzalez, R. C. & Woods, R. E. (1992). *Digital Image Processing*, Addison-Wesley.

Jansson, P. (1997). *Deconvolution of image and spectra*, Academic Press.

Jiang, D. & Guoping, Q. (2004). Fast tone mapping for high dynamic range images, *Proc. of 17th Intl. Conf. on Pattern Recognition (ICPR)*, Vol. 2, pp. 847–850.

Konika Minolta Inc. (2003). Anti-Shake Technology, *www.konicaminolta.com/ products/consumer/digital camera/dimage/dimage-a2/02.html* .

Liu, X. & Gamal, A. E. (2003). Synthesis of high dynamic range motion blur free image from multiple captures, *IEEE Transaction on Circuits and Systems-I* **50**(4): 530–539.

Lucas, B. D. & Kanade, T. (1981). An Iterative Image Registration Technique with an Application to Stereo Vision, *Proc. of 7th Intl Conf on Artificial Intelligence (IJCAI)*, Vancouver,Canada, pp. 674–679.

Mitsunaga, T. & Nayar, S. K. (1999). Radiometric self calibration, *Proc. of Conference on Computer Vision and Pattern Recognition*.

Nakamura, J. (2006). Basics of image sensors, *in* J. Nakamura (ed.), *Image Sensors and Signal Processing for Digital Still Cameras*, CRC Press, pp. 53–94.

Thevenaz, P. & Unser, M. (1998). A Pyramid Approach to Subpixel Registration Based on Intensity, *IEEE Transactions on Image Processing* **7**(1): 27–41.

Tico, M. (2008a). Adaptive block-based approach to image stabilization, *Proc. of the IEEE International Conference of Image Processing (ICIP)*, Vol. 1, San Diego, CA, USA, pp. 521–524.

Tico, M. (2008b). Multiframe image denoising and stabilization, *Proc. of the 15th European Signal Processing Conference (EUSIPCO)*, Lausanne, Switzerland.

Tico, M. & Kuosmanen, P. (2003). Fingerprint matching using an orientation-based minutia descriptor, *IEEE Trans. on Pattern Analysis and Machine Intelligence* **25**(8): 1009–1014.

Tico, M., Trimeche, M. & Vehviläinen, M. (2006). Motion blur identification based on differently exposed images, *Proc. of the IEEE International Conference of Image Processing (ICIP)*, Atlanta, GA, USA, pp. 2021–2024.

Tico, M. & Vehviläinen, M. (2005). Constraint motion filtering for video stabilization, *Proc. of the IEEE International Conference of Image Processing (ICIP)*, Vol. 3, Genova, Italy, pp. 569–572.

Tico, M. & Vehviläinen, M. (2007a). Image stabilization based on fusing the visual information in differently exposed images, *Proc. of the IEEE International Conference of Image Processing (ICIP)*, Vol. 1, San Antonio, TX, USA, pp. 117–120.

Tico, M. & Vehviläinen, M. (2007b). Robust image fusion for image stabilization, *IEEE International Conference on Acoustics, Speech, and Signal Processing (ICASSP)*, Honolulu, USA.

Wang, Y., Ostermann, J. & Zhang, Y.-Q. (2002). *Video Processing and Communications*, Prentice Hall.

You, Y.-L. & Kaveh, M. (1996). A regularization approach to joint blur identification and image restoration, *IEEE Trans. on Image Processing* **5**(3): 416–428.

Yuan, L., Sun, J., Quan, L. & Shum, H.-Y. (2007). Image deblurring with blurred/noisy image pairs, *ACM Transactions on Graphics* **26**(3).

Zitova, B. & Flusser, J. (2003). Image registration methods: a survey, *Image and Vision Computing* **21**: 977–1000.

2

About array processing methods for image segmentation

J. Marot, C. Fossati
Institut Fresnel (Ecole Centrale Marseille)
France
Y. Caulier
Fraunhofer Institute IIS
Germany

1. Introduction

Shape description is an important goal of computational vision and image processing. Giving the characteristics of lines or distorted contours is faced in robotic way screening, measuring of wafer track width in microelectronics, aerial image analysis, vehicle trajectory and particle detection. Distorted contour retrieval is also encountered in medical imaging. In this introduction, we firstly present classical methods that were proposed to solve this problem, that is, Snakes and levelset methods (Kass et al., 1988; Xu & Prince, 1997; Zhu & Yuile, 1996; Osher & Sethian, 1988; Paragios & Deriche, 2002). We secondly present original methods which rely on signal generation out of an image and adaptation of high resolution methods of array processing (Aghajan & Kailath, 1993a; Aghajan, 1995; Bourennane & Marot, 2006; Marot & Bourennane, 2007a; Marot & Bourennane, 2007b; Marot & Bourennane, 2008).

A Snake is a closed curve which, starting from an initial position, evolves towards an object of interest under the influence of forces (Kass et al., 1988; Xu & Prince, 1997; Zhu & Yuile, 1996; Xianhua & Mirmehdi, 2004; Cheng & Foo 2006; Brigger et al., 2000) Snakes methods are edge-based segmentation schemes which aim at finding out the transitions between uniform areas, rather than directly identifying them (Kass et al., 1988; Xu & Prince, 1997). Another model of active contour is geodesic curves or "levelset". Its main interest with respect to Snakes is to be able to face changes in topology, to the cost of a higher computational load (Osher & Sethian, 1988; Paragios & Deriche 2002; Karoui et al., 2006).

We describe here more precisely Snakes type methods because they are edge-based methods as well as the proposed array processing methods. Edge-based segmentation schemes have improved, considering robustness to noise and sensitivity to initialization (Xu & Prince, 1997). Some active contour methods were combined with spline type interpolation to reduce the number of control points in the image (Brigger et al. 2000). This increases the robustness to noise and computational load. In particular, (Precioso et al., 2005) uses smoothing splines in the B-spline interpolation approach of (Unser et al. 1993). In (Xu & Prince, 1997) the proposed "Gradient Vector Flow" (GVF) method provides valuable results, but is prone to shortcomings: contours with high curvature may be skipped unless an elevated computational load is devoted. Concerning straight lines in particular, in (Kiryati & Brucktein, 1992; Sheinval & Kiryati, 1997) the extension of the Hough transform retrieves the main direction of roughly aligned points. This method gives a good resolution even with noisy images. Its computational load is elevated. Least-squares fit of straight lines seeks to minimize the summation of the squared error-of-fit with respect to measures (Gander et al., 1994; Connel & Jain, 2001). This method is sensitive to outliers.

An original approach in contour estimation consists in adapting high-resolution methods of array processing (Roy & Kailath, 1989; Pillai & Kwon, 1989; Marot et al., 2008) for straight line segmentation (Aghajan & Kailath, 1993a; Aghajan, 1995; Aghajan & Kailath, 1993b; Halder et al., 1995; Aghajan & Kailath, 1994; Aghajan & Kailath, 1992). In this framework, a straight line in an image is considered as a wave-front. Now, high-resolution methods of array processing have improved for several years (Roy & Kailath, 1989; Bourennane et al., 2008). In particular, sensitivity to noise has improved, and the case of correlated sources is faced by a "spatial smoothing" procedure (Pillai & Kwon 1989). To adapt high-resolution methods of array processing to contour estimation in images, the image content is transcripted into a signal through a specific generation scheme, performed on a virtual set of sensors located along the image side. In (Abed-Meraim & Hua, 1997), a polynomial phase model for the generated signal is proposed to take into account the image discretization, for an improved straight line characterization. The ability of high-resolution methods to handle correlated sources permitted to handle the case of parallel straight lines in image understanding (Bourennane & Marot, 2006; Bourennane & Marot, 2005). Optimization methods generalized straight line estimation to nearly straight distorted contour estimation (Bourennane & Marot, 2005; Bourennane & Marot, 2006b; Bourennane & Marot, 2006c).

Circular and nearly circular contour segmentation (Marot & Bourennane, 2007a; Marot & Bourennane, 2007b) was also considered. While straight and nearly straight contours are estimated through signal generation on linear antenna, circular and nearly circular contour segmentation is performed through signal generation upon circular antenna. We adapt the shape of the antenna to the shape of the expected contours so we are able to apply the same high-resolution and optimization methods as for straight and nearly straight line retrieval. In particular array processing methods for star-shaped contour estimation provide a solution to the limitation of Snakes active contours concerning contours with high concavity (Marot & Bourennane, 2007b). The proposed multiple circle estimation method retrieves intersecting circles, thus providing a solution to levelset-type methods.

The remainder of the chapter is organized as follows: We remind in section 2 the formalism that adapts the estimation of straight lines as a classical array processing problem. The study dedicated to straight line retrieval is used as a basis for distorted contour estimation (see section 3). In section 4 we set the problem of star-shaped contour retrieval and propose a circular antenna to retrieve possibly distorted concentric circles. In section 5 we summarize the array processing methods dedicated to possibly distorted linear and circular contour estimation. We emphasize the similarity between nearly linear and nearly circular contour estimation. In section 6 we show how signal generation on linear antenna yields the coordinates of the center of circles. In section 7 we describe a method for the estimation of intersecting circles, thereby proposing a solution to a limitation of the levelset type algorithms. In section 8 we propose some results through various applications: robotic vision, omni directional images, and medical melanoma images.

2. Straight contour estimation

2.1 Data model, generation of the signals out of the image data

To adapt array processing techniques to distorted curve retrieval, the image content must be transcripted into a signal. This transcription is enabled by adequate conventions for the representation of the image, and by a signal generation scheme (Aghajan, 1995; Aghajan & Kailath, 1994). Once a signal has been created, array processing methods can be used to retrieve the characteristics of any straight line. Let I be the recorded image (see Fig.1 (a).).

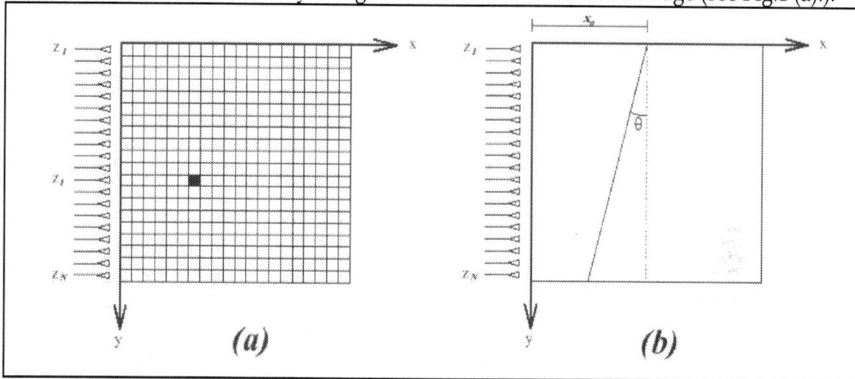

Fig. 1. The image model (see Aghajan & Kailath, 1992):

(a) The image-matrix provided with the coordinate system and the linear array of N equidistant sensors,
(b) A straight line characterized by its angle θ and its offset x_0.

We consider that I contains d straight lines and an additive uniformly distributed noise. The image-matrix is the discrete version of the recorded image, compound of a set of $N * C$ pixel values. A formalism adopted in (Aghajan & Kailath, 1993) allows signal generation, by the following computation:

$$z(i) = \sum_{k=1}^{C} I(i,k) exp(-j\mu k), \quad i = 1,.......,N \tag{1}$$

Where $\{I(i,k); i \in \{1,...,N\}; k \in \{1,...,C\}\}$ denote the image pixels. Eq. (1) simulates a linear antenna: each row of the image yields one signal component as if it were associated with a sensor. The set of sensors corresponding to all rows forms a linear antenna. We focus in the following on the case where a binary image is considered. The contours are composed of 1-valued pixels also called "edge pixels", whereas 0-valued pixels compose the background. When d straight lines, with parameters angle $\{\theta_k\}$ and offset x_{0k} $(k = 1,...,d)$, are crossing the image, and if the image contains noisy outlier pixels, the signal generated on the ith sensor, in front of the ith row, is (Aghajan & Kailath, 1993):

$$z(i) = \sum_{k=1}^{d} exp(j\mu(i-1)tan(\theta_k)) exp(-j\mu x_{0k}) + n(i) \tag{2}$$

Where μ is a propagation parameter (Aghajan & Kailath, 1993b) and $n(i)$ is due to the noisy pixels on the ith row.
Defining $a_i(\theta_k) = exp(j\mu(i-1)tan\,\theta_k),\quad s_k = exp(-j\mu x_{0k})$, Eq. (2) becomes:

$$z(i) = \sum_{k=1}^{d} a_i(\theta_k) s_k + n(i), \quad i = 1,...,N \tag{3}$$

Grouping all terms in a single vector, Eq. (3) becomes:
$\mathbf{z} = \mathbf{A}(\theta)\mathbf{s} + \mathbf{n}$, with $\mathbf{A}(\theta) = [\mathbf{a}(\theta_1),...,\mathbf{a}(\theta_d)]$ where $\mathbf{a}(\theta_k) = [a_1(\theta_k), a_2(\theta_k),..., a_N(\theta_k)]^T$, with $a_i(\theta_k) = exp(j\mu(i-1)tan\,\theta_k),\quad i = 1,...,N$, superscript ^{T} denoting transpose. SLIDE (Subspace-based Line DEtection) algorithm (Aghajan & Kailath, 1993) uses TLS-ESPRIT (Total-Least-Squares Estimation of Signal Parameters via Rotational Invariance Techniques) method to estimate the angle values.
To estimate the offset values, the "extension of the Hough transform" (Kiryati & Bruckstein, 1992) can be used. It is limited by its high computational cost and the large required size for the memory bin. (Bourennane & Marot, 2006a; Bourennane & Marot, 2005) developed another method. This method remains in the frame of array processing and reduces the computational cost: A high-resolution method called MFBLP (Modified Forward Backward Linear Prediction) (Bourennane & Marot, 2005) is associated with a specific signal generation method, namely the variable parameter propagation scheme (Aghajan & Kailath, 1993b). The formalism introduced in that section can also handle the case of straight edge detection in gray-scale images (Aghajan & Kailath, 1994).
In the next section, we consider the estimation of the straight line angles and offsets, by reviewing the SLIDE and MFBLP methods.

2.2 Angle estimation, overview of the SLIDE method

The method for angles estimation falls into two parts: the estimation of a covariance matrix and the application of a total least squares criterion.
Numerous works have been developed in the frame of the research of a reliable estimator of the covariance matrix when the duration of the signal is very short or the number of realizations is small. This situation is often encountered, for instance, with seismic signals. To cope with it, numerous frequency and/or spatial means are computed to replace the temporal mean. In this study the covariance matrix is estimated by using the spatial mean (Halder & al., 1995). From the observation vector we build K vectors of length M with $d < M \leq N - d + 1$. In order to maximize the number of sub-vectors we choose $K=N+1-M$. By grouping the whole sub-vectors obtained in matrix form, we obtain : $\mathbf{Z}_K = [\mathbf{z}_1,...,\mathbf{z}_K]$, where $\mathbf{z}_l = \mathbf{A}_M(\theta)s_l + \mathbf{n}_l,\quad l = 1,...,K$. Matrix $\mathbf{A_M}(\theta) = [\mathbf{a}(\theta_1),...,\mathbf{a}(\theta_d)]$ is a Vandermonde type one of size M x d. Signal part of the data is supposed to be independent from the noise; the components of noise vector $\mathbf{n}_l$ are supposed to be uncorrelated, and to have identical variance. The covariance matrix can be estimated from the observation sub-vectors as it is performed in (Aghajan & Kailath, 1992). The eigen-decomposition of the covariance matrix is, in general, used to characterize the sources by subspace techniques in array processing. In the frame of image processing the aim is to estimate the angle θ of the d straight lines. Several high-resolution methods that solve this problem have been proposed (Roy & Kailath, 1989). SLIDE algorithm is applied to a particular case of an array consisting of two

identical sub-arrays (Aghajan & Kailath, 1994). It leads to the following estimated angles (Aghajan & Kailath, 1994):

$$\hat{\theta}_k = tan^{-1}\left[\frac{1}{(\mu * \Delta)} Im\left(ln\left(\frac{\lambda_k}{|\lambda_k|}\right)\right)\right] \tag{4}$$

where $\{\lambda_k, k = 1,...,d\}$ are the eigenvalues of a diagonal unitary matrix that relates the measurements from the first sub-array to the measurements resulting from the second sub-array. Parameter μ is the propagation constant, and Δ is the distance between two sensors. TLS-ESPRIT method used by SLIDE provides the estimated parameters in closed-form, in opposite to the Hough transform which relies on maxima research (Kiryati & Bruckstein, 1992). Offset estimation exploits the estimated straight lines angles.

2.3 Offset estimation

The most well-known offset estimation method is the "Extension of the Hough Transform" (Sheinvald & Kiryati, 1997). Its principle is to count all pixel aligned on several orientations. The expected offset values correspond to the maximum pixel number, for each orientation value. The second proposed method remains in the frame of array processing: it employs a variable parameter propagation scheme (Aghajan, 1993; Aghajan & Kailath, 1993b; Aghajan & Kailath, 1994) and uses a high resolution method. This high resolution "MFBLP" method relies on the concept of forward and backward organization of the data (Pillai & Kwon, 1989; Halder, Aghajan et al., 1995; Tufts & Kumaresan, 1982). A variable speed propagation scheme (Aghajan & Kailath, 1993b; Aghajan & Kailath, 1994), associated with "MFBLP" (Modified Forward Backward Linear Prediction) yields offset values with a lower computational load than the Extension of the Hough Transform. The basic idea in this method is to associate a propagation speed which is different for each line in the image (Aghajan & Kailath, 1994). By setting artificially a propagation speed that linearly depends on row indices, we get a linear phase signal. When the first orientation value is considered, the signal received on sensor i $(i = 1,...N)$ is then:

$$z(i) = \sum_{k=1}^{d_1} exp(-j\tau x_{0k}) exp(j\tau(i-1)tan(\theta_1)) + n(i) \tag{5}$$

d_1 is the number of lines with angle θ_1. When τ varies linearly as a function of the line index the measure vector $\mathbf{z}$ contains a modulated frequency term. Indeed we set $\tau = \alpha(i-1)$.

$$z(i) = \sum_{k=1}^{d_1} exp(-j\alpha(i-1)x_{0k}) exp\left(j\alpha(i-1)^2 tan(\theta_1)\right) + n(i) \tag{6}$$

This is a sum of d_1 signals that have a common quadratic phase term but different linear phase terms. The first treatment consists in obtaining an expression containing only linear terms. This goal is reached by dividing $z(i)$ by the non zero term $a_i(\theta_1) = exp\left(j\alpha(i-1)^2 tan(\theta_1)\right)$. We obtain then:

$$w(i)=\sum_{k=1}^{d_1} exp(-j\alpha(i-1)x_{0k})+n'(i) \tag{7}$$

The resulting signal appears as a combination of d_1 sinusoids with frequencies:

$$f_k=\frac{\alpha x_{0k}}{2\pi}, \quad k=1,...,d_1 \tag{8}$$

Consequently, the estimation of the offsets can be transposed to a frequency estimation problem. Estimation of frequencies from sources having the same amplitude was considered in (Tufts & Kumaressan, 1982). In the following a high resolution algorithm, initially introduced in spectral analysis, is proposed for the estimation of the offsets.
After adopting our signal model we adapt to it the spectral analysis method called modified forward backward linear prediction (MFBLP) (Tufts & Kumaresan, 1982) for estimating the offsets: we consider d_k straight lines with given angle θ_k, and apply the MFBLP method, to the vector $\mathbf{w}$. Details about MFBLP method applied to offset estimation are available in (Bourennane & Marot, 2006a). MFBLP estimates the values of $f_k, k=1,...,d_1$. According to Eq. (8) these frequency values are proportional to the offset values, the proportionality coefficient being $-\alpha$. The main advantage of this method comes from its low computational load. Indeed the complexity of the variable parameter propagation scheme associated with MFBLP is much less than the complexity of the Extension of the Hough Transform as soon as the number of non zero pixels in the image increases. This algorithm enables the characterization of straight lines with same angle and different offset.

3. Nearly linear contour retrieval

In this section, we keep the same signal generation formalism as for straight line retrieval. The more general case of distorted contour estimation is proposed. The reviewed method relies on constant speed signal generation scheme, and on an optimization method.

3.1 Initialization of the proposed algorithm

To initialize our recursive algorithm, we apply SLIDE algorithm, which provides the parameters of the straight line that fits the best the expected distorted contour. In this section, we consider only the case where the number d of contours is equal to one. The parameters angle and offset recovered by the straight line retrieval method are employed to build an initialization vector $\mathbf{x}_0$, containing the initialization straight line pixel positions:

$$\mathbf{x}_0=[x_0,x_0-tan(\theta),...,x_0-(N-1)tan(\theta)]^T$$

Fig.2 presents a distorted curve, and an initialization straight line that fits this distorted curve.

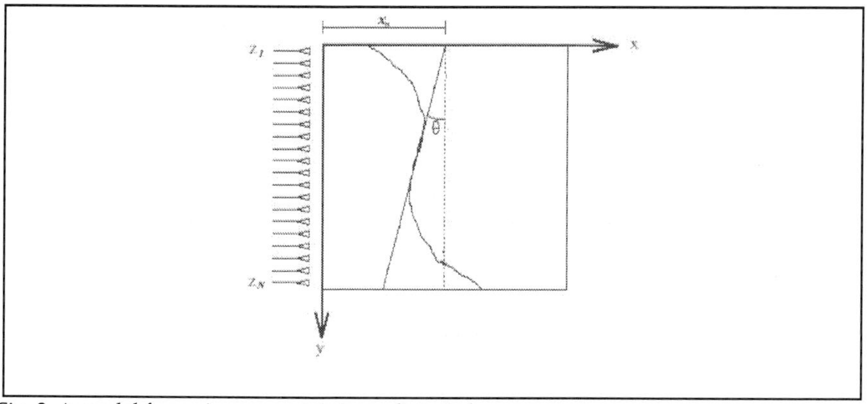

Fig. 2. A model for an image containing a distorted curve

3.2 Distorted curve: proposed algorithm

We aim at determining the N unknowns $x(i), \quad i=1,...,N$ of the image, forming a vector $\mathbf{x_{input}}$, each of them taken into account respectively at the ith sensor:

$$z(i)=exp(-j\mu x(i)), \quad \forall i=1,...,N \tag{9}$$

The observation vector is

$$\mathbf{z_{input}}=[exp(-j\mu x(1)),...,exp(-j\mu x(N))]^T \tag{10}$$

We start from the initialization vector $\mathbf{x_0}$, characterizing a straight line that fits a locally rectilinear portion of the expected contour. The values $x(i), \quad i=1,...,N$ can be expressed as: $x(i)=x_0-(i-1)tan(\theta)+\Delta x(i), \quad i=1,...,N$ where $\Delta x(i)$ is the pixel shift for row i between a straight line with parameters θ and the expected contour. Then, with k indexing the steps of this recursive algorithm, we aim at minimizing

$$J(\mathbf{x_k})=\left\|\mathbf{z_{input}}-\mathbf{z_{estimated\ for\ x_k}}\right\|^2 \tag{11}$$

where $\|.\|$ represents the C^N norm. For this purpose we use fixed step gradient method: $\forall k \in N$: $\mathbf{x_{k+1}}=\mathbf{x_k}-\lambda\nabla(J(\mathbf{x_k}))$, λ is the step for the descent. At this point, by minimizing criterion J (see Eq. (11)), we find the components of vector $\mathbf{x}$ leading to the signal $\mathbf{z}$ which is the closest to the input signal in the sense of criterion J. Choosing a value of μ which is small enough (see Eq. (1)) avoids any phase indetermination. A variant of the fixed step gradient method is the variable step gradient method. It consists in adopting a descent step which depends on the iteration index. Its purpose is to accelerate the convergence of gradient. A more elaborated optimization method based on DIRECT algorithm (Jones et al., 1993) and spline interpolation (Marot & Bourennane, 2007a) can be adopted to reach the global minimum of criterion J of Eq. (11). This method is applied to modify recursively signal $\mathbf{z_{estimated\ for\ x_k}}$: at each step of the recursive procedure vector $\mathbf{x_k}$ is computed by making an interpolation between some "node" values that are retrieved by DIRECT. The

interest of the combination of DIRECT with spline interpolation comes from the elevated computational load of DIRECT. Details about DIRECT algorithm are available in (Jones et al., 1993). Reducing the number of unknown values retrieved by DIRECT reduces drastically its computational load. Moreover, in the considered application, spline interpolation between these node values provides a continuous contour. This prevents the pixels of the result contour from converging towards noisy pixels. The more interpolation nodes, the more precise the estimation, but the slower the algorithm.
After considering linear and nearly linear contours, we focus on circular and nearly circular contours.

4. Star-shape contour retrieval

Star-shape contours are those whose radial coordinates in polar coordinate system are described by a function of angle values in this coordinate system. The simplest star-shape contour is a circle, centred on the origin of the polar coordinate system.
Signal generation upon a linear antenna yields a linear phase signal when a straight line is present in the image. While expecting circular contours, we associate a circular antenna with the processed image. By adapting the antenna shape to the shape of the expected contour, we aim at generating linear phase signals.

4.1 Problem setting and virtual signal generation

Our purpose is to estimate the radius of a circle, and the distortions between a closed contour and a circle that fits this contour. We propose to employ a circular antenna that permits a particular signal generation and yields a linear phase signal out of an image containing a quarter of circle. In this section, center coordinates are supposed to be known, we focus on radius estimation, center coordinate estimation is explained further. Fig. 3(a) presents a binary digital image I. The object is close to a circle with radius value r and center coordinates (l_c, m_c). Fig. 3(b) shows a sub-image extracted from the original image, such that its top left corner is the center of the circle. We associate this sub-image with a set of polar coordinates (ρ,θ), such that each pixel of the expected contour in the sub-image is characterized by the coordinates $(r+\Delta\rho,\theta)$, where $(\Delta\rho)$ is the shift between the pixel of the contour and the pixel of the circle that roughly approximates the contour and which has same coordinate θ. We seek for star-shaped contours, that is, contours that can be described by the relation: $\rho = f(\theta)$ where f is any function that maps $[0,2\pi]$ to R_+. The point with coordinate $\rho = 0$ corresponds then to the center of gravity of the contour.
Generalized Hough transform estimates the radius of concentric circles when their center is known. Its basic principle is to count the number of pixels that are located on a circle for all possible radius values. The estimated radius values correspond to the maximum number of pixels.

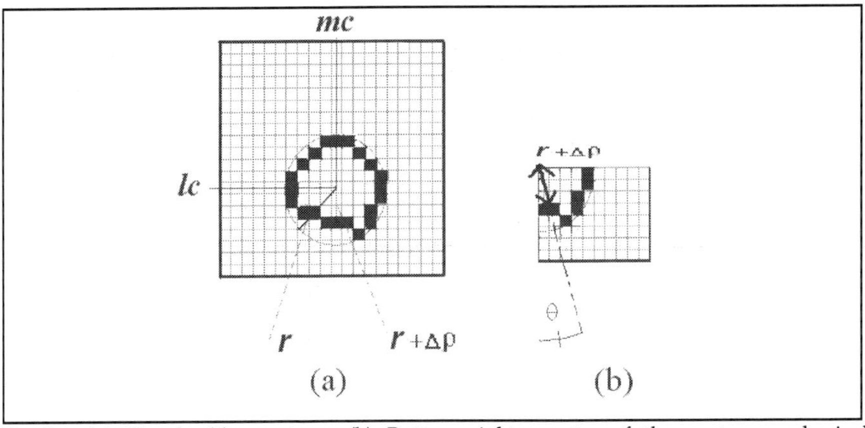

Fig. 3. (a) Circular-like contour, (b) Bottom right quarter of the contour and pixel coordinates in the polar system (ρ,θ) having its origin on the center of the circle. r is the radius of the circle. $\Delta\rho$ is the value of the shift between a pixel of the contour and the pixel of the circle having same coordinate θ

Contours which are approximately circular are supposed to be made of more than one pixel per row for some of the rows and more than one pixel per column for some columns. Therefore, we propose to associate a circular antenna with the image which leads to linear phase signals, when a circle is expected. The basic idea is to obtain a linear phase signal from an image containing a quarter of circle. To achieve this, we use a circular antenna. The phase of the signals which are virtually generated on the antenna is constant or varies linearly as a function of the sensor index. A quarter of circle with radius r and a circular antenna are represented on Fig.4. The antenna is a quarter of circle centered on the top left corner, and crossing the bottom right corner of the sub-image. Such an antenna is adapted to the sub-images containing each quarter of the expected contour (see Fig.4). In practice, the extracted sub-image is possibly rotated so that its top left corner is the estimated center. The antenna has radius R_α so that $R_\alpha = \sqrt{2}N_s$ where N_s is the number of rows or columns in the sub-image. When we consider the sub-image which includes the right bottom part of the expected contour, the following relation holds: $N_s = max(N - l_c, N - m_c)$ where l_c and m_c are the vertical and horizontal coordinates of the center of the expected contour in a cartesian set centered on the top left corner of the whole processed image (see Fig.3). Coordinates l_c and m_c are estimated by the method proposed in (Aghajan, 1995), or the one that is detailed later in this paper.
Signal generation scheme upon a circular antenna is the following: the directions adopted for signal generation are from the top left corner of the sub-image to the corresponding sensor. The antenna is composed of S sensors, so there are S signal components.

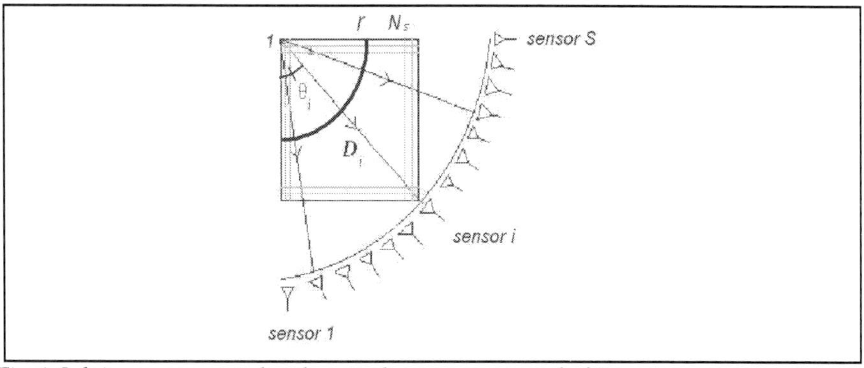

Fig. 4. Sub-image, associated with a circular array composed of S sensors

Let us consider D_i, the line that makes an angle θ_i with the vertical axis and crosses the top left corner of the sub-image. The ith component $(i=1,...,S)$ of the $\mathbf{z}$ generated out of the image reads:

$$z(i)=\sum_{\substack{l,m=1\\(l,m)\in D_i}}^{l,m=N_s} I(l,m)exp\left(-j\mu\sqrt{l^2+m^2}\right) \tag{12}$$

The integer l (resp. m) indexes the lines (resp. the columns) of the image. j stands for $\sqrt{-1}$. μ is the propagation parameter (Aghajan & Kailath, 1994). Each sensor indexed by i is associated with a line D_i having an orientation $\theta_i=\frac{(i-1)\pi/2}{S}$. In Eq. (2), the term $(l\ ,m\ )$ means that only the image pixels that belong to D_i are considered for the generation of the ith signal component. Satisfying the constraint $(l\ ,m\ )\in D_i$, that is, choosing the pixels that belong to the line with orientation θ_i, is done in two steps: let $setl$ be the set of indexes along the vertical axis, and $setm$ the set of indexes along the horizontal axis. If θ_i is less than or equal to $\pi/4$, $setl=[1:N_s]$ and $setm=\lfloor[1:N_s]tan(\theta_i)\rfloor$. If θ_i is greater than $\pi/4$, $setm=[1:N_s]$ and $setl=\lfloor[1:N_s]tan(\pi/2-\theta_i)\rfloor$. Symbol $\lfloor.\rfloor$ means integer part. The minimum number of sensors that permits a perfect characterization of any possibly distorted contour is the number of pixels that would be virtually aligned on a circle quarter having radius $\sqrt{2}N_s$. Therefore, the minimum number S of sensors is $\sqrt{2}N_s$.

4.2 Proposed method for radius and distortion estimation

In the most general case there exists more than one circle for one center. We show how several possibly close radius values can be estimated with a high-resolution method. For this, we use a variable speed propagation scheme toward circular antenna. We propose a method for the estimation of the number d of concentric circles, and the determination of each radius value. For this purpose we employ a variable speed propagation scheme (Aghajan & Kailath, 1994). We set $\mu = \alpha(i-1)$, for each sensor indexed by $i = 1,...,S$. From Eq. (12), the signal received on each sensor is:

$$z(i) = \sum_{k=1}^{d} exp(-j\alpha(i-1)r_k) + n(i), \quad i = 1,...,S \tag{13}$$

where $r_k, k = 1,...,d$ are the values of the radius of each circle, and $n(i)$ is a noise term that can appear because of the presence of outliers. All components $z(i)$ compose the observation vector $\mathbf{z}$. TLS-ESPRIT method is applied to estimate $r_k, k = 1,...,d$, the number of concentric circles d is estimated by MDL (Minimum Description Length) criterion. The estimated radius values are obtained with TLS-ESPRIT method, which also estimated straight line orientations (see section 2.2).

To retrieve the distortions between an expected star-shaped contour and a fitting circle, we work successively on each quarter of circle, and retrieve the distortions between one quarter of the initialization circle and the part of the expected contour that is located in the same quarter of the image. As an example, in Fig.3, the right bottom quarter of the considered image is represented in Fig. 3(b). The optimization method that retrieves the shift values between the fitting circle and the expected contour is the following:

A contour in the considered sub-image can be described in a set of polar coordinates by : $\{\rho(i), \theta(i), i = 1,...,S\}$. We aim at estimating the S unknowns $\rho(i), i = 1,...,S$ that characterize the contour, forming a vector:

$$\rho = [\rho(1), \rho(2),..., \rho(S)]^T \tag{14}$$

The basic idea is to consider that ρ can be expressed as: $\rho = [r + \Delta\rho(1), r + \Delta\rho(2),..., r + \Delta\rho(S)]^T$ (see Fig. 3), where r is the radius of a circle that approximates the expected contour.

5. Linear and circular array for signal generation: summary

In this section, we present the outline of the reviewed methods for contour estimation.

An outline of the proposed nearly rectilinear distorted contour estimation method is given as follows:

- Signal generation with constant parameter on linear antenna, using Eq. 1;
- Estimation of the parameters of the straight lines that fit each distorted contour (see subsection 3.1);
- Distortion estimation for a given curve, estimation of $\mathbf{x}$, applying gradient algorithm to minimize a least squares criterion (see Eq. 11).

The proposed method for star-shaped contour estimation is summarized as follows:

- Variable speed propagation scheme upon the proposed circular antenna : Estimation of the number of circles by MDL criterion, estimation of the radius of each circle fitting any expected contour (see Eqs. (12) and (13) or the axial parameters of the ellipse;
- Estimation of the radial distortions, in polar coordinate system, between any expected contour and the circle or ellipse that fits this contour. Either the

gradient method or the combination of DIRECT and spline interpolation may be used to minimize a least-squares criterion.

Table 1 provides the steps of the algorithms which perform nearly straight and nearly circular contour retrieval. Table 1 provides the directions for signal generation, the parameters which characterize the initialization contour and the output of the optimization algorithm.

	Straight	Circular
Direction for signal generation	row i	D_i
Initialization parameters	θ, x_0	r, center
Pixel shift	$\Delta x(i)$	$\Delta \rho(i)$

Table 1. Nearly straight and nearly circular distorted contour estimation: algorithm steps.

The current section presented a method for the estimation of the radius of concentric circles with *a priori* knowledge of the center. In the next section we explain how to estimate the center of groups of concentric circles.

6. Linear antenna for the estimation of circle center parameters

Usually, an image contains several circles which are possibly not concentric and have different radii (see Fig. 5). To apply the proposed method, the center coordinates for each feature are required. To estimate these coordinates, we generate a signal with constant propagation parameter upon the image left and top sides. The lth signal component, generated from the lth row, reads: $z_{lin}(l) = \sum_{m=1}^{N} I(l,m)exp(-j\mu m)$ where μ is the propagation parameter. The non-zero sections of the signals, as seen at the left and top sides of the image, indicate the presence of features. Each non-zero section width in the left (respectively the top) side signal gives the height (respectively the width) of the corresponding expected feature. The middle of each non-zero section in the left (respectively the top) side signal yields the value of the center l_c (respectively m_c) coordinate of each feature.

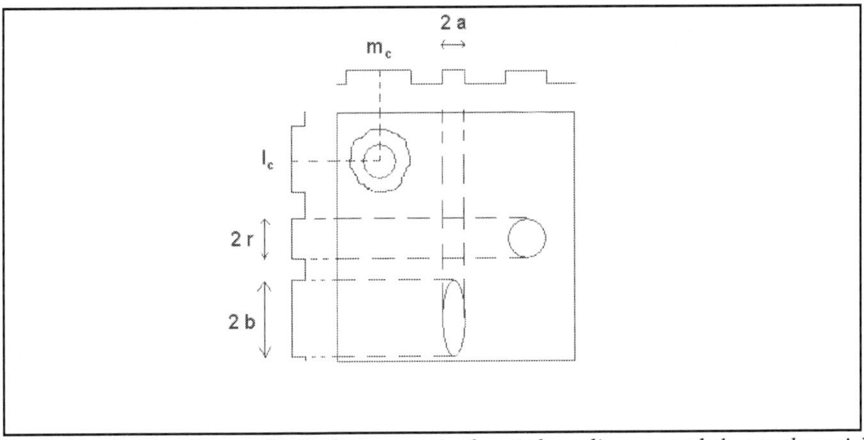

Fig. 5. Nearly circular or elliptic features. r is the circle radius, a and b are the axial parameters of the ellipse.

7. Combination of linear and circular antenna for intersecting circle retrieval

We propose an algorithm which is based on the following remarks about the generated signals. Signal generation on linear antenna yields a signal with the following characteristics: The maximum amplitude values of the generated signal correspond to the lines with maximum number of pixels, that is, where the tangent to the circle is either vertical or horizontal. The signal peak values are associated alternatively with one circle and another. Signal generation on circular antenna yields a signal with the following characteristics: If the antenna is centered on the same center as a quarter of circle which is present in the image, the signal which is generated on the antenna exhibits linear phase properties (Marot & Bourennane, 2007b)

We propose a method that combines linear and circular antenna to retrieve intersecting circles. We exemplify this method with an image containing two circles (see Fig. 6(a)). It falls into the following parts:

- Generate a signal on a linear antenna placed at the left and bottom sides of the image;
- Associate signal peak 1 (P1) with signal peak 3 (P3), signal peak 2 (P2) with signal peak 4 (P4);
- Diameter 1 is given by the distance P1-P3, diameter 2 is given by the distance P2-P4;
- Center 1 is given by the mid point between P1 and P3, center 2 is given by the mid point between P2 and P4;
- Associate the circular antenna with a sub-image containing center 1 and P1, perform signal generation. Check the phase linearity of the generated signal;
- Associate the circular antenna with a sub-image containing center 2 and P4, perform signal generation. Check the linearity of the generated signal.

Fig. 6(a) presents, in particular, the square sub-image to which we associate a circular antenna. Fig. 6(b) and (c) shows the generated signals.

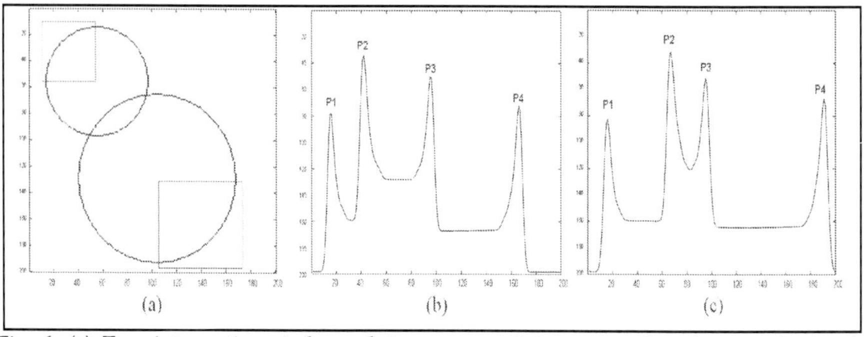

Fig. 6. (a) Two intersecting circles, sub-images containing center 1 and center 2; signals generated on (b) the bottom of the image, (c) the left side of the image.

8. Results

The proposed star-shaped contour detection method is first applied to a very distorted circle, and the results obtained are compared with those of the active contour method GVF (gradient vector flow) (Xu & Prince, 1997). The proposed multiple circle detection method is applied to several application cases: robotic vision, melanoma segmentation, circle detection in omnidirectional vision images, blood cell segmentation. In the proposed applications, we use GVF as a comparative method or as a complement to the proposed circle estimation method. The values of the parameters for GVF method (Xianghua & Mirmehdi, 2004) are the following. For the computation of the edge map: 100 iterations; $\mu_{GVF} = 0,09$ (regularization coefficient); for the snakes deformation: 100 initialization points and 50 iterations; $\alpha_{GVF} = 0.2$ (tension); $\beta_{GVF} = 0.03$ (rigidity); $\gamma_{GVF} = 1$ (regularization coefficient); $\kappa_{GVF} = 0.8$ (gradient strength coefficient). The value of the propagation parameter values for signal generation in the proposed method are $\mu = 1$ and $\alpha = 5\ 10^{-3}$.

8.1 Hand-made images

In this subsection we first remind a major result obtained with star-shaped contours, and then proposed results obtained on intersecting circle retrieval.

8.1.1 Very distorded circles

The abilities of the proposed method to retrieve highly concave contours are illustrated in Figs. 7 and 8. We provide the mean error value over the pixel radial coordinate $M\,E_{\rho}$. We notice that this value is higher when GVF is used, as when the proposed method is used.

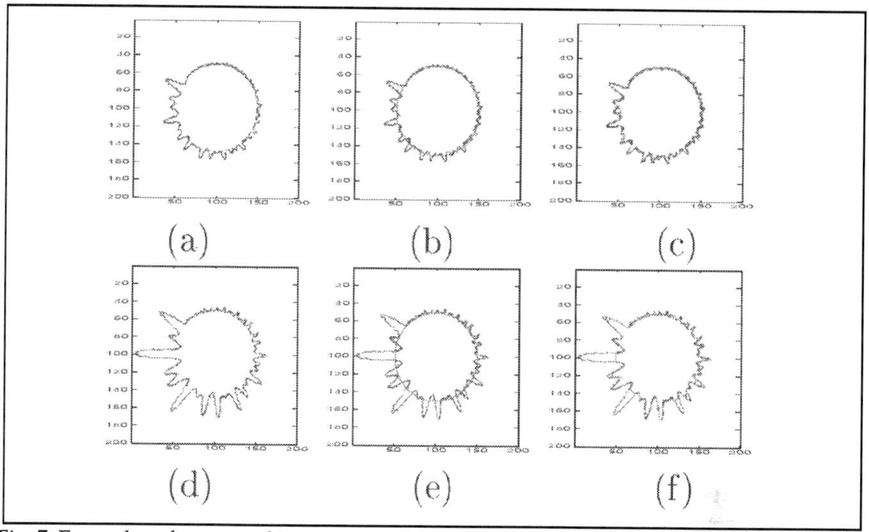

Fig. 7. Examples of processed images containing the less (a) and the most (d) distorted circles, initialization (b,e) and estimation using GVF method (c,f). ME_{ρ} =1.4 pixel and 4.1 pixels.

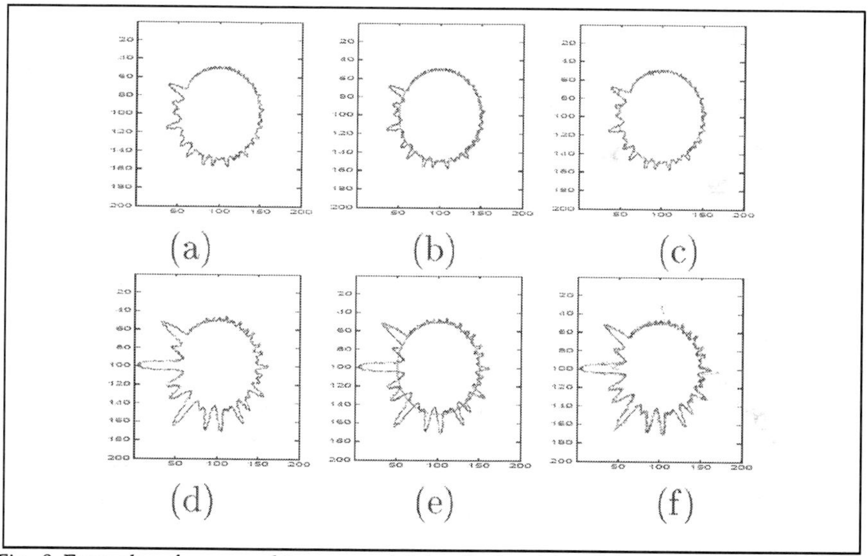

Fig. 8. Examples of processed images containing the less (a) and the most (d) distorted circles, initialization (b,e) and estimation using GVF method (c,f). ME_{ρ} =1.4 pixel and 2.7 pixels.

8.1.2 Intersecting circles

We first exemplify the proposed method for intersecting circle retrieval on the image of Fig. 9(a), from which we obtain the results of Fig. 9(b) and (c), which presents the signal generated on both sides of the image. The signal obtained on left side exhibits only two peak values, because the radius values are very close to each other. Therefore signal generation on linear antenna provides a rough estimate of each radius, and signal generation on circular antenna refines the estimation of both values.

The center coordinates of circles 1 and 2 are estimated as $\{l_{c1}, m_{c1}\} = \{83,41\}$ and $\{l_{c2}, m_{c2}\} = \{83,84\}$. Radius 1 is estimated as $r_1 = 24$, radius 2 is estimated as $r_2 = 30$.

The computationally dominant operations while running the algorithm are signal generation on linear and circular antenna. For this image and with the considered parameter values, the computational load required for each step is as follows:

- signal generation on linear antenna: 3.8 10^{-2} sec.;
- signal generation on circular antenna: 7.8 10^{-1} sec.

So the whole method lasts 8.1 10^{-1} sec. For sake of comparison, generalized Hough transform with prior knowledge of the radius of the expected circles lasts 2.6 sec. for each circle. Then it is 6.4 times longer than the proposed method.

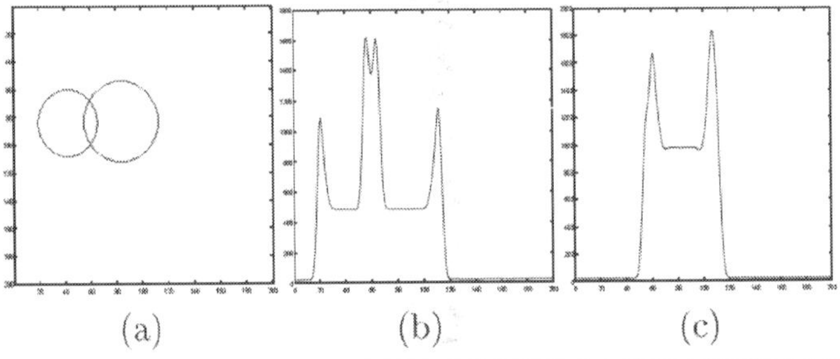

Fig. 9. (a) Processed image; signals generated on: (b) the bottom of the image; (c) the left side of the image.

The case presented in Figs. 10(a) and 10(b), (c) illustrates the need for the last two steps of the proposed algorithm. Indeed the signals generated on linear antenna present the same peak coordinates as the signals generated from the image of Fig. 7(a). However, if a subimage is selected, and the center of the circular antenna is placed such as in Fig. 7, the phase of the generated signal is not linear. Therefore, for Fig. 10(a), we take as the diameter values the distances P1-P4 and P2-P3. The center coordinates of circles 1 and 2 are estimated as $\{l_{c1}, m_{c1}\} = \{68,55\}$ and $\{l_{c2}, m_{c2}\} = \{104,99\}$. Radius of circle 1 is estimated as $r_1 = 87$, radius of circle 2 is estimated as $r_2 = 27$.

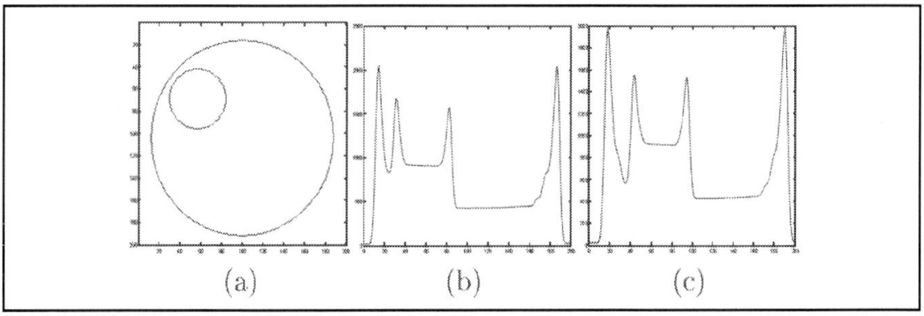

Fig. 10. (a) Processed image; signals generated on: (b) the bottom of the image; (c) the left side of the image.

Here was exemplified the ability of the circular antenna to distinguish between ambiguous cases.

Fig. 11 shows the results obtained with a noisy image. The percentage of noisy pixels is 15%, and noise grey level values follow Gaussian distribution with mean 0.1 and standard deviation 0.005. The presence of noisy pixels induces fluctuations in the generated signals, Figs. 11(b) and 11(c) show that the peaks that permit to characterize the expected circles are still dominant over the unexpected fluctuations. So the results obtained do not suffer the influence of noise pixels. The center coordinates of circles 1 and 2 are estimated as $\{l_{c1}, m_{c1}\} = \{131,88\}$ and $\{l_{c2}, m_{c2}\} = \{53,144\}$. Radius of circle 1 is estimated as $r_1 = 67$, radius of circle 2 is estimated as $r_2 = 40$.

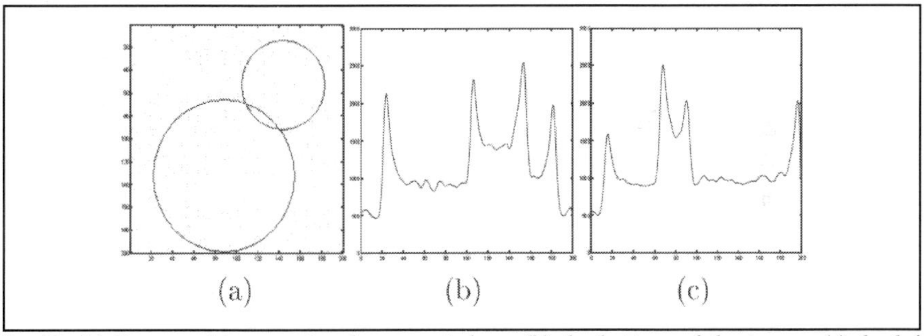

Fig. 11. (a) Processed image; signals generated on: (b) the bottom of the image; (c) the left side of the image.

8.2 Robotic vision

We now consider a real-world image coming from biometrics (see Fig. 12(a)). This image contains a contour with high concavity.

Fig. 12(b) gives the result of the initialization of our optimization method. Fig. 12(c) shows that GVF fails to retrieve the furthest sections of the narrow and deep concavities of the hand, that correspond to the two right-most fingers. Fig. 12(d) shows that the proposed method for distortion estimation manages to retrieve all pixel shift values, even the elevated ones. We also noticed that the computational time which is required to obtain this result with GVF is 25-fold higher than the computational time required by the proposed method: 400 sec. are required by GVF, and 16 sec. are required by our method.

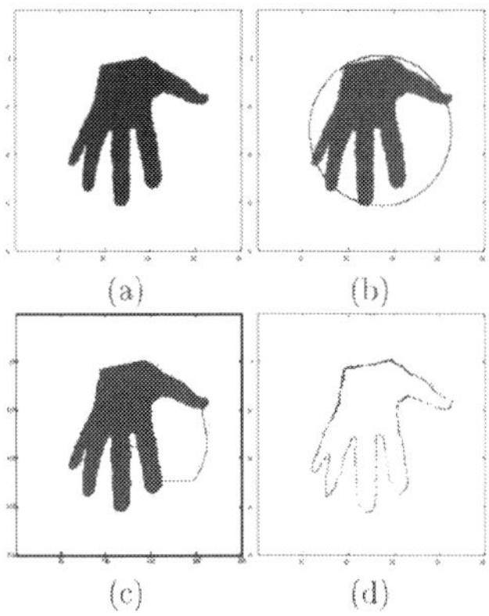

Fig. 12. Hand localization: (a) Processed image, (b) initialization, (c) final result obtained with GVF, (d) final result obtained with the proposed method

8.3 Omnidirectionnal images

Figures 13(a), (b), (c) show three omnidirectional images, obtained with a hyperbolic mirror. For some images it is useful to remove to parasite circles due to the acquisition system.
The experiment illustrated on Fig. 14 is an example of characterization of two circles that overlap. Figures 14(a), (b), (c), show for one image the gradient image, the threshold image, the signal generated on the bottom side of the image (Marot & Bourennane, 2008). The samples for which the generated signal takes none zero values (see Fig. 14(c)) delimitate the external circle of Fig. 13(a).
The diameter of the big circle is 485 pixels and the horizontal coordinate of its center is 252 pixels. This permits first to erase the external circle, secondly to characterize the intern circle by the same method.

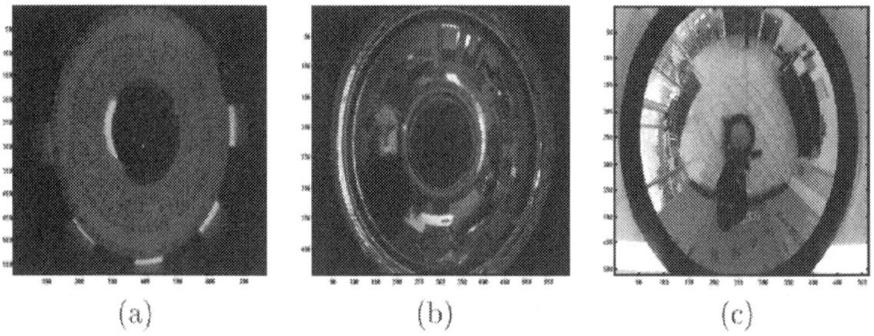

Fig. 13. Omnidirectional images

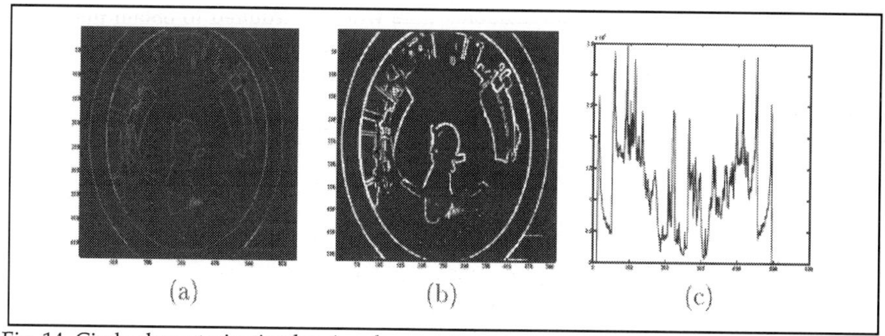

Fig. 14. Circle characterization by signal generation

8.4 Cell segmentation

Fig. 15 presents the case of a real-world image. It contains one red cell and one white cell. Our goal in this application is to detect both cells. The minimum value in the signal generated on bottom side of the image corresponds to the frontier between both cells. The width of the non-zero sections on both sides of the minimum value is the diameter of each cell. Each peak value in each generated signal provides one center coordinate.

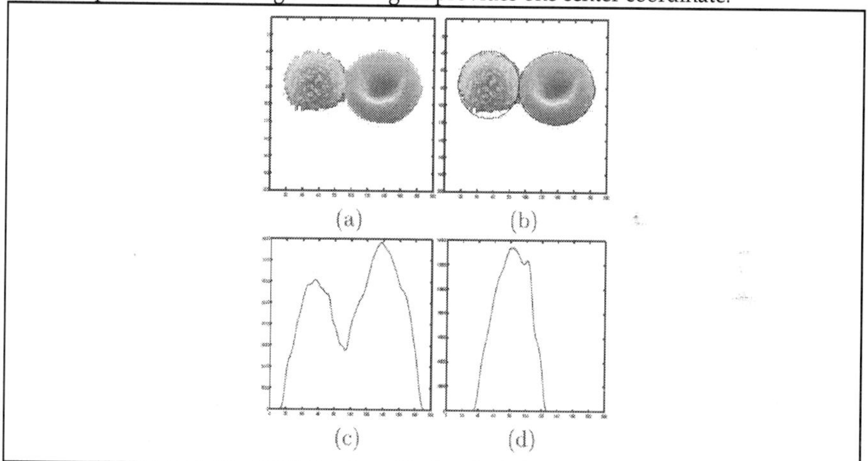

Fig. 15. Blood cells: (a) processed image; (b) superposition processed image and result; signals generated on: (c) the bottom of the image; (d) the left side of the image.

8.5 Melanoma segmentation

Fig. 16 concerns quantitative analysis in a medical application. More precisely, the purpose of the experiment is to detect the frontier of a melanoma. The melanoma was chosen randomly out of a database (Stolz et al., 2003).

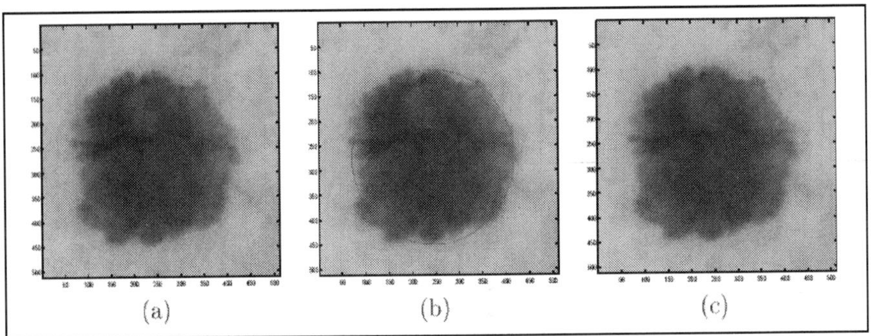

Fig. 16. Melanoma segmentation: (a) processed image, (b) elliptic approximation by the proposed array processing method, (c) result obtained by GVF.

The proposed array processing method detects a circular approximation of the melanoma borders (Marot & Bourennane, 2007b; Marot & Bourennane, 2008) (see Fig 16(b)). A few iterations of GVF method (Xu & Prince, 1997) yield the contour of the melanoma (see Fig 16(c)). Such a method can be used to control automatically the evolution of the surface of the melanoma.

9. Conclusion

This chapter deals with contour retrieval in images. We review the formulation and resolution of rectilinear or circular contour estimation. The estimation of the parameters of rectilinear or circular contours is transposed as a source localization problem in array processing. We presented the principles of SLIDE algorithm for the estimation of rectilinear contours based on signal generation upon a linear antenna. In this frame, high-resolution methods of array processing retrieve possibly close parameters of straight lines in images. We explained the principles of signal generation upon a virtual circular antenna. The circular antenna permits to generate linear phase signals out of an image containing circular features. The same signal models as for straight line estimation are obtained, so high-resolution methods of array processing retrieve possibly close radius values of concentric circles. For the estimation of distorted contours, we adopted the same conventions for signal generation, that is, either a linear or a circular antenna. For the first time, in this book chapter, we propose an intersecting circle retrieval method, based on array processing algorithms. Signal generation on a linear antenna yields the center coordinates and radii of all circles. Circular antenna refines the estimation of the radii and distinguishes ambiguous cases. The proposed star-shaped contour estimation method retrieves contours with high concavities, thus providing a solution to Snakes based methods. The proposed multiple circle estimation method retrieves intersecting circles, thus providing a solution to levelset-type methods. We exemplified the proposed method on hand-made and real-world images. Further topics to be studied are the robustness to various types of noise, such as correlated Gaussian noise.

10. References

Abed-Meraim, K. & Hua, Y. (1997). Multi-line fitting and straight edge detection using polynomial phase signals, *ASILOMAR31*, Vol. 2, pp. 1720-1724, 1997.

Aghajan, H. K. & Kailath, T. (1992). A subspace Fitting Approach to Super Resolution Multi-Line Fitting and Straight Edge Detection, *Proc. of IEEE ICASSP*, vol. 3, pp. 121-124, 1992.

Aghajan, H. K. & Kailath, T. (1993a). Sensor array processing techniques for super resolution multi-line-fitting and straight edge detection, *IEEE Trans. on IP*, Vol. 2, No. 4, pp. 454-465, Oct. 1993.

Aghajan, H.K. & Kailath, T. (1993b). SLIDE: subspace-based line detection, *IEEE int. conf. ASSP*, Vol. 5, pp. 89 - 92, April 27-30, 1993.

Aghajan, H. & Kailath, T. (1995). SLIDE: Subspace-based Line detection, *IEEE Trans. on PAMI*, 16(11):1057-1073, Nov. 1994.

Aghajan, H.K. (1995). Subspace Techniques for Image Understanding and Computer Vision, PhD Thesis, Stanford University, 1995

Bourennane, S. & Marot, J. (2005). Line parameters estimation by array processing methods, *IEEE ICASSP*, Vol. 4, pp. 965-968, Philadelphie, Mar. 2005.

Bourennane, S. & Marot, J. (2006a). Estimation of straight line offsets by a high resolution method, *IEE proceedings - Vision, Image and Signal Processing*, Vol. 153, issue 2, pp. 224-229, 6 April 2006.

Bourennane, S. & Marot, J. (2006b). Optimization and interpolation for distorted contour estimation, *IEEE-ICASSP*, vol. 2, pp. 717-720, Toulouse, France, April 2006.

Bourennane, S. & Marot, J. (2006c). Contour estimation by array processing methods, *Applied signal processing*, article ID 95634, 15 pages, 2006.

Bourennane, S.; Fossati, C. & Marot, J., (2008). About noneigenvector source localization methods *EURASIP Journal on Advances in Signal Processing* Vol. 2008, Article ID 480835, 13 pages doi:10.1155/2008/480835

Brigger, P. ; Hoeg, J. & Unser, M. (2000). B-Spline Snakes: A Flexible Tool for Parametric Contour Detection, *IEEE Trans. on IP*, vol. 9, No. 9, pp. 1484-96, 2000.

Cheng, J. & Foo, S. W. (2006). Dynamic directional gradient vector flow for snakes, *IEEE Trans. on Image Processing*, vol. 15, no. 6, pp.1563-1571, June 2006.

Connell, S. D. & Jain, A. K. (2001). Template-based online character recognition, *Pattern Rec.*, vol. 34, no 1, pp: 1-14, 2001.

Gander, W.; Golub, G.H. & Strebel, R. (1994). Least-squares fitting of circles and ellipses , *BIT*, n. 34, pp. 558-578, 1994.

Halder, B. ; Aghajan, H. & T. Kailath (1995). Propagation diversity enhancement to the subspace-based line detection algorithm, *Proc. SPIE Nonlinear Image Processing VI* Vol. 2424, p. 320-328, pp. 320-328, March 1995.

Jones, D.R. ; Pertunen, C.D. & Stuckman, B.E. (1993). Lipschitzian optimization without the Lipschitz constant, *Journal of Optimization and Applications*, vol. 79, no. 157-181, 1993.

Karoui, I.; Fablet, R.; Boucher, J.-M. & Augustin, J.-M. (2006). Region-based segmentation using texture statistics and level-set methods, *IEEE ICASSP*, pp. 693-696, 2006.

Kass, M.; Witkin, A. & Terzopoulos, D. (1998). Snakes: Active Contour Model, *Int. J. of Comp. Vis.*, pp.321-331, 1988

Kiryati, N. & Bruckstein, A.M. (1992). What's in a set of points? [straight line fitting], *IEEE Trans. on PAMI*, Vol. 14, No. 4, pp.496-500, April 1992.

Marot, J. & Bourennane, S. (2007a). Array processing and fast Optimization Algorithms for Distorted Circular Contour Retrieval , *EURASIP Journal on Advances in Signal Processing*, Vol. 2007, article ID 57354, 13 pages, 2007.

Marot, J. & Bourennane, S. (2007b). Subspace-Based and DIRECT Algorithms for Distorted Circular Contour Estimation, *IEEE Trans. On Image Processing*, Vol. 16, No. 9, pp. 2369-2378, sept. 2007.

Marot, J., Bourennane, S. & Adel, M. (2007). Array processing approach for object segmentation in images, *IEEE ICASSP'07*, Vol. 1, pp. 621-24, April 2007.

Marot, J. & Bourennane, S. (2008). Array processing for intersecting circle retrieval, *EUSIPCO'08*, 5 pages, Aug. 2008.

Marot, J.; Fossati, C.; & Bourennane, S. (2008) Fast subspace-based source localization methods *IEEE-Sensor array multichannel signal processing workshop*, Darmstadt Germany, 07/ 2008

Osher, S. & Sethian, J. (1998). Fronts propagating with curvature-dependent speed: algorithms based on Hamilton-Jacobi formulations, *J. Comput. Phys.* , Vol. 79, pp. 12-49, 1988.

Paragios, N. & Deriche, R. (2002). Geodesic Active Regions and Level Set Methods for Supervised Texture Segmentation, *Int'l Journal of Computer Vision*, Vol. 46, No 3, pp. 223-247, Feb. 2002.

Pillai, S.U. & Kwon, B.H. (1989). Forward/backward spatial smoothing techniques for coherent signal identification, *Proc. of IEEE trans. on ASSP*, vol. 37 (1), pp. 8-15, 1989.

Precioso, F. ; Barlaud, M. ; Blu, T. & Unser, M. (2005). Robust Real-Time Segmentation of Images and Videos Using a Smooth-Spline Snake-Based Algorithm, *IEEE Trans. on IP*, Vol. 14, No. 7, pp. 910-924, July 2005.

Roy, R. & Kailath, T. (1989). ESPRIT: Estimation of signal parameters via rotational invariance techniques, *IEEE Trans. on ASSP*, vol. 37, no. 7, pp. 984-995, 1989.

Sheinvald, J. & Kiryati,N. (1997). On the Magic of SLIDE, *Machine Vision and Applications*, Vol. 9, pp. 251-261, 1997.

Stolz, W. ; Horsch, A. ; Pompl, R. ; Abmayr, W. ; Landthaler, M. (2003) Datensatz Dermatology Skin Surface Microscopy Melanocytic Lesions 749, Version 1.0, October 2003 (D-SSM-ML-749 V1.0).

Tufts, D.W. & Kumaresan, R. (1982). Estimation of frequencies of multiple sinusoids: making linear prediction perform like maximum likelihood, *Proc. IEEE*, vol. 70, pp. 975-989, sept. 1982.

Unser, M. ; Aldroubi, A. & Eden, M. (1993). B-spline signal processing: Part I-theory; part II-efficient design and applications, *IEEE Trans. on SP*, Vol. 41, No. 2, pp. 821-848, Feb. 1993.

Xianghua X. & Mirmehdi, M. (2004). RAGS: region-aided geometric snake , *IEEE Trans. IP*, Vol. 13, no. 5, pp: 640-652, May 2004.

Xu, C. & Prince, J.L. (1997). Gradient vector flow: a new external force for snakes, *Proceeding of IEEE Computer Society Conference on Computer -Vision and Pattern Recognition* pp. 66-71, Jun. 1997.

Zhu, S. C. & Yuille, A. (1996). Region Competition: Unifying Snakes, Region Growing, and Bayes /MDL for Multiband Image Segmentation, *IEEE Trans. on PAMI*, Vol. 18, No. 9, pp. 884-900, Sept. 1996.

3

Locally Adaptive Resolution (LAR) codec

François Pasteau, Marie Babel, Olivier Déforges,
Clément Strauss and Laurent Bédat
IETR - INSA Rennes
France

1. Introduction

Despite many drawbacks and limitations, JPEG is still the most commonly-used compression format in the world. JPEG2000 overcomes this old technique, particularly at low bit rates, but at the expense of a significant increase in complexity. A new compression format called JPEG XR has recently been developed with minimum complexity. However, it does not outperform JPEG 2000 in most cases (De Simone et al., 2007) and does not offer many new functionalities (Srinivasan et al., 2007). Therefore, the JPEG normalization group has recently proposed a call for proposals on JPEG-AIC (Advanced Image Coding) in order to look for new solutions for still image coding techniques (JPEG normalization group, 2007). Its requirements reflect the earlier ideas of Amir Said (Said & Pearlman, 1993) for a good image coder i.e. compression efficiency, scalability, good quality at low bit rates, flexibility and adaptability, rate and quality control, algorithm unicity (with/without losses), reduced complexity, error robustness (for instance in wireless transmission) and region of interest decoding at decoder level. Additional functionalities such as image processing at region level, both in the coder or the decoder, could be explored. One other important feature is complexity, in particular for embedded systems such as cameras or mobile phones, in which power consumption restriction is more critical nowadays than memory constraints. The reconfiguration ability of the coding sub-system can then be used to dynamically adapt the complexity to the current consumption and processing power of the system. In this context, we proposed the Locally Adaptive Resolution (LAR) codec as a contribution to the relative call for technologies, since it suited all previous functionalities. The related method is a coding solution that simultaneously proposes a relevant representation of the image. This property is exploited through various complementary coding schemes in order to design a highly scalable encoder.
The LAR method was initially introduced for lossy image coding. This efficient and original image compression solution relies on a content-based system driven by a specific quadtree representation, based on the assumption that an image can be represented as layers of basic information and local texture. Multiresolution versions of this codec have shown their efficiency, from low bit rates up to lossless compressed images. An original hierarchical self-extracting region representation has also been elaborated, with a segmentation process realized at both coder and decoder, leading to a free segmentation map. The map can then be further exploited for color region encoding or image handling at region level. Moreover,

the inherent structure of the LAR codec can be used for advanced functionalities such as content securization purposes. In particular, dedicated Unequal Error Protection systems have been produced and tested for transmission over the Internet or wireless channels. Hierarchical selective encryption techniques have been adapted to our coding scheme. A data hiding system based on the LAR multiresolution description allows efficient content protection. Thanks to the modularity of our coding scheme, complexity can be adjusted to address various embedded systems. For example, a basic version of the LAR coder has been implemented onto an FPGA platform while respecting real-time constraints. Pyramidal LAR solution and hierarchical segmentation processes have also been prototyped on heterogeneous DSP architectures.
Rather than providing a comprehensive overview that covers all technical aspects of the LAR codec design, this chapter focuses on a few representative features of its core coding technology. Firstly, profiles will be introduced. Then functionalities such as scalability, hierarchical region representation, adjustable profiles and complexity, lossy and lossless coding will be explained. Services such as cryptography, steganography, error resilience, hierarchical securized processes will be described. Finally application domains such as natural images, medical images and art images will be described.
An extension of the LAR codec is being developed with a view to video coding , but this chapter will not describe it and will stay focused on still image coding.

2. Design characteristics and profiles

The LAR codec tries to combine both efficient compression in a lossy or lossless context and advanced functionalities and services as described before. To provide a codec which is adaptable and flexible in terms of complexity and functionality, various tools have been developed. These tools are then combined in three profiles in order to address such flexibility features (Fig. 1).

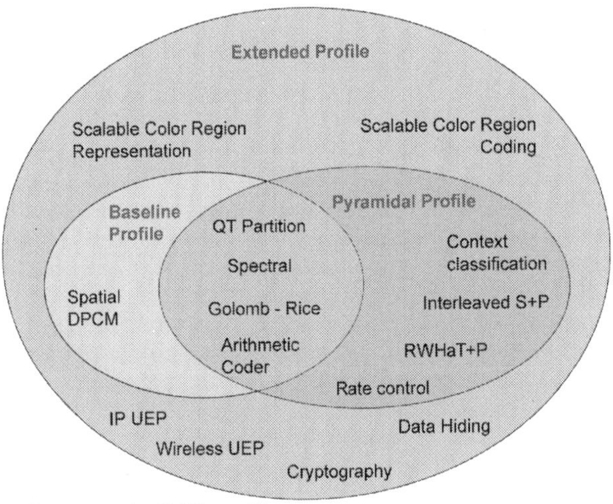

Fig. 1. Specific coding parts for LAR profiles

Therefore, each profile corresponds to different functionalities and different complexities:

- Baseline profile: low complexity, low functionality,
- Pyramidal profile: higher complexity but new functionalities such as scalability and rate control,
- Extended profile: higher complexity, but also includesscalable color region representation and coding, cryptography, data hiding, unequal error protection.

3. Technical features

3.1 Characteristics of the LAR encoding method

The LAR (Locally Adaptive Resolution) codec relies on a two-layer system (Fig. 2) (Déforges et al., 2007). The first layer, called Flat coder, leads to the construction of a low bit-rate version of the image with good visual properties. The second layer deals with the texture. It is encoded through a texture coder, to achieve visual quality enhancement at medium/high bit-rates. Therefore, the method offers a natural basic SNR scalability.

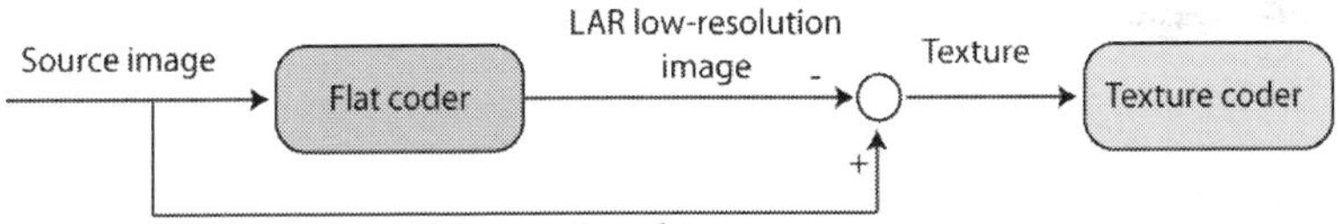

Fig. 2. General scheme of a two-layer LAR coder

The basic idea is that local resolution, in other words pixel size, can depend on local activity, estimated through a local morphological gradient. This image decomposition into two sets of data is thus performed in accordance with a specific quadtree data structure encoded in the Flat coding stage. Thanks to this type of block decomposition, their size implicitly gives the nature of the given block i.e. the smallest blocks are located at the edges whereas large blocks map homogeneous areas. Then, the main feature of the FLAT coder consists of preserving contours while smoothing homogeneous parts of the image (Fig. 3).

This quadtree partition is the key system of the LAR codec. Consequently, this coding part is required whatever the chosen profile.

Fig. 3. Flat coding of "Lena" picture without post processing

3.2 Baseline Profile

The baseline profile is dedicated to low bit-rate encoding (Déforges et al., 2007). As previously mentioned, the quadtree partition builds a variable block size representation of the image and the LAR low-resolution image is obtained when filling each block by its mean luminance value. Moreover, in a lossy context, this semantic information controls a quantization of the luminance. Large blocks require fine quantization (in uniform areas, human vision is highly sensitive to brightness variations) while coarse quantization (low sensitivity) is sufficient for small blocks. Block values are encoded through a DPCM scheme, adapted to our block representation.
The flat LAR coder is clearly dedicated to low bit-rate image coding. To obtain higher image quality, the texture (whole error image) can be encoded through the spectral coder (second layer of the LAR coding scheme) which uses a DCT adaptive block size approach. In this case, both the size and the DC components are provided by the flat coder. The use of adapted block size naturally allows for a semantic scalable encoding process. For example, edge enhancement can be achieved by only transmitting the AC coefficients of small blocks. Further refinements can be envisaged by progressively sending larger block information.
With regard to the entropy coder, we simply adapted the classical Golomb-Rice coder for low complex applications, and the arithmetic coder for better compression results.

3.3 Pyramidal Profile

To both increase scalability capacity and address lossless compression, we have proposed multiresolution extensions of the basic LAR called Interleaved S+P (Babel et al., 2005) and RWHaT+P (Déforges et al., 2005). The overall approach used in these two techniques is identical; the only difference lies in the decomposition step. To fit the Quadtree partition, dyadic decomposition is carried out. The first and second layers of the basic LAR are replaced by two successive pyramidal decomposition processes. However the image representation content is preserved. The first decomposition reconstructs the low-resolution image (block image) while the second one processes local texture information (Fig. 2). These methods provide both increasing scalability and an efficient lossy to lossless compression solution.

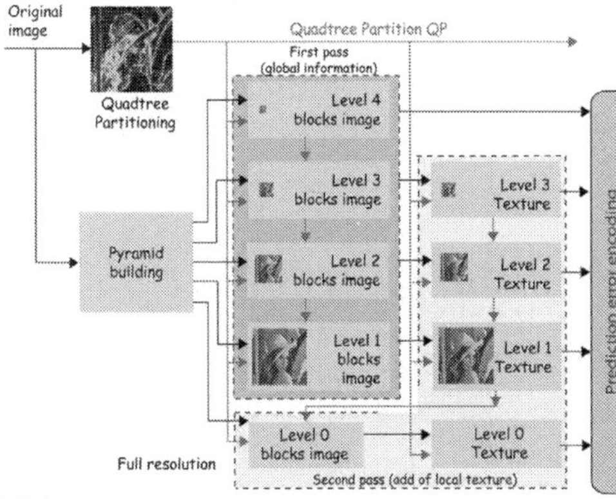

Fig. 4. LAR pyramidal decomposition

In the pyramidal profile, we use mainly the arithmetic coding scheme for prediction error encoding. The original structure of the LAR codec automatically produces context modelling, reducing zeroth order entropy cost. By adding specific inter-classification methods, the compression efficiency can be greatly increased (Pasteau et al.,2008);(Déforges et al., 2008).

3.4 Hierarchical region representation and coding - Extended Profile

For color images, we have designed an original hierarchical region-based representation technique adapted to the LAR coding method. An initial solution has already been proposed in (Déforges et al., 2007). To avoid the prohibitive cost of region shape descriptions, the most suitable solution consists of performing the segmentation directly, in both the coder and decoder, using only a low bit-rate compressed image resulting from the flat coder (or first partial pyramidal decomposition). Natural extensions of this particular process have also made it possible to address medium and high quality encoding and the region-level encoding of chromatic images. Another direct application for self-extracting region representation is found in a coding scheme with local enhancement in Regions Of Interest (ROI). Current work is aimed at providing a fully multiresolution version of our segmentation process. Indeed, this region representation can be connected to the pyramidal decomposition in order to build a highly scalable compression solution.
The extended profile also proposes the use of dedicated steganography and cryptography processes, which will be presented in the next sections.
To sum up, the interoperability of coding and representation operations leads to an interactive coding tool. The main features of the LAR coding parts are depicted on Fig. 5.

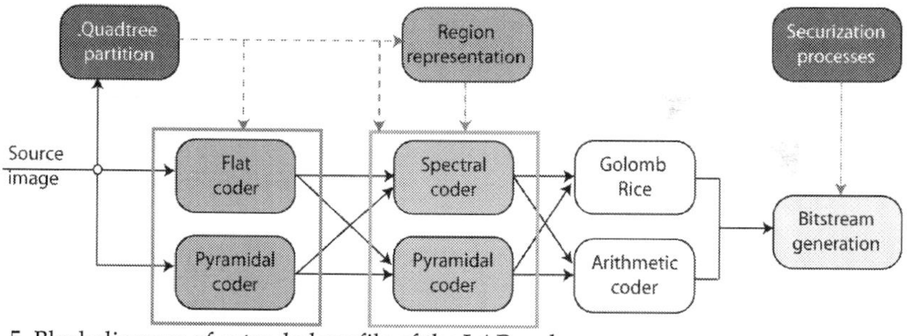

Fig. 5. Block diagram of extended profile of the LAR coder

4. Functionalities

4.1 Scalable lossy to lossless compression

The pyramidal description of the images resulting from Interleaved S+P or RWHaT+P encoding provides various scalability levels. The conditional decomposition (the constraint of two successive descent processes by the initial quadtree partition of the image) provides a highly scalable representation in terms of both resolution and quality.
This scalable solution allows compression from lossy up to lossless configuration. The pyramidal profile codec has been tested and has shown its efficiency on natural images as

depicted on Fig. 6 and Table 1, as well as medical images (Babel et al., 2008) and high resolution art images (Babel et al., 2007).

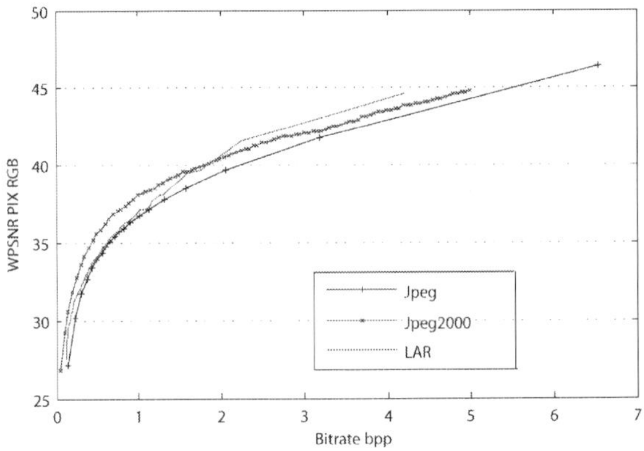

Fig. 6. Objective comparisons of Jpeg, Jpeg2000 and LAR Interleaved S+P codec for WPSNR PIX RGB metric (De Simone et al., 2008) on the lena image

Image	RGB	YDbDr	JPEG 2000
Lena	13.21 bpp	13.22 bpp	13.67 bpp
Mandrill	17.98 bpp	17.99 bpp	18.18 bpp
Pimento	14.60 bpp	14.87 bpp	14.92 bpp
Fruit	10.42 bpp	10.46 bpp	9.58 bpp

Table 1. JPEG 2000 / LAR coder comparison of color lossless compression of natural images with different color spaces.

4.2 Region level handling

Through the definition of a Region of Interest (ROI), images can be lossly compressed overall and losslessly encoded locally as shown on Fig. 7. Combined with a progressive encoding scheme, region scalability allows faster access to significant data. The LAR scheme enables more flexible solutions in terms of ROI shape and size. Indeed, an ROI can be simply described at both the coder and decoder as a set of blocks resulting from the quadtree partition. As the ROI is built from the variable block size representation, its enhancement (texture coding) is straightforward - it merely requires execution of the Interleaved S+P or RWHaT codec for the validated blocks, i.e. ROI internal blocks. Unlike traditional compression techniques, the LAR low resolution image does not introduce strong distortions on the ROI contours. Such distortion usually makes the image too unreliable to be used (Babel et al., 2007); (Babel et al., 2003).

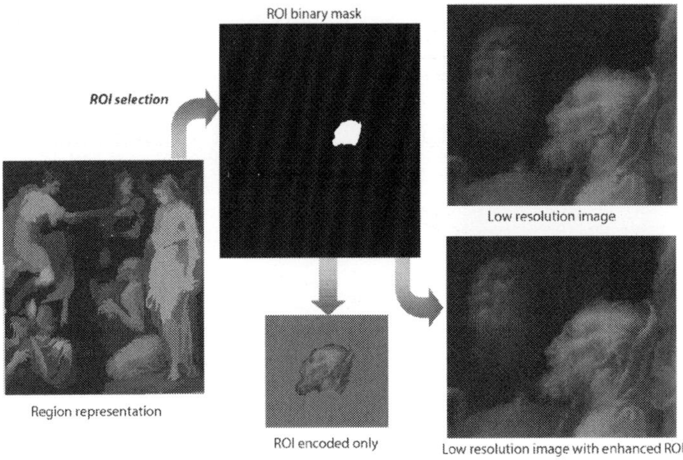

Fig. 7. ROI enhancement scheme of LAR codec

4.3 Adjustable complexity

The modularity of our scheme produces a new level of scalability in terms of complexity, closely related to the chosen profile. The IETR laboratory also aims to provide automatic solutions of fast prototyping onto heterogeneous architecture (DSPs, FPGAs), using Algorithm Architecture Matching methodology. Consequently, although the LAR codec has been developed on PCs, we can easily implement various LAR versions on embedded systems.

Previous work focused on fast development and the implementation of the distributed LAR image compression framework on multi-components for flat LAR (Raulet et al., 2003), or for extended profiles with the proper region description, using cosimulation approaches (Flécher et al., 2007). For these embedded versions, we used the Golomb-Rice coder as the entropy coder, because of its lower complexity.

We presented in (Déforges & Babel, 2008) a dedicated FPGA implementation of the FLAT LAR image coder. This coding technique is particularly suitable for low bit-rate compressions. From an image quality point of view, the FLAT LAR presents better results than JPEG, while implementation resources requirements are similar. Internal architecture has been designed as a set of parallel and pipelined stages, enabling full image processing during a single regular scan. The architecture latency is extremely low as it is determined by the data acquisition for one slice of 8 lines.

5. Services

5.1 Error resilience

Protecting the encoded bit-stream against error transmission is required when using networks with no guaranteed quality of service (QoS). In particular, the availability of the information can be ensured by the Internet protocol (IP). We focused our studies on two topics, namely the loss of entire IP packets and transmission over wireless channels.

Limited bandwidth and distortions are the main features of a wireless channel. Therefore, both compression and secured transmission of sensitive data are simultaneously required. The pyramidal version of the LAR method and an Unequal Error Protection strategy are applied respectively to compress and protect the original image. The UEP strategy takes account of the sensitivity of the substreams requiring protection then optimizes the redundancy rate. In our application, we used the Reed Solomon Error Correcting Code RS-ECC, combined with symbol block interleaving for simulated transmission over the COST27 TU channel (W. Hamidouche et al., 2009). When comparing this to the JPWL system, we show that the proposed layout is better than the JPWL system, especially when transmission conditions are poor (SNR<21 dB).
With regard to the other topic, compensating IP packet loss also requires an UEP process. This is done by using an exact and discrete Radon transform, the Mojette transform (Babel et al., 2008). The frame-like definition of this transform allows redundancies that can be further used for image description and image communication (Fig. 8), for QoS purposes.

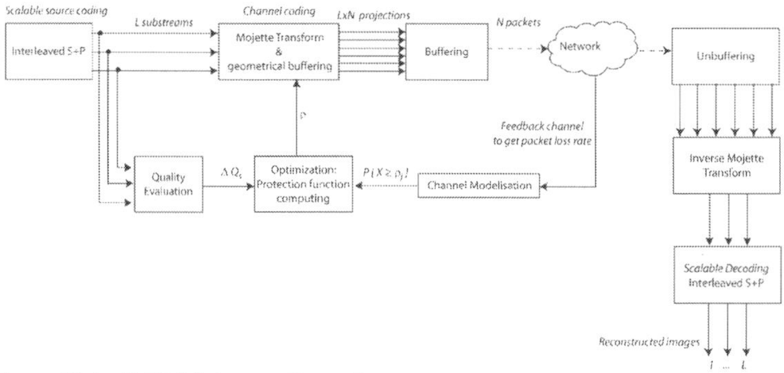

Fig. 8. General joint LAR-Mojette coding scheme

5.2 Content securization: cryptography and steganography

Besides watermarking, steganography, and techniques for assessing data integrity and authenticity, providing confidentiality and privacy for visual data is one of the most important topics in the area of multimedia security. Our research focuses on fast encryption procedures specifically tailored to the target environment. For that purpose, we use the pyramidal profile with Interleaved S+P configuration.
As the representation relies entirely on knowledge of the quadtree partition, this partition needs to be transmitted without any error. Previous work on error resilience dealt with that aspect and has shown that the decoder was still able to decode erroneous bit-streams. In that case, visual quality was very poor as depicted on Fig. 10, even when only a few bits of the quadtree were wrongly transmitted. Consequently, we propose to encrypt different levels of the quadtree partition description, as depicted on Fig. 9 (Fonteneau et al., 2008). This scheme is equivalent to a selective encryption process. Indeed, the encryption of a given level of the partition prevents the recovery of any additional visually-significant data. From a distortion point of view, it appears that encrypting higher levels (smaller blocks) increases the PSNR, and at the same time, the encrypting cost. From a security point of view, as the level increases, so the search space for a brute force attack increases drastically.

Moreover, we propose a method based on using the quadtree decomposition as a way to protect the content of the image. The main idea is to transmit the data without quadtree decomposition, using the quadtree as the key to decrypt the image (Motsch et al., 2006). This system has the following properties: embedded in the original bit-stream at no cost, allowing multilevel access authorization combined with state-of-the-art still picture codec. Multilevel quadtree decomposition provides a way to select the quality of the picture decoded.

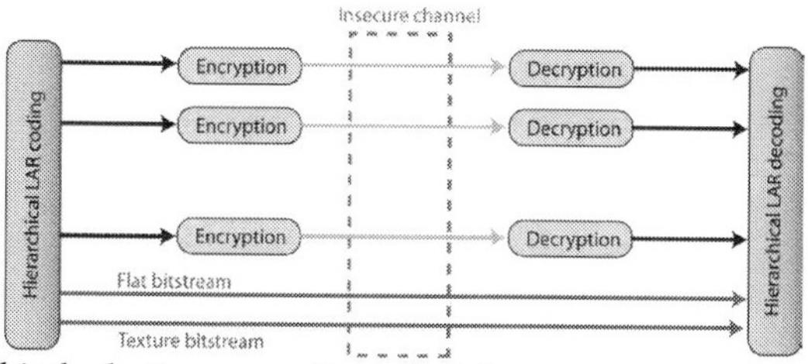

Fig. 9. LAR hierarchical selective encryption principle

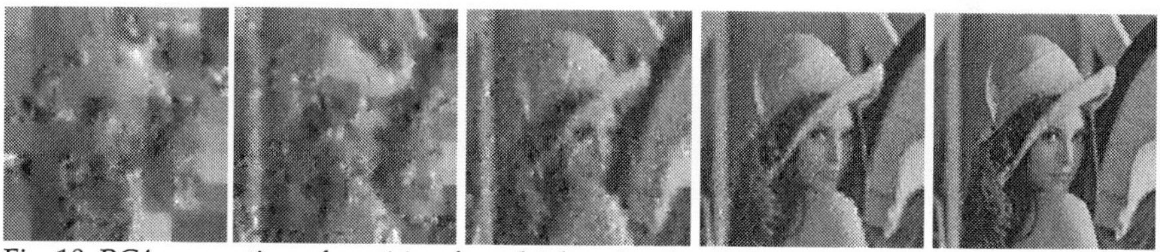

Fig. 10: RC4 encryption of partition from highest level to full resolution of the lena image

For the steganography point of view, we have adapted a fast and efficient reversible data embedding algorithm for the LAR-Interleaved S+P compression framework, namely the Difference Expansion, as the two techniques are based on the S-transform. Both this codec and the data embedding algorithm explore the redundancy in the digital picture to achieve either better than state-of-the-art compression rates or reversible data embedding respectively. The resultant capacity-distortion rates for embedded images were among the best in the literature on lossless data embedding (Motsch et al., 2009),(Fig. 11).

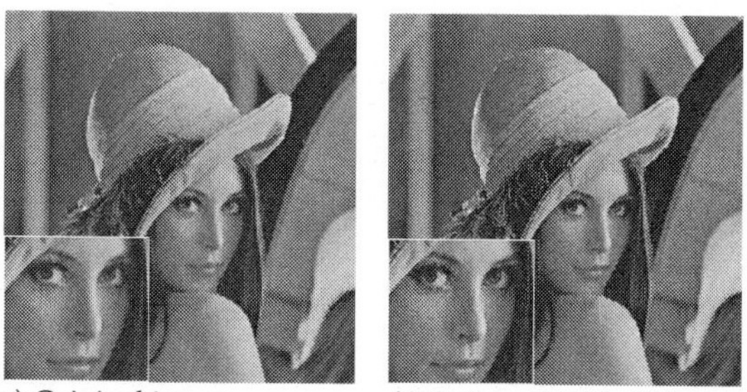

a) Original image b) Data embedded image

Fig. 11. Data embedding of 100,000 bits in the lena image

5.3 Client-server application and hierarchical access policy

In France, the C2RMF laboratory connected to the Louvre museum has digitized more than 300,000 documents taken from French museums, in high resolution (up to 20000 × 30000 pixels). The resulting EROS database is, for the moment, only accessible to researchers whose work is connected with the C2RMF. The TSAR project (Secure Transmission of high-Resolution Art images) is supported by the French National Research Agency. The idea is to integrate another scalable coding solution able to achieve a high lossy and lossless compression ratio. A second area of research concerns the secure access of images. The objective is to design an art image database accessible through a client-server process that includes and combines a hierarchical description of images and a hierarchical secured access.

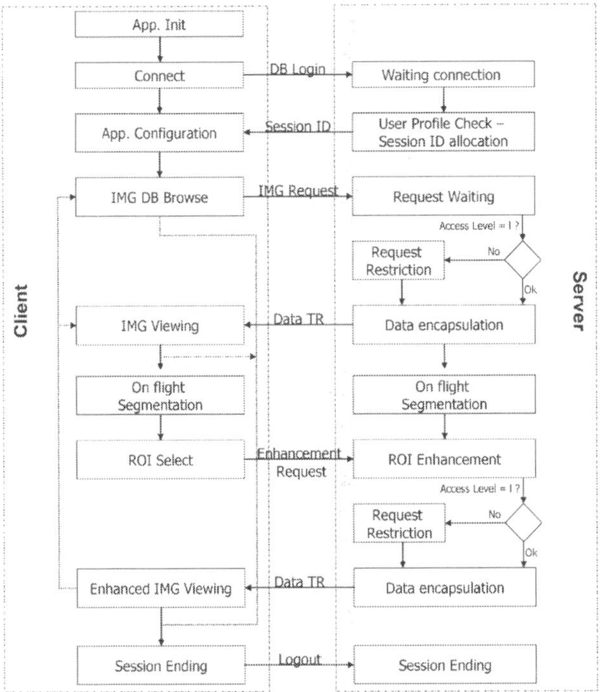

Fig. 12. Exchange protocol for client-server application

We are currently working on a corresponding client-server application (Babel et al., 2007). Every client will be authorized to browse the low-resolution image database and the server application will verify the user access level for each image and ROI request. If a client application sends a request that does not match the user access level, the server application will reduce the image resolution according to access policy. The exchange protocol is depicted in Fig. 12.

6. Conclusion

In this chapter, we focused on a few representative features of the LAR coding technology and its preliminary associated performances. This algorithm fulfills different functionalities and services, such as scalability, region-level handling, steganography, cryptography, robustness and adjustable complexity. These functionalities have yet to be evaluated with ad-hoc tools that have to be defined in the JPEG-AIC context. Furthermore, some of the results presented have revealed better than state-of-the-art performances.

As the LAR coder provides good results in terms of both compression, representation and functionnalities, an extension of the LAR codec aimed at video compression with associated services is being worked on.

7. References

Babel, M.; Déforges, O. & Ronsin, J. (2003). Adaptive Multiresolution Scheme for Efficient Image Compression, *Proceedings of Picture Coding Symposium*, April, 2003, pp. 23-25.

Babel, M.; Déforges, O. & Ronsin, J. (2005). Interleaved S+P pyramidal decomposition with refined prediction model, *Proceedings of Image Processing, ICIP 2005, IEEE International Conference on*, pp. II-750-3, 0-7803-9134-9, Genova Swiss, September 2005, Genova.

Babel, M.; Déforges, O.; Bédat, L. & Motsch, J. (2007). Context-Based Scalable Coding and Representation of High Resolution Art Pictures for Remote Data Access, *Multimedia and Expo, 2007 IEEE International Conference on*, 2007, pp. 460-463.

Babel, M.; Parrein, B.; Déforges, O.; Normand, N.; Guédon, J. & Coat V. (2008). Joint source-channel coding: Secured and progressive transmission of compressed medical images on the Internet, In: *Computerized Medical Imaging and Graphics*, vol. 32, June. 2008, pp. 258-269.

Déforges, O.; Babel, M. & Motsch, J. (2006). The RWHT+P for an improved lossless multiresolution coding, proceedings of EUSIPCO 2006, August 2006, p. nc , Florence Italy

Déforges, O.; Babel, M.; Bédat, L. & Ronsin, J. (2007). Color LAR Codec: A Color Image Representation and Compression Scheme Based on Local Resolution Adjustment and Self-Extracting Region Representation, *Circuits and Systems for Video Technology , IEEE Transactions on*, Vol. 17, Issue. 8, August 2007, 974-987, 1051-8215

Déforges, O.; Babel, M.; Bédat, L. & Coat, V. (2008). Scalable lossless and lossy image coding based on the RWHaT+P pyramid and the inter-coefficient classification method, *Proceedings of Multimedia and Expo, 2008 IEEE International Conference on*, pp. 185-188, 978-1-4244-2570-9, Hanover Germany, June 2008,Hanover.

Déforges O. & Babel M. (2008). LAR method: from algorithm to synthesis for an embedded low complexity image coder, *3rd International Design and Test Workshop 3rd International Design and Test Workshop, IDT'08* , Monastir Tunisia : 2008, pp. 1-4 .

De Simone, F.; Ticca, D.; Dufaux, F.; Ansorge, M.; Ebrahimi, T. (2008). A comparative study of color image compression standards using perceptually driven quality metrics, *Proceedings of SPIE 2008*, vol. 7073, San Diego, CA USA, August 11-14, 2008.

De Simone, F.; Ouaret, M.; Dufaux, F ; Tescher, A. G. and Ebrahimi, T (2007). A comparative study of JPEG 2000, AVC/H264, and HD Photo, *Proceedings of SPIE 2007,* San Diego, vol. 6696, August 2007

Flécher, E.; Raulet, M.; Roquier, G.; Babel, M. & Déforges, O. (2007). Framework For Efficient Cosimulation And Fast Prototyping on Multi-Components With AAA Methodology: LAR Codec Study Case, *Proceedings of 15th European Signal Processing Conference (Eusipco 2007),* Poznan; Poland : 2007, pp. ISBN: 978-83-921340-2-2 .

Fonteneau, C.; Motsch, J.; Babel, M. & Déforges, O. (2008). A Hierarchical Selective Encryption Technique in a Scalable Image Codec, *Proceedings of International Conference in Communications International Conference in Communications* , Bucharest Romania : 2008, pp. 1-4 .

Hamidouche, W.; Olivier, C.; Babel, M.; Deforges, O.; Boeglen, H. and Lorenz, P (2009). LAR Image Transmission over Fading Channels: a Hierarchical Protection Solution, *in 2nd Int. Conf. on Communication Theory, Relaibility and Quality of Service,* IEEE Xplore, Colmar (France), july 2009.

JPEG normalization group (2007). Jpeg-aic: scope and evaluation. *International Standards Organization working document,* ISO/IEC SC29/WG 1/N4326, 2007

Motsch, J.; Déforges, O. & Babel, M. (2006). Embedding Multilevel Image Encryption in the LAR Codec, *Proceedings of IEEE Communications International Conference* , 2006, p. 4

Motsch, J.; Déforges, O. & Babel, M. (2009). Joint lossless coding and reversible data embedding in a multiresolution still image coder, *Proceedings of the EUSIPCO'09 European Signal Processing Conference,* pp. 1-5, EUSIPCO , Glasgow Scotland, August 2009

Pasteau, F.; Babel, M.; Déforges, O. & Bédat, L. (2008). Interleaved S+P Scalable Coding with Inter-Coefficient Classification Methods, *Proceedings of the EUSIPCO'08 European Signal Processing Conference,* pp. 1-5, EUSIPCO , Lausanne Swiss, August 2008

Raulet, M.; Babel, M.; Déforges, O.; Nezan, J. & Sorel, Y. (2003). Automatic coarse-grain partitioning and automatic code generation for heterogeneous architectures, *Signal Processing Systems, SIPS 2003. IEEE Workshop on,* 2003, pp. 316-321.

Said, A. and Pearlman, W. (1993). Reversible image compression via multiresolution representation and predictive coding. In *Visual Communication and Image Processing,* volume 209, pages 664-674. SPIE, Novembre 1993

Srinivasan, S.; Tu, C.; Zhou, Z.; Ray, D.; Regunathan, S. and Sullivan, G. (2007). *An Introduction to the HD Photo Technical Design,* Microsoft Corporation WG 1/N4183, 2007

4

Methods for Nonlinear Intersubject Registration in Neuroscience

Daniel Schwarz and Tomáš Kašpárek
Masaryk University
Czech Republic

1. Introduction

The human body is an amazingly complex system. Acquiring data about its static and dynamic properties yields massive amounts of information. The use of images is the most effective way to manage, present and interpret the vast quantities of that information in the clinical medicine and in the supporting biomedical research. Computational neuroanatomy is a new growing field of powerful applications in neuroscience. It promises an automated methodology to characterize neuroanatomical configuration of structural magnetic resonance imaging (MRI) brain scans. One of the crucial techniques in this methodology is image registration. It performs the task of spatial normalization of images according to a common reference anatomy termed as a brain atlas. It allows interpreting results of an image analysis in a standard anatomical coordinate system. Further, an atlas of brain makes it possible to find out how different is a subject brain compared with the common reference anatomy which represents certain population. Many approaches to registration of brain images assume same or functionally dependent intensities in the images across subjects. Thus, they allow the registration process to be driven by differences in intensities. They however do not count on intensity variations caused by various imaging conditions or tissue atrophy and degradation induced by neurological diseases. On the other hand, the image registration methods which are robust to such intensity variations enable only low-dimensional parametric transformations, which make it impossible to detect localized image differences without additional efforts. This chapter mainly contributes to the field of registration with the use of nonlinear locally adaptive transformations. Particularly, problems connected to matching brain image data obtained from various subjects and with various imaging conditions are solved here. Difficulties lie in the complex brain structure which varies widely from one individual to another. Other difficulties lie in the complex and unknown relations between intensities in images to be registered. A solution of a specific clinical task from the field of computational neuroanatomy is further presented.
Magnetic resonance imaging (MRI) is a highly successful diagnostic imaging modality, largely due to its rich set of contrast mechanisms. The signal intensity is a multivariable function, depending on many parameters. Partial listing includes proton spin density PD, spin lattice relaxation time T1, spin spin relaxation time T2, proton flow and diffusion. Due to its exceptionally high soft tissue contrast, MRI lends itself well to morphometric studies in the brain where clear distinction between structures is required (Ali et al., 2005).

1.1 Image registration in computational neuroanatomy

Recently the importance of new methods for image analysis has been growing due to the rapid development of medical imaging modalities. In the field of computational neuroanatomy, automated whole-brain methods for morphometry are utilized intensively for structural MRI brain volumetry besides the gold standard methods based on regions of interest (ROI) in the last decade. The automated whole-brain methods are voxel-based (VBM - voxel-based morphometry) or deformation-based (DBM - deformation-based morphometry). While the ROI-based methods need manual segmentation, which is time-consuming and subjective, the whole-brain methods use semi-automated or automated processing of images including their segmentation. Detection of pathological changes with the use of this type of methods is not limited by arbitrarily predefined borders. This fact is advantageous in disorders with progression of morphological changes during its duration.

Spatial normalization is a necessary step, which reduces an impact of individual variability in brain shape on the resulting assessment of its local characteristics. Spatial normalization of images in the stereotaxic space (Ashburner & Friston, 2000; Mechelli et al., 2005) with the use of deformable image registration is a common kernel of both VBM and DBM. In the VBM case, the registration suppresses only global shape differences, whereas DBM needs an image registration method, which covers complex anatomical variability including subtle local changes (Gaser C. et al. 2001; 2004). The endpoint of any morphometry method in computational neuroanatomy is usually a statistical parametric map which locates regions of significant anatomical differences between two groups of subjects. The map is a result of a standard parametric significance tests performed independently at each point of scalar fields or vector fields which describe the differences among the subject's anatomies.

An ongoing development of the morphomery methods lies in new designs for deformable registration methods (Ashburner, 2007; Schwarz et al. 2007) and in extending and refining the statistical apparatus which is used for computing statistical parametric maps destined for anatomical abnormality detection (Friston et al., 2007; Xu et al. 2008).

2. Registration of medical images

Image registration is a process of estimating a spatial transformation which maps each point of an image onto its corresponding point of another image (Rohr, 2001). Image registration is a fundamental problem in medical image analysis. A universal method does not exist due to the diversity of registration tasks. There are various approaches to the classification of image registration methods in surveys (Maintz & Viergever, 1998; Rohr, 2001; Zitova & Flusser, 2003; Gholipour et al, 2007).

2.1 Optimal registration

Optimal registration can be defined as an optimization problem with the goal of finding the spatial mapping that will bring the floating image N into alignment with the reference image M. Fig. 1 shows its basic steps.

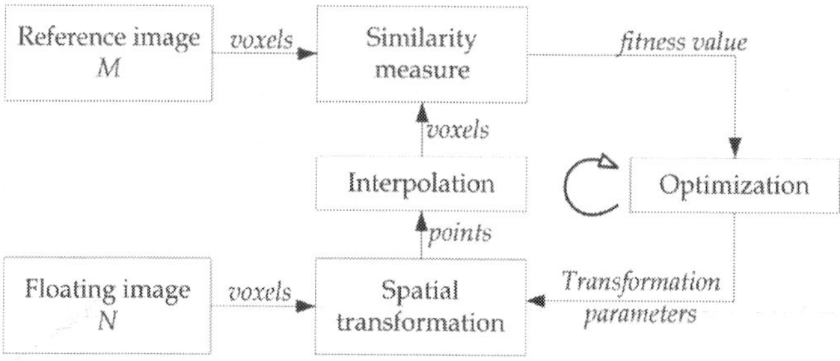

Fig. 1. Basic components of an optimal registration framework (Ibanez et al., 2003).

The spatial transformation φ_a^{-1} maps points from the reference image space to points in the floating image space. It is parameterized by a vector of parameters **a**. It is in fact an inverse mapping which is preferable as it avoids problems of holes with the forward mapping. The transformation is directly connected to interpolation which serves for evaluation of floating image intensities at non-grid positions. The similarity measure $S(M, N \circ \varphi_{\mathbf{a}})$ or its negative forms a criterion of optimality - a cost function which is minimized in the optimization over the search space defined by parameters of the spatial transformation.

The affine transformation is one of the most popular transformations used in image registration. It can be described by a single 4 × 4 matrix computed as a product of matrices representing translation, rotation, shearing and scaling.

The choice of an appropriate similarity measure is determined by the character of intensities in the floating and the reference image. Popular choices are based on intensity, correlation and mutual information. Supposing the image intensities to be discrete random variables, their mutual information (MI) is defined as (Ibanez et al., 2003):

$$I(M,N) = H(M) + H(N) - H(M,N) = \\ = \sum_{m,n} p_{MN}(m,n) \log_2 \frac{p_{MN}(m,n)}{p_M(m) p_N(n)}, \quad (1)$$

where $I(M,N)$ is the mutual information of random variables M and N, $H(M)$ and $H(N)$ are entropies of M and N respectively and $H(M,N)$ is the joint entropy of M and N. It is rewritten to a form containing marginal probability density functions (PDF) $p_M(m)$, $p_N(n)$ and joint PDF $p_{MN}(m,n)$. MI gives a measure of the strength of the dependence between the random variables. The major advantage of using MI is that the actual form of the dependency does not have to be specified. Therefore, MI is well suited as a criterion of multimodal registration. The marginal and joint PDFs are estimated from image data by Parzen windowing (Viola, 1995; Studholme et al., 1999; Modersitzki, 2004) or by normalizing the joint histogram (Maes, 1998; Maintz et al., 1998).

An optimization technique is needed to find the spatial transformation defined by a vector of transformation parameters $\mathbf{a}=[a_1, \ldots, a_D]$. The number of parameters D ranges from six, for rigid body transformation, to twelve, for general affine transformation. In the case of deformable registration techniques, there are hundreds or even thousands of parameters. Optimization methods with no gradient computation requirement are typical for

correlation-based and mutual information based criterions. Powell's directions set method (Maintz et al., 1998; Pluim et al., 2001), downhill simplex method (Collins et al., 1994) and simulated annealing (Čapek et al., 2001; Kubečka & Jan, 2004) are most often examples.
To alleviate the problems associated with direct intensity interpolation methods, partial volume interpolation was proposed in (Maes, 1998) for mutual information based registration. It was further extended to a scheme called generalized partial volume (GPV) joint histogram estimation (Chen & Varshney, 2003).

2.2 Deformable registration

In many medical imaging applications, the global linear alignment does not provide a sufficient solution. A nonlinear transformation is necessary to correct the local differences in the images. Here, the process of finding such a transformation is termed as deformable registration. The reference image M and a floating image N are expected to be aligned by the global rigid body or affine transformation. The central idea behind deformable registration is to find local forces which will deform the floating image to make it more similar to the reference image, see Fig. 2. The transformation $\varphi(\mathbf{x})$ is usually split into the trivial identity part and a so called displacement field $\mathbf{u}(\mathbf{x})$ (Modersitzki, 2004):

$$\varphi(\mathbf{x}) = \mathbf{x} + \mathbf{u}(\mathbf{x}). \tag{2}$$

Computation of the displacement field involves local forces together with regularization provided by a spatial deformation model. Regularized mapping function ensures realistic registration results without tearing or folding of the image.

2.2.1 Parametric deformable registration

Parametric transformation (sometimes termed as low-dimensional) can be expanded in terms of some parameters a_i and basis functions ψ_i. The registration task is to determine the parameters of the transformation. Methods based on radial basis function (RBF) interpolation are used widely. Wendland's functions (Fornefett et al., 2001) and thin-plate splines (Kostelec et al., 1998; Pauchard et al., 2004) are examples of RBFs used in image registration. Other functions used for parametric deformations are B-splines (Rueckert et al., 1999; Rohlfing et al., 2003; Schnabel et al., 2003), components of discrete cosine transform (Ashburner & Friston, 2000) or wavelet basis functions (Downie & Silverman, 2001).
In the case of image deformation with the use of RBFs, the displacement field $\mathbf{u}(\mathbf{x})$ is controlled by a finite number of movable control points. The interpolation problem is solved separately for each coordinate of the displacement field:

$$u_k(\mathbf{x}) : \mathrm{R}^d \to \mathrm{R}, \quad u_k(\mathbf{p}_i) = f_{i,k}, \quad i = 1 \ldots n, \quad k = 1 \ldots d. \tag{3}$$

where d is the image dimension, $\mathbf{p}_i$ constitute a given set of n control points and $\mathbf{f}_i$ are their translations. Using RBFs, the interpolant is constructed:

$$u_k(\mathbf{x}) = \sum_{j=1}^{m} b_j \phi_j(\mathbf{x}) + \sum_{i=1}^{n} a_i \psi(\|\mathbf{x} - \mathbf{p}_i\|), \tag{4}$$

where the first term is a linear combination of polynomials and the second term is a linear combination of RBFs. Here, ϕ_j are m polynomial components, ψ denotes a RBF and $\|\mathbf{x}-\mathbf{p}_i\|$ is the Euclidean distance from $\mathbf{x}$ to $\mathbf{p}_i$ and a_i, b_i are coefficients. A RBF is a function depending only on the distance from the origin: $\psi(\|\mathbf{x}-\mathbf{p}_i\|)=\psi(\mathbf{r})$. By inserting (4) into (3) and using constraints that guarantee polynomial precision (Amidror, 2002), a following system of linear equations for the coefficients $\mathbf{a}=[a_1, ..., a_n]^T$ and $\mathbf{b}=[b_1, ..., b_m]^T$ is obtained:

$$\begin{pmatrix} \mathbf{K} & \mathbf{P} \\ \mathbf{P}^T & 0 \end{pmatrix} \begin{pmatrix} \mathbf{a} \\ \mathbf{b} \end{pmatrix} = \begin{pmatrix} \mathbf{f}_k \\ 0 \end{pmatrix}, \tag{5}$$

where $\mathbf{K}$ is a $n \times n$ sub-matrix given by $K_{ij}=\psi(\|\mathbf{p}_i-\mathbf{p}_j\|)$, P is a $n \times m$ sub-matrix given by $P_{ij}=\phi_j(\mathbf{p}_i)$ and $\mathbf{f}_k=[f_{k,1}, ..., f_{k,n}]^T$ is a vector of the kth coordinate of the control points' translations $\mathbf{f}_i$. The polynomial sub-matrix $\mathbf{P}$ depends on the type of RBF. For thin plate splines, it has its ith row of the form $[1, x_{pi}, y_{pi}, z_{pi}]$, which are x, y and z-components of $\mathbf{p}_i$ (Donato & Belongie, 2002). Hence, there is a global influence of a control point on the resulting displacement field $\mathbf{u}(\mathbf{x})$. Compactly supported RBFs are another recent choice. Due to their positive definiteness, the regularity of the matrix $\mathbf{K}$ is ensured. Therefore, no polynomial part is needed and (5) reduces to:

$$\mathbf{K}\mathbf{a} = \mathbf{f}_k. \tag{6}$$

One of Wendland's functions (Wendland, 1995) is proposed for deformable image registration in (Fornefett et al., 2001):

$$\psi_{CP}(r) = (1-r)_+^4(4r+1). \tag{7}$$

Its mathematical properties hold for various spatial supports s, such that: $\psi_{CP}(r;s)=\psi_{CP}(\mathbf{r}/s)$. Compared to other RBFs, the use of compactly supported RBFs is highly efficient, as the matrix $\mathbf{K}$ is rather sparse and no transcendental functions are involved in the calculation. The support length s cannot be set arbitrary, as there is a fundamental condition of topology preservation. This requirement is satisfied if the determinant of the Jacobian of the deformation is non-negative.

2.2.2 Non-parametric deformable registration

Non-parametric deformable registration methods (sometimes termed as high dimensional) directly compute a displacement in every point most often by imitating real world transformations of deformable materials. One of the first proposed methods based on continuum mechanics was elastic matching (Ferrant et al., 2001; Alterovitz et al., 2004; Modersitzki, 2004). Only small deformations are assumed, thus linear elastic model can be used. In (Christensen et al., 1996), a viscous fluid model is used to control the deformation. The floating image is modelled as a thick fluid that flows out to match the reference image under the control of the local forces. Convolution filter methods for solving associated PDE were proposed in (Gramkow & Bro-Nielsen, 1997). A considerable piece of work is presented in (Rogelj et al., 2003; Rogelj & Kovačič, 2004), where Gaussian filters are used for modelling the spatial deformation. The Gaussian filters are used to approximate the elastic as well as the fluid model. It is also successfully used for a so-called incremental model, which is used for image registration in (Peckar et al., 1998). A spatial deformation model made up from the elastic and the incremental model is proposed, in order to combine their advantages and thus improve the registration. The model consists of two convolution filters (Rogelj & Kovačič, 2004):

$$\mathbf{u}_f = k\mathbf{f}, \tag{8}$$

$$\mathbf{u}^i = \left(\mathbf{u}^{i-1} + \mathbf{u}_f * \mathbf{G}_I\right) * \mathbf{G}_E, \tag{9}$$

see the scheme in Fig. 2. The first part follows the Hooke's law to compute unregularized displacements $\mathbf{u}_f$ of image points. It says that the points move proportionally to the applied forces with a constant k. The filter $\mathbf{G}_I$ regularizes displacement improvements $\mathbf{u}_f$ and the second filter $\mathbf{G}_E$ regularizes the overall displacement field $\mathbf{u}$.

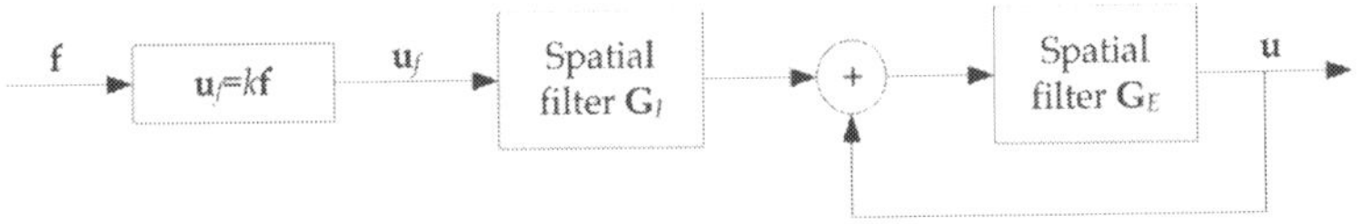

Fig. 2. The combined elastic-incremental model (Rogelj & Kovačič, 2004).

2.2.3 Local forces estimation and similarity measures

Local forces are obtained either by optimization or they are computed directly, depending on a particular registration method. In the former case, the registration is usually based on a global similarity measure which detects improvement of local image correspondence (Rueckert et al., 1999; Rohlfing et al., 2003), or block matching techniques are performed (Kostelec et al., 1998; Maintz et al., 1998). Most suitable translations are found in an optimization procedure with the use of monomodal as well as multimodal similarity measures. In the latter case, the forces are estimated in every point as the derivative of a similarity measure. The resulting dense field of the forces is used to compute a high dimensional deformation, often based on some physical interpretation. The registration methods which perform the high-dimensional warping are typically limited to monomodal data, e.g. (Gramkow & Bro-Nielsen, 1997; Christensen et al., 1996; Thirion, 1998). However, the effort to develop registration algorithms focused on high-dimensional matching of multimodal data recently emerged. In (Rogelj et al., 2003), point similarity measures are proposed for high dimensional deformable registration of multimodal data. The point similarity measures are derived from global similarity measures based on the joint PDF estimated from the joint histogram.

The point similarity measure $S_{MI}(\mathbf{x})$ derived from the global mutual information is defined as (Rogelj & Kovačič, 2003):

$$S_{MI}(\mathbf{x}) = \log_2 \frac{p_{MN}(m(\mathbf{x}), n(\mathbf{x}))}{p_M(m(\mathbf{x}))p_N(n(\mathbf{x}))} \tag{10}$$

The negative joint entropy $H(M,N)$, which is the most informative part of MI can be used as a global multimodal similarity measure and a point similarity measure S_H can be derived. In (Maintz et al., 1998), conditional probability densities are used for a region similarity measure, which is here rewritten as another point similarity measure:

$$S_{PC}(\mathbf{x}) = p(n(\mathbf{x})|m(\mathbf{x})), \tag{11}$$

In (Rogelj et al., 2003), other measures are proposed:

$$S_U(\mathbf{x}) = \frac{p_{MN}(m(\mathbf{x}), n(\mathbf{x}))^2}{p_M(m(\mathbf{x}))p_N(n(\mathbf{x}))}, \tag{12}$$

$$S_{UH}(\mathbf{x}) = \log_2 p_{MN}(m(\mathbf{x}), n(\mathbf{x})) + \log_2 \frac{p_{MN}(m(\mathbf{x}), n(\mathbf{x}))}{p_M(m(\mathbf{x}))p_N(n(\mathbf{x}))} = S_H + S_{MI}. \tag{13}$$

There are measures expressed in the terms of probability (S_{PC}, S_U) and uncertainty (S_{MI}, S_H, S_{UH}). It was shown in the previous work (Schwarz et al., 2007) that better performance of the proposed registration methods is achieved involving the probability similarity measures and another point similarity measure depending on the probability was proposed there:

$$S_{PMI}(\mathbf{x}) = \frac{p_{MN}(m(\mathbf{x}), n(\mathbf{x}))}{p_M(m(\mathbf{x}))p_N(n(\mathbf{x}))}. \tag{14}$$

Any point similarity measure can be used to compute a region similarity measure by simply averaging the point similarities over the region. The averaging over a region can also be viewed as convolution filtering with some spatial filter (Rogelj & Kovačič, 2003). Convolution spatial filtering was previously described as a method for modeling spatial deformations. The regularization provided directly by region similarity measures is substantial for large regions. The concept of local forces based on the derivative of a point similarity measure is further extended in (Rogelj & Kovačič, 2003), where symmetric local forces are proposed to improve registration consistency.

3. Multimodal deformable registration in stereotaxic space

Two algorithms for atlas-based deformable registration of MRI brain images are proposed. The use of various multimodal similarity measures is explored. Their computation requires knowledge of the joint PDF of the images being registered. Its estimation is a common part in both algorithms. The algorithms differ in the other parts including extraction of local forces and spatial deformation models. The subjects' image data are supposed to be transformed into stereotaxic space by a previous linear registration step.

3.1 Low-dimensional deformable registration by enhanced block matching

The first registration algorithm produces low-dimensional deformations which are suitable for coarse spatial normalization which is an essential step in VBM. On the contrary to the widely used spatial normalization implemented in (Ashburner & Friston, 2000), the proposed algorithm is applicable for matching multimodal image data. It is in fact an enhanced block matching technique. The scheme of the algorithm is in Fig. 3. A multilevel subdivision is applied on a floating image N. Obtained rectangular image blocks are matched with a reference image M. The resulting displacement field $\mathbf{u}$ is made up from local translations of the image blocks by RBF interpolation. The translations representing warping forces $\mathbf{f}$ are found by maximizing symmetric regional similarity measures.

3.1.1 Symmetric regional matching

Conventional block matching techniques measure the similarity of the floating image regions with respect to the reference image. Here, inspired by the symmetric forces introduced for high dimensional matching (Rogelj & Kovačič, 2003), the regional similarity measure is computed by:

$$S_W^{sym} = S_W^{forward}\left[M(\mathbf{x}_W + \mathbf{u}_W(\mathbf{x}_W)), N(\mathbf{x}_W)\right] + S_W^{reverse}\left[M(\mathbf{x}_W), N(\mathbf{x}_W - \mathbf{u}_W(\mathbf{x}_W))\right], \tag{15}$$

where the first term corresponds to the similarity measure computed over all K_W voxels $\mathbf{x}_W=[\mathbf{x}_1, \mathbf{x}_2, ..., \mathbf{x}_{Kw}]$ of a region W of the floating image according to the reference image. The second term corresponds to the reverse direction. The terms $M(\mathbf{x}_W)$ and $N(\mathbf{x}_W)$ denotes all voxels of the region W in the reference image and in the floating image respectively. The displacements $\mathbf{u}_W(\mathbf{x}_W)=[\mathbf{u}(\mathbf{x}_1), \mathbf{u}(\mathbf{x}_2), ..., \mathbf{u}(\mathbf{x}_{Kw})]$ are computed in foregoing iterations and they moves the voxels $N(\mathbf{x}_W)$ of the floating image from their undeformed positions $\mathbf{x}_W$ to new positions $\mathbf{x}_W+\mathbf{u}_W(\mathbf{x}_W)$, where they get matched with the voxels $M(\mathbf{x}_W+\mathbf{u}_W(\mathbf{x}_W))$ of the reference image. In the case of the reverse similarity measure, the displacements $\mathbf{u}_W(\mathbf{x}_W)$ are applied on the reference image M, as it would be deformed by the inversion of the so far computed deformation. The voxels $M(\mathbf{x}_W)$ of the reference image are thus moved to get matched with the voxels $N(\mathbf{x}_W-\mathbf{u}_W(\mathbf{x}_W))$ of undeformed floating image, see the illustration in Fig. 4.
It is impossible to uniquely describe correspondences of regions in two images by multimodal similarity measures, due to their statistical character. When the local translations are searched in complex medical images, suboptimal solutions are obtained frequently with the use of the forward similarity measure only. Using the symmetric similarity measure, additional correspondence information is provided and the chance of getting trapped in local optima is thus reduced.
Due to the subvoxel accuracy of performed deformations, the point similarities have to be computed in points that are not positioned on the image grid. Point similarity functions (10)-(14) are defined for a finite number of intensity values due to histogram binning performed in the joint histogram computation. Conventional interpolation of voxel intensities is therefore inapplicable, because the point similarity functions are not defined for new values which would arise. Thus, the GPV method, which was originally designed for computation of joint intensity histogram, is used here. The computation of point pair similarity requires knowledge of the intensities m and n in the points of the images M and N respectively. The intensity n on a grid point of the deformed grid of the floating image is straight-forward, whereas the intensity m on a point off the regular grid of the reference

image is unknown. Their similarity is computed as a linear combination of similarities of intensity pairs corresponding to the points in the neighbour-hood of the examined point.

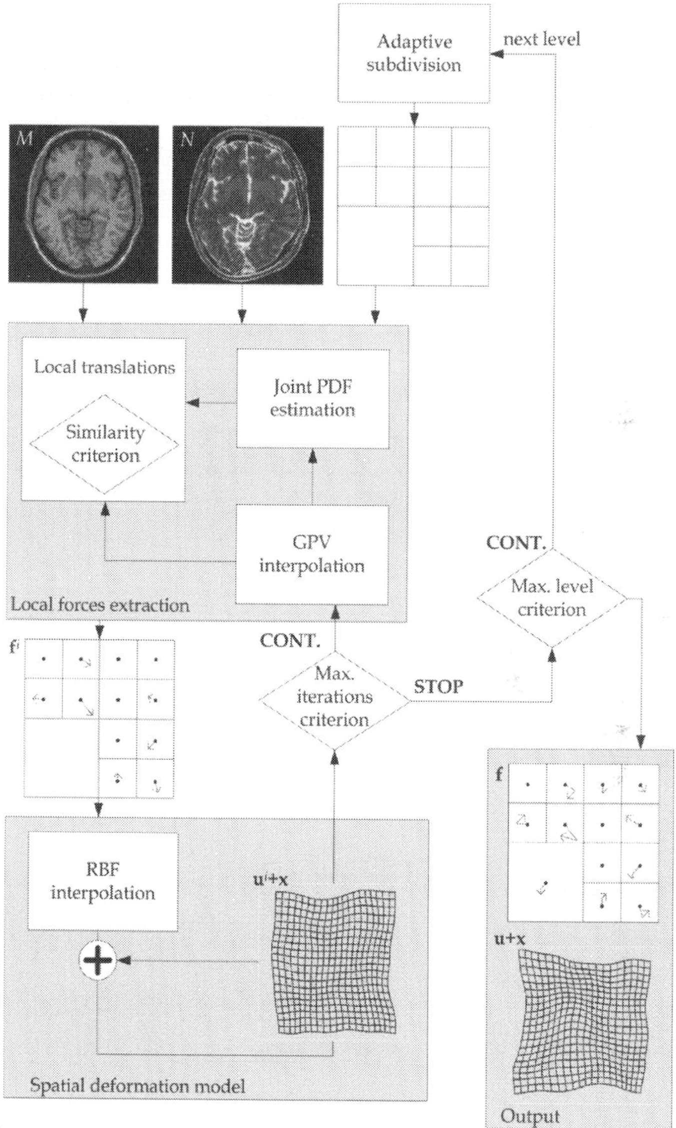

Fig. 3. The scheme of the block matching algorithm proposed for coarse spatial normalization.

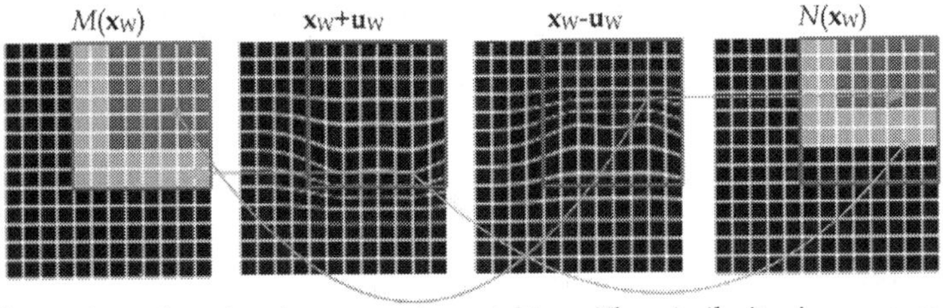

Fig. 4. Illustration of regional symmetric matching. The similarity is measured in the forward (the blue line) as well as in the reverse (the green line) direction of registration. In the forward direction, the displacement field computed so far is applied on the floating image voxels. In the reverse direction, the inverse displacement field is applied on the reference image voxels.

The extent of the neighbourhood depends on the chosen kernel function. Here, the first-order, the second-order and the third-order B-spline functions with 8, 27 and 64 grid points in neighbourhood for 3-D tasks or 4, 9 and 16 points in neighbourhood for 2-D tasks are used. The particular choice of the kernel function affects the smoothness of the behaviour of the regional similarity measure, see Fig. 5. The number of local optima is the lowest in the case of the third-order B-spline. As the evaluation of the B-splines increases the computational load, their values are computed only once and stored in a lookup table with increments equal to 0.001.

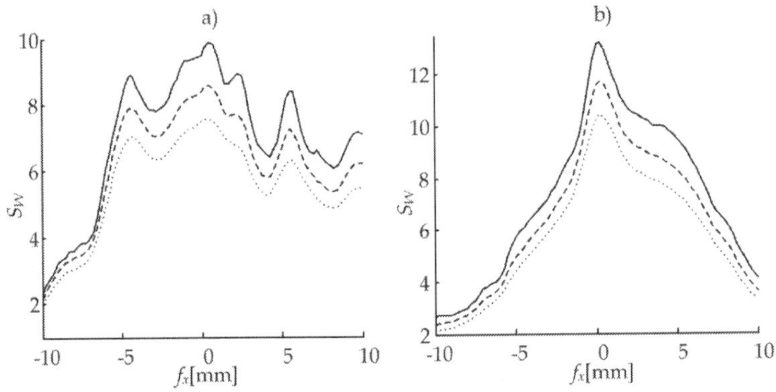

Fig. 5. Comparison of the regional similarity measure computed with the use of GPV and the first-order B-spline (solid line), the second-order B-spline (dashed line) and the third-order B-spline (dotted line). A region of the size a) 10x10 mm, b) 20x20 mm was translated by f_x=±10mm in the x direction.

Local translations which maximize a matching criterion are searched in optimization procedures. Here, the symmetric regional similarity measure is used as the matching criterion which has to be maximized:

$$S_W(\mathbf{f}_W) = S_W^{forward}\left(M(\mathbf{x}_W + \mathbf{u}_W(\mathbf{x}_W) + \mathbf{f}_W), N(\mathbf{x}_W)\right) + \\ + S_W^{reverse}\left(M(\mathbf{x}_W), N(\mathbf{x}_W - \mathbf{u}_W(\mathbf{x}_W) - \mathbf{f}_W)\right), \tag{16}$$

where $\mathbf{f}_W = [\mathbf{f}_1, \mathbf{f}_2, \ldots, \mathbf{f}_{Kw}]$, $\mathbf{f}_1 = \mathbf{f}_2 = \ldots \mathbf{f}_{Kw} = [f_x, f_y, f_z]^T$ is a translation of all voxels in a region W along x, y and z axis. The use of the symmetric regional similarity measure and the GPV interpolation with the use of the second-order B spline or the third order B-spline leads to well-behaved criterion function in the case of large regions. In the case of small regions, the uncertainty about the best translation is still high and many local maxima occur near the optimal solution. A combination of extensive search and hillclimbing algorithms is used here to find the global maximum. First, a space of all possible translations is determined by absolute maximum translation $|\mathbf{f}_{max}|$ in all directions. Then, the space of all possible translations is searched with a relatively big step s_e. The q best points are then used as starting points for the following hillclimbing with a finer step s_h. The maximum of q local maxima obtained by the hillclimbing is then declared as the global maximum, see Fig. 6. All the parameters of the optimization procedure depend on the size of the region which is translated. In this way, fewer criterion evaluations are done for larger regions when the chance of getting trapped into local maxima is reduced and more evaluations of the criterion is performed for smaller regions.

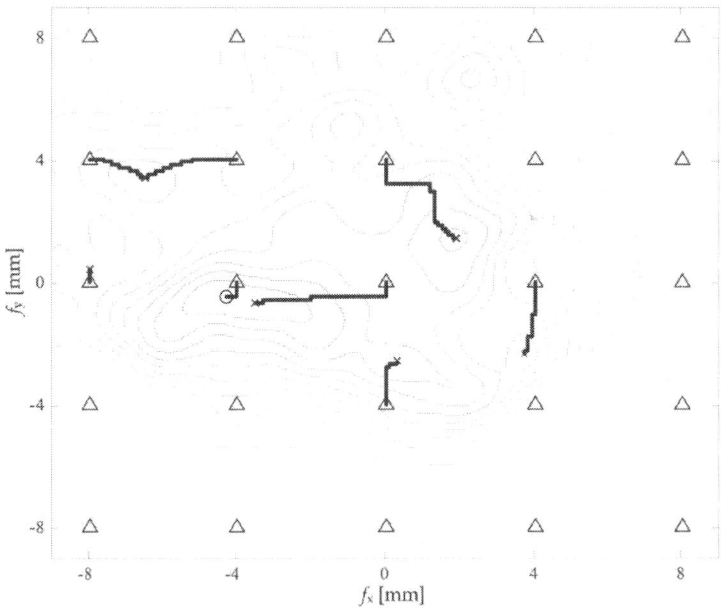

Fig. 6. A trajectory of 2-D optimization performed by an extensive search (triangles) combined with hillclimbing (bold lines). The optimization procedure was set for this illustration as follows: $|f_{max}|=[8, 8]$, s_e=4 mm, s_h=0.1 mm, q=8. The local maxima are marked by crosses and the global one is marked by the circle.

Image deformation based on interpolation with the use of RBFs is used here. The control points $\mathbf{p}_i$ are placed into the centers of the regions and their translations $\mathbf{f}_i$ are obtained by symmetric regional matching. Substituting the translations into (6), three systems of linear equations are obtained and three vectors of w coefficients, where w is the number of the regions, $\mathbf{a}_k=(a_{1,k}, \ldots, a_{w,k})^T$ computed. The displacement of any point $\mathbf{x}$ is then defined separately for each dimension by the interpolant:

$$u_k(\mathbf{x}) = \sum_{i=1}^{w} a_{i,k}\psi_{CP}\left(\left\|\mathbf{x}-\mathbf{p}_i\right\|\right), \quad k=1\ldots3. \tag{17}$$

The values of spatial support s for various regions sizes are set empirically.
Optimal matches can be hardly found in a single pass composed of the local translations estimation and the RBF-based interpolation, since features in one location influence decisions at other locations of the images. Iterative updating scheme is therefore proposed here. A multilevel strategy is incorporated into the proposed algorithm. The deformation is iteratively refined in the coarse to fine manner. The size of the regions cannot be arbitrarily small, because the local translations are determined independently for each region and voxel interdependecies are introduced only by the regional similarity measure. The regions containing poor contour or surface information can be eliminated from the matching process and the algorithm can be accelerated in this way. The subdivision is performed only if at least one voxel in the current region has its normalized gradient image intensity bigger then a certain threshold.

3.2 High-dimensional deformable registration with the use of point similarity measures and wavelet smoothing

The second registration algorithm produces high dimensional deformations involving gross shape differences as well as local subtle differences between a subject and a template anatomy. As multimodal similarity measures are used, the algorithm is suitable for DBM on image data with different contrasts. There are two main parts repeated in an iterative process as it was in the block matching algorithm: extraction of local forces $\mathbf{f}$ by measurements of similarity and a spatial deformation model producing the displacement field $\mathbf{u}$. The main difference is that these parts are completely independent here, whereas the regional similarity measure used in the block matching technique constrains the deformation and thus it acts as a part of the spatial deformation model. Another difference is in the way of extraction of the local forces. No local optimization is done here and the forces are directly computed from the point similarity measures.
The registration algorithm is based on previous work and it differs from the one presented in (Schwarz et al., 2007) namely in the spatial deformation model. The scheme of the algorithm is in Fig. 7. The displacement field $\mathbf{u}$ which maximizes global mutual information between a reference image and a floating image is searched in an iterative process which involves computation of local forces $\mathbf{f}$ in each individual voxel $\mathbf{x}$ and their regularization by the spatial deformation model. The regularization has two steps here. First, the displacements proportional to forces are smoothed by wavelet thresholding. These displacements are integrated into final deformation, which is done iteratively by summation. The second part of the model represents behaviour of elastic materials where

displacements wane if the forces are retracted. This is ensured by the overall Gaussian smoother.

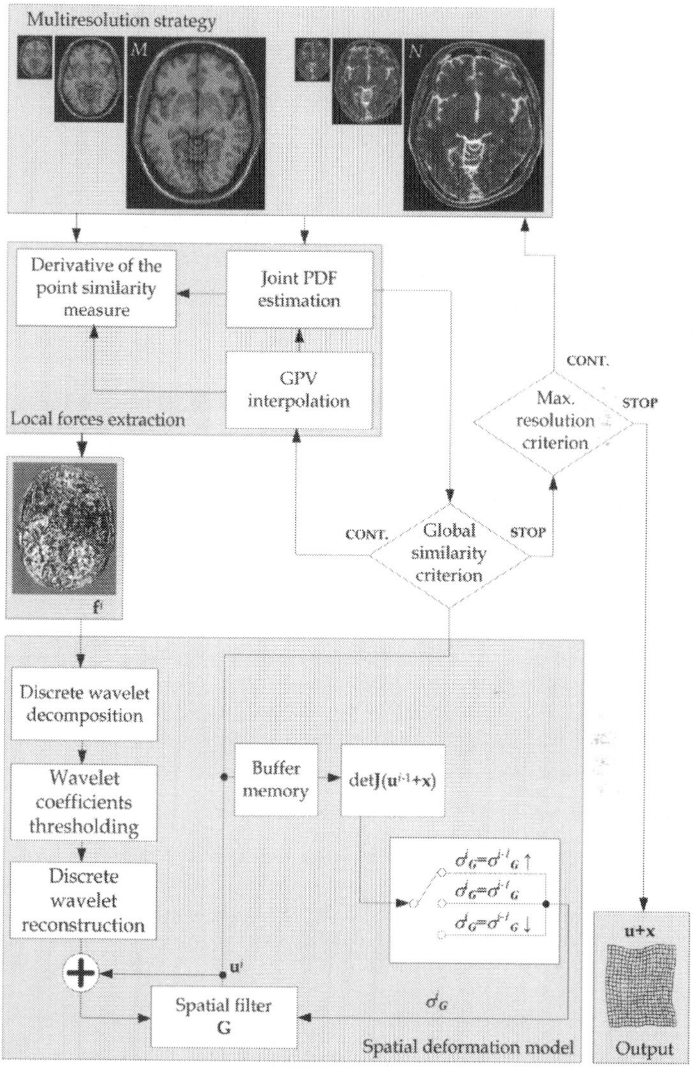

Fig. 7. The scheme of the high-dimensional registration algorithm proposed for DBM. The spatial deformation model consists of two basic components. First, the dense force field is smoothed by wavelet thresholding and then the displacements are regularized by Gaussian filtering to prevent breaking the topological condition of diffeomorphicity.

Nearly symmetric orthogonal wavelet bases (Abdelnour & Selesnick, 2001) are used for the decomposition and the reconstruction, which are performed in three levels here. All detail coefficients in the first and in the second level of decomposition are set to zero in the thresholding step of the algorithm. The initial setup of the standard deviation σ_G of the Gaussian filter is supposed to be found experimentally. The deformation has to preserve the topology, i.e. one-to-one mappings termed as diffeomorphic should only be produced. This requirement is satisfied if the determinant of the Jacobian of the deformation is held above zero:

$$\det \mathbf{J}(\varphi) \geq 0, \qquad \mathbf{J}(\varphi) = \begin{pmatrix} \frac{\partial \varphi_1}{\partial x} & \frac{\partial \varphi_1}{\partial y} & \frac{\partial \varphi_1}{\partial z} \\ \frac{\partial \varphi_2}{\partial x} & \frac{\partial \varphi_2}{\partial y} & \frac{\partial \varphi_2}{\partial z} \\ \frac{\partial \varphi_3}{\partial x} & \frac{\partial \varphi_3}{\partial y} & \frac{\partial \varphi_3}{\partial z} \end{pmatrix}. \tag{18}$$

where φ_1, φ_2 and φ_3 are components of the deformation over x, y and z axes respectively. The values of the Jacobian determinant are estimated by symmetric finite differences. The image is undesirably folded in the positions, where the Jacobian determinant is negative. In such a case, the deformation is not invertible. The σ_G-control block therefore ensures increments in σ_G if the minimum Jacobian determinant drops below a predefined threshold. On the other hand, the deformation should capture subtle anatomical variations among studied images. The σ_G-control block therefore ensures decrements in σ_G if the minimum Jacobian determinant starts growing during the registration process.

Local forces are computed for each voxel independently as the difference between forward forces and reverse forces, using the same symmetric registration approach as in the previously described block-matching technique. The forces are estimated by the gradient of a point similarity measure. The derivatives are approximated by central differences, such that the kth component of a force at a voxel $\mathbf{x}$ is defined here as:

$$\begin{aligned} f_k(\mathbf{x}) &= f_k^{forward}(\mathbf{x}) - f_k^{reverse}(\mathbf{x}) = \\ &= \frac{S(M(\mathbf{x}+\mathbf{u}(\mathbf{x})+\varepsilon_k), N(\mathbf{x})) - S(M(\mathbf{x}+\mathbf{u}(\mathbf{x})-\varepsilon_k), N(\mathbf{x}))}{2\varepsilon_k} - \\ &- \frac{S(M(\mathbf{x}), N(\mathbf{x}-\mathbf{u}(\mathbf{x})+\varepsilon_k)) - S(M(\mathbf{x}), N(\mathbf{x}-\mathbf{u}(\mathbf{x})-\varepsilon_k))}{2\varepsilon_k}, \quad k = 1 \ldots D, \end{aligned} \tag{19}$$

where ε_k is a voxel size component. The point similarity measure is evaluated in non-grid positions due to the displacement field applied on the image grids. Thus, GPV interpolation from neighboring grid points is employed here. For more details on computation and normalization of the local forces see (Schwarz et al., 2007).

3.3 Evaluation of deformable registration methods

The quality of the presented registration algorithms is assessed here on recovering synthetic deformations. The synthetic deformations based on thin-plate spline simulator (TPSsim) and Rogelj's spatial deformation simulator (RGsim) were applied to 2-D realistic T2-weighted MRI images with 3% noise and 20% intensity nonuniformity from the Simulated Brain Database (SBD) (Collins et al., 1998). The deformation simulators are described in detail in (Schwarz et al., 2007). The deformed images were then registered to artifact-free T1-weighted images from SBD and the error between the resulting and the initial deformation was measured. The appropriate evaluation measures are the root mean-squared residual displacement and the maximum absolute residual displacement. In the ideal case, the composition of the resulting and initial deformation should give an identity transform with no residual displacements.

Based on preliminary results and previous related works, the similarity measure S_{PMI} was used for both registration algorithms and the maximum level of subdivision in the block matching technique was set to 5. This level corresponds to the subimage size of 7x7 pixels. Although the next level of subdivision gave an increase in the global mutual information, the alignment expressed by quantitative evaluation measures and also by visual inspection was constant or worse.

The results expressed by root mean squared error displacements are presented in Table 1 and Table 2. The high-dimensional deformable registration technique gives more precise deformations with the respect to the lower residual error. The obtained results showed its ability to recover the smooth deformations generated by TPSsim as well as the complex deformations generated by RGsim.

$\|e_0^{MAX}\|$ [mm]	e_0^{RMS} [mm]	e^{RMS} [mm]					
		o_1 = 1, o_2 = 1	o_1 = 2, o_2 = 1	o_1 = 3, o_2 = 1	o_1 = 2, o_2 = 2	o_1 = 3, o_2 = 2	o_1 = 3, o_2 = 3
TPSsim							
5	2.47	0.59	0.57	0.56	**0.51**	0.52	**0.51**
8	3.95	0.74	0.71	0.69	0.68	**0.67**	**0.67**
10	4.93	0.91	0.89	0.86	0.85	**0.82**	**0.82**
12	5.92	1.17	1.38	1.34	**1.16**	1.36	1.35
RGsim							
5	2.30	0.93	0.87	0.85	0.79	0.77	**0.75**
8	3.67	1.47	1.41	1.37	1.39	1.33	**1.27**
10	4.59	2.19	2.17	2.09	2.05	2.07	**1.98**
12	5.51	3.09	2.93	**2.92**	3.05	2.93	2.99

Table 1. Root mean squared error displacements achieved by the multilevel block matching technique on various initial misregistration levels expressed by $|e_0^{MAX}|$ and e_0^{RMS} and with various setups in GPV interpolation kernel functions. The order of B-splines used in joint PDF estimate construction is signed as o_1 and the order of B-splines used in regional matching is signed as o_2.

$\mid e_0^{MAX} \mid$ [mm]	e_0^{RMS} [mm]	e^{RMS} [mm]				
		σ_G=2.0 mm	σ_G=2.5 mm	σ_G=3.0 mm	σ_G=3.5 mm	σ_G=4.0 mm
RGsim						
2.30	2.47	1.10	0.73	**0.69**	0.93	0.93
3.67	3.95	1.87	**1.07**	1.09	1.70	1.72
4.59	4.93	2.70	**1.46**	1.52	2.56	2.62
5.51	5.92	3.69	**2.02**	2.19	3.65	3.73
TPSsim						
2.47	2.30	0.84	0.60	**0.53**	0.61	0.58
3.95	3.67	1.26	0.74	**0.68**	1.00	0.96
4.93	4.59	1.77	0.84	**0.78**	1.48	1.43
5.92	5.51	2.42	1.16	**0.98**	2.20	2.18

Table 2. Root mean squared error displacements achieved by the highdimensional deformable registration method on various initial misregistration levels expressed by $\mid e_0^{MAX} \mid$ and e_0^{RMS} and with various setups in σ_G . Highlighted values show the best results achieved with the registration algorithm.

4. Deformation-based morphometry on real MRI datasets

In this section the results of high-resolution DBM in the first-episode and chronic schizophrenia are presented, in order to demonstrate the ability of the high-dimensional registration technique to capture the complex pattern of brain pathology in this condition. High-resolution T1-weighted MRI brain scans of 192 male subjects were obtained with a Siemens 1.5 T system in Faculty Hospital Brno. The group contained 49 male subjects with first-episode schizophrenia (FES), 19 chronic schizophrenia subjects (CH) and 124 healthy controls. The template from SBD which is based on 27 scans of one subject was used as the reference anatomy and 192 template-to-subject registrations with the use of the presented high-dimensional technique were performed. The resulting displacement vector fields were converted into scalar fields by calculating Jacobian determinants in each voxel of the stereotaxic space. The scalar fields were put into statistical analysis which included assessing normality, parametric significance testing. The Jacobian determinant can be viewed as a parameter which characterizes local volume changes, i.e. local shrinkage or enlargement caused by a deformation. The analysis of the scalar fields produced spatial map of t statistic which allowed to localize regions with significant differences in volumes of anatomical structures between the groups. Complex patterns of brain anatomy changes in schizophrenia subjects as compared to healthy controls were detected, see Fig. 8.

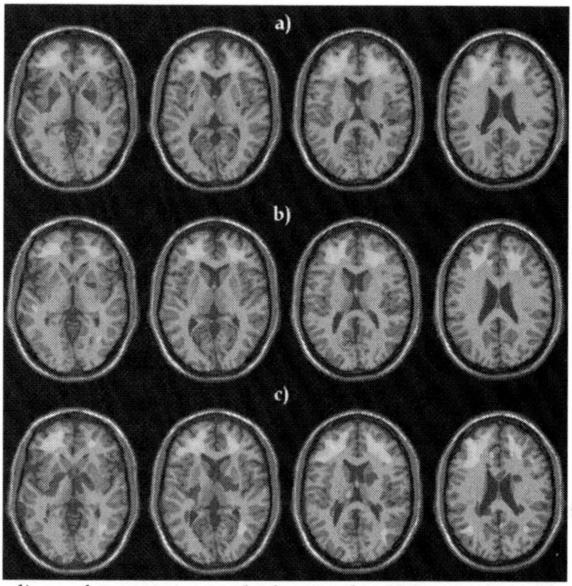

Fig. 8. Selected slices of t statistic overlaid over the SBD template. The t values were thresholded at the levels of significance α=5% corrected for multiple testing by the False Detection Rate method. The yellow regions represent local volume reductions in schizophrenia subjects compared to healthy controls and the red regions represent local volume enlargements. Compared groups: a) FES$\cup$CH vs. NC, b) FES vs. NC, c) CH vs. NC.

5. Conclusion

In this chapter two deformable registration methods were described: 1) a block matching technique based on parametric transformations with radial basis functions and 2) a high-dimensional registration technique with nonparametric deformation models based on spatial smoothing. The use of multimodal similarity measures was insisted. The multimodal character of the methods make them robust to tissue intensity variations which can be result of multimodality imaging as well as neuropsychological diseases or even normal aging.

One of the described algorithms was demonstrated in the field of computational neuroanatomy, particularly for fully automated spatial detection of anatomical abnormalities in first-episode and chronic schizophrenia based on 3-D MRI brain scans.

Acknowledgement

The work was supported by grants IGA MH CZ NR No. 9893-4 and No. 10347-3.

References

Abdelnour, A. F. & Selesnick, I. W. (2001). Nearly symmetric orthogonal wavelet bases. *Proc. IEEE Int. Conf. Acoust., Speech, Signal Processing (ICASSP)*, May 2001, IEEE, Salt Lake City

Ali, A. A.; Dale, A. M.; Badea, A. & Johnson, G. A. (2005). Automated segmentation of neuroanatomical structures in multispectral MR microscopy of the mouse brain. *NeuroImage*, Vol. 27, No. 2, 425–435, ISSN 1053-8119

Alterovitz, R.; Goldberg, K.; Kurhanewicz, J.; Pouliot, J. & Hsu, I. (2004). Image registration for prostate MR spectroscopy using biomechanical modeling and optimization of force and stiffness parameters. *Proceedings of 26th Annual International Conference of IEEE Engineering in Medicine and Biology Society*, 2004, pp. 1722–1725, ISBN 0-7803-8440-7, IEEE, San Francisco

Amidror, I. (2002). Scattered data interpolation methods for electronic imaging systems: a survey. *Journal of Electronic Imaging*, Vol. 11, No. 2, pp.157–176, ISSN 1017-9909

Ashburner, J. & Friston, K. J. (2000). Voxel-based morphometry - the methods. *NeuroImage*, Vol. 11, No. 6, 805–821, ISSN 1053-8119

Ashburner, J. (2007). A fast diffeomorphic image registration algorithm. *NeuroImage*, Vol. 38, No. 1, 95–113, ISSN 1053-8119

Chen, H. & Varshney, P. K. (2003). Mutual information-based CT-MR brain image registration using generalized partial volume point histogram estimation. *IEEE Transactions on Medical Imaging*, Vol. 22, No. 9, 1111–1119, ISSN 0278-0062

Christensen, G. E.; Rabbitt, R. D. & Miller M. I. (1996). Deformable templates using large deformation kinematics. *IEEE Transactions on Image Processing*, Vol. 5, No. 10, 1435–1447, ISSN 0278-0062.

Clatz, O. et al. (2005). Robust nonrigid registration to capture brain shift from intraoperative MRI. *IEEE Transactions on Medical Imaging*, Vol. 24, No. 11, 1417–1427, ISSN 0278-0062.

Collins, D. L. et al. (1998). Design and construction of a realistic digital brain phantom.*IEEE Transactions on Medical Imaging*, Vol. 17, No. 3, 463–468, ISSN 0278-0062

Collins, D. L.; Neelin, P.; Peters, T. M. & Evans, A. C. (1994). Automatic 3D inter-subject registration of MR volumetric data in standardized Talairach space. *Journal of Computer Assisted Tomography*, Vol. 18, No. 2, 192–205, ISSN 0363-8715.

Čapek, M.; Mroz, L. & Wegenkittl, R. (2001). Robust and fast medical registration of 3D-multi-modality data sets. *Proceedings of the International Federation for Medical & Biological Engineering*, pp. 515–518, ISBN 953-184-023-7, Pula

Donato, G. & Belongie, S. (2002). Approximation methods for thin plate spline mappings and principal warps. *Proceedings of European Conference on Computer Vision*, pp. 531–542

Downie, T. R. & Silverman, B. W. (2001). A wavelet mixture approach to the estimation of image deformation functions. *Sankhya: The Indian Journal Of Statistics Series B*, Vol. 63, No. 2, 181–198, ISSN 0581-5738

Ferrant, M.; Warfield, S. K.; Nabavi, A.; Jolesz, F. A. & Kikinis, R. (2001). Registration of 3D intraoperative MR images of the brain using a finite element biomechanical model. In: *IEEE Transactions on Medical Imaging*, Vol. 20, No. 12, 1384–97, ISSN 0278-0062

Fornefett, M.; Rohr, K. & Stiehl, H. S. (2001). Radial basis functions with compact support for elastic registration of medical images. *Image and Vision Computing*, Vol. 19, No. 1, 87–96, ISSN 0262-8856

Friston, K. J. et al. (2007). *Statistical Parametric Mapping: The Analysis of Functional Brain Images*, Elsevier, ISBN 0123725607, London

Gaser, C. et al. (2001). Deformation-based morphometry and its relation to conventional volumetry of brain lateral ventricles in MRI. *NeuroImage*, Vol. 13, No. 6, 1140–1145, ISSN 1053-8119

Gaser, C. et al. (2004). Ventricular enlargement in schizophrenia related to volume reduction of the thalamus, striatum, and superior temporal cortex. *American Journal of Psychiatry*, Vol. 161, No. 1, 154–156, ISSN 0002-953X

Gholipour, A. et al. (2007). Brain functional localization: a survey of image registration techniques. *IEEE Transactions on Medical Imaging*, Vol. 26, No. 4, 427–451, ISSN 0278-0062.

Gramkow, C. & Bro-Nielsen, M. (1997). Comparison of three filters in the solution of the Navier-Stokes equation in registration. *Proceedings of Scandinavian Conference on Image Analysis SCIA'97*, 1997, pp. 795–802, Lappeenranta

Ibanez, L.; Schroeder, W.; Ng, L. & Cates, J. (2003). *The ITK Software Guide*. Kitware Inc, ISBN 1930934106

Kostelec, P.; Weaver, J. & Healy D. Jr. (1998). Multiresolution elastic image registration. *Medical Physics*, Vol. 25, No. 9, 1593–1604, ISSN 0094-2405

Kubečka, L. & Jan, J. (2004). Registration of bimodal retinal images - improving modifications. *Proceedings of 26th Annual International Conference of IEEE Engineering in Medicine and Biology Society*, pp. 1695–1698, ISBN 0-7803-8440-7, IEEE, San Francisco

Maes, F. (1998). Segmentation and registration of multimodal medical images: from theory, implementation and validation to a useful tool in clinical practice. Catholic University, Leuven

Maintz, J. B. A. & Viergever, M. A. (1998). A survey of medical image registration. *Medical Image Analysis*, Vol. 2, No. 1, 1–37, ISSN 1361-8415

Maintz, J. B. A.; Meijering, E. H. W. & Viergever, M. A. (1998). General multimodal elastic registration based on mutual Information. In: *Medical Imaging 1998: Image Processing*, Kenneth, M. & Hanson, (Ed.), 144–154, SPIE

Mechelli, A., Price, C. J., Friston, K. J. & Ashburner, J. (2005). Voxel-based morphometry of the human brain: methods and applications. *Current Medical Imaging Reviews*, vol. 1, No. 2, 105–113, ISSN 1573-4056

Modersitzki, J. (2004). *Numerical Methods for Image Registration*. Oxford University Press, ISBN 0198528418, New York.

Pauchard, Y.; Smith, M. R. & Mintchev, M. P. (2004). Modeling susceptibility difference artifacts produced by metallic implants in magnetic resonance imaging with point-based thin-plate spline image registration. *Proceedings of 26th Annual International Conference of IEEE Engineering in Medicine and Biology Society*, pp. 1766–1769, ISBN 0-7803-8440-7, IEEE, San Francisco

Peckar, W.; Schnörr, C.; Rohr, K.; Stiehl, H. S. & Spetzger, U. (1998). Linear and incremental estimation of elastic deformations in medical registration using prescribed displacements. *Machine Graphics & Vision*, Vol. 7, No. 4, 807–829, ISSN 1230-0535

Pluim, P. W. J.; Maintz J. B. A. & Viergever M. A. (2001). Mutual information matching in multiresolution contexts. *Image and Vision Computing,* Vol. 19, No. 1, 45–52, ISSN 0262-8856

Rogelj, P.; Kovačič, S. & Gee, J. C. (2003). Point similarity measures for non-rigid registration of multi-modal data. *Computer Vision and Image Understanding,* Vol. 92, No. 1, 112–140, ISSN 1077-3142

Rogelj, P. & Kovačič, S. (2003). Point similarity measure based on mutual information. In: *Biomedical Image Registration: Revised Papers,* Gee, J. C.; Maintz, J. B. A. & Vannier, M. W. (Ed.), 112–121, Springer-Verlag, ISBN 978-3-540-20343-8

Rogelj, P. & Kovačič, S. (2003). Symmetric image registration. *Medical Image Analysis,* Vol. 10, No. 3, 484–493, ISSN 1361-8415

Rogelj, P. & Kovačič, S. (2004). Spatial deformation models for non-rigid image registration. *Proceedings of 9th Computer Vision Winter Workshop CVWW'04,* 2004, pp. 79–88, Slovenian Pattern Recognition Society, Piran.

Rohlfing, T.; Maurer, C. R.; Bluemke, D. A. & Jacobs, M. A. (2003). Volume-preserving nonrigid registration of MR breast images using free-form deformation with an incompresibility constraint. *IEEE Transactions on Medical Imaging,* Vol. 12, No. 6, 730–741, ISSN 0278-0062.

Rohr, K. (2001). Elastic registration of multimodal medical images: a survey. *Künstliche Intelligenz,* Vol. 14, No. 3, 11–17, ISSN 0933-1875

Rueckert, D. et al. (1999). Nonrigid registration using free-form deformations: application to breast MR images. *IEEE Transactions on Medical Imaging,* Vol. 18, No. 8, 712–721, ISSN 0278-0062

Schnabel, J. A. et al. (2003). Validation of non-rigid image registration using finite element methods: application to breast MR images. *IEEE Transactions on Medical Imaging,* Vol. 22, No. 2, 238–247, ISSN 0278-0062.

Schwarz, D.; Kašpárek, T., Provazník, I. & Jarkovský, J. (2007). A deformable registration method for automated morphometry of MRI brain images in neuropsychiatric research. *IEEE Transactions on Medical Imaging,* Vol. 26, No. 4, 452-461, ISSN 0278-0062.

Studholme, C.; Hill, D. L. G.; & Hawkes, D. J. (1999). An overlap invariant entropy measure of 3D medical image alignment. *Pattern Recognition,* Vol. 32, No. 1, 71–86, ISSN 1054-6618

Thirion, J. P. (1998). Image matching as a diffusion process: an analogy with Maxwell's demons. *Medical Image Analysis,* Vol. 2, No. 3, 243–260, ISSN 1361-8415

Viola, P. & Wells, W. M. (1995). Alignment by maximization of mutual information. *International Journal of Computer Vision,* Vol. 24, No. 2, 137–154, ISSN 0920-5691

Wendland, H. (1995). Piecewise polynomial, positive definite and compactly supported radial functions of minimal degree. *Advances in Computational Mathematics,* Vol. 4, No. 1, 389–396, ISSN 1019-7168

Xu, L.; Groth, K. M.; Pearlson, G.; Schretlen, D. J.; Calhoun, V. D. (2008). Source-based morphometry: the use of independent component analysis to identify gray matter differences with application to schizophrenia. *Human Brain Mapping,* Vol. 30, No. 3, 711–724, ISSN 1065-9471

Zitova, B. and Flusser J. (2003). Image registration methods: a survey. *Image and Vision Computing,* Vol. 21, No. 11, 977–1000, ISSN 0262-8856

5

Functional semi-automated segmentation of renal DCE-MRI sequences using a Growing Neural Gas algorithm

Chevaillier Beatrice[(1)], Collette Jean-Luc[(1)], Mandry Damien[(2)], Claudon Michel[(2)] & Pietquin Olivier[(1,2)]

[(1)]SUPELEC-Metz campus, IMS Research Group
[(2)]IADI, INSERM, ERI 13 ; Nancy University
France

1. Introduction

In this chapter we describe a semi-automatic segmentation method for dynamic contrast-enhanced magnetic resonance imaging (DCE-MRI) sequences for renal function assessment. Among the different MRI techniques aiming at studying the renal function, DCE-MRI with gadolinium chelates injection is the most widely used (Grenier et al., 2003). Several parameters like the glomerular filtration rate or the differential renal function can be non-invasively computed from perfusion curves of different Regions Of Interest (ROI). So segmentation of internal anatomical kidney structures like cortex, medulla and pelvo-caliceal cavities is crucial for functional assessment detection of diseases affecting different parts of this organ. Manual segmentation by a radiologist is fairly delicate because images are blurred and highly noisy. Moreover the different compartments are not visible during the same perfusion phase because of contrast changes: cavities are enhanced during late perfusion phase, whereas cortex and medulla can only be separated near the cortical peak, when the contrast agent enters the kidney (figure 1); consequently they cannot be delineated on a single image. Radiologists have to examine the whole sequence in order to choose the two most suitable frames: the operation is time-consuming and functional analysis can vary greatly in case of misregistration or through-plane motion. Some classical semi-automated methods are often used in the medical field but few of them have been tested on renal DCE-MRI sequences (Michoux et al., 2006). In (Coulam et al., 2002), cortex of pig kidneys is delineated by simple intensity thresholding during cortical enhancement phase, but precision is limited essentially because of noise. In (Lv et al., 2008), a three-dimensional kidney extraction and a segmentation of internal renal structures are performed using a region-growing technique. Anyway only few frames are used, so problems due frames selection and non corrected motion remain. As the contrast temporal evolution is different in every compartment for physiological reasons, pixels can be classified according to their time-intensity curves: such a method can improve both noise robustness and reproducibility. In (Zoellner et al., 2006), independent component analysis allows recovering

some functional regions but does not result in segmentations comparable to morphological ones: any pixel can actually be attributed to zero, one or more compartment. In (Sun et al., 2004), a multi-step approach including successive registrations and segmentations is proposed: pixels are classified using a K-means partitioning algorithm applied to their time-intensity curves. Nevertheless a functional segmentation using some unsupervised classification method and resulting in only three ROIs corresponding to cortex, medulla and cavities seems to be hard to obtained directly. This is mainly due to considerable contrast dissimilarities between pixels in a same compartment despite some common characteristics (Chevaillier et al., 2008a).
Concerning validation, very few results for real data have been exposed. In (Rusinek et al., 2007), a segmentation error is defined in connection with a manual segmentation as the global volume of false-positive (oversegmented) and false-negative (undersegmented) voxels. Nevertheless assessment consists mostly in qualitative consistency with manual segmentations or in comparisons between the corresponding compartment volumes or between the induced renograms (Song et al., 2005).

We propose to test a semi-automated split (2.1) and merge method (2.2) for renal functional segmentation. The kidney pixels are first clustered according to their contrast evolution using a vector quantization algorithm. These clusters are then merged thanks to some characteristic criteria of their prototype functional curves to get the three final anatomical compartments. Operator intervention consists only in a coarse tuning of two independent thresholds for merging, and is thus easy and quick to perform while keeping the practitioner into the loop. The method is also relatively robust because the whole sequence is used instead of only two frames as for traditional manual segmentation. In the absence of ground truth for results assessment, a manual anatomical segmentation by a radiologist is considered as a reference. Some discrepancy criteria are computed between this segmentation and functional ones. As a comparison, the same criteria are evaluated between the reference and another manual segmentation.
This book chapter is an extended version of (Chevaillier et al., 2008b).

2. Method for functional segmentation

2.1 Vector quantization of time-intensity curves

The temporal evolution of contrast for each of the N pixels of a kidney results from a DCE-MRI registered sequence: examples of three frames for different perfusion phases can be seen in figure 1.
Let I_{ip} be the intensity at time p for the pixel x_i, I_B the mean value for baseline and I_L the mean value during late phase for the time-intensity curve of entire kidney. Let $\xi_i = (\xi_{i1},\ldots,\xi_{iN_T})$ be the N_T-components vector associated with each pixel, where $\xi_{ip} = (I_{ip} - I_B)/(I_L - I_B)$ (intensity normalization is performed in order to have similar dynamic for any kidney). The N vectors ξ_i are considered as samples of an unknown probability distribution over a manifold $X \subseteq R^{N_T}$ with a density of probability $p(\xi)$.

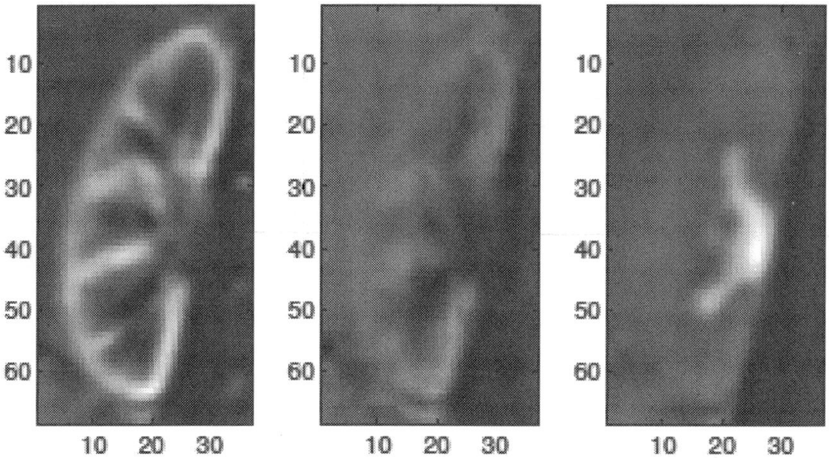

Fig. 1. Examples of frames from a DCE-MRI sequence during arterial peak (left), filtration (middle) and late phase (right)

The aim is to find a set $\{w_j\}_{1 \le j \le K} \subset X$ of prototypes (or nodes) that maps the distribution with a given distortion. Let be $w(\xi) = \arg\min_{w_j} \|\xi - w_j\|^2$. The Growing Neural Gas with targeting (GNG-T) (Frezza-Buet, 2008), which is a variant of the classical Growing Neural Gas algorithm (Fritzke, 1995), minimizes a cost function that tends towards the distortion:

$$E = \int_X \|w((\xi) - \xi\|^2 p(\xi) d\xi = \sum_{j=1}^{K} E_j \tag{1}$$

where

$$E_j = \int_{V_j} \|w_j - \xi\|^2 p(\xi) d\xi \text{ and } V_j = \{\xi \in X : w(\xi) = w_j\} \tag{2}$$

V_j is the so-called Voronoï cell of w_j and consists of all points of X that are closer to w_j than to any other w_i. The set of $\{V_j\}_{1 \le j \le K}$ is a partition of X.

More precisely, GNG-T algorithm builds iteratively a network consisting in both:

- a set of prototypes,
- a graph structure preserving the topology of the underlying probability distribution.

This graph is made up of a set of connections between nodes defining a topological neighbourhood relation in the parameter space. It approximates the induced Delaunay triangulation of the set $\{w_j\}_{1 \le j \le K}$ on the manifold X (Martinetz et al., 1993). Edges are drawn up according to a competitive Hebbian learning rule: the basic principle is, for each input ξ_i, to connect the two best matching prototypes. Two prototypes that are directly

linked in the final graph should thus have similar temporal behaviour. Both the winner, i.e. the closest prototype of the current data point, and all its topological neighbours are adjusted after each iteration. Influence of initialization is thus reduced for GNG-T compared to on-line K-means for instance.
The number K of prototypes is iteratively determined to reach a given average node distortion T. While a prior lattice has to be chosen for other algorithms like self-organising map (Kohonen, 2001), no topological knowledge is required here: the graph adapts automatically to any distribution structure during the building process.
GNG-T is an iterative algorithm that processes successive epochs. During each epoch, N samples $(\xi_j)_{1\leq i\leq N}$ are presented as GNG-T inputs. An accumulation variable e_j is associated with each node w_j: it is initialized to zero at the beginning of the epoch and is updated every time w_j actually wins by adding the error $\left\|\xi_i - w_j\right\|^2$. When the cost function defined in equation (1) is minimal, all the E_j reach the same value, denoted T'. For a given epoch, E_j can be estimated by:

$$E_j \approx \frac{e_j}{N} \tag{3}$$

T' helps to adapt the number of nodes at the end of each epoch. It is then compared to the desired target T. If $T' > T$, vector quantization is not accurate enough: a new node is thus added between the node w_{j_0} with the strongest accumulated error e_{j_0} and its topological neighbour w_{j_1} with the strongest error e_{j_1}, and the edges are adapted accordingly. If $T' < T$, the node with the weakest accumulated error is eliminated to reduce accuracy. All implementation details can be found in (Frezza-Buet, 2008).
Let us note that the aim of the algorithm is not to classify pixels but to perform vector quantization. For this reason it tends to give a fairly large K value. A given class is actually represented by a subset of connected nodes, and all points that belong to the union of their associated Voronoï cells are attributed to this class. As an example, the quantization results and the boundaries of the clusters for a two-dimensional Gaussian mixture distribution are given in figure 2 (notice that our problem is N_T-dimensional). Nevertheless, for real cases, a single connected network is obtained most of the time because of noise and because the distributions are not straightforwardly separable. So an additional merging step is mandatory in order to break non significant edges and then obtain the final segmentation in three anatomical compartments.

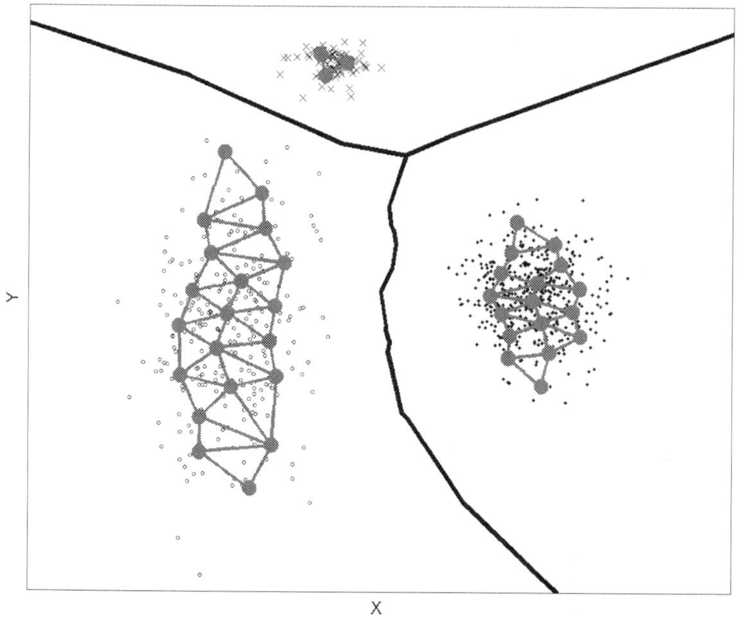

Fig. 2. Results of a vector quantization by GNG-T procedure with final partition (large solid lines): small dots represent samples of the distribution, large dots are the resulting nodes linked with edges.

2.2 Formation of the three final compartments for real data

Each node has then to be assigned to one of the three anatomical compartments. Typical time-intensity curves with the main perfusion phases (baseline, arterial peak, filtration, equilibrium and late phase) are shown in figure 3.

Nevertheless, for a given kidney, noticeable differences can be observed inside each compartment (see figure 4). The Euclidean distance between curves is therefore not a criterion significant and robust enough to aggregate nodes. Indeed the distance between two prototypes of two distinct ROIs may often be smaller than disparity within a single compartment. This is true even if distance is evaluated only for points of filtration, during which contrast evolutions should be the most different. It is why some physiology related characteristics of the contrast evolution have to be used to get the final compartments.

We proceed as follows:

- First, as cavities should be the brighter structure in the late phase (see figure 3) due physiological reasons, nodes whose average intensity during this stage is greater than a given threshold t_1 and that are directly connected to each other in the GNG graph are considered as cavities.

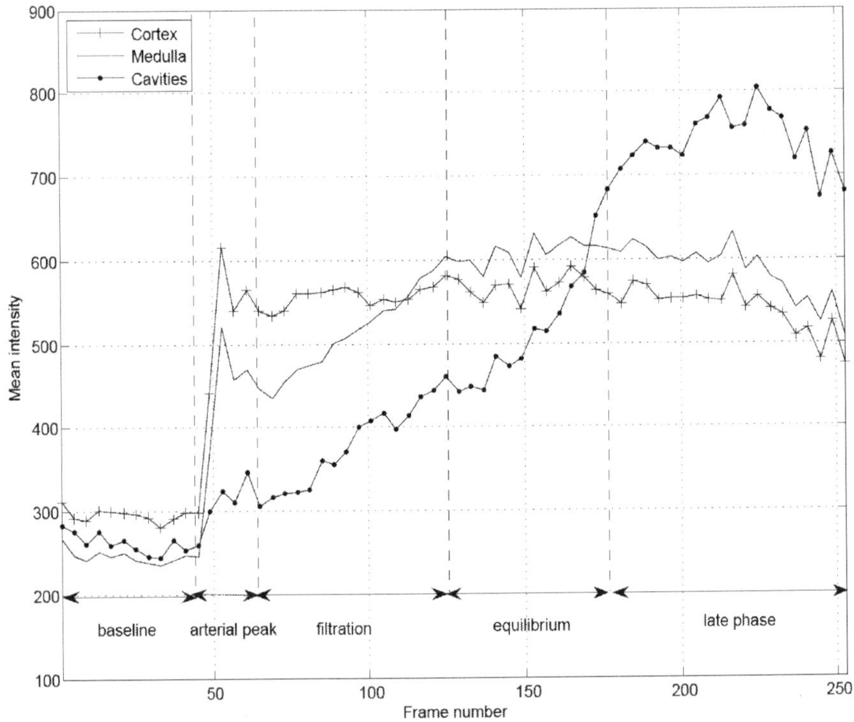

Fig. 3. Typical time-intensity curves for cortex, medulla and cavities

- In a second step, filtration phase is used to separate cortex and medulla. Filtration rate depends on the tissue nature. So the slope of time-intensity curves during filtration (see figure 3) is evaluated using standard linear regression for all remaining prototypes: a node is attributed to the cortex if the corresponding slope is less than a given threshold t_2, else it is assigned to the medulla.

The two thresholds t_1 and t_2 are initialized so that cortex represents approximately 50% and cavities about 20% of kidney area and are adjusted by an observer. This is the only manual intervention of the whole operation. As the algorithm is very fast, the tuning step can be done in real time. Let us stress that the second criterion would not be sufficient to distinguish cavities from cortex and medulla because of a theoretically unexpected but fairly high arterial peak that can be observed in figure 4(c): this peak is induced by the great vascularization of the whole kidney and may appear in all ROIs. Furthermore the use of topological edges for cavities determination avoids classifying in this compartment some nodes that have a similar contrast in late phase but whose behaviour differs sufficiently in other filtration phases.

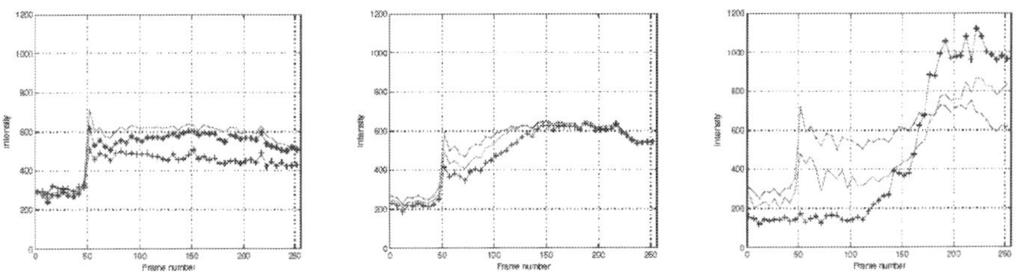

(a) (b) (c)

Fig. 4. Some examples of time-intensity curves for prototypes attributed to cortex (a), medulla (b) and cavities (c) of a given kidney

3. Experiment

3.1 Materials

Eight two-dimensional low resolution DCE-MRI sequences of normal kidney perfusion with 256 images were used (acquisition duration: about 12 minutes, temporal resolution: about 3 s). The examinations were performed on a whole-body 1.5T MR-scanner (General Electric Healthcare). A 3D ultrafast gradient echo LAVA sequence was used with the following parameters: 15° flip angle, TR/TE 2.3 ms/1.1 ms. The slice that contained the largest surface of renal tissue was then selected. The initial matrix size was 256×256 with pixel size between 1.172 mm and 1.875 mm (slice thickness: 10 mm). A rectangular area containing kidney was delineated (size between 47×35 and 84×59). In-plane movements due to respiration were corrected by a rigid registration algorithm including translations and rotation. Because of rapid and high contrast changes during perfusion mutual information was chosen as a similarity criterion (Pluim et al., 2003). Anyway through-plane motions remained and frames were highly noisy. An example of frames for three different perfusion phases is shown in figure 1.

3.2 Manual segmentations by radiologists

The different sequences were presented to two experienced radiologists (OP1 and OP2) after automatic registration. They had to delineate three ROIs, namely the cortex, the medulla and the pelvo-caliceal cavities as well as a global kidney mask. To do so, the following procedure was set up:

1. visualization of the complete sequence,
2. selection of a late phase frame were cavities contrast is maximum and manual segmentation of the cavities,
3. identification of the frame corresponding to the cortical enhancement peak and manual segmentation of the cortex,
4. segmentation of medulla by difference with cortex and cavities already segmented.

A global mask was then extracted as the common area of the two manual segmentations, including the three ROIs delineated by the two radiologists. This mask was subsequently used for functional segmentation (only pixels inside this mask were used by the GNG-T algorithm). Two examples of manual segmentations can be seen in figure 5.

3.3 Discrepancy criteria for segmentation comparison

For each of the eight cases a manual segmentation is considered as a reference. The functional segmentation obtained thanks to the proposed method or another manual one will be both compared to this reference.

Every segmentation can be considered as a binary map, with label 1 inside the ROI and label~0 outside. Let be R the reference segmentation and T the tested one. Four types of pixels can then be defined, according to their labels in R and T:

Pixel type	Label in R	Label in T
True Positive (TP)	1	1
False Negative (FN)	1	0
False Positive (FP)	0	1
True Negative (TN)	0	0

Four discrepancy measures between R and T are evaluated for each ROI:

- percentage overlap $PO = 100 \times TP/(TP + FN)$, i.e. percentage of pixels of the reference ROI that are in the test ROI too,
- percentage extra $PE = 100 \times FP/(TP + FN)$, i.e. the number of pixels that are in the test ROI while they are out of reference ROI, divided by the number of pixels in the reference ROI. Perfect segmentation would give $PO = 100\%$ and $PE = 0\%$. High values for both PO and PE for a given segmentation tend to point out some oversegmentation of the corresponding compartment. A high PE associated to a weak PO may indicate that the ROI is globally wrong positioned.
- similarity index $SI = 2 \times TP/(TP + FN + FP)$. SI is sensitive to both differences in size and location (Zijdenbos et al., 1994). For instance two equally sized ROIs that share half of their pixels would yield $SI = 1/2$. A ROI covering another that is twice as little would give $SI = 2/3$. For a perfect segmentation the SI value would be 1.
- mean distance MD (in pixel) between contours of test and reference segmentation: MD is the average distance between every pixel of the contour in the test segmentation and the closest pixel of the reference contour.

SI is the only selected criterion that is independent of the chosen reference, however its values appear twice in the tables in order to facilitate comparisons.

4. Results

Examples of two manual segmentations and of a functional semi-automated one can be seen in figure 5. For this case, size of ROIs varies between 532 and 700 pixels for cortex, 375 and 559 for medulla, 161 and 217 for cavities. The delineated contours are superimposed on MR images of the renal pixels (region out of the global kidney mask is black). Frames correspond to perfusion phases during which each compartment is visible at best:

- arterial peak for cortex and medulla
- late phase for cavities.

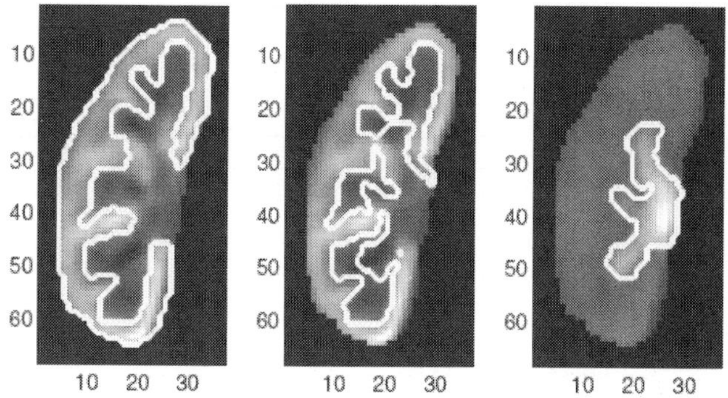

(a) Anatomical manual segmentation (OP1)

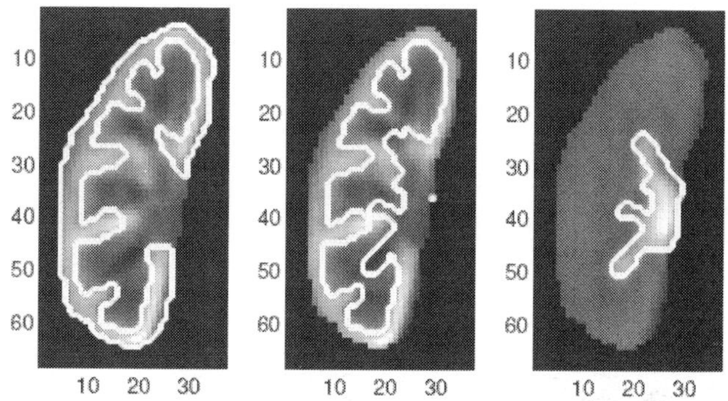

(b) Anatomical manual segmentation (OP2)

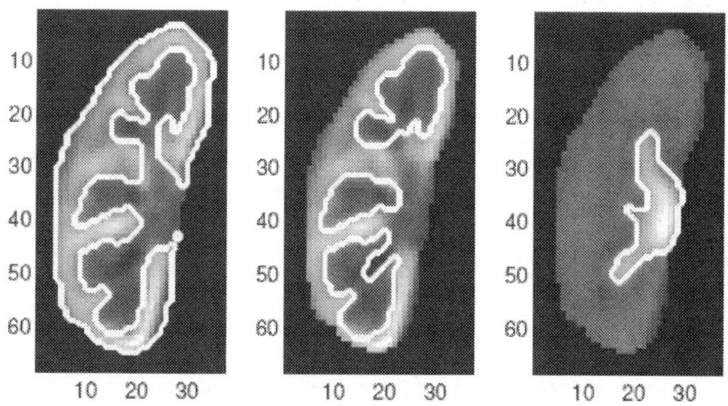

(c) Functional semi-automated segmentation

Fig.5. Example of cortex (left), medulla (middle) and cavities (right) segmentations

For almost all the tested kidneys, a very good visual qualitative consistency between these frames and functional segmentation is obtained.
For quantitative comparisons the manual segmentation OP1 is first considered as the reference. Table 1 Part 1 shows for each type of ROI, means over the eight cases of discrepancy measures between:

- the semi-automated segmentation (GNG-T) and OP1,
- the second manual segmentation (OP2) and OP1.

In table 1 Part 2, on the other hand, the reference is OP2. The percentage of well classified pixels for a given compartment is the sum of TP pixels over the eight cases divided by the total number of pixels for this type of ROI. For global kidney it is the sum of TP pixels for all ROIs over the eight cases divided by the total number of pixels of all kidney global masks. Results for small kidneys have less influence on this percentage than on mean overlap.

Part 1

Segmentation by	OP2	GNG-T
Well classified pixels (%)	69.8	83.7
Overlap (%)	71.8	83.2
Extra pixels(%)	9.2	21.9
Similarity index	0.79	0.81
Mean distance to reference contour	0.6	0.8

(a) Cortex

Segmentation by	OP2	GNG-T
Well classified pixels (%)	84.8	73.0
Overlap (%)	84.0	73.0
Extra pixels(%)	56.6	33.7
Similarity index	0.70	0.71
Mean distance to reference contour	1.0	0.8

(b) Medulla

Segmentation by	OP2	GNG-T
Well classified pixels (%)	74.9	68.7
Overlap (%)	73.9	69.8
Extra pixels(%)	16.1	11.1
Similarity index	0.77	0.77
Mean distance to reference contour	0.8	0.7

(c) Cavities

Segmentation by	OP2	GNG-T
Well classified pixels (%)	74.9	77.6

(d) Global kidney

Part 2

Segmentation by	OP1	GNG-T
Well classified pixels (%)	89.7	85.8
Overlap (%)	89.0	85.7
Extra pixels(%)	36.1	34.8
Similarity index	0.79	0.78
Mean distance to reference contour	0.7	0.9

(a) Cortex

Segmentation by	OP1	GNG-T
Well classified pixels (%)	60.3	69.7
Overlap (%)	60.5	69.9
Extra pixels(%)	11.8	16.3
Similarity index	0.70	0.75
Mean distance to reference contour	1.0	0.9

(b) Medulla

Segmentation by	OP1	GNG-T
Well classified pixels (%)	81.8	74.9
Overlap (%)	82.2	76.4
Extra pixels(%)	32.4	12.6
Similarity index	0.77	0.80
Mean distance to reference contour	0.9	0.5

(c) Cavities

Segmentation by	OP1	GNG-T
Well classified pixels (%)	74.9	76.7

(d) Global kidney

Table 1. Discrepancy measures for segmentations of the three ROIs when OP1 (Part 1) or OP2 (Part 2) are considered as a reference.

Similarity measures between functional segmentation and any manual segmentation are very similar to those computed between the two manual ones. A better score for overlap is always compensated by an increase of extra pixels. The percentage of globally well classified pixels is even higher for the proposed method, and the similarity index and the mean distance between contours are most of the time better. This was not the case for k-means clustering of the time-intensity curves, where scores were lower for functional segmentation (Chevaillier et al., 2008a): for instance an increase of 3 to 6% in the percentage of globally well classified pixels can be noted for the new method. Furthermore results do not depend significantly on the type of ROI. The quality of functional segmentation does not change with the region size: cavities that are much smaller than the two other ROIs are recovered as correctly as those. Moreover this technique is fast and user-friendly. The size of the prototype set stemming from GNG-T varies between 10 and 30 nodes: it depends essentially on temporal evolution complexity induced in particular by vascularization artefacts and highly noisy acquisition but little on kidney size. Nevertheless operator has only to adjust two thresholds: the first allows extracting cavities by adding or taking off the most relevant nodes, whereas the second is used in the same way to set relative areas of cortex and medulla. The splitting step with GNG-T allows to consider first the global time-intensity evolution and to reduce noise effect; the threshold adjustment is then easier because at each tuning level a relatively numerous set of pixels with homogenous temporal evolution is added.

5. Conclusion and perspectives

A semi-automated method for functional segmentation of internal kidney structures using DCE-MRI sequences was tested and compared with manual segmentations by radiologists. Good qualitative consistency between the two types of segmentation is observed. Similarity measures between a manual segmentation and a functional one are comparable and often better than the same criteria evaluated between two manual segmentations. Results are better than those obtained with the k-means algorithm applied on the same data: for instance the percentage of well classified pixels is 3 to 6% higher. Let us note that the derived time-intensity curves of each compartment are almost identical for functional or manual segmentation. Thus the method is suitable for renal segmentation from DCE-MRI. Moreover this technique is user friendly because the only manual intervention during the whole segmentation process consists in the coarse real-time tuning of two independent thresholds. It offers more reproducibility and is also greatly faster than manual segmentation: the latter requires 12 to 15 minutes for one sequence, versus about 30 seconds for the former, including threshold adjustment. To validate the method further tests will be performed on a larger database including both healthy and pathological kidneys. In the latter case, an adaptation of the physiological criteria previously used to obtain the final compartments can be needed because new temporal behaviours may appear.

6. References

Chevaillier, B. ; Ponvianne, Y. ; Collette, J.L. ; Mandry, D. ; Claudon, M. & Pietquin, O. (2008a). Functional semi-automated segmentation of renal DCE-MRI sequences, *Proceedings of the IEEE International Conference on Acoustics, Speech and Signal Processing (ICASSP 2008)*, pp. 525-528, ISBN 1-4244-1484-9, Las Vegas (NV, USA), March 2008..

Chevaillier, B. ; Ponvianne, Y. ; Collette, J.L. ; Mandry, D. ; Claudon, M. & Pietquin, O. (2008b). Functional semi-automated segmentation of renal DCE-MRI sequences using a Growing Neural Gas algorithm, *Proceedings of the 16th European Signal Processing Conference (EUSIPCO 08)*, EURASIP, Lausanne (Switzerland), August 2008.

Coulam, C.H.; Bouley, D.M. & Sommer, F.G. (2002). Measurement of renal volumes with contrast-enhanced MRI. *Journal Of Magnetic Resonance Imaging,* Vol. 15, No. 2, February 2002, pp. 174-179, ISSN 1053-1807

Frezza-Buet, H. (2008). Following non-stationary distributions by controlling the vector quantization accuracy of a growing neural gas network. *Neurocomputing,* Vol. 71, No7-9., March 2008, pp. 1191-1202, ISSN 0925-2312

Fritzke, B. (1995). A growing neural gas network learns topologies, *Advances in Neural Information Processing Systems, Proceedings of 1995 Conference,* pp. 625-632, ISBN 0-262-20107-0, Denver CO, November 1995, D. S. Touretzky, M. C. Mozer, M. E. Hasselmo, eds. MIT Press, Cambridge

Grenier, P.; Basseau, F. ; Ries, M. ; Tyndal, B. ; Jones, R. & Moonen, C. (2003). Functional MRI of the kidney, *Abdominal Imaging,* Vol. 28, No.2, March 2003, pp. 164-175, ISSN 0942-8925

Kohonen, T. (2001). *Self-organizing maps,* Springer, ISBN 9783540679219, New York

Lv, D.; Zhuang, J.; Chen, H.; Wang, J.; Xu, Y.; Yang, X.; Zhang, J.; Wang, X. & Fang, J. (2008). Dynamic contrast-enhanced magnetic resonance images of the kidney. *IEEE Engineering in Medicine and Biology Magazine,* Vol. 27, No. 5, September 2008, pp. 36-41, ISSN 0739-5175

Martinetz, T.; Berkovich, S. & Schulten, K. (1993). Neural-gas Network for Vector Quantization and its Application to Time-Series Prediction. *IEEE-Transactions on Neural Networks,* Vol. 4, No. 4, July 1993, pp. 558-569, ISSN 1045-9227

Michoux, N.; Vallee, J.P. ; Pechere-Bertschi, A. ; Mintet,X. ; Buehler, L. & Beers, B. (2006). Functional MRI of the kidney, *Abdominal Imaging,* Vol. 28, No.2, march 2003, pp. 164-175, ISSN: 0942-8925

Pluim, J.P.W.; Maintz, J.B.A. & Viergever, M.A. (2003). Mutual-information-based registration of medical images: a survey. *IEEE Trans. Med. Imaging,* Vol. 22, No. 8, (2003) pp. 986-1004, ISSN 0278-0062

Song, T.; Lee, V.S.; Rusinek, H.; Sajous, J.B. & Laine, A.F. (2005). Registration and Segmentation of Dynamic Three-dimensional MR Renography Based on Fourier Representations and K-Means Clustering, *Proceedings of ISMRM 13th Scientific Meeting,* ISSN 1545-4428, Miami Beach (FL, USA), May 2005.

Sun, Y.; Moura, J.M.F. & Chien Ho. (2004). Subpixel registration in renal perfusion MR image sequence, *2nd IEEE International Symposium on Biomedical Imaging: Macro to Nano (IEEE Cat No. 04EX821),* pp. 700-3, ISBN 0-7803-8388-5, Arlington (VA, USA), April 2004

Zijdenbos, A.P.; Dawant, B.M.; Margolin, R.A. & Palmer, A.C. (1994). Morphometric analysis of white matter lesions in MR images: method and validation. *IEEE Trans. Med. Imaging,* Vol. 13, No. 4, December 1994, pp. 716-24, ISSN 0278-0062

Zoellner, F.G.; Sance, R.; Anderlik, A.; Roervik, J.; Kocinski, M. & Lundervold, A. (2006). Towards quantification of kidney function by clustering volumetric MRI perfusion time series. *Magnetic Resonance Materials in Physics, Biology and Medicine,* Vol. 19, September 2006, pp. 103-104, ISSN 0968-5243

6

Combined myocardial motion estimation and segmentation using variational techniques

N. Carranza-Herrezuelo[1], A. Bajo[2,3], C. Santa-Marta[4], G. Cristóbal[1], A. Santos[2,3] and M. J. Ledesma-Carbayo[2,3]

[1] *Instituto de Óptica (CSIC)*

[2] *Biomedical Image Technologies, ETSI Telecomunicación. Universidad Politecnica de Madrid*

[3] *Centro de Investigación Biomédica en Red en Bioingeniería, Biomateriales y Nanomedicina (CIBER-BBN)*

[4] *Departamento de Física Matemática y Fluidos. Universidad Nacional de Educación a Distancia*

Spain

1. Introduction

One of the most important challenges in the last few years in the medical imaging analysis field has been automatic cardiac motion estimation, to obtain indicators of heart disease. The visualization and quantification of the heart motion is an important aid for an early diagnosis of heart pathologies (Santos & Ledesma-Carbayo, 2006).

In the last few years, there have been numerous technological progresses in non-invasive cardiac imaging methods (Axel & Dougherty, 1989; McVeigh & Atalar, 1992; Fischer et al., 1993; Atalar & McVeigh, 1994; Fischer et al., 1994; Zerhouni et al., 1998). Therefore, there are new clinical options for cardiac illnesses diagnosis (Thomson et al., 2004). Coronary angiography, nuclear imaging, echocardiography and computerized tomography provide most of the information required by the cardiologist and cardiovascular surgeon (Sinitsyn, 2001). In the 80s, magnetic resonance imaging (MRI) was only used for the evaluation of the heart anatomy. Lately, great advances have been achieved, which have totally changed the possibilities of the diagnosis in this area (de Roos et al., 1999; Pohost et al., 2000; Duerden et al., 2006). Some of the facts that have made magnetic resonance imaging a functional and flexible modality are the increment in temporal and spatial resolution, the improvement in signal to noise ratio and the removal of motion artefacts due to motion. Currently, cardiac magnetic resonance (CMR) is considered the reference gold standard to evaluate ventricular function. The acquisition is dynamic, so several frames are acquired in a cardiac cycle. Tissues can be clearly defined without the use of contrast agents, and unlike other tomographic techniques, it can provide images in the desired plane without limitations due to the body anatomy. There are no limitations for the angulation of the images.

Nevertheless, there are still limitations obtaining cardiac function measurements because the myocardial tracking is hindered as there are no intramural features (Axel et al., 2005). With conventional magnetic resonance imaging (MRI) or ultrasound imaging, a qualitative estimation of the local cardiac motion can be done. Nevertheless, it is quite difficult to compare the results obtained among different modalities even by experts. The reference technique to evaluate quantitatively the contractile myocardial function is tagged magnetic resonance imaging (tagged MRI) (Axel & Dougherty, 1989; Prince & McVeigh, 1992; Dornier et al., 2004; Sampath & Prince, 2007). Changing the tissue magnetization, a lineal grid can be superimposed to the myocardium. The tagged grid acts as an intramural intrinsic feature of the tissue until it vanishes due to the T1 relaxation is the process by which the longitudinal magnetization attains its equilibrium value. The time constant to approach the equilibrium value is called T1 of the cardiac muscle. Therefore, the grid moves with the myocardium during the cardiac cycle and cardiac motion can be tracked by means of the grid. As the grid is deforming during the cardiac cycle, the material coordinates can be tracked and motion can be quantified inside the myocardium. The myocardial displacement field and the parameters derived from it, such as strain, have revealed to be very useful for the diagnosis of different pathologies (Lelieveldt et al., 2004).

The most important clinical application for the local functional cardiac analysis is the assessment of the affected but recoverable regions of an ischemic heart (Picano et al., 1991; Nagel et al., 1999). This is usually done by measuring the width of the cardiac wall on CINE images of the myocardium (Lieberman et al., 1981; Götte et al., 2001). However, the myocardial strain calculation implies the accurate computation of the myocardial displacement field.

The methods proposed for motion estimation from tagged images are based on the use of different aspects of the heterogeneity of the myocardium intensity (Axelo et al., 2005). These methods include: tracking the lines of minimum intensity (Guttman et al., 1994; Chen & Amini, 2001; Quian et al., 2003), optical flow (Prince & McVeigh, 1992; Denney & Prince, 1994; Dougherty et al., 1999) or harmonic phase methods (HARP) (Osman et al., 1999).

The methods based on tracking the tags with minimum intensity use an intensity profile model of a grid line. These methods are normally very time consuming, and depend on a user who manually starts to identify the location of the taging lines in the first frame. Afterwards, the most probable location is searched, or a segmentation using approximations such as morphological operators (Guttman et al., 1994; Young, 1998; Chen & Amini, 2001), tuned filters (Young, 1998; Chen & Amini, 2001), Gabor filters (Quian et al., 2003), deformable grids (Kumar & Goldof, 1993) and manually identified points (Young & Axel, 1992). Although the techniques using tuned filters and Gabor filters are relatively robust to the intensity loss of the tag lines, the limitation of the methods which perform the tracking of lines is that the temporal correspondences are only valid for those pixels belonging to the lines and not for those within them (Axel et al., 2005).

The advantage of the optical flow methods is that they provide a dense estimation of the motion field in two dimensions, and not only a sparse set of data. Technical details about this type of methods will be explained later. Nevertheless, there have been several strategies to perform the tracking of lines in the myocardium using such techniques (Prince & McVeigh, 1992; Gupta & Prince, 1995; Gupta et al., 1997; Dougherty et al., 1999). The main limitation of these methods is the difficulty to follow large displacements.

Phase harmonic methods are based upon the fact that tagged magnetic resonance imaging typically presents a set of different spectral peaks in the Fourier domain corresponding to the spatial frequency of the tag lines. Each peak contains information about the motion perpendicular to the tag line (Zhang et al., 1996). The inverse Fourier transform of one of those peaks is a complex image whose phase is directly related to a directional component of the real motion (Osman et al., 1999; Osman et al., 2000).

Nevertheless, the assessment of myocardial function not only requires the motion estimation but also the segmentation of the myocardium over a cardiac cycle (Chenoune et al., 2005). Identifying the heart chambers, the endocardium and the epicardium is of great importance for clinical applications. Such information can be used to improve the diagnostics of cardiovascular diseases, to estimate the ventricular blood volume, wall mass, wall motion and wall thickening properties (Paragios, 2002). Numerous cardiac segmentation methods have been developed and used to estimate the myocardial boundaries accurately and efficiently. Among these, the two main approaches for cardiac segmentation are based on boundaries, either of an explicit implementation (Montagnat & Delingette, 2005) or an implicit approach such as level sets (Paragios, 2002; Chenoune et al., 2005) or regions (Blekas et al., 2005).

Active contour models have also been very effective in segmenting and tracking moving objects in image sequences, such as cardiac image sequences. Leymarie et al. (Leymarie & Levine, 1993) used the previously segmented contour as an initial seed contour for the current frame to track the contour through a sequence of images. Inspired on this, Gupta et al. (Gupta et al., 1993) proposed an automatic contour propagation scheme throughout the entire slices and frames in their four-dimensional cardiac analysis study using image sequences from MRI. Chalana et al. (Chalana et al., 1996) investigated the dependency of the accuracy of cardiac segmentation on the initial seed contour and proposed a multiple active contour model to reduce the propagation error in sequential segmentation of myocardial boundaries on echocardiographic sequences, by adding temporal smoothness and monotonic motion constraints to the internal and external energy formulation. Li et al (Li et al., 2002) also proposed a similar approach to take into account a temporal smoothness of the contour.

Regarding the coupling of segmentation and motion estimation, many researchers have addressed this problem. In (Wang & Adelson, 1994), they first estimate local motion and subsequently segment regions with respect to estimated motion. In (Nagel & Enkelmann, 1986; Black & Anandan, 1996; Kornprobst et al., 1999; Weickert & Schnörr, 2001), they propose to model motion discontinuities implicitly by non-quadratic robust estimators. Others tackled the problem of segmenting motion by treating first the motion estimation in disjoint sets and then by optimizing the motion boundaries separately (Schnörr, 1992; Black, 1994; Caselles & Coll, 1996; Paragios & Deriche, 2000). Other approaches are based on Markov Random Field formulations and optimization schemes, such as stochastic relaxation by Gibbs sampling, split-and-merge techniques, deterministic relaxation, graph cuts or expectation maximization (Cremers & Soatto, 2005). A novel variational approach for segmenting an image plane into a set of regions of parametric motion, based on a conditional probability for the spatio-temporal image gradient is presented in (Cremers & Soatto, 2005). In the case of segmentation of cardiac images, several examples can be mentioned where the optical flow has been included into the segmentation process (Giachetti et al., 1996; Mikic et al., 1998).

In this chapter, a new approach is presented which combines the advantages of the variational technique for motion estimation with the segmentation process of the endocardial and epicardial borders by means of a variational-based approach: the well-known level set technique (Li et al., 2005). For endocardial and epicardial border segmentation, dual CINE and tagged cardiac magnetic resonance sequences have been used. A idea was not to develop a new segmentation technique but to implement a hybrid approach that would benefit from the motion estimation of the variational technique, in order to build a more robust implementation for both tagged and conventional cardiac magnetic resonance imaging. The motion estimation technique is based on a variational approach, improved by taking into account the particular features of tagged magnetic resonance sequences. Specifically, this variational method has been enhanced by adding a robustness term based on the accurate tracking at some control points by means of their phase stability. The main idea of the integration of the two sub-systems is to minimize computational cost of the segmentation process together with a better accuracy of the segmentation.
In section 2, we describe the method implemented for segmentation (level sets), for motion estimation (variational techniques) and the hybrid technique for motion estimation and segmentation. Section 3 explains the experiments performed to evaluate and validate the method, and the results obtained. Finally, in section 4, the main conclusions are presented.

2. Methods

2.1 Level Set Segmentation

The level set method technique was introduced by Osher and Sethian (Osher & Sethian, 1988), and later it has been investigated to cope with different image segmentation problems in several publications. The method proposed for the segmentation of the temporal sequence of tagged cardiac magnetic resonance images is a modified version of the variational formulation of the geometric active contours principle proposed by (Li et al., 2005). The main idea is to evolve the boundary C from some initial curve in the direction of the negative energy gradient. This is done by implementing the gradient descent equation (Cremers et al., 2007):

$$\frac{\partial C}{\partial t} = -\frac{\partial E(C)}{\partial C} = F \cdot \mathbf{n} \tag{1}$$

and modelling the evolution along the normal $\mathbf{n}$ with a speed function F. In the implicit contour representation theory, the contour C is represented as the zero level line of some embedding function ϕ such as

$$C(t) = \{(x,y) | \phi(t,x,y) = 0\} \tag{2}$$

In the method proposed by Osher and Sethian in (Osher & Sethian, 1988), a contour is propagated by evolving a time-dependent embedding function ϕ according to an appropriate partial differential equation. Having a contour C evolving along the normal $\mathbf{n}$ with a speed F and since $\phi(C(t),t) = 0$, this equation can be derived as

$$\frac{d}{dt}\phi(C(t),t) = \nabla\phi\frac{\partial C}{\partial t} + \frac{\partial \phi}{\partial t} = \nabla\phi(F \cdot \mathbf{n}) + \frac{\partial \phi}{\partial t} = 0 \tag{3}$$

The evolution equation of the level set function ϕ can be written in the following general form, inserting the definition of the normal $n = \frac{\nabla \phi}{|\nabla \phi|}$

$$\frac{\partial \phi}{\partial t} = -|\nabla \phi| F \tag{4}$$

which is called the level set equation (Osher & Sethian, 1988). Nevertheless, the level set function ϕ can suffer of transients, very sharp and/or flat shape during the evolution. For this reason, it is necessary to initialize the function ϕ as a signed distance function before the evolution starts, and then "reshape" (or "re-initialize") the function ϕ to be a signed distance function periodically during the evolution. Re-initialization has been extensively used as a numerical remedy in traditional level set methods (Caselles et al., 1993; Malladi et al., 1995). The standard re-initialization method solving the following equation is

$$\frac{\partial \phi}{\partial t} = sign(\phi_0)(1 - |\nabla \phi|) \tag{5}$$

where ϕ_0 is the function to be re-initialized, and $sign(\phi)$ is the sign function. There has been copious literature on re-initialization methods (Peng et al., 1999; Sussman & Fatemi, 1999), and most of them are variants of the above partial differential equation (PDE)-based method. Unfortunately, if ϕ_0 is not smooth or ϕ_0 is much steeper on one side of the border than the other, the zero level set of the resulting function ϕ can be moved incorrectly with respect to the original function. Moreover, when the level set function is far away from a signed distance function, these methods may not be able to re-initialize properly the level set function to a signed distance function. In practice, the evolving level set function can deviate greatly from its value as signed distance in a small number of iteration steps, especially when the time step is not chosen small enough. So far, re-initialization has been extensively used as a numerical remedy for maintaining stable curve evolution and ensuring desirable results. From the practical point of view, the re-initialization process can be quite complicated, expensive, and have subtle side effects.

In this chapter we have used the variational approach explained in (Li et al., 2005), which can be easily implemented by a simple finite difference scheme without the need of re-initialization. Provided that a signed distance function must satisfy the desirable property of $|\nabla \phi| = 1$, the minimization of the following integral is proposed

$$P(\phi) = \int_{\Omega} \frac{1}{2}(|\nabla \phi| - 1)^2 \, dxdy \tag{6}$$

With the above defined functional $P(\phi)$, it is proposed the following variational formulation

$$E(\varphi) = \mu P(\phi) + E_m(\varphi) \tag{7}$$

where $\mu > 0$ is a parameter controlling the effect of penalizing the deviation of ϕ from a signed distance function, and $E_m(\phi)$ is a certain energy that would drive the motion of the zero level curve of ϕ (Li et al., 2005).

2.2 Proposed Method for Motion Estimation of Tagged Cardiac Magnetic Resonance Images

The method proposed for the study of the motion in tagged CMR is one of the well-known differential techniques. The basis of these methods is the constancy of the intensity structures of local time-varying image regions under motion, at least for a short duration time (Horn & Schunk, 1981). The use of this method actually assumes intensity conservation between consecutive frames, that can be admitted in the case of tagged MR image frames separated by short time intervals as compared with T1 recovery (Ledesma-Carbayo et al., 2008). However, if required, the T1 signal modulation could also be included in the criterion (Ledesma-Carbayo et al., 2008). Let us remember the optical flow constraint equation:

$$\mathbf{v}(x_1,x_2)\cdot\nabla I(x_1,x_2,t_0)+I_t(x_1,x_2,t_0)=0 \qquad (8)$$

where $\mathbf{v}=(v_1,v_2)$, $I_t=\partial I/\partial t$ and $v_1=\partial x_1/\partial t$ and $v_2=\partial x_2/\partial t$ are the components of the velocity field. This equation needs an additional constraint, as the problem is undetermined (ill posed). The one adopted here is based on the regularization of the velocity fields (Aubert, 1999).The problem originally proposed has to deal with the following energy minimization, proposed by Horn & Schunk in (Horn and Schunk, 1981)

$$\min_{v} \int_{\Omega}(\mathbf{v}\cdot\nabla I+I_t)^2\,dx+\alpha^r\int_{\Omega}\left(\|\nabla v_1\|^2+\|\nabla v_2\|^2\right)dx \qquad (9)$$

and modified later on with more robust norms to cope with optical flow discontinuities (Aubert & Kornprobst, 2006)

$$\int_{\Omega}\phi(\|\nabla v_1\|)dx+\int_{\Omega}\phi(\|\nabla v_2\|)dx \qquad (10)$$

where the functions ϕ allow noise removal and edge preservation. Among the different ϕ functions (Deriche et al., 1995), in this approach the norm L^1 has been chosen. It is also called Total Variation (TV), $\phi(t)=t$. Very good anisotropic denoising properties of the TV semi-norm are well known (Sroubek & Flusser, 2005). Since TV is highly nonlinear and non continuous, a special attention must be paid to its discretization. Several relaxed linearization schemes were proposed. We follow the half-quadratic regularization scheme describe in (Charbonnier et al., 1997) that introduces an auxiliary variable.

On the other hand in homogeneous areas characterized by low image gradients magnitude, no visible motion can be locally detected. To minimize this undesirable motion, an extra term is added to equation (11) such as

$$\int_{\Omega}c(x)\|v\|_2^2\,dx \qquad (11)$$

where $\|\ \|_2$ is the Euclidean norm, and

$$c(x)=\frac{1}{\sqrt{\left(\frac{\partial}{\partial x_1}I\right)^2+\left(\frac{\partial}{\partial x_2}I\right)^2+eps}} \qquad (12)$$

represents a penalizing function, which is small for high image gradients and big for low image gradients. Finally, including the different terms, the energy minimization equation that we propose to use has the following form:

$$\min_{v}\int_{\Omega}(\mathbf{v}\cdot\nabla I+I_t)^2\,dx+\alpha^r\int_{\Omega}\phi(\|\nabla\mathbf{v}\|)dx+\alpha^c\int_{\Omega}c(x)|\mathbf{v}|_2^2\,dx \qquad (13)$$

In the same way that the homogeneous term $c(x)$ has been added, it is easy to add other terms in order to adapt the algorithm to the problem. The main idea of the improved version described here has been introducing a regularization term in order to find a more accurate optical flow based on prior robust estimates in given control points. The new term is going to have information of the displacement of several points inside the myocardium with a very low phase difference with respect to the following frame (estimated below 10^{-3}). For the sequel, we will name these points as control points. Such term has the following form,

$$\beta \sum_i (v_i - p_i) \tag{14}$$

where $\mathbf{p}_i$ is the set of control points. The parameter β is a mask, with non-zero values only for the control point position. The final equation yields as

$$\min_v \int_\Omega (\mathbf{v} \cdot \nabla I + I_t)^2 \, dx + \alpha^r \int_\Omega \phi(\|\nabla \mathbf{v}\|) dx + \alpha^c \int_\Omega c(x) |\mathbf{v}|_2^2 \, dx + \beta \sum_i (\mathbf{v}_i - \mathbf{p}_i)^2 \tag{15}$$

With this equation, a compromise agreement is reached. The regularization term is going to provide a more accurate optical flow in the neighbourhood of the control points. In those regions without any control point, this term does not have any effect.Although the equation (15) seems to have an easy implementation, obtaining the control points is a challenging task. The tags of the image are an essential property which will allow obtaining such points. There are some papers which propose tracking the dark lines as finding points of minimum intensity (Guttman et al., 1994; Young, 1998; Chen & Amini, 2001). In this case, several tag line points could be chosen as control points. However, the tag fading is a limitation for these techniques, as the error allowed in the displacement estimation of those points has to be very small.

In contrast, techniques using the phase of the images (for instance, the Harmonic Phase or HARP technique reported in (Osman et al., 1999; Osman et al., 2000)) turn out to be very accurate for tracking a selected number of points, that is those points whose phases are not affected by noise and where tag jumping is avoided. As we only need a reduced set of points and not a dense optical flow for these control points, the control points will be a set of points with high stability of phase.

In 1-1 SPAMM (Spatial Modulation of Magnetization) tagging pulse sequences, tags are created with a sinusoidal cross-sectional intensity profile. At any point on or between the tags, the tissue has both the magnetization intensity and the spatial phase of the periodic tag magnetization pattern, which are dependent on position (Axel et al., 2005). So, when the heart moves, a particular piece of tissue has the same phase in the deformed state as it has in the reference state. The phase of those images is an intrinsic invariant property that can be tracked.

As the phase of the tagged images is restricted to be in the range $[-\pi, +\pi]$, the control points will be selected among a set of points in the myocardium having a certain phase, using the criterion explained before to reject the points which phase difference with respect to the following frame is higher than 10^{-3}. This process is fully automatic and it does not need any manual interaction. We are going to select one point per tag intersection, forming a grid of selected points in the myocardium. An example can be seen in Fig. 1.

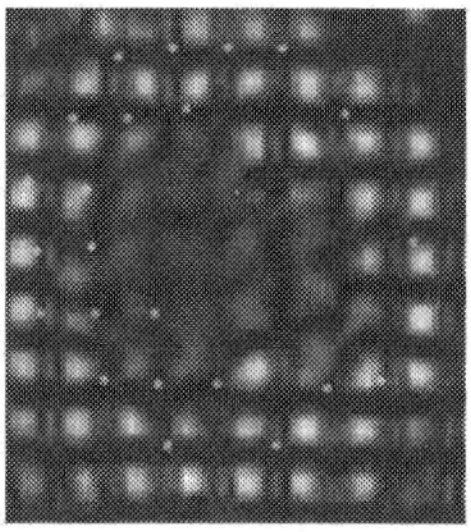

Fig. 1. Example of the control points manually chosen in one of the sequences tested.

From those points, a similar procedure as reported in (Osman et al., 1999) and (Osman et al., 2000) is established for tracking the points, using the Newton-Raphson method. The Newton-Raphson method is a well-known technique to find the root of a function. We are going to apply it in a small region centered in the point of interest, to find the roots in the difference of phase images. To avoid tag jumping, the Newton-Raphson method is only run in a small window around each point, taking into account tag spacing. In addition to that, those points whose difference of phases has an error higher than 10^{-3} have been rejected. Therefore, only points with very good phase stability have been chosen as control points. This automatic selection provides control points with robust tracking estimates including prior information very valid to enhance the method. In principle it does not matter which points are selected, although it is desirable that they are evenly distributed. It is also important to note that the computational time does not increase very much as only a few points are going to be selected.

Another important point is that the control points are different for each pair of images. Thus, the errors which could have been made in previous images of the sequence will not been propagated.

The motion estimation method has been validated with a simulated sequence without noise and with four different levels of Gaussian noise, and also with five real sequences. According to the standardized myocardial division of segments (Cerqueira, Weissman et al. 2002), the myocardium has been divided into six regions, and four points of each region have been manually tracked. Overall, 24 points have been selected along each sequence. The results obtained with the motion estimation method have been compared with the points tracked manually. The error has been computed, as the average root mean square error for each segment. The average root mean square error for synthetic sequences is 0.49 pixels/frame and for real sequences it is 0.62 pixel/frame. Results have been compared to a reference method (HARP), achieving always better results (Carranza-Herrezuelo, 2009a; Carranza-Herrezuelo et al, 2009b).

2.3 Integration of the Motion Estimation and Segmentation Approach

This algorithm has been applied on four sequences where both CINE and tagged CMR images are available (see an example in Fig. 2). The motion field has been extracted for each pair of tagged CMR images. This motion field has been computed with the enhanced variational method, and integrated with the segmentation technique.

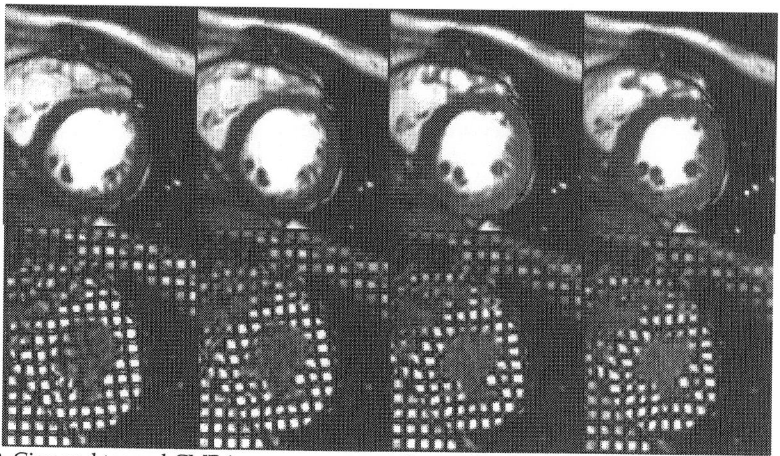

Fig. 2. Cine and tagged CMR images corresponding to the same patient.

To starting the algorithm, the segmentation of the first image is performed being initialized with a manually drawn curve. All the rest operations are automatically accomplished. After the first image is segmented, the next step is to estimate the motion field that applied to this first segmentation will provide the new contour in the next image of the sequence. When the curve for the next image is estimated, the level set technique is run only to refine the solution and for smoothing the first approach. The segmentation algorithm is run on the CINE sequences, while the motion estimation is run on the tagged sequences. The block diagram of the previous steps is shown in Fig. 3

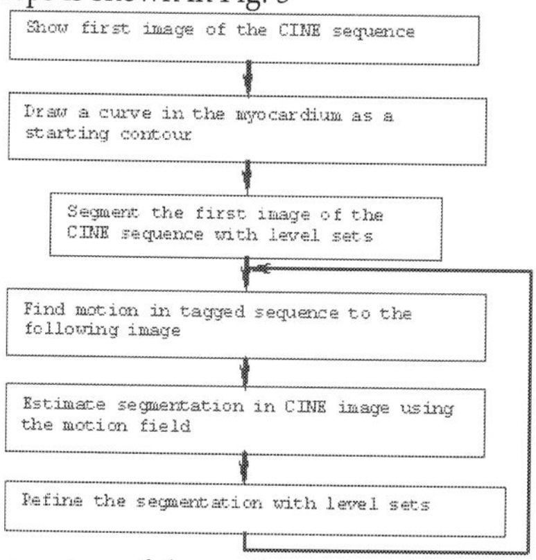

Fig. 3. Block diagram of the system of the motion estimation and segmentation for dual sequences

By means of this algorithm, the computational time of the segmentation is considerably reduced, because we only need to compute the segmentation for the first image of the sequence. For the rest, the iterative process of the segmentation is stopped when the evolution of the level-set implementation is below a given threshold.

3. Experimental Results

3.1 Experiments

The four sequences were acquired with a Philips Intera 1.5 T (Philips Medical Systems, The Netherlands) using a five element phased-array coil dedicated to cardiac imaging. CINE MR scans were acquired using a breath hold Balanced Fast Field Echo (B-FEE) sequence, obtaining images with a pixel size between 1 mm^2 and 1.3 mm^2. As in the previous experiment the tagging sequence used consists of an enhanced version of the SPAMM sequence provided by the manufacturer for our Phillips Intera scanner (Santa-Marta et al., 2006). Both CINE and Tagged MR sequences were acquired using exactly the same acquisition geometry in order to have precise alignment and pixel correspondence between both datasets. Some small rigid misalignments due to the acquisitions in different respiratory positions have been corrected between both sequences before applying the segmentation approach.
The values of the parameters used in the program have been selected manually, choosing the parameters which provided better results. For the motion estimation, the parameters used for the tagged CMR sequences are $\alpha^c = 10^{-8}$, $\alpha^r = 10^{-7}$ and $\beta = 10^{-7}$. The parameter that controls the number of iterations explained in the previous section has been set as 3.8 pixels for the endocardium and 0.5 for the epicardium segmentation. The rest of the parameters employed in the algorithm are the same as stated in (Li et al., 2005).
The computational time has been tested in this experiment. On the other hand, the accuracy of the segmentation has been evaluated. For this purpose the endocardium and epicardium have been manually segmented, independently on each sequence. Four sequences have been analysed selecting the systolic period, and 46 curves from 23 images were manually segmented. To compare the results obtained with the automatic algorithm, the metrics proposed in (Chalana & Kim, 1997) have been used, as described in the following paragraphs.
Let us suppose that we have two curves A and B where the former A is obtained by the segmentation algorithm and the later B is the one manually segmented. Both curves are divided into a set of points, a_i and b_i. In our case, we have used all the points of the contour. The minimum distance of each of the points to the other curve is computed, which is the distance to the closer point in the other curve.

$$d(a_i, B) = \min_j \left\| b_j - a_i \right\| \tag{16}$$

In each image of the sequence, the following measures are obtained:

- Mean distance between curves. It is obtained from the distances of all the points

$$d(A, B) = \frac{1}{m} \sum_{i=1}^{n} d(a_i, B) \tag{17}$$

- Hausdorff distance. Maximum distance of one curve to the other, measured as the maximum value between the distances of all the points.

$$e(A, B) = \max\left(\max_j \{d(a_i, B)\}, \max_j \{d(b_i, A)\}\right) \tag{18}$$

- Overlapping. From the surfaces defined by the curves, the overlapping degree is the division of the number of coincident pixels in both surfaces, and the number of pixels belonging to one or another.

$$Overlapping(A,B) = \frac{A \cap B}{A \cup B} \quad (19)$$

An example of the manually and automatic segmentation in two different frames is shown in Figs. 4-5. It can be seen how the contours are smoother in the case of the automatic segmentation (see e.g. Fig. 4c-d).

a) b) c) d)

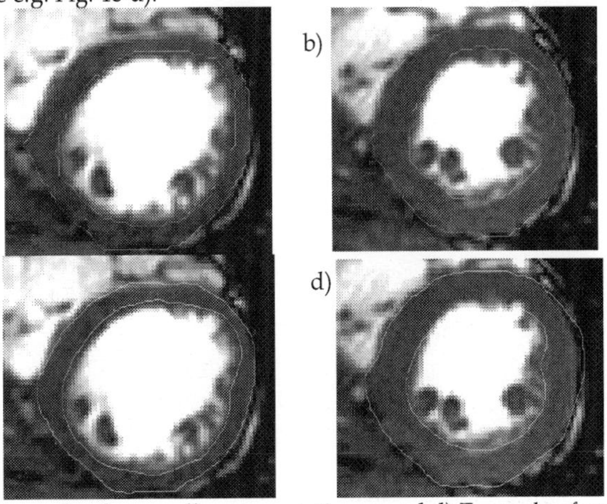

Fig. 4. a) and b) Example of manually segmentation. c and d) Example of automatic segmentation.

3.2 Results

The results obtained for one of the sequences are visualized in Fig. 5., where the segmentation result (left column) and the optical flow (right column) on the tagged images are shown.

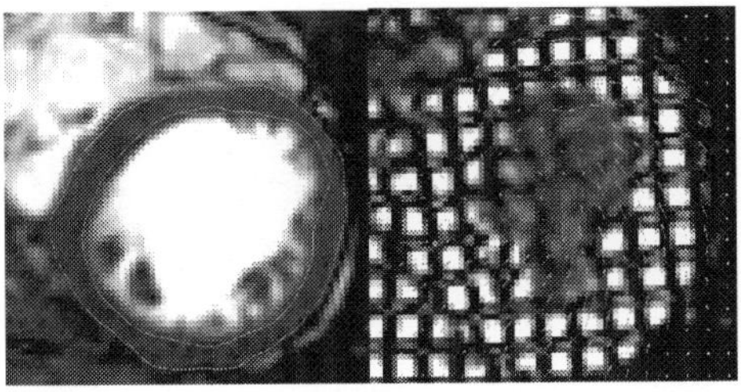

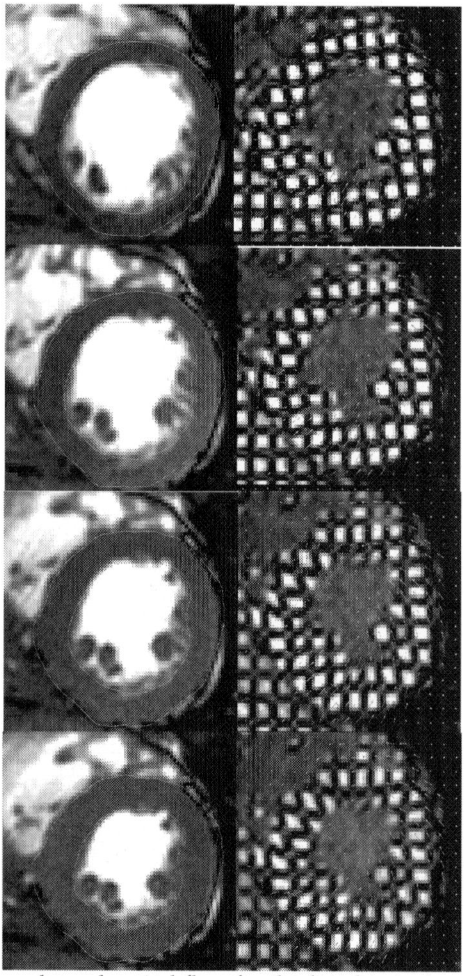

Fig. 5. Segmentation results and optical flow for the first five images of the sequence. The first column shows the CINE images with the segmentation and the second column shows the optical flow obtained with the tagged CMR images.

As it can be seen, the results obtained adjust well to the endocardium and epicardium. The contour fit perfectly to the myocardial border, avoiding the inclusion of the papillary muscles which can not be achieved so easily on the tagged images. Fig. 6 shows the results of the computational time. As it can be seen in figure 6, the computational time for the integrated solution is smaller than the one needed if the sequence were segmented frame by frame. Fluctuations on the computational time for the integrated method are due only to the refinement of the segmentation needed for each frame; this fact explains the increase of the computational time between frames forth and fifth.

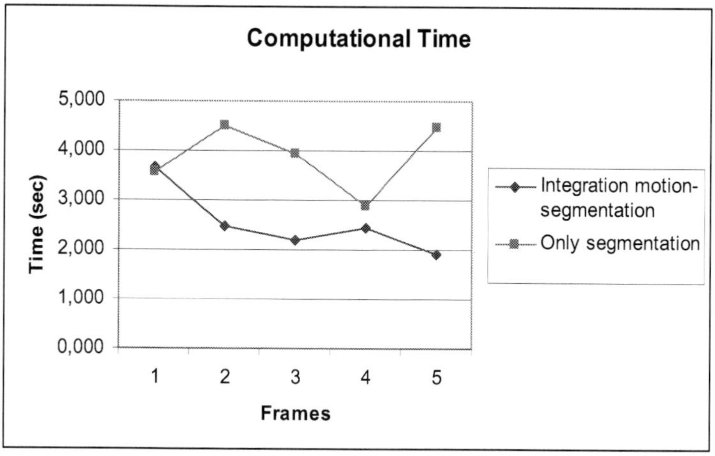

Fig. 6. Computational time for the proposed integrated solution compared with the time obtained segmenting each image for the dual sequence.

The results of the evaluation of the 46 curves tested are shown in Table 1. Resultant parameters show that the segmentation performance is very accurate.

		Mean Distance (pixels) Mean ± SD	*Haussdorf Distance (pixels) Mean ± SD*	*Overlapping degree (%) Mean ± SD*
Sequence 1	Endocardium	0.94 ± 0.9	2.71 ± 1.44	90 ± 3.84
	Epicardium	1.01 ± 0.04	2.80 ± 0.21	93 ± 1.85
Sequence 2	Endocardium	1.25 ± 0.16	3.75 ± 0.97	88 ± 4.04
	Epicardium	0.96 ± 0.00	2.65 ± 0.40	94 ± 0.59
Sequence 3	Endocardium	0.87 ± 0.18	2.82 ± 0.33	87 ± 3.12
	Epicardium	0.82 ± 0.31	2.60 ± 0.70	92 ± 2.93
Sequence 4	Endocardium	0.88 ± 0.43	2.35 ± 1.09	90 ± 6.01
	Epicardium	1.24 ± 0.22	3.54 ± 0.74	90 ± 1.62

Table 1. Evaluation results of the segmentation (mean distance, Haussdorf distance and overlapping degree) for the four sequences tested in comparison to manual delineations.

The mean distance between pixels is always below 1.25 pixels, and the Haussdorf distance is smaller than 4 pixels. In the first sequence, results for the endocardium and epicardium segmentation are similar. In the second sequence, the results obtained for the epicardium are better. This is due to the fact the manual segmentation of the endocardium is generally quite difficult. In the second sequence, the resolution of the images was lower than in the first case, and the error obtained with the segmentation algorithm is a bit higher than those obtained in the first sequence.

4. Conclusions

A method for segmentation and motion estimation of the myocardium based on level sets and variational techniques has been presented. The segmentation method uses a level set method implemented through a variational formulation, which has been integrated with a motion estimation algorithm, also based on variational techniques. This approach applied to dual sequences takes advantage of the appealing features from each type of images (detail resolution form CINE CMR and motion estimation from Tagged MR). The segmentation has been proved to be feasible in real images, having a low computational cost. On the other hand the accuracy of the segmentation has been tested in dual CINE + Tagged MR sequences in comparison to manual delineation of the endocardium and epicardium. Results show a good performance of the algorithm with a mean error between curves of approximately one pixel. The proposed approach constitutes a very interesting framework for the measurement of global and regional functional parameters from both types of data (CINE+tagged MRI).

5. Acknowledgments

This research has been supported by the following grants: TEC2007-67025/TCM, TEC2006-28009-E, TEC2007-30709E TIN2007-68048-C02-01, CDTI-CDTEAM and SINBAD (PS-010000-2008-1) by the Spanish Ministry of Science and Innovation.

6. References

Atalar, E. & McVeigh, E. R. (1994). Minimization of desd-periods, *Magnetic Resonance in Medicine,* Vol. 32, No. 6, (773-777), 0740-3194

Aubert, G. & Kornprobst, P. (2006). *Mathematical Problems in Image Processing. Partial Differential Equations and the Calculus of Variations*, Springer, 978-0-387-32200-1

Aubert, G.; Deriche, R. & Kornprobst, P. (1999). Computing optical flow via variational techniques, *Siam Journal on Applied Mathematics,* Vol. 60, No. 1, (156-182), 0036-1399

Axel, L. & Dougherty, L. (1989). MR imaging of motion with spatial modulation of magnetization, *Radiology,* Vol. 171, (841-845), 1527-1315

Axel, L.; Montillo, A. & Kim, D. (2005). Tagged magnetic resonance imaging of the heart: a survey, *Medical Image Analysis,* Vol. 9, No. 4, (376-393), 1361-8415

Black, M. J. (1994). Recursive non-linear estimation of discontinuous flow fields, *Proceedings of the European Conference of Computer Vision*, Vol. 800, (138-145).

Black, M. J. & Anandan, P. (1996). The robust estimation of multiple motions: Parametric and piecewise-smooth flow fields, *Computer Vision of Graphical Image Processing,* Vol. 63, No. 1, (75-104), 0734-189X

Blekas, K.; Likas, A.; Galatsanos, N. & Lagaris, I. (2005). A spatially constrained mixture model for image segmentation, *IEEE Transactions on Neural Networks,* Vol. 16, No. 2, (494-498), 1045-9227

Carranza-Herrezuelo, N. (2009a). *New Contributions on Motion Estimation through Optical Flow Techniques Applied to Cardiac Magnetic Resonance Imaging,* PhD Thesis, Universidad Politécnica de Madrid

Carranza-Herrezuelo, N. ; Bajo, A.; Sroubek, F.; Santa-Marta, C.; Cristóbal, G.; Santos, A. & Ledesma-Carbayo, M. J. (2009b). Motion estimation of Tagged Cardiac Magnetic Resonance Images using Variational Techniques, *Computerized Medical Imaging and Graphics*, 0895-6111, under review

Caselles, V.; Catte, F.; Coll, T. & Dibos, F. (1993). A Geometric Model for Active Contours in Image Processing, *Numerische Mathematik,* Vol. 66, No.1, (1-31), 0945-3245

Caselles, V. & Coll, B. (1996). Snakes in movement, *SIAM Journal on Numerical Analysis,* Vol. 33, (2445-2456), 0036-1429

Cerqueira, M. D.; Weissman, N. J.; Dilsizian, V.; Jacobs, A. K.; Kaul, S.; Laskey, W. K.; Pennell, D. J.; Rumberger, J. A.; Ryan, T. & Verani, M. S. (2002). Standardized Myocardial Segmentation and Nomenclature for Tomographic Imaging of the Heart: A Statement for Healthcare Professionals from the Cardiac Imaging Committee of the Council on Clinical Cardiology of the American Heart Association, *Journal of the American Heart Association,* Vol. 105, (539-542), 0194911X

Cremers, D.; Rousson, M. & Deriche, R. (2007). A review of statistical approaches to level set segmentation: Integrating color, texture, motion and shape, *International Journal of Computer Vision,* Vol. 72, No. 2, (195-215), 0920-5691

Cremers, D. & Soatto, S. (2005). Motion Competition: A Variational Approach to Piecewise Parametric Motion Segmentation, *International Journal of Computer Vision,* Vol. 62, No. 3, (249-265), 0920-5691

Chalana, V. & Kim, Y. (1997). A methodology for evaluation of boundary detection algorithms on medical images, *IEEE Transactions on Medical Imaging,* Vol. 16, No. 5, (642-652), 0278-0062

Chalana, V.; Linker, D. T.; Haynor, D. R. & Kim, Y. M. (1996). A multiple active contour model for cardiac boundary detection on echocardiographic sequences, *IEEE Transactions on Medical Imaging,* Vol. 15, No. 3, (290-298), 0278-0062

Charbonnier, P.; BlancFeraud, L.; Aubert, G. & Barlaud, M. (1997). Deterministic edge-preserving regularization in computed imaging, *IEEE Transactions on Image Processing,* Vol. 6, No. 2, (298-311), 1057-7149

Chen, Y. S. & Amini, A. A. (2001). A MAP framework for tag line detection in SPAMM data using Markov random fields on the B-spline solid, *Proceedings of IEEE Workshop on Mathematical Methods in Biomedical Image Analysis,* 9780818673672

Chenoune, Y.; Delechelle, E.; Petit, E.; Goissen, T.; Garot, J. & Rahmouni, A. (2005). Segmentation of cardiac cine-MR images and myocardial deformation assessment using level set methods, *Computerized Medical Imaging and Graphics,* Vol. 29, No.8, (607-616), 0895-6111

de Roos, A.; Kunz, P.; Lamb, H.; Kroft, L.; Langerak, S.; Doornbos, J. & van der Wall, E. (1999). Magnetic resonance imaging of ischemic heart disease: Why cardiac magnetic resonance imaging will play a significant role in the management of patients with coronary artery disease, *Journal of Computer Assisted Tomography,* Vol. 23, (S135-S141), 03638715

Denney, T. & Prince, J. L. (1994). Optimal brightness functions for optical flow estimation of deformable motion, *IEEE Transactions on Image Processing,* Vol. 3, No. 2, (178-191), 1057-7149

Deriche, R.; Kornprobst, P. and Aubert, G. (1995). Optical-Flow Estimation while Preserving its Discontinuities: A Variational Approach, *Invited Session Papers from the Second*

Asian Conference on Computer Vision: Recent Developments in Computer Vision, Vol. 1035, (71 - 80)

Dornier, C.; Somsen, A.; Ivancevic, M. K.; Osman, N. F.; Didier, D.; Righetti, A. & Vallée, J. P. (2004). Comparison between tagged MRI and standard cine MRI for evaluation of left ventricular ejection fraction, *Radiology,* Vol. 14, (1348-1352), 1527-1315

Dougherty, L.; Asmuth, J.; Blom, A.; Axel, L. & Kumar, R. (1999). Validation of an optical flow method for tag displacement estimation, *IEEE Transactions on Medical Imaging,* Vol. 18, No. 4, (359-363), 0278-0062

Duerden, R. M.; Pointon, K. S. & Habib, S. (2006). Review of clinical cardiac MRI, *Imaging,* Vol. 18, (178-186), 0942-8925

Fischer, S. E.; McKinnon, G. C.; Maier, S. E. & Boesiger, P. (1993). Improved myocardial tagging contrast, *Magnetic Resonance in Medicine,* Vol. 30, (191-200), 0740-3194

Fischer, S. E.; McKinnon, G. C.; Scheidegger, M. B.; Prins, W.; Meier, D. & Boesiger, P. (1994). True myocardial motion tracking, *Magnetic Resonance in Medicine,* Vol. 31, (401-413), 0740-3194

Giachetti, A., Gigli, G. & Torre, V. (1996). Computer assisted analysis of echocardiographic image sequences, *Medical Image Analysis,* Vol. 2, No. 4, (261-284), 1361-8415

Götte, M. J. W.; van Rossum, A. C.; Twisk, J. W. R.; Kuijer, J. P. A.; Marcus, J. T. & Visser, C. A. (2001). Quantification of regional contractile function after infarction: strain analysis superior to wall thickening analysis in discriminating infarct from remote myocardium, *Journal of American College of Cardiology,* Vol. 37, (808-817), 0735-1097

Gupta, A.; Vonkurowski, L.; Singh, A.; Geiger, D.; Liang, C. C.; Chiu, M. Y.; Adler, L. P.; Haacke, M. & Wilson, D. L. (1993). Cardiac Mr Image Segmentation Using Deformable Models, *Proceedings of Computers in Cardiology,* (747-750), 0276-6574

Gupta, S. N. & Prince, J. L. (1995). On variable brightness optical flow for tagged MRI, *Information Processing in Medical Imaging: 14th International Conference.,* (323-334), Dordrecht: Kluwer, June 1995

Gupta, S. N.; Prince, J. L. & A-Theotokis, S. (1997). Bandpass optical flow for tagged MR imaging, *Proceedings of IEEE International Conference of Image Processing,* (364-367), San Diego, October 1997

Guttman, M. A.; Prince, J. L. & McVeigh, E. R. (1994). Tag and Contour-Detection in Tagged MR-Images of the Left-Ventricle, *IEEE Transactions on Medical Imaging,* Vol. 13, No. 1, (74-88), 0278-0062

Horn, B. K. P. & Schunk, B. G. (1981). Determining Optical-Flow, *Artificial Intelligence,* Vol. K17, No. 1-3, (185-203), 1989-1660

Kornprobst, P.; Deriche, R. & Aubert, G (1999). Image sequence analysis via partial differential equations, *Journal of Mathematical Image Vision,* Vol. 11, No. 1, (5-16), 1573-7683

Kumar, S. & Goldof, D. (1993). Automatic tracking of SPAMM grid and the estimation of deformation parameters from cardiac MR images, *IEEE Transactions on Medical Imaging,* Vol. 13, No. 1, (122-132), 0278-0062

Ledesma-Carbayo, M. J.; Derbyshire, J. A.; Sampath, S.; Santos, A.; Desco, M. & McVeigh, E. R. (2008). Unsupervised estimation of myocardial displacement from tagged MR sequences using nonrigid registration, *Magnetic Resonance in Medicine*, Vol. 59, (181-189), 0740-3194

Lelieveldt, B. P. F., Van der Geest, R. J. & Reiber, J. H. C. (2004). Towards 'One-Stop' Cardiac MR Image Analysis, *Image Decisions MRI,* Vol. 8, No.2, (2-12), 1433-3317

Leymarie, F. & Levine, M. D. (1993). Tracking Deformable Objects in the Plane Using an Active Contour Model, *IEEE Transactions on Pattern Analysis and Machine Intelligence,* Vol. 15, No. 6, (617-634), 0018-9340

Li, C. M.; Xu, C. Y.; Gui, C. & Fox, M. D. (2005). Level set evolution without re-initialization: A new variational formulation, *Proceedings of IEEE Computer Society Conference on Computer Vision and Pattern Recognition,* Vol. 1, (430-436), 0-7695-2372-2

Li, M.; Kambhamettu, C. & Stone, M. (2002). Motion-based post processing of deformable contours, *Proceedings of The Indian Conference on Computer Vision, Graphics and Image Processing (ICVGIP),* Ahbedamad (India), December 2002.

Lieberman, A. N.; Weiss, J. L.; Jugdutt, B. I.; Becker, L. C.; Bulkley, B. H.; Garrison, J. G.; Hutchins, G. M.; Kallman, C. A. & Weisfeldt, M.L. (1981). Two-dimensional echocardiography and infarct size: relationship of regional wall motion and thickening to the extent of myocardial infarction in the dog, *Circulation,* Vol. 63, (739-746), 0009-7322

Malladi, R.; Sethian, J. A. & Vemuri, B. C. (1995). Shape Modeling with Front Propagation - A Level Set Approach, *IEEE Transactions on Pattern Analysis and Machine Intelligence,* Vol. 17, No. 2, (158-175), 0018-9340

McVeigh, E. R. & Atalar E. (1992). Cardiac tagging with breath hold cine MRI, *Magnetic Resonance in Medicine,* Vol. 28, (318-327), 0740-3194

Mikic, I.; Krucinski, S. & Thomas, J. D. (1998). Segmentation and tracking in echocardiographic images: Active contours guided by optical flow estimates, *IEEE Transactions on Medical Imaging,* Vol. 17, No. 2, (274-284), 0278-0062

Montagnat, J. & Delingette, H. (2005). 4D deformable models with temporal constraints: applications to 4d cardiac image segmentation, *Medical Image Analysis,* Vol. 9, No. 1, (87-100), 1361-8415

Nagel, E.; Lehmkuhl, H. B.; Bocksch, W.; Klein, C.; Vogel, U.; Frantz, E.; Ellmer, A.; Dreysse, S. & Fleck, E. (1999). Noninvasive Diagnosis of Ischemia-Induced Wall Motion Abnormalities with the Use of High-Dose Dobutamine Stress MRI: Comparison With Dobutamine Echocardiography Stress, *Circulation,* Vol. 99, (763-770), 0009-7322

Nagel, H. H. & Enkelmann, W. (1986). An investigation of smoothness constraints for the estimation of displacement vector fields from image sequences, *IEEE Transactions in Pattern Analysis and Machine Intelligence,* Vol. 8, No. 5, (565-593), 0018-9340

Osher, S. & Sethian, J. A. (1988). Fronts Propagating with Curvature-Dependent Speed - Algorithms based on Hamilton-Jacobi Formulations, *Journal of Computational Physics,* Vol. 79, No. 1, (12-49), 1090-2716

Osman, N. F.; Kerwin, W. S.; McVeigh, E. R. & Prince, J. L. (1999). Cardiac motion tracking using CINE harmonic phase (HARP) magnetic resonance imaging, *Magnetic Resonance in Medicine,* Vol. 42, No. 6, (1048-1060), 0740-3194

Osman, N. F.; McVeigh, E. R. & Prince, J. L. (2000). Imaging heart motion using harmonic phase MRI, *IEEE Transactions on Medical Imaging,* Vol. 19, No. 3, (186-202), 0278-0062

Paragios, N. (2002). A variational approach for the segmentation of the left ventricle in cardiac image analysis, *International Journal of Computer Vision,* Vol. 50, No.3, (546-362), 0920-5691

Paragios, N. & Deriche R. (2000). Geodesic active contours and level sets for the detection and tracking of moving objects, *IEEE Transactions in Pattern Analysis and Machine Intelligence*, Vol. 22, No.3, (266-280), 0018-9340

Peng, D.; Merriman, B.; Osher, S.; Zhao, H. & Kang, M. (1999). A PDE-based fast local level set method, *Journal of Computational Physics,* Vol. 155 (410-438), 1090-2716

Picano, E.; Lattanzi, F.; Orlandini. A; Marini, C. & L'Abbate, A. (1991). Stress echocardiography and the human factor: the importance of being expert, *Journal of American College of Cardiology* , Vol. 17, (666-669), 0735-1097

Pohost, G. M.; Biederman, R. W. & Doyle, M. (2000). Cardiovascular magnetic resonance imaging and spectroscopy in the new millennium, *Current Problems in Cardiology,* Vol. 25, No. 8, (525-620), 0146-2806

Prince, J. L. & McVeigh, E. R. 1992. Motion Estimation from Tagged MR Image Sequences, *IEEE Transactions on Medical Imaging,* Vol. 11, No. 2, (238-249), 0278-0062

Quian, Z.; Montillo, A.; Metaxas, D. & Axel, L. (2003). Segmenting cardiac MRI tagging lines using Gabor filter banks. *Proceedings of International Conference of the Engineering in Medicine and Biology Society,* Cancun, Mexico

Sampath, S. & Prince, J. L. (2007). Automatic 3D tracking of cardiac material markers using slice-following and harmonic-phase MRI, *Magnetic Resonance Imaging,* Vol. 25. No. 2, (197-208), 1796-2234

Santa-Marta, C.; Ledesma-Carbayo, M. J.; Bajo, A.; Pérez-David, E.; Santos, A. & Desco, M. (2006). Respiratory Gated SPAMM Sequence for Magnetic Resonance Cardiac Tagging, *Proceedings of Computers in Cardiology*, September 2006, Valencia (Spain).

Santos, A. & Ledesma-Carbayo, M. J. (2006). *Cardiac Imaging.* New Yersey, Wiley Encyclopedia of Biomedical Engineering, John Wiley & Sons Inc, 9783131477811

Schnörr, C. (1992). Computation of discontinuous optical flow by domain decomposition and shape optimization, *International Journal of Computer Vision,* Vol. 8, No. 2, (153-165), 0920-5691

Sinitsyn, V. (2001). Magnetic resonance imaging in coronary heart disease, *European Journal of Radiology,* Vol. 38, No. 3, (191-199), 1527-1315, 0720-048X

Sroubek, F. & Flusser, J. (2005). Multichannel blind deconvolution of spatially misaligned images, *IEEE Transactions on Image Processing,* Vol. 14, No. 7, (874-883), 1057-7149

Sussman, M. & Fatemi, E. (1999). An efficient, interface preserving level set redistancing algorithm and its application to interfacial incompressible fluid flow, *SIAM Journal on Scientific Computing,* Vol. 20, (1165-1191), 1095-7197

Thomson, L. E. J.; Kim, R. J. & Judd, R. M. (2004). Magnetic resonance imaging for the assessment of myocardial viability, *Journal of Magnetic Resonance Imaging,* Vol. 19, No. 6, (771-788), 1749-8023

Wang, J. Y. A. & Adelson, E. H. (1994). Representing moving images with layers, *IEEE Transactions on Image Processing,* Vol 3, No. 5, (625-638), 1057-7149

Weickert, J. & Schnörr, C. (2001). A theoretical framework for convex regularizers in PDE-based computation of image motion, *International Journal of Computer Vision,* Vol. 45, No. 3, (245-264), 0920-5691

Young, A. A. (1998). Model tags: Direct 3D tracking of heart wall motion from tagged MR images. *Medical Image Computing and Computer-Assisted Intervention - Miccai'98*. W. M. Wells, A. Colchester and S. Delp., Vol. 1496, (92-101)

Young, A. A. & Axel, L. (1992). Three-dimensional motion and deformation of the heart wall: Estimation with spatial modulation of magnetization -- A model-based approach, *Radiology,* Vol. 185, (241-247), 1527-1315

Zhang, S.; Douglas, M.; Yaroslavsky, L.; Summers, R.; Dilsizen, V.; Fananapazir, L. & Bacharach, S. (1996). A Fourier based algorithm for tracking SPAMM tags in gated magnetic resonance cardiac images, *Medical Physics,* Vol. 23, No.8, (1359-1369)

7

Protecting the color information by hiding it

Marc CHAUMONT and William PUECH
University of Nîmes, University of Montpellier 2, CNRS UMR 5506- LIRMM, France

1. Introduction

Few work have been proposed for image color protection. A color protection algorithm should give some comprehensive information about the image (such as its grey-level version) but should hide securely the color information. The proposed algorithms are thus specific but take into account recent signal processing concepts such as quantization, compression and data-hiding. Figure 1 illustrates a possible use of the color protection where only secret key owners may rebuild the color image.

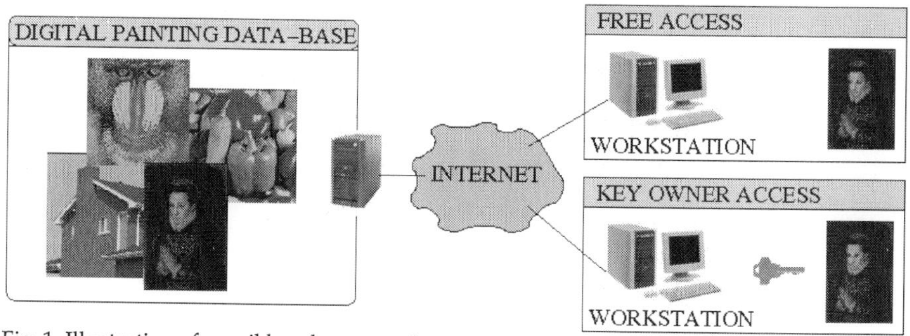

Fig. 1. Illustration of possible color protection use.

This chapter presents some previously published solutions and proposes new solutions built on data-hiding methods. Remember that many methods propose solutions to hide information by using the decomposition of a color image in an *index* image and a color palette (Fridrich, 1998, Wu et al., 2003, Tzeng et al., 2004). The data-hiding may occur in the *index* image (Fridrich, 1998) or in the color palette (Wu et al., 2003, Tzeng et al., 2004). Nevertheless, none of those techniques tries to protect the color information by hiding the color palette in the *index* image. Other approaches such that (Campisi et al., 2002, Queiroz & Braun, 2006) based on wavelet decomposition and sub-band substitution propose solutions to embed the color information in a grey-level image. Their areas are image printing for (Queiroz & Braun, 2006), and perceptive compression for (Campisi et al., 2002). Even if those

techniques embed the color information, their approaches and their purposes are clearly different since they do not try to preserve the best color quality while ensuring security.
In previous work (Chaumont & Puech, 2007a, Chaumont & Puech, 2007b), we presented two new approaches in order to protect the color information by hiding the color palette in the *index* image. In (Chaumont & Puech, 2007a) we propose to sort the colors of the color palette in order to get an *index* image which is near of the luminance of the original color image. In the same time, we get a color palette whose consecutive colors are close. In (Chaumont & Puech, 2007b) the approach is completely different and relies on a function optimization of the global problem formulation. In those two previous work, the security and the color quality requirements were not fully addressed. In this chapter, we give new directions of analysis and improve the security and the quantized color image quality.
This chapter will first remind two solutions quite close from the image color protection problem: the image printing algorithm (Queiroz & Braun, 2006) and the perceptive compression algorithm (Campisi et al., 2002). We will then remind the two specific solutions: the fuzzy approach (Chaumont & Puech, 2007b) and the re-ordering approach (Chaumont & Puech, 2007a). Finally, we will present a better solution for this problem which consists to hide a 512 color palette in an 8-bit-grey-level image.

2. Two substitution-based approaches in the wavelet domain

2.1. Queiroz & Braun color hiding

The solution proposed by (Queiroz & Braun, 2006) is specific to the image printing problem. When a document owning color images has to be distributed in a society, it is still often printed onto black-and-white printers. Graphics, pie charts, or other color images may then become unreadable. The proposed solution is to transform a color image in a readable *grey-level* image even in presence of colors of same luminance. What is interesting us in the (Queiroz & Braun, 2006) solution is not the readability aspect but the reversibility of their transformation from grey-level to color. Indeed, it is possible to recover a visually close approximation of the original color image from the *grey-level* image.

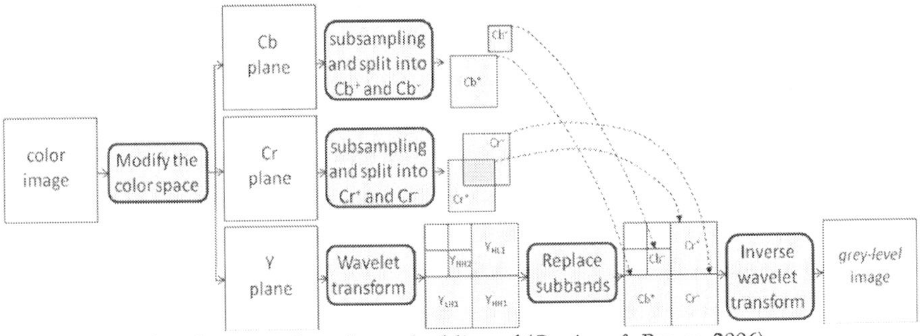

Fig. 2. Sub-band replacement for color embedding of (Queiroz & Braun, 2006).

The technique, illustrated in Figure 2, is very simple and consists:

a) to express the color image into the Y, Cr, Cb color space,
b) to subsample by four the two planes Cr and Cb,

c) to derive two planes Cr^+ and Cr^- (resp. Cb^+ and Cb^-) from the subsampled Cr (resp. Cb) plane; The plane Cr^+ (resp. Cb^+) is a copy of the subsampled Cr (resp. Cb) plane where negative values are set to 0 and the plane Cr^- (resp. Cb^-) is a copy of the subsample Cr (resp. Cb) plane where positive values are set to 0,
d) to decompose the Y plane with a 2-levels discrete wavelet transform,
e) to substitute the LH1 by Cb^+, HL1 by Cr^+, HH1 by Cr^- and HH2 by a ¼ subsampling of Cb^-,
f) to inverse the wavelet transform in order to produce a *grey-level* image embedding its color information.

To recover the embedded color information i.e the Y, Cr, Cb planes, from the *grey-level* image and then rebuild a color image, one should:

a) apply a 2-levels wavelet transform,
b) extract Cb^+, Cr^+, Cr^-, and Cb^-.
c) up-sample the Cb^- plane,
d) retrieve Cr and Cb planes such that $Cr = |Cr^+| - |Cr^-|$ and $Cb = |Cb^+| - |Cb^-|$, and up-sample them,
e) set sub-bands coefficients of HL1, LH1, HH1 and HH2 to 0 and apply the invert wavelet transform.

Figure 3 illustrates the recovering principle.

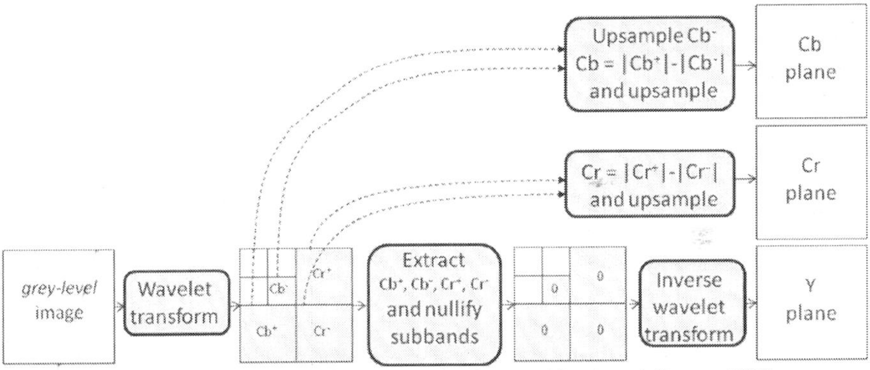

Fig. 3. Recovering of a color image from a *grey-level* image (Queiroz & Braun, 2006).

This substitution approach in the wavelet domain is interesting for its potential for hiding the color information into a grey-level image. Figure 4 shows some key images of the process for the baboon image. One could nevertheless remark that the retrieved color image (Figure 4.e) from the *grey-level* image has a poor visual quality. We could note some blurring and strong ringing effects. Those artefacts are due to the poor quality of the retrieve Y plane since lots of wavelet sub-bands are nullify. In Table 1 we should essentially remark that PSNRs between the original color image and the rebuild color image are below 31 dB. In conclusion, this approach is only useful for printing applications. We will see in the next section another similar approach (Campisi et al., 2002) which gives higher PSNR and images visually more pleasant.

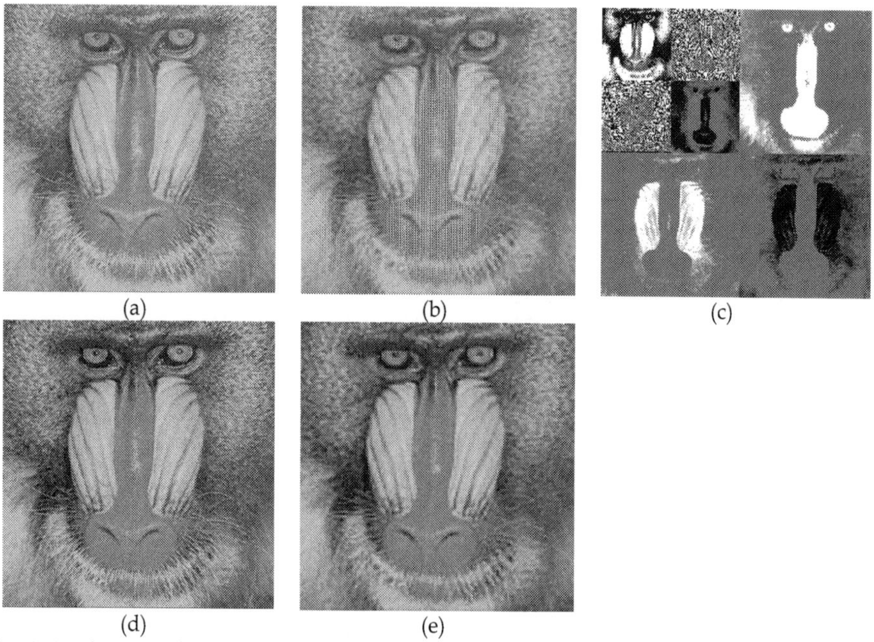

Fig. 4. Application of the *substitution-based approach* of (Queiroz & Braun 2006): a) Luminance of the original color image, b) *Grey-level* image embedding the chrominance planes, c) Wavelet decomposition of the *grey-level* image, d) Original color image, e) Rebuilt color image from the *grey-level* image.

Images	$\text{PSNR}_{(luminance,\ grey\text{-}level)}$	$\text{PSNR}_{(original\ color,\ rebuilt)}$
baboon	21.03 dB	23.93 dB
barbara	23.93 dB	26.33 dB
airplane	26.47 dB	28.56 dB
peppers	21.24 dB	28.82 dB
lena	21.02 dB	30.31 dB
house	25.18 dB	30.75 dB

Table 1. PSNR between the luminance image and the *grey-level* image and PSNR between the original color image (RGB space) and the rebuilt color image (RGB space) using the *grey-level* image embedding its color information.

2.2. Campisi et al. color hiding

The objective of the solution proposed by (Campisi et al., 2002) is to improve the compression efficiency of a color image. The idea is to transform a color image into a single grey-level image which embeds the chrominance planes. The solution principle is thus very similar to (Queiroz & Braun 2006) approach. Nevertheless, the distortion between the original color image and the rebuilt one is smaller.

The approach, illustrated in Figure 5, consists in:

a) expressing the color image into the Y, I, Q color space,

b) sub-sampling by 16 the two planes I and Q in order to obtain I_{LL2} and Q_{LL2} planes; Note that this sub-sampling is process by applying a 2-levels wavelet Daubechies 9/7 (Daubechies & Sweldens, 1998) decomposition and keeping the low-pass sub-band of I and Q,

c) applying a 1-level wavelet Daubechies decomposition to the Y plane and re-apply a 1-level wavelet decomposition to the sub-bands HL and LH; The decomposition of sub-band HL (resp. LH) give four sub-bands and the low-pass one is noted $Y_{ll,HL}$ (resp. $Y_{ll,LH}$),

d) normalizing the two planes I_{LL2} and Q_{LL2} with values N_I and N_Q; those values will be transmitted as side information,

e) substitute the sub-band $Y_{ll,HL}$ (resp. $Y_{ll,LH}$) by I_{LL2} (resp. Q_{LL2}),

f) compress the data.

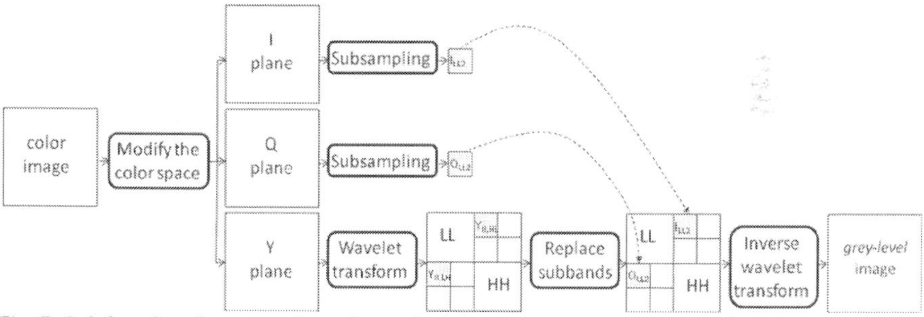

Fig. 5. Sub-band replacement for color embedding of (Campisi et al., 2002).

To recover the embedded color information i.e Y, I, Q planes, from the *grey-level* image and then rebuild a color image, one should:

a) apply the wavelet transforms,

b) extract I_{LL2} and Q_{LL2} and rescale them thanks to normalizing values N_I and N_Q,

c) up-sample the I_{LL2} and Q_{LL2} in order to retrieve I and Q planes,

d) set sub-bands coefficients of $Y_{ll,HL}$ and $Y_{ll,LH}$ to 0 and apply the invert wavelet transforms.

Figure 6 illustrates the recovering principle.

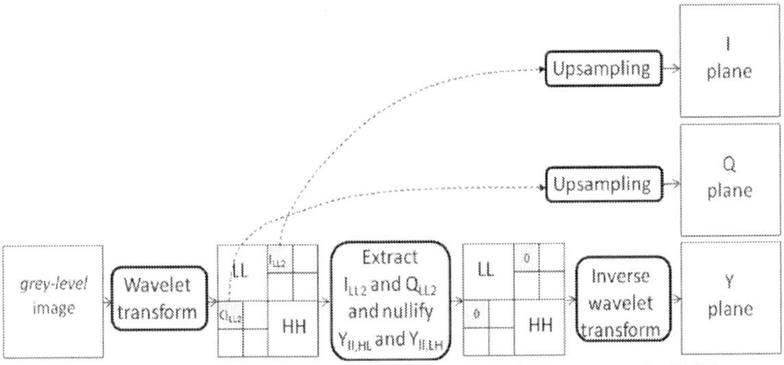

Fig. 6. Recovering of a color image from a *grey-level* image (Campisi et al., 2002).

Figure 7 shows some key images of the process for the baboon image. One could remark that the reconstructed color image (Figure 7.d) from the *grey-level* image has a good visual quality. Since, the Campisi et al. approach does not degrade too much the Y component and that chrominance planes are good enough, the rebuilt color image is visually pleasant. We just notice some small ringing effects. In Table 2 we should essentially remark that the PSNRs between the original color image and the rebuild color image are above 29 dB. Thus, the Campisi et al. approach performs better objective and subjective results than (Queiroz & Braun 2006). We will see in the next section, that the palette based approach gives rebuilt color images of even better quality.

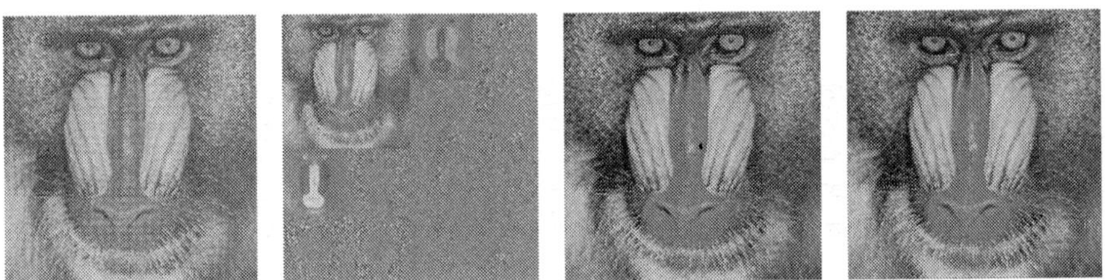

(a) (b) (c) (d)

Fig. 7. Application of the *substitution-based approach* of (Campisi et al., 2002): a) *Grey-level* image embedding the chrominance planes, b) Wavelet decomposition of the *grey-level* image, c) Original color image, d) Rebuilt color image from the *grey-level* image.

Images	PSNR *(luminance, grey-level)*	PSNR *(original color, rebuilt)*
baboon	27.37 dB	29.8 dB
barbara	30.61 dB	31.75 dB
peppers	25.82 dB	32.36 dB
airplane	34.12 dB	32.58 dB
house	30.76 dB	31.76 dB
lena	26.91 dB	36.75 dB

Table 2. PSNR between the luminance image and the *grey-level* image and PSNR between the original color image (RGB space) and the rebuilt color image (RGB space) using the *grey-level* image embedding its color information.

3. Two palette-based approaches

In order to obtain a grey-level image embedding its color information, we decompose a color image in an *index* image and a color palette. Figure 8 illustrates a decomposition of the Baboon color image into an *index* image and a color palette. Note that the decomposition is a quantization since the total number of colors is reduced. The color palette is then hidden in the *index* image. The *index* image should be similar to the luminance of the color image, the embedding process should be of week magnitude and the color palette should be cleverly ordered. We proposed in previous work two solutions for this problem: **the fuzzy approach** (Chaumont & Puech, 2007b) and the **reordering approach** (Chaumont & Puech, 2007a).

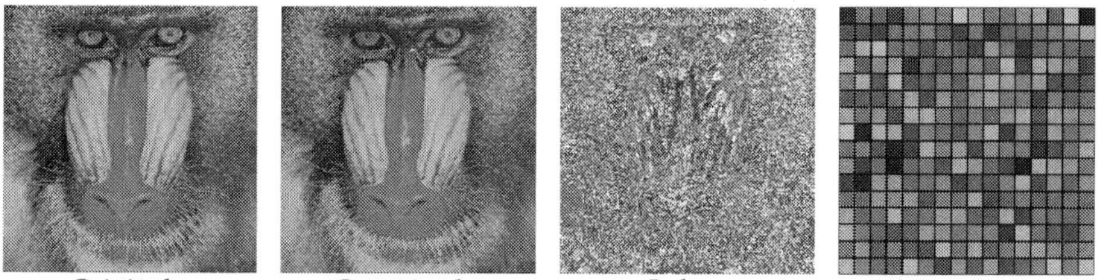

Fig. 8. Decomposition of a color image into an *Index* image and a color palette.

3.1. The fuzzy approach

The originality of the fuzzy approach is to propose a solution for the very constrained decomposition problem. Thus, the main contribution of this work is the proposition of an energetic function in order to model the decomposition of the color image. The optimization of the energetic function leads to the obtaining of a well suit *index* image and a well sorted color palette. The fuzzy approach is then decomposed in two parts: the energetic function optimisation and the data-hiding.

3.1.1. The problem formulation and its resolution

The goal of the first step is to find an *index* image and a color palette with the following constraints:

- the *index* image should be close from the luminance of the original color image,
- the color quantized image should be close from the color image,
- and, for data-hiding purpose, the color palette should own consecutive couples of close color.

The problem of the computation of a color palette made of couples of close colors and an *index* image similar to the luminance may be expressed by three constraints. Mathematically this comes to found the K colors $C(k)$ (C is the color palette) and the $P_{i,k}$ ownership values giving the degree of belongingness of a pixel i to the kth color. Note that $P_{i,k}$ belongs to $[0,1]$ and are named fuzzy membership values in fuzzy c-mean clustering approach (Dunn, 1974). Also note that the $P_{i,k}$ give indirectly the *index* image such that: $Index(i) = \arg_k \max_k P_{i,k}$.

Thus, we are looking to minimize the above energetic model in order to obtain

$\forall i \in [1, N], \forall k \in [1, K]$, $P_{i,k}$ and *C(k)*:

$$E = \underbrace{\sum_{i=1}^{N}\sum_{k=1}^{K} P_{i,k}^{m}(C(k) - I(i))^2}_{first\ term} + \underbrace{\lambda_1 \sum_{i=1}^{N}\sum_{k=1}^{K} P_{i,k}^{m}(Y(i) - k)^2}_{second\ term} + \underbrace{\lambda_2 \sum_{k|k\in[1..K]\ and\ k\ is\ odd} (C(k) - C(k+1))^2}_{third\ term}, \quad (1)$$

with *I* the color image, *Y* the luminance image, λ_1 and λ_2 two scalar values and $m \in]1, \infty[$ the fuzzy coefficient tuning the equi-probability. Note that m is set to 2 for computational complexity reduction.

The first term is expressing the constraint of color quantization. The aim is to found the best representative *K* colors. The second term stands for getting the *index* image the nearest to the luminance image *Y*. The last term constrain couples of consecutive color from the palette to be close.

The minimization of Equation (1) such that:

$$\{P_{i,k}, C(k)\} = \underset{\{P_{i,k}, C(k)\}}{\arg} \min E,$$

is performed iteratively in a two steps loop as in conventional fuzzy c-mean algorithms. In the first step, colors *C(k)* are updated, given $P_{i,k}$, by solving the linear system below:

$$\underline{\forall k\ odd:}$$
$$(\lambda_2 + \sum_{i=1}^{N} P_{i,k}^{m}) \times C(k) - \lambda_2 \times C(k+1) = \sum_{i=1}^{N} P_{i,k}^{m} I(i),$$

$$\underline{\forall k\ even:}$$
$$-\lambda_2 \times C(k-1) + (\lambda_2 + \sum_{i=1}^{N} P_{i,k}^{m}) \times C(k) = \sum_{i=1}^{N} P_{i,k}^{m} I(i).$$

In the second step, $P_{i,k}$ (with m=2) are updated given the colors *C(k)* with:

$$P_{i,k} = \frac{\left(\sum_{l=1}^{l=K} \frac{1}{2\times((C(l)-I(i))^2+\lambda_1(Y(i)-l)^2)}\right)^{-1}}{2 \times ((C(k) - I(i))^2 + \lambda_1(Y(i) - k)^2)}$$

Mathematical details are given in (Chaumont & Puech, 2007b).

3.1.2. Spatial data hiding

For this approach, we have used an algorithm to embed the color palette information in the Least Significant Bit (LSB) of an image of *N* pixels. The objective is thus to embed a message *M* made up of *m* bits b_j ($M = b_1 b_2 ... b_m$). The embedding factor, in bit/pixel, is $E_f = m / N$.

The original image is then divided in areas of size $\lfloor 1/E_f \rfloor$ pixels. Each area is used to hide **only one bit** b_j of the message. This splitting procedure guarantees that the message is spread homogeneously over the whole *index* image. In order to hide the color palette, we need to embed 3 × 256 × 8 = 6144 bits (the number of colors is K=256) in the *index image.*

Consequently, the embedding factor E_f, only depends on the image size N. In our process, a Pseudo-Random Number Generator (PRNG) selects randomly, for each region, a pixel *Index(i)*. In order to get a marked pixel $Index_M(i)$, the LSB of this selected pixel *Index(i)* is then modified according to the message bit b_j (the formula is given for *index* values belonging to *[0,K-1]*):

$$Index_M(i) = Index(i) - Index(i) \ mod \ 2 + b_j,$$

This way to embed the color palette ensures that each marked pixel is at worst modified by one grey-level and in the same time that the rebuilt color pixel would not be very far from the right color value. Indeed, the third term of Equation (1) ensures that consecutive couples of color are close.

3.1.3. Evaluation of the fuzzy approach

In order to illustrate the performance of the fuzzy approach, we present results on few color images of size 256×256 pixels. For all the experiments, $\lambda_1 = 1$ and $\lambda_2 = 0.01 \times N/(K+1)$ (see Equation (1)). The obtained results show that the approach is efficient whatever the image type. Below, the different steps of the algorithm are commented on the baboon image.

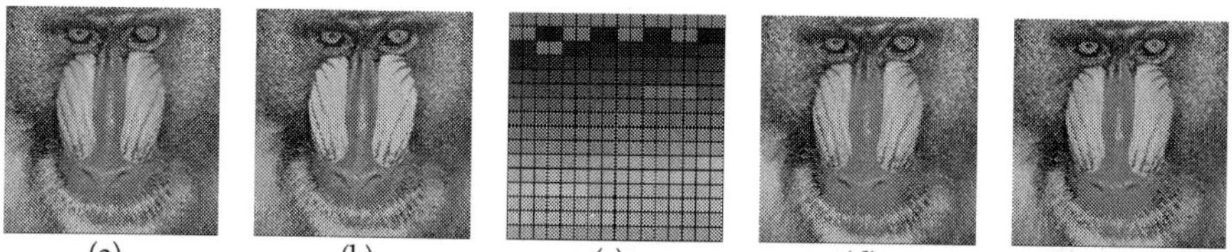

(a) (b) (c) (d) (e)

Fig. 9. Application of the *fuzzy approach*: a) Luminance of the original color image, b) *Index* image, c) Color palette, d) Original color image, e) Rebuilt color image from the *index*-marked image.

After achieving the minimization of Equation (1) on the baboon image with *K=256* colors, we obtain an *index* image, illustrated in Figure 9.b, and its color palette illustrated in Figure 9.c. The luminance image of the original color image is given in Figure 9.a. One could observe the good similarity between *index* image and luminance image. The good PSNR value of 29.74 dB confirms this subjective feeling. We can notice that lots of *index* values are unused which explain the presence of some useless colors on the color palette of Figure 9.c. Also note that in the color palette in Figure 9.c, consecutive couples of color are colorimetricly close as expressed by the third term of Equation (1). Finally, we should precise that the computational cost for the minimization Equation (1) is very high. The article (Chaumont & Puech, 2007c) proposes a solution to reduce this cost but in counterpart, the results are less good.

The length of our embedded message (color palette) is *6144* bits which gives an embedding factor for an image of *256* × *256* pixels of $E_f = 6144 / (256 \times 256) = 0.093$ *bit/pixel*. The *index* image is then cut in block of *10* pixels. In each *10*-pixel block, **one** bit of the color palette is embedded at the position selected by the PRNG. The secured is obtained through the use of a secret key of 128 bits as a seed for the PRNG. The distribution of the message over the image is then key-related.

Figure 9.e shows the rebuilt color image from the *index*-marked one. This image is not visually far from the original color image even if the PSNR value of 27.90 dB is of middle quality. Note that the degradation due to the data-hiding method is weak because it disturbs *index* values of a maximum of one. This is made possible thanks to the color palette property to own consecutive couples of close colors.

PSNRs values are given in Table 3. Rebuilt color images are of middle quality (over 27 dB) but visually pleasant. Compared to the substitution-based approach of (Campisi et al., 2002) the rebuilt color images, with the fuzzy approach, are sometimes better and sometimes worse. On the other side, the *index* image is extremely close to the luminance image. We will see, in the next section, with the reordering approach, that if we reduce the strong constraint on the luminance, the rebuilt color images are of better quality.

PSNR values for *index*-marked images are over 29 dB. Since the grey-level images (i.e. the *index*-marked images) are of good quality, images may be colorized semi-automatically (Chaumont & Puech, 2008). This colorization may be seen as an indirect attack since an attacker is able to retrieve a pleasant color image and then fraudulently use it. Next section will expose a solution where *index* image have a weak quality and the rebuilt color image of have a better quality.

Images	PSNR *(luminance, index-marked)*	PSNR *(original color, rebuilt)*
baboon	29.74 dB	27.90 dB
barbara	34.86 dB	30.74 dB
peppers	35.03 dB	31.68 dB
airplane	35.95 dB	33.66 dB
lena	37.87 dB	34.78 dB
house	35.40 dB	35.45 dB

Table 3. PSNR between the luminance image and the *index*-marked image and PSNR between the original color image (RGB space) and the rebuilt color image (RGB space) using the *index*-marked image embedding its color palette.

3.2. The reordering approach

3.2.1. The image decomposition

Reducing the color number of a color image is a classical quantization problem. The optimal solution, to extract the *K* colors, is obtained by solving:

$$\{P_{i,k}, C(k)\} = \arg \min_{P_{i,k}, C(k)} \sum_{i=1}^{N} \sum_{k=1}^{K} P_{i,k}.dist^2(I(i), C(k)),\ and\ \forall i, \exists! k', \left[P_{i,k'} = 1\ and\ \forall k \neq k', P_{i,k} = 0\right], \quad (2)$$

where I is a color image of dimension N pixels, $C(k)$ is the kth color of the research K colors, *dist* is a distance function in the color space (L2 in the RGB color space), and $Pi,k \subset \{0, 1\}$ is the membership value of pixel i to color k.

A well known solution to minimize the Equation (2), and then to obtain the K colors, is to use the ISODATA k-mean clustering algorithm (Ball & Hall, 1966). $P_{i,k}$ is defined as:

$$\forall i, \forall k, P_{i,k} = \begin{cases} 1 \text{ if } k = \arg\{\min\limits_{\{k'\}\ k' \in [1,K]} dist(I(i), C(k'))\}, \\ 0 \text{ otherwise,} \end{cases}$$

with $C(k) = \frac{\sum_{i=1}^{N} P_{i,k} \times I(i)}{\sum_{i=1}^{N} P_{i,k}}$.

Nevertheless, in our approach the K number is significant (K=256). If we proceed with a classical k-mean algorithm, the number of colors extracted will often be below K. Indeed, it is the well known problem of *death classes*. Moreover, the k-mean algorithm is quite long in CPU time in comparison to non optimal but faster algorithms such that *octree color quantization algorithm* of Gervautz and Purgathofer (Gervautz & Purgathofer, 1990), *Median Cut algorithm* (Heckbert, 1982)... To overcome those two problems ("death classes" and "CPU time"), we are using the *octree color quantization algorithm* as an initialization to the k-mean algorithm: $P_{i,k}$ are set from the result obtained with the *octree color quantization algorithm*.

3.2.2. The Layer Running Algorithm

Once the color quantization has been processed, the obtained K color image could be represented by an *index image* and a color palette. The *index* image is noted down *Index* and is defined such that:

$$\forall i \in [1, N], Index(i) = \arg \max_{k \in [1,K]} P_{i,k}.$$

The color palette is noted down *Palette* and $\forall k \in [1, K], Palette(k) = C(k)$.

Our goal is to get an *index* image where each grey-level is not too far from the luminance of the original color image. A second weakest constraint is that in the color palette, two consecutive colors should be close. Thanks to the color quantization, we already own an *index* image and a color palette. Our problem is then to find a permutation function which permutes in the same time the values of the *index* image and the values of the color palette. The best permutation function Φ is found by solving:

$$\Phi = \arg\min_{\Phi} \sum_{i=1}^{N} dist^2(Y(i), \Phi(Index(i))) + \lambda \sum_{k=1}^{K-1} dist^2(Palette(\Phi^{-1}(k)), Palette(\Phi^{-1}(k+1))), \quad (3)$$

where Y is the luminance of the original color image, and λ a constant value. The Φ permutation function is a bijective function in $\mathbb{N}$ defined such that Φ: [1..K] → [1..K].

In a first approximation, Equation (3) is solved thanks to an heuristic algorithm: the *layer running algorithm* (Chaumont & Puech, 2007a). The aim of this algorithm is to find an ordering for the K colors such that consecutive colors are close and such that colors are ordered from the darkest to the lightest. This ordering defines for each kth color a k' position which gives us the Φ function such that Φ (k) = k'.

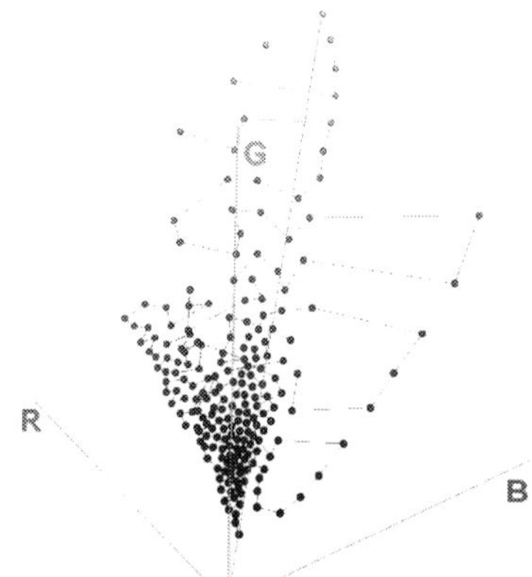

Fig. 10. A view of the layer running in the RGB cube.

To find an ordering of the *K* colors, the algorithm runs the color space to build the ordered suite of colors, illustrated Figure 10. This running is obtained by jumping from color to color, into the color space, by choosing the closer color from the current one. The first color of this suite is chosen as the darkest one among the *K* colors. An additional constraint to this running is that we limit the color research to colors which are very close in luminance. This signifies that the running in the color space is limited to a layer defined on luminance information. This *layer running algorithm* could then be seen as a kind of *3D spiral run* in the color space. A description of the algorithm may be found in (Chaumont & Puech, 2007a).

This *layer running algorithm* owns an implicit hidden parameter which is the *layer size* used during the color running in the color space. Since our goal is to minimize the Equation (3), a satisfying way to automatically set this parameter is to test all the possible values for this *layer size* parameter and to keep the *layer size* value minimizing the equation. Knowing that the possible values of the *layer size parameter* belong to the range [1, K] and that it is very fast to make just one run in the color space, this gives an elegant and fast solution to approximate the Equation (3).

Another problem still unsolved is the tuning of the lambda parameter. The equation below gives more details on the way lambda is expressed: $\lambda = \alpha \times N / (3 \times (K-1))$, with α the value balancing the two constraints evoke above and expressed by Equation (3). For example, α value set to *1* means giving the same weight to the two constraints, an α value set to *0.5* signifies an *index image* nearest to the luminance image, *a contrario* an α value set to *2* means a color palette more continuous.

3.2.3. Spatial data hiding

Similarly to the fuzzy approach, we embed the color palette information by modifying pixels of 0 or +1 or – 1. The embedding approach is also substitutive but it is not a simple

LSB approach. The objective is again to embed a message M made up of m bits b_j ($M = b_1 b_2 ... b_m$). The original image is divided in areas of equal sizes and each area is used to hide **only one bit** b_j of the message.

A Pseudo-Random Number Generator (PRNG) selects randomly, for each region, a pixel *Index(i)*. In order to get a marked pixel $Index_M(i)$, the selected pixel *Index(i)* is modified according to the message bit b_j:

$$Index_M(i) = \begin{cases} Index(i) \text{ if } b_j = Index(i) \bmod 2, \\ \arg\min_{k} {}_{k \in \{Index(i)-1, Index(i)+1\} \cap \{1,...,K\}} (Palette(Index(i)) - Palette(k))^2 \text{ otherwise.} \end{cases}$$

Thus, the *index* value *Index(i)* is modified of +1 or -1 when $b_j \neq Index(i) \bmod 2$. The best choice for this modification is then to choose the closest color between *Palette(Index(i)+1)* and *Palette(Index(i)-1)* in order to minimize the distance to the color *Palette(Index(i))*. This way to embed the color palette ensures that each marked pixel is at worst modified by one grey-level and in the same time that the rebuilt color pixel would not be very far from the right color value.

3.2.4. Evaluation of the reordering approach

In order to illustrate the performance of the reordering approach, we present results on few color images of size 256×256 pixels. The obtained results show that the approach is efficient whatever the image type. Below, the different steps of the algorithm are commented on the baboon image.

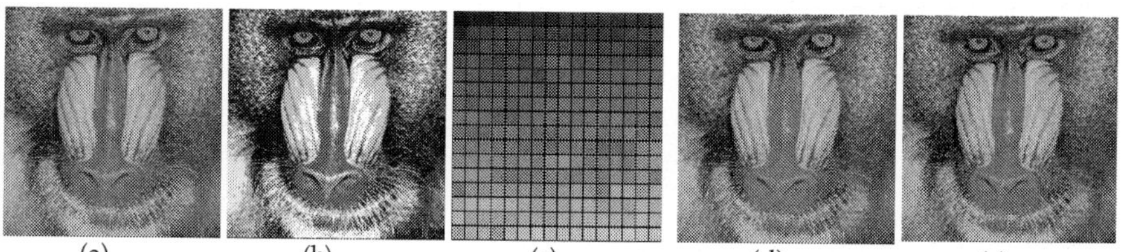

(a) (b) (c) (d) (e)

Fig. 11. Application of the *layer running algorithm*: a) Luminance of the original color image, b) *Index* image after color ordering, c) Color palette after color ordering, d) Original color image, e) Rebuilt color image from the *index*-marked image.

After the fast quantization step (with K=256 colors) and the optimized *layer running algorithm* step, we obtain an *index image* and its color palette shown in Figures 11.b and 11.c. Note that the *index* image (Figure 11.b) is more contrasted than the luminance of the original color image (Figure 11.a) but keeps its semantic intelligibility. Also note that in the color palette, Figure 11.c, consecutive colors are colorimetricly close.

In order to be able to recover the embedded color-palette at the receiver, the embedding factor for an image of 256×256 pixels, is set to $E_f = 6144 / (256 \times 256) = 0.093$ *bit/pixel*. The *index* image after color ordering is then cut in block of *10* pixels. In each *10*-pixel block, a bit of the color palette is embedded at the position selected by the PRNG. The secured is obtained through the use of a secret key of 128 bits as a seed for the PRNG. The distribution of the message over the image is then key-related.

Figure 11.e shows the rebuilt color image from the *index*-marked one. This image is visually near from the original quantified one and the $PSNR_{(quantized\ ,\ rebuilt)}$ of 42.3 dB confirms this feeling. Some PSNRs values are given in Table 4. We could notice that rebuilt color images are of good quality (over 33 dB). PSNR values for *index* images are below 20 dB which is in general a poor result but in our case, it helps us to counter-attack the colorization attack (Chaumont & Puech, 2008). Moreover, *index* images are still semantically understandable.

Images	$PSNR_{(luminance,\ index-marked)}$	$PSNR_{(original\ color,\ rebuilt)}$
baboon	16.75 dB	33.31 dB
peppers	19.76 dB	36.32 dB
lena	19.11 dB	38.63 dB
house	18.64 dB	39.27 dB
airplane	12.87 dB	39.9 dB

Table 4. PSNR between the luminance image and the *index*-marked image and PSNR between the original color image (RGB space) and the rebuilt color image (RGB space) using the *index*-marked image embedding its color palette.

4. The 512 colors into an 8-bit-grey-level image approach

In this section we present a new approach based on a reversible data-hiding method allowing us to hide a color palette of 512 colors in the *index* image (Chaumont & Puech, 2008). Compared to the previous work of (Chaumont & Puech, 2007a, Chaumont & Puech, 2007b) presented in Section 3, the three main contributions of this approach are:

- the used of 512 colors (*index* values belongs to [0, 511]; *index* image is thus a 9-bit coded image; and there are 512 colors in the palette) but a resultant grey-level image owning values belonging to [0, 255]. The stored image (grey-level image) is then a classical 8-bit grey-level image and embeds a color palette plus a bitplane.
- the compression of a bitplane and the color palette,
- and the use of a high capacity reversible watermarking algorithm.

The overview of the embedding/extraction scheme is given in Figure 12. During the embedding scheme, the color image is quantized in a 512 color image. The 9-bit *index* image is split into an 8-bit grey level image and a bitplane. The extracted bitplane and the color palette are then embedded in the 8-bit grey level image.

The quantization of a color image into an *index* image and a color palette is achieved similarly to the color image decomposition detailed in Section 3.2.1. One applies the *octree color quantization algorithm* of Gervautz and Purgathofer (Gervautz & Purgathofer, 1990) follows-up with a k-mean clustering (Ball & Hall, 1966). Note that we decompose the image in 512 colors and not in 256 colors.

The palette re-ordering uses the *Layer Running Algorithm* which is detailed in Section 3.2.2. This re-ordering produces an *index* image visually similar to the luminance image and also give a color palette whose consecutive color values are very close. Note that those two properties are necessary for the compression and data hiding parts.

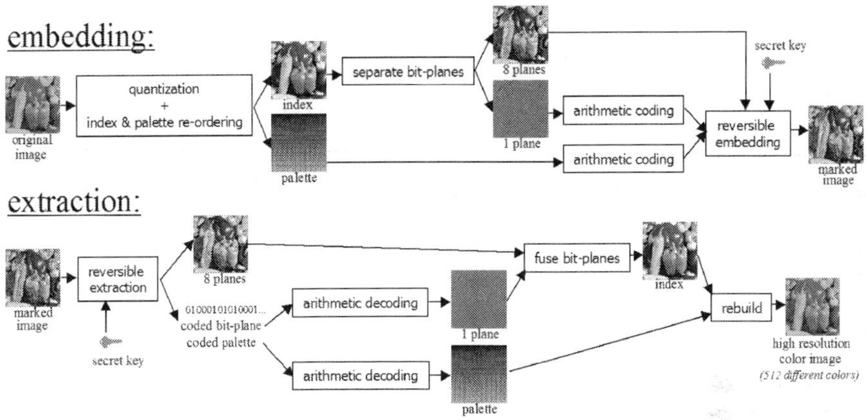

Fig. 12. The general embedding/extraction scheme.

Once *index* image and color palette are computed and re-ordered, the data hiding is achieved. Section 4.1 explains what is the message to embed, how to format it and how the reversible-watermarking algorithm works. After the watermarking process, the resultant grey-level image may be stored on a public website. The reversible extraction scheme, illustrated in Figure 12, is the exact inverse of the embedding scheme.

4.1. Data-hiding

4.1.1. Message construction

Once the color image decomposition (into 512 colors) and its re-arrangement (*layer running algorithm*) have been achieved, one bitplane of the *index* image is removed in order to create the cover image. The extracted bitplane and the color palette are then compressed in order to be embedded into the cover image (see Figure 12). The solution retained to compress the color palette is to statistically encode the error of prediction (differential encoding + arithmetic encoding) of each color belonging to the color palette.

The compression rate of the chosen bitplane is not enough efficient if directly achieved. One has to modify the statistics in order to reduce the entropy (theoretical rate cost). Thus, the bitplane vector (noted **bp**) is transformed in a prediction error vector (noted **e**) owning three possible values: $\{-1, 0, 1\}$. Each bit $\mathbf{bp}(i)$, $i \in [0, N]$, of the bitplane vector is then substituted by $\mathbf{e}(i) \in \{-1, 0, 1\}$ before the lossless coding.

For each pixel $I(i)$ at position i, we first compute a prediction $Pred_{pixel}(i)$:

$$Pred_{pixel}(i) = \begin{cases} C \; if \; |A-B| < |A-C| \\ B \; otherwise, \end{cases}$$

with A, B and C the neighbors pixels of current pixel *I(i)* as defined below:

previous line	*A*	*B*
current line	*C*	*I(i)*

This kind of prediction is used in the Differential Pulse Code Modulation (DPCM) approach. It essentially takes into account the edges in order to predict more cleverly than with a simple mean. Note that some more sophisticated predictions may be explored in particularly by looking at lossless compression techniques. Nevertheless, this predictor is enough efficient for our approach. Also note that for image border the prediction is achieved with the available values.

The second step is to find the best prediction for the bit **bp**(i) of the bitplane vector. At the coder and the decoder sides, the information of all the other bitplanes is known. Thus, one have two possible prediction solutions: either predict a 0 knowing the other bitplanes, either predict a 1 knowing the other bitplanes. Knowing the prediction $Pred_{pixel}(i)$, one have to decide which is the best hypothesis: having a 0 in the bitplane (in this case the pixel value is noted $I_0(i)$) or having a 1 (in this case the pixel value is noted $I_1(i)$). This best hypothesis (best prediction) is chosen in accordance to the maximum of the two probabilities p($Pred_{pixel}(i)$ | $I_0(i)$) and p($Pred_{pixel}(i)$ | $I_1(i)$). This is a classical two hypothesis choice and with Gaussian pdf assumptions the best choice is:

$$Pred_{bit}(i) = \begin{cases} 0 \; if \; (Pred_{pixel}(i) - I_0(i))^2 < (Pred_{pixel}(i) - I_1(i))^2 \\ 1 \; otherwise. \end{cases}$$

The last step in order to obtain the **e** prediction error vector is to compute the prediction error (error values are either -1, 0 or 1):

$$e(i) = bp(i) - Pred_{bit}(i).$$

The prediction **e** error vector may now be encoded and because of the good prediction behaviour, the entropy is low and then the encoding cost is low.

4.1.2. Reversible watermarking scheme

The algorithm used for the reversible embedding is one of the three most efficient for its embedding capacity. A brief description is given below; for more details see (Chaumont & Puech, 2009). The algorithm lies on congruence computations. The congruence properties allow defining three possible states for a pixel:

- the state ***embedding*** which corresponds to a pixel *embedding* an integer coefficient belonging to *[1, n]*,
- the state ***to-correct*** which corresponds to a pixel that has been modified but *does not embed* any information; this pixel will be *corrected* during the reverting process,
- the state ***original*** which corresponds to an *original* pixel (i.e unchanged).

Let's define a constant integer value n greater or equals to 3. Let's also define the T transform which takes two integers x_1 and x_2 as input and return an integer:

$$T : \mathbb{N} \times \mathbb{N} \rightarrow \mathbb{N}$$
$$T(x_1, x_2) = (n+1).x_1 - n.x_2.$$

We will name the coding process, the act of embedding a message into an image and the decoding process, the act of extracting the message and rebuilding the original image. Let's now define the three possible states and the coding-decoding algorithms.

Embedding state

A pixel i in the *embedding* state is a pixel such that:

$$0 \leq T(I(i), I(i+1)) \quad and \quad T(I(i), I(i+1)) + n \leq L, \tag{4}$$

with I the original image (of N pixel size) whose grey-levels belongs to $[0,L]$. In the case of 8-bits images, L equals to 255. All pixels i in the *embedding* state:

- are T transformed such that $I_T(i) = T(\ I(i),\ I(i+1)\ )$, with $I_T(i)$ the resulting transformed pixel,
- **must** then embed **a** coefficient w **belonging to $[1, n]$** such that $I_w(i) = I_T(i) + w$.

Note that after the embedding of a coefficient w belonging to $[1, n]$, it is impossible to recover $I(i)$ with the only knowledge of $I(i+1)$. Indeed $I_w(i) = (n+1).I(i) - n.I(i+1) + w$ with $w \neq 0$, thus $I(i) = \frac{I_w(i)+n.I(i+1)-w}{n+1}$ and so:

$$(I_w(i) + n.I(i+1)) \ mod \ (n+1) \neq 0. \tag{5}$$

The **congruence property** of Equation (5) allows detecting an **embedding** pixel during the decoding process. Note that during the decoding process, the $I_w(i+1)$ pixel should have been previously reverted to $I(i+1)$ in order to compute this congruence. This implies that the image scan order used during the decoding process is the opposite of the one used during the coding process.

To-correct state

A pixel i in the *to-correct* state is a pixel such that the negation of Equation (4) is true:

$$T(I(i), I(i+1)) < 0 \quad or \quad T(I(i), I(i+1)) + n > L.$$

All pixels that are in this *to-correct* state are then modified such that:

$$\begin{aligned} &c \leftarrow (I(i) + n.I(i+1)) \ mod \ (n+1); \\ &if \ (I(i) - c) < 0 \ \ then \ \ c \leftarrow -(n+1-c); \\ &I_w(i) \leftarrow I(i) - c. \end{aligned} \tag{6}$$

The c coefficients belong to $[-n, n]$ and are embedded (into the *embedding* pixels) in order to enable the reversibility of the *to-correct* pixels during the decoding process. We name the c coefficients the **corrective codes**. Note that after the modification expressed by Equation (6), pixel $I_w(i)$ checks the property:

$$(I_{w}(i) + n.I(i+1)) \; mod \; (n+1) = 0. \tag{7}$$

The **congruence property** of Equation (7) allows detecting a *to-correct* pixel at the reverting process. Note that at the decoding process the $I_w(i+1)$ pixels should have been previously reverted to $I(i+1)$ in order to compute this congruence.

Original state

Given an image order scan for the coding, a pixel in the *original* state (i.e. unmodified pixel) must always be present just before a pixel in the *to-correct* state. For a top-bottom-left-right scan order, if a pixel at position *i* is in the *to-correct* state, then the pixel at position *i-1* **must be** in the *original* state. In order to ensure this strong property (*original* and *to-correct* pixels go by pairs), during the scan, when a pixel at position *i* is detected as a *to-correct* one, a forward research is achieved in order to find the next *embedding* position (noted *next*). *Original* and *to-correct* states are then alternates between the *i* (or *i-1*) position and the *next-1* position.

This grouping constraint breaks the problematic dependencies during the decoding process. Remember that during the decoding, the image scan order is inverted. A *to-correct* pixel at position *i* may not be reverted immediately if its associated corrective code is still not extracted. Nevertheless, because the pixel at position *i-1* is an *original* pixel, the pixel at position *i-2* may be treated immediately and the decoding process may continue (pixel at position *i* will be corrected later, in a second pass).

Coding and decoding algorithms

The **coding** process is composed of two steps:

- classify each pixel in one of the three states: *embedding, to-correct, original,*
- embed into the *embedding* pixels, the watermark made of corrective codes plus the message.

For the **decoding** process, the image scan order is inverted. The decoding process is also composed of two steps:

- extract the watermark from the *embedding* pixels, revert (during the scan) all those pixels and localize the *to-correct* pixels,
- from the extracted watermark retrieve the corrective codes and the message, and correct the *to-correct* pixels.

Note that the security is ensured by the secrecy of the scan order. The user secret key is used as a seed of a pseudo-random number generator. The obtained pseudo-random number sequence is used to generate an adapted scan order. Thus, no information about the message (color palette + bitplane) may be extracted by an attacker. Moreover, an attack by colorization (Chaumont & Puech, 2008), which consists in retrieving semi-automatically (a small human intervention is necessary) the colors of each pixels, is difficult since the final grey-level image has a poor quality. Also note, that this reversible watermarking scheme is not robust to any signal processing but it is not a deficiency for this application.

4.2. Evaluation of the 512 colors into an 8-bit-grey-level image approach

We have applied the "512 colors approach" on well known color images of size 256×256 pixels. For all the experiments, $n = 4$ for the reversible watermarking. The obtained results show that the approach is efficient whatever the image type. In Figure 13, the main steps of our approach are comment for the *peppers* image.

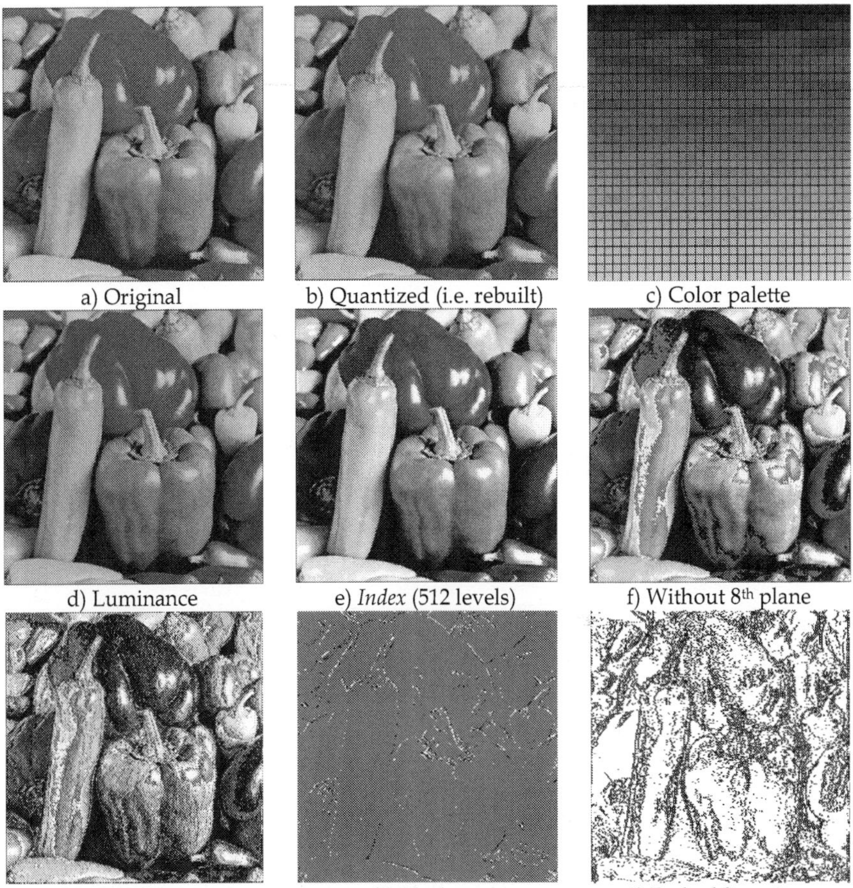

a) Original b) Quantized (i.e. rebuilt) c) Color palette
d) Luminance e) *Index* (512 levels) f) Without 8th plane
g) Marked image h) 8th plane i) Embedding sites

Fig. 13. Steps of the "512 colors" approach.

After achieving the color decomposition of the *peppers* image (Figure 13.a) we obtain an *index* image whose *index* values belongs to *[0, 511]* (Figure 13.e), and a color palette made of *K=512* colors (Figure 11.c). The quantized image, which is rebuilt with the knowledge of the *index* image and the color palette, is illustrated in Figure 13.b. The PSNR of this quantized image equals to 38.95 dB. The best PSNR obtained with a palette-based approach was 36.32

dB with the re-ordering one (Chaumont & Puech, 2007a). The obtained **gain** with the "512 colors" approach is more than to **2 dB** for the rebuilt color image.
The luminance image of the original color image is illustrated Figure 13.d. One could observe the good visual similarity between this luminance image and the *index* image. The *index* image is more contrasted but keeps its semantic intelligibility.
Once color image decomposition has been achieved, the *index* image is split into an 8-bit image (Figure 13.f) and a one bitplane image (a binary image). The chosen bitplane is the 8th for *peppers* image. The binary image is then modified in order to obtain a ternary error prediction image of very low entropy. This error prediction image is illustrated in Figure 13.h (in grey the 0 value, in black the -1 value, and in white the 1 value). The error prediction image and the color palette are then encoded with an arithmetic coder (Said, 2003). The embedded message is then made of the two bitstreams concatenations. Figure 13.i is a map giving the localization of the embedding site (white pixels) with the reversible watermarking approach of (Chaumont & Puech, 2009). Figure 13.g shows the final 8-bit image embedding a color palette (of 512 colors) and a bitplane image (the 8th bitplane of the *index* image).
The quality of the watermarked image (see Figure 13.g) is poor but as previously explains this is a good property. Indeed, this image yields difficult the colorization attack (Chaumont & Puech, 2008). On the contrary, the rebuilt color image (knowing the secret key) gives a very good quality color image (PSNR = 38.95 dB).

a) Original b) Watermarked c) Rebuilt (i.e quantized)

Fig. 14. Example on barbara image.

Another result is shown for *barbara 315×230* image in Figure 14. Figure 14.a is the original image, Figure 14.b is the watermarked image and Figure 14.c is the rebuilt (i.e quantized) image with a PSNR of 38.75 dB. Note that the semantic content is preserved in this watermarked image.

Images	Queiroz & Braun	Campisi et al.	Fuzzy	Re-ordering	512 colors
baboon	23.93 dB	29.8 dB	27.90 dB	33.31 dB	35.86 dB
peppers	28.82 dB	32.36 dB	31.68 dB	36.32 dB	38.95 dB
lena	30.31 dB	36.75 dB	37.87 dB	38.63 dB	40.93 dB
house	30.75 dB	31.76 dB	35.45 dB	39.27 dB	41.67 dB
airplane	28.56 dB	32.58 dB	33.66 dB	39.90 dB	42.96 dB

Table 5. PSNR between the original color image and the rebuilt color image.

In Table 5, few PSNRs are computed between the original color image and the rebuilt one. For all the images, the 512 colors approach is 2 dB greater than the second best approach of (Chaumont & Puech, 2007a).

5. Conclusion

In this chapter, we discussed about various solutions in order to protect the color information. First, we remind two quite far-off techniques usable for protecting the color (Queiroz & Braun, 2006, Campisi et al., 2002). Those techniques are based on wavelet sub-bands substitutions. They provide good solutions for a first approach. Second, we talk about two palette-based approaches: the re-ordering approach (Chaumont & Puech, 2007a) and the fuzzy approach (Chaumont & Puech 2007b). We conclude that the solution using the re-ordering layer running algorithm (Chaumont & Puech, 2007a) gives the best results in term of quality for the rebuilt color image, in term of security facing the colorization attack (Chaumont & Puech, 2008a) and in term of CPU computational complexity. Third, we present a new proposition: the 512 colors approach (Chaumont & Puech, 2008b).
The 512 colors approach consists to hide a 512 color palette in an 8-bit-grey-level image. The method is based on a decomposition of a color image in an *index* image and a color palette with 512 colors. The *index* image is then split in an 8-bit image and a binary image. The binary image and the color palette are then reversibly embedded in the 8-bit image. The resultant watermarked image is still semantically understandable.
Some objective PSNR measures are given and show that the 512 colors approach improves the general rebuilt color image quality compared to other approaches. Moreover, the security (only confidentiality is of interest: color retrieving should be difficult without the key) is reinforced by reducing the grey-level quality. Finally, the computational complexity is low.
semantically understandable, and a rebuilt color image of good quality is possible. Improvements are probably also possible by mixing the different approaches or with prior knowledge from both embedding and extracting sides.

6. References

Ball, G. H. & Hall, D. J. (1996). "ISODATA, A novel Method of Data Analysis and Pattern Classification," *in Proceedings of the International Communication Conference*, June 1966.

Campisi, P.; Kundur, D.; Hatzinakos, D. & Neri, A. (2002). "Compressive Data Hiding: An Unconventional Approach for Improved Color Image Coding," *EURASIP Journal on Applied Signal Processing*, Vol. 2002, No. 2, pp. 152–163, 2002.

Chaumont, M. & Puech, W. (2007a). "A Fast and Efficient Method to Protect Color Images," *in IS&T/SPIE 19th Annual Symposium on Electronic Imaging, Visual Communications and Image Processing, VCIP'2007, SPIE'2007*, vol. 6508, San Jose, California, USA, Jan. 2007.

Chaumont, M. & Puech, W. (2007b). "A Grey-Level Image Embedding its Color Palette," *in IEEE International Conference on Image Processing, ICIP'2007*, Vol. I, pp. 389–392, San Antonio, Texas, USA, Sept. 2007.

Chaumont, M. & Puech, W. (2007c). "Fast Protection of the Color of High Dimension Digital Painting Images," *in the 8th International Workshop on Image Analysis for Multimedia Interactive Services, WIAMIS'2007*, Santorini, Greece, 6-8 June 2007.

Chaumont, M. & Puech, W. (2008a), "Attack By Colorization of a Grey-Level Image Hiding its Color Palette," *in IEEE International Conference on Multimedia & Expo, ICME'2008*, Hannover, Germany, June 2008.

Chaumont, M. & Puech, W. (2008b). "A 8-Bits-Grey-Level Image Embedding its 512 Color Palette," *in the 16th European Signal Processing Conference, EUSIPCO'2008*, Lausanne, Switzerland, 25-29 August, 2008.

Chaumont, M. & Puech, W. (2009). "A High Capacity Reversible Watermarking Scheme, " *in IS&T/SPIE 21th Annual Symposium on Electronic Imaging, Visual Communications and Image Processing, VCIP'2009, SPIE'2009*, Paper 7257-54, San Jose, California, USA, 18–22 Jan. 2009.

Queiroz, De R. L. & Braun, K. (2006). "Color to Gray and Back: Color Embedding Into Textured Gray Images," *IEEE Transaction on Image Processing*, Vol. 15, No. 6, pp. 1464–1470, 2006.

Daubechies, I. & Sweldens, W. (1998). "Factoring wavelet transforms into lifting steps," *Journal of Fourier Analysis and Applications*, Vol. 4, No. 3, pp. 247–269, 1998.

Dunn, J. C. (1974). "A Fuzzy Relative of the ISODATA Process and its Use in Detecting Compact Well-Separated Clusters," *Journal of Cybernetics*, Vol. 3, pp. 32–57, 1974.

Fridrich, J. (1998). "A New Steganographic Method for Palette-Based Images," *in proceedings of the IS&T PICS conference*, Apr. 1998.

Gervautz, M. & Purgathofer, W. (1990). "A Simple Method for Color Quantization: Octree Quantization," *Graphics Gems*, A.S. Glassner, pp. 287–293, 1990.

Heckbert, P. (1982). "Color Image Quantization for Frame Buffer Display," *Computer Graphics*, Vol. 16, No. 3, pp. 297–303, 1982.

Said, A. (2003), Chapter about Arithmetic Coding, In : *Lossless Compression Handbook*, Academic Press, 2003.

Tzeng, C.H.; Yang, Z.F. & Tsai, W.H. (2004). "Adaptative Data Hiding in Palette Images by Color Ordering and Mapping With Security Protection," *IEEE Transaction on Communications*, Vol. 52, No. 5, pp. 791–800, 2004.

Wu, M.-Y.; Ho, Y.-K. & Lee, J.-H. (2003). "An Iterative Method of Palette-Based Image Steganography," *Pattern Recognition Letters*, Vol. 25, pp. 301–309, 2003.

8

JPEG2000-Based Data Hiding and its Application to 3D Visualization

Khizar Hayat[a], William Puech[a] & Gilles Gesquière[b]
a.LIRMM, UMR CNRS 5506, University of Montpellier II
b.LSIS, UMR CNRS 6168, Aix-Marseille University
France

1. Introduction

This first decade of twenty-first century is witnessing revolution in the form of memory and network speeds as well as computing efficiencies. Simultaneously, the platform and client diversity base is also expanding, with powerful workstations on one extreme and handheld portable devices, like smart-phones on the other. The range of networks, even if we narrow it down, may end up at optical fiber to EDGE. Still versatile are the clients whose needs evolve with every passing moment. The technological revolution notwithstanding, dealing the accompanying diversity is always a serious challenge that must certainly require some scalable strategies. When it comes to scalability, one is compelled to think of the multi-resolution characteristic of wavelets as far as multimedia data is concerned. With the wavelets comes the JPEG2000 standard which has added newer dimensions to the concept of scalability. The scalability challenge is more glaring in the case of applications where disparate and large data is involved. An example application is the area of 3D visualization that requires more than one set of the data. Here, issues like data security, data authentication and data unification then emerge. All these form part and parcel of the field of data hiding. The emergence of the wavelet oriented JPEG2000 codec has brought with it the challenge of when, where and how to hide the data for watermarking or steganography while keeping in view the requirements of hiding capacity, robustness and imperceptibility. Even before the advent of the codec, wavelet transformations were commonplace in the field of signal processing. For the last few years, several techniques to embed data inside a host signal in the wavelet transform domain have been proposed. Few of the methods are compatible with the JPEG2000 standard and that is why one comes across methods exclusively proposed for the codec after the latter's inception. In today's world, data hiding is not limited to just watermarking, steganography or authentication but some non-traditional prospects are also there. One such area is the field of 3D visualization wherein data hiding can be employed as a tool for the synchronous and scalable unification of the disparate data in the JPEG2000 coding pipeline.
The rest of this chapter is arranged as follows. Section 2 is dedicated to the background concepts wherein a brief account of the wavelet transformations is being given, followed by the presentation of the salient features of the JPEG2000 codec. After introducing information

hiding concepts, Section 3 focuses on the when and where to embed in the JPEG2000 coding pipeline, which leads us to introduce a context level classification of the JPEG2000-based data hiding methods presented in the literature in Section 4. In Section 5 we present an application of the JPEG2000-based data hiding for a scalable and synchronous 3D visualization in a client/server environment. Section 6 sums up this chapter.

2. Discrete Wavelet Transform and JPEG2000

In standard image compression techniques, one of the essential steps is the domain transformation. The transform results in the decorrelation of the pixels. Pixel energy is thus compacted into a small number of coefficients. The idea is to enable the quantization step to trim the samples selectively, i.e. irrelevant samples must be quantized more heavily than the relevant ones [Taubman and Marcellin, 2002]. One aspect of the success of JPEG [Pennebaker and Mitchell, 1992] is in the efficiency of its transform, i.e. discrete cosine transformation (DCT) applied to each image block of 8 x 8. But the use of block-based transforms rests on the unrealistic assumption of the independence of blocks.
Of the alternatives available to the block-based transforms the one that got the approval of JPEG2000 [ISO/IEC, 2004] proponents is the discrete wavelet transform (DWT). The key being its multi-resolution nature resulting in sub-bands containing some level of detail derived from the whole image or at least a considerably large tile if the image is of very large size. The quality in such a situation is incremental as the lowest sub-band has the most important and relevant information and the higher sub-bands have finer details. Most of the energy is thus compacted into a few large transform coefficients -- an entropy coder easily locates these coefficients and encodes them.
DWT offers better energy compaction than the DCT without any blocking artifact after coding. In addition, the DWT decomposes the image into an L-level dyadic wavelet pyramid. The resultant wavelet coefficient can be easily scaled in resolution as one can discard the wavelet coefficients at levels finer to a given threshold and thus reconstruct an image with less detail.

(a) (b) (c)

Fig. 1. DWT; a) Sub-band structure, b) Lena, c) Lena at level 2 DWT decomposition.

The multi-resolution nature of DWT, therefore, makes it ideal for scalable image coding. After the color transformation, the DWT decomposes each component (luminance Y and chrominance Cr and Cb) into numerous frequency bands called sub-bands. For each level,

DWT is applied twice, once row-wise and once column-wise and hence four sub-bands result:

1. horizontally and vertically low-pass (LL),
2. horizontally low-pass and vertically high-pass (LH),
3. horizontally high-pass and vertically low-pass (HL) ,
4. horizontally and vertically high-pass (HH).

Let us consider the input image signal (or tile-component signal if image is large) as the LL_0 band. A (R−1)-level wavelet decomposition is associated with R resolution levels. Each sub-band of the decomposition is identified by its orientation (i.e. LL, LH, HL, and HH) and its corresponding decomposition level (0, 1, . . .R − 1). At each resolution level (except the lowest) the LL band is further decomposed. Thus the LL_0 band is decomposed to yield the LL_1, LH_1, HL_1 and HH_1 bands. Then, at the next level, as illustrated in Fig. 1.a, the LL_1 band is decomposed. This process is repeated until the LL_{R-1} band is obtained. If no transform is applied (R = 1) then there is only one sub-band: the LL_0 sub-band. A level-2 wavelet decomposition of the image Lena, given in Fig. 1.b is illustrated in Figure. 1.c.

Right from the beginning, JPEG2000 has been supporting two kinds of transforms: the reversible integer-to-integer Daubechies (5/3) and the irreversible real-to-real Daubechies (9/7) [Daubechies and Sweldens, 1998, Sweldens, 1995] with the former being lossless and the latter being lossy. The 2D transformation can then be carried out by separately applying the 1D version horizontally and vertically one after the other. Let the 1D (pixel row or pixel column) input signal be $S_1,...S_n$ then for the reversible 5/3 wavelet transform the low-pass sub-band signal $L_1,...L_{n/2}$ and high-pass sub-band signal $H_1,...H_{n/2}$ are given by:

$$\begin{cases} H_i = S_{2i+1} - \left\lfloor \frac{1}{2}(S_{2i+2} + S_{2i}) \right\rfloor \\ L_i = S_{2i} + \left\lfloor \frac{1}{4}(H_i + H_{i-1}) + \frac{1}{2} \right\rfloor \end{cases} \quad (1)$$

For the lossy version we define a new set of variables $S'_1,...S'_n$ where the odd numbered variables (S'_{2n+1}) will hold the first stage lifting outcomes and the even numbered (S'_{2n}) will hold those of second stage lifting. Let a, b, c and d are the first, second third and fourth stage parameters, respectively, then for bi-orthogonal 9/7 wavelet transform:

$$\begin{cases} S'_{2i-1} = S_{2i-2} + a.(S_{2i} + S_{2i-2}) \\ S'_{2i} = S_{2i} + b.(S'_{2i-1} + S'_{2i-1}) \\ H_i = \beta'.(S'_{2i-1} + c.(S'_{2i} + S'_{2i-2})) \\ L_i = \beta.(S'_{2i} + d.(H_{i-1} + H_i)), \end{cases} \quad (2)$$

where

$$a \approx -1.586134 \qquad b \approx -0.052980$$
$$c \approx 0.882911 \qquad d \approx 0.443506,$$

with β and β', being the scaling parameters, having the values:

$$\beta \approx 0.812893 \qquad \beta' \approx 1/\beta$$

The boundaries in both types of transforms are handled by utilizing symmetric extension[1]. In a simplified way, a typical JPEG2000 encoder[2] consists of the following steps [Taubman and Marcellin, 2002] which are illustrated in Fig. 2:

---

[1] http://research.microsoft.com/~jinl/paper_2002/msri_jpeg.htm

1. Preprocessing such as tiling and shifting the origin of the pixel values to 0 by subtracting 128.
2. Inter-component transform in the form of irreversible or reversible color transform to pass from RGB space to YCrCb space.
3. Intra-component transform that may be lossy or lossless DWT.
4. Quantization which decreases the size of the large coefficients and nullifies the small ones.
5. Tier 1 coding when the quantized coefficients are partitioned into rectangular code blocks and each is subjected independently to three coding passes. This step involves entropy coding too.
6. Tier 2 coding which is the packetization step whereby the code-pass data is converted to packets – these packets are combined to get the final image in the JPEG2000 format.

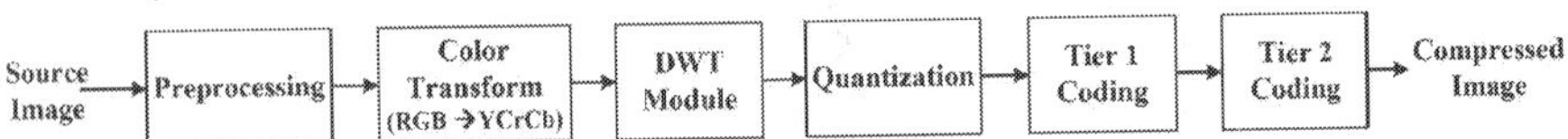

Fig. 2. A generalized scheme of the JPEG2000 encoder.

It must be noted that in a JPEG2000 coding pipeline there are two primary sources of data loss. One is obviously quantization and the other is the stage in tier-1 coding when a decision is made that which coding passes must be excluded from the final JPEG2000 file. For the application proposed in this chapter, the scalability prospects offered by JPEG2000 in the form of multi-resolution are to our advantage, especially in the client/server environment.

3. The When and Where of Information Hiding in JPEG2000

Data hiding deals with embedding information, called *message*, inside some host signal, like image, sound or video, called *cover* or *carrier*. The message may be small and robust as in the case of copyright protection in the form of watermarking or it may be large, critical and statistically invisible as in steganography. Four factors [Bender et al., 1996] characterize the effectiveness of a data hiding method, namely the *hiding capacity*, the *perceptual transparency*, the *robustness* and the *tamper resistance*. Hiding capacity refers to the maximum payload that can be held by the cover. Perceptual transparency ensures the retention of visual quality of the cover after data embedding. Robustness is the ability of the cover to withstand various signal operations, transformations and noise whereas tamper resistance means to remain intact in the face of malicious attacks. The relative importance of these four factors depends on the particular data hiding application. For example, for visually sensitive applications perceptual transparency becomes very important. Domain-wise, embedding can be carried out in both the frequency domain and the transform domain. Pixel or coefficient allocation for data embedding may be regular (e.g. every k^{th} pixel or coefficient) or irregularly distributed (e.g. pseudo-random). Probably the most preferred pixel allocation is by running a pseudo-random number generator (PRNG) using some secret key as a seed. Finally, an

[2] http://www.ece.uvic.ca/~mdadams/jasper

embedding method is blind if data extraction by the recipient does not require the original cover.

Being an active research area for the last two decades, data hiding is now an established field and that is why a lot has been written about it [Cox et al., 2008]. We, therefore, focus on the literature about wavelet-based data hiding which is again very extensive and one is compelled to be brief and limit oneself to JPEG2000, as far as possible. Looking at the structure of JPEG2000 codec, as explained in Section 2, makes one think about when and where to interrupt the coding flow in order to embed the message. Theoretically, you can interrupt the codec anywhere for embedding but, at the periphery, the embedding capacity is lower, accompanied by relatively higher distortion.

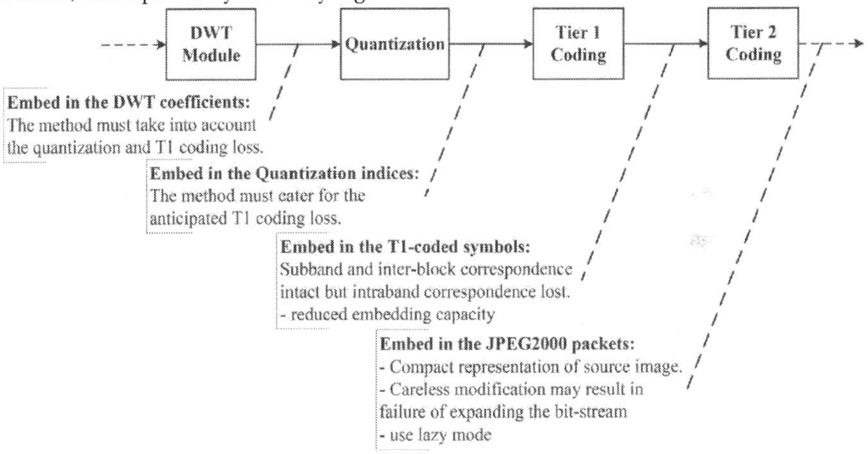

Fig. 3. Interrupting the JPEG2000 coding pipeline for information hiding.

Fig. 3 illustrates the potential interruption stages during the JPEG2000 coding to embed data in the to-be-encoded image[3]. Every type of intervention has its advantages and limitations.

- Embedding immediately after the DWT step would have the advantage of larger word size of the coefficients leading to high capacity. All the components are easily available one can allocate coefficients at will. This strategy may be especially convenient for JPEG2000 in lossless mode. The problem is however that steganalysis is easier since there is a high probability of unusual coefficient values. This is particularly true of coefficients belonging to high frequency sub-bands. Moreover embedding must be at least robust enough to resist the ensuing steps of quantization and T1-coding.
- Just after quantization, one can embed in the clipped coefficients with reduced capacity. The overhead of anticipating the loss, due to quantization, is eliminated with this type of embedding. Strictly speaking, however, the technique is the same as the last one and shares its pros and cons.
- As already stated T1-coding operates on the independence of blocks and comprises bit-plane coding with three passes in each bit-plane, namely significance,

[3] http://www.cs.nthu.edu.tw/~yishin

refinement and cleanup passes. This followed by the arithmetic coding (MQ coder). One way to intervene is to take advantage of the fact that the partitioned code blocks are coded independently using the bit-plane coder thus generating a sequence of symbols with some or all of these may be entropy coded. The T1 coded symbols from a given block vary in energy and the low index symbols are more energetic than the higher index ones. What can be done, for example, is to use the least energetic of these symbols, from the tail of the stream for each code block, for embedding implying non-random allocation. There is, however one problem in that the T1 coded symbols have smaller word size resulting in smaller embedding capacity and higher rate of distortion in quality as a result of embedding. This policy is not, however, advised in the lossless case since wordsizes of the coefficients are longer at the earlier steps thus leading to lesser distortions as result of embedding. In addition the embedding capacity is limited for such an embedding strategy and the rate of degradation is still larger.
An alternative approach could be to go for lazy mode and bypass arithmetic coding for most of the significance and refinement passes, except 4 MSBs, however. There would be no substantial benefit from entropy coding in such a scenario. The refinement pass carries subsequent bits after the MSB of each sample hence modification should not cause problems. The significant bits would act as masking which should make the modification of the subsequent bits less obvious. Hence the lazy mode mostly involves raw coding. Care must be taken in selecting potential raw coded magnitude refinement passes for embedding; otherwise there may be high degradation in quality. This may involve close examination of the bit-planes. The limitations are escalation in the size of the coded image and suspicion in the form of unusual bit stuffing and unusual appearance of error resilience marker.

- Subsequent to lazy mode encoding, one can also embed in the T2-coded bit-stream. This approach may be simple but has problems in the form of low capacity and high degradation wherein careless modification may result in failure of the expanding bit-stream. The easiest way for a novice may be to intervene here and that is why this intervention may be popular but this popularity makes it an easy target of steganalysis.

4. Context-Based Classification of JPEG2000 Data Hiding Methods

The wavelet-based information hiding can be classified in various ways depending on the criteria employed. Many criteria, like decomposition strategy, embedding technique, goal, application, extraction method and many others can be employed for classification. But for our purpose we will use classification where we will be taking into account the *when and where* factor to embed in the JPEG2000 coding pipeline. We call this a *context-based criterion* for classification. Before the advent of JPEG2000, many methods existed in the literature. A very elaborate compilation of these methods can be found in the form of [Meerwald, 2001a]. Not all of these methods are compatible with the JPEG2000 scheme. According to [Meerwald and Uhl, 2001], data hiding methods for JPEG2000 images must process the code blocks independently and that is why methods like inter-sub-band embedding [Kundur, 1999] and those based on hierarchical multi-resolution relationship [Kundur and

Hatzinakos, 1998] have not been recommended. In the same breath they reject the correlation-based method [Wang and Kuo., 1998] as well as non-blind methods. The reason for they give is the limited number of coefficients in a JPEG2000 code-block that are likely to fail in reliably detecting the hidden information in a single independent block.
The fact to classify in the context of JPEG2000 is driven by its coding structure as well as the multi-resolution character of DWT.

4.1 Embedding in the DWT coefficients

We further classify these methods into lowest sub-band methods, high or detail sub-band methods, trans-sub-band methods and methods exploiting the coefficient relationships in sub-band hierarchy.

4.1.1 Lowest sub-band methods

Embedding in lowest sub-band coefficient is suited for cases where the image has to be authenticated at every resolution level. The problem is however the size of the sub-band which is a dyadic fraction of the total, thus leading to reduced capacity. Moreover, since most of the energy is concentrated in the lowest sub-band, the embedding would definitely lead to low perceptual transparency. As an example of this type of embedding can be found in [Xiang and Kim, 2007] which uses the invariance of the histogram shape to rely on time-frequency localization property of DWT to propose a watermarking scheme that is resistant to geometric deformations. A geometrically invariant watermark is embedded into the low-frequency sub-band of DWT in such a way that the watermark is not only invariant to various geometric transforms, but also robust to common image processing operations.

4.1.2 High or detail sub-band methods

In contrast to low sub-bands, higher sub-bands may provide larger capacity. But this is accompanied by escalation in the final image size as the detail sub-band coefficients hover around zero. While explaining their method of embedding biometric data in fingerprint images, Noore *et al.* argue against the modification of the lowest sub-band to avoid degradation of the reconstructed image as most of the energy is concentrated in this band [Noore et al., 2007]. Instead they propose to redundantly embed information in all the higher frequency sub-bands. There are methods for embedding invisible watermarks by adding pseudo-random codes to large coefficients of the high and middle frequency bands of DWT but these methods have the disadvantage of being non-blind [Xia et al., 1997, Kundur and Hatzinakos, 1997]. An additive method transforms the host image into three levels of DWT and carry out embedding with the watermark being spatially localized at high-resolution levels [Suhail et al., 2003].

4.1.3 Inter sub-band methods

To avoid high computational cost for wavelet-based watermarking Woo *et al.* propose a simplified embedding technique that significantly reduces embedding time while preserving the performance of imperceptibility and robustness by exploiting implicit features of discrete wavelet transform (DWT) sub-bands, i.e. the luminosity information in the low pass band, and the edge information in the high pass bands [Woo et al., 2005]. The method of Kong *et al.* embeds watermark in the weighted mean of the wavelets blocks, rather than in the individual coefficient, to make it robust and perceptually transparent [Kong et al., 2004]. One blind method transforms the original image by one-level wavelet transform and sets the three higher sub-bands to zero before inverse transforming it to get the modified image [Liu et al., 2006]. The difference values between the original image and the modified image are used to ascertain the potential embedding locations of which a subset is selected pseudo-randomly for embedding. The concept of Singular Value Decomposition (SVD) has been employed [Yavuz and Telatar, 2007] for their watermarking scheme wherein the $m \times n$ image matrix A is decomposed into a product of three matrices (USV^T); the $m \times m$ matrix U and $n \times n$ matrix V are orthogonal ($U^TU = I$, $V^TV = I$) and the $m \times n$ diagonal matrix S has r (rank of A) nonzero elements called singular values (SVs) of the matrix A. The SVs of the watermark are embedded into SVs of the LL and HL sub-bands of the cover image from level-3 DWT domain while components of U matrix of the watermark are embedded into LH and HH sub-bands. In extraction, first the similarity of extracted U matrix is checked with the original one. If it is found similar, the watermark is constructed by using extracted SVs and original U and V matrices of the watermark. Another DWT-SVD based method employs particle swarm optimizer (PSO) for watermarking [Aslantas et al., 2008]. Agreste *et al.* put forward a strong wavelet-based watermarking algorithm, called WM2.0 [Agreste et al., 2007]. WM2.0 embeds the watermark into high frequency DWT components of a specific sub-image and it is calculated in correlation with the image features and statistical properties. Watermark detection applies a re-synchronization between the original and watermarked image. The correlation between the watermarked DWT coefficients and the watermark signal is calculated according to the Neyman-Pearson statistic criterion just like the blind chaotic method of DWT oriented watermarking [Dawei et al., 2004]. The spread spectrum (SS) method by Maitya *et al.* embeds watermark information in the coefficients of LL and HH sub-bands of different decompositions [Maitya et al., 2007]. In two-band system, to increase embedding rate, the cover image is decomposed in different directions using biorthogonal wavelets (BiDWT). For embedding each watermark symbol bit, pseudo-random noise (PN) matrix of size identical to the size of LL sub-band coefficient matrix is generated and modulated by Hadamard matrix. This modulated code pattern is used to embed data in the LL sub-band while its bit-wise complement gives an orthogonal code pattern which is used for data embedding in the HH sub-band. To decode message bit for binary signaling, two correlation values (one from LL and the other from HH) are calculated. The overall mean of these correlation values serves as the threshold for watermark decoding.

4.1.4 Methods exploiting coefficient relationships in the sub-band coefficient hierarchy

Such methods may suitable for embedding resolution scalable messages. An example is image fusion when a small image is embedded in the larger one. Similarly 3D meshes can be embedded by hiding coarse meshes in low and finer details in high frequency coefficients. One can employ data structures like the embedded zero-tree wavelets (EZW [Shapiro, 1993]) or its improved form, the set partitioning in hierarchical trees (SPIHT [Said and Pearlman, 1996]). These structures enable to effectively remove the spatial redundancy across multi-resolution scales. The additional advantage is the provision of fine scalability. There is a method [Inoue et al., 1998] that exploits zero-tree structure by replacing the insignificant coefficients with the addition/subtraction of small values. Uccheddu *et al.* adopt a wavelet framework in their blind watermarking scheme for 3D models under the assumption that the host meshes are semi-regular, thus paving the way for wavelet decomposition and embedding of the watermark at a suitable resolution level [Uccheddu et al., 2004]. For the sake of robustness the host mesh is normalized by a Principal Component Analysis (PCA) before embedding. Watermark detection is accomplished by computing the correlation between the watermark signal and the *to-be-inspected* mesh. Yu *et al.* propose a robust 3D graphical model watermarking scheme for triangle meshes that embeds watermark information by perturbing the distance between the vertices of the model to the center of the model [Yu et al., 2003]. With robustness and perceptual transparency in focus, the approach distributes information corresponding to a bit of the watermark over the entire model. The strength of the embedded watermark signal is adaptive with respect to the local geometry of the model. A method adopts Guskov's multi-resolution signal processing method for meshes and uses a 3D non-uniform relaxation operator to construct a Burt-Adelson pyramid for the mesh, and then watermark information is embedded into a suitable coarser mesh [Yin et al., 2001]. The algorithm is integrable with the multi-resolution mesh processing toolbox and watermark detection requires registration and resampling to bring the attacked mesh model back into its original location, orientation, scale, topology and resolution level.

Besides above there may be methods involving specialized wavelets. Vatsa *et al.* present a 3-level redundant DWT (RDWT) biometric watermarking algorithm to embed the voice biometric Mel Frequency Cepstral (MFC) coefficients in a color face image of the same individual for increased robustness, security and accuracy [Vatsa et al., 2009]. Green channel is not used and after transforming the red and blue channels, watermarking is carried out followed by the inverse transform. Phase congruency model is used to compute the embedding locations which preserves the facial features from being watermarked and ensures that the face recognition accuracy is not compromised. The proposed watermarking algorithm uses adaptive user-specific watermarking parameters for improved performance. Yen and Tsai put forward an algorithm based on Haar DWT for the gray scale watermark by proposing visual cryptographic approach to generate two random shares of a watermark: one is embedded into the cover-image, another one is kept as a secret key for the watermark extraction later [Yen and Tsai, 2008].

4.2 Quantization-based methods

The authentication scheme described in [Piva et al., 2005] embeds an image digest in a subset of the sub-bands from the DWT domain. The image digest is derived from the DCT of the level 1 DWT LL sub-band of the image. The resultant DCT coefficients are scaled down by quantization and ordered from most to least significant through a zig-zag scan. A most significant subset, after discarding the DC coefficient, is quadruplicated for redundancy and then rescaled and scrambled by using two different keys. This gives the message which is substituted to the sub-bands selected from a set obtained by the further wavelet decomposition of the level 1 HL and LH sub-bands of the original image. Based on the significant difference of wavelet coefficient quantization, a blind algorithm groups every seven non-overlap wavelet coefficients of the host image into a block [Lin et al., 2008]. The two largest coefficients, in a given block, are referred to as significant coefficients and their difference as significant difference. The local maximum wavelet coefficient in a block is quantized by comparing the significant difference value in a block with the average

significant difference value in all blocks. The maximum wavelet coefficients are so quantized that their significant difference between watermark bit 0 and watermark bit 1 exhibits a large energy difference which can be used for watermark extraction. During the extraction, an adaptive threshold value is designed to extract the watermark from the watermarked image under different attacks. To determine the watermark bit, the adaptive threshold value is compared to the block-quantized significant difference. Jin *et al.* employ modulo arithmetic to constrain the noise resulted from the blind embedding into the quantized DWT coefficients directly. Ohyama *et al.* extract a least significant bit (LSB) plane of the quantized wavelet coefficients of the Y color component in a reversible way. They then embed the secret data and a JBIG2 bit-stream of a part of the LSB plane as well as the bit-depth of the quantized coefficients on some code-blocks [Ohyama et al., 2008]. Based on the compression ratio Li and Zhang propose an adaptive watermarking with the strength of watermark being proportional to the compression ratio to enable the embedded watermark survive the following code-stream rate allocation procedure without degrading the image quality [Li and Zhang, 2003].
There are methods that employ quantization index modulation (QIM). The idea is to quantize the host signal with a quantizer indexed by the message, i.e. if S is the embedded signal, M the message, and C the cover or host signal, then $S(C,M) = QM(C)$. The embedded signal should then be composed only of values in the set of quantizer outputs [Sullivan et al., 2004]. In the method of Ishida *et al.*, the QIM-JPEG2000 steganography, QIM is exploited with two different quantizers (one for embedding a '0' and other for a '1') to embed bit at the quantization step of DWT coefficients under the assumption that the probabilities of '0' and '1' are same in the message [Ishida et al., 2008]. A JPEG2000-based image authentication method employs extended scalar quantization and hashing for the protection of all the coefficients of the wavelet decomposition [Schlauweg et al., 2006]. The process involves feature extraction by wavelets to result in digital signature which, after encryption and error correction coding, is embedded as a removable watermark using the well-known QIM technique called dither modulation. The embedded watermark information is removable during the decompression process which is important for the improved image quality in the context of visualization. Traditionally, correlation analysis has been an integral part of the SS methods reported in various works - the principal difference being in the manner they ascertain the threshold for decoding.

4.3 Embedding in the compressed bit-stream

These methods usually involve partial or complete roll back of some coding steps, lazy mode coding. The blind scheme proposed in [Su et al., 2001] integrates data hiding with the embedded block coding with optimized truncation (EBCOT) and embed data during the formation of compressed bit stream. The method of Su and Kuo employs lazy coding to speed up the encoding process by skipping the 4 lowest bit planes during arithmetical encoding [Su and Kuo, 2003] . The authors maintain their software by the name stegoJasper, as reported in [Kharrazi et al., 2006] in which the bits are modified in function to their contribution in the reconstructed image at the decoder side, i.e. bits with least level of contributions are modified first. With this backward embedding approach they try to minimize the embedding artifact on the final embedded image. A similar method rolls back the JPEG2000 encoding process until the dequantization stage [Noda et al., 2003]. The method relies on the fact that the data has already passed the rate controller during the first encoding and an aspired bitrate has already been established. Hence the second rate control should not be able to remove further information, so the additional information can be embedded after the quantization stage and the manipulated image data are again processed by the remaining parts of the JPEG2000 pipeline. To ensure the fidelity of the embedded data to further processing, the target bitrate may be set at a lower value for initial processing and set to the desired value for the second and final run. The technique is applicable during encoding as well as to already encoded JPEG2000 bit streams. One particular technique embeds watermark in the JPEG2000 pipeline after the stages of quantization and region of interest (ROI) scaling but before the entropy coding [Meerwald, 2001b]. A window sliding approach is adopted for embedding and for the sake of reliability the finest resolution subbands are avoided while the lowest frequencies carry higher payload.

5. An Application for Scalable Synchronized Surface-Based 3D Visualization

Volumes have been written on the traditional use of watermarking and steganography, in the form of copyrighting, authentication, security and many other applications. The JPEG2000 data hiding is not only valid for these as any generic technique but offers the additional advantage of multi-resolution to embed the message or the watermark in a scalable fashion. This aspect may have a particular value in the case, e.g. image fusion, where the message is not some plain text. We deviate, therefore, from the traditional course, to present a very interesting use of the JPEG2000 based data hiding in the field of surface-based 3D visualization.

5.1 Introduction

A typical 3D surface visualization is based on at least two sets of data: a 2D intensity image, called texture, with a corresponding 3D shape rendered in the form of a range image, a shaded 3D model and a mesh of points. A range image, also sometimes called a depth image, is an image in which the pixel value reflects the distance from the sensor to the imaged surface [Bowyer et al., 2006]. The underlying terminology may vary from field to field, e.g. in terrain visualization height/depth data is represented in the form of discrete altitudes which, upon triangulation, produce what is called a digital elevation model (DEM): the texture is a corresponding aerial photograph which is overlaid onto the DEM for visualization [Abdul-Rahman and Pilouk, 2008]. Similarly in 3D facial visualization the 2D color face image represents the texture but the corresponding depth map is usually in the form of what is called a 2.5D image. The latter is usually obtained by the projection of the 3D polygonal mesh model onto the image plane after its normalization [Conde and Serrano, 2005].

With the evolution of existing technologies, even if the quality of 3D visualization becomes very high, the client/server environments are very diverse in terms of network, computation and memory resources. Therefore, to cater each of the perspective clients, it is advisable to encode the data in a scalable way, unified into one standard format file. The JPEG2000 format offers the scalability thanks to the multi-resolution nature of its discrete wavelet transform (DWT). For the integration of all the data into one file one can rely on the technique of data hiding due to the smaller size of the depth map file as it can be embedded in the bulky texture image. But this embedding must be carried out in such a way that the JPEG2000 file format is conserved. In addition, the embedding must not interfere with the

multi-resolution hierarchy of the JPEG2000. As a consequence, for each of the possible resolutions, the corresponding texture and its depth map must be recoverable at the decoder.
In this section, the synchronized unification of the range data with the corresponding texture is realized by the application of perceptually transparent DWT domain data hiding strategies. In order to conserve the high quality of visualization we are relying on the LSB-based embedding. At the beginning we interrupt immediately after the DWT stage for embedding but then discuss the prospects of some other type of interventions too. The proposed methods are blind in the sense that only a secret key, if any and the size of the range image are needed to extract the data from the texture image.

5.2 The proposed strategy

A precursor of this method can be found in [Hayat et al., 2008b] wherein the method was developed for 3D terrain visualization. In that scenario we had the luxury of choosing the potential carrier coefficients from a large population of texture coefficient since due to considerable disparity between the texture and its depth map in the context of size. For the work in perspective we have chosen the worst case scenario, i.e. same size of texture and the depth map. This should have an additional advantage to have a clearer idea of the embedding capacity. As a case study we are taking a 3D face visualization example.

5.2.1 Background

Transmitting digital 3D face data in real-time has been a research issue for quite a long time. When it comes to the real-time, two main areas, viz. conferencing and surveillance, suddenly come to mind. In the earlier videoconference applications, the aim was to change the viewpoint of the speaker. This allowed, in particular, recreating a simulation replica of a real meeting room by visualizing the "virtual heads" around a table [Weik et al., 1998]. Despite the fact that many technological barriers have been eliminated, thanks to the availability of cheap cameras, powerful graphic cards and high bitrate networks, there is still no commercial product that offers a true conferencing environment. Some companies, such as Tixeo in France[4], propose a 3D environment where interlocutors can interact by moving an avatar or by presenting documents in a perspective manner. Nevertheless, the characters remain artificial and do not represent the interlocutors' real faces. In fact, it seems that changing the viewpoint of the interlocutor is considered more as a gimmick than a useful functionality. This may be true of a videoconference between two people but in the case of a conference that would involve several interlocutors spread over several sites that have many documents, it becomes indispensable to replicate the conferencing environment. Another application consists in tracking the 3D movement of the face in order to animate a clone, i.e. a model of the user's face. In fact, the transmission of only a small number of parameters of movement or expression can materialize the video through low speed networks. However, recent technologies have increased the bandwidth of conventional telephone lines to several Mbps. This has led to a slowing down of research activities on the subject in recent years. Nevertheless, the bitrate limitation still exists in the case of many devices like PDA or mobile phones. It becomes even critical, in particular in remote video-

[4] www.tixeo.com

surveillance applications which are gaining increasing economic importance. Some companies offer to send surveillance images on the mobile phones/PDAs of authorized persons but these are only 2D images whereby the identification of persons is very difficult, especially in poor light conditions.
The objective over here is to reduce the data considerably for optimal real-time 3D facial visualization in a client/server environment. As already stated, 3D face data essentially consists of a 2D color image called texture and its corresponding depth map in the form of what is called 2.5D image. For 3D visualization one would thus have to manipulate at least two files. It would be better to have a single file rather than two. We propose to unify the two files into a single standard JPEG2000 format file. The use of DWT-based JPEG2000 will give us two specific advantages, aside from the compression it offers. One, the multi-resolution nature of wavelets would offer the required scalability to make for the client diversity. Two, we will not be introducing any new file format but conform to a widely known standard. To ensure highest quality for a resource rich client we would use the JPEG2000 codec in the lossless mode. For the unification of the 2D texture and 2.5D model, a scalable data hiding strategy is proposed wherein the 2.5D data is embedded in the corresponding 2D texture in the wavelet transform domain. This would allow transmitting all the data in a hierarchical and synchronized manner. The idea is to break down the image and its 3D model at different levels of resolution. Each level of resolution of the image will contain the associated 3D model without reducing the image quality and without any considerable increase the file size.

5.2.2 The embedding step

For an $N \times N$ pixel facial texture and its corresponding $M \times M$ point depth map (2.5D) we propose our data hiding strategy presented in Fig. 4. The face texture is subjected to the level-L JPEG2000 encoding in the lossless mode. The encoding process is interrupted after the DWT step to get the three transformed YCrCb face texture components. The corresponding grayscale ($k-1$ bit) depth map is also subjected to level-L lossless DWT in parallel. To ensure the accuracy we expand the word-size for each of the transformed depth map coefficient by one additional bit and represent it in k bits. The DWT domain depth map coefficients are then embedded in the DWT domain YCrCb face texture components while strictly following the spatial correspondence, i.e. low frequency 2.5D coefficients in low while higher in higher frequency YCrCb coefficients. This step strictly depends on the ratio, $M{:}N$, where $M \leq N$. In the worst case, where $M = N$, the k bit transformed 2.5D coefficient is equally distributed among the three components and each of the transformed YCrCb texture coefficient carries $\lfloor k \rfloor$ to $\lfloor k \rfloor + 1$ bits. If $M < N$ then, rather than a face texture coefficient, a whole face texture block corresponds to one depth map coefficient and one has the choice of selecting the potential carrier coefficients. This is especially true when $M < N/3$ as one has the facility to run a PRNG to select the potential carrier coefficients.

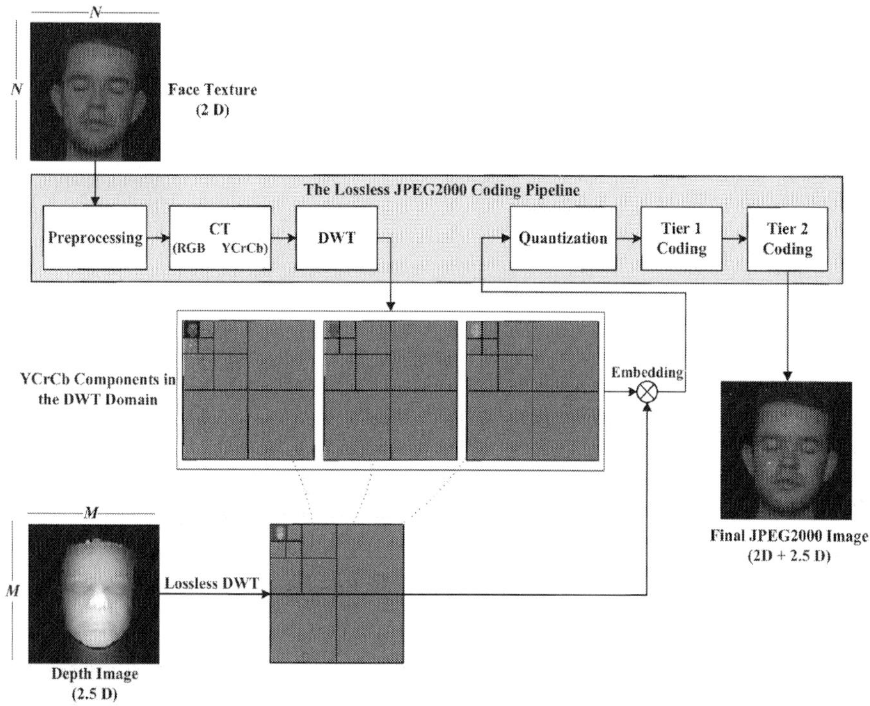

Fig. 4. Description of the method.

To keep the method blind, the embedding process involves the substitution of the least significant bit (LSBs) of the carrier coefficient with the bit(s) from the 2.5D coefficient. After embedding, the YCrCb components are re-inserted into the JPEG2000 coding pipeline. The result is a monolithic JPEG2000 format face texture image that has the depth map hidden in it. A raw description of the embedding strategy is outlined in Algorithm 1. The use of nested loop may be misleading for some readers but it must be borne in mind that the loops are finite and does not imply by any means a cubic complexity. We have written this algorithm for the sake of comprehension.

Algorithm 1 The embedding strategy.

begin
read the level-L DWT-domain carrier texture C from the JPEG2000 coding pipeline, such that $C \subseteq \{Y, Cr, Cb\}$
read the corresponding depth map file
apply lossless DWT to the depth map at level L to get M and optimize if needed
initialize a PRNG with a seed K
for each subband of C and its counterpart in M **do**
  partition the C subband into square blocks in relation to the M subband
  for each correspondence of C subband block $B_{u,v}$ and its M subband k-bit coefficient $d_{u,v}$ **do**
    for $p = 0$ to k **do**
      generate the index which is the next pseudo-random number to get i, j
      get the C subband coefficient $t_{i,j}$
      substitute the LSB of $t_{i,j}$ with the pth bit of $d_{u,v}$
    end for
  end for
end for
label the block-wise marked C as C'
end

5.2.3 Optimization in embedding

In the embedding step, a given k-bit transformed depth map coefficient is to be substituted into the *[k/3]* LSBs each of the corresponding Y, Cr and Cb transformed coefficients. To reduce the payload we have optimized our method to some extent. One of the important characteristics of DWT is the high probability of 0 coefficients in higher frequency subbands. Hence one can always use a flag bit to differentiate this case from the rest. In addition, the use of kth additional bit for transform domain coefficients is a bit too much. Thus, for example, for an 8 bit spatial domain 2.5D coefficient the initial range of [−128, 127] may not be enough in the DWT domain and needs to be enhanced but not to the extent to warrant a range of [−256, 255]. A midway range of [−192, 192] ought to be sufficient. For such a 8-bit scenario one may then have four possibilities for the value of a coefficient viz. zero, normal ([−128, 127]), extreme negative ([−192, −128]) and extreme positive ([128, 192]). Keeping all these possibilities in view, we decided to pre-process the transformed depth coefficient set, before embedding. In our strategy, we keep the first bit exclusively as a flag bit. The next two bits are data cum flag bits and the last six bits are strictly data bits. For a coefficient in the range [−128, 127], the first bit is set to 0, with the rest of eight bits carrying the value of the coefficient, otherwise it is set to 1. For a zero coefficient, the first two bits are set to 1 and thus only 11 is inserted. The absolute difference of an extreme negative coefficient and −128 is carried by the last six bits with the first three bits carrying 101. For extreme positives the first three bits have 100 and the rest of six bits have the absolute difference of the coefficient with +127. In essence we are to embed either two or nine bits according to the following policy:

- **if** *coeff* $\in [-128, 127]$ then concatenate *coeff* to 0 and embed as 9bits;
- **else if** *coeff* = 0 then embed binary 11;
- **else if** *coeff* $\in [-192,-128]$ then concatenate $|-128 - coeff|$ to 101 & embed as 9 bits;
- **else** concatenate (*coeff* − 128) to 100 and embed as 9 bits;

The above coded image can be utilized like any other JPEG2000 image and sent across any communication channel. The blind decoding is the reverse of the above process.

5.2.4 Decoding and reconstruction

Just before the inverse DWT stage of the JPEG2000 decoder, the DWT domain depth map can be blindly extracted by reversing the embedding process mentioned above. In the reconstruction phase, by the application of *0-padding*, one can have $L+1$ different approximation images of facial texture/depth map pair. And this is where one can achieve the scalability goal. Our method is based on the fact that it is not necessary that all the data is available for reconstruction. This is one of the main advantages of the method since the depth map and facial texture can both be reconstructed with even a small subset of the transmitted carrier coefficients. The resolution scalability of wavelets and the synchronized character of our method enable a 3*D* visualization even with fewer than original resolution layers as a result of partial or delayed data transfer. The method thus enables to effect visualization from a fraction of data in the form of the lowest sub-band, of a particular resolution level since it is always possible to stuff 0's for the higher bands. The idea is to have a 3D visualization utilizing lower frequency sub-bands at level L', with $L' \leq L$. For the rest of $3L'$ parts one can always pad a 0 for each of their coefficient as shown in Algorithm 2. The inverse DWT of the 0-stuffed transform components will yield what is known as image of approximation of level L0. A level-L' approximate image is the one that is constructed with $(1/4^{L'})\times 100$ percent of the total coefficients that corresponds to the available lower $3(L-L')+1$ sub-bands. For example, level-0 approximate image is constructed from all the coefficients and level-2 approximate image is constructed from 6.12% of the count of the initial coefficients. Before being subjected to inverse DWT, data related to depth map must be extracted from the transformed face texture whose size depends on both L and L'. Thus if $L' = L$ one will always have the entire set of the embedded DEM coefficients since all of them will be extractable. We would have a level 0 approximate final DEM after inverse DWT, of the highest possible quality. On the other hand if $L' < L$, one would have to pad 0's for all coefficients of higher $3L'$sub-bands of transformed DEM before inverse DWT that would result in a level L'-approximate DEM of an inferior quality.

Algorithm 2 The reconstruction process via 0-padding.

begin
read the coded texture data corresponding to level-L'' subbands
decode to extract the range data which may correspond to L'' or a larger level $L'' + \Delta$, where $\Delta \geq 0$ depends on the extent of adaptation
for both the texture and the extracted range data **do**
  initialize c_l to L'' if dealing with texture or to $L'' + \Delta$, otherwise
  stuff a '0' for every coefficient of the subbands with level$\neq c_l$
  apply inverse DWT to the result
  add the result with the $(c_l - 1)$ approximation to get the (c_l) approximation
end for
end

5.3 Example Simulation

We have applied our method to a number of examples from FRAV3D[5] database. One such example is given in that consists of a 120×120 point 2.5D depth map (Fig. 5.a) corresponding to a 120 × 120 pixel colored 2D face image given n Fig. 5.b. Each point of the 2.5D depth map is coded with 8 bits. A 3D visualization based on the two images is depicted by a view given in Fig. 5.c. Lossless DWT is applied in isolation to the depth map at level-3 to get the image given in Fig. 6.a. To ensure the accuracy we represent each of the transformed depth map coefficients in 9 bits. The corresponding 2D face image is subjected to level-3 lossless JPEG2000 encoding and the process is interrupted just after the DWT step. What we get are the level-3 transformed luminance and chrominance components given in Fig. 6.b-d. The transformed depth map is embedded in the three components according to the scheme outlined above. The resultant components are reintroduced to the JPEG2000 pipeline at quantization step. The final result is a single JPEG2000 format 2D image.

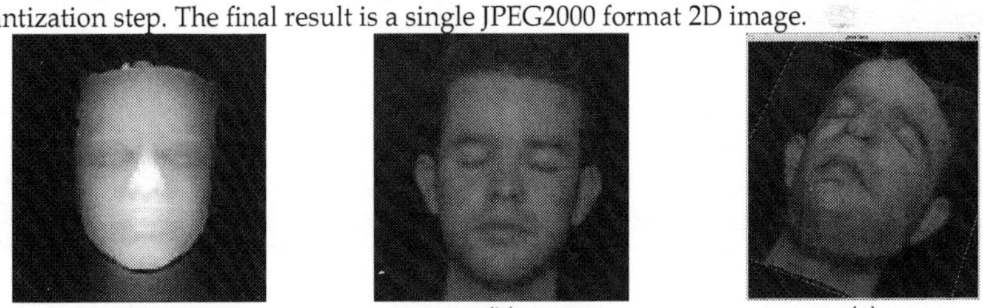

(a) (b) (c)

Fig. 5. Original data: a) a 120 × 120 depth map (2.5D), b) the corresponding 120 × 120 2D face image, c) a 3D face view obtained from (a) and (b)

5 http://www.frav.es/databases/FRAV3d

(a) 2.5D (b) Y (c) Cr (d) Cb

Fig. 6. Level-3 DWT domain images: a) depth map, b-d) components of the transformed 2D face image from the lossless JPEG2000 coding pipeline.

As already stated, level-L' approximate image is the one that is constructed with $(1/4^{L'})\times 100$ percent of the total coefficients that corresponds to the available lowest frequency $3(L-L') + 1$ sub-bands. The level-3 encoded image with our method can give us four different quality 2D/2.5D pairs upon decoding and reconstruction. In terms of increasing quality, these are level-3, 2, 1 and 0 images reconstructed from 1.62%, 6.25%, 25% and 100% of the transmitted coefficients, respectively. The number of lowest sub-bands involved being 1, 4, 7 and 10 out of the total of 10 sub-bands, respectively. For visual comparison, the approximation 2D images are given in Fig. 7 while the approximation depth maps are shown in Fig. 8.

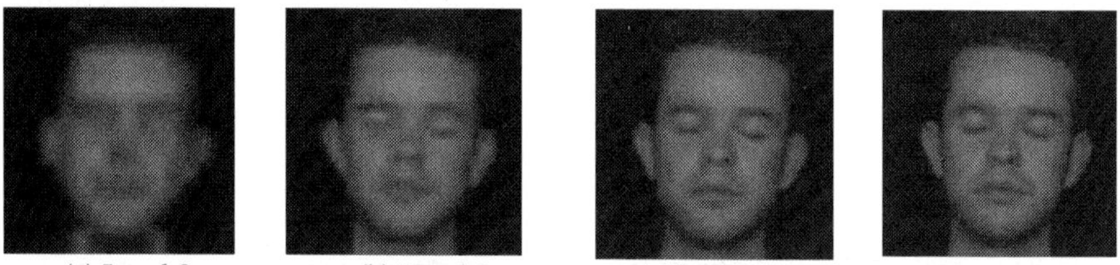

(a) Level-3 (b) Level-2 (c) Level-3 (d) Level-3

Fig. 7. Approximation 2D images obtained after the decoding and reconstruction.

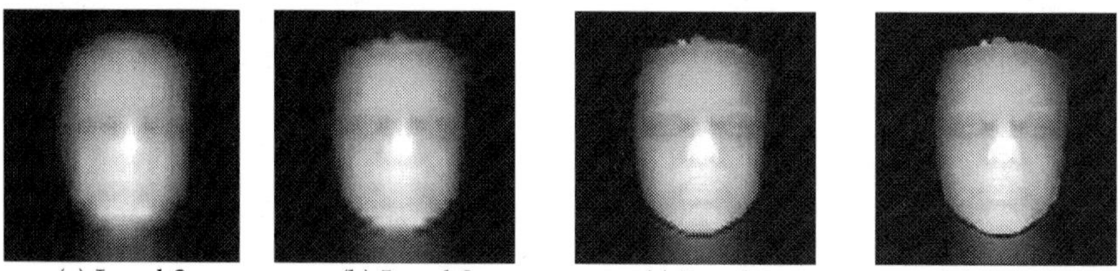

(a) Level-3 (b) Level-2 (c) Level-3 (d) Level-3

Fig. 8. Approximation 2.5D images obtained after the decoding and reconstruction.

For the purpose of quantitative comparison the mean results over all the FRAV3D *2D/2.5D* pairs subjected to our method are tabulated in the form of Table 1. Results obtained for 2D face image after the extraction and reconstruction as a function of the transmitted data. and Table 2.

Approximation image	lev. 3	lev. 2	lev. 1	lev. 0
Bitrate (*bpp*)	0.41	1.10	3.55	8.38
MSE	120.25	43.35	21.17	20.16
PSNR (*dB*)	27.33	31.76	34.87	35.09

Table 1. Results obtained for 2D face image after the extraction and reconstruction as a function of the transmitted data.

Approximation image	lev. 3	lev. 2	lev. 1	lev. 0
Bits per coefficient (theoretical)	0.14	0.56	2.25	9
Bits per coefficient (optimized)	0.14	0.44	1.49	4.98
MSE	11.33	7.76	4.73	0
PSNR (*dB*)	27.05	30.33	34.63	∞

Table 2 Results obtained for the depth map after the extraction and reconstruction as a function of the transmitted data.

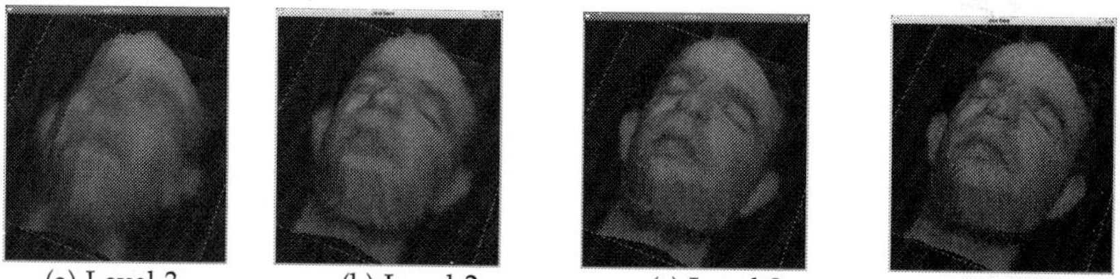

(a) Level-3 (b) Level-2 (c) Level-3 (d) Level-3

Fig. 9. 3D views from the visualization with different 2D/2.5D Approximation pairs

For the 2D face images it can be observed that the level-3 approximate image is the lowest quality having a mean PSNR of 27.33 *dB* which is not bad in the face of the fact that it is constructed from just 0.25% of the transmitted coefficients. The level-0 approximate face image has a mean PSNR of 35.09 *dB* despite the fact that we are treating the worst case, i.e. both the 2D and 2.5D have the same dimensions. Even doubling the 2D dimensions, i.e. one depth map point corresponds to four 2D pixels, gave us a PSNRs in the order of 45 *dB*. For 2.5D approximations we are comparing the theoretical or worst case compression to that obtained by the application of our method in Table 5.4. It can be seen that for very high frequency the probability of zero is high and that is why for level-0 approximation we observed a mean bitrate of 4.98 against the expected value of 9. Since level-3 approximation has only the lowest frequency sub-band, the bitrate stays at 0.14 for both. We have used root mean square error (RMSE) as an error measure in length units for 2.5*D*. The 3D visualization obtained from the approximation *2D/2.5D* pairs is depicted in the form of a 3D view at a particular angle in Fig. 9.

5.4 Innovations

We have applied this work to many examples of terrain visualization without the optimization step [Hayat et al., 2008b]. Taking another terrain case study we changed the codec to the lossless mode and interrupted after the quantization stage [Hayat et al., 2008a].

In T1 coding, which is the first of the two coding stages of JPEG2000, the quantizer indices for each sub-band are partitioned into rectangular code blocks with its nominal dimensions being dyadic and their product not exceeding 4096. The partitioned code blocks are coded independently using the bit-plane coder thus generating a sequence of symbols with some or all of these may be entropy coded. Due to this independent encoding of code blocks, the correspondence between the lossless DWTed DEM and lossy DWTed Y plane of texture is maintainable. The T1 coded symbols from a given block vary in energy and the low index symbols are more energetic than the higher index ones. What we do is to use the least energetic of these symbols, from the tail of the stream for each code block, for LSB embedding implying non-random allocation. There is, however one problem in that the T1 coded symbols have smaller word-size resulting in smaller embedding capacity and higher rate of distortion in quality as a result of embedding. This policy is not, however, advised in the lossless case since word-sizes of the coefficients are longer at the earlier steps thus leading to lesser distortions as result of embedding. Hence one can embed immediately after the DWT step at the earliest.

Another possible innovation is to adapt the synchronization in the method by employing lower level of DWT for the decomposition of the depth map due to the latter's critical nature. That would imply that, rather than utilizing all the texture sub-bands for embedding, utilize a subset on the low frequency side. For the details of this strategy, with an LSB based embedding and for a terrain example, consult [Hayat et al., 2008c].

In all of the above, LSB based embedding technique has been employed which makes these technique perceptually transparent but at the cost of robustness. A spread spectrum technique may improve the robustness. An adaptive strategy with SS embedding has been presented in [Hayat et al., 2009]. The additional advantage of this strategy is its highest possible imperceptibility due to its removable nature.

6. Summary

We started this chapter with a brief description of the DWT with a focus on the Daubechies' algorithms supported by the JPEG2000 codec. This was followed by a stepwise introduction to the structure of the JPEG2000 encoding. The structure served as the foundation to analyse various stages where one can embed the data to be hidden. This analysis led us to classify, on the basis of context, the large number of JPEG2000-based embedding methods presented in the literature in the past few years. In the end, a novel application of the JPEG2000-based information hiding, for synchronized and scalable 3D visualization, was presented.

In a nutshell, this chapter not only presented a non-traditional application of wavelet based data hiding but also a detailed, though compact, survey of the state-of-the-art techniques in this context. Our approach to classify the methods on the base of context must be helpful to readers to understand recent JPEG2000 data hiding approaches. Coming back to the non-traditional application, the results of our simulation have been interesting in the sense that even with a depth map of the same dimensions as the 2D face image one got good quality visualization. Usually the sizes are not the same and one depth map coefficient corresponds to a square block of 2D face texture pixels. Even for a 2 × 2 block the PSNR for level-0 jumps from 35.09 dB to a maximum of 49.05 dB. The trend in our results shows that an effective visualization is possible even with a 0.1% of the transmitted coefficients, i.e. level-5. This must bode well for videoconferencing and video-surveillance applications when frames would replace the still image. Hence for a client with meager computing, memory or network resources a tiny fraction of the transmitted data should do the trick. The scalability aspect can then hierarchically take care of resourceful clients.

7. Acknowledgement:

This work is in part supported by the Higher Education Commission (HEC), Pakistan as well as by VOODDO (2008-2011), a project of ANR and the region of Languedoc Roussillon, France."

8. References

Abdul-Rahman and Pilouk, 2008] A. Abdul-Rahman and M. Pilouk. *Spatial Data Modelling for 3D GIS*. Springer, 2008.

Agreste *et al.*, 2007] S. Agreste, G. Andaloro, D. Prestipino, and L. Puccio. An Image Adaptive, Wavelet-Based Watermarking of Digital Images. *Journal of Computational and Applied Mathematics*, 210(1-2):13-21, 2007.

Aslantas *et al.*, 2008] V. Aslantas, A .L. Dogan, and S. Ozturk. DWT-SVD Based Image Watermarking Using Particle Swarm Optimizer. In *Proc. ICME'08, IEEE International Conference on Multimedia & Expo*, pages 241-244, June 2008.

Bender *et al.*, 1996] W. Bender, D. Gruhl, N. Morimoto, and A. Lu. Techniques for Data Hiding. *IBM Systems Journal*, 35(3-4):313-336, February 1996.

Bowyer *et al.*, 2006] K. W. Bowyer, K. Chang, and P. Flynn. A Survey of Approaches and Challenges in 3D and Multi-modal 3D + 2D Face Recognition. *Computer Vision & Image Understanding*, 101(1):1-15, 2006.

Conde and Serrano, 2005] C. Conde and A. Serrano. 3D Facial Normalization with Spin Images and Influence of Range Data Calculation over Face Verification. In *Proc. 2005 IEEE Computer Society Conference on Computer Vision and Pattern Recognition*, volume 16, pages 115-120, June 2005.

Cox *et al.*, 2008] I. J. Cox, M. L. Miller, and J. A. Bloom. *Digital Watermarking*. Morgan Kaufmann Publishers, 2008.

Daubechies and Sweldens, 1998] I. Daubechies and W. Sweldens. Factoring Wavelet Transforms into Lifting Steps. *Fourier Anal. Appl.*, 4(3), 1998.

Dawei *et al.*, 2004] Z. Dawei, C. Guanrong, and L. Wenbo. A Chaos-Based Robust Wavelet-Domain Watermarking Algorithm. *Chaos, Solitons & Fractals*, 22(1):47-54, 2004.

Hayat *et al.*, 2008a] K. Hayat, W. Puech, and G. Gesquière. A Lossy JPEG2000-Based Data Hiding Method for Scalable 3D Terrain Visualization. In *Proc. EUSIPCO'08: the 16th European Signal Processing Conference*, Lausanne, Switzerland, August 2008.

Hayat *et al.*, 2008b] K. Hayat, W. Puech, and G. Gesquière. Scalable 3D Visualization Through Reversible JPEG2000-Based Blind Data Hiding. *IEEE Trans. Multimedia*, 10(7):1261-1276, November 2008.

Hayat *et al.*, 2008c] K. Hayat, W. Puech, and G. Gesquière. Scalable Data Hiding for Online Textured 3D Terrain Visualization. In *Proc. ICME'08, IEEE International Conference on Multimedia & Expo*, pages 217-220, June 2008.

Hayat *et al.*, 2009] K. Hayat, W. Puech, and G. Gesquière. An Adaptive Spread Spectrum (SS) Synchronous Data Hiding Strategy for Scalable 3D Terrain Visualization. In *Proc.*

SPIE, Electronic Imaging, Visualization and Data Analysis, volume 7243, San Jose, CA, USA, January 2009.

Inoue *et al.*, 1998] H. Inoue, A. Miyazaki, A. Yamamoto, and T. Katsura. A digital watermark based on the wavelet transform and its robustness on image compression. In *Proc. ICIP 98. the 1998 International Conference on Image Processing*, volume 2, pages 391-395 vol.2, October 1998.

Ishida *et al.*, 2008] T. Ishida, K. Yamawaki, H. Noda, and M. Niimi. Performance Improvement of JPEG2000 Steganography Using QIM. In *Proc. IIH-MSP '08: the 2008 International Conference on Intelligent Information Hiding and Multimedia Signal Processing*, pages 155–158, Washington, DC, USA, 2008.

ISO/IEC, 2004] ISO/IEC. *ISO/IEC 15444-1: Information Technology, JPEG2000 Image Coding System, Part 1: Core Coding System.* ISO Central Secretariat: CH-1211 Geneva, Switzerland, 2004.

[Kharrazi *et al.*, 2006] M. Kharrazi, H. T. Sencar, and N. Memon. Performance Study of Common image Steganography and Steganalysis Techniques. *Journal of Electronic Imaging*, 15(4):041104, 2006.

Kong *et al.*, 2004] X. Kong, Y. Liu, H. Liu, and D. Yang. Object Watermarks for Digital Images and Video. *Image and Vision Computing*, 22:583–595, 2004.

Kundur and Hatzinakos, 1997] D. Kundur and D. Hatzinakos. A Robust Digital Image Watermarking Scheme Using the Wavelet-Based Fusion. In *Proc. IEEE International Conference on Image Processing (IEEE ICIP 97)*, volume 1, pages 544–547, Santa Barbara, CA, USA, October 1997.

[Kundur and Hatzinakos, 1998] D. Kundur and D. Hatzinakos. Digital Watermarking Using Multiresolution Wavelet Decomposition. In *Proc. IEEE International Conference on Acoustic, Speech and Signal Processing (IEEE ICASSP 98)*, volume 5, pages 2969–2972, Seattle, WA, USA., May 1998.

Kundur, 1999] D. Kundur. Improved Digital Watermarking Through Diversity and Attack Characterization. In *Proc. ACM Workshop on Multimedia Security'99*, pages 53–58, Orlando, FL, USA, October 1999.

[Li and Zhang, 2003] K. Li and X. P. Zhang. Reliable Adaptive Watermarking Scheme Integrated with JPEG2000. In *Proc. of 3rd International Symposium on Image and Signal Processing and Analysis (ISPA 2003)*, Rome, Italy, September 2003.

Lin *et al.*, 2008] W.-H. Lin, S.-J. Horng, T.-W. Kao, P. Fan, C.-L. Lee, and Y. Pan. An Efficient Watermarking Method Based on Significant Difference of Wavelet Coefficient Quantization. *IEEE Trans. Multimedia*, 10(5):746–757, 2008.

Liu *et al.*, 2006] J. L. Liu, D. C. Lou, M. C. Chang, and H. K. Tso. A Robust Watermarking Scheme Using Self-Reference Image. *Computer Standards & Interfaces*, 28:356–367, 2006.

Maitya *et al.*, 2007] S. P. Maitya, M. K. Kundub, and T. S. Das. Robust SS Watermarking with Improved Capacity. *Pattern Recognition Letters*, 28(3):350–356, 2007.

Meerwald and Uhl, 2001] P. Meerwald and A. Uhl. A Survey of Wavelet-Domain Watermarking Algorithms. In *Proc. SPIE, Electronic Imaging, Security and Watermarking of Multimedia Contents III*, volume 4314, pages 505–516, San Jose, CA, USA, January 2001.

[Meerwald, 2001a] P. Meerwald. Digital Image Watermarking in the Wavelet Transform Domain. Master's thesis, Department of Scientific Computing, University of Salzburg, Austria, January 2001.

[Meerwald, 2001b] P. Meerwald. Quantization Watermarking in the JPEG2000 Coding Pipeline. In *Proc. Communications and Multimedia Security Issues of The New Century, IFIP TC6/TC11 Fifth Joint Working Conference on Communications and Multimedia Security, CMS '01*, pages 69–79, May 2001.

[Noda *et al.*, 2003]H. Noda, J. Spaulding, M. N. Shirazi, M. Niimi, and E. Kawaguchi. Bit-plane decomposition steganography combined with jpeg2000 compression. In *IH '02: Revised Papers from the 5th International Workshop on Information Hiding*, pages 295–309, London, UK, 2003.

[Noore *et al.*, 2007] A. Noore, R. Singh, M. Vatsa, and M. M. Houck. Enhancing Security of Fingerprints through Contextual Biometric Watermarking. *Forensic Science International*, 169(2–3):188–194, 2007.

[Ohyama *et al.*, 2008] S. Ohyama, M. Niimi, K. Yamawaki, and H. Noda. Reversible data hiding of full color jpeg2000 compressed bit-stream preserving bit-depth information. In *Proc. ICPR'08: the 19th International Conference on Pattern Recognition*, pages 1–4, December 2008.

[Pennebaker and Mitchell, 1992] W. B. Pennebaker and J. L. Mitchell. *JPEG: Still Image Data Compression Standard*. Springer, 1992.

[Piva *et al.*, 2005] A. Piva, F. Bartolini, and R. Caldelli. Self Recovery Authentication of Images in the DWT Domain. *Int. J. Image Graphics*, 5(1):149–166, 2005.

[Said and Pearlman, 1996] A. Said and W.A. Pearlman. A new, fast, and efficient image codec based on set partitioning in hierarchical trees. *Circuits and Systems for Video Technology, IEEE Transactions on*, 6(3):243–250, June 1996.

[Schlauweg *et al.*, 2006] M. Schlauweg, D. Pröfrock, and E. Müller. JPEG2000-Based Secure Image Authentication. In *Proc. MM&Sec '06: the 8th Workshop on Multimedia and Security*, pages 62–67, New York, NY, USA, 2006.

[Shapiro, 1993] J.M. Shapiro. Embedded Image Coding using Zerotrees of Wavelet Coefficients. *IEEE Trans. Signal Processing*, 41(12):3445–3462, 1993.

[Su and Kuo, 2003] P. C. Su and C .-C .J. Kuo. Steganography in jpeg2000 compressed images. *IEEE Trans. Consumer Electronics*, 49(4):824–832, November 2003.

[Su *et al.*, 2001] P. C. Su, H. J. Wang, and C. C. J. Kuo. An Integrated Approach to Image Watermarking and JPEG-2000 Compression. *Journal of VLSI Signal Processing Systems, Special Issue on Multimedia Signal Processing*, 27(1-2):35–53, June 2001.

[Suhail *et al.*, 2003] M. A. Suhail, M. S. Obaidat, S. S. Ipson, and B. Sadoun. A Comparative Study of Digital Watermarking in JPEG and JPEG 2000 Environments. *Inf. Sci. Inf. Comput. Sci.*, 151:93–105, 2003.

[Sullivan *et al.*, 2004] K. Sullivan, Z. Bi, U. Madhow, S. Chandrasekaran, and B.S. Manjunath. Steganalysis of quantization index modulation data hiding. In *IEEE International Conference on Image Processing*, pages 1165–1168, October 2004.

[Sweldens, 1995] W. Sweldens. The Lifting Scheme: a New Philosophy in Biorthogonal Wavelet Constructions. In *Proc. SPIE, Electronic Imaging, Wavelet Applications in Signal and Image Processing*, volume 2569, pages 68–79, San Jose, CA, USA, September 1995.

[Taubman and Marcellin, 2002] D. S. Taubman and M. W. Marcellin. *JPEG2000: Image Compression Fundamentals; Standards and Practice.* Springer, 2002.

[Uccheddu *et al.*, 2004] F. Uccheddu, M. Corsini, and M. Barni. Wavelet-Based Blind Watermarking of 3D Models. In *Proc. MM&Sec '04: Workshop on Multimedia and Security*, pages 143–154, New York, NY, USA, 2004.

[Vatsa *et al.*, 2009]M. Vatsa, R. Singh, and A. Noore. Feature Based RDWT Watermarking for Multimodal Biometric System. *Image and Vision Computing*, 27(3):293–304, 2009.

[Wang and Kuo., 1998] H. J. Wang and C. C. Kuo. An Integrated Approach to Embedded Image Coding and Watermarking. In *Proc. IEEE International Conference on Acoustic, Speech and Signal Processing (IEEE ICASSP 98)*, pages 3271–3275, Seattle, WA, USA, May 1998.

[Weik *et al.*, 1998] S. Weik, J. Wingbermuhle, and W. Niem. Automatic Creation of Flexible Antropomorphic Models for 3D Videoconferencing. In *Proc. CGI'98: Computer Graphics International*, pages 520–527, 1998.

[Woo *et al.*, 2005] C. S. Woo, J. Du, and B. Pham. Performance Factors Analysis of a Wavelet-Based Watermarking Method. In *Proc. ACSW Frontiers '05: the Australasian Workshop on Grid Computing and e-Research*, pages 89–97, Darlinghurst, Australia, 2005.

[Xia *et al.*, 1997] X. G. Xia, C. G. Boncelet, and G. R. Arce. A Multiresolution Watermark for Digital Images. In *Proc. IEEE International Conference on Image Processing (IEEE ICIP 97)*, pages 548–551, Santa Barbara, CA, USA, October 1997.

[Xiang and Kim, 2007] S. Xiang and H. J. Kim. Geometrically Invariant Image Watermarking in the DWT Domain. In *WISA*, volume 4867 of *Lecture Notes in Computer Science*, pages 76–90, 2007.

[Yavuz and Telatar, 2007] E. Yavuz and Z. Telatar. Improved SVD-DWT Based Digital Image Watermarking Against Watermark Ambiguity. In *Proc. SAC '07: the ACM Symposium on Applied Computing*, pages 1051–1055, New York, NY, USA, 2007.

[Yen and Tsai, 2008] E. Yen and K. S. Tsai. HDWT-Based Grayscale Watermark for Copyright Protection. *Expert Systems with Applications*, 35(1–2):301–306, 2008.

[Yin *et al.*, 2001] K. Yin, Z. Pan, J. Shi, and D. Zhang. Robust Mesh Watermarking Based on Multiresolution Processing. *Computers & Graphics*, 25(3):409–420, 2001.

[Yu *et al.*, 2003] Z. Yu, H. H. S. Ip, and L. F. Kwok. A Robust Watermarking Scheme for 3D Triangular Mesh Models. *Pattern Recognition*, 36(11):2603–2614, 2003.

9

Content-Based Image Retrieval as Validation for Defect Detection in Old Photos

Edoardo Ardizzone, Haris Dindo and Giuseppe Mazzola
Dipartimento di Ingegneria Informatica - Università degli Studi di Palermo
Palermo,Italy

1. Introduction

The art of photography is more than 150 years old, but it has quickly absorbed technological innovations of the following years. Methods, cameras, techniques changed and improved, and so supports changed, from physical (e.g. paper) to digital ones. Even if the discussion about advantages and drawbacks of digital and film cameras is still open, the need for digital preservation of old documents became more and more pressing. Their economic worth and high cultural value induced the use of digital techniques to protect and preserve them. Old photographic prints may present several types of defects, due to many different factors. In most cases, damages are originated by an inaccurate handling and/or storage of the original image, by chemical factors, or by decomposition of the support caused by age. While the origin of a damage is an essential information for the analysis of defects on the physical support, different defects may look similar once the document had been digitized. Furthermore, once a photo is digitally acquired, defects become part of the image, and their features change.

We proposed our own defect taxonomy, which is based on digital features (shape, color, texture, etc.) of a defect rather than considering its origin. With respect to defects in our taxonomy, several works rely on the analysis of damages in old documents by the study of their digital copies. Cracks, scratches, global fading are defects which have been studied, and digital detection algorithms have been proposed to analyze them. Defect detection means the ability to locate the position of corrupted pixels. Digital detection techniques are designed to analyze images which are affected by a specific defect. They typically give as output a mask into which pixels are labelled as good or bad. However they may sometimes extract misleading information, if they are applied to images which are not affected by the damage they have been designed for.

Content-based Image Retrieval techniques can be used to validate the output of a detection algorithm. The goal is to understand if an image is affected by a specific damage, giving an interpretation to the information extracted by the corresponding detection method. Manual annotation cannot be a solution. It is expensive and time consuming, because of the typical huge amount of data to be analyzed. Automatic or semiautomatic methods are needed to help users in this task.

2. Digital Defect Taxonomy

A first interesting attempt to classify defects in old photos was proposed in [De Polo et al., 2003]. Defects were classified on the basis of their physical-chemical origin. We noted that the proposed taxonomy was incomplete. Many defects we observed in our image database could not be easily classified in one of the proposed classes. In [Ardizzone et al., 2006] we extended this taxonomy, starting from one used by expert manual restorers of old photos. New defects were added and a more detailed description was given. However, we observed that it was not suitable for "digital" restoration purposes, since it was as well based on the defect physical-chemical origin. For example, an observer won't be able to discriminate an abrasion from a tear, if their digital versions have similar aspect (see fig. 1).

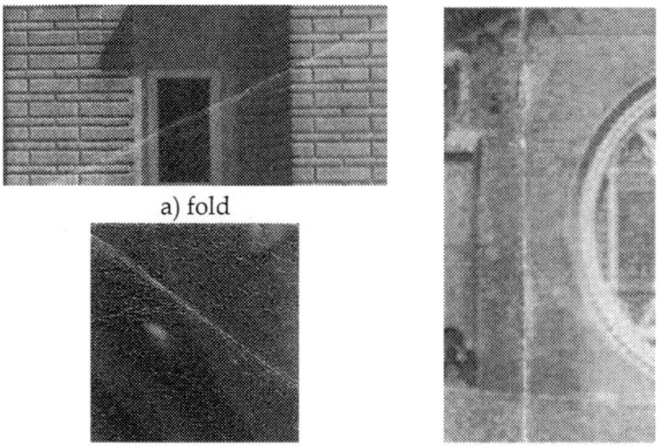

a) fold

b) abrasion

c) tear

Fig. 1. A comparison between three defects, which have similar digital aspects, but that are caused by different physical factors.

Therefore we proposed a new digital taxonomy[Ardizzone et al., 2009a], which focuses on the digital features of a defect (shape, color, texture, etc.).

DIGITAL DEFECTS	TYPE
Spots	Local
Semi-Transparent Spots	Local
Scratches	Local
Foxing	Local/Diffuse
Folds	Local
Cracks	Local
Deformations	Local
Blotches	Diffuse
Fading	Global
Yellowing	Global
Lacking Color	Local
Lacking Portions	Local
Handwritings	Local

Table 1. The digital defect taxonomy

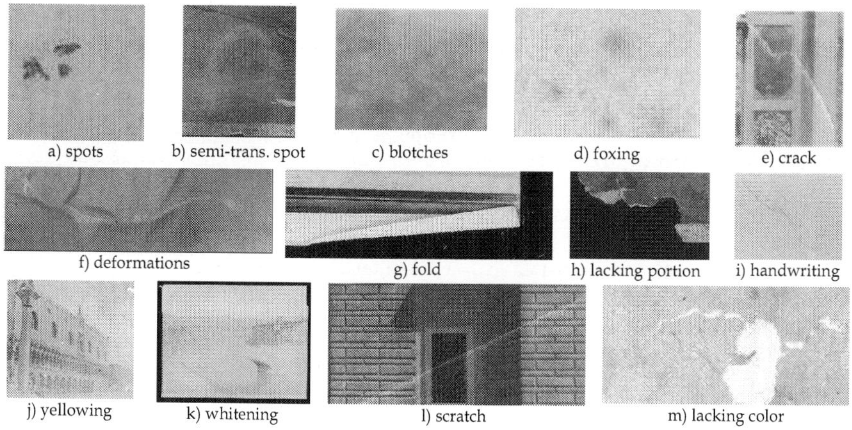

Fig. 2. Some examples of defects classified according to the digital taxonomy (courtesy of Fratelli Alinari Museum Collections (RFMA) in Florence).

Within the proposed digital taxonomy (table 1), a damage can be **global**, if it affects every pixel in the image, **diffuse**, if distributed overall the image, without affecting all the pixels, and **local**, if it is located in a limited portion of the image. According to their digital aspect, defects may be classified as:

- Spots: local defects. Fig. 2.a. Underlying information is lost and must be fully substituted. No specific colors. More or less rounded shaped.
- Semi-Transparent Spots: local defects. Fig. 2.b. Similar to spots, residual information can be recovered with restoration techniques.
- Scratches: local defects. Fig. 2.l. Thin lines, with a preferential direction. Usually lighter than the rest of the image. Can have a darker kernel. Possible limited changing in width and slope.
- Foxing: local/diffuse defects. Fig. 2.d. Covering or semi-transparent spots. It is composed by a dark red- brown kernel, surrounded by a lighter red area, which is usually semi-transparent.
- Folds: local defects. Fig. 2.g. Located near the edges of the photo. It is composed by a lighter central area (the verso side) and darker edges, depending on the acquisition operation.
- Cracks: local defects. Fig. 2.e. Undefined orientation. In some cases they can have branches. Cracks are usually composed by a darker kernel surrounded by a lighter area.
- Deformations (lifting): local defects. Fig. 2.f. Due to the digital acquisition of a non planar support. They look like the negative of a branched crack.
- Blotches: diffuse defects. Fig. 2.c. Semi-transparent spots which can be seen all over the image. Usually lighter than the rest of the image.
- Whitening: global defect. Fig. 2.k. Overall fading.
- Yellowing: global defect. Fig. 2.j. Distortion in the chromaticity (to yellow) of the whole image.

- Lacking color: local defect. Fig. 2.m. Undefined shape (some similar to scratches, some other to spots). Usually white, because of the exposition of the color of the support. Information is totally lost.
- Lacking Portions: local defect. Fig. 2.h. Usually black, but it depends on the acquisition condition. In most cases lacking portions have jaggy edges.
- Handwritings: writings and scrawls. Fig. 2.i. Complex curve lines, darker than the rest of the image.

Note that according our taxonomy a digital defect is no more univocally determined by the cause that generated it. That is, a "digital" spot can be caused by the digital acquisition of defects such as garbage, abrasions or chemical factors. On the other hand, if a printed photo was partially scraped by something, once digitized its digital counterpart may look like a spot, a lacking color, or a scratch.

3. Damage Detection in Old Photos

Several works rely on the analysis and restoration of damages in digitized/digital pictures. The problem of detecting, analyzing and removing cracks from digitized paintings has been widely examined in literature [Giakoumis et al., 2006][Abas & Martinez, 2002][Barni et al., 2000]. [Stanco et al., 2005] proposed a method to restore vintage photos affected by water blotches and foxing spots. This method will be further described in section 6.2. [Ramponi & Bruni, 2006] presented a fast technique for enhancing faded images. This method decompose the luminance channel of a faded image in a smooth and in a detail components, using a non linear edge-preserving filter. The two components are then separately processed, to exploit the best available dynamic range, without emphasizing unwanted noise. [Chang et al, 2005] developed a mechanism to automatically detect superimposed defect in a digital photo, including damages by color ink spray and scratch drawing. Their method tried to find inconsistencies in the color properties of a damaged image, working in the HSI space, and proposed an adaptive filter to remove these inconsistencies. In [Ardizzone et al., 2007] we proposed a method to detect and remove quasi-horizontal scratches in digitized aerial photos. We used a pass-band oriented filter, to enhance the horizontal components of the image, the Hough transform, to detect scratch orientation and position, and we proposed a new restoration inpainting technique to remove damaged detected pixels. The detection step was improved in [Ardizzone et al., 2009b], in order to find scratches with any orientation and color, and then a new correlation-based method was proposed to trace the scratch contour. Nevertheless scratches are typical defects of old movie films. In fact many papers dealt with the problem of detecting and removing vertical scratches in vintage movies. [Bruni & Vitulano, 2004] presented a generalized model for scratch detection on digital film materials, on the hypothesis that a scratch is not purely additive to a given image. The proposed detector performs on a hierarchical representation of the degraded image, and successive selections are performed considering both scratch width and height as well as the Weber's law [Joyeux et al., 1999] dealt scratch degradation problem by means of a temporal representation, using all frames of the degraded sequence. In the detection phase the Radon's transform and the combination of the Kalman's filter and the Hough transform are used. Line artifacts are removed using a an interpolation technique, dealing with both low and high frequencies.

4. Validation of Detection Algorithms by CBIR

Content-Based Image Retrieval (CBIR) applications deals with the problem of searching for digital images in a large database. Content-based means that image retrieval is made using information that can be extracted from the image itself, rather than using tags, keywords or annotations by hand. For a complete overview of the existing works in the field of content-based multimedia retrieval see [Lew et al., 2006]. Our idea is to use a CBIR application, in order to compare a damaged image with a dataset of images, affected by several types of degradation. The goal is to understand if an image is affected by a specific damage, using the corresponding detection algorithm.

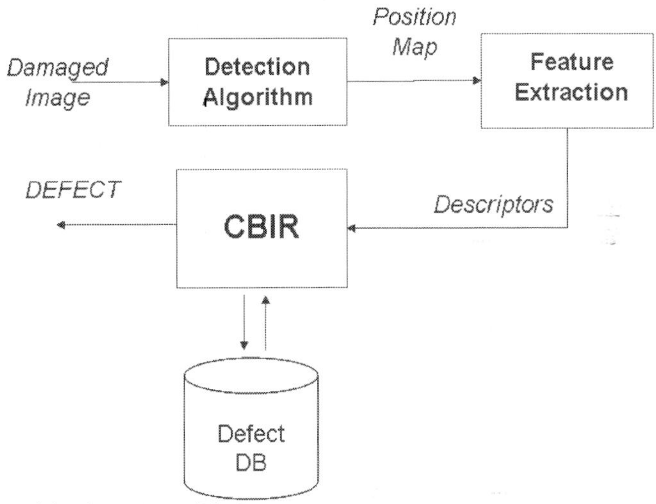

Fig. 3. Scheme of the detection validation process.

In fig.3 the scheme of the detection validation process is shown. A damaged image is processed by a detection algorithm which is designed for a specific defect. Note that the input image could be not affected by that damage. Once we know the position of the damaged pixels, according to the selected detection algorithm, the second step is to extract relevant features from the detected area. That is, we must compute suitable image descriptors, that are the representation of one or more features of an image. The choice of the appropriate descriptors is the critical point of every content-based analysis application. Standard and ad-hoc descriptors can be used in this step. We have observed that pixel statistics (mean, standard deviation, maximum and minimum values, etc) computed on one or more properties (intensity, RGB values, etc.) over the damaged area, can be used as ad hoc descriptors with good results.

Descriptors are then compared, by CBIR, to those extracted from a dataset of images, whose defects have been previously (manually or automatically) annotated. The idea is that, by using suitable metrics to compare the descriptors' values, similar images should have similar values:

- if the most similar image is affected by the selected damage, the detection output is validated, and the area in the image, which had been labelled by the detection algorithm, can be reasonably considered affected by that damage.
- if the most similar image is affected by a defect which is not that corresponding to the detection algorithm, the output is not validated, and the damaged image cannot be classified.

5. A case study: detection of foxing spots

A case study for the proposed methodology is presented in [Ardizzone et al., 2008]: Foxing. Foxing is a typical chemical damage which can be seen in old books, documents, postage stamps, and so forth. The term "foxing" was used for the first time in the 18th century, to indicate those red-brown (the color of the fox fur) spots in the surface of the paper of old documents. Actually causes are not clean. Two are the most reliable theories about the chemical origin of these spots[Beckwith et al., 1940]. One is that spots are caused by the growth of some fungoid microorganisms on the surface of the paper. Other one asserts that foxing would be caused by the oxidation of iron, cop or other substances of which the photographic support is made. Probably multiple factors are involved. Foxing spots are composed by a dark red-brown kernel, surrounded by an area into which colors are smoothed. Information in the center of the spot is totally damaged and must be considered lost. Surrounding area can have some residual information, that could be enhanced with manual or digital techniques. However a discussion about the restoration techniques for documents affected by foxing is out of the scope of this paper.

5.1 Foxing detection

In this section we briefly present the foxing detection algorithm proposed by [Stanco et al., 2005] which will be used in the feature extraction process.
Due to the particular nature of the foxing defect, this algorithm is based on color of the spots, and its distribution. The algorithm works in two steps:
- image is decomposed in the YC_bC_r color space and only the C_r chrominance is processed. It has been shown that C_r histogram of foxed images presents a tail on the right, formed by a set of bins having almost the same small height, and with the peak on the left. The bins on the right tail rep-resent the points damaged by foxing.
- finding all the pixels where the original information is only partially affected by foxing. They are characterized by a lighter coloring than the center of the foxing and their position is near the reddish-brown spot.
Fig. 4 shows an image affected by foxing, the corresponding tail in the Cr histogram, and the detected mask using the described algorithm. We noted that even if it works very well in locating damaged pixels in images affected by foxing, it may sometimes detect small foxed areas in non-foxed images. Figg. 5.a and 5.b show other two examples: in the first case the algorithm correctly detects foxed pixels in a slightly damaged image; in the second case it is applied to a non-foxed image and it wrongly detects a foxed area. Comparing the two examples we noted that the two output masks are very similar, so that the described algorithm cannot be used as a classification method. Extracted information needs to be further analyzed.

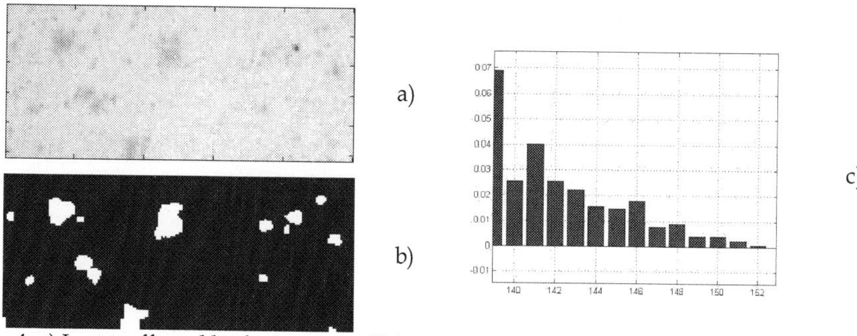

Fig. 4. a) Image affected by foxing spots. b) histogram of the Cr chrominance (zoom on the tail). c) detected damaged area.

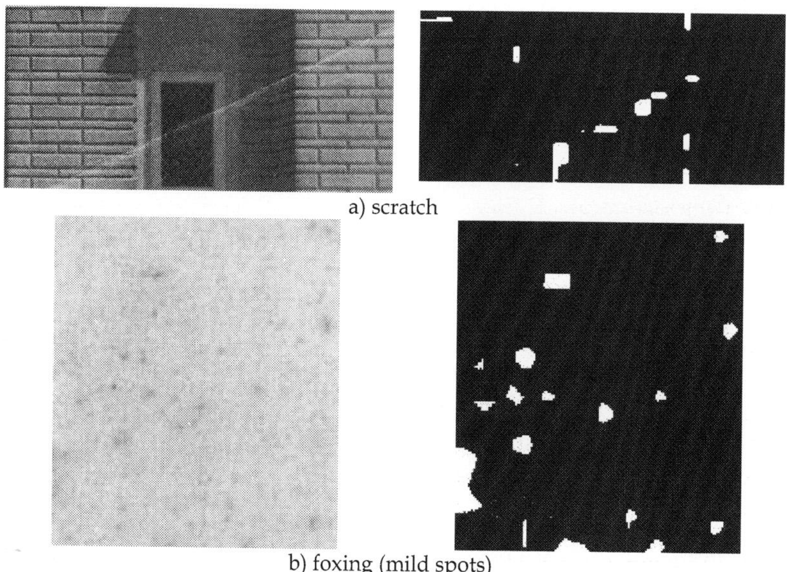

Fig.5. a) Image affected by scratch and the corresponding output mask. b) image slightly damaged by foxing and the corresponding output mask.

5.2 Feature extraction

For an automated application for the analysis and the inspection of an image, some local and global information must be extracted. That is, we must extract some meta-data from the image, which will be used by some specific operators to analyze the image content. "Descriptor" is the representation of one or more features of an image. The definition of new descriptors for a specific damage of an image can be functional for the development of damage oriented applications (restoration, classification, etc.).

For foxing description, the choice of the best set of descriptors must depend on two aspects:

- the specific features of the foxing spots (color and its distribution);
- the definition of relevant distance metrics, designed for an image retrieval application.

In this paper we focus on three different set of features, to describe a digital foxing spot: the C_r chrominance histogram, the statistical values of the damaged pixels, and the spot size. Each of these elements is used to analyze a specific aspect of the spot.

The first proposed descriptor is the tail of the C_r chrominance histogram, detected as described in section 5.1 (see fig. 4.b). Bins and heights of the histogram, from the right to the left of the tail, are stored,

$$d_1 = \{(B_i, h(B_i)) | B_i \geq B_l\} \qquad i = 1...256 \tag{1}$$

where B_i are the bins of the histogram, $h(B_i)$, the corresponding heights and B_l the left value of the tail. This descriptor gives us information about the length, the minimum value, and the distribution of the heights of the tail. That is information about the shade of the color of the spot.

The second proposed descriptor is a set of statistical values of the C_r chrominance component: mean, variance, minimum and maximum value. Values are computed only into the damaged area, detected with the algorithm described in section 5.1 (see fig. 4.c).

The third descriptor is based on the average size of the spots. This is computed by considering the ratio of the number of damaged pixels in the detected area to the number of the distinguishable spots, located with a 8-connection labelling process(see fig. 4.c)..

The next section presents an image retrieval application, based on the information extracted by these descriptors.

5.3 Content-based foxing retrieval

The goal of the proposed CBIR is to discriminate if an image is affected by foxing. That is, given a new image, we compare its content to that of all the images in the dataset. If the most similar image, according to some distance metrics, is affected by foxing, the new image can be reasonably sup-posed to be "foxed". In this section we presents three different metrics, based on the proposed descriptors.

The first one is based on the histogram tail descriptor. It is obtained as the difference, point to point, of the heights of the corresponding bins of the tails. Since tails can have different supports, starting and ending point, that with the lower maximum is shifted rightward to align the two maxima, and that with the shorter support is zero-padded to have the same support of the other one. Given d_{11} and d_{12}, the descriptors of the two different tails, supposed d_{11} to have a maximum value n-units higher than that of d_{12}, the distance of the two tails is:

$$D_1(d_1^1, d_1^2) = \sum_{B_i = B_{\min}}^{B_{\max}} |h(B_{i-n}^1) - h(B_i^2)| \tag{2}$$

where B_{min} is the lowest of the two minima and B_{max} is the highest of the two maximum bins. This distance is used to compare information about the different "trends" of the color in the two images (only damaged pixels), regardless of their absolute values.

The second proposed metric is based on the statistical values of the damaged pixels. It is obtained as the sum of the absolute differences of the corresponding components of the statistical descriptors in the two images:

$$D_2\left(d_2^1, d_2^2\right) = \left|d_2^{1mean} - d_2^{2mean}\right| + \left|\sqrt{d_2^{1\,var}} - \sqrt{d_2^{2\,var}}\right| + +\left|d_2^{1\min} - d_2^{2\min}\right| + \left|d_2^{1\max} - d_2^{2\max}\right|. \quad (3)$$

Note that standard deviation is considered rather than variance. This distance is used to compare the absolute values of the color of the spot. That means the "general" color aspect of the defect.

The third proposed distance is based on the average size of the spots in the image. It is the absolute difference of the size descriptors of the two images:

$$D_3\left(d_3^1, d_3^2\right) = \left|d_3^1 - d_3^2\right|. \quad (4)$$

Many combinations of the three distances has been tested, e.g. a combined distance with different weights. Experiments showed that the best solution is a multi-step classifier. Given a new image, it is compared with all the images in the dataset using only one of the proposed distances. The N most similar images in the dataset, according to this distance, are selected. Matching is then made using one of the other two distances within this image subset, and the M (M<N) best images are extracted. A final comparison is made, within this new subset, using the last metric, and the best image is shown. If this image is affected by foxing, the new image is classified as foxed.

results\distance		HIST	STAT	SIZE	3-STEP	CCV	DC	CS
Correct classification(%)		84,3	87,6	71,4	90,3	88,5	89,4	81,6
False positives(%)		8,3	6,4	13,4	5,1	7,4	5,1	9,2
False negatives(%)		7,4	6	15,2	4,6	4,1	5,5	9,2
Avg exec time (s)	feat extract	1,3				3,9	3,7	9,1
	matching	0,1	<0,1	<0,1	0,1			

Table 2. Experimental results

5.4 Experimental results

Tests have been made on an image dataset composed by about 220 images from the Alinari Photographic Archives in Florence. Images in the dataset are affected by several typical defects of old photos (scratches, spots, cracks, foxing, etc.) and has been manually classified by a restoration expert of the Archives. For our experiments, the whole dataset has been used for testing. Each image has been used as a test image and it has been matched to the other images in the dataset. About the 30% of the image is affected by foxing. In table 2 we show our experimental results, for each distance discussed in section 5.3 and for the 3- step classifier. Tests suggested the best configuration as follows: step 1, histogram distance and N=8; step 2, statistical distance and M=4; step 3, size distance.

Results are compared to those obtained with distances based on three standard color descriptors: Color Coherence Vector (CCV), Dominant Color (DC) and Color Structure (CS).

[Sikora, 2000] [Pass et al., 1996]. For each distance we show the percentage of correct classifications, of false positives (images without foxing, classified as foxed) and of false negatives (images with foxing, classified as not foxed). Average execution time is also shown to compare the efficiency of the classification methods. For our distances, time is shown for the all-at-once feature extraction and for each matching process. We observed that:
- the statistical descriptor, among our proposed, gives best results, which are comparable to those obtained with standard CCV and DC, but it takes much less execution time;
- the size descriptor gives, as we expect, no good results, because it is not color-based; its role is to refine the retrieve in the last step of the classifier;
- CCV and DC give very similar results;
- CS descriptor gives worst results and is less efficient than the two other standard ones.

The multi-step classifier improves results obtained with the statistical descriptor, with no significant increment in the execution time. Results are slightly better than those obtained by standard descriptors, with much less execution time. Further combinations with the standard descriptors may improve the results.
A multi-step classifier has been implemented using the standard descriptors, with no significant improvements in the results, with respect of the single-descriptor classifiers.

6. Conclusions

Digital analysis is the first step in the preservation process of degraded documents.
Our purpose is not to propose new detection methods, i.e. to find which pixels are affected by a specific damage. We aimed to understand if an image is affected by a damage, giving an interpretation to the information extracted by an existing detection methods. In fact detection algorithms may sometimes extract misleading information, if they are applied to images which are not affected by the damage they are designed for. For this purpose new ad-hoc descriptors are needed for each specific defect.
Our idea is to analyze information extracted by specific detection algorithms, and to use Content-Based-Image-Retrieval applications, to compare it to a set of images which are affected by several defects (our dataset has been previously annotated by hand). Comparing ad-hoc features, we find the most similar image according to these selected features. If it is affected by the defect related to the detection algorithm, the input image can be reasonably considered affected by this defect. That is, information extracted from the input image is similar to that of other images which is affected by that damage. Otherwise input image cannot be considered affected by that damage, because its information is different from what we expected to have.
We presented a study case: images affected by foxing. A set of low-level descriptors has been presented, to extract information from damaged images, starting from a state-of-the-art detection algorithm. A CBIR-based classifier gives an interpretation to this information, comparing it with that extracted from a dataset of images, affected by several types of degradation. The goal is to discriminate whether the image is affected by foxing or not.
Experiments showed that the proposed application gives same results compared to those obtained using standard descriptors, while our improves the execution time.

Actually we plan to apply our methodology for other typical defects of which old documents are affected (scratches, cracks, spots, fading) in order to find appropriate descriptors for each type of defect.

7. Acknowledgement

The authors wish to thank the Fratelli Alinari Museum Collections (RFMA) in Florence (http://www.alinari.com) for having permitted the use of their photos and their material in this research.

8. References

Abas F. S., and Martinez K. (2002) "Craquelure Analysis for Content-Based Retrieval", In *14th International Conf. on Digital Signal Processing*, July 1-3, 2002, Santorini, Greece

Ardizzone E., De Polo A., Dindo H., Mazzola G., Nanni C. (2009a)"A Dual Taxonomy for Defects in Digitized Historical Photos", *Proceedings of International Conference on Document Analysis and Recognition*, Barcelona, Spain, July 26-29 2009 (in press)

Ardizzone E., Dindo H., Mazzola G., Scriminaci M., Vitali M. (2009b) "Multi-Directional Detection of Scratches in Digitized Images" in *Proceedings of European Signal Processing Conference*, Glasgow, Scotland, August 24-28 2009 (in press)

Ardizzone E., Dindo H., Mazzola G. (2008) "A Set of Low-Level Descriptors for Images Affected by Foxing" in *Proceedings of European Signal Processing Conference* , Lausanne, Switzerland, August 25-29, 2008

Ardizzone E., Dindo H., Gambino O., Mazzola G. (2007) "Scratches Removal in Digitised Aerial Photos Concerning Sicilian Territory", *14th Int. Conf. on Systems, Signals and Image Processing IWSSIP*, Maribor, Slovenia .27-30 June 2007.

Ardizzone E., Dindo H., Maniscalco U., Mazzola G. (2006) "Damages of Digitized Historical Images as Objects for Content Based Applications," in *Proc. European Conference on Signal Processing*, 4-8 Sept. 2006, Florence, Italy. EURASIP

Barni, M., Bartolini, F., and Cappellini, V. 2000. "Image Processing for Virtual Restoration of Artworks". *IEEE MultiMedia* 7, 2 (Apr. 2000), 34-37.

Beckwith T. D., Swanson W. H., and Iiams T. M. (1940) "Deterioration of Paper: the Cause and Effect of Foxing", *University of California Publications in Biological Science* 1(13):299-356, 1940.

Bruni V., Vitulano D. (2004) "A Generalized Model for Scratch Detection", *IEEE Transactions on Image Processing*, Vol. 13, No. 1, January 2004.

Chang, R., Sie, Y., Chou, S., and Shih, T. K. (2005) "Photo Defect Detection for Image Inpainting", In *Proceedings of the Seventh IEEE international Symposium on Multimedia*, December 12 - 14, 2005, Irvine, California, USA.

De Polo A., Stanco F., Ramponi G.(2003), "Towards the Automated Restoration of Old Photographic Prints: A Survey", In *Proc. of IEEE EUROCON 2003*, pp. 370-374, Ljubljana, Slovenia, September, 2003.

Giakoumis I., Nikolaidis N. and Pitas I. (2006) "Digital image processing techniques for the detection and removal of cracks in digitized paintings" *IEEE Transactions on Image Processing*, vol. 15, no. 1, January, 2006.

Joyeux L., Buisson O., Besserer B., Boukir S. (1999) "Detection and removal of line scratches in motion picture films", *CVPR'99, International Conference on Computer Vision and Pattern Recognition*, Fort Collins, Colorado, June 1999.

Lew, M. S., Sebe, N., Djeraba, C., and Jain, R. (2006) "Content-based multimedia information retrieval: State of the art and challenges". *ACM Trans. Multimedia Comput. Commun. Appl.* 2, 1 (Feb. 2006), 1-19.

Pass G., Zabih R. and Miller J. (1996) "Comparing Images Using Color Coherence Vectors"', *ACM Conference on Multimedia*, Boston, Massachusetts, Nov. 1996, pp. 65-74.

Ramponi G. and Bruni V. (2006) "Virtual Restoration of Faded Photographic Prints", *Proc. EUSIPCO-06, 14th European Signal Processing Conf.*, 4-8 Sept. 2006, Florence, Italy.

Sikora T. (2001) "The MPEG-7 Visual standard for content description - an overview". *IEEE Trans. on Circuits and Systems for Video Technology, special issue on MPEG-7,* vol.11 pp:696--702, June 2001.

Stanco F., Tenze L. and Ramponi G. (2005) "Virtual Restoration of Vintage Photographic Prints Affected by Foxing and Water Blotches", *J. of Electronic Imaging,* vol.14, no.4, Oct.-Dec. 2005.

10

Supervised Crack Detection and Classification in Images of Road Pavement Flexible Surfaces

Henrique Oliveira[1,2] and Paulo Lobato Correia[1]
[1]*Instituto de Telecomunicações - Instituto Superior Técnico, Univ. Técnica de Lisboa*
[2]*Escola Superior de Tecnologia e Gestão - Instituto Politécnico de Beja*
Portugal

1. Introduction

Roads are important man-made infrastructures that exhibit distresses due to their constant usage, its maintenance being an essential task to ensure a correct pavement performance. To this end, good road maintenance policies are required, relying on adequate rehabilitation management procedures. Periodic road pavement surveys provide the necessary collection of data about pavement surface condition, an essential tool to decide on the appropriate maintenance techniques to be applied in pavement rehabilitation (restoration and repairs).

During periodic road pavement surveys, human visual inspection aims to provide a good structural and functional quality evaluation. This type of inspection is traditionally done by skilled technicians (inspectors) that travel along the surveyed road, acquiring images (the most important source of information for quantitative and qualitative distresses evaluation) and annotating them about pavement surface distresses types (cracks and other degradations) and their location.

The analysis of distresses relies on the inspector's experience on pavement surface observation. Some major drawbacks of this procedure are (Meignen et al., 1997; Chen & Miyojim, 1998): it is labor-intensive, since usually less than 10km per day can be surveyed and a considerable effort is required from those skilled technicians to manually analyze the full set of acquired images; it is prone to subjectivity, since two inspectors can produce different analysis results over similar distress situations. An automatic crack detection system based on the analysis of road pavement surface images, as proposed here, can significantly speed up the process and reduce results' subjectivity.

The methodologies reported so far, mainly deal with automatic crack detection and classification using techniques such as neural networks, including fuzzy sets and the computation of moment invariants, Markov random fields and edge detectors, among others, as discussed in Section 2. This text explores a novel approach for automatic crack distresses detection and classification in images taken over road pavement flexible surfaces, relying on image processing and pattern recognition techniques, envisaging a simple framework based on local statistics computed over non-overlapping image regions.

For the automatic detection of crack distresses (the first task of the proposed system), this chapter describes supervised classification strategies, composed of two main steps: training and testing. To supply adequate input data to these steps, the entire image database is split into two subsets, resorting to an automatic selection of training images. The training image subset is used for classifier training, in which a human expert manually selects image regions containing crack pixels. The test image subset is composed by images to be automatically classified, here used also for crack detection evaluation.

All the images are pre-processed using normalization techniques to reduce the effects of non-uniform illumination and to mitigate the influence of noise and some irrelevant properties of pavement upper layer aggregates. In training and test steps, six supervised classification strategies, three parametric and three non-parametric, are confronted to infer about their crack detection suitability (Oliveira & Correia, 2008). These classification strategies explore a 2D feature space, relying on the mean value of pixel intensities in non-overlapping image regions, together with the corresponding standard deviations. The 2D feature space is subsequently normalized to reduce feature value scattering among database images, leading to a better classifier performance.

The results obtained in the crack detection task are subsequently used as input for a crack type classification task, where images are labeled as containing longitudinal, transversal and miscellaneous or no cracks, a subset of the crack distress types identified in the Portuguese Distress Catalogue (JAE, 1997). This second task explores another 2D feature space, computed for this purpose.

The proposed automatic system is evaluated over an image database composed by real flexible pavement surface images, acquired during a survey over a Portuguese road (following the visual inspection method), using a set of well-know metrics and exploiting the availability of ground truth data manually provided (human labeling) for the entire image database. Promising results are obtained in both crack detection and classification tasks.

This chapter is structured as follows. Section 2 reviews the most relevant literature addressing automatic crack detection and classification systems. Section 3 discusses image acquisition, the automatic selection of training images, image normalization and saturation, followed by feature extraction and normalization. Section 4 describes the classification strategies used for crack detection and the associated parameters while Section 5 presents the approach for crack distress type classification. Section 6 discusses the experimental results. Conclusions and some hints for future work are addressed in Section 7.

2. Literature Review

In the scientific literature, not so many papers dealing with the automatic detection of pavement surface distresses are available. A good starting point can be found in (Chen & Miyojim, 1998), which reviews the techniques applied for the development of automatic pavement distress detection and classification systems. They also propose a novel approach according to the following major steps: region based image enhancement, to correct nonuniform background illumination and a skeleton analysis algorithm to classify pavement surface distress types. Experimental results for forty two crack samples are analyzed, corresponding to six different distress types, notably transversal, diagonal, longitudinal, block, combination and alligator pattern cracks. They claim 100% accuracy in the distress type classification results, but no evaluation of the crack detection step is included.

(Chou et al., 1994) proposed the use of moment invariant features and trained neural networks, again focusing on crack type classification. The same crack distress types of (Chen & Miyojim, 1998) are considered plus right diagonal, left diagonal non-distress types. The authors claim 100% accuracy for crack distress type classification, but crack detection results are not reported.

A multi-scale approach using Markov Random Fields for crack detection is presented in (Chambon et al., 2009). Cracks are enhanced using a Gaussian function and then processed by a 2D matched filter to detect cracks. Another approach, based on a nonsubsampled contourlet transform for pavement distress crack detection, is proposed in (Ma et al., 2008) but very few experimental results are provided.

An artificial living system is proposed in (Zhang & Wang, 2004). This work includes a pre-processing step to exclude bright points in images and enhance the contrast between crack and non-crack pixels (based on top-hat and bottom-hat procedures). No ground truth information is provided here and experimental results are mainly qualitative.

The use of edge detectors for pavement distress evaluation is proposed in (Li et al., 1991), while a pavement image segmentation technique is presented in (Qingquan & Xianglong, 2008) to identify image cracks. A novel thresholding technique is used, the authors claiming to achieve better experimental results than with well-known thresholding methods. Another thresholding-based technique is presented in (Liu et al., 2008), where the resulting binary images are processed by a connected domain algorithm to find cracks. No information about the use of ground truth information is provided.

Also the problem of pavement image acquisition and the related hardware is discussed in some papers. (Wang, 2000) describes new hardware acquisition systems as well as their applicability to the automation of pavement distress evaluation. Also (Huang & Xu, 2006) describes a system where images are acquired using a time delay integration line-scan camera.

3. Crack Detection Supervised Strategies

The proposed system architecture for automatic crack detection and classification is shown in Fig. **1**. The first step aims to split the image database into two subsets: the Training Image Set (TIS), used to train classifiers with manually labeled samples (image regions) containing crack pixels; the Testing Image Set (TTIS), the remaining images to be automatically processed by the system for crack detection and crack types classification. A set of procedures (image normalization and saturation and feature normalization) are implemented to ensure the computation of adequate decision boundaries, aiming better crack detection performance.

Two main tasks are identified: detection, where image regions are labeled as containing crack pixels or not; and crack type classification, where 'longitudinal', 'transversal', 'miscellaneous' or 'no cracks' labels are assigned to each detected crack.

Detailed discussion on training images selection, feature extraction, normalization (for both image and feature space data) and saturation procedures is given in the following sub-sections.

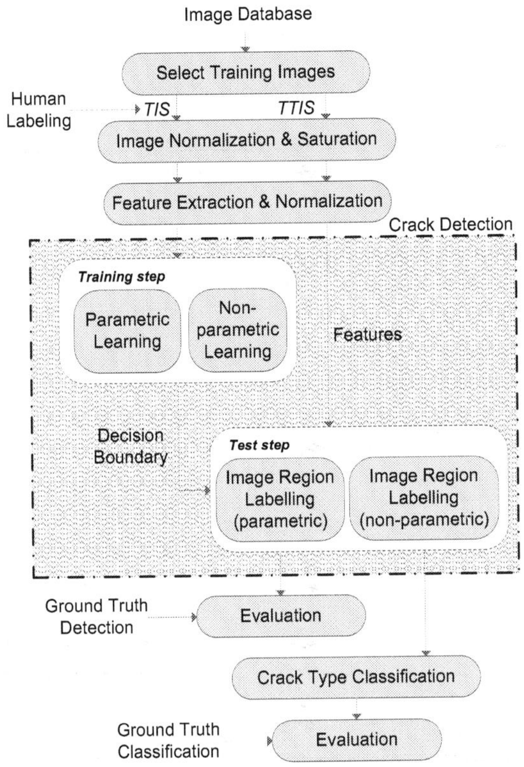

Fig. 1. System architecture.

3.1 Image Acquisition

The image database considered in this research work is composed by grayscale images, acquired during a pavement surface visual survey over a Portuguese road. A digital camera was manually positioned by the inspector with its optical axis perpendicular to the road surface, at a distance of approximately 1.2 m. Images with different sizes are obtained (2048×1536 pixels and 1858×1384 pixels), according to different camera setup procedures. The digital camera is oriented in such a way that the images only contain areas belonging to the road pavement surface. Moreover, the database includes images with several types of cracks (longitudinal, transversal and miscellaneous), as well as images without any cracks.

Instead of processing the images at a pixel level in all the steps of the proposed system, each image is divided into a set of non-overlapping regions of size 75×75 pixels. These dimensions were empirically chosen, leading to a faster processing time and lower memory storage requirements, while providing a good compromise between complexity and accuracy. Database images can then be represented by smaller matrices, where each of their values corresponds to the computation of region local statistics, as described next.

3.2 Selection of Training Images

Dealing with supervised classification strategies, training data (images for the envisaged application) is necessary for classifiers learning. This section describes a technique for the automatic selection of images, to be included in TIS, from the entire image database acquired during the visual road pavement survey.

To allow a correct learning stage, training images should contain road pavement cracks. Therefore, in a preliminary classification phase, all images are pre-processed in order to detect the regions with most evident crack pixels, by exploiting the knowledge that regions with crack pixels are supposed to have lower average intensities, when compared to regions without crack pixels. The images are then sorted, starting from those where the longest cracks were detected, the TIS being chosen from the top of this sorted list. The number of images to be included in TIS is an option controlled by the system operator. Moreover, the operator can edit the TIS, i.e., he can manually reject images automatically labeled by the system as 'training image' or add additional ones. Images definitely labeled as 'training images' are finally presented to the system operator, for manual identification of regions containing crack pixels.

In this preliminary classification phase, image regions revealing evident crack pixels are automatically labeled '1', or '0' otherwise. The result is a binary matrix (M_{bm}) with dimensions nl_{bm} and nc_{bm}, given by:

$$nl_{bm} = fix\left(\frac{nl_{img}}{nl_r}\right) \text{ and } nc_{bm} = fix\left(\frac{nc_{img}}{nc_r}\right) \tag{1}$$

where nl_{img} and nc_{img} stand for the number of lines and columns of an image, respectively; nl_r and nc_r are the number of lines and columns of regions (here square regions of 75x75 are used, as referred in Section 3.1), and *fix* is an operator which rounds a number towards zero.

Automatic image region labeling, in the preliminary classification phase, starts with the computation of a regions' mean values matrix - M_{rm}, with dimensions $nl_{bm} \times nc_{bm}$, each of its elements representing the region's pixel intensities average. This matrix is vertically and horizontally scanned to find regions with evident crack pixels, by analyzing the variation of the average region values when compared to those of the nearest neighbors, also taking into account all the values along the line or column under analysis.

Starting with the vertical scanning of M_{rm}, a region is considered a candidate of containing cracks when the following logical decision, $ld^{(V)}$, holds true:

$$ld^{(V)} = \left[\mathrm{std}(\mathrm{Av}^{(i,j)}) > k_1 \times \mathrm{std}(\mathrm{Bv}^{j}) + k_2 \times \mathrm{mean}(\mathrm{Bv}^{j})\right] \wedge \left[\left(\mathrm{Av}^{(i,j)}[1] - \mathrm{Av}^{(i,j)}[2]\right) > 0\right] \tag{2}$$

with

$$\mathrm{Av}^{(i,j)} = \begin{bmatrix} \dfrac{rm_{(i-1,j)} + rm_{(i+1,j)}}{2} \\ rm_{(i,j)} \end{bmatrix}, \mathrm{Bv}^{j} = \begin{bmatrix} 0 \\ \mathrm{std}\left(\mathrm{Av}^{(2,j)}\right) \\ \vdots \\ \mathrm{std}\left(\mathrm{Av}^{(nl_{bm}-1,j)}\right) \\ 0 \end{bmatrix}, \tag{3}$$

where $rm_{(i,j)}$ corresponds to the average pixel intensity of a region at position (i,j), k_1 and k_2 are parameters controlled by the system operator (set by default to an empirically chosen value) and $\mathrm{Av}^{(i,j)}$ and Bv^{j} are column vectors with dimensions 2×1 and nlbm×1, respectively. Elements of Bv^{j} represent the standard deviation between region average intensities along row i and column j (i.e. rm(i,j)) and the corresponding values of its nearest vertical

neighboring regions ($[rm_{(i-1,j)} + rm_{(i+1,j)}]/2$). Bv^j is used to gather some knowledge about the expected variations along the columns of M_{rm}, highlighting the presence of relevant dark pixels in regions, to be accounted for in equation (2). Regions with relevant crack pixels have higher std(Bv^j) values, due to higher $Av^{(i,j)}$ values when compared to regions without crack pixels. Additionally, the values of $Av^{(1,j)}$ and $Av^{(nl_{bm},j)}$, i.e. the extreme regions of each column (top and bottom edges), take value zero. After the vertical scanning of M_{rm}, a binary matrix, $M_{bm}^{(V)}$, is build with the computed $ld^{(V)}$ values; it has the same dimensions of M_{rm}.
Fig. **2** is used to illustrate the behavior of std(Bv^j) in the presence of cracks. It shows a sample column of Mrm matrix (12th column) in two road pavement surface images. The std(Bv^j) value computed for the regions of the left image is lower (0.5696) than the corresponding value for the right image (1.1895), due to the existence of an higher std($Av^{(11,12)}$) value when compared to std($Av^{(i,12)}$) for the remaining regions. The same tendency is observed for mean(Bv^j), presenting a lower value for the left image (0.9405) than for the right image (1.3788).

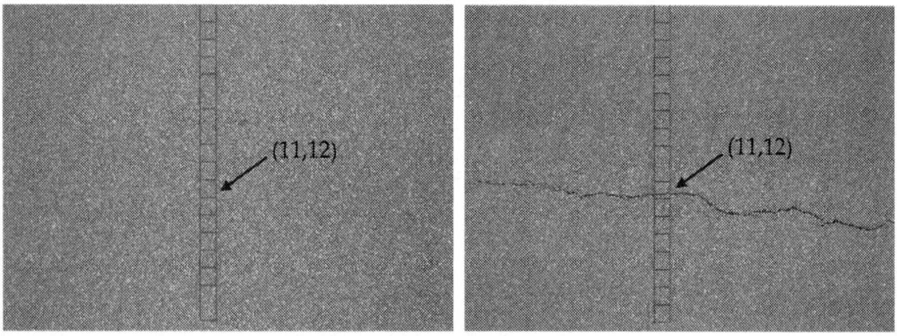

Fig. 2. Two sample images, with 1536x2048 pixels, from the pavement survey database. The left image shows a pavement surface without cracks, while the right image includes a transversal crack. Processed 75x75 pixel regions are marked with squares.

After the vertical scan, a horizontal scan proceeds in a similar way, acquainting for longitudinal cracks, which would be difficult to detect in a vertical scan. Expressions (4) and (5), for the horizontal scan, are similar to (2) and (3), with Av and Bv being replaced by Ah and Bh, respectively:

$$ld^{(H)} = \left[\text{std}(\text{Ah}^{(i,j)}) > k_1 \times \text{std}(\text{Bh}^i) + k_2 \times \text{mean}(\text{Bh}^i)\right] \wedge \left[\left(\text{Ah}^{(i,j)}[1] - \text{Ah}^{(i,j)}[2]\right) > 0\right] \quad (4)$$

$$\text{Ah}^{(i,j)} = \left[\frac{rm_{(i,j-1)} + rm_{(i,j+1)}}{2};\ \ rm_{(i,j)}\right],\ \text{Bh}^i = \left[0;\ \ \text{std}\left(\text{Ah}^{(i,2)}\right);\ \ \ldots\ \ \text{std}\left(\text{Ah}^{(i,nc_{bm}-1)}\right);\ \ 0\right]' \quad (5)$$

with $Ah^{(i,j)}$ and Bh^i being vectors with dimensions 2×1 and ncbm×1, respectively, and the values for $Ah^{(i,1)}$ and $Ah^{(i,nc_{bm})}$, i.e. the extreme regions of each row (left and right edges), taking value zero. After the horizontal scanning of M_{rm}, a new binary matrix with the computed $ld^{(H)}$ values is build, $M_{bm}^{(H)}$ (with the same dimensions of M_{rm}).

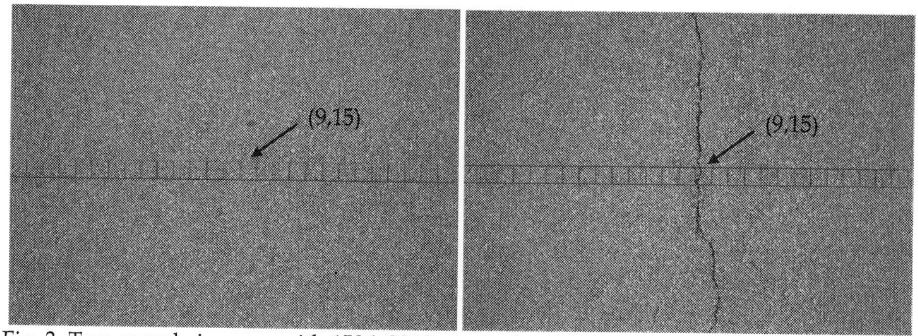

Fig. 3. Two sample images, with 1536x2048 pixels, from the pavement survey database. The left image shows a pavement surface without cracks, while the right image includes a longitudinal crack. Processed 75x75 pixel regions are marked with squares.

As an example, a horizontal scanning for the Mrm matrix 9th row of the images in Fig. **3** is considered. Lower values for std(Bhi) and mean(Bhi) are obtain for the left image (0.6002 and 1.0681, respectively) than for the right image (0.9298 and 1.2171, respectively), due to the existence of an higher std($Ah^{(9,15)}$) value when compared to std($Ah^{(9,j)}$) of the remaining regions.

The next step of the preliminary detection of regions containing cracks is to merge the two binary matrices $M_{bm}^{(V)}$ and $M_{bm}^{(H)}$ into a new binary matrix, M_{bm}, to retain the results of both the horizontal and vertical scans. The connected components of M_{bm} are identified, considering a 8-neighbourhood, and only those containing more than one region are kept as crack region candidates; isolated crack region candidates are discarded (relabeled to '0'), as they are likely to correspond to oil spots or other types of noise.

Finally, the length of each retained connect component is computed and, for each image, the length of longest connected component (*llcc*) is stored. The selection of a given number of training images (controlled by the system operator) is achieved by sorting the entire image database in descending order of the computed *llcc* values – the TIS is chosen from the top of this sorted list. This procedure ensures that the images selected for training the classifiers effectively contain cracks.

Sample results of the binary matrices corresponding to images selected for the training step are shown in Fig. **4**, using k_1 and k_2 values equal to 0.4 and 2.0 respectively (empirically chosen by the system operator). More detailed results and the corresponding analysis are included in Section 6.1.

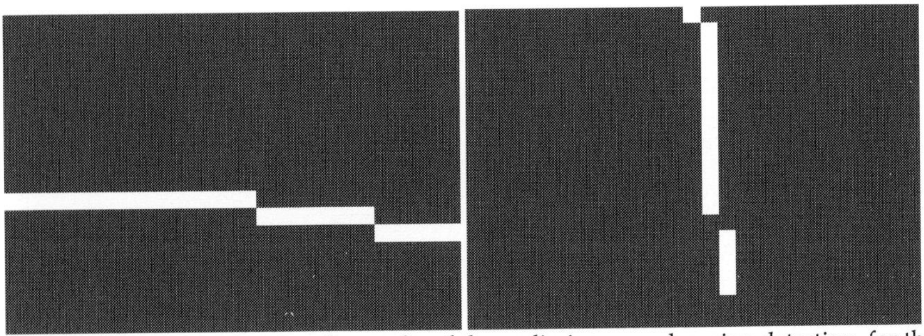

Fig. 4. Binary matrices showing the results of the preliminary crack region detection, for the right images of Fig. **2** and Fig. **3**, respectively. Regions in white are those preliminary classified as containing relevant crack pixels.

3.3 Image Normalization and Saturation

As stated in Section 3.1, pavement surface images were acquired during a survey over a Portuguese road using a digital camera. These images are free from shadows or other kind of occlusions, caused for instance by trees near road footpaths, but they present a non-uniform background illumination due to the type of sensor used, causing slight variations on the regions' pixel intensities average even in images without cracks.

To reduce this effect, an image normalization procedure is proposed. It consists in computing a base intensity level value (bil_{img}) for each image, equal to the average of the elements of M_{rm} corresponding to regions preliminary classified as not containing crack pixels, i.e., those labeled with value '0' in matrix M_{bm}. The need to use M_{bm} values for image normalization is the reason why this step is performed after the selection of training images.

Based on the bil_{img} value, a normalization constants matrix M_{nc} (with the same dimension of M_{rm}) is computed for each image, its elements being real values lower or higher than 1.0. The computation of M_{nc} elements is different depending if the corresponding label in M_{bm} is '0' or '1'.

For regions previously labeled with '0', i.e. regions preliminary classified as not containing cracks, the corresponding M_{nc} elements are computed using the expression in (6):

$$M_{nc}(i,j)^{'0'} = \frac{bil_{img}}{M_{rm}(i,j)^{'0'}} \quad (6)$$

where $M_{nc}(i,j)^{'0'}$ stands for the normalization constant to be applied to region (i,j), which has a M_{bm} label '0' and $M_{rm}(i,j)^{'0'}$ is the corresponding element in M_{rm}.

As an example, for a region with average pixel intensity of 163 and a M_{nc} value of 0.92, all that region's original pixel values are affected by this normalization constant. The resulting region average intensity will be 163×0.92=150.

For regions previously labelled with '1', i.e. regions preliminary classified as containing relevant cracks, the corresponding M_{nc} elements are computed using the expression in (7):

$$M_{nc}(\mathrm{i},\mathrm{j})^{'1'} = \frac{bil_{img}}{\frac{1}{k^{(0)}}\sum_{p=-a}^{a}\sum_{q=-b}^{b} M_{rm}(\mathrm{i}+\mathrm{p},\mathrm{j}+\mathrm{q})^{'0'}} \quad (7)$$

where $k^{(0)}$ is the number of regions with label '0' in a neighbourhood around the (i,j) region under analysis and the double sum accounts for all the corresponding M_{rm} elements. The search for regions with label '0' starts in 3×3 neighborhood (corresponding to a=b=1 in (7)). A larger neighborhood is adopted (e.g., 5×5 which corresponds to a=b=2 in (7)) only if no regions labeled '0' are found in the previous one. For instance, a region with label '1' and average pixel intensity of 152, with four neighbors labeled '0' and region averages of 148, 159, 140 and 153, has its original pixel intensities changed by a normalization constant of *152/150.*

Expression (7) only considers regions with label '0' for the computation of $M_{nc}(\mathrm{i,j})^{'1'}$. This is done to prevent strong changes in pixel intensities of normalized regions with label '1', preventing dark pixels to become brighter than expected during the normalization step, thus avoiding to loose the information that this region is likely to contain a crack.

Sample results using the proposed normalization procedure are shown in Fig. **5**. The graph on the left shows M_{rm} original values, for the regions of the row considered in the right side of Fig. **3**; the graph on the right of Fig. **5** shows the normalized average intensity levels. As can be seen from Fig. **5**, the normalization procedure tends to equalize the average intensities for those regions preliminary classified as not containing cracks, while maintaining the average intensity of regions expected to contain crack pixels below bil_{img}.

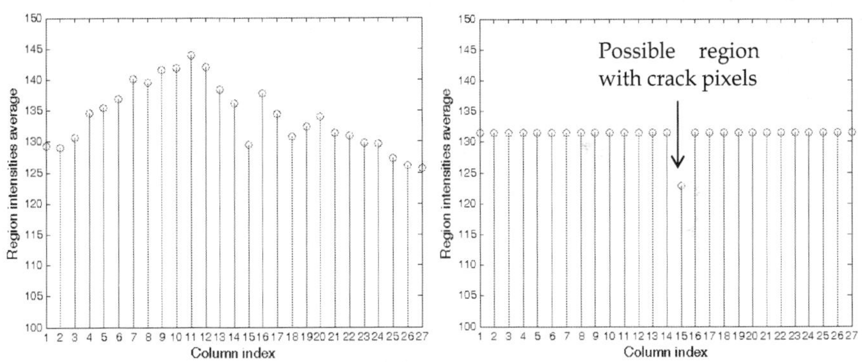

Fig. 5. Region average intensity values along the row selected in the right side of Fig. **3** before (left) and after (right) normalization.

Besides non-uniform background illumination, pavements surface images also frequently reveal the presence of white pixels due to specular reflectance of some surface materials. These pixels do not correspond to cracks but lead to higher intensity standard deviation values, even for regions without cracks. Higher standard deviation of region intensities are expected to be found in regions containing cracks (now due to higher differences between dark crack pixels and the corresponding average computed for the entire region). Therefore, white pixels may hinder detection performance, as different types of regions would present similar local statistics.

In order to eliminate the undesired influence of white pixels, a region saturation algorithm is proposed. For this purpose, the average of all pixel intensities of each normalized image is computed (*api*) and all image pixels having intensities higher than *api* assume that value. The pixel intensity saturation function is illustrated in Fig. **6**. The effect of applying the pixel intensity saturation algorithm to a normalized image is illustrated in Fig. **7**.

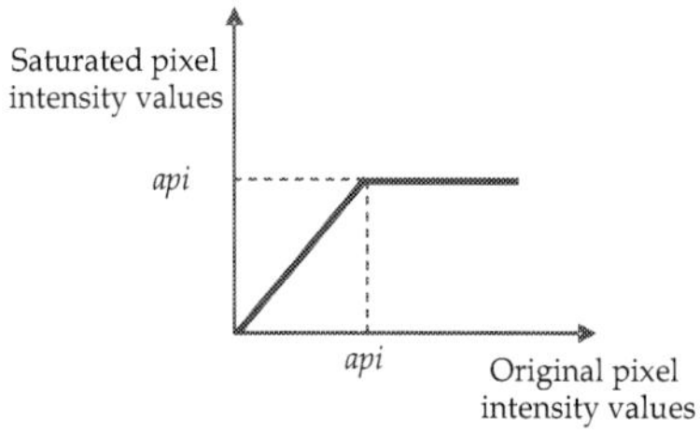

Fig. 6. Pixel intensity saturation function.

Fig. 7. Normalized image containing a longitudinal crack before (left) and after (right) applying the intensity saturation algorithm.

The proposed saturation function efficiently simplifies normalized images, reducing noise and also the standard deviation of regions without crack pixels, while keeping all relevant crack information.

To clarify the effect of applying the pixel saturation algorithm, which slightly changes the regions' average intensities, an example is shown in Fig. **8** for the row considered in the right image of Fig. **3**. At a first glance, comparing the right graph of Fig. **5** with the one on top of Fig. **8**, the region average intensities are globally lower for the second case. Moreover, the corresponding standard deviations are also lower after applying the saturation algorithm as seen in the bottom graphs of Fig. **8**. In fact, the average standard deviation value for the image regions preliminary classified as not containing cracks (26 out of the 27 regions in the example of Fig. **8**) is 26.8, while after applying the saturation algorithm it is reduced by approximately 54%, to 12.4. Still, for the region likely to contain cracks, the reduction is only 29% (31.5 against 44.1 in the non-saturated case).

Thus, the saturation algorithm achieves a strong standard deviation reduction for regions without cracks, creating a good separation to the standard deviation values of crack regions, and allowing to consider it, together with the region average intensities, as the features to be exploited by the classifier used for crack regions detection, as discussed in the next section.

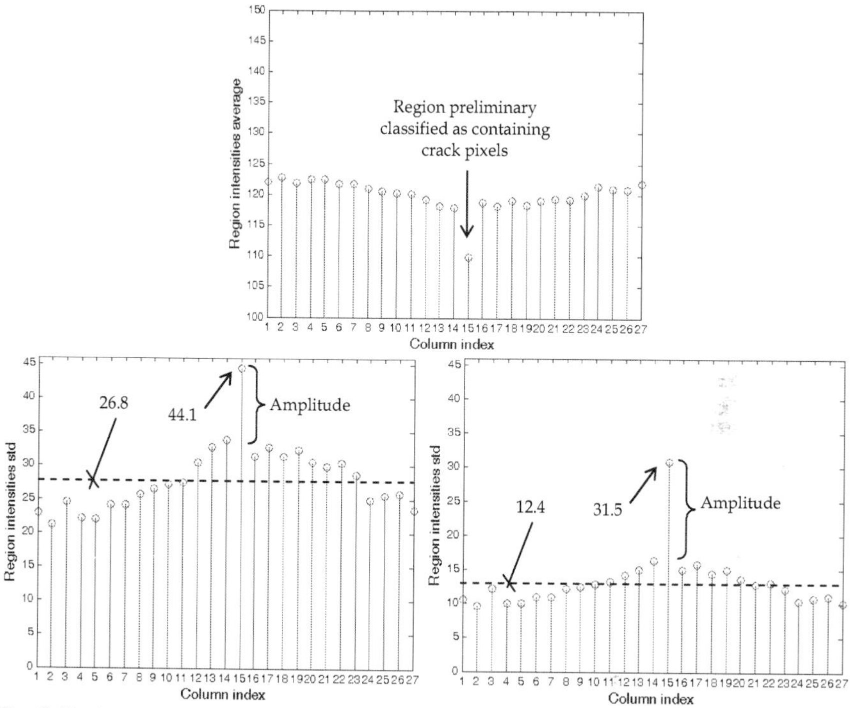

Fig. 8. Region average intensity values along the row selected in the right side of Fig. 3 after normalization and saturation (top) and standard deviation of region intensities for the normalized images before (bottom left) and after applying the saturation algorithm (bottom right).

3.4 Feature Extraction and Normalization

To automatically label regions as containing cracks or not, a pattern recognition system operating over a simple feature space is proposed. The feature space is two dimensional, being constructed using regions' local statistics, computed for normalized and saturated images. The first feature is the mean value of all pixel intensities in a region; the second is the standard deviation of the region's pixel intensities. Images can then be represented in the feature space - see example in Fig. 9, where each point identifies a region of an image.

Since different images present different average values, as can be observed by the scattering of points in Fig. 9 top-right and bottom-left images, a further normalization step is needed to allow a better classifier performance.

This additional feature space normalization starts with the computation of each image's two dimensional feature space centroid, together with a global centroid computed for all the database images. Then, for each individual image, the two dimensional feature space points are translated to align the respective centroid with the global one. The corresponding result is illustrated in the bottom-right image of Fig. **9**. Table 1 complements these results with the values of the intraclass and interclass distances (Heijden et al., 2004), computed for a TIS image set composed of five images, as discussed in Section 6.

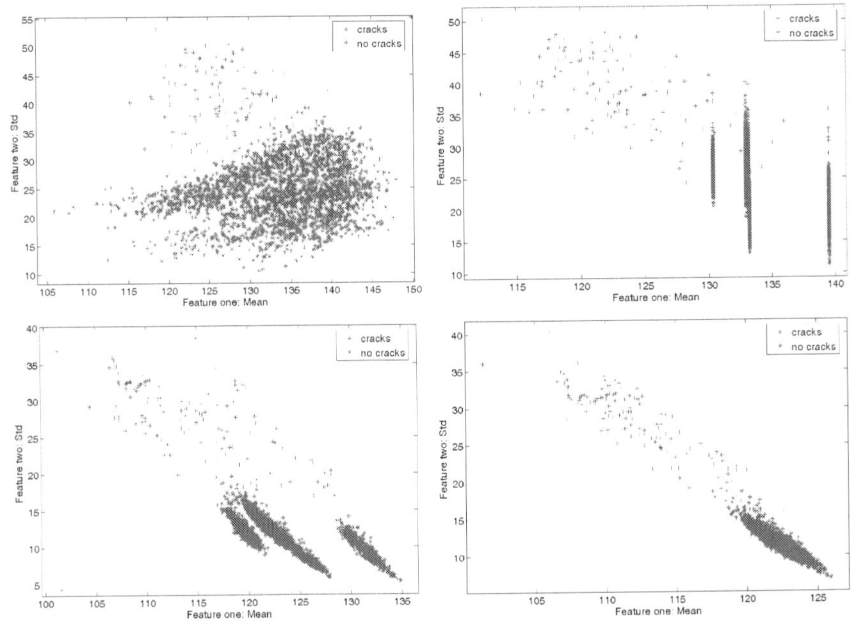

Fig. 9. Feature space representation, using a TIS composed of five images, for the original image (top-left), after image normalization (top-right), after normalization and saturation (bottom-left) and after the additional feature space normalization (bottom-right).

Implementations	**Intraclass distance** (crack regions)	**Intraclass distance** (no crack regions)	**Interclass distance**	**Crack region's intra/ interclass ratio** (%)	**No crack region's intra/interclas s ratio** (%)
Original images	147.9	145.0	395.8	37.4	36.6
Norm.	150.4	59.1	371.4	40.5	15.9
Norm. + Satur.	138.7	45.5	423.9	32.7	10.7
Norm. + Satur. + Trans.	87.2	8.7	402.4	21.7	2.2

Table 1: Interclass and intraclass distances computed using TIS set.

As can be seen in the first line of Table 1, high intraclass and interclass distance values are obtained for the original images, denoting a very scattered feature space where class separation would be a difficult task, as illustrated by the top-right graph of Fig. 9.
After region normalization (top-right graph of Fig. **9**), non crack regions points become aligned along vertical lines (each vertical alignment corresponding to an image), with very little variation along the horizontal axis. For these points, the values of the second line of Table 1 show a better class compactness. The distribution of crack region's points is not significantly affected by this task.
Applying the saturation algorithm to the normalized images (see bottom-left graph in Fig. **9**) a reduction of the intraclass to interclass distance ratio is obtained for both classes.
With feature space normalization a further improvement is observed in the results. The intraclass to interclass distance ratios is the best (21.7% and 2.2%), revealing a more separable feature space and more compact point distributions.

4. Training and Classification

This section describes the classification strategies being evaluated, which are based on two supervised learning approaches: parametric (Section 4.1) and nonparametric (Section 4.2). Parametric approaches are based on a bivariate class-conditional normal density, as it provides a good data description (Oliveira & Correia, 2007).

4.1 Parametric Learning and Classification

Points obtained by applying the described feature extraction and normalization procedures to the training image set (TIS) are manually labeled by a skilled system operator, providing a training data set for which the labels are a priori known.
From a fully automatic application point-of-view this is a drawback, as a human operator is required to manually label image regions. However, since the aim here is to develop parametric supervised strategies for crack region detection, the manual labeling is required to create the training data to be used by the classifiers' parameter learning step.
All TIS feature points compose a pattern vector **x**, representing a sample of the random variable **X**, taking values on a sample space **X**. For each element x_i of pattern vector **x**, one possible class y_i is assigned, where **Y** is the class set, .i.e. $y_i \in \mathbf{Y}$. Thus, the training set is:

$$\mathrm{T} = \{(x_1, y_1)\ldots(x_n, y_n) : x_i \in \Re^2; y_i \in \{c_1, c_2\}\} \tag{8}$$

where n is the number of points of the pattern vector **x**. Only two classes are used: regions with crack pixels, labeled as class c_1, and regions without crack pixels, labeled as class c_2.
Assigning a loss penalty to misclassified measurements, the minimal expectation of the resulting cost is taken as an acceptable optimization criterion for the Bayesian classifier presented here (Heijden et al., 2004):

$$\hat{y}_i = \arg\max_{y_i} \ln\left(p(\mathbf{x} \mid y_i)p(y_i)\right) \tag{9}$$

where $p(y_i)$ are the class priors, computed by:

$$p(y_i = c_k) = \frac{\#\,\text{points labeled into class } c_k}{\text{total number of points for all classes}}. \tag{10}$$

with k being the class index. A loss function $L(s,a) : \mathbf{S}\times\mathbf{A} \rightarrow \mathbf{R}$ is constructed to quantify the cost of each classification action, where **S** is the state space, *s* is the true state of nature, **A** is the action space and *a* is the action (classification) taken by the classifier (Figueiredo, 2004). The decision rule is to take the action that minimizes the associated risk, i.e., take action a_1 if $R(a_1 | x)$ is lower than $R(a_2 | x)$, where a_k means classifying measurement x_i into class c_k with $k\in\{1,2\}$, symbolically represented by (Duda et al., 2004):

$$p(\mathbf{x} \mid y_i = c_1)P(y_i = c_1) \underset{c_2}{\overset{c_1}{\gtrless}} \left(\frac{L_{12} - L_{22}}{L_{21} - L_{11}}\right) p(\mathbf{x} \mid y_i = c_2)P(y_i = c_2) \quad (11)$$

where L_{pq} is the loss resulting from classifying a measurement into class c_p, while the true state of nature is class c_q, i.e. $L(\hat{y}_i = c_p \mid y_i = c_q)$. Since a uniform loss function is used here, i.e. $L_{11}= L_{22}=1$ and $L_{12}= L_{21}=0$, the expression in (10) identifies a *maximum a posteriori* probability classifier. Ground truth for the training set is known, thus the parameters for both classes are learned from TIS feature points, $\mathbf{X}\sim N(\mu_k,\Sigma_k)$, with (Bishop, 2006):

$$\hat{\mu}_k = \frac{1}{n_k}\sum_{i=1}^{n_k} x_{ki} \quad \text{and} \quad \hat{\Sigma}_k = \frac{1}{n_k - 1}\sum_{i=1}^{n_k}(x_{ki} - \hat{\mu}_k)(x_{ki} - \hat{\mu}_k)^{\mathrm{T}} \quad (12)$$

where $\hat{\mu}_k$ is the sample unbiased vector mean, $\hat{\Sigma}_k$ is the sample unbiased covariance matrix, k is the class index and n_k is the total number of k class points.

Three ways to compute the decision boundaries are considered. The first one, denoted as linear, assumes a joint sample covariance matrix (Σ), with the boundary being computed by a weighted average (according to the class prior probabilities) of each class' covariance matrix, which results in a **linear decision boundary** (Duda et al., 2004; Heijden et al., 2004) given by:

$$\alpha + \mathbf{x}^{\mathrm{T}}\beta = 0 \quad (13)$$

$$\alpha = 2\ln\frac{P(y_i = c_2)}{P(y_i = c_1)} - \mu_2^{\mathrm{T}}\,\Sigma^{-1}\,\mu_2 + \mu_1^{\mathrm{T}}\,\Sigma^{-1}\,\mu_1 \quad (14)$$

$$\beta = 2\Sigma^{-1}(\mu_2 - \mu_1) \quad (15)$$

The second way to compute the decision boundary, denoted as quadratic, assumes a general covariance matrix resulting in the **quadratic boundary** (Heijden et al., 2004) defined by:

$$\alpha + \mathbf{x}^{\mathrm{T}}\beta + \mathbf{x}^{\mathrm{T}}\varphi\,\mathbf{x} = 0 \quad (16)$$

$$\alpha = +\ln|\Sigma_1| - \ln|\Sigma_2| + 2\ln\frac{P(y_i = c_2)}{P(y_i = c_1)} - \mu_2^{\mathrm{T}}\,\Sigma_2^{-1}\,\mu_2 + \mu_1^{\mathrm{T}}\,\Sigma_1^{-1}\,\mu_1 \quad (17)$$

$$\beta = 2\left(\Sigma_2^{-1}\,\mu_2 - \Sigma_1^{-1}\,\mu_1\right) \quad \text{and} \quad \varphi = -\Sigma_2^{-1} + \Sigma_1^{-1} \quad (18)$$

The third decision boundary, denoted as **independent**, is computed assuming independent features, i.e. the covariance matrices in (12) are now diagonal matrices computed as:

$$\hat{\Sigma}_{k_{l,l}} = \mathrm{E}\left[\left(\mathbf{x}_{k_l} - \mu_{k_l}\right)\left(\mathbf{x}_{k_l} - \mu_{k_l}\right)\right] \tag{19}$$

and $\hat{\Sigma}_{k_{l,m}}$ takes value zero whenever $l \neq m$; E stands for the expected value and l and m are feature identifiers, taking value 1 or 2 for class regions without or with crack pixels, respectively. Using these new covariance matrices, equations from (16) to (18) are used to compute the target decision boundary.

A sample result using the three types of decision boundaries, computed for the TIS, is illustrated in Fig. **10**.

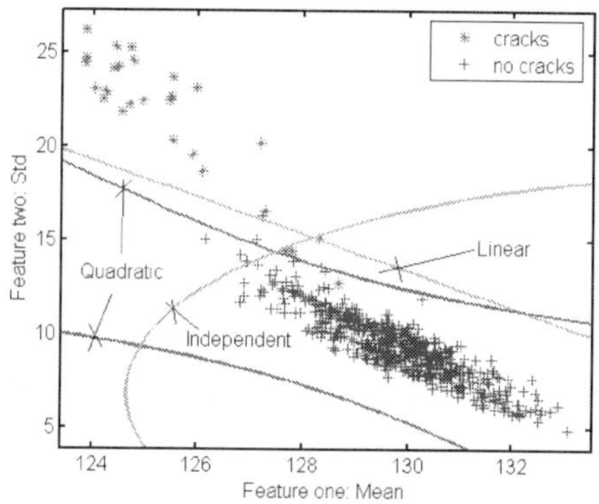

Fig. 10. Three parametric decision boundaries computed for the TIS.

4.2 Non-parametric Learning and Classification

This subsection deals with classifiers that operate when both conditional probability distributions are unavailable. This is different from the parametric case, where the only unknowns were the probability density parameters modeling the data.

In general, one advantage of non-parametric learning, when compared with parametric learning, is that not so much prior knowledge about the data to be processed is required, but, on the other hand, a large amount of data is needed to compensate the lack of knowledge about probability density functions, although it can be reduced when certain computational constrains of the classifiers apply (for example, the use of a linear boundary decision instead of a non-linear one) and they match the inherent distributions (Heihjen et al., 2004; Webb, 2002).

Here, three non-parametric techniques are considered: Parzen windows, k-Nearest Neighbor and Fisher's Least Square Linear classifiers.

The implemented **Parzen** algorithm for learning and classification follows the descriptions in (Heijden et al., 2004). Considering a labeled training vector **x** according to (8) and an unlabelled test set, the probability density estimation for an arbitrary test vector **z** is achieved by:

$$\hat{p}(\mathbf{z} \mid y_i = c_k) = \frac{1}{n_k} \sum_{q=1}^{n_k} \underbrace{\frac{1}{2\pi \times fs^2} \exp\left(-\frac{\|\mathbf{z} - \mathbf{x}_\mathbf{q}\|^2}{2 fs^2} \right)}_{\mathbf{A}} \tag{20}$$

where **A** is a kernel that represents the knowledge about the distance between a test measurement **z** and the training measurement x_q, corresponding to a Gaussian interpolation distance function, n_k is the total number of measurements for class k and fs is a constant that controls the size of the kernel influence zone, computed such that it maximizes:

$$\sum_{k=1}^{2} \sum_{q=1}^{n_k} \ln\left(\hat{p}\left(\mathbf{x}_{k,q} \mid y_i = c_k \right) \right) \tag{21}$$

where $x_{k,q}$ is the sample q of the class k which is left out by the leave-one-out method when computing the estimation of the posterior probability density. A measurement is classified into class c_k with the maximum posterior probability:

$$\hat{k} = \underset{k=1,2}{\operatorname{argmax}} \left[\hat{p}(\mathbf{z} \mid y_i = c_k) \hat{P}(y_i = c_k) \right] \tag{22}$$

where $\hat{P}(y_i = c_k)$ represents class priors according to (10).

For **k-Nearest Neighbors** classification (*k-nn*), the estimated posterior probability density may have different resolutions when the training data is not homogeneous, i.e., it's resolution is higher when the training data is more dense. The posterior probability density for an arbitrary test vector **z** is computed by (Duda et al., 2001; Theodoridis & Foutroumbas, 2003):

$$\hat{p}(\mathbf{z} \mid y_i = c_k) \approx \frac{N_k}{n_k \mathbf{V}(\mathbf{z})} \tag{23}$$

where N_k is the number of samples inside the volume V(**z**)—which represents a sphere centered in **z**—belonging to class k and n_k is the total number of training samples belonging to class k. Thus, a measurement is classified into the class (c_1 or c_2) that contains more training measurements in the N_k neighborhood of **z**:

$$\hat{k} = \underset{k=1,2}{\arg\max} \left\{ \hat{p}(\mathbf{z} \mid y_i = c_k) \hat{P}(y_i = c_k) \right\} = \underset{k=1,2}{\arg\max} \left\{ N_k \right\} \tag{24}$$

where $\hat{P}(y_i = c_k)$ again represents the class priors according to (10).

The aim of the **Fischer**'s linear classification strategy is to find the linear discriminant function between both classes, which corresponds to the projection that maximizes the class separability (Bishop, 2006; Duda et. al., 2001). Class separability in a direction $d \in \Re^n$ is defined by:

$$R(d) = \frac{d^T J_B d}{d^T J_W d} \tag{25}$$

which is also denoted as the ratio of the between-class covariance matrix (J_B) to the within-class covariance matrix (J_K), defined as:

$$J_B = (\mu_1 - \mu_2)(\mu_1 - \mu_2)^T \tag{26}$$

$$J_W = J_{W_{c_1}} + J_{W_{c_2}} \ , \ J_{W_{c_k}} = \sum_{k=1}^{2} (\mathbf{x}_k - \mu_k)(\mathbf{x}_k - \mu_k)^T \tag{27}$$

where μ_k denotes the vector mean for class k, computed according to (12) and $\mathbf{x}_k$ is class k measurements vector data. An estimate of d is obtained maximizing (25) according to:

$$\hat{d} = \underset{d}{\mathbf{argmax}} \left(\frac{d^T J_B d}{d^T J_W d} \right) \tag{28}$$

Thus, a measurement from a vector **z** is classified into class c_1 when $y(x_i) \geq y_0$ for $y_0 = K.\mathbf{z}$ (**z** is classified into class c_2 otherwise).

A sample result using the three types of decision boundaries, computed using the TIS, is illustrated in Fig. **11**.

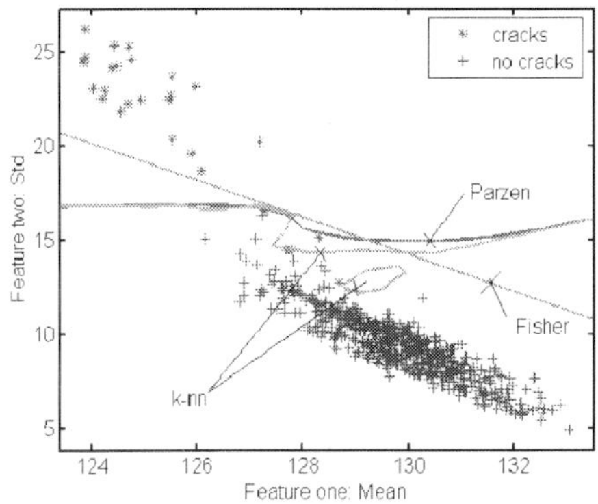

Fig. 11. Three non-parametric decision boundaries computed for the TIS. For *k-nn*, the boundary shown corresponds to a neighborhood of 1 point.

5. Crack Type Classification

Detection results are stored in binary matrices (one for each TTIS image) with the same dimensions as (1), where '1' means regions labeled as containing crack pixels and '0' the opposite case. All binary matrices are then processed to identify connect components and the resulting connected crack regions are finally classified into one of the crack types considered in the scope of this research work, following the specifications of the Portuguese Distress Catalog (JAE, 1997): longitudinal (c_L), transversal (c_T) or miscellaneous (c_M).

Crack type classification uses another pattern classification system exploiting a new 2D feature space. A crack type label is assigned to each connected crack region and cumulatively added to each TTIS image.

The 2D feature space used for crack type classification is composed by the standard deviations of the column (feature one) and row (feature two) coordinates of connected crack regions. A sample representation of this feature space is given in Fig. **12**.

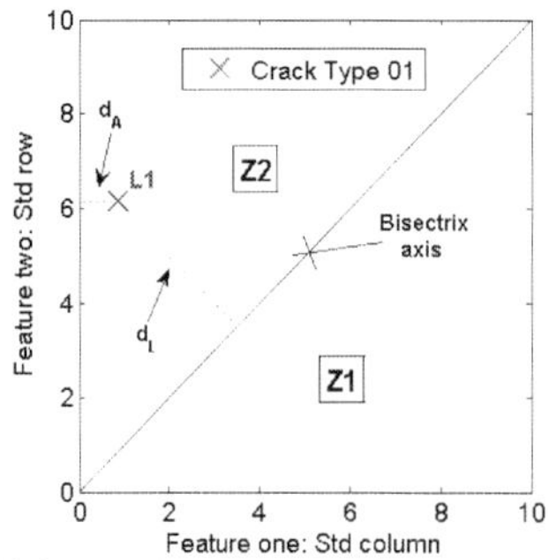

Fig. 12. 2D feature space used for crack type classification. Point L_1 represents a connected crack region classified as a 'longitudinal crack'.

The bisectrix sectioning the 2D feature space into two zones, 'Z1' and 'Z2', represents the points where connected components have equal column and row standard deviation values, identifying perfect miscellaneous cracks. Points positioned over the horizontal or vertical axes correspond to perfect transversal or longitudinal cracks, respectively.
Crack type classification is performed by computing two distances for each connected crack region point representation in the 2D feature space: d_L and d_A, where d_L is the distance from the point to the bisectrix axis and d_A corresponds to the distance to nearest axis (horizontal or vertical). The example in Fig. **12** shows the classification of one connected crack region (point L_1) as a 'longitudinal crack' ($d_L > d_A$). This crack type classification is fully automatic and unsupervised, no training stage being required.
The probability of a crack belonging to class c_L or c_T is computed, according to:

$$P(y_i = c_{cr} \mid r_i) = 1 - \frac{d_{Ai}}{d_{Ai} + d_{Li}} \tag{29}$$

while the probability of a crack belonging to the miscellaneous cracks class (c_M) is computed according to:

$$P(y_i = c_M \mid r_i) = 1 - \frac{d_{Li}}{d_{Ai} + d_{Li}} \tag{30}$$

where the index $_{cr}$ is one of the class indexes T or L, d_{Ai} is the distance from point i to the nearest axis, d_{Li} is the distance from point i to the bisectrix and r_i is the observation (region i).
Thus, a connected crack region is classified into the class presenting a probability above 0.5:

- a crack is classified as 'longitudinal' (class c_L) if $d_L > d_A$ and the nearest axis is the vertical one;
- a crack is classified as 'transversal' (class c_T) if $d_L > d_A$ and the nearest axis is the horizontal one;
- a crack is classified as 'miscellaneous' (class c_M) if $d_A > d_L$, independently of the nearest axis.

6. Experimental Results and Performance Evaluation

The proposed classification strategies are evaluated over the TTIS, which is composed by real flexible pavement surface images, eventually containing cracks with linear development. These images were acquired during a survey over a Portuguese road and ground truth data has been manually constructed. Part of the algorithmic development was supported by the PRtools toolbox (Duin et al., 2004). Experimental results are firstly presented for crack regions detection (Section 6.1) and then for crack type classification (Section 6.2).

6.1 Crack Regions Detection Results and Evaluation

Sample results for one TTIS image using the available classifiers are shown in Fig. **13**. For the k-nn strategy, one nearest neighbor (*1-nn*) is considered, as this is the neighborhood that optimizes the leave-one-out error for the target image.
An evaluation of the different strategies, by comparison with the ground truth data, is included in Table 2. A global Error-rate is computed ($e\text{-}r_G$ being the classification error for classes c_1 and c_2), as well as some metrics related only to regions with crack pixels: Crack Error-rate ($e\text{-}r_{Cr}$), Precision (pr), Recall (re) as well as a Performance Criterion (pc) reflecting the overall classifier performance, according to (Tax, 2006):

$$e - r_G = \frac{\text{Number of regions wrongly classified for classes } c_1 \text{ and } c_2}{\text{Total number of regions}} \tag{31}$$

$$e - r_{Cr} = \frac{\text{Number of regions wrongly classified for class } c_1}{\text{Total number of crack regions (ground truth)}} = 1 - re \tag{32}$$

$$pr = \frac{\text{Number of regions correctly classified for class } c_1}{\text{Total number of crack regions detected}} \tag{33}$$

$$re = \frac{\text{Number of regions correctly classified for class } c_1}{\text{Total number of crack regions (ground truth)}} \tag{34}$$

$$pc = \frac{2 \times pr \times re}{pr + re}. \tag{35}$$

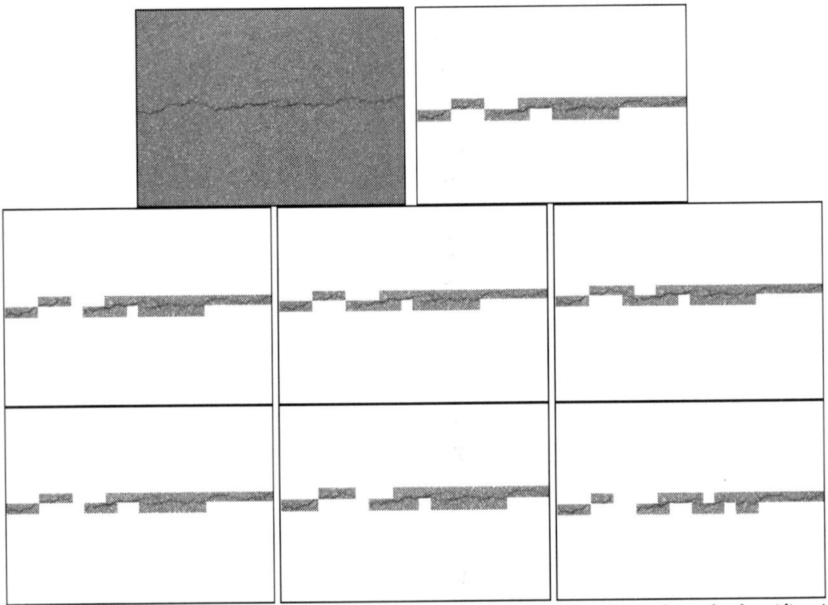

Fig. 13. Experimental results for a test image: original (top left), ground truth classification (top right). Parametric classification results (2nd line): linear classifier (left), quadratic classifier (middle), classifier with independent features (right). Non-parametric results (3rd line): Parzen windows (left), 1-nn nearest neighbors (middle) and Fischer's linear classifier (right).

Strategy	**Global Error-rate** ($e\text{-}r_G$)	**Crack Error-rate** ($e\text{-}r_{Cr}$)	**Precision** (pr)	**Recall** (re)	pc
Linear	0.68%	8.90%	97.1%	91.2%	94.0%
Quadratic	**0.64%**	**2.96%**	92.5%	**97.0%**	**94.7%**
Independ.	0.85%	6.87%	92.4%	93.1%	92.7%
Parzen	0.73%	10.79%	**98.2%**	89.2%	93.3%
k-nn	0.78%	5.38%	92.5%	94.6%	93.5%
Fischer	1.00%	15.45%	98.1%	84.6%	90.7%

Table 2. Detection results for regions with crack pixels case. Best results for each metric are underlined.

The best overall classifier performance is achieved by the quadratic classifier, according to pc values and confirmed by the best Recall value, meaning that this classifier produces the best true positive detection performance.

An interesting observation is that the features used seem to have some degree of dependence, which can be seen by comparing the quadratic and the independent parametric classifier results, but a worst classification performance is achieved when a diagonal covariance matrix is assumed. The use of parametric classifiers seems to be a good strategy, producing better *pc* values and taking into account that Recall is more important than Precision for this type of application.

It is important to note that although the use of *k-nn* classifier produces good results (see *pc* and Recall), it may be difficult to obtain a fixed neighborhood size. For different training images, values between 1 and 10 were observed as the best, with an average of 4. Using a small neighborhood may produce some over fitting problems, with the decision boundary adapted to the training set, thus leading to a poor generalization of the classifier performance.

Additionally, all classifiers seem to perform very well according to false positives detection (i.e., regions without crack pixels being classified as containing cracks), with the corresponding computed errors always below 1%.

Looking in more detail to the quadratic classifier results, some samples computed for TTIS images and the respective ground truths are shown in Fig. **14**, emphasizing the good performance of the classifier.

It is also interesting to compare these results with those obtained in the preliminary classification stage for selecting images for the TIS (see Section 3.2). The corresponding results for the same metrics reported in Table 2 are included in Table 3.

Comparing the values reported in Table 2 and Table 3, it can be noticed that at the preliminary classification strategy achieves very good precision results (95.7%). This means that the great majority of crack regions preliminary detected do correspond to image regions containing crack pixels, which is important at that stage as it effectively finds good images for the training set.

Apart from that, crack detection using a Normal based density quadratic classifier significantly raises the system performance (from 66.1% to 97.0% for recall), although more false positives are detected in this case (precision drops from 95.7% to 92.5%).

Global Error-rate ($e\text{-}r_G$)	**Crack Error-rate** ($e\text{-}r_{Cr}$)	**Precision** (*pr*)	**Recall** (*re*)	*pc*
1.7%	33.9%	95.7%	66.1%	76.7%

Table 3. Results for crack regions preliminary classification.

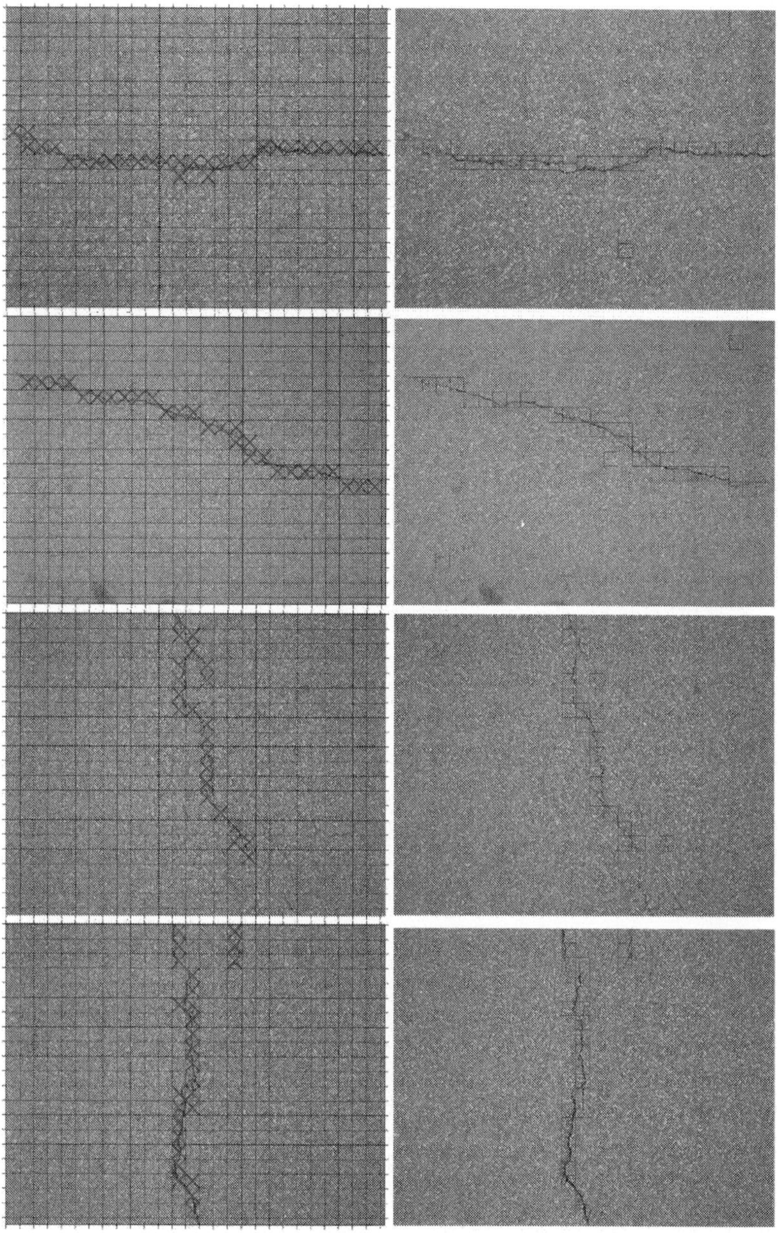

Fig. 14. Images on left column correspond to detection results using the quadratic classifier. The right column includes the corresponding ground truth.

Fig. 15 shows ground truth, preliminary classification and crack detection results (first, second and third column respectively) for the same images presented in Fig. **14**.

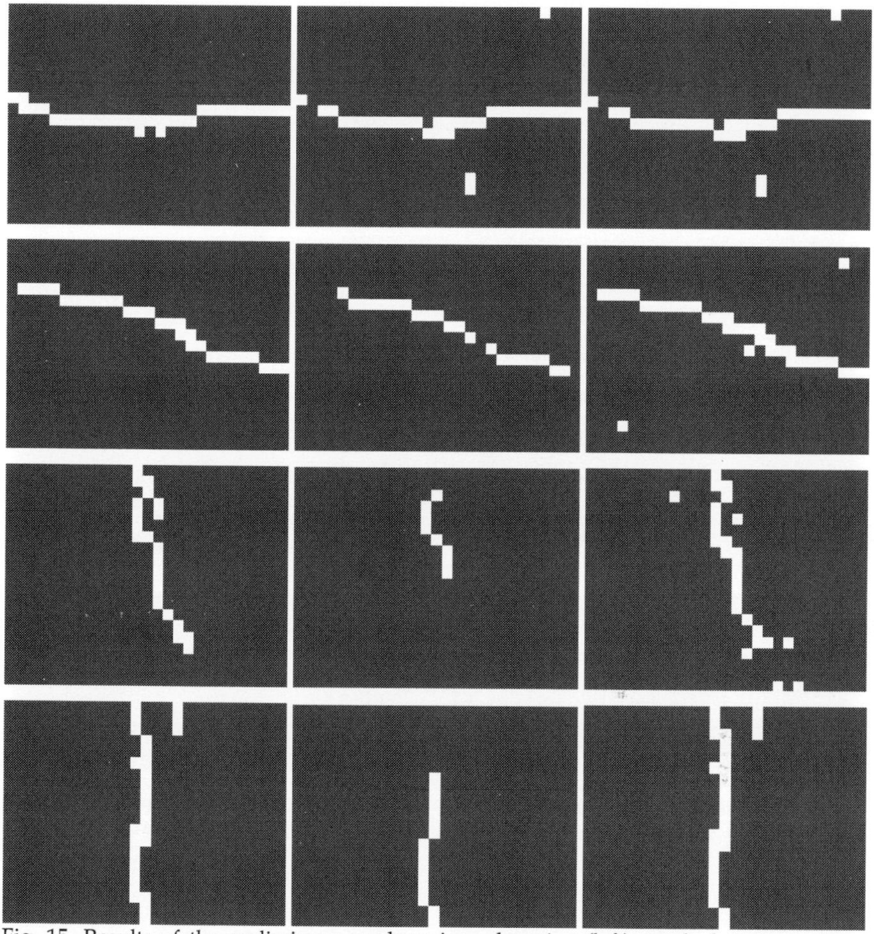

Fig. 15. Results of the preliminary crack regions detection (left), crack detection using a quadratic classifier (middle) and the corresponding ground truth (right).

6.2 Crack Type Classification Results and Evaluation

Crack type classification is performed on the resulting binary images produced by the crack detection task. Crack type classification labels are used to annotate database images and can later be used by a search engine to retrieve images containing a given type of crack. Fig. **16** shows crack classification results for the sample images shown in Fig. **14**.

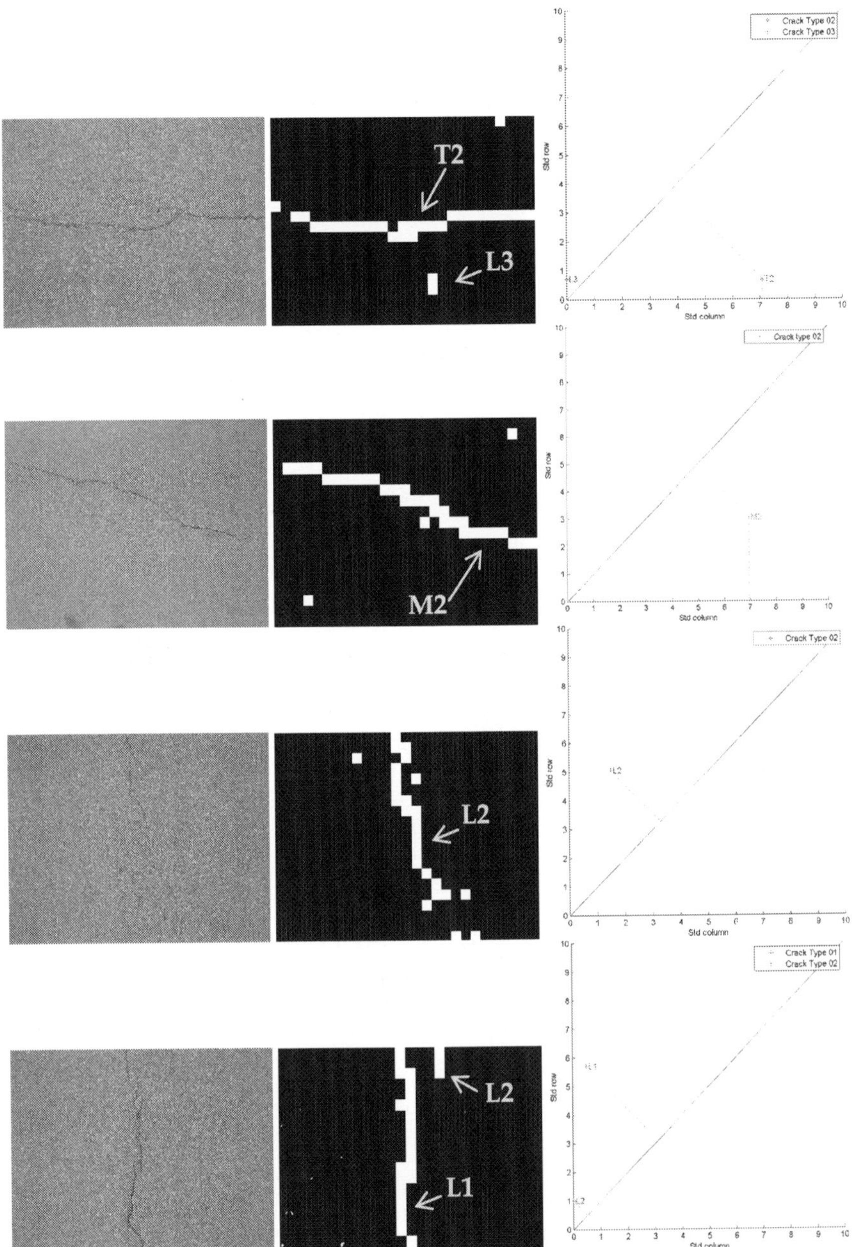

Fig. 16. Crack type classification results: original images (left), crack detection results (middle) and the corresponding crack type classification feature space (right).

From top to bottom, the first line shows an image containing a transversal crack and a short longitudinal crack. The second contains a miscellaneous crack. The third and fourth lines show images containing longitudinal cracks. The column on the right shows the crack's representation in the 2D feature space used for crack type classification. Regions with length equal to '1' (isolated regions) are not considered in the classification process, as they are likely to correspond to oil spots or similar occurrences in pavement surface images.
Using the crack type classification ground truth constructed for the TTIS, 100% recall and precision are obtained for all the cracks, emphasizing a very good classifier performance.

7. Conclusions and Future Work

This chapter proposes a supervised system for crack regions detection and classification. The proposed system automates the selection of training images, splitting the image database into training and test sets.
Six supervised classification strategies (three parametric and three non-parametric) were tested and analyzed. All six obtain an acceptable performance, with parametric classifiers, and especially the quadratic one, achieving the best classification results.
All detected cracks were correctly classified into types, considering a set of crack types listed in the Portuguese Distress Catalogue (JAE, 1997).
In terms of future developments, filtering techniques may be introduced to preprocess images before the classification stage, notably for reducing falloff and specular reflection problems. Also unsupervised approaches may be developed and confronted with those presented in this chapter, notably investigating the use of one class classifiers, as regions with crack pixels may be seen it as outliers of a well defined cluster of points in the feature space.
Additionally, a reject-option for the Bayesian approach and a non uniform loss function will be explored, since false positive detections have less impact than false negatives detection. Also a deeper study of windows size, to maximize class separability, will be performed.

8. References

Bishop, C. (2006). Pattern Recognition and Machine Learning, Springer, ISBN: 0-387-31073-8, USA

Chambon, S., Subirats, P. & Dumoulin, J. (2009). Introduction of a wavelet transform based on 2D matched filter in a Markov random field for fine structure extraction: application on road crack detection, in Proceedings of IS&T/SPIE Electronic Imaging, - Image Processing: Machine Vision Applications II, San José, USA

Chen, H. & Miyojim, M. (1998). Automatic pavement distress detection system. Journal of Information Sciences, Vol., 108, (July 1998) pp. 219-240

Chou, J., O'Neill, W. & Cheng, H.D. (1994), Pavement distress classification using neural networks, IEEE International Conference on Systems, Man, and Cybernetics - "Humans, Information and Technology", pp. 397 – 401, October 1994

Duda, R., Hart, P. & Stork, D. (2001). Pattern Classification, John Wiley & Sons Ltd, ISBN: 0-471-70350-8, Canada

Duin, R., Juszczak, P., Paclik, P., Pekalska, P., Ridder, D. & Tax, D. (2004). PRTools 4 - A MatLab Toolbox for Pattern Recognition - version 4.0.23, http://www.prtools.org/, Netherlands

Figueiredo, M. (2004). Lecture Notes on Bayesian Estimation and Classification, http://www.lx.it.pt/~mtf/learning/, Portugal

Heijden, F., Van der, Dwin, R.P.W., Ridder, D. & Tax, D.M.J. (2004). Classification, Parameter Estimation and State Estimation: An Engineering Approach using Matlab, John Wiley & Sons Ltd, ISBN: 0-470-09013-8

Huang, Y. & Xu, B. (2006). Automatic inspection of pavement cracking distress, Journal of Electronic Imaging, Vol. 15, N.1, (Jan-Mar 2006), SPIE and IS&T

JAE. (1997). Catálogo de Degradações dos Pavimentos Rodoviários Flexíveis - 2ª Versão, Ex-Junta Autónoma das Estradas, Portugal

Li, L., Chan, P., Rao, A. & Lytton, R.L. (1991). Flexible pavement distress evaluation usin image analysis, in Proceedings of the Second International Conference on Applications of Advanced Technologies in Transportation Engineering, pp. 66-70, 18-21 August

Liu, F., G. Xu, Yang, Y., Niu, X. & Pan, Y. (2008). Novel approach to pavement cracking automatic detection based on segment extending, in International Symposium on Knowledge Acquisition and Modeling. KAM '08, pp. 610-614, 21-22 December

Ma, C., Zhao, C. & Hou, Y. (2008). Pavement distress detection based on nonsubsampled contourlet transform, in International Conference on Computer Science and Software Engineering, pp. 28-31, 12-14 December

Meignen, D., Bernadet, M. & Briand, H. (1997). One application of neural networks for detection of defects using video databases: identification of road distresses, Proceedings of 8th Int. Workshop on Database and Expert Systems Applications, pp. 459-464, 1-2 September 1997

Oliveira, H. & Correia, P.L. (2007). Automatic crack pavement detection using a Bayesian stochastic pattern recognition system, Proceedings of RECPAD2007, Portugal, October 2007, Lisbon

Oliveira, H. & Correia, P.L. (2008). Supervised strategies for crack detection in images of road pavement flexible surfaces, Proceedings of EUSIPCO2008, Switzerland, August 2008, Lausanne

Qingquan, L. & Xianglong, L. (2008). Novel approach to pavement image segmentation based on neighboring difference histogram method, in Congress on Image and Signal Processing CISP '08, pp. 792 - 796, Volume 2, 27-30 May 2008

Tax., D. (2006). Data Description Toolbox, http://ict.ewi.tudelft.nl/~davidt/dd_tools.html, Netherlands

Theodoridis, S. & Foutroumbas., K., (2003). Pattern Recognition - 3nd edition, Elsevier - Academic Press, ISBN: 0-123-69531-7, USA

Wang, K.C.P. (2000). Designs and implementations of automated systems for pavement surface distress survey, Journal of Infrastructure Systems, Vol. 6, N.1, (March 2000), ASCE, ISSN 1076-0342/00/0001-0024-0032

Webb, A. (2002). Statistical Pattern Recognition - 2nd edition, John Wiley & Sons, ISBN: 0-470-84514-7, England

Zhang, H. G. & Wang Q. (2004). Use of artificial living system for pavement distress survey, The 30th Annual Conference of IEEE Industrial Electronics Society, Korea, November 2004, Busan

11

Contact-free hand biometric system for real environments based on geometric features

Aythami Morales and Miguel A. Ferrer
Universidad de Las Palmas de Gran Canaria
Spain

1. Introduction

The Biometrics plays an increasingly important part in authentication and identification systems. The processes of biometric recognition allow the identification of individual based on the physical or behavioral characteristics. Various technologies were developed such as fingerprint, iris, face, voice, signature and hand. This last method is based on a study of hand shape and texture. It has many advantages compared to other technologies. Firstly, the capture device is less expensive than that for iris recognition, the hand characteristics are more numerous than those of fingerprints and they can be specified with low resolution images. Moreover, this system is well accepted by users (Jain et al., 2001).

Most of the existing hand involved techniques require pegs or contact-based image acquisition devices. This causes some increasing user acceptance issues and system reliability issues. In this paper we propose a contact-free biometric system based on the hand geometry.

A contact-free system is composed by a pc and a camera. The users put the hand in the free space in front of the camera. In these systems there are two main tasks to solve: the segmentation problems associated to a real environment and the projective distortions associated to the absence of contact plane.

Working with non controlled backgrounds and illumination conditions, the segmentation is not an obvious task. We propose the use of infrared illumination to solve the segmentation problem. The uses of templates guide the user to minimize the projective distortions.

So, in the next section we will review the hand based biometric technology, in order to locate our development in the biometric area. Afterwards we will describe our proposal: segmentation in section 3, the extraction of geometric features will be described in sections 4. Section 5 describes the verification scheme and Section 6 gives our experimental results. The paper is closed with conclusions and the references.

2. State of the art

Traditionally, hand geometry technology is based on analysis of the shape of a hand. The shape has been exclusively characterized by either its geometric sizes or the contour of the hand, or sometimes both. The geometric sizes include measurements of lengths and widths of the fingers, thickness of the fingers and palm, and widths of the palm, etc. A hand contour is formed either by the boundary of the entire hand or by the boundaries of the fingers. In recent research works, (Tantachun et al., 2006) represent a hand pattern by an eigenhand obtained from principle component analysis (PCA) or a mesh constructed from feature points. Accordingly, various techniques have been proposed to obtain and mathematically represent these hand features (Zheng et al., 2007).

Intuitively, geometric sizes of some particular regions of a hand should be used for the hand geometry biometrics. For that purpose, the regions being measured should be the same for each hand each time. This requires a hand to be placed on the exactly the same position on the measuring device. This is accomplished by some guiding pegs mounted on a flat surface of the imaging device. (Jain et al., 1999) developed such a hand geometry authentication system. Five pegs were used to guide the placement of a hand. Both top view and side view images of a hand were taken. Various geometric sizes, including widths, lengths, and thicknesses of fingers, as well as the widths of the palm at different positions were measured. With 16 geometric sizes of a hand, an equal error rate (EER) of 6% was reported. (Sanchez-Reillo et al., 2000) used six pegs in their hand geometry implementation. They measured 25 geometrical sizes of a hand, including widths of fingers and the palm, thicknesses, deviations of fingers, and angles created by the valley points. They obtained an EER less than 3%.

Although the guiding pegs provide consistent measuring positions, they cause some problems as well:

1) The pegs can deform the shape of a hand in which the performance of both size-based and contour-based hand geometry largely relies on. The deformation of hand shapes can increase the variation between hand images of the same hand, which results in false identification [7].

2) The pegs add more complexity to the device. Both the system supervisors and the users must be well trained to cooperate with the system. This increases the responsibility of the users; therefore degrading the reliability of the system.

3) The contact-based devices are becoming an issue due to hygiene and public-health concerns.

Therefore, size-based peg-free hand geometry techniques were under consideration. A typical peg-free hand geometry technique uses optical devices, such as an optical scanner, to capture the images of a hand. The removal of the pegs gives the hand, some motion freedom. To overcome the inconsistent positions of a hand due to the hand motion, the finger tip points and the finger valley points were commonly used as the landmark points for image alignment. (Wong & Shi, 2002) proposed a peg-free hand geometry authentication system using a flatbed optical scanner for hand image capturing. The hand sizes and shape of the fingertip regions were measured. They achieved a genuine acceptance rate of 88.9% and a false acceptance rate (FAR) of 2.2% with 30 hand features. (Bulatov et al.,2004) measured 30 geometric sizes on a hand image. Circles were fitted into different areas of fingers and the palm. The radiuses, perimeters, and areas of the circles, together with the lengths and widths of fingers, were measured. They achieved an FAR of 1% and a false rejection rate (FRR) of 3% for verification. (Boreki & Zimmer, 2005) and (Hashemi & Fatemizadeh, 2005) measured the lengths and widths of each individual finger as well. Boreki et al. profiled curvatures along the hand contour and found landmark points to separate each finger. An FAR of 0.8% and FRR of 3.8% were reported based on 360 images of 80 users. Heshemi and Fatemizadeh separated each finger from the palm using the distances from the hand contour to a fixed point. In other research efforts, researchers were trying to combine the geometric sizes with other recognition methods, such as palmprint (Wei et al., 2005), hand contour (Oden et al., 2003), or neural-network classifiers (Faundez, 2005) in order to improve system performance.

After trying to remove the effect of the guiding pegs, contact-free hand geometry techniques were also attempted by researchers. (Haeger, 2003) exhibited his work in a project presentation at University of South Florida. In this work, hand images were taken in a free space by a digital camera. The centroid of a segmented hand was detected. A number of concentric circles were drawn around the centroid passing through the fingers. Then different sizes of the fingers were measured by these circles. Using 124 geometric sizes of the fingers, they reached a 45.7% genuine matching rate and 8.6% false matching rate. The poor performance mainly resulted from the hand motions in a free space. Slight changes of viewpoint could tremendously ruin the hand shape.

Several other research works used different ways to create hand descriptors. (Garrison et al., 2001) developed a peg-free and contact-free hand-based authentication system. Hand images were taken using a digital camera from a distance. An eigenhand created by PCA was used as the identifier. But this method suffers from the viewpoint changing due to the perspective distortion on the hand shape. (Doi & Yamanaka, 2003) created a mesh on a hand image captured by an infrared CCD camera. The mesh was created by 20 to 30 feature points extracted from the principal creases of fingers and the palm. Root-mean-square (rms) deviation was used to measure the alignment distance between the meshes. This method is sensitive to the perspective distortion too. (Zheng et al., 2007) present an invariant hand features for contact-free hand biometric systems. An EER of 0% was reported on 52 hand images in a non real environment.

In previous works (Morales et al., 2008), we shows different prototypes based in contact-free hand biometric systems. Using laboratory databases the error rates obtained encourage us to continue the research. In this paper we present our experience working with contact-free systems in real environments.

3. Segmentation

We work with a video sequence and fast background segmentation is important. Usually there are two different video segmentation approaches, shot-based segmentation that uses a set of key-frames to represent a video shot and object-based segmentation that partitions a video shot into objects and background (Lijie & Guoliang, 2005). We use an object-based segmentation because the user hand is in close-up. The uses of direct illumination give the necessary contrast between hand and background. The segmentation problem is not obvious working in real environments.

We tried to use face detection techniques for solve the hand segmentation problem. The most common techniques are the skin based methods (Ruiz & Verschae, 2004). Skin detection is not robust enough for dealing with complex environments. Changing lighting conditions, and complex background containing surfaces and objects with skin-like colors are major problems, limiting its use in practical "real world" applications.

In a real application without controlled illumination and unknown background, the segmentation is not a trivial problem. In the beginning, the webcam was used with a lighting system composed for a standard bulb of 60W that emits in the visible light range. The system was placed at a vertical position and the right hand palm had to be placed at about 30 cm of the system, facing the web-cam.

After a study of the captured hands, it was observed that the system performance decreased in the following situations:

1) when direct light fell in the web-camera lens.
2) with a non uniform background.
3) when there was an object in close-up.
4) when there was a reflection object in the background.

The decreasing of the system performance was due to segmentation problems, being impossible to extract the hand from background. Therefore, the performance of the verification process was not enough good because for a correct verification a good segmentation is needed.

Before discard the skin segmentation techniques, we studied the infra-red illumination. With a correct illumination, the problem of segmentation can be solved. In the Fig. 1.a we can see an example of a captured image in a real non controlled environment. The background segmentation is a hard task with this kind of environment. In the Fig. 1.b we can see the problems to use the skin segmentation methods with two near skin objects. A solution to this problem was proposed. Use infra-red illumination. The visible light system was replaced for an infrared system.

To obtain an adequate image acquisition, the web-cam specifications have to be set in this way: maximum contrast and brightness with a low value to achieve a very high contrast between hand and background, low gain and exposure to enhance the close-up. The low exposure is important in order to eliminate the background. We can see an example in the Fig. 1.c. The Fig. 1.d shows the near skin objects example.

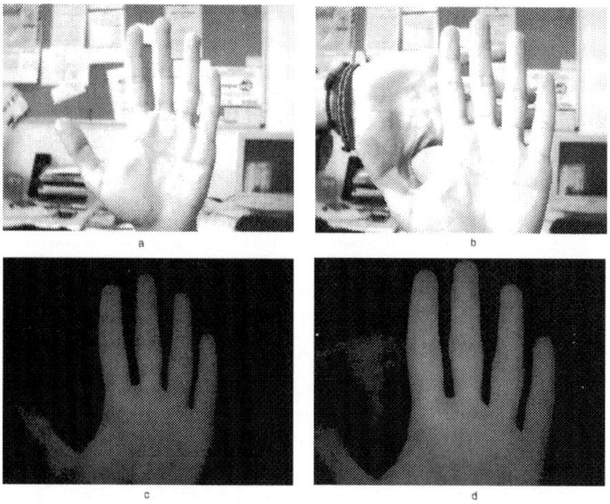

Fig. 1. a) Captured image in visible range; b) Near skin objects in visible range; c) Image a in infrared domain; d) Image b in infrared domain

This system is composed for a set of GaAs infrared emitting diode (CQY 99) with a peak wavelength emission of 925 nm and a spectral half bandwidth of 40 nm. The diodes were placed in an inverted U shape with the webcam in the middle. The number of diodes used is 16 and the current is 110 mA for each diode pair. The user can observe the correct positioning in a 12″ screen.

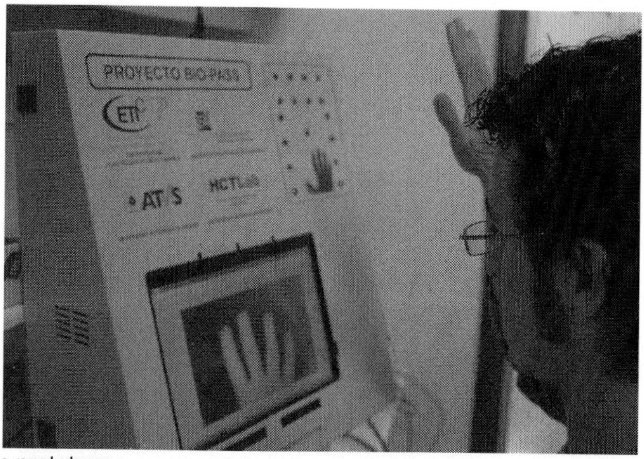

Fig. 2. System prototype

The web-cam was modified in order to adapt it to receive infrared emissions: the infrared filter was removed (normal in the commercial webcams) and two cascade filters were added. The added filters are Kodak No 87 FS4-518 and No 87c FS4-519 visible opaque infrared filters, with no transmittance between 400-700 nm.

The user in our system can place the hand palm freely in the 3D space in front of the camera. We do not use surface, the system is contact-free. We use a template for a correct positioning of the hands to reduce the projective distortions associated to the absence of contact plane, see Fig. 3.

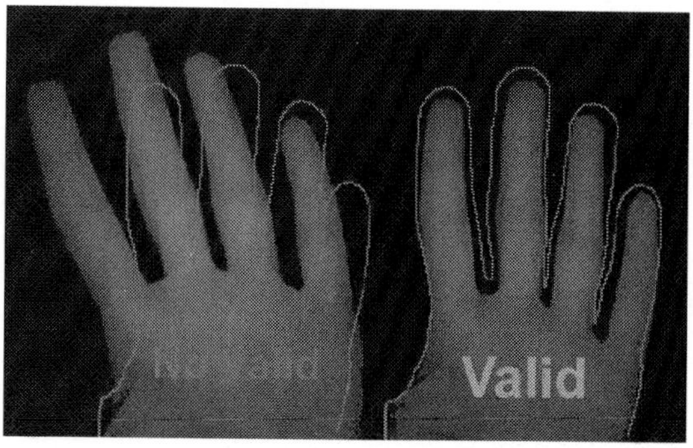

Fig. 3. Template and hand positioning

Once obtained the infrared image, the segmentation is simple. We use a low-pass filter to obtain the binary image from the gray scale IR image. This is a fast method in computational terms. The filter uses two-dimensional Hamming window to form an approximately circularly symmetric window using Huang's method. The cut frequencies are $\omega_1 = \pi$ all pass filter and $\omega_2 = 0.5\pi$ low-pass filter. This filter enhances the vertical lines to improve the contrast between hand and background.
The filtered image is normalized in amplitude and binarized by the Otsu's method. This method chooses the threshold to minimize the intraclass variance of the thresholded black and white pixels. Once we apply the binarization, we obtain hand image in white colour and background in black.
The last step is performing of a flood-fill operation on the binary image to fill small hand holes that can appear in the binarization phase.

4. Parameterization

The hand's contour is obtained from the black and white image. To work out the ends and valleys between the fingers we convert the Cartesian coordinates of the hand contour to polar coordinates (radius and angle) considering as coordinates origin the center of the hand base. The peaks of the radius locate the finger ends and the minimums of the radius indicate the valleys between fingers.
To obtain the exterior base of the index and little finger, we work out the slope of the line going from the index-heart fingers valley to the ring-little fingers valley (Ferrer et al., 2007). The exterior of the thumb is worked out as the intersection of the contour and the line going from the heart-ring fingers valley to the index-thumb fingers valley.
Once located the most important points of the hand, we can obtain the geometric features by means of measures. We use the geometrical features of the little, the index, middle and ring fingers, see Fig. 4. The reason for no uses the thumb finger is the great variance of the positioning in this finger.

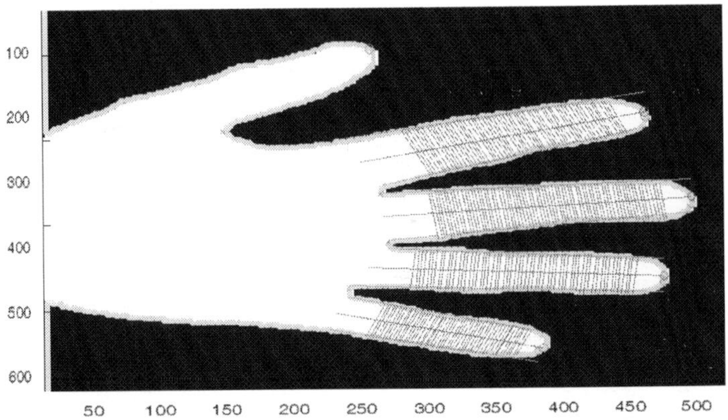

Fig. 4. Feature extraction

To obtain the geometric feature vector is immediate once the ends and valleys between fingers have been detected. Each finger is characterized as a triangle. The three vertexes of the triangle are the end and the two side valleys of the finger. We take approximately 60 wide measures to parameterize the little, the index, middle and ring fingers. We discard the first 20% of the finger to solve rings problems. Each hand is characterized by 240 measures vector.

The Fig. 5 shows ten parameter vectors for two different users, five acquisition for each user. The geometric features are normalized. We can observe the inter-class and intra-class variance.

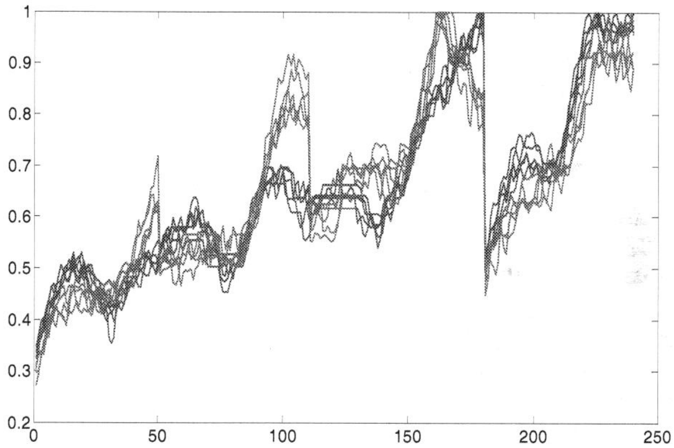

Fig. 5. Intra-class and inter-class variance example

In a contact-free system, the user can put the hand freely in a 3D space. To minimize the intra-class variance produced by the projective distortions we applied the DCT transform, equation 1.

$$DCT(u,v) = \frac{1}{\sqrt{2n}} C(u)C(v) \sum_{x=0}^{n-1} \sum_{y=0}^{n-1} f(x,y) \cos\left[\frac{(2x+1)u\pi}{2N}\right] \cdot \cdot \cos\left[\frac{(2y+1)v\pi}{2N}\right] \tag{1}$$

$$C(u), C(v) = \begin{cases} \frac{1}{\sqrt{2}} & u,v = 0 \\ 1 & rest \end{cases} \qquad u,v = 0,1,\ldots,N-1$$

Where *f(x,y)* is the array of N original values and *DCT(u,v)* are the DCT coefficients. We use the first 45 coefficients to characterize each hand. In Fig 6, we can observe the transformed vectors obtained from exaples showed in previous figures.

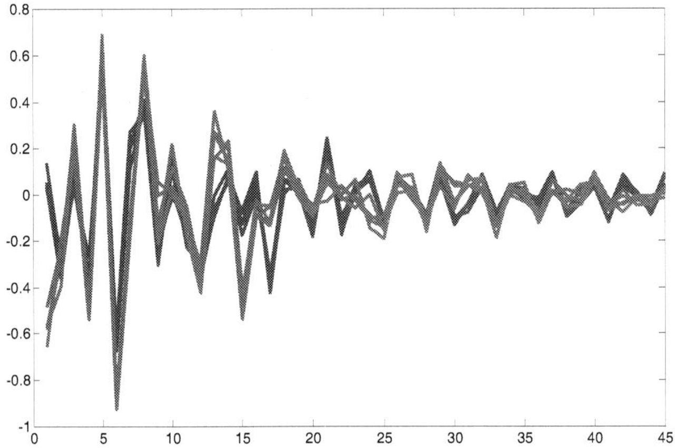

Fig. 6. DCT transform of geometric features

5. Verification

During four months, 102 people (70 genuine and 32 impostors) use the system. More than 900 unsupervised accesses were achieved. The total of the images have been taken from the user's right hand. Most of the users are within a selective age range from 21 to 33 years old. In the database, 63% of the users are males. The database was acquired in "Real World" conditions. No supervised and non controlled environments conditions.

The verification scheme depends on the feature vector. We have used a support vector machine (SVM) for classify the features. We have used for modeling the geometric hand features the technique of Support Vector Machines (SVM) because it generally provides better generalization performance. SVM learning machine seeks for an optimal separating hyperplane between classes. In order to achieve a good level of generalization performance, we maximize the margin between the separator hyperplane and the data.

The software used to train and test the model is the LS-SVM[24]. To verify that an input hand belongs to the identity claimed, we calculate the distance of the input hand features to the separator hyperplane of the SVM that model the hands of the identity claimed. If the distance is greater than a threshold, the identity is accepted.

6. Experiments

Four hands were used for train, the rest were used for test purpose. Fig.7 presents the False Acceptance Rate versus the False Rejection Rate. The Equal Error Rate is the point where the two error rates are equals.

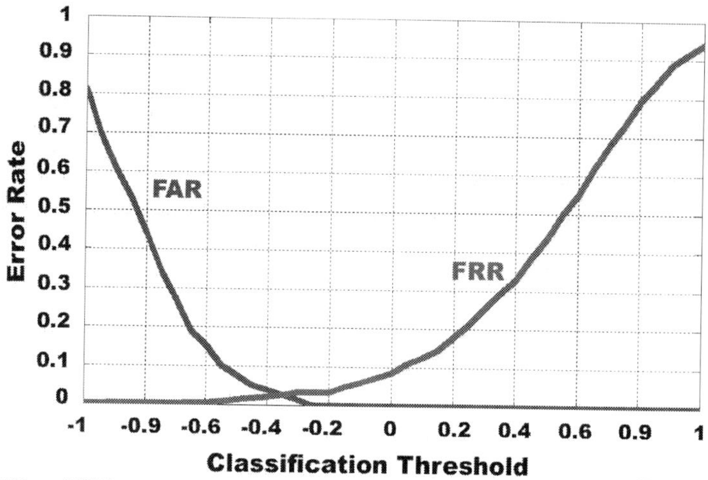

Fig. 7. FAR and FRR results

7. Conclusions

This chapter has presented a contact-free biometric identification system based on the geometrical hand features. A "real world" database, composed by 102 users and more than 4000 images was used. The results reports an EER of 3.2% encourage to us to follow the present research. With the segmentation problem solved, we should to improve the parameterization methods. Minimize the projective distortions associates to the contact-free biometric systems and elaborate a more extensive database will be the principal tasks.

8. References

Boreki, G. & A. Zimmer. (2005) Hand geometry: A new approach for feature extraction. *Proc. 4th IEEE Workshop on Automatic Identification Advanced Technologies*, Oct. 2005, pp. 149–154.

Bulatov, Y.; S. Jambawalikar, P. Kumar, & S. Sethia. (2004). Hand recognition using geometric classifiers. *Proc. 1st Int. Conf. Biometric Authentication,* Hong Kong, China, Jul. 2004, pp. 753-759.

Doi, J. & M. Yamanaka, (2003). Personal authentication using feature points on finger and palmer creases. *32nd Applied Imagery Pattern Recognition Workshop*, Washington, D.C., 2003.

Faundez, M. (2005). Biometric verification of humans by means of hand geometry. *Proc. 39th Annu. Int. Carnahan Conf. Security Technology*, 2005, pp. 61–67.

Ferrer, M.A.; Morales, A.; Travieso, C.M.; Alonso, J.B. (2007). Low Cost Multimodal Biometric identification System Based on Hand Geometry, Palm and Finger Print Texture. *Security Technology, 2007 41st Annual IEEE International Carnahan Conference.* 8-11 Oct. 2007 Page(s):52 - 58.

Garrison, K.; A. Sorin; Z. Liu & S. Sarkar. (2001). Hand Biometrics From Image at a Distance Dept. *Compu. Sci. Eng.*, Univ. South Florida, Tampa, Tech. Rep.: USF-Nov-2001-Palm.

Haeger, S. (2003) .Feature Based Palm Recognition, *Univ. South Florida*. Tampa, FL, Dec. 2003.

Hashemi, J. & E. Fatemizadeh, (2005). Biometric identification through hand geometry. *Proc. Int. Conf. Comput. Tool*, 2005, vol. 2, pp. 1011–1014.

Jain, A. K.; Ross, & S. Pankanti. (1999). A prototype hand geometry-based verification system. *Proc. 2nd Int. Conf. Audio- and Video-Based Biometric Person Authentication*, Mar. 1999, pp. 166–171.

Jain A. K.; R. Bolle, & S. Pankanti. (2001). *Biometrics: Personal Identification in Networked Society*, Kluwer Academic Publishers.

Morales A.; Ferrer M. A.; Díaz F. D.; Alonso J. B. & Travieso C. M. (2008). Contact-free hand biometric system for real environments. *16th Euopean Signal Processing Conference (EUSIPCO 2008)*, 4 pages, Laussane, September 2008.

Lijie Liu & Guoliang Fan. (2005). Combined key-frame extraction and object-based video segmentation. *Circuits and Systems for Video Technology*, IEEE Transactions on, Volume 15, Issue 7, July 2005 Page(s):869 – 884.

Tantachun, S.; Pintavirooj, C.; Lertprasart, P.; Bunluechokchai, S. (2006). Biometrics with Eigen-Hand. *Industrial Electronics and Applications 2006 1ST IEEE Conference* on 24-26 May 2006 Page(s):1 – 4.

Oden C.; A. Ercil, & B. Buke, (2003). Combining implicit polynomials and geometric features for hand recognition, *Pattern Recognit. Letter.*, 2003, vol. 24, no. 13, pp. 2145–2152.

Ruiz del Solar, J. and Verschae, R. (2004). Skin detection using neighbourhood information. *Automatic Face and Gesture Recognition 2004 Proceedings*. Sixth IEEE International Conference on 17-19 May 2004 Page(s):463 – 468.

Sanchez-Reillo, R.; C. Sanchez-Avila, and A. Gonzalez-Marcos, (2000). Biometric identification through hand geometry measurements. *IEEE Trans. Pattern Analysis*. March. Intell., vol. 22, no. 10, pp. 1168–1171, Oct. 2000.

Suykens J.A.K. and Vandewalle J. (1999) Least squares support vector machine classifiers. *Neural Processing Letters*, vol. 9, no. 3, Jun. 1999, pp. 293-300.

Wei, X.; D. Xu, & C. Ngo. (2005). Multibiometrics based on palmprint and hand geometry. *Proc. 4th Annu. Int. Conf. Computer Information Science*, 2005, pp. 495–500.

Wong, A. & P. Shi. (2002). Peg-free hand geometry recognition using hierarchical geometry and shape matching. *Proc. IAPRWorkshop on Machine Vision Applications*, Nara, Japan, Dec. 2002, pp. 281–284.

Zheng, G.; Wang, C.-J.; Boult, T. E. (2007) Application of Projective Invariants in Hand Geometry Biometrics. *Information Forensics and Security, IEEE Transactions* on Volume 2, Issue 4, Dec. 2007 Page(s):758 – 768.

12

Gaze prediction improvement by adding a face feature to a saliency model

MARAT Sophie, GUYADER Nathalie and PELLERIN Denis
Gipsa-Lab
France

1. Introduction

To understand how human observers move their eyes when viewing videos and why some locations are more often gazed at than others is of great importance for much research. Many computational models compute a *saliency map* that attributes high values to the locations that predict where humans should direct their gaze when viewing the stimulus freely. To compute saliency maps, models are generally based on low-level properties of the visual stimulus. These bottom-up models, like the human visual system, break down the visual stimulus into elementary feature maps: a colour map, spatial frequency maps, orientation maps and a motion map (motion feature is often processed separately from other static features). Hence, the visual stimulus is split into a static saliency map, a dynamic saliency map (Marat et al., 2009), and some models add a colour saliency map (Itti et al., 1998; Le Meur et al. 2006). These maps are then added together to create the master saliency map of the visual stimuli. In the research cited, models only used low-level properties of the visual stimuli, although the role of high-level (e.g. semantic information) properties is undisputed. We know, for example, that live subjects and objects play a significant role in the visual perception of static stimulus.

In this research, we focus our interest on human faces. In a recent paper, Cerf, Harel, Einhäuser and Koch (Cerf et al., 2007) showed that in images containing frontal shots of people, faces were fixated on by subjects within the first saccades and this was true independently of the task subjects were asked to complete. For this reason, they integrated into their static saliency model a special "face-detection" channel (using the Viola and Jones algorithm (Viola & Jones, 2004)). They found that this additional channel improved the performance of their static saliency model.

In this research, we show that faces are very salient even in natural dynamic stimuli. We found that when asking subjects to look at videos faces were fixated on within the first saccades as was the case for static images. We also show that to add a face saliency map to a classical saliency model, using only static and dynamic features, improves eye movement predictions. In fact, even if faces are emphasized with a static saliency map, eyes or the mouth, and with a dynamic saliency map, moving faces, adding a face saliency map considerably improves model prediction. Moreover, model predictions are improved by computing a face saliency map inversely proportional to the number of faces in the scene.

We also proposed a fusion that takes into account the special feature of each saliency map: static, dynamic and face features.
Section 2 describes the eye movement experiment. The static and dynamic pathways are presented in section 3. Section 4 tests whether faces are salient in dynamic stimuli and section 5 deals with the choice of a face detector. Section 6 describes the face pathway, and finally, the fusion of the different saliency maps and the evaluation of the model are presented in section 7.

2. Eye movement experiment

Our purpose is to analyse whether faces influence human gaze and to understand how this influence occurs. The video database was built in order to obtain videos with various contents, with and without faces, with textured backgrounds, with moving and static objects, with a moving camera etc. We were only interested in the first eye movements of subjects when viewing videos. In fact, we know that after a certain time (quite short) it is much more difficult to predict eye movements without taking into account top-down processes. In order to remove top-down effects as much as possible, we did not use classical videos. Instead, we created small concatenated clips as was done in (Carmi & Itti, 2006). We put small parts of videos together with unrelated semantic contents. In this way, we minimized potential top-down confounds without sacrificing real world relevance.

2.1.1 Participants

Fifteen human observers (3 women and 12 men, aged from 23 to 40 years old) participated in the experiment. They had normal or corrected to normal vision and were not aware of the purpose of the experiment. They were asked to look at the videos freely.

2.1.2 Apparatus

Eye tracking was performed by an Eyelink II eye tracker (SR Research[1]). During the experiment, participants were sitting, with their chin supported, in front of a 21" colour monitor (75 Hz refresh rate) at a viewing distance of 57 cm (40°x 30° usable field of view). A 9-point calibration was carried out every five trials and a corrected-drift was done before each trial.

2.1.3 Stimuli

The stimuli were inspired by an experiment proposed in (Carmi & Itti, 2006). Fifty-three videos (25 frames per seconds, 720 x 576 pixels per frame) were selected from heterogeneous sources including movies, TV shows, TV news, animated movies, commercials, sport and music clips. The fifty-three videos were cut every 1-3 seconds (1.86 ± 0.61) into *305 clip-snippets*. The length of these clip-snippets was chosen randomly with the only constraint being to obtain snippets without any shot cut. These clip-snippets were strung together to make up *twenty clips* of 30 seconds (30.20 ± 0.81). Each clip contained at most one clip-snippet from each of the fifty-three continuous sources. The choice of the clip-snippets and their duration were random to prevent subjects from anticipating shot cuts. We used grey

[1] http://www.eyelinkinfo.com/

level stimuli (14155 frames) without audio signal because the model did not consider colour and audio information. Stimuli were seen in random order.

2.1.4 Human eye position density maps

The eye tracker records eye positions at 500 Hz. We recorded twenty eye positions (10 positions for each eye) per frame and per subject. The median of these positions (X-axis median and Y-axis median) was taken for each frame and for each subject. Then, for each frame, we had fifteen positions (one per subject). Because the final aim was to compare these positions to a saliency map, a two-dimensional Gaussian was added to each position. The standard deviation at mid-height of the Gaussian was equal to 0.5° of visual angle, which is close to the size of the maximum resolution of the fovea. Therefore, for each frame k, we got a human eye position density map $M_h(x,y,k)$.

2.1.5 Metric used for model evaluation

We used the Normalized Scanpath Saliency (NSS) (Peters & Itti, 2008). This criterion was especially designed to compare eye fixations and the salient locations emphasized by a model saliency map. We computed the *NSS* metric as follows (1):

$$NSS(k) = \frac{\overline{M_h(x,y,k) \times M_m(x,y,k)} - \overline{M_m(x,y,k)}}{\sigma_{M_m(x,y,k)}} \tag{1}$$

where $M_h(x,y,k)$ is the human eye position density map normalized to unit mean and $M_m(x,y,k)$ a model saliency map for a frame k. The *NSS* is null if there is no link between eye position and salient regions. The *NSS* is negative if eye position tends to be in non-salient regions. The *NSS* is positive if eye position tends to be in salient regions. To summarize, a saliency map is a good predictor of human eye fixations if the corresponding *NSS* value is positive and high. In the next sections, we computed the *NSS* average over several frames.

3. The static and the dynamic pathways of the saliency model

We based ourselves on the biology of the human visual system to propose a saliency model that decomposes the visual signal into a static and a dynamic saliency maps. The static and the dynamic pathways, described in detail in (Marat et al., 2008; Marat et al., 2009), were built in two common stages: a retina-like filter and a cortical-like bank of filters.

3.1 The retina and the visual cortex models

The retina model proposed split visual stimuli into different frequency bands: the high spatial frequencies simulate a "Parvocellular-like" output and the low spatial frequencies simulate a "Magnocellular-like" output. These outputs correspond to the two main outputs of the retina with a parvocellular output that conveys detailed information and a magnocellular output that responds rapidly and conveys global information about the visual scene.

V1 cortical complex cells are modelled using a bank of Gabor filters, into six different orientations and four frequency bands in the Fourier domain. The energy output of each filter corresponds to an intermediate map, m_{ij}, which is the equivalent of an elementary feature of Treisman's Theory (Treisman & Gelade, 1980).

3.2 The static pathway

The static pathway is dedicated to the extraction of the static features of the visual stimulus. This pathway corresponds to the ventral pathway of the human visual system and processes detailed visual information. It starts with the parvocellular output of the retina and is then, processed by the bank of Gabor filters. Two types of interactions between filter outputs were implemented: short interactions reinforce objects belonging to a specific orientation and long interactions allow contour facilitation.
After the interactions and after being normalized between [0,1], each map m_{ij} was multiplied by $(\max(m_{ij})-\overline{m_{ij}})^2$ where $\max(m_{ij})$ is the maximum value and $\overline{m_{ij}}$ is the average of the elementary feature map m_{ij} (Itti et al., 1998). Then, for each map, values smaller than 20% of the maximum value $max(m_{ij})$ were set to 0. Finally, the intermediate maps were added together to obtain a static saliency map $M_s(x,y,k)$ for each frame *k* (Fig. 1).

3.3 The dynamic pathway

The dynamic pathway, which is equivalent to the dorsal pathway of the human visual system, is fast and carries global information. Because we assumed that human gaze is attracted by motion contrast (the motion of a region against the background), we applied a background motion compensation (2D motion estimation, Odobez & Bouthemy, 1995) before the retina process. This allowed us to estimate the relative motion of regions against the background. The compensated frames were filtered by the retina model described above to form the "Magnocellular-like" output. Because this output only contains low spatial frequencies, its information would be processed by the Gabor filters with the three lowest frequency bands. For each frame, the classical optical flow constraint was applied to the Gabor filter outputs in the same frequency band. The solution of this flow constraint defined a motion vector per pixel of a frame. Then we computed for each pixel the motion vector module, corresponding to the speed, and its angle, corresponding to the motion direction. Hence, the motion saliency of a region is proportional to its speed against the background. Then, a temporal median filter was applied to remove possible noise (if a pixel had a motion in one frame but not in the previous ones). The filter was applied to five successive frames (the current frame and the four previous ones) and it was reinitialised after each shot cut. A dynamic saliency map $M_d(x,y,k)$ was obtained for each frame *k* (Fig. 1).

(a) (b) (c)

Fig. 1. Static and dynamic saliency maps: (a) Input video frame, (b) Static saliency map M_s and (c) Dynamic saliency map M_d..

4. Face an important feature

Faces are one of the most important visual cues for communication. A lot of research has examined the complex issue of face perception (Kanwisher & Yovel, 2006; Thorpe, 2002; Palermo & Rhodes, 2007; Tsao & Livingstone, 2008; Goto & Tobimatsu, 2005), for a complete review see (Dekowska et al., 2008). In this research, we just wanted to test whether faces were gazed at during free viewing of dynamic scenes. Hence, to test if a face is an important feature in the prediction of human eye movements, we hand-labelled the frames of the videos used in the experiment described in section 2 with the position and the size of faces. We manually created a face saliency map by adding a two dimensional Gaussian to the top of each marked face: we called this saliency map the "true" face saliency map (Fig. 3). We call "face" any kind of face (frontal or profile) as long as the face is big enough for the eyes (at least one) and the mouth to be distinguished. Because it takes times to hand label all the frames and because we wanted to test the influence of faces we only used a small part of the whole database and we chose frames with at least one face (472 frames). Then, we computed the mean NSS over these 472 frames between the human eye position density maps and the different saliency model: the static saliency map, the dynamic saliency map and the "true" face saliency map (Fig. 2). As noted above a saliency map is a good predictor of human eye fixations if the corresponding *NSS* value is positive and high.

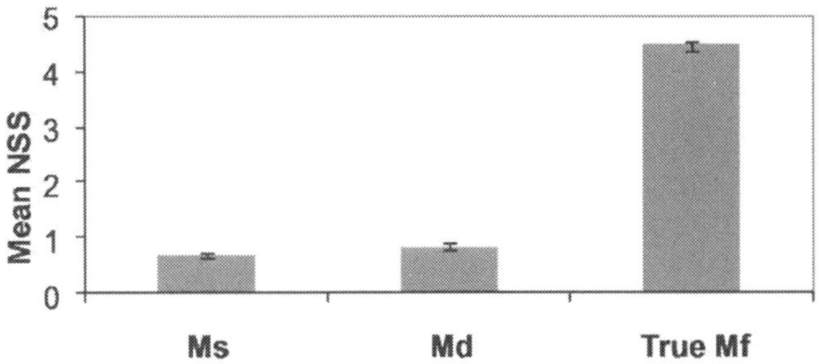

Fig. 2. Mean *NSS* values for the different saliency map: the static M_s, the dynamic M_d and the "true" face saliency map M_f.

As we can see on figure 2 the mean NSS value for the true face saliency map is higher than for the mean NSS for the static and the dynamic saliency maps (F(2,1413)=1009.81; p#0). The large difference is due to the fact that we only study frames with at least one face.

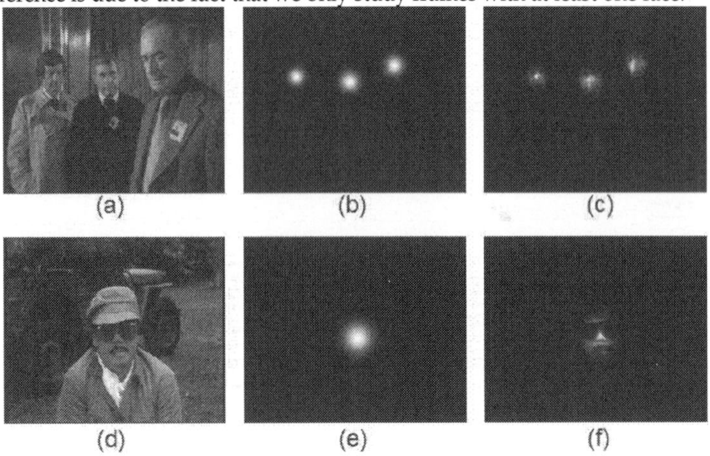

Fig. 3. Examples of the "true" face saliency maps obtained with the hand-labelled faces: (a) and (d) Input video frames, (b) and (e) Corresponding "true" face saliency maps M_f, (c) and (f) Superposition of the input frame and the "true" face saliency map.

We experimentally found that faces attract human gazes and hence computing saliency models that highlight faces improves the predictions of a more traditional saliency model considerably. We still want to answer different questions. Is a face on its own inside a scene more or less salient than a face with other faces? Is a large face more salient than a small one? To answer these questions we chose some clips according to the number of faces and according to the size of faces.

4.1 Impact of the number of faces

To see the influence of the number of faces, we split the database according to the number of faces inside the frames: three clip-snippets (121 frames) with only one face and three others (134 frames) with more than one face. We computed the *NSS* value for each frame using the "true" face saliency map and the subject's eye position density maps. Figure 4 presents the mean *NSS* value for the frames with only one face and for the frames with more than one face. A high NSS value means a good correspondence between human eye position density maps and "true" face saliency maps.

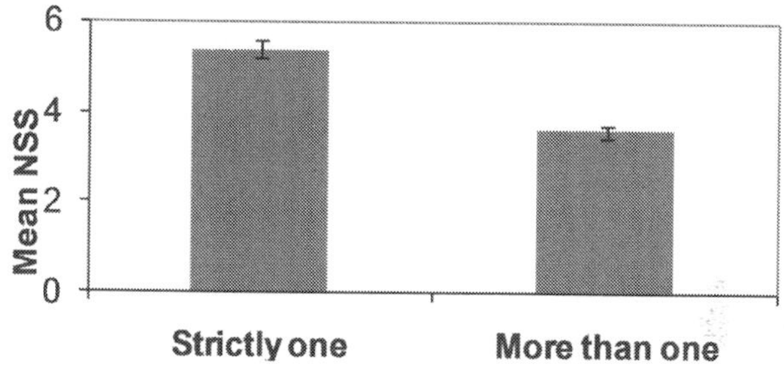

Fig. 4. Mean NSS values for the "true" face saliency maps compared with human eye positions as a function of the number of faces in frames: for frames with strictly one face (121) and for frames with more than one faces (134).

The *NSS* value is higher when there is only one face than when there are more than one face (F(1,253) =52.25; p#0). There is a better correspondence between the saliency map and eye positions. This could be predicted by the fact that if there is only one face, all the subjects would gaze at this single face whereas if there are several faces on the same frame some subjects would gaze at a particular face and other subjects would gaze at another face. Hence, a frame with only one face is more salient than a frame with more than one face, in the sense that it is easier to predict subjects' eye positions. To take this result into account, we chose to compute the face saliency map using an inversely proportional coefficient to the number of faces. That means that if there is only one face on a frame the corresponding saliency map would have higher values than the saliency map of a frame with more than one face.

An example of the eye position on a frame with three faces is presented in figure 5. Subjects' gazes are more spread out over the frame with three faces than over the frames with only one face.

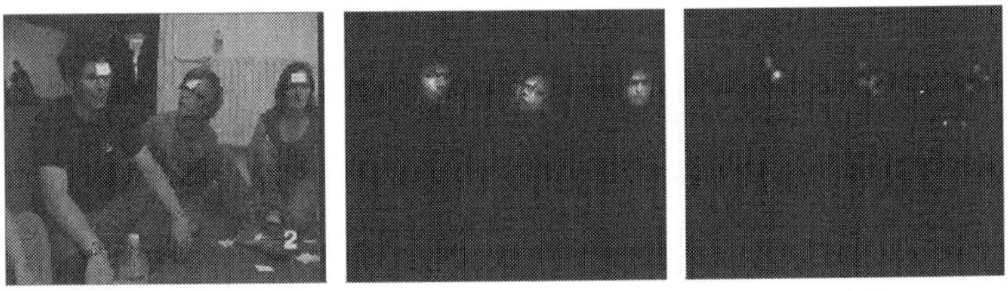

(a) (b) (c)

Fig. 5. Examples of eye positions on a frame with three faces: (a) Input video frame, (b) Superimposition of the input frame and the "true" face saliency map and (c) Eye positions of the fifteen subjects.

As we can see in figure 5 (c) subjects gazed at the different faces. To test how much subjects gazed at different positions in a frames we computed a criterion to measure the dispersion of eye positions between subjects using the equation (2):

$$D = \frac{1}{N^2} \sum_{i,j<i} d_{i,j}^2 \tag{2}$$

where N is the number of subjects and $d_{i,j}$ is the distance between the eye positions of subjects i and j. Table 1 presents the mean dispersion value for frames with strictly one face and for frames with more than one face.

Number of faces	**Strictly one**	**More than one**
Mean dispersion	1 252.3	7 279.9

Table 1. Mean dispersion values of eye positions between subjects on frames as a function of the number of faces: strictly one and more than one.

As expected, the dispersion is significantly higher for frames with more than one face, than for frames with only one face ($F(1,253)=269.7$; p#0). This is consistent with a higher NSS for frames with only one face than more than one.

4.2 Impact of face size

The previous observations are made for faces with almost the same size (See Fig. 5). But what happen if there is one big face and two small ones? It is difficult to understand exactly how size influences eye movements as many configurations can occur: for example, if there are two faces, one may be large and the other may be small, or the two faces may be large or small, one may be in the foreground etc. Hence it is difficult to understand exactly what happens for eye movements. Let us consider clips with only one face. These clips are then split according to the size of the face: three clip snippets with only one small face (141 frames), three with a medium face (107 frames) and three with a large face (90 frames). The diameter of the small face is around 30 pixels, the diameter of the medium face is around 50 pixels and the diameter of the large face is around 80 pixels. The mean *NSS* value was computed for the frames with a small, a medium and a large face (Fig. 6).

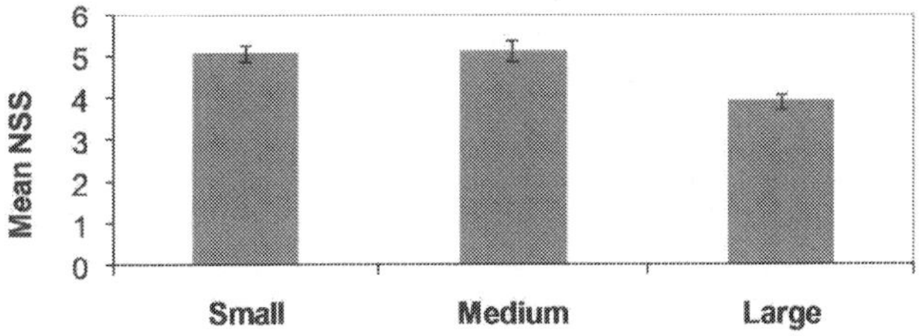

Fig. 6. Mean *NSS* value for "true" face saliency maps compared with human eye positions for frames of nine clip snippets as a function of face size.

Large faces give significantly lower results than small or medium faces (F(1,336)=18.25; p=0.00002). The difference between small and medium faces is not significant (F(1,246)=0.04; p=0.84). This could be expected in fact: when a face is small, all subjects will gaze at the same position, that is, the small face, and if the face is large, then some subjects will gaze at the eyes, other will gaze at the mouth etc. To verify this, we computed the mean dispersion of subject eye positions for the frames with small, medium or large faces in Table 2.

Face size	Small	Medium	Large
Mean dispersion	2 927.6	1 418.4	904.24

Table 2. Mean dispersion values of eye positions between subjects on frames as a function of face size.

The dispersion of eye positions is significantly higher for small faces (F(2,335)=28.44; p#0). The dispersion of eye positions for frames with medium faces is not significantly different from the frames with large faces (F(1,195)=2.89; p=0.09). These results are apparently in contradiction with the mean NSS values found. Hence, two main questions arise: (1) why do frames with one small face lead to a higher dispersion than frames with a larger face? And (2) why do frames that lead to more spread out eye positions give a higher NSS?
Most of the time, when a small face is on a frame it is because the character is filmed in a wide view; the frame shows the whole character and the scene behind him which may be complex. If the character moves his hand, or if there is something interesting in the foreground, some subjects will tend to gaze at the moving or the interesting thing after viewing the face of the character. On the other hand, if a large face is on a frame, this corresponds to a close-up view of the character being filmed. Hence, there is little information outside the character 's face and hence, subjects will tend to keep their focus on the only interesting area: the face, and access in more detail the different parts of the face.
A small face could lead to a high dispersion value if some subjects gaze at other areas after having gazed at the face, and a large face could lead to a low dispersion value as subject gazes tend to be spread over the face area. This is illustrated in figure 7, where eye positions were shown for a large face and for a small one. In this example a subject gazed at the device at the bottom of the frame, increasing the dispersion of eye positions. This is why we observed a high dispersion value of eye positions even for frames with a high NSS value (example of frames with a small face). A small face with few eye positions outside of the

face, will lead to a high dispersion, but can thus have a higher NSS than a large face with more eye positions on the face, so lower dispersion. Hence, the NSS tends to reward fixations that are less due to chance more strongly: as the salient region for a small face is small, the eye positions that are in this region will be more strongly rewarded than the ones on a larger face.

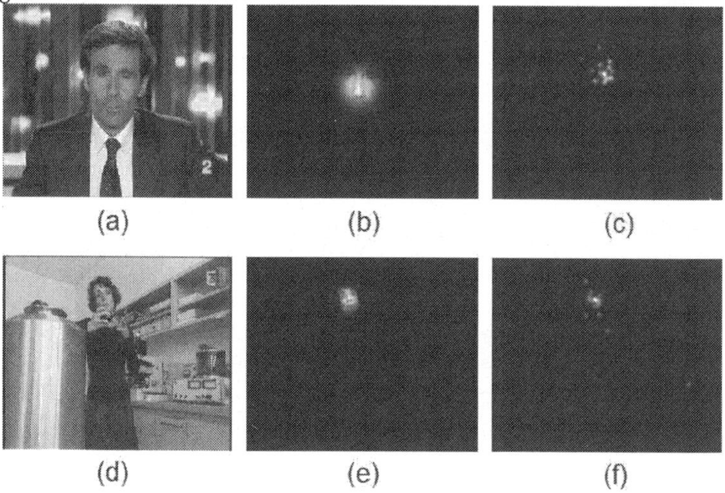

Fig. 7. Examples of eye positions on frames with a face of different sizes: (a) and (d) Input video frames, (b) and (e) Superimposition of the input frame and the face saliency map and (c) and (f) Eye positions of the fifteen subjects corresponding to the input frame.

Considering the case of only one face, face size influences eye positions. If more than one face is present, too many configurations can occur, and so, it is much more difficult to generalize the size effect. That is why for this study, the size information was not integrated to build the face saliency map from the face detector output.

5. Face detection algorithms

Various methods have been proposed to detect faces in images (Yang et al., 2002). We tested three algorithms available on the web: the one proposed by Viola[2] and Jones (Viola & Jones, 2004), the one proposed by Rowley[3] (Rowley et al., 1998) and the one proposed by Nilsson[4] (Nilsson et al., 2007) which is called the Split-up SNoW face detector. In our study, the stimuli are different from classical databases used to evaluate algorithm performance for face detection. We chose stimuli which were very different from one to another, and most faces are presented with various and textured backgrounds. The different algorithms were

2 Viola & Jones - http://sourceforge.net/projects/openlibrary/

3 Rowley - http://vasc.ri.cmu.edu/NNFaceDetector/

4 Nilsson - http://www.mathworks.com/matlabcentral/fileexchange/loadFile.do?objectId=13701&objectType=FILE

compared on one of the twenty clips presented to subjects (Table 3). This clip was hand-labelled: 429 faces were marked.

Algorithms	Number of correct detections	Number of false positives
Viola & Jones, 2004	146 (34%)	77
Rowley et al., 1998	87 (20.3%)	25
Nilsson et al., 2007 Split-up SNoW[5]	97 (22.6%)	6

Table 3. Three face detection algorithms: number of correct detections (also called true positives) and false positives for one clip (745 frames with 429 faces present).

Because the videos chosen are different from traditional stimuli used to evaluate face detection algorithm, the three algorithms detected less than half the faces. During the snippets, characters are moving, can turn to profile view, can sometimes be occluded or can have tilted faces. Faces can also be blurred as the characters move fast. All these cases complicate the task of the face detection algorithms. The Viola and Jones algorithm has the highest correct detection rate but also the highest false positive rate. Most of the time, false positives are on textured regions. Because we wanted to create a face saliency map that emphasizes only areas with a face, and we wanted to prevent the highlighting of false positives, we chose to use the split-up SNoW face detector which has the lowest false positive rate.

5.1 The split-up SNoW face detector

SNoW (Sparse Network of Winnows) is a learning architecture framework designed to learn a large number of features. It can be used for a more general purpose as a multi-class classifier. SNoW has been used successfully in several applications in the natural language and visual processing domains.
If a face is detected, the algorithm returns the position and the size of a squared bounding box containing the face detected. The algorithm detects faces with frontal views, even partially occluded faces (i.e. faces with glasses) and slightly tilted faces, but it cannot retrieve faces which are too occluded or profile views. We tested the efficiency of the SNoW face detector algorithm on the whole database (14155 frames). As it takes time and it is fastidious to hand-label all the faces for all the frames, we counted the number of frames that contained at least one face and we found 6623 frames. The split-up SNoW face detector gave 1566 frames with at least a correct detection and only 147 false positives. As already said, the number of correct detections is quite low but, what is more important for our purpose is that the number of false positive is very low. Hence, using this face detection algorithm ensures that we will only emphasize areas with a very high probability of containing a face. Examples of results for the split-up SNoW face detector are given in figure 8.

[5] Results are given setting the parameter *sens* to 9 in the Matlab program.

Fig. 8. Examples of correct detections (true positives) (marked with a white box) and missed detections (false negatives) for the split-up SNoW face detector.

6. Saliency model: The face pathway

The face detection algorithm output needs to be converted into a saliency map. The algorithm returns the position and the size of a squared bounding box containing the face detected. How can this information be translated into a face saliency map? The face detector gives a binary result: A pixel is equal to 1 if it is part of a face (the corresponding bounding box) and 0 otherwise. In the few papers that dealt with face saliency maps, the bounding boxes used to mark the face detected are replaced by a two-dimensional Gaussian. This induced the centre of a face to be more salient than its border. For example, in (Cerf et al., 2007) the "face conspicuity map" is normalized to a fixed range, in (Ma et al., 2005) the face saliency map values are weighted by the position of the face, enhancing faces in the centre of the frame.

As the final aim of our model is to provide a master saliency map by computing the fusion of the three saliency maps, face M_f, static M_s and dynamic M_d, the face saliency map was normalized to give values in the same range as static and dynamic saliency map values. As stated above, the face saliency map is intrinsically different from the static and the dynamic saliency maps. On one hand, the face detection algorithm returns binary information: presence or absence of face. On the other hand, static or dynamic saliency maps are weighted "by nature": more or less textured for the static saliency map and more or less rapid for moving areas of the dynamic saliency map. The face saliency map was built by replacing the bounding box of the algorithm output by a two-dimensional Gaussian. To be in the same range as the static and the dynamic saliency maps, the maximum value of the two-dimensional Gaussian was set to 5. Moreover, as stated above, a frame with only one face is more salient than a frame with more than one face. To lessen the face saliency map when more than one face is detected, the maximum of the Gaussian (after been multiplied by five) was divided by $N^{1/3}$ where N is the number of faces detected on the frame. To sum up, the Gaussian that replaced the bounding box that marked a detected face was set to $\frac{5}{N^{1/3}}$. We used the cube root of N to attenuate the effect of a high N value.

7. Evaluation

7.1. Fusions

Static, dynamic and face saliency maps do not have the same appearance. On one hand, the static saliency map exhibits a large number of salient areas, corresponding to textured areas that are spread over the whole image. On the other hand, the dynamic saliency map can exhibit only small and compact areas corresponding to moving objects. Finally, the face saliency map can be null when no face is detected.

A previous study detailed the analysis of the static and the dynamic pathways (Marat et al., 2009). This study showed that a frame with a high maximum static saliency map value is more salient than a frame with a lower maximum static saliency map value. Moreover, a frame with high skewness of the dynamic saliency map is more salient than a frame with a lower skewness value of the dynamic saliency map. A high skewness value corresponds to a frame with only one compact moving area. To add the static saliency map multiplied by its maximum to the dynamic saliency map multiplied by its skewness creating the master saliency map provides better eye movement prediction than a simple sum. The face saliency map was designed to reduce the maximum saliency value with the number of faces detected. Hence, this maximum is characteristic for the face pathway. The fusion proposed considers the particular features of each saliency map by weighting the raw saliency maps by their relevant parameters (maximum or skewness) and provides better results. The weighted saliency maps are defined as:

$$M_{s'} = \max(M_s) \times M_s \tag{3}$$

$$M_{d'} = skewness(M_d) \times M_d \tag{4}$$

$$M_{f'} = \max(M_f) \times M_f \tag{5}$$

To study the importance of the face pathway, we computed two different master saliency maps: one using only the static and the dynamic maps (6) and another using the three maps (7).

$$M_{sd} = M_{s'} + M_{d'} \tag{6}$$

$$M_{sdf} = M_{s'} + M_{d'} + M_{f'} \tag{7}$$

Note that if the face saliency map is null for a frame the master saliency map would depend only on the static and the dynamic saliency maps. Moreover, to strengthen regions that are salient in two different maps (static and dynamic, static and face or dynamic and face), a more elaborate fusion, called "reinforced" fusion (M_{Rsdf}), was proposed (8):

$$M_{Rsdf} = M_{s'} + M_{d'} + M_{f'} + M_{s'} \times M_{d'} + M_{s'} \times M_{f'} + M_{d'} \times M_{f'} \tag{8}$$

This fusion reinforces the weighted fusion M_{sdf} by adding multiplicative terms. We chose multiplicative terms with only two maps because if we chose a multiplicative term with the three maps when the face saliency map is null the multiplicative term would be null. If the face saliency map is null the "reinforced" fusion takes advantage of the static and the dynamic maps. In that case, the face saliency map does not improve the result but it does not penalize the result either. Examples of these fusions integrating the face pathway are proposed in figure 9. In figure 9 (a), the face on the right of the frame is moving, whereas the two faces on the left are not moving. In figure 9 (b) the three faces are almost equally salient, but in figure 9 (c) the multiplicative reinforcement terms increase the saliency of the moving face on the right of the frame.

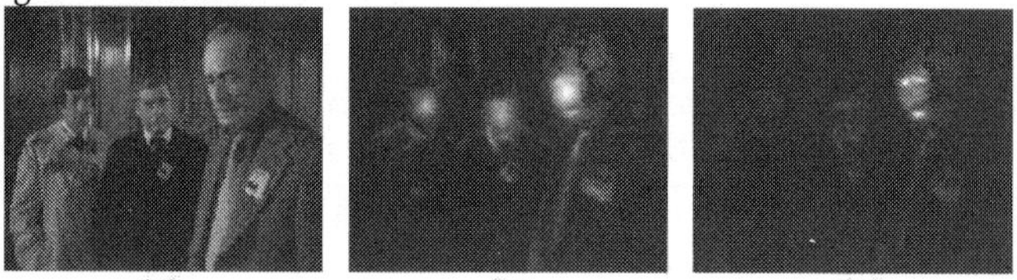

(a) (b) (c)

Fig. 9. Example of master saliency maps: (a) Input video frame, (b) Corresponding master saliency map computed using a weighted fusion of the three pathways M_{sdf}, (c) Corresponding master saliency map using the "reinforced" fusion of the three pathways M_{Rsdf}.

7.2. Evaluation of different saliency maps

The first evaluation was done on the database of "true" face saliency maps which were hand-labelled. Each saliency map was weighted as explained in section 6.1. The results are presented in Table 4.

Saliency maps	M_s	M_d	M_f	M_{sd}	M_{sdf}	M_{Rsdf}
Mean *NSS*	0.68	0.84	4.46	1.00	3.38	3.99
Standard deviation	0.72	1.03	2.19	0.80	1.63	2.05

Table 4. Evaluation of the different saliency map and the fusion, on the database where a "true" face saliency map was hand-labelled.

As stated above, the face saliency map gives better results than the static or the dynamic ones ($F(2,1413)=1009.81$; $p\#0$). The fusion which did not take face saliency maps into account gives a lower result than the fusions with face saliency maps ($F(2,1413)=472.33$; $p\#0$), and the reinforced fusion is even better than a more classical fusion ($F(1,942)=25.63$; $p=4.98\times10^{-7}$). Subsequently, the *NSS* was computed for each frame of the whole database (14155 frames) using the different model saliency maps and the eye movement data. The face saliency map is obtained using the split-up SNoW face detector and the weighting and fusion previously explained. In order to test the contribution of face pathway, the mean *NSS* value was calculated using the saliency map given by each pathway independently and the different possible fusions. The mean NSS value is plotted for six models of saliency maps (M_s, M_d, M_f, M_{sd}, M_{sdf}, M_{Rsdf}) in comparison with human data in figure 10. The *NSS* values are given for the saliency maps (M_s, M_d and M_f) but note that the *NSS* results would be the same for the weighted saliency maps ($M_{s'}$, $M_{d'}$ and $M_{f'}$), as multiplying the saliency map by a constant did not change the NSS value.

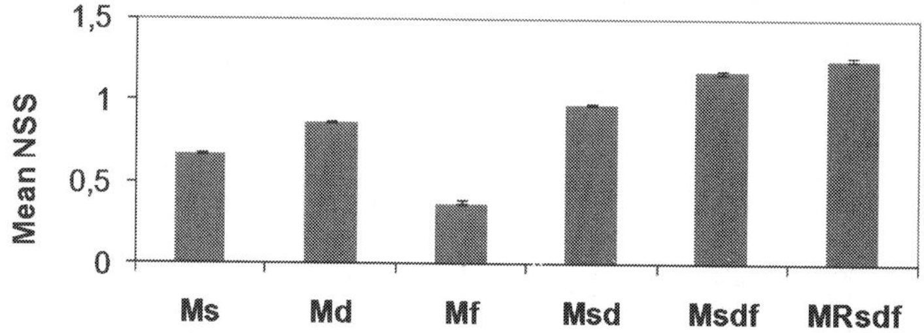

Fig. 10. Mean NSS values on the whole database (14155 frames) for six models of saliency maps (static, dynamic, face, weighted fusion of the static and dynamic pathways M_{sd}, weighted fusion of the static, the dynamic and the face pathway M_{sdf} and a "reinforced" weighted fusion M_{Rsdf}).

As presented in (Marat et al., 2009), the dynamic saliency maps are more predictive than the static ones. The fusion of the static and the dynamic saliency maps improves the prediction of the model: the static and the dynamic information needs to be considered to improve the model prediction. The results of the face pathway should not be considered; in fact, it gives the lowest results but only because a small number of frames contain at least one face detected compared to the total number of frames (12% of the whole database).The weighted fusion integrating the face pathway (M_{sdf}) is significantly better than the weighted fusion of the static and the saliency maps (M_{sd}), ($F(1,28308)=255.39$; $p\#0$). Integrating the face pathway increases the model prediction; hence, as already observed, faces are crucial information to predict eye positions. The "reinforced" fusion integrating multiplicative terms (M_{Rsdf}), increasing saliency in regions that are salient in two maps, gives the best results, outperforming the previous fusion (M_{sdf}), ($F(1,28308)=25.91$; $p=3.6\times10^{-9}$). The contribution of the face pathway in attracting our gaze is undeniable. The face pathway improves the results greatly, faces have to be integrated into a saliency model to make the results of the model match the experimental results more closely.

8. Conclusion

When viewing scenes, faces are almost immediately gazed on. This was shown in static images (Cerf et al., 2007). We report in this research the same phenomenon using dynamic stimuli. This means that even if there are moving objects, faces rapidly attracted gazes. To study the influence of faces on gaze, we ran an experiment to record the eye movements of subjects when looking freely at videos. We used videos with various contents, with or without faces with textured backgrounds and with or without moving objects. This experiment enabled us to check that faces are fixated on within the first milliseconds and independently of the scenes (presence or not of moving objects etc.). Moreover, we showed that a face is more salient if it is the only face on the frame. In order to take this into account, we added a "face pathway" to a bottom-up saliency model inspired by the biology. The "face pathway" uses the Split-up Snow face detector algorithm. Hence, the model splits the visual signal into static, dynamic, and face saliency maps. The static saliency map emphasizes orientation and spatial frequency contrasts. The dynamic saliency map emphasizes motion contrasts and the face saliency map emphasizes faces proportionally to the number of faces. Then, these three maps are originally fuzzed by taking into account the specificity of each saliency map. The fusion showed that the "face pathway" significantly increases the predictions of the model.

9. References

Carmi R. & Itti L. (2006). Visual causes versus correlates of attentional selection in dynamic scenes. *Vision Research,* Vol. 46, No. 26, pp. 4333-4345

Cerf M.; Harel J.; Einhäuser W. & Koch C. (2007). Predicting gaze using low-level saliency combined with face detection, *in Proceedings of Neural Information System NIPS 2007*

Dekowska M.; Kuniecki M. & Jaskowski P. (2008). Facing facts: neuronal mechanisms of face perception. *Acta Neurobiologiae Experimentalis,* Vol. 68, No. 2, pp. 229-252

Goto Y. & Tobimatsu S. (2005). An electrophysiological study of the initial step of face perception. *International Congress Series,* Vol. 1278, pp. 45-48

Itti L.; Koch C. & Niebur E. (1998). A model of saliency-based visual attention for rapid scene analysis. *IEEE Trans. on PAMI,* Vol. 20, No. 11, pp. 1254-1259

Kanwisher N. & Yovel G. (2006). The fusiform face area: a cortical region specialized for the perception of faces. *Philosophical transactions of the royal society Biological sciences,* Vol. 361, No. 1476, pp. 2109-2128

Le Meur O.; Le Callet P. & Barba D. (2006). A coherent computational approach to model bottom-up visual attention. *IEEE Trans. on PAMI,* Vol. 28, No. 5, pp. 802-817

Marat S.; Ho Phuoc T.; Granjon L.; Guyader N.; Pellerin D. & Dugué-Guérin A. (2009). Modelling spatio-temporal saliency to predict gaze direction for short videos. *International Journal of Computer Vision,* Vol. 82, No. 3, pp. 231-243

Marat S.; Ho Phuoc T.; Granjon L.; Guyader N.; Pellerin D. & Dugué-Guérin A. (2008). Spatio-temporal saliency model to predict eye movements in video free viewing, *in Proceedings of Eusipco 2008,* Lausanne, Switzerland

Odobez J.-M. & Bouthemy P. (1995). Robust multiresolution estimation of parametric motion models. *Journal of visual communication and image representation,* Vol. 6, pp. 348-365

Palermo R. & Rhodes G. (2007). Are you always on my mind? A review of how face perception and attention interact. *Neuropsychologia,* Vol. 45, No. 1, pp. 75-92

Peters R. J. & Itti L. (2008). Applying computational tools to predict gaze direction in interactive visual environments. *ACM Trans. On Applied Perception,* Vol. 5, No. 2

Thorpe S. J. (2002). Ultra-rapid scene categorization with a wave of spikes, *in Proceedings of the Second International Workshop on Biologically Motivated Computer Vision,* Vol. 2525, pp. 1-15

Treisman A. M. & Gelade G. (1980). A feature-integration theory of attention. *Cognitive Psychology,* Vol. 12, No. 1, pp. 97-136

Tsao D. Y. & Livingstone M. S. (2008). Mechanisms of face perception. *Annu. Rev. Neuroscci.,* Vol. 31, pp. 411-437

Viola P. & Jones M. J. (2004). Robust real time face detection. *International Journal of Computer Vision,* Vol. 57, No. 2, pp. 137-154

Yang M.-H.; Kriegman D. J. & Ahuja N. (2002). Detecting faces in images: a survey. *IEEE Trans. on PAMI,* Vol. 24, No. 1, pp. 34-58

13

Suppression of Correlated Noise

Jan Aelterman, Bart Goossens, Aleksandra Pizurica and Wilfried Philips
Ghent University, TELIN-IPI-IBBT
Belgium

1. Introduction

Many signal processing applications involve noise suppression (colloquially known as denoising). In this chapter we will focus on image denoising. There is a substantial amount of literature on this topic. We will start by a short overview:

Many algorithms denoise data by using some transformation on the data, thereby considering the signal (the image) as a linear combination of a number of atoms. For denoising purposes, it is beneficial to use such transformations, where the noise-free image can be accurately represented by only a limited number of these atoms. This property is sometimes referred to as sparsity. The aim in denoising is to detect which of these atoms represent significant signal energy from the large amount of possible atoms representing noise.

A lot of research has been performed to find representations that are as sparse as possible for 'natural' images. Examples of such representations are the Fourier basis, the Discrete Wavelet Transform (DWT) (Donoho, 1995), the Curvelet Transform (Starck, 2002), the Shearlet transform (Easley, 2006), the dual-tree complex wavelet transform (Kingsbury, 2001; Selesnick, 2005), ... Many denoising techniques designed for one such representation can be used in others, because the principles (exploiting sparsity) are the same. Without exception, these denoising methods try to preserve the small amount of significant transform coefficients, i.e the ones carrying the information, while suppressing the large amount of transform coefficients that only represent noise. The sparsity property of natural images (in its proper transform domain) ensures that there will be only a very small amount of significant transform coefficients, which allows to suppress a large amount of the noise energy in the insignificant transform coefficients. Multiresolution denoising techniques range from rudimentary approaches such as hard or soft thresholding of coefficients (Donoho, 1995) to more advanced approaches that try to capture some statistical significance behind atom coefficients by imposing appropriate prior models (Malfait, 1997; Romberg, 2001; Portilla, 2003; Pizurica, 2006; Guerrero-Colon, 2008; Goossens, 2009;).

Another class of algorithms try to exploit image (self-) similarity. It has been noted that many images have repetitive features on the level of pixel blocks. This was exploited in recent literature through the use of statistical averaging schemes of similar blocks (Buades 2005; Buades, 2008; Goossens, 2008) or grouping of similar blocks and 3d transform domain denoising (Dabov, 2007).

In practice, processes that corrupt data can often not be described using a simple additive white gaussian noise (AWGN) model. Many of these processes can be modelled as linear filtering process of a white Gaussian noise source, which results into correlated noise. Some correlated noise generating processes are described in section 2. The majority of the mentioned denoising techniques are only designed for white noise and relatively few techniques have been reported that are capable of suppressing correlated noise. In this chapter, we present some techniques for noise estimation in section 4 and image modelling in section 3, which form the theoretical basis for the (correlated) noise removal techniques explained in section 5. Section 6 contains demonstration denoising experiments, using the explained denoising algorithms, and presents a conclusion.

2. Sources of Correlated Noise

2.1 From white noise to correlated noise

In this section, the aim is to find a proper description of correlated noise. Once established, we will use it to describe several correlated noise processes in the remainder of this section. Since the spatial correlation is of interest, rather than time/spatially-varying noise statistics, we will assume stationarity throughout this chapter. Stationarity means that the autocorrelation function only depends on the relative displacement between two pixels, rather than their absolute positions. This is evident from (1), a random process generating samples f(n) is called white if it has zero mean and a delta function as autocorrelation function $r_f(n)$:

$$\begin{aligned} &E[f(n)] = 0 \\ &r_f(n) = E[f(m)\overline{f(n+m)}] = \partial(n) \end{aligned} \tag{1}$$

The Wiener-Khinchin theorem states that the power spectral density (PSD) of a (wide-sense stationary) random signal f(n) is the Fourier transform of the corresponding autocorrelation function r(n):

$$R(\omega) = \sum_{n=-\infty}^{\infty} r(n) e^{-j\omega n} \tag{2}$$

This means that for white noise, the PSD is equal to a constant value, hence the name white (white light has a flat spectrum). When a linear filter h(n), with Discrete Time Fourier Transform (DTFT) H(ω) is applied (often inadvertently) to the white noise random signal, the resulting effect on the autocorrelation function and PSD of $f'(n) = f(n) * h(n)$ is:

$$\begin{aligned} &r'(n) = E[f'(m)\overline{f'(n+m)}] = \sum_{m=-\infty}^{\infty} h(m)\overline{h(n+m)} \\ &R'(\omega) = H(\omega)\overline{H(\omega)} = |H(\omega)|^2 \end{aligned} \tag{3}$$

This result shows that the correlated noise PSD R′(ω) is the squared magnitude response of the linear filter DTFT, hence one can think of correlated noise as white noise subjected to linear filtering. In analogy with the term 'white noise' this is sometimes referred to as 'colored noise'. In the following sections, some real world technologies will be explained from the perspective of noise correlation.

2.2 Phase Alternating Line (PAL) Television

PAL is a transmission standard used in colour analogue broadcast television systems. Dating back to the 1950s, there are several bandwidth saving techniques that are very nice in their own right, but are responsible for the noise in PAL television. One is the deinterlacing mechanism (Kwon, 2003). Another is the use of a different modulation and filtering schemes. We will restrict us here to show the PSD of a patch of noise from a PAL signal broadcast:

Fig. 1. noisy PAL broadcast of a sports event and PSD of noise in a green color channel of the PAL broadcast.

It is clear that the noise here is almost cut off horizontally, leading to stripe like artifacts and there is significant energy in the lower vertical frequencies, leading to vertical streaks. It is therefore naive to assume noise in PAL/NTSC television to be white.

2.3 Demosaicing

Modern digital cameras use a rectangular arrangement of photosensitive elements. This matrix arrangement allows the interleaving of photosensitive elements of different color sensitivity. This interleaving allows sampling of full color images without the use of three matrices of photosensitive elements. One very popular arrangement is the Bayer pattern (Bayer, 1976), shown in figure 2.

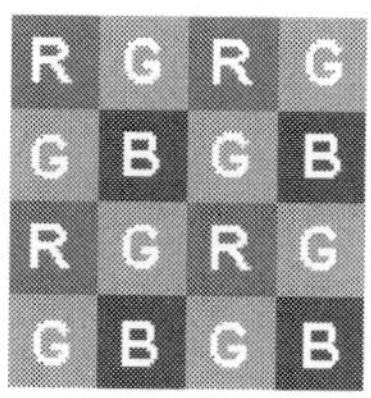

Fig. 2. Bayer mosaic pattern of photosensitive elements in a camera sensor

There exist a wide range of techniques for reconstructing the full color image from mosaiced image data. A thorough study of these techniques is beyond the scope of this chapter. Instead, we compare the simplest approach with one state of the art technique, from the viewpoint of noise correlation.

Since all of these techniques perform interpolation in some way, we are confident that the conclusion will be similar for all demosaicing techniques. When using patches of white noise as input data for an image mosaic sensor, the PSD of the demosaicing noise is shown in figure (3)-(4). Because white noise is used as input for a demosaicing system, the reconstruction will be a color image of correlated noise. Since we are assuming additive noise, this will be a good model for type of noise that is encountered in color digital camera images. In figure (3), we compared the simplest demosaicing approach, bilinear demosaicing, for both the green and the red color plane. Since the red data is subsampled more, the demosaicing treats both color planes differently, explaining the difference in PSD bandwidth. Figure (4) shows the result using a state-of-the-art demosaicing technique (Aelterman, 2009). There is no visible difference between the green and blue plane PSD here, because the algorithm works in a luminance/chrominance approximation rather than red/green/blue space.

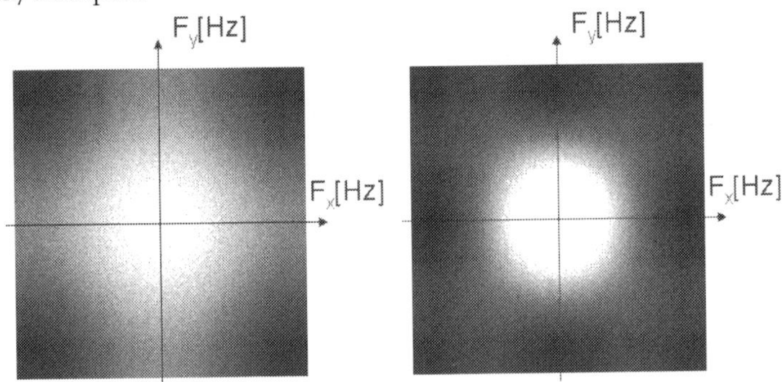

Fig. 3. PSD of the green channel (left) and a red/blue channel(right) from the demosaiced white noise patch using bilinear demosaicing.

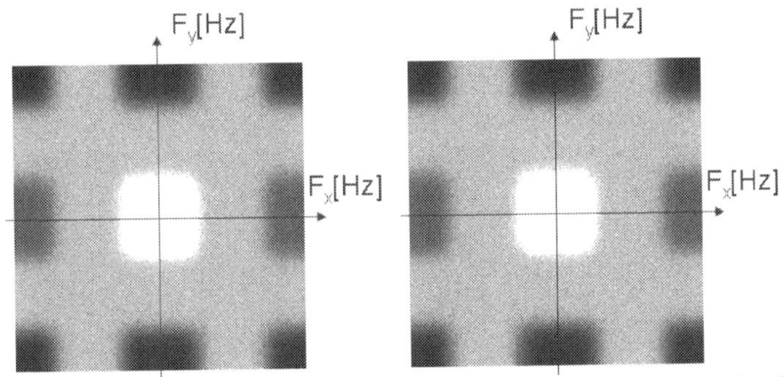

Fig. 4. PSD of the green channel (left) and a red/blue channel(right) from the demosaiced white noise patch using the technique described in (Aelterman, 2009)

The demosaicing experiments in figure 4 and 5 also show that the low pass part of the PSD is brighter, meaning it represents more noise energy. This is explained through the tendency of demosaicing algorithms to favour smooth color patches, as this is an accurate model for natural images.

Fig. 5. The full color lighthouse image (left) corrupted with white noise (middle) and with correlated noise due to bilinear demosaicing (right)

2.3 Thermal Camera's

Many thermal cameras are based on the push broom or whisk broom principle. Only very few infrared sensors are used, which have to be reused through an optics system in order to scan the different pixels positions, creating the complete image. This raster scan principle is illustrated in figure 6.

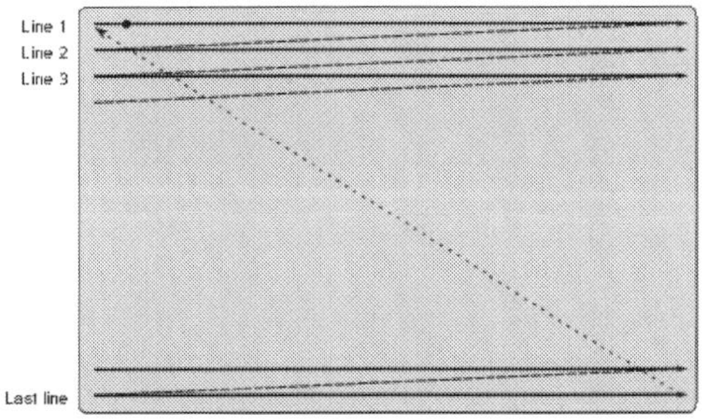

Fig. 6. Example of a raster scanned image pattern (whisk broom imaging)

The downside of such imaging principles is that they sometimes exhibit streaking noise artifacts, which can be attributed to the sensor and sampling circuitry. Since pixel intensities at different spatial positions are acquired using the same sensor, temporal correlation in the noisy sensor data results in spatial noise correlation in the acquired image. For thermal cameras, noise can be approximated using a $1/f$ frequency dependency of the noise (Borel, 1996). This type of 'pink' noise is very common in electronic devices and becomes apparent when reusing image sensors for different pixels in the image at high sample rates.

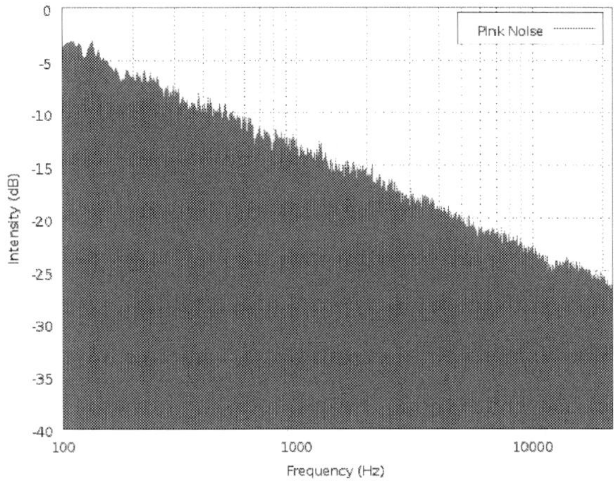

Fig. 7. PSD of 'pink noise', an approximate model of noise in some types of electronic devices through time

Pink noise can easily be simulated, by filtering a time sequence of white pseudorandom numbers with a 1/f filter characteristic and then adding those noise samples to the signal values in a raster scan pattern. Figure 8 shows this type of noise on the Einstein image.

Fig. 8. The Einstein image with simulated whisk broom imaging 1/f noise.

The streaking noise artifacts are clearly visible.

2.4 Magnetic Resonance Imaging

Magnetic Resonance Imaging is a non-invasive imaging technique. The Signal to Noise ratio (SNR) is heavily dependent on scan time. Longer scans are not only less comfortable for the patient, it is also less economical for the scanner operator and it increases the chance of involuntary patient movement. Because MRI technology acquires a Fourier transformed version of the image, rather than the image itself, patient movement during a scan translates

to 'echo'-like artifacts in the image, which is much more detrimental to the diagnostic image quality than simple blurring in conventional photography.
These facts are a major motivation for scanner manufacturers, who have created a wide range of tricks and technologies that allow an MRI scan to be made faster or less susceptible to motion artifacts. Noise in MRI is traditionally considered white (e.g. Nowak, 1999; Pizurica, 2003), and this is indeed a good noise model for theoretical MRI, but in practice, almost all clinical MRI acquisition devices use one or more acceleration techniques. As an illustration we now explain a few:
In K-space subsampling, bands of the spectrum of the signal are simply not scanned. Elliptical filtering is similar, where only elliptical area around the K-space center is sampled. An illustration and example of this principe is shown in figure 9.

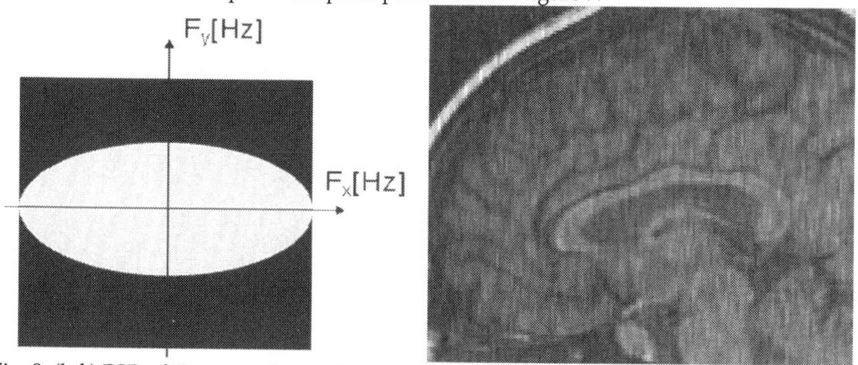

Fig. 9. (left) PSD of K-space subsampled and elliptically filtered noise (right) Brain MRI with simulated K-space subsampled and elliptically filtered MRI noise

It is clearly visible that for this situation, the noise creates stripe-like artifacts rather than being statistically independent from one pixel to another.

3. Describing natural images

3.1 Sparsity

When generating an image using purely random generators, chances are it will look like random noise. To the authors' knowledge, nobody ever succeeded in generating an image this way that looks like a 'natural' picture, which could have come from a camera. This is because what people consider 'natural' images is a very small subset of all possible images. Natural images have specific properties. These properties have been the object of intensive study throughout the years and are of interest here, as it is what will enable the statistical separation of noise from signal in images.
An easily verifiable, intuitive, property of natural images is that they are smoothly varying signals, which give low frequency responses, delineated by lines (edges). This is somewhat quantified by the inverse power scaling law, natural image PSD's are inversely proportional in magnitude to the squared modulus of the spatial frequency variable (Ruderman, 1994; Field, 1987):

$$R'(\omega) \propto \frac{1}{\omega^{2+\eta}} \tag{4}$$

Where η is a small number (|η|<1). This observation, coupled with the mathematical elegance of the Gaussian distribution, motivated early image processing engineers to model both image and noise as Gaussian distributed, in some transform domain. The Minimization of the Mean Squared Error Bayesian risk estimator (MMSE) denoising solution is the well known Wiener filter. However, the Gaussian distribution does not account for the relatively large number of outliers when considering e.g. wavelet filter responses. In fact, as a consequence of thinking of images as smooth regions delineated by edges, most coefficients will be far smaller than predicted by the Gaussian model and a small number will be really big.

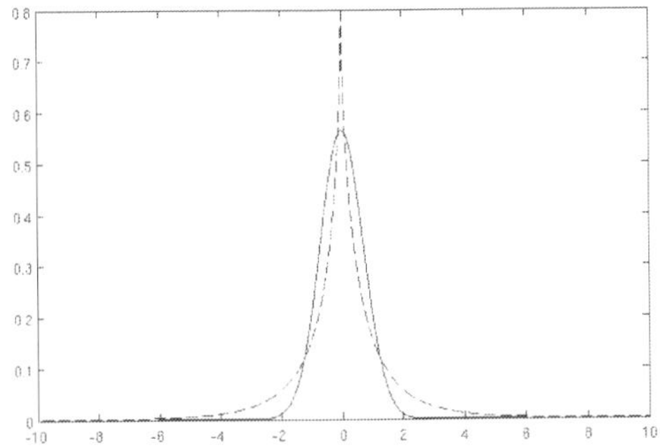

Fig. 10. Comparison of a Gaussian distribution (full line) with a more heavily tailed distribution, which is a better model for the transform coefficient distribution of natural images

This property, sometimes referred to as sparsity, is better modeled by a more heavily tailed distribution model, a comparison between both types of prior distributions is shown in figure 11. The next section gives some examples.

3.2 Marginal statistics of multiresolution image transformation coefficients

It is clearly visible in multiresolution decompositions that marginals distributions of coefficients exhibit highly non Gaussian behaviour. In fact, more leptokurtic distributions account better for the heavy tailed marginal distributions that one encounters in practice. For this reason, other distributions, such as the Laplacian (also known as the exponential power distribution) or Generalized Laplacian (Mallat, 1989; Pizurica, 2006) have been applied in more effective techniques. The Generalized Laplacian distribution is described in (5), with λ and υ called the scale and shape parameter and Γ() the gamma function.

$$p(\beta) = \frac{\lambda \upsilon}{2\Gamma\left(\frac{1}{\upsilon}\right)} \exp\left(-\left|\lambda\beta\right|^{\upsilon}\right) \tag{5}$$

The Gaussian Scale Mixtures (GSM) (Wainwright, 2000) is a more elegant alternative, because it can be extended more easily to the multivariate situation, which is advantageous when considering spatial noise correlation. A random vector $\boldsymbol{\beta}$ is a GSM when it can be written as:

$$\beta \overset{d}{=} \sqrt{z}U \qquad (6)$$

Where $\mathbf{U}$ is a Normally distributed random vector with mean $\mathbf{0}$ and covariance matrix $\mathbf{C}$, $z>0$ is a random scalar variable, independent of $\mathbf{U}$ and superscript d means 'equal in distribution'. The marginal distribution of $\boldsymbol{\beta}$ can then be written as:

$$p(\beta) = \int_{-\infty}^{\infty} \frac{1}{(2\pi)^{N/2} \left| z\, C \right|^{1/2}} \phi(z) \exp\left(-\frac{\beta^t C^{-1} \beta}{2z} \right) dz \qquad (7)$$

Both the Generalized Laplacian and the GSM model are parameterized, which means that some (often empirical) parameter estimation is required for the parameters. For the Generalized Laplacian, this can be done by fitting the sample kurtosis and variance, while for the GSM covariance matrix and hidden multiplier z distribution, there exist an expectation maximization (EM) solution (Portilla, 2003). It is also possible to assume a fixed distribution for the hidden multiplier z, which will enhance the kurtosis of the marginal distribution $p(\beta)$ in order to have a more heavily tailed distribution that corresponds more to the model from section 3.1 e.g. Jeffey's prior ($p(z)=1/z$).

3.2 Selfsimilarity

Another property of natural images is that they often contain a lot of redundant information. Natural images contain a lot of repeating structures and texture. Often, similarity can also be encountered at different scales. Some images of plants or art can be surprisingly well described using fractals, meaning that they can be described as built up of downscaled copies of themselves. This suggests that there is a lot of similarity in an image, a property called selfsimilarity. Since noise is typically more spatially independent, it is a good idea to find a description for self similarity, which can then be exploited in a denoising algorithm. This is done by finding similar image patches for every pixel in the image.

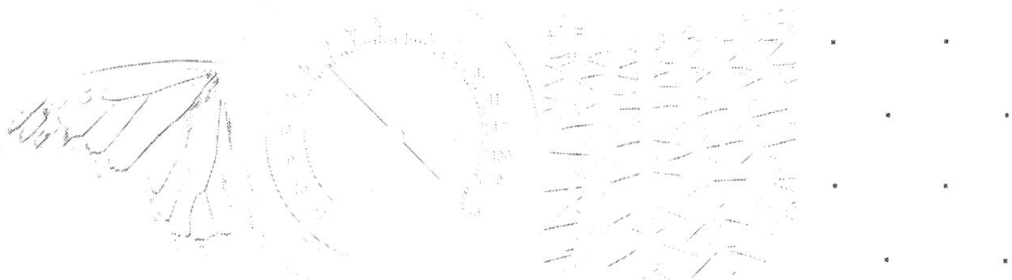

Fig. 11. Several natural images (top), with a similarity map (MSE) for the cyan pixel (bottom). Note how there is a large number of similar pixels for natural images.

Finding similar patches in an image can be done by block matching: For some neighborhood window size L, the mean squared error is taken between every neighborhood in the image and the neighborhood around the current pixel. Similar pixels exhibit a low MSE and the selfsimilarity property ensures that there will be plenty of such similar patches in a natural image. Figure 11 shows the similarity values for every pixel in the image, with respect to the image indicated by the arrow for a neighborhood size of 3x3. Black means a high similarity (low MSE). Note that for the cactus image, all the needles are found to be similar, even though the perspective causes the needles on the top of the image to be smaller versions of the needles at the bottom, which is an example of where similarity can be found at different scales.

4. Estimating noise Correlation

4.1 Signal-free data

In many applications, noise can be considered additive. Additive noise means that even after linear image transformations, the noise remains additive. In this case, the noise statistics are not signal dependent, and could just as well be estimated from signal-free data. In fact, this is easier, because the estimation will not be hindered by the signal. Many applications allow for the acquisition of signal-free data. This is the case for MRI images, where physical limitations ensure the existence of signal-free regions next to the scanned subject in the MRI image. For an unknown thermal camera type, one could photograph a surface of even temperature. Similar techniques can be used for optical photography and many other imaging modalities. When presented with such signal-free, noisy data, the autocorrelation function can be calculated in a straightforward way.

Since the Discrete Fourier Transform (DFT) can be used as a good approximation for the Discrete Time Fourier Transform (DTFT) in (2) for finite data, it is possible to obtain the autocorrelation function from the power spectral density, which can be estimated from the finite noisy, signal-free input data f(n):

$$F(k)=\sum_{n=0}^{N-1} f(n)e^{-\frac{j2\pi kn}{N}}$$

$$r(n)=\sum_{k=0}^{N-1} F(k)\overline{F(k)}e^{\frac{j2\pi kn}{N}} \tag{8}$$

This way of using the DTFT to estimate the autocorrelation function of a stationary process is computationally more efficient than calculating the autocorrelation function or covariance matrix explicitly through e.g. convolution in the image domain.

4.3 Estimating correlated noise in transform domains

Calculating the pixel (voxel) autocorrelation function / covariance matrix is just part of the solution. Since many denoising algorithms operate in a transform domain, it is necessary to transform the autocorrelation function / covariance matrix as well. A transformed covariance matrix enables the whitening of transform coefficients, which allows the use of a white noise denoising algorithm.

One obvious way to obtain the transformed covariance matrices, is through Monte Carlo simulations. First patches of noise are generated, then transformed into the transform domain and then the noise covariance matrix are calculated for every obtained subband. Doing this for multiresolution transforms with a lot of scales either results in heavy memory requirements or high computational requirements, in order to get meaningful results.

In (Goossens, 2009), a different approach is presented. Many transformations can be viewed as banks of linear filters. Applying a transform filter $G(\omega)$ to the signal $f'(n)$ from (3), the PSD $R''(\omega)$ becomes:

$$R''(\omega)=G(\omega)R'(\omega)\overline{G(\omega)} \tag{9}$$

When also taking the subsampling step from many shift-variant transformations (such as the discrete wavelet transform) into account, the transform becomes less trivial:

$$R''(2\omega)=\left(G(\omega)F'(\omega)+G(\omega+\pi)F'(\omega+\pi)\right)\overline{\left(G(\omega)F'(\omega)+G(\omega+\pi)F'(\omega+\pi)\right)} \tag{10}$$

In (10) we see the appearance of crosscorrelation terms $F'(\omega)\overline{F'(\omega+\pi)}$ which seem to indicate that it is not possible to simply filter the autocorrelation function such as in (9). However, considering the stationarity assumption, the following should also hold:

$$R''(2\omega)=\left(G(\omega)F'(\omega)-G(\omega+\pi)F'(\omega+\pi)\right)\overline{\left(G(\omega)F'(\omega)-G(\omega+\pi)F'(\omega+\pi)\right)} \tag{11}$$

The minus sign is caused by a one sample shift prior to subsampling. Now the crosscorrelation terms appear with an inverted sign with respect to (10). Since the stationarity assumption implies equality between (11) en (10) it follows that the crosscorrelation are zero. This means that the calculation of the transform autocorrelation function simplifies to:

$$R''(2\omega)=G(\omega)R'(\omega)\overline{G(\omega)}+G(\omega+\pi)R'(\omega+\pi)\overline{G(\omega+\pi)} \tag{12}$$

Again, the transform autocorrelation functions are simply filtered and subsampled versions of the original autocorrelation function. Noise covariance in subbands of a separable, decimated wavelet transform with an arbitrary number of scales can hence be calculated.

4.4 Full Blind GSM estimation

Many scenarios exist where there is no (sufficient) signal-free data. For this situation, the problem of obtaining accurate noise covariance estimations is not so trivial. The median absolute deviation (MAD) of the image transform coefficients in the finest scale (Donoho, 1994) is a robust estimator for the noise variance for white noise. The reason for using the finest resolution scale is that it contains the smallest signal contribution, which is in turn explained by the tendency of natural images to contain predominantly low frequency content. However, correlated noise is by its very definition frequency dependent, which means an estimate from a high frequency subband cannot be used for other transform subbands. Lower frequency subbands have a larger signal contribution, making noise covariance estimations less accurate.

Since the mentioned image transformations are designed to yield sparse responses for natural images, there are still substantial signal-free regions inside each subband. From these areas, an estimate for the noise covariance could be made in the respective transform subband.

There has been some research to put this principle in practice, through a maximum likelihood formulation of the signal estimation problem (Portilla, 2004). The algorithm relies on the different statistical properties of (correlated) Gaussian noise and natural image signal, which is modelled as a GSM (section 3.2). Considering the signal as a series of neighbourhood vectors of arbitrary size, the vector of noisy coefficients is then written as **y=x+w**. Considering the GSM model, one can also write: **y=** $\sqrt{z}$ **.U+w.** Using conditional distributions on the hidden GSM multiplier z, these observed vectors can be written as:

$$p_y(y) = \int_0^\infty p_{y|z}(y \mid z) p_z(z) dz \tag{13}$$

Now consider, without loss of generality, E[z]=1. This means that the underlying signal covariance $C_x = C_u$. Note that the Gaussianity of the scale mixture components and of the noise means it is very easy to write the conditional probability of the observed vector on the hidden GSM multiplier z:

$$p_{y|z}(y \mid z) = \frac{\exp\left(-y^t \left(zC_u + C_w\right)^{-1} y/2\right)}{(2\pi)^{N/2} \left|zC_u + C_w\right|^{1/2}} \tag{14}$$

From this model, we need to obtain the noise covariance matrix. Note that C_x can be estimated as $\lfloor C_y - C_w \rfloor_+$ where the '+' sign signifies an operation to only preserve positive eigenvalues since covariance matrices need to be positive semidefinite in order to keep the marginal probability values lower than 1. Consider the case for small values of z in equation (17), then $p_{y|z}(y \mid 0 \le z < dz)dz$ approaches the Gaussian noise distribution. The conditional $p_{z|y}(0 \le z < dz \mid y)dz$ can then be considered the conditional probability that an observed vector **y** was generated by this noise process. Then, the weighted sample covariance calculation (15) will automatically exclude neighborhoods which are likely to contain signal contributions.

$$C_w^{new} = \frac{\sum_{m=1}^{M} p_{z|y}(0 \le z < dz \mid y_m; C_w^{old}) y_m . y_m^t dz}{\sum_{m=1}^{M} p_{z|y}(0 \le z < dz \mid y_m; C_w^{old}) dz} \tag{15}$$

Note that the calculation of the conditionals on z requires knowledge of C_w. This equation needs to be iterated in an Generalized Expectation Maximization (GEM) (Hastie, 2001) style until convergence to reach the ML estimate for the noise covariance matrix. The weights in (15) are visualized in figure 12 for one subband of a noisy version of the Einstein image.

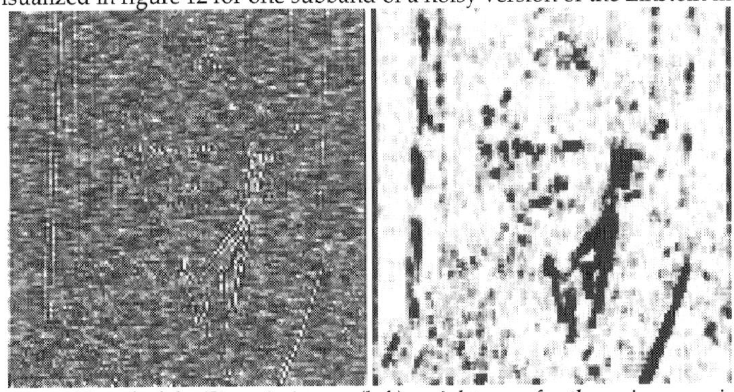

Fig. 12. Noisy subband of the Einstein image (left) weight map for the noise covariance estimation (right) Black corresponds to low weights, note how all the visible image features are detected and excluded from the covariance estimation.

Where the hidden multiplier distribution $p_z(z)$ is unknown, i.e. when a fixed prior distribution, such as Jeffrey's prior or others are not assumed, it is also necessary to estimate $p_z(z)$. Here the choice is to use the classical EM solution for Gaussian scale mixtures:

$$p_z^{new}(z) = \frac{1}{M}\sum_{m=1}^{M} p_{z|y}\left(z \mid y_m; p_z^{old}(z)\right) \tag{16}$$
$$= p_z^{old}(z)\frac{1}{M}\sum_{m=1}^{M}\frac{p_{y|z}(y_m \mid z)}{\int_0^\infty p_{y|z}(y_m \mid \alpha)p_z^{old}(\alpha)d\alpha}$$

The combination of (15) and (16) allows to estimate the noise covariance matrices for the subband representations of an image in a transform domain. These can be combined into the pixel domain covariance matrix or autocorrelation functions using the filter bank technique from section 4.3 and (18) and subsequently be used in correlated noise denoising algorithms.

5. Denoising Algorithms

In this section, some state-of-the-art denoising algorithms are presented. It should be noted that the all of them, except for the NLMS algorithm are designed for use in a multiresolution transform domain. These are often presented in an implementation using one type of multiresolution transform. The basic principles however, are general enough to allow the techniques to be used with any multiresolution image decomposition. That is why it was chosen to explain the algorithms for a general image transformation and refer to the multiresolution image decomposition transform coefficients as 'transform coefficients' or just simply 'coefficients'. Examples of possible image transforms are the Discrete Wavelet Transform (DWT) (Donoho, 1995), the Curvelet Transform (Starck, 2002), the Shearlet transform (Easley, 2006), the dual-tree complex wavelet transform (Kingsbury, 2001; Selesnick, 2005), Steerable pyramids (Simoncelli, 1992), ... Since this chapter deals with the difficulties of handling correlated noise, an investigation into the differences between the mentioned image transforms is beyond the scope of this work.

5.1 Noise Whitening

A convenient way to deal with the problem of correlated noise is to start from existing denoising techniques. Most existing denoising techniques assume that noise is uncorrelated. One way to be able to reuse existing denoising techniques is to use a prewhitening transform that decorrelates the image noise. Arranging the noise measurements in a vector **f**, the decorrelating transform matrix **W** needs to satisfy the whiteness property:

$$\begin{aligned} &E\left[f.f^*\right]=C \\ &E[W.f.f^*.W^*]=I \\ &W.C.W^*=I \\ &C=(W^*.W)^{-1} \\ &W=C^{-1/2} \end{aligned} \tag{17}$$

The result from (17) shows that the decorrelating transform can be calculated as the matrix square root of the matrix inverse of the covariance matrix **C**. The covariance matrix **C** and the autocorrelation function r(n) are closely related through their respective definitions (again, a zero mean noise process f() is assumed):

$$\begin{aligned} &r(n)=E[f(m)\overline{f(n+m)}] \\ &C=E[f.f^t] \end{aligned} \tag{18}$$

The ability to whiten transform coefficients with respect to the noise indicates it is possible to use the techniques for covariance estimation from section 4 and the whitening transformation in combination white noise denoising algorithms.

In practice, for many types of correlated noise, it is not necessary to take correlation between samples across the entire image into account. In fact, this would make the whitening procedure (17) intractable. When considering a size N for the neighbourhood vector **f**, it means that the noise covariance matrix **C** is of size N^2. That is why in practice, the neighbourhood size N is kept low, often just 9=3x3 or 25=5x5. The approximation means that all correlation with pixels not included in the neighbourhood window is set to zero, but this is usually not problematic in practice.

The whitening operation in (17) can become quite computationally expensive, as a naïve implementation would mean vectorizing an image into a one neighbourhood vector per pixel, causing huge memory requirements and then one matrix multiplication per pixel. Since the interest is in decorrelating the center pixel in the neighbourhood vector from its neighbours, actually only the corresponding row **w** of the decorrelating transform matrix **W** is of interest. The image now just needs to be filtered by this linear filter **w**, which has an interpretation as a prewhitening linear filter. In fact, given the PSD $R(\omega)$, the prewhitening filter $w(\omega)$ can also be obtained as:

$$w(\omega) = \frac{1}{\max(\varepsilon, \sqrt{R(\omega)})} \tag{19}$$

Where ε is a small constant to enforce stability against small values of the PSD $R(\omega)$. Note that the prewhitening filter (19) can be different when compared to the one derived from the autocovariance matrix **C**. The definition of **C** does not assume stationarity of the noise, which means that e.g. the diagonal elements can differ from each other. In this case the PSD $R(\omega)$ does not exist and (19) and (17) are not equivalent. In this chapter, we avoided that situation by assuming noise stationarity.

5.2 Bayesian Least Squares – GSM

The BLS-GSM denoising algorithm, proposed in (Portilla, 2005), is a multiresolution minimum mean square error estimator under multivariate GSM prior, explained in section 4. This makes it very suitable for correlated noise. It starts from the very generic Bayesian Least Squares (or MMSE) estimate for a noise free vector of transform coefficients:

$$E[x \mid y] = \int_x x p_{x|y}(x \mid y) dx \tag{20}$$

The conditional probability can be quite hard to calculate, but since the algorithm works in the multiresolution transform domain, it is possible to use the GSM prior model to simplify the calculation:

$$E[x \mid y] = \int_x x \int_z p_{x|z,y}(x \mid z, y) p_{z|y}(z \mid y) dz dx$$
$$= \int_z E[x \mid z, y] p_{z|y}(z \mid y) dz \tag{21}$$

Under the assumption of (multivariate) Gaussian noise, the expectations in (21) reduce to the Wiener estimate:

$$E[x \mid z, y] = zC_u.(zC_u + C_w)^{-1} y \tag{22}$$

In order to evaluate (21), it is also necessary to estimate the conditional probability of the hidden GSM multiplier z on the observed coefficient vector **y** where C_w is estimated as explained in section 4 and $C_u = E[z]^{-1}[C_y - C_w]_+$. With knowledge of the hidden multiplier pdf p(z), as explained in section 4, this is possible:

$$p_{z|y}(z \mid y) = \frac{p(y \mid z)p(z)}{p(y)} = \frac{p(y \mid z)p(z)}{\int_z p(y \mid z) dz} \tag{23}$$

where $p(y \mid z)$ is the multivariate Gaussian distribution, given by (14). Implementation of these equations for the subbands of a multiresolution decomposition constitutes a BLS-GSM denoising algorithm.

5.3 Probshrink

Probshrink was first developed in (Pizurica, 2006), for white noise. In a more recent work (Aelterman, 2008) it has been extended to 3D correlated noise for denoising noise volumes. In section 3, it was explained how natural images consist of edges and smooth areas, giving rise to the heavy-tailed transform coefficient distributions. This model led to the idea of classifying transform coefficients into two classes. Transform coefficients are either large, meaning they represent an edge and arose from the tail of the distribution, or they are small, meaning they represent a smooth area (or the noise floor) and arose from the main body of the distribution:

$$\begin{aligned} H_1 &= \mid y \mid > T \\ H_0 &= \mid y \mid \le T \end{aligned} \tag{24}$$

with T a threshold value. T is often chosen to comply with the noise floor, related to the noise variance. In fact, this noise variance is often simply equal to the noise variance in the image, because some wavelet transforms are unitary with respect to white Gaussian noise. Conditioned on these two classes, the MMSE estimator becomes:

$$E[x \mid y] = E[x \mid y, H_1] P_{H|y}(H_1 \mid y) + E[x \mid y, H_0] P_{H|y}(H_0 \mid y) \tag{25}$$

Probshrink handles the transform coefficients coefficient-wise. It does not handle neighbourhood vectors of transform coefficients, as BLS-GSM does. In fact, this is not a problem for the decimated wavelet transform, as one can prove that the noise in the wavelet domain is white when the input noise was white. For redundant image transforms, this is

not the case, and an approach as in section 4.3 would show that the noise is in fact correlated in the transform domain. A proper approach for correlated noise is then needed, using a whitening transform to whiten coefficients to obtain better results.
The calculation of (25) is facilitated through some simplifying assumptions: It is assumed that $E[x \mid y, H_0] = 0$ because the model suggests that small transform coefficients, corresponding to hypothesis H_0, are attributed to noise. Similarly, large wavelet coefficients are attributed to the signal with very high SNR, and since this corresponds to hypothesis H_1, the assumption $E[x \mid y, H_1] = y$ is made. This leads to the Probshrink denoising estimator:

$$E[x \mid y] = P_{H|y}(H_1 \mid y)y \tag{26}$$

The Probshrink estimator can be seen as a soft shrinkage wavelet denoising operator, where the shrinkage factor is determined as $P_{H|y}(H_1 \mid y)$ through the Bayesian interpretation (25). Evaluation is done by rewriting:

$$E[x \mid y] = \frac{p_{y|H}(y \mid H_1)P_H(H_1)}{p_{y|H}(y \mid H_1)P_H(H_1) + p_{y|H}(y \mid H_0)P_H(H_0)}y \tag{27}$$

Assuming additive noise (with distribution $p_w(w)$), this expression can be evaluated quite easily. With knowledge of the prior model $p_x(x)$, the conditional probabilities in (27) are written as in (28).

$$\begin{aligned} p_{y|H}(y \mid H_0) &= \int p_w(y-x)p_{x|H}(x \mid H_0)dx \\ p_{y|H}(y \mid H_1) &= \int p_w(y-x)p_{x|H}(x \mid H_1)dx \end{aligned} \tag{28}$$

Hence, the conditional probabilities of $p_{y|H}$ in (28) are the convolved prior conditional probabilities $p_{x|H}$ with the noise distribution p_w. This is illustrated in figure 13.

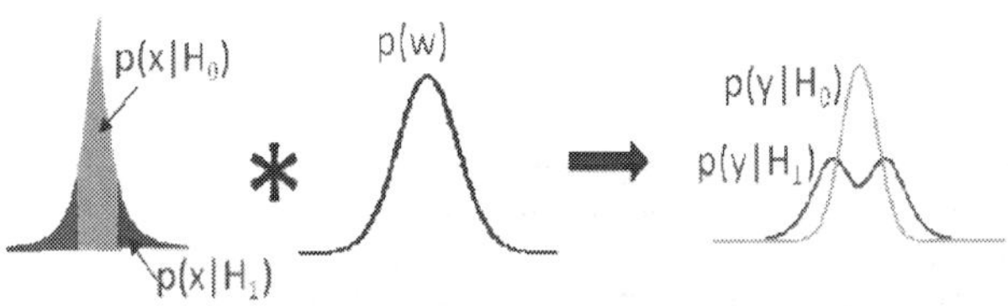

Fig. 13. Example of the estimation of the conditional probabilities $p_{y|H}$ from the prior probabilities $p_{x|H}$ and noise distribution p_w

Note how the conditional prior probability distributions $p_{x|H}$ can easily be calculated by imposing (24) and renormalizing the prior, also illustrated in figure 13. Again using (24), it is possible to estimate p_H through integrating this function over the threshold interval:

$$p_H(H_0) = \int_{-T}^{T} p_x(x)dx \qquad (29)$$
$$p_H(H_1) = 1 - p_H(H_0)$$

With knowledge of the exact prior model, it becomes possible to evaluate the Probshrink equations numerically (Pizurica, 2006), it is even possible to calculate (27) empirically, from the data (Pizurica, 2003) or analytically, for the Laplacian Prior (Pizurica, 2007). Together, these equations constitute the white noise Probshrink denoising method.

5.4 3D Probshrink for correlated noise

There exist several adaptations for the Probshrink estimator with the aim of handling correlated noise. In (Goossens, 2007; Goossens, 2009), such methods were proposed, which use a prewhitening filter before the classification step (24). In (Aelterman, 2008) the approach was extended to 3D, with the practical application of MRI denoising in mind. As both approaches are extensions of the Probshrink estimator, both approaches make use of multiresolution image decompositions (in this case, the dualtree complex wavelet transform (Kingsbury, 2001)). Instead of the classification (24), (30) is used:

$$H_1 = \left\| W.\overline{x_n} \right\| > T \qquad (30)$$
$$H_0 = \left\| W.\overline{x_n} \right\| \le T$$

With **W** the whitening transform matrix (8) and $\overline{y_n}$ the neighborhood coefficient vector of the coefficient at spatial location **n.** This will ensure that only coefficients are selected that are sufficiently distant from the noise in the succeeding Probshrink steps.

Multiresolution decompositions do not decorrelate the image features through the scales, a large transform coefficient in one scale increases the possibility of finding another in the subsequent scales. These interscale dependencies have been studied thoroughly for the wavelet transform. In (Mallat, 1998), it is shown that the wavelet coefficient magnitude increases with increasing scale (i.e. decreases with increasing spatial frequency) for natural, sufficiently regular signals, like natural images. Improvements to the Probshrink approach are made by exploiting this. In (Goossens, 2007), this is exploiting by fitting a Hidden Markov Tree model to the interscale dependencies of complex wavelet coefficients. In (Aelterman, 2008), this has been exploited by changing (30) by its interscale product:

$$H_1 = \left\| W_{j+1}.\overline{y_{j,n}} \right\| \cdot \left\| W_j.\overline{y_{j,n}} \right\| > T \qquad (31)$$
$$H_0 = \left\| W_{j+1}.\overline{y_{j,n}} \right\| \cdot \left\| W_j.\overline{y_{j,n}} \right\| \le T$$

With j the scale indicator. This way, a coefficient is only selected as significant coefficient if both it is large, as well as its whitened 'parent' coefficient, in compliance with the interscale dependency model.
These adaptations will make sure that only significant (with respect to the noise covariance) transform coefficients are selected, which will in the end lead to a better Probshrink denoising.

5.5 Non Local Means

The Non Local Means Algorithm (NLMS) is an algorithm that tries to exploit the self-similarity (section 3.2) in images. An overview is given in (Buades, 2008). A very intuitive way to look at this algorithm is through its relationship with the simpler Bilateral Filtering scheme (Tomasi, 1998). The simplest image denoising algorithms apply some kind of linear filter. The Bilateral Filtering modifies this principle by making the filter data-adaptive:

$$\widehat{x}(n) = \sum_{m} h(m,n)c(y(m), y(n))y(n) \tag{32}$$

In short, noise-free pixel estimate $\widehat{x}$ is a linear combination of noisy pixel values y with the weights depending on both the spatial position of the pixels (most of the time just the relative distance), and the actual value of the pixel. This way, through a clever choice of the weighing function, it is possible to reinforce statistical averaging of only similar pixel values, avoiding blurring of image edges.
The NLMS algorithm improves on this concept, by performing block matching on blocks (neighbourhoods) of pixels. Block matching uses the Euclidian distance between two vectors $\overline{y_n}$ and $\overline{y_m}$, containing the neighbourhood pixel values of a region around a pixels $y(n)$ and $y(m)$. It essentially compares image patches instead of pixels. This allows to find similar pixel values more accurately:

$$\widehat{x}(n) = k_n^{-1} \sum_{m} \exp\left(-\frac{\| \overline{y_n} - \overline{y_m} \|^2}{2h^2} \right) y(n) \tag{33}$$

With k_n a normalization constant. An important difference with the bilateral filter is that the NLMS theory allows to look beyond the linear filter mask for similar image patches. The block matching concept will ensure that similar pixels are found from a similar textured patch or image structure, even when the blocks come from the other side of the image. In practice this search space size condition will often be relaxed for computational reasons. The NLMS algorithm can hence be seen as an algorithm that exploits the self-similarity in an image.
The block matching approach means that the weights are calculated on neighbourhood vectors. From this it is conceptually a small step to do it on whitened neighbourhood vectors, using the noise whitening procedures from section 5.1. This decreases the influence of spatial noise correlation on the distance/similarity measure. The Euclidian distance in (33) is transformed into what is known as the Mahalanobis distance. This was one improvement over the classical NLMS scheme proposed in (Goossens, 2008).

$$\hat{x}(n) = k_n^{-1} \sum_m \exp\left(-\frac{\left(\overline{y_n} - \overline{y_m}\right)^T C_w^{-1} \left(\overline{y_n} - \overline{y_m}\right)}{2h^2} \right) y(n) \tag{34}$$

Using the Mahalanobis distance, the measure will actually take the correlation structure of the noise into account when calculating the distance between two image patches.

6. Results

The next few figures show a comparison of the two classes of algorithms, with different types of noise. Peak signal to noise ratio (PSNR) comparisons are given in table 1.
Figure 14 shows the result of white noise denoising on the Einstein image. For white noise it can be seen that the denoising algorithms perform similar with only a relatively small difference in PSNR. A visible difference is that the NLMS algorithm suffers less from the typical wavelet artifacts (small very local oscillations in image intensity).

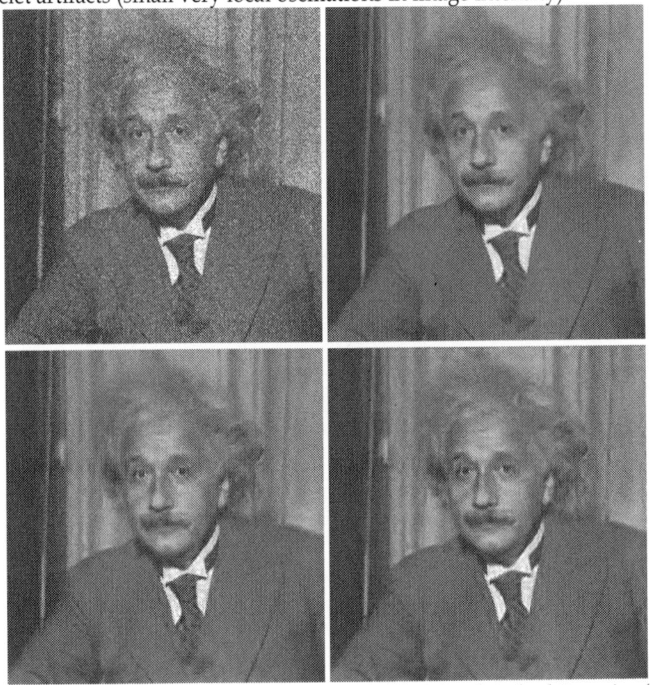

Fig. 14. Denoising results of Einstein image corrupted by simulated white noise (top left): by NLMS denoising (top right), by BLS-GSM denoising (bottom left), by Probshrink for white noise (bottom right)

In a second experiment, thermal noise was simulated on the House image. This is correlated noise, which behaves as stripes. It can be seen that an algorithm for correlated noise denoising has some advantage in PSNR. A qualitative comparison can be made in figure 15. Clearly, the Probshrink algorithm, which has very good results for white noise, has problems with properly discerning image details from the noise structure. Even though the correlated noise algorithms succeed in preserving the horizontal brick structure of the house to some degree, the white noise Probshrink algorithm completely suppresses those details while preserving the vertical stripes noise pattern.

Fig. 15. Denoising results of House image corrupted by simulated thermal noise (top left): by NLMS denoising (top right), by BLS-GSM denoising (bottom left), by Probshrink for white noise (bottom right)

In a third denoising experiment, a fictional type of correlated noise was used, high frequency noise, combined with diagonal streaks. It is referred to as 'streak' noise in Table 1. The qualitative comparison can be seen in figure 16. As expected, the white noise denoising algorithm Probshrink does not succeed in suppressing the diagonal streak noise structures. It does succeed in suppressing the high frequency noise, because even for white noise the high frequency parts of the noisy image PSD typically have a very low SNR, because of the fact that natural images predominantly have energy in low frequency parts of the PSD, as explained in section 3.

Fig. 16. Denoising results of Goldhill image corrupted by heavily correlated streak noise (top left): by NLMS denoising (top right), by BLS-GSM denoising (bottom left), by Probshrink denoising for white noise (bottom right)

In a fourth denoising experiment, the Stonehenge image was used. It was treated as a color image, and used as input for a mosaicing/demosaicing experiment using the bilinear demosaicing algorithm. This results in low frequency noise structures. Then the red channel of the resulting color image was used as input for the denoising experiment. Again, it is visible that the white noise denoising algorithm Probshrink does not succeed in suppressing the noise artifacts, while the algorithms for correlated noise do. It is also visible that the BLS-GSM algorithm suffers from ringing near the top edge of the Stonehenge structure. This type of artifacts is common in wavelet-base denoising experiments and is a result from incorrectly suppressing the small coefficients that make up the edge in higher frequency scales, while keeping their respective counterparts in lower frequency scales.

Fig. 17. Denoising results of Stonehenge image corrupted by simulated red channel demosaicing noise (top left): by NLMS denoising (top right), by BLS-GSM denoising (bottom left), by Probshrink denoising for white noise (bottom right)

From the experiments, some conclusions can be made. White noise denoising algorithms, such as Probshrink, work well enough as long as the image is corrupted by white noise. It fails when presented with correlated noise. One reason is that the Donoho MAD estimator is often a very bad choice, leading to underestimated noise power (for low frequency noise) or severely overestimated noise power (for high frequency noise). Because of this failure of the MAD estimator, the choice was made to choose the noise variance parameter heuristically for the white noise Probshrink algorithm, in order to obtain the highest possible PSNR. It can be concluded from figures 14-17 and table 1, that for situations where image noise is correlated, a simple white noise denoising algorithm will not perform optimally and there is need for the techniques and ideas explained in this chapter.

	Noisy	ProbShrink	BLS-GSM	NLMS
White	22dB	29.22dB	29.76dB	29.88dB
Demosaicing	27.9dB	29.8dB	32.6dB	31.4dB
Thermal	24.5dB	26.0dB	31.6dB	31.5dB
Streaks	16.1dB	22.8dB	25.7dB	25.9dB

Table 1. PSNR table for the different denoising experiments

In a last experiment, we used the 3D dual tree complex wavelet denoising algorithm for MRI (Aelterman, 2008) to illustrate the denoising performance on practical MRI images. A qualitative comparison can be seen in figure 18.

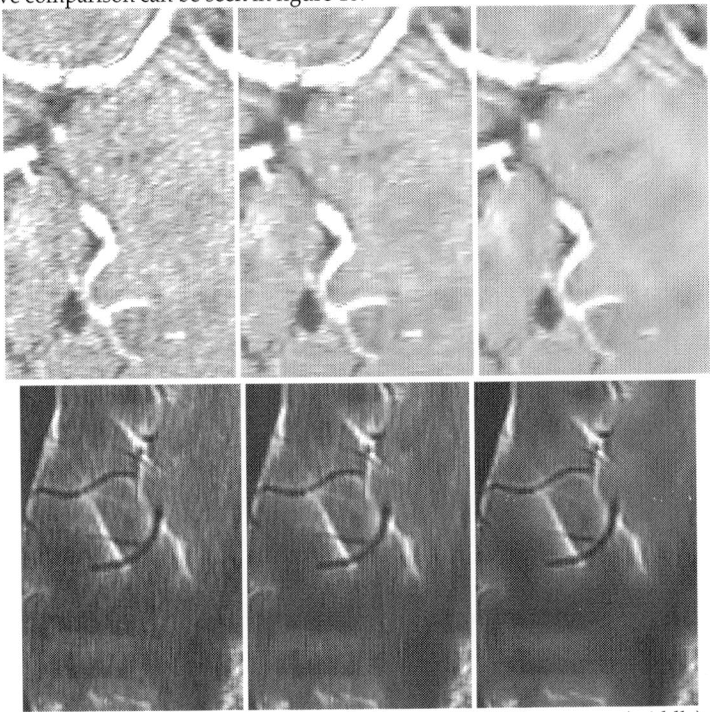

Fig. 18. Denoising results of noisy MRI data. (left) noisy 3D MRI sequence (middle) denoised by 2D per-slice Probshrink (right) denoised by 3D correlated noise Probshrink for MRI

7. Conclusion

From the results in the previous section, it is clear that one needs to make use of specialized denoising algorithms for situations in which one encounters correlated noise in images. The short overview in section 2 shows that there are many such situations in practice. Correlated noise manifests itself as stripes, blobs or other image structures that cannot be modelled as spatially independent. Several useful noise estimation techniques were presented that can be used when creating or adapting a white noise denoising algorithm for use with correlated noise. To illustrate this, some state-of-the-art techniques were explained and compared with techniques designed for white noise.

8. References

Aelterman, J.; Goossens, B.; Pizurica, A. & Philips, W. (2008) Removal of Correlated Rician Noise in Magnetic Resonance Imaging *Proceedings of European Signal Processing Conference (EUSIPCO, Lausanne, 2008*

Aelterman, J.; Goossens, B.; Pizurica, A. ; Philips, W. (2009) Locally Adaptive Complex Wavelet-Based Demosaicing for Color Filter Array Images *Proceedings of SPIE Electronic Imaging 2009, San Jose, CA*, Vol. 7248, no. 0J

Bayer, B. (1976) Color Imaging Array *US Patent 3,971,065*

Borel, C.; Cooke, B.; Laubscher, B. (1996) Partial Removal of Correlated noise in Thermal Imagery *Proceedings of SPIE*, Vol. 2759, 131

Buades, A., Coll B. & Morel J. M. (2005) Image Denoising by Non-Local Averaging, *Proc. IEEE Int. Conf. on Acoustics, Speech, and Signal Processing*, vol. 2, pp. 25-28

Buades, A.; Coll, B & Morel, J.M (2008) Nonlocal Image and Movie Denoising *Int Journal on Computer vision* Vol. 76, pp. 123-139

Dabov, K.; Foi, A.; Katkovnik, V. & Egiazarian K. (2006) Image Denoising with Block-Matching and 3D Filtering, *Proc. SPIE Electronic Imaging: Algorithms and Systems V*, no. 6064A-30

Dabov, K.; Foi, A.; Katkovnik, V. & Egiazarian K. (2007) Image denoising by sparse 3D transform-domain collaborative filtering, *IEEE Trans. on Im. Processing*, vol. 16, no. 8

Donoho, D. & Johnstone, I. (1994) Adapting to Unknown Smoothness via Wavelet Shrinkage *Journal of the American Statistics Association*, Vol. 90

Donoho, D. L. (1995) De-Noising by Soft-Thresholding, *IEEE Transactions on Information Theory*, vol. 41, pp. 613-62.

Easley, G.; Labate, D.; Lim, Wang-Q, (2006) Sparse Directional Image Representation using the Discrete Shearlet Transform *Preprint submitted to Elsevier Preprint*

Elad, M.; Matalon, B.; & Zibulevsky, M. (2006) Image Denoising with Shrinkage and Redundant Representations *Proc. IEEE Conf. on Computer Vision and Pattern Recognition* vol. 2, pp. 1924-1931

Field, D. (1987) Relations between the statistics of natural images and the response properties of cortical cells *J. Opt. Soc. Am.* A 4, p. 2379-2394

Goossens, B.; Pizurica, A. & Philips, W. (2007) Removal of Correlated Noise by Modeling Spatial Correlations and Interscale Dependencies in the Complex Wavelet Domain *Proceedings of International Conference on Image Processing (ICIP)* pp. 317-320

Goossens, B.; Luong, H., Pizurica, A. Pizurica & Philips, W. (2008) An Improved Non-Local Denoising Algorithm *Proceedings of international Workshop on Local and Non-Local Approximation in Image Processing*, Lausanne, 2008

Goossens, B.; Pizurica, A. & Philips W. (2009) Removal of correlated noise by modelling the signal of interest in the wavelet domain *IEEE Transactions on Image Processing* in press

Guerrero-Colon, J. ; Simoncelli, E. & Portilla, J. (2008) Image Denoising using Mixtures of Gaussian Scale Mixtures, *Proc. IEEE Int. Conf. on Image Processing (ICIP)*, San Diego, 2008.

Hastie, Trevor; Tibshirani, Robert & Friedman, J. (2001) The Elements of Statistical Learning *New York: Springer* 8.5 The EM algorithm pp. 236–24

Kingsbury, N. G. (2001) Complex Wavelets for shift Invariant analysis and Filtering of Signals, *Journal of Applied and Computational Harmonic Analysis*, vol. 10, no. 3, pp. 234-253

Kwon, O.; Sohn, K. & Lee, C. (2003) Deinterlacing using Directional Interpolation and Motion Compensation *IEEE Transactions on Consumer Electronics*, vol. 49, no. 1

Malfait, M. & Roose, D. (1997) Wavelet-Based image denoising using a Markov random field a priori model. *IEEE Transactions on Image Processing*, vol. 6, no. 4, pp. 549-565

Mallat, S. (1989) A theory for multiresolution signal decomposition: the wavelet representation *IEEE Pat. Anal. Mach. Intell.*, Vol. 11, pp. 674-693

Mallat, S. (1998) A Wavelet Tour of Signal Processing, *Academic Press, 1998*, p. 174

Nowak, R. (1999) Wavelet-based Rician noise removal for Magnetic Resonance Imaging *Transactions on Image Processing*, vol. 10, no. 8, pp. 1408-1419

Pizurica, A.; Philips, W.; Lemahieu, I. & Acheroy, M. (2003) A Versatile Wavelet Domain Noise filtration Technique for Medical Imaging *IEEE Transactions on Medical Imaging*, vol. 22, no. 3, pp. 323-331

Pizurica, A. & Philips, W. (2006) Estimating the Probability of the Presence of Signal of Interest in Multiresolution Single- and Multiband Image Denoising *IEEE Transactions on Image Processing*, Vol. 15, No. 3, pp. 654-665

Pizurica, A. & Philips, W. (2007) Analysis of least squares estimators under Bernoulli-Laplacian priors *Twenty eighth Symposium on Information Theory in the Benelux* Enschede, The Netherlands, May 24-25 2007

Portilla, J.; Strela, V.; Wainwright, M.J. & Simoncelli, E.P. (2003) Image Denoising using Scale Mixtures of Gaussians in the Wavelet Domain *IEEE Transactions On Image Processing*, vol. 12, no. 11., pp. 1338-1351

Portilla, J. (2004) Full Blind Denoising through Noise Covariance Estimation using Gaussian Scale Mixtures in the Wavelet Domain, *Proc. IEEE Int. Conf. on Image Processing (ICIP)*, pp. 1217-1220

Portilla, J. (2005) Image Restoration using Gaussian Scale Mixtures in Overcomplete Oriented Pyramids *SPIE's 50th Annual Meeting, Proc. of the SPIE*, vol. 5914, pp. 468-82

Romberg, J; Choi, H. & Baraniuk R. (2000) Bayesian Tree-Structured Image Modeling using Wavelet-domain Hidden Markov Models *IEEE Transactions on Image Processing*, vol. 10, no. 7

Ruderman, D (1994) The statistics of natural images *Network: Computation in Neural Systems*, Vol. 5, pp. 517-548

Selesnick, I.W.; Baraniuk, R.G. & Kingsbury, N.G. (2005) The Dual-Tree Complex Wavelet Transform, *IEEE Signal Processing Magazine*, pp 123-151

Simoncelli, E.; Freeman, W.; Adelson, E. & Heeger D. (1992) Shiftable Multi-Scale Transforms or, "What's Wrong with Orthonormal Wavelets" *IEEE Trans. Information Theory, Special Issue on Wavelets Vol. 38, No. 2, pp. 587-607*

Starck, J.-L; Candès, E. J. & Donoho, D. L. (2002) The Curvelet Transform for Image Denoising, *IEEE Transactions on Image Processing*, vol. 11, no. 6, pp. 670-684

Tomasi, C. & Manduchi, R. (1998) Bilateral Filtering for Gray and Color Images *Proceedings of the 1998 IEEE International Conference on Computer Vision, Bombay,India, 1998*

Wainwright, J. & Simoncelli, E. (2000) Scale Mixtures of Gaussians and the Statistics of Natural Images *Advances in Neural Information Processing Systems*, Vol. 12, pp. 855-861

Noise Estimation of Polarization-Encoded Images by Peano-Hilbert Fractal Path

Samia Ainouz-Zemouche[1] and Fabrice Mériaudeau[2]
[1]*Laboratoire d'Informatique, de Traitement de l'Information et des systèmes, (LITIS, EA4108), INSA de Rouen, 76000 Rouen*
[2]*Laboratoire Electronique Informatique et Image (LE2I, UMR CNRS 5158), IUT le Creusot, 71200 Le Creusot*
France.

1. Introduction

Polarization-sensitive imaging systems have emerged as a very attractive vision technique which can reveal important information about the physical and geometrical properties of the targets. Many imaging polarimeters have been designed in the past for several fields, ranging from metrology (Ferraton et al., 2007), (Morel et al., 2006) to medical (Miura et al., 2006) and remote sensing applications (Chipman, 1993).

Imaging systems that can measure the polarization state of the outgoing light across a scene are mainly based on the ability to build effective Polarization State Analyzers (PSA) in front of the camera enabling to acquire the Stokes vectors (Chipman, 1993), (Tyo et al., 2006). These Stokes polarimeters produced four images called "Stokes images" corresponding to the four Stokes parameters. Accordingly, polarization-encoded images have a multidimensional structure; i.e. multi-component information is attached to each pixel in the image. Moreover, the information content of polarization-encoded images is intricately combined in the polarization channels making awkward their proper interpretation in the presence of noise.

Noise is inherent to any imaging systems and it is therefore present on Stokes images. It is of additive nature when the scene is illuminated by incoherent light and multiplicative when the illumination is coherent (Bénière et al., 2007), (Corner et al., 2003). Its presence degrades the interpretability of the data and prevents from exploring the physical potential of polarimetric information. Few works in the literature addressed the filtering of polarimetric images. We note nevertheless the use of optimization methods by (Zallat et al., 2006) to optimize imaging system parameters that condition signal to noise ratio, or the improvement of the accuracy of the degree of polarization by (Bénière et al., 2007) with the aim of reducing the noise in Stokes images.

The main problem in filtering polarization-encoded images so as to remove their noise content is to respect their physical content. Indeed, mathematical operations which are performed on polarization information images while processing them alter in most cases the physical meaning of the images. The same problem has been encountered for polarization

images segmentation in (Ainouz, 2006a) and (Ainouz, 2006b). Therefore, because of the duality between the polarization images filtering and their physical constraint, a trade-off is to be reached in order to minimize the effect of the noise affecting polarimetric images and to preserve their physical meaning.
In this chapter, we present a technique which, estimate the additive noise (images acquired under incoherent illumination), and eliminate it such that the physical content of the polarimetric images is preserved as much as possible. Our technique combines two methods; Scatter plot (Aiazzi et al., 2002) and data masking (Corner et al., 2003) previously used in the field of multispectral imaging and to take advantage of both them.
As the information content of polarization-encoded images is intricately combined in several polarization channels, Peano-Hilbert fractal path is applied on the noisy image to keep the connectivity of homogeneous areas and to minimize the impact of the outliers. The performances and the bias of our method are statistically investigated by Bootstrap method.
The rest of this chapter is organized as follows: the next section deals with the principle of polarisation images acquisition, the third part details our noise estimation technique whereas part 4 presents the results obtained while filtering polarization encoded images. The chapter ends with a short conclusion.

2. Polarization images acquisition

The next two subsections respectively present the principle of a Stoke's imaging system as well as the model for the additive noise resulting from the acquisition set-up.

2.1 Stokes imaging

The general polarization state of a light wave can be described by the so called Stokes vector S which fully characterizes the time-averaged polarization properties of a radiation. It is defined by the following combination of complex-valued components E_x and E_y of the electric field, along two orthogonal directions x and y as (Chipman, 1993):

$$S = \begin{pmatrix} S_0 \\ S_1 \\ S_2 \\ S_3 \end{pmatrix} = \begin{pmatrix} \langle E_x E_x^* \rangle + \langle E_y E_y^* \rangle \\ \langle E_x E_x^* \rangle - \langle E_y E_y^* \rangle \\ 2\,Re\left(\langle E_x E_y^* \rangle\right) \\ 2\,Im\left(\langle E_x E_y^* \rangle\right) \end{pmatrix} \tag{1}$$

The first parameter (S_0) is the total intensity of the optical field and the other three parameters (S_1, S_2 and S_3) describe the polarization state (Chipman, 1993). S_1 is the tendency of the wave to look like a linear horizontal vibration (S_1 positive) or a linear vertical vibration (S_1 negative). S_2 and S_3 reflect the nature and the direction of rotation of the wave. It is straightforward to show that

$$S_0^2 \geq S_1^2 + S_2^2 + S_3^2 \tag{2}$$

This condition is known as the physical condition of Stokes formalism. An arbitrary vector that does not satisfy this condition is not a Stokes vector and doesn't possess any physical meaning.
The general scheme of Stokes images acquisition is illustrated in Figure.1 (Chipman, 1993). The device used for the acquisition is named a classical polarimeter. The wave reflected from the target, represented by a Stokes vector S_{in} , is analyzed by a polarization-state analyzer (PSA) by measuring its projections over four linearly independent states. A PSA consists of a linear polarizer (LP) and a quarter wave (QW) rotating about four angles $(\theta_i)_{i=1,4}$. Incoming intensities are then measured with a standard CCD camera.

The complete set of 4 measurements can be written in a vectorial form as:

$$I = AS_{in} \tag{3}$$

I is a 4×1 intensity matrix measured by the camera. The Stokes vector S_{in} can then easily be extracted from the raw data matrix I provided that the modulation matrix A of the PSA, is known from calibration. For the ideal case (theory), matrix A can be given as (Chipman, 1993):

$$A(\theta_i) = \begin{bmatrix} 1 & -cos^2 2\theta_i & -\frac{1}{2} sin 4\theta_i & sin^2 2\theta_i \\ -1 & cos^2 2\theta_i & \frac{1}{2} sin 4\theta_i & -sin^2 2\theta_i \\ 0 & 0 & 0 & 0 \\ 0 & 0 & 0 & 0 \end{bmatrix} \tag{4}$$

The angles θ_i are chosen such that the matrix A is invertible to easily recover the Stokes parameters from the intensity matrix. Each of the four intensity component corresponds to one image, leading to four images carrying information about the Stokes vector.

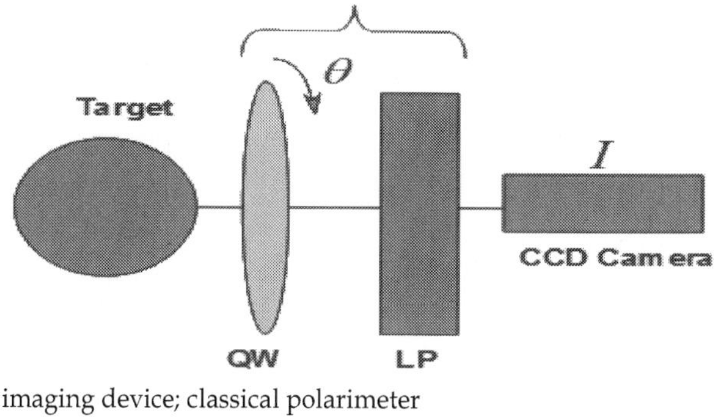

Fig. 1. Stokes imaging device; classical polarimeter

Figure. 2 shows an example of a set of Stokes images obtained with the Stokes imaging device. In order to test the performances of our algorithm, Stokes images were acquired in strong noisy conditions. In order to have these strong noisy conditions, addition to the natural noise, a hair dryer is turned between the PSA and the camera. The scene is made of 4 small elements of different composition glued on a cardboard. Objects A and D are transparents whereas objects B and C are darks.

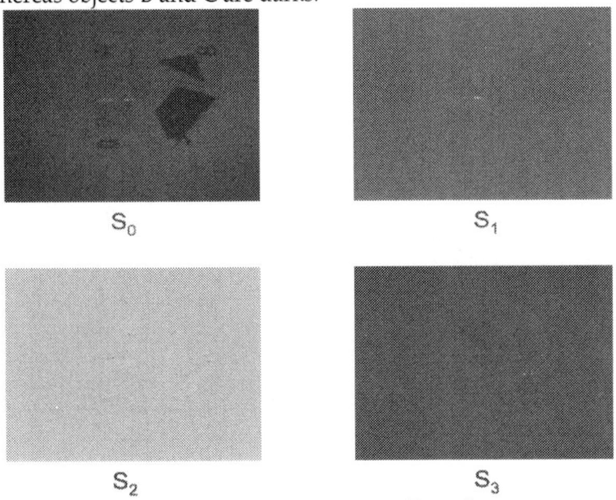

Fig. 2. Stokes image of four small objects glued on a cardboard

The following subsection describes the noise model which was used through out this study.

2.1 Noise in Stokes images

It has been established that under incoherent illumination, the noise affecting the images can be modelled as additive and independent (Corner et al., 2003). This type of noise can be modelled by a zero mean random Gaussian distribution which probability density function (PDF) is expressed as follows (Aiazzi et al., 2002):

$$f_x(x) = \frac{1}{\sigma_n \sqrt{2\pi}} exp\left(-\frac{x^2}{2\sigma_n^2} \right) \tag{5}$$

Where σ_n^2 is the noise variance. The effect of an additive noise n_a on a digital image g at the pixel position (i,j) is expressed as the sum of the noise free image I and the noise in the form :

$$g = I + n_a \tag{6}$$

In perfect acquisition conditions, the Stokes vector is recovered from equation (3) such that:

$$S(i,j) = A^{-1} I(i,j) \tag{7}$$

In the presence of noise, equation (7) becomes:

$$\begin{aligned}\hat{S}(i,j) &= A^{-1}\left(I(i,j)+n_a(i,j)\right) \\ &= A^{-1}I(i,j)+A^{-1}n_a(i,j) \\ &= S(i,j)+\delta S(i,j)\end{aligned} \tag{8}$$

The estimated Stokes vector $\hat{S}$ is an independent sum of the theoretical Stokes vector (noise free) S and the term δS due to the additive noise effects. The estimation of the noise distribution is then needed to reconstruct the noisy image δS and minimize its effects on the estimated Stokes image $\hat{S}$.

However, as explained above, in the introduction, direct filtering of polarimetric measurements can induce a non physical meaning of the filtered Stokes image $\hat{S}-\delta S$. This means that for an important number of pixels, the vector $\hat{S}-\delta S$ does not satisfy the physical constraint stated in equation (2) and therefore cannot be considered as a Stokes vector which fully fulfils physical constraints. In such conditions, these images have no interest and additional steps have be taken to obtain a trade-off between filtering and physical meaning for as many pixels as possible. The following section presents three methods for noise estimation in the case of additive Gaussian noise.

3. Parametric noise estimation

Inasmuch as the estimated noised Stokes image is an independent sum of the noise and the noise free image, the estimation of the δS distribution is sufficient to have information about the additive noise. Two multi-spectral filtering methods: Scatter plot method (SP) (Aiazzi et al., 2002) and data masking method (DM) (Corner et al., 2003) were used to process the images. The proposed filtering algorithm takes advantages of both methods.

In order to eliminate the impact of non relevant data, the image is first transformed to a Peano-Hilbert fractal path. This method is applied onto gray level images and the results are compared to the results obtained with SP and DM methods.

3.1 Scatter plot and Data masking methods reminder

3.1.1 Scatter plot method (SP)

In the SP method, the standard deviation of the noisy observed image can be evaluated in homogeneous areas (Aiazzi et al., 2002). Under the assumption that the noise is Gaussian with zero mean, local means μ and local standard deviations σ are calculated in a sliding small window within the whole image. The scatter plot plane of local standard deviations (σ) versus local means (μ) is plotted and then partitioned into rectangular blocks of size $L \times L$ (100×100 for example). After sorting the blocks by decreasing number of points, denser blocks are considered as the homogeneous areas of the image. The estimated standard deviation of the noise, $\hat{\sigma}$, is found as the intersection between the linear regression of the data set corresponding to homogenous areas with the ordinate (y) axis.

3.1.2 Data masking method (DM)

DM method deals by first filtering the image to remove the image structure, leaving only the noise (Corner et al., 2003). The Laplacian Kernel presented in equation.9 is used for that purpose. The image obtained after the convolution with the Laplacian kernel (Laplacian image) mainly contains the noise as well as the edges of the objects present in the original image. The Laplacian image is further filtered with a Sobel detector (Kazakova et al., 2004), followed by a threshold in order to create a binary edge map. This edge map is subtracted to the Laplacian image (to produce the Final Image) in order to reduce the contribution of the edges to the noise estimation.
The optimal threshold is established by varying the threshold and choosing the one for which the variance in the final image (Laplacian - edge map) is maximum
Then, on the final image, standard deviations are calculated on 9x9 blocks and the median value of the histogram of the standard deviation is used as the estimate of the noise standard deviation.

$$L = \begin{pmatrix} 1 & -2 & 1 \\ -2 & 4 & -2 \\ 1 & -2 & 1 \end{pmatrix} \tag{9}$$

The outline of the noise estimation procedure can be summarized by the following algorithm:

1-Start
2-Acquire Image
3-Apply Laplacian Kernel
4-Apply Sobel Kernel
5-Select the optimal threshold
6-Subtract edges map to the Laplacian Image
7-Calculate the variance in a 9x9 blocks
8-Create the histogram of the standard deviation
9-Select the median value as the noise standard deviation estimate.
10-Stop

3.2 Fractal vectorization filtering algorithm (FVFA)

The two previous methods have limitations which can be summarized as follows:

- SP method is not appropriate for rich textured images. It is time effective because of the calculation of local statistics within the image.
- DM method overestimates the noise parameters due to edges points which remain in the final image.

In order to estimate the final noise parameters, our algorithm keeps the idea of calculating the residual image and the use of the local statistics. The remaining limitations of these combined ideas will be compensated by a vectorization of the residual image by the Peano-Hilbert fractal path.
As for the DM method, operations 1 to 6 (with a fixed filter) are applied to the original image. The resulting image is then transformed on a vector following a fractal path as presented in an 9×9 image example of Figure.3. The path deals with the Peano-Hilbert

fractal path and the vector is designed in the same way as the numbering of Figure.3, from 1 to 81.

1	6	7	48	49	54	55	60	61
2	5	8	47	50	53	56	59	62
3	4	9	46	51	52	57	58	63
16	15	10	45	40	39	70	69	64
17	14	11	44	41	38	71	68	65
18	13	12	43	42	37	72	67	66
19	24	25	30	31	36	73	78	79
20	23	26	29	32	35	74	77	80
21	22	27	28	33	34	75	76	81

Fig. 3. Peano-Hilbert fractal path

Local means μ and standard deviations σ are calculated on the resulting vector by using a shifting interval. The local mean and non-biased standard deviation are respectively defined as:

$$\mu_v(i) = \frac{1}{2m+1} \sum_{k=-m}^{m} v(i+k) \qquad (10)$$

$$\sigma_v(i) = \left(\frac{1}{2m} \sum_{k=-m}^{m} \left(v(i+k) - \mu_v(i)\right)^2 \right)^{1/2}$$

where v is the portion of the Laplacian image vector limited by the shifting interval of size $2m+1$. These local statistics are the vectorial version of those calculated in SP algorithm applied on the residual no-edges image.

The plane (μ, σ) is then plotted. Two types of points are formed in that plane (Aiazzi et al., 2002). The first type is a dense cloud and the second is an isolated set of points corresponding to the remaining edges pixels that are not eliminated by the Sobel filtering. The intersection of linear regression of the cloud points and the y axis gives the better estimation of the noise standard deviation. Similarly, the mean of the noise may be estimated by applying the same instructions on the plotted plane (σ, μ).

The advantage of the fractal path is double: it eases the task of calculating the local statistics within the image with keeping at most the neighbourhood of image pixels. Moreover, the vectorization of the image disperses so much the isolated points of the plane (μ, σ)

preventing the regression process from taking them into account. This fact decreases the overestimation of the noise as in the DM method.

3.3 Application to gray level images

To prove the efficiency of the proposed algorithm, three experiments were carried out on two 256x256 gray level images (Figure.4). The first image is a chessboard image and the second image is a section of the 3D MRI (Magnetic Resonance Imaging) of the head. Additive noises of zero mean with variances 5, 10, 30 and 60 are added to these two images. The noise variance is then estimated by the three methods exposed previously: SP method, DM method, and our proposed algorithm (FVFA). In order to have robust statistical results, the estimated standard deviation $\hat{\sigma}$ is the empirical mean of 200 estimations found by the re-sampling Bootstrap method (Cheng, 1995). The dispersion σ_d is then estimated showing that the exact value of the standard deviation lies in the interval $[\hat{\sigma}-3\sigma_d, \hat{\sigma}+3\sigma_d]$ with a probability of 99,73%.

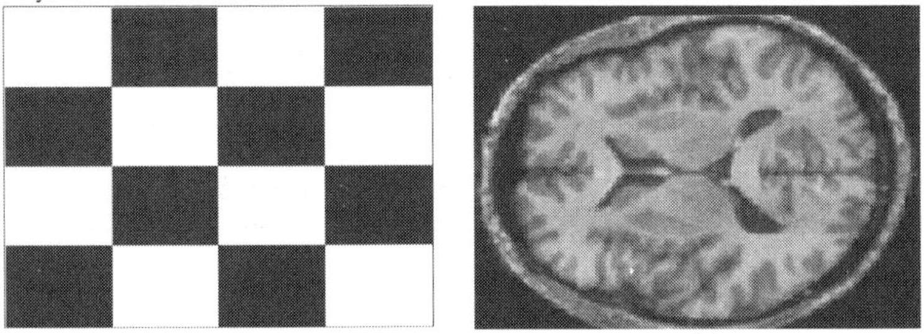

(a) (b)

Fig.4. Gray level images used to the validation of the proposed algorithm, (a) chessboard, (b) section of a 3D MRI of the head.

The results of the estimation are summarized in Table 1 for the Figure.4. (a) and in Table 2 for the Figure. 4. (b). The dispersion σ_d is displayed between brackets.

Our algorithm proved to exhibit better performances than the two other methods. As expected our method is even better when dealing with textured image (table 1).

Combined with some physical considerations, in the next section this method is applied to estimate the noise present in polarimetric images.

Simulated noise	SP method	DM method	FV method
σ^2	$\hat{\sigma}^2$	$\hat{\sigma}^2$	$\hat{\sigma}^2$
5	10.23[0.5]	9.3[0.41]	5.8[0.04]
10	16.84[0.45]	11.45[0.32]	10.97[0.02]
30	35.09[0.3]	32.75[0.27]	29.59[0.01]
60	63.75[0.27]	62.04[0.12]	60.75[0.01]

Table 1 - Comparison of the noise estimation parameters using SP, DM and FVFA methods on the image of Figure.4. (a).

Simulated noise	SP method	DM method	FV method
σ^2	$\hat{\sigma}^2$	$\hat{\sigma}^2$	$\hat{\sigma}^2$
5	9.13[0.48]	7.8[0.41]	5.4[0.01]
10	13.12[0.41]	11.23[0.3]	9.38[0.01]
30	32.45[0.29]	31.01[0.15]	30.25[0.009]
60	57.41[0.16]	61.08[0.2]	60.09[0.007]

Table 2 - Comparison of the noise estimation parameters using SP, DM and FVFA methods on the image of Figure. 4. (b).

4. Polarimetric images filtering

4.1 Polarization-based filtering

As seen in section 2 the measured Stokes vector $\hat{S}$ attached to the pixel (i,j) is given as an independent sum of the perfect Stokes vector S_p and an attached noise term δS by:

$$\hat{S}(i,j) = S_p(i,j) + \delta S(i,j) \tag{11}$$

The term δS is equal to $A^{-1}\delta I$ ($\delta I = n_a$). Under Gaussian assumption of the additive noise, noise parameters are estimated by FVFA method. The intensity noise δI is reconstructed and the polarimetric noise attached term δS is calculated.

Naturally, the real Stokes vector S_p can be derived from equation (11) by:

$$S_p(i,j) = \hat{S}(i,j) - \delta S(i,j) \tag{12}$$

Furthermore, the richness information of our images is extremely conditioned by the physical content, .i.e. the vector S_p must satisfy equation (2). However, the direct application of equation (12) to filter polarimetric image may induce the non physical

behaviour of a large amount of image pixels. Mathematically, this is due to the fact that the set of physical Stokes vectors is not a space vector. Therefore, any addition or subtraction of two Stokes quantities may lead to a no physical result.
In order to handle this fundamental limitation, a new tool is needed to find the best trade-off between the filtering and the physical constraint of Stokes images.
The Stokes vector S_p must satisfy equation (2), which is equivalent to the following formula:

$$S_p^T G S_p \geq 0, \qquad G = diag(1,-1,-1,-1) \tag{13}$$

Where *diag* refers to the diagonal. To control the physical condition on the vector S_p, a parameter α which lies in the interval $[0,1]$ is inserted into equation (12) such that:

$$S_p = \hat{S} - \alpha \delta S \tag{14}$$

If this parameter is too large the physical condition will not be respected whereas if it is too small the filtering is not efficient. The parameter α cannot take negative values; it will result in noise amplification.
Combining equations (13) and (14), one has to search the parameter α that satisfies:

$$\left(\hat{S} - \alpha \delta S\right)^T G\left(\hat{S} - \alpha \delta S\right) \geq 0 \tag{15}$$

Developing equation (15), one has to search the parameter α that respects the inequality:

$$\begin{aligned} f(\alpha) &= \left(\hat{S} - \alpha \delta S\right)^T G\left(\hat{S} - \alpha \delta S\right) = \\ &\hat{S}^T G \hat{S} - \left(\delta S^T G \hat{S} + \hat{S}^T G \delta S\right)\alpha + \left(\delta S^T G \delta S\right)\alpha^2 \geq 0 \end{aligned} \tag{16}$$

Assuming that $a = \delta S^T G \delta S$, $b = \delta S^T G \hat{S} + \hat{S}^T G \delta S$, $c = \hat{S}^T G \hat{S}$, equation (16) is written in the simplified form as:

$$f(\alpha) = a\alpha^2 + b\alpha + c \geq 0 \tag{17}$$

Two real solutions are given by:

$$\alpha = \frac{-b - \sqrt{\Delta}}{2a}, \quad or \quad \alpha = \frac{-b + \sqrt{\Delta}}{2a}, \text{ with } \Delta = b^2 - 4ac$$

Assume that α_1 always refers to the smallest solution and α_2 to the greatest one. For an infinitesimal ε such that if α_i is positive, $\alpha_i - \varepsilon$ is still positive and after the classical resolution of the inequality (17), three cases arise depending on the sign of a:

$sign(a) > 0$

- If $1 \in [\alpha_1, \alpha_2]$ thus $\alpha = 1$
- If $1 \in [\alpha_1, \alpha_2]$ and $\alpha_1 > 0$ thus $\alpha = \alpha_1 - \varepsilon$
- Otherwise there is no α between 0 and 1

$sign(a) < 0$

- If $1 \in [-\infty, \alpha_1] \cup [\alpha_2, +\infty]$ thus $\alpha = 1$
- If $0 < \alpha_2 < 1$ thus $\alpha = \alpha_2 - \varepsilon$

- Otherwise there is no α between 0 and 1

$a = 0$

- One solution exists $\alpha_1 = \alpha_2 = \frac{c}{b}$
- If $0 < \alpha_1 < 1$ thus $\alpha = \alpha_1 - \varepsilon$
- If $\alpha_1 > 1$ thus $\alpha = 1$
- Otherwise there is no α between 0 and 1

These three cases take in account the fact that α must belong to [0,1]. Finally the algorithm can be summarized as:

1. Construct the noise term δS attached to each image pixel by the FVFA method Compute equation (10) for each pixel
2. If the pixel's Stokes vector is physically realisable (equation (2) verified for the pixel), set α to 1
3. Otherwise, search the parameter α by following the above instructions.
4. If the discriminate Δ is negative or if there is no α in [0,1], choose the Stokes vector satisfying the maximum between $\hat{S}^T G \hat{S}$ and $S_p^T G S_p$

4.2 Illustration and discussion

Our algorithm is run on two images: one simulated Stokes image for which the noise additive contents is known and a real Stokes image. The synthetic image is built as follows: the Stokes vector at the image center is set to $S = \begin{bmatrix} 1 & 1/\sqrt{3} & 1/\sqrt{3} & 1/\sqrt{3} \end{bmatrix}$ (white elliptical part) and to zero elsewhere. Stokes images are multiplied by the modulation matrix A as in equation (3) in order to have the corresponding intensity channels. Then, a Gaussian noise of zero mean and variance 0.2 is added to each intensity channel. Noisy images are inverted as in equation (7) to get the noisy Stokes image (Figure. 5).

The estimated variances using FVFA filtering algorithm on the four intensity channels corresponding to S_0, S_1, S_2 and S_3 are respectively 0.18, 0.19, 0.194 and 0.187.

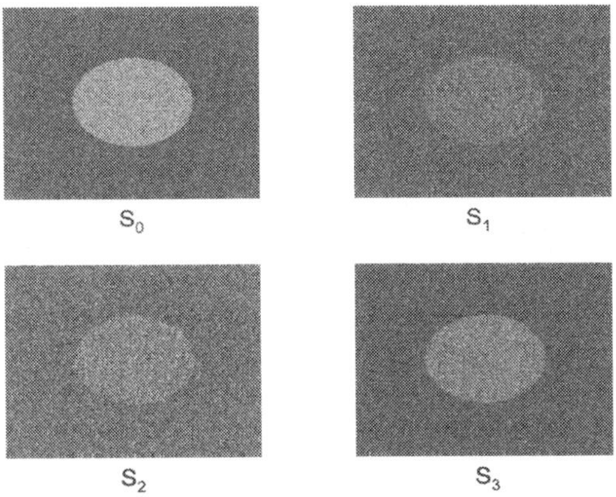

Fig. 5 . Noisy Stokes channels. Gaussian zero-mean noise and of variance 0.2 is added to the correspondent intensity channels

These values are very close to the simulated variance. The results also show that the noise affecting the four polarimetric measurements is roughly the same. The regularization parameter α is calculated for each pixel. Figure. 6 shows the binary values of this parameter. Pixels for which α is found between 0 and 1 appear white otherwise black.

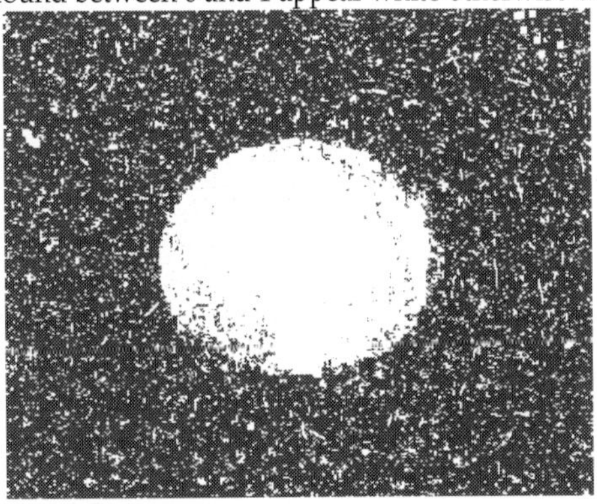

Fig. 6. Binary values of the regularization parameter α

The use of the regularization parameter allows the processing of an important amount of pixels in the image. Indeed without this parameter (equation 12), the image is well filtered but only 10% of the pixels in S_p have physical meaning whereas it reaches 70% with the use of parameter α (equation 14). The amount of remaining pixels having no physical meaning is less important. It is due to the fact that conditions 1 to 4 of the algorithm are not satisfied and neither $\hat{S}^T G\hat{S}$ nor $S_p^T GS_p$ are positive (step 4). The result of the two filtering processes is illustrated in Figure. 7.

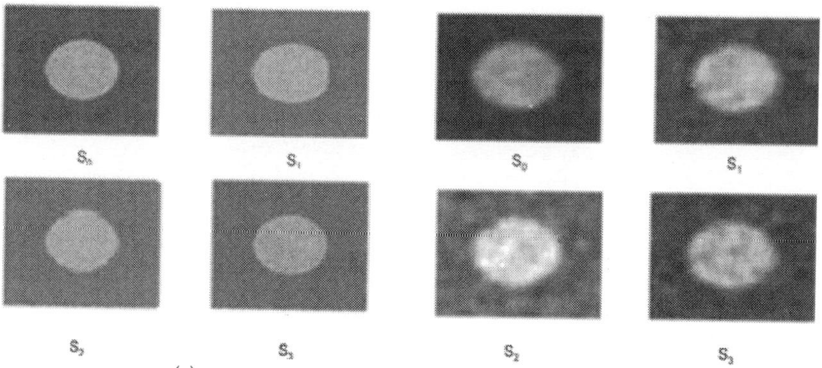

(a) (b)

Fig.7. Filtered Stokes images with: (a) regularization parameter (equation 10), (b) without regularization parameter (equation 12)

As shown in Figure.7. (a), our algorithm ensures an improvement in polarimetric information carried by Stokes image preserving its physical constraint for most of the pixels. The real measurement case deals with the Stokes image of Figure. 2. The inherent noise variances estimated on the correspondent intensity images are respectively up to 10.75, 10.52, 9.78 and 9.88 on a gray scale value of 8 bits. Results of the physical filtering on noisy Stokes images are presented in Figure. 8. The new filtering ensures 64% of physical pixels whereas the classical filtering ensures only 7% of physical pixels. Again, real experiment shows the performances of our method. The proposed algorithm is thus a trade-off between a fully filtered image and a physical constrained (of the most pixels) image. Only additive independent noie is considered herein. Consequently, most of the imperfections remaining after the physical filtering (Figure. 8. b) arise from other sources of noise. This problem will be addressed in future works.

5. Conclusion

A new algorithm to filter polarimetric images is introduced in this chapter. Based on the filtering methods of multispectral images and combined with a fractal vectorization of the image, the new algorithm is a trade-off between a classical filtering (noise smoothing) and preserving the physcial meaning of the data. No comparison with other methods is done in this paper, because in the best of our knowledge, this work is the first dealing with the trade-off between filtering of polarimetric images and preserving the physical condition. Our methods are tested on simulated and on real images acquired with a classical polarimeter. Promising results were presented at the end of the chapter. As the additive noise in not the only noise affecting polarimetric measurement, other sources of noise are currently being investigated especially multiplicative noise.

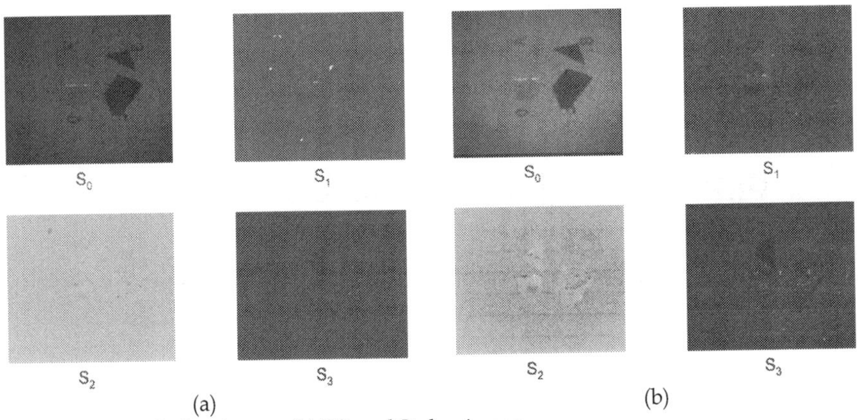

Fig. 8. (a) Noisy Stokes image, (b) Filtered Stokes image

6. References

B. Aiazzi, L. Alparone, A. Barducci, S. Baronti & I. Pippi. (2002). Estimating noise and information of multispectral imagery, In *Opt. Eng*, vol.41, pp. 656–668.

S. Ainouz, J. Zallat & A. De Martino. (2006a). Clustering and color preview of polarization-encoded images. *Eusipco 2006*, Firenze, September 2006, Italy.

S. Ainouz, J. Zallat, A. De Martino & C. Collet. (2006b). Physical interpretation of polarization-encoded images by color preview, *Opt. Express*, Vol. 14, pp. 5916-5927.

A. Bénière, F. Goudail, M. Alouini & D. Dolfi. (2007). Precision of degree of polarization estimation in the presence of additive Gaussian detector noise, *Optics Communication*, vol. 278, pp. 264–269, October 2007.

R. C. H. Cheng. (1995). Bootstrap methods in computer simulation experiments, in *Simulation Conference Proc.* vol.2, pp. 71–177.

R.A. Chipman. (1993). Polarimetry, In: *Handbook of Optics*, M. Bass, ed (McGraw-Hill, New York), pp. 22.1-22.36.

A. B. Corner, R. M. Narayanan & S. E. Reichenbach. (2003). Noise estimation in remote sensing imagery using data masking, In *Int. J. Remote sensing*, vol.4, pp. 689–702.

M. Ferraton, C. Stolz & F. Meriaudeau. (2007). 3D reconstruction of transparent objects using image polarization, *EOS topical meeting*, pp. 110-111, Lille, France.

N. Kazakova, M. Margala & N. G. Durdle. (2004). Sobel edge detection processor for a real-time volume rendering system, in *ISCAS'04*, vol.2, pp. 913–916.

M. Miura et al. (2006). Imaging Polarimetry in Central Serous Chorioretinopathy, *American Journal of Ophtamology*, 40 (6), pp. 1014-1019.

O. Morel, C. Stolz, F. Meriaudeau & P. Gorria. (2006). Active Lighting Applied to 3D Reconstruction of Specular Metallic Surfaces by Polarization Imaging, *Applied Optics*, 45 (17), pp. 4062-4068

S. Tyo, et al. (2006). Review of passive imaging polarimetry for remote sensing applications, Vol. 45, No. 22 , *Applied Optics*, pp 4553-5469.

J. Zallat, S. Ainouz & M-P. Stoll. (2006). Optimal configuration for imaging polarimeters : impact of image noise and systematic errors, in *J. Opt.* vol.8, pp. 807–814.

15

Speech Enhancement based on Iterative Wiener Filter using Complex LPC Speech Analysis

Keiichi Funaki
University of the Ryukyus
Japan

1. Introduction

In these days, the speech enhancement plays an important role to improve the performance of the speech coding or speech recognition since cellular phone or the car navigation system are being widely used more and more. These systems are often used in noisy environment. Therefore, the quality of speech coding or the performance of speech recognition is deteriorated due to the surrounding noise. In order to avoid the deterioration, technology that removes noise from the noisy speech viz., speech enhancement is strongly desired. Especially, speech enhancement is an important factor for speech coding to keep the quality even under noisy environment. 3GPP (The 3rd Generation Partnership Project) thus provides the minimum performance requirement and the evaluation procedure for AMR-NB [1]. Several speech enhancement methods such as [2] have already satisfied the requirement. Moreover, speech enhancement is being sincerely demanded for wide band speech coding such as [3] since the additive noise in wide band speech can be percept by human auditory system. Traditional approaches for speech enhancement have been proposed from the end of 1970's to 1980's [4][5][6]. Spectrum subtraction (SS) method [4] is widely adopted since it can be implemented easily and it can offer some degree of effect. However, the SS generates unpleasant artificial sound called musical noise so that it is not suitable for speech coding. In MMSE-STSA (Minimizing Mean Squared Error-Short Term Spectral Amplitude) method [5], under an assumption of Gaussian distribution of Fourier coefficient for speech, speech enhancement is realized by minimizing the mean squared error for Short Term Spectral Amplitude (STSA) spectrum. On the other hand, MAP (Maximum a Posterior) method [7] has been proposed, in which the parametric function that differs from that for the MMSE-STSA, is adopted as a criterion. Wiener filter method has been proposed by J.S.Lim [6], and the method designs the optimal filter minimizing the mean squared error (MSE) in the frequency domain. The musical noise is reduced by the Wiener filter method than the SS method. If accurate power spectrum for clean speech and accurate power spectrum of additive noise can be estimated, the Wiener filter can be designed accurately. However, the power spectrum of clean speech cannot be observed directly. Therefore, the iterative Wiener filter (IWF) method is adopted to estimate the power spectrum more accurately. First, the power spectrum for noise is estimated in silent segment of speech and the speech power spectrum is estimated by LPC analysis for noisy speech. Next, the Wiener filter is designed by using the estimated two spectra and speech enhancement is carried out by filtering the noisy speech with the Wiener filter to obtain the enhanced speech. Next, LPC analysis is operated for the enhanced speech and the Wiener filter is designed again and the filter is operated for the noisy speech to obtain enhanced speech. These procedures are repeated to obtain more accurate speech power spectrum and to design more optimal Wiener filter. However, it is known that the spectrum of the enhanced speech is distorted after several iterations and the optimal number of iteration cannot be determined [8][9].

On the other hand, the complex LPC speech analysis methods have already been proposed for an analytic signal [10][11][12]. An analytic signal is a complex signal having an observed signal in real part and a Hilbert transformed signal for the observed signal in imaginary part. Since the analytic signal provides the spectrum only on positive frequencies, the signals can be decimated by a factor of 2 with no degradation. As a result, the complex speech analysis offers attractive features, for example, more accurate spectral estimation in low frequencies. The remarkable feature is feasible to design more appropriate Wiener filter in the IWF and it is expected that it can lead to higher performance of speech enhancement especially for the additive noise whose energy is concentrated in low frequencies, for example, babble noise or car internal noise.

In this paper, we propose an improved IWF method by adopting the MMSE based time-varying complex AR (TV-CAR) speech analysis [12] instead of LPC analysis. The TV-CAR speech analysis introduces the TV-CAR speech model, in which the AR model parameters are represented by complex basis expansion.

The reminder of this paper is organized as follows. We will explain the TV-CAR speech analysis in Section 2 and we will explain the iterative Wiener filter method and the proposed algorithm in Section 3. The benefit of complex speech analysis will be explained in Section 4. We will explain the experiments evaluating the performance for additive white Gaussian, pink, babble, or car internal noise in Section 5.

2. TV-CAR Speech Analysis

2. 1 Analytic speech signal

Target signal of the time-varying complex AR (TV-CAR) method is an analytic signal that is complex-valued signal defined by

$$y^c(t) = \frac{y(2t) + j \cdot y_H(2t)}{\sqrt{2}} \tag{1}$$

where $j = \sqrt{-1}$ and $y^c(t)$, $y(t)$, and $y_H(t)$ denote an analytic signal at time t, an observed signal at time t, and a Hilbert transformed signal for the observed signal, respectively. Since analytic signals provide the spectra only over the range of $(0, \pi)$, analytic signals can be decimated by a factor of two. The term of $1/\sqrt{2}$ is multiplied in order to adjust the power of an analytic signal with that of the observed one. Note that superscript **c** denotes complex value in this paper.

2. 2 Time-Varying Complex AR (TV-CAR) model

Conventional LPC model is defined as

$$Y_{LPC}(z^{-1}) = \frac{1}{1+\sum_{i=1}^{I} a_i z^{-i}} \tag{2}$$

where $\{a_i\}$ and I are i-th order LPC coefficient and LPC order, respectively. Since the conventional LPC model cannot express the time-varying spectrum, LPC analysis cannot extract the time-varying spectral features from speech signal. In order to represent the time-varying features, the TV-CAR model employs a complex basis expansion shown as

$$a_i^c(t) = \sum_{l=0}^{L-1} g_{i,l}^c f_l^c(t) \tag{3}$$

where $\{a_i^c(t)\}$, I, L, $\{g_{i,l}^c\}$ and $f_l^c(t)$ are taken to be i-th complex AR coefficient at time t, AR order, finite order of complex basis expansion, complex parameter, and a complex-valued basis function, respectively. By substituting Eq.(3) into Eq.(2), one can obtain the following transfer function.

$$Y_{TVCAR}(z^{-1}) = \frac{1}{1+\sum_{i=1}^{I}\sum_{l=0}^{L-1} g_{i,l}^c f_l^c(t) z^{-i}} \tag{4}$$

The input-output relation is defined as

$$y^c(t) = -\sum_{i=1}^{I} a_i^c(t) y^c(t-i) + u^c(t) = -\sum_{i=1}^{L}\sum_{l=0}^{L-1} g_{i,l}^c f_l^c(t) y^c(t-i) + u^c(t) \tag{5}$$

where $u^c(t)$ and $y^c(t)$ are taken to be complex-valued input and analytic speech signal, respectively. In the TV-CAR model, the complex AR coefficient is modelled by a finite number of arbitrary complex basis expansion. Note that Eq.(3) parameterizes the AR coefficient trajectories that continuously change as a function of time so that the time-varying analysis is feasible to estimate continuous time-varying speech spectrum. In addition, as mentioned above, the complex-valued analysis facilitates accurate spectral estimation in the low frequencies, as a result, the TV-CAR analysis allows for more accurate spectral estimation in low Frequencies. Since more optimal Wiener filter can be designed, it assigns better performance on speech enhancement.

Eq.(5) can be represented by vector-matrix notation as

$$\begin{aligned}
\bar{y}_f &= -\bar{\Phi}_f \bar{\theta} + \bar{u}_f \\
\bar{\theta}^T &= [\bar{g}_0^T, \bar{g}_1^T, \ldots, \bar{g}_l^T, \ldots, \bar{g}_{L-1}^T] \\
\bar{g}_l^T &= [g_{1,l}^c, g_{2,l}^c, \ldots, g_{i,l}^c, \ldots, g_{I,l}^c] \\
\bar{y}_f^T &= [y^c(I), y^c(I+1), y^c(I+2), \ldots, y^c(N-1)] \\
\bar{u}_f^T &= [u^c(I), u^c(I+1), u^c(I+2), \ldots, u^c(N-1)] \\
\bar{\Phi}_f &= [\bar{D}_0^f, \bar{D}_1^f, \ldots, \bar{D}_l^f, \ldots, \bar{D}_{L-1}^f] \\
\bar{D}_l^f &= [\bar{d}_{1,l}^f, \ldots, \bar{d}_{i,l}^f, \ldots, \bar{d}_{I,l}^f] \\
\bar{d}_{i,l}^f &= [y^c(I-i) f_l^c(I), y^c(I+1-i) f_l^c(I+1), \ldots, y^c(N-1-i) f_l^c(N-1)]^T
\end{aligned} \tag{6}$$

where N is analysis interval, $\bar{y}_f$ is (N-I,1) column vector containing analytic speech signal, $\bar{\theta}$ is (LI ,1) column vector containing complex parameters, $\bar{\Phi}_f$ is (N-I, LI) matrix containing weighted analytic speech signal by the complex basis. Superscript T denotes transposition.

2. 3 MMSE-based algorithm [12]

Fig.1 shows the block diagram of MMSE estimation. In the estimation, parameters are estimated so as to minimize the mean-square-error of equation error, or residual. MSE criterion is defined as

$$\bar{r}_f = [r^c(I), r^c(I+1), \ldots, r^c(N-1)]^T = \bar{y}_f + \bar{\Phi}_f \bar{\theta}_f \tag{7}$$

$$r^c(t) = y^c(t) + \sum_{i=1}^{I} \sum_{l=0}^{L-1} \hat{g}_{i,l}^c f_l^c(t) y^c(t-i) \tag{8}$$

$$E = \bar{r}_f^H \bar{r}_f = \left(\bar{y}_f + \bar{\Phi}_f \bar{\theta}\right)^H \left(\bar{y}_f + \bar{\Phi}_f \bar{\theta}\right) \tag{9}$$

where $\{\hat{g}_{i,l}^c\}$ is the estimated complex parameter, $r^c(t)$ is an equation error, or complex AR residual and E is Mean Squared Error (MSE) for the equation error. To obtain optimal complex AR coefficients, we minimize the MSE criterion. Minimizing the MSE criterion of Eq.(9) with respect to the complex parameter leads to the following MMSE algorithm.

$$\left(\bar{\mathbf{\Phi}}_f^H \bar{\mathbf{\Phi}}_f\right)\hat{\boldsymbol{\theta}} = -\bar{\mathbf{\Phi}}_f^H \bar{\mathbf{y}}_f \tag{10}$$

Superscript H denotes Hermitian transposition. After solving the linear equation of Eq.(10), we can get the complex AR parameter at time t , $\hat{a}^c(t)$, by calculating the Eq.(3) with the estimated complex parameter, $\{\hat{g}_{i,l}^c\}$.

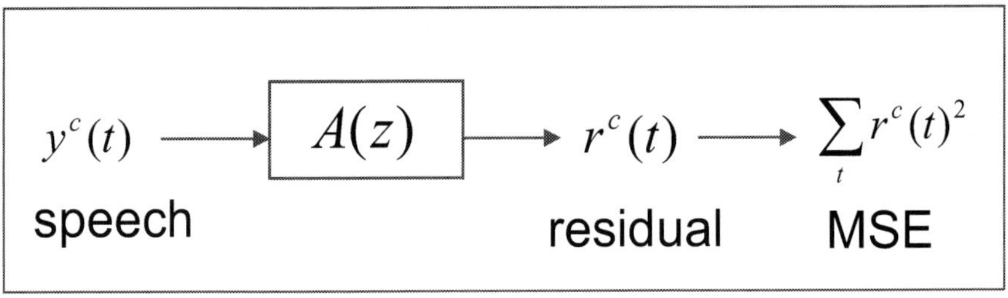

Fig. 1. Block diagram of MMSE estimation

3. Wiener Filter Algorithm

3.1 Wiener filter

Assuming that the clean speech, $s(t)$, degraded by an additive noise, $w(t)$, the noisy speech, $x(t)$, is defined by

$$x(t) = s(t) + w(t) \tag{11}$$

Wiener filter is an optimal filter that minimizes the Mean Squared Error (MSE) criterion. In the case of Eq.(11), the filter can be defined by

$$S(\omega) = H(\omega)X(\omega) \tag{12}$$

where ω is the frequency index, $S(\omega), X(\omega), H(\omega)$ are the discrete Fourier transform of the clean speech, that of noisy speech and that of Wiener filter, respectively. The MSE can be defined as follows. The error is defined as

$$E(\omega) = S(\omega) - \hat{S}(\omega) = S(\omega) - H(\omega)X(\omega) \tag{13}$$

The Mean-Squsre-Error of Eq(11) is defined by

$$E[|E(\omega)|^2] = E[|S(\omega) - H(\omega)X(\omega)|^2] \tag{14}$$

where $E[\bullet]$ stands for an expectation operator. By minimizing the MSE, the Wiener filter $H(\omega)$ can be estimated

$$\frac{\partial E[|E(\omega)|^2]}{\partial H(\omega)} = 2H(\omega)E[|X(\omega)|^2] - 2E[X(\omega)S^*(\omega)] = 2H(\omega)P_{XX}(\omega) - 2P_{XS}(\omega) = 0 \tag{15}$$

where $P_{XX}(\omega), P_{XS}(\omega)$ are the power spectrum of noisy speech and cross power spectrum between noisy speech and clean speech, respectively. If there is no correlation between the speech signal $s(t)$ and additive noise $w(t)$, the power spectrum of the noisy speech and the cross power spectrum can be transformed as follows.

$$\begin{aligned} P_{XX}(\omega) &= E[|X(\omega)|^2] = E[|S(\omega)|^2] + E[|2S(\omega)W(\omega)|] + E[|W(\omega)|^2] \\ &= E[|S(\omega)|^2] + E[|W(\omega)|^2] = P_{SS}(\omega) + P_{WW}(\omega) \\ P_{XS}(\omega) &= E[(S(\omega) + W(\omega))S^*(\omega)] = E[|S(\omega)|^2] = P_{SS}(\omega) \end{aligned} \tag{16}$$

Consequently, the Wiener filter can be derived as follows.

$$H(\omega) = \frac{P_{SS}(\omega)}{P_{SS}(\omega) + P_{WW}(\omega)} \tag{17}$$

From Eq.(12) and (15), the enhanced speech is estimated in the frequency domain by

$$S(\omega) = \frac{P_{ss}(\omega)}{P_{ss}(\omega) + P_{ww}(\omega)} X(\omega) \tag{18}$$

and then inverse FFT is operated to obtain enhanced speech as:

$$s(t) = IFFT(S(\omega)) \tag{19}$$

Finally, the OLA (OverLap Add) procedure is carried out in the time domain between adjacent frames to avoid click sound.

3.2 Iterative Wiener Filter (IWF) algorithm [8][9]

The performance of the Wiener filter depends on the accuracy of speech power spectral estimation, $P_{SS}(\omega)$. It is possible to make the estimated spectrum close to the true one by repeating the Wiener filter processing. Fig.2 shows the block diagram of the iterative Wiener filter algorithm. The two kinds of power spectra can be estimated by LPC analysis as follows. Noise power spectrum, $P_{WW}(\omega)$, are estimated in the first non-speech segment. Speech power spectrum, $P_{SS}(\omega)$, is estimated by LPC analysis for input noisy speech, $x(t)$. By the Wiener filtering in the frequency domain and Inverse FFT operation, enhanced speech is estimated and then it is analyzed in order to estimate more accurate speech power spectrum, $P_{SS}(\omega)$, by means of LPC analysis and the Wiener filter is operated again. The iterative procedure is repeated to obtain more clean speech.

3.3 Proposed Method

The block diagram of the proposed method is shown in Fig.3. The proposed method employs the estimated two spectra, $P_{SS}(\omega)$ and $P_{WW}(\omega)$, estimated by the TV-CAR speech analysis [12] instead of LPC analysis. The two spectra can be estimated as

$$P_{SS}(\omega) = \frac{G_S^2}{|1 + \sum_{i=1}^{I} \sum_{l=0}^{L-1} \hat{g}_{si,,l}^c f_l^c(t) e^{-ji\omega}|^2}$$

$$P_{WW}(\omega) = \frac{G_W^2}{|1 + \sum_{i=1}^{I} \sum_{l=0}^{L-1} \hat{g}_{wi,,l}^c f_l^c(t) e^{-ji\omega}|^2} \tag{20}$$

$\{\hat{g}_{si,l}^c\}$ is estimated by Eq.(10) from analytic speech for the enhanced speech at previous iteration (input speech at first iteration) and G_s is energy of the corresponding residual. $\{\hat{g}_{wi,l}^c\}$ is estimated by Eq.(10) from analytic speech for the input speech in first silent

segment and G_w is energy of the corresponding residual. Note that these two power spectra provide only one side of spectrum, thus, mirroring is operated to apply to Eq.(17) .
As mentioned above, complex speech analysis can estimate more accurate speech spectrum in low frequencies. It is expected that the feature leads to higher performance of the IWF algorithm. In this paper, time-invariant complex speech analysis (L=1), is equivalent to complex LPC analysis, is adopted.

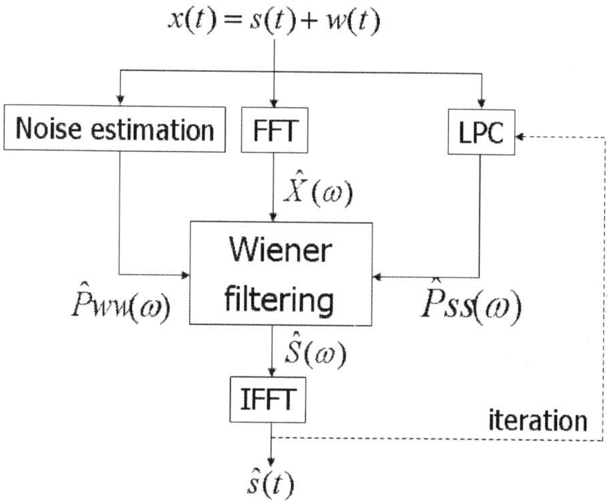

Fig. 2. Block diagram of the IWF algorithm

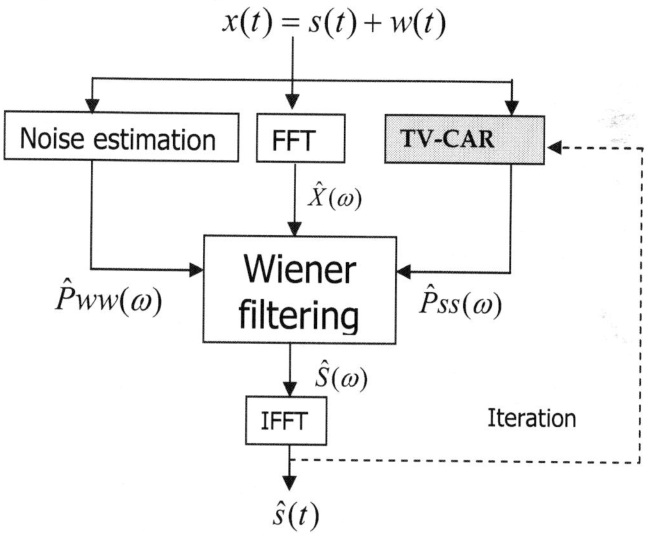

Fig. 3. Block diagram of the proposed IWF algorithm

4. Benefit of Complex Speech Analysis

Fig.4 shows example of the estimated speech spectra of natural Japanese vowel /o/ for analytic signal by complex LPC [11] and conventional LPC analysis for speech signal.

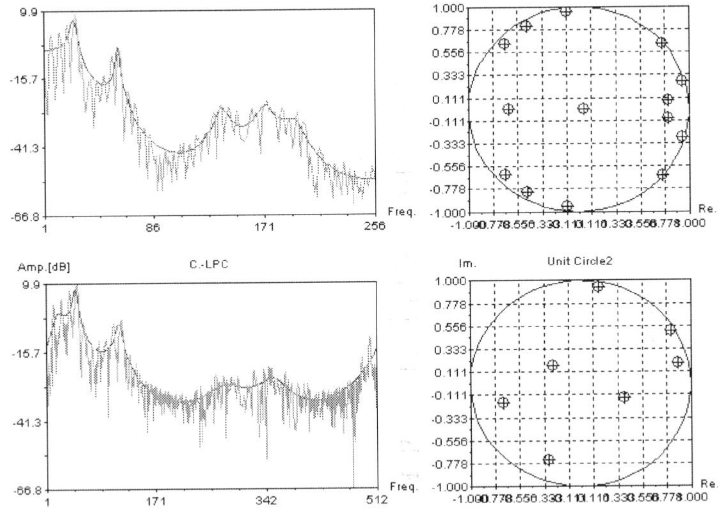

Fig. 4. Estimated Spectra of vowel /o/ with complex and conventional LPC analysis

In Fig.4, left side denote the estimated spectra. Upper is for real-valued LPC analysis. Lower is for complex-valued LPC analysis. Blue line means estimated spectrum by LPC analysis and green line means estimated DFT spectrum. Right side means estimated poles from the estimated AR filter. Fig.5 and 6 show the estimated running spectrum for clean natural speech /arayu/ and for the speech corrupted by white Gaussian (10[dB]), respectively. In Fig.5 and 6, (1) means speech waveform, (2),(3),(4),(5) and (6) mean the estimated spectrum by auto-correlation LPC speech analysis, by time-varying complex AR (TV-CAR) speech analysis (L=2), by time-invariant complex AR (CAR) speech analysis (L=1), by time-varying real AR (TV-RAR) speech analysis (L=2), and by time-invariant real AR (RAR) speech analysis (L=1), respectively. Analysis order I is 14 for real analysis and 7 for complex analysis. Basis function is 1st order polynomial function (1,t).

One can observe that the complex analysis can estimate more accurate spectrum in low frequencies whereas the estimation accuracy is down in high frequencies. Since speech spectrum provides much energy in low frequencies, it is expected that the high spectral estimation accuracy in low frequencies makes it possible to improve the performance on the IWF.

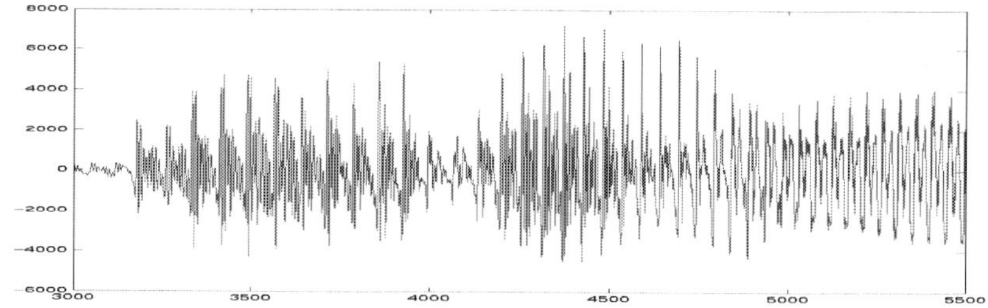

(1) clean speech waveform /arayu/

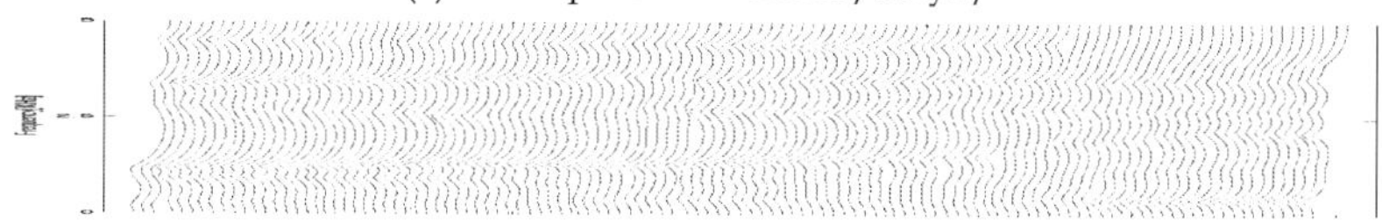

(2) LPC spectrum

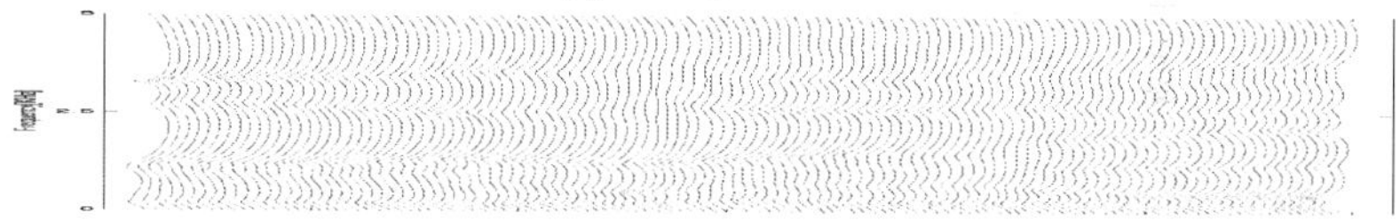

(3) TV-CAR spectrum (L=2)

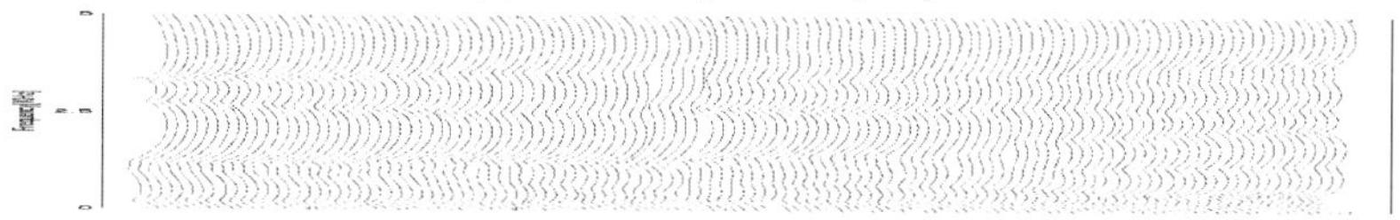

(4) CAR spectrum (L=1)

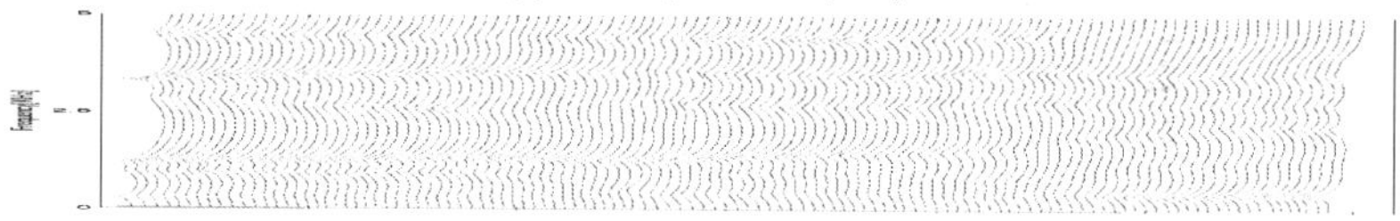

(5) TV-RAR spectrum (L=2)

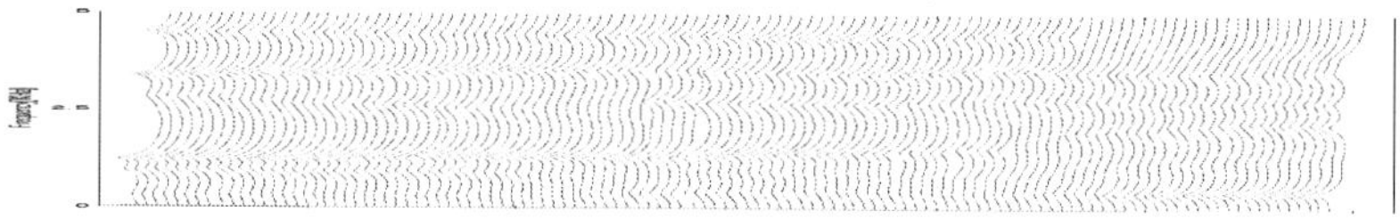

(6) RAR spectrum (L=1)

Fig. 5. Estimated spectrum for clean speech /arayu/

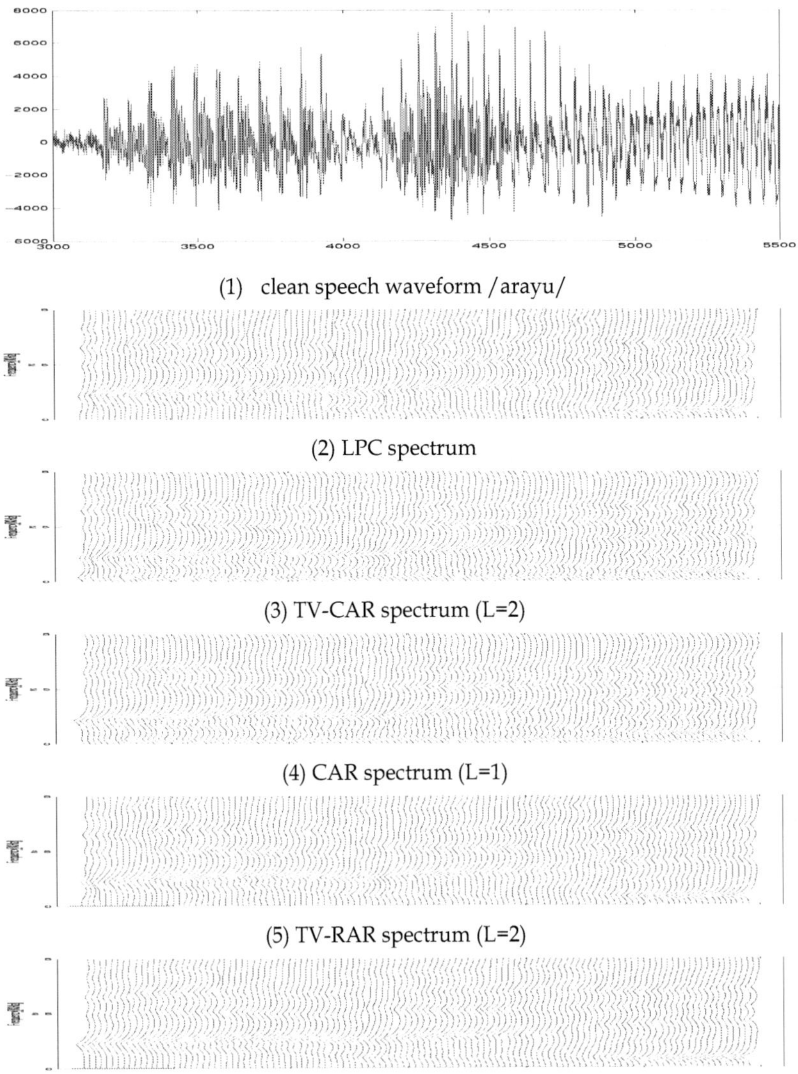

(1) clean speech waveform /arayu/

(2) LPC spectrum

(3) TV-CAR spectrum (L=2)

(4) CAR spectrum (L=1)

(5) TV-RAR spectrum (L=2)

(6) RAR spectrum (L=1)

Fig. 6. Estimated spectrum for noise corrupted speech /arayu/ (10[dB])

5. Experiments

We have already carried out the experiments to compare the performance of the proposed method (TV-CAR) for analytic speech with that for the conventional one (LPC method) for observed speech by means of objective evaluation of LPC Cepstral distance (CD). Since the IWF is based on filtering in the frequency domain, spectral distance such as LPC cepstral distance is appropriate measure for objective evaluation. Table 1 shows the experimental conditions. Sampling rates were 16KHz or 8KHz. Additive noises were white Gauss noise, pink noise, babble noise or car internal noise [13]. Noise levels were -5, 0, 5, 10 or 20[dB]. In the TV-CAR speech analysis, L is set to be one, thus the TV-CAR speech analysis is equivalent to non-time varying, complex LPC analysis. Figures 7 and 8 show the experimental results. Fig.7 means the results for 8 KHz of speech. Fig.8 means the results for 16 KHz of speech. In these figures, (1),(2),(3) and (4) means CDs for additive white Gauss noise, those for additive pink noise, those for additive babble noise, and those for additive car internal noise, respectively.

In these figures, X-axis means noise level (20, 10, 5, 0, -5 [dB]) and Y-axis means CD. **LPC** denotes the CDs by means of the conventional method based on LPC analysis. **CLPC** denotes the CDs by means of the proposed method based on complex LPC analysis. The results demonstrate that the proposed method can perform better than the conventional one for additive pink, babble or car internal noise whereas the proposed method does not perform better for additive white Gauss noise. The reason why the proposed method can perform better for additive pink, babble or car internal noise is as follows. The complex speech analysis can estimate more accurate speech spectrum in low frequencies for these noises whose energy is concentrated in low frequencies.

Speech data	Male 10 sentences Female 10 sentences ATR database set B
Sampling	8KHz/16bit 16KHz/16bit
Window Length/ Shift Length	20ms/10ms
FFT	1024 samples
LPC analysis	I=14, L=1(time-invariant)
Pre-emphasis	None
Complex LPC analysis	I=7, L=1(time-invariant)
Noise	(1) White Gauss noise (2) Pink noise [13] (3) Babble noise [13] (4) Car internal noise [13]
Noise Level	20,10,5,0,-5[dB]
Cepstral Distance (CD) Window Length/ Shift Length LPC order Cepstral order	LPC Cepstral Distance 20[msec]/ 20[msec] 16 for 8KHz, 32 for 16KHz 16 for 8KHz, 32 for 16KHz

Table 1. Experimental Conditions

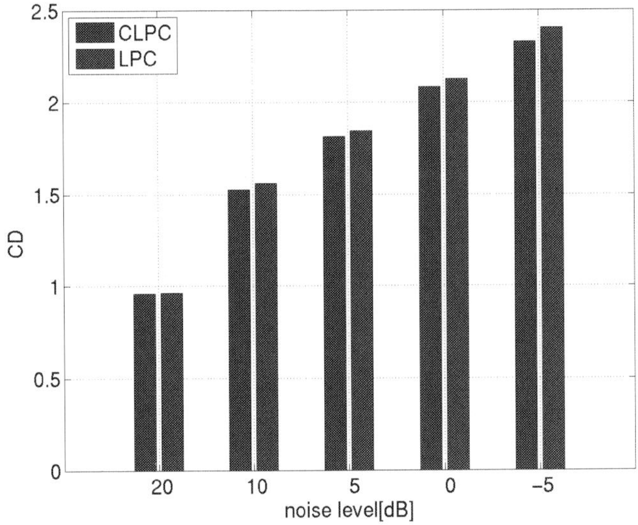

(1) CDs for additive white Gauss noise (8KHz)

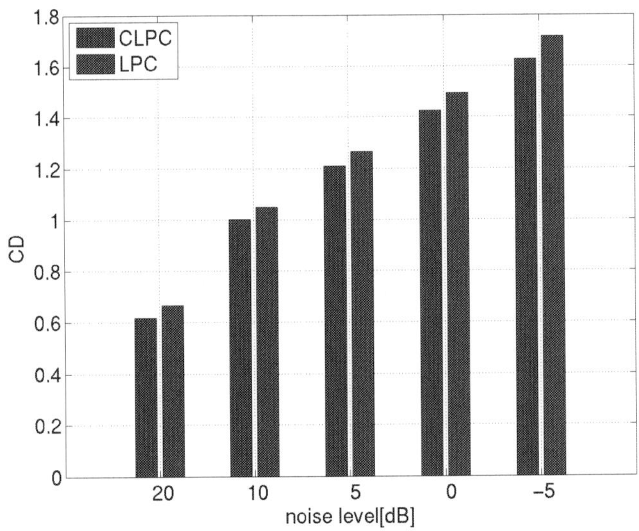

(2) CDs for additive Pink noise (8KHz)

Fig. 7. CDs for 8KHz speech

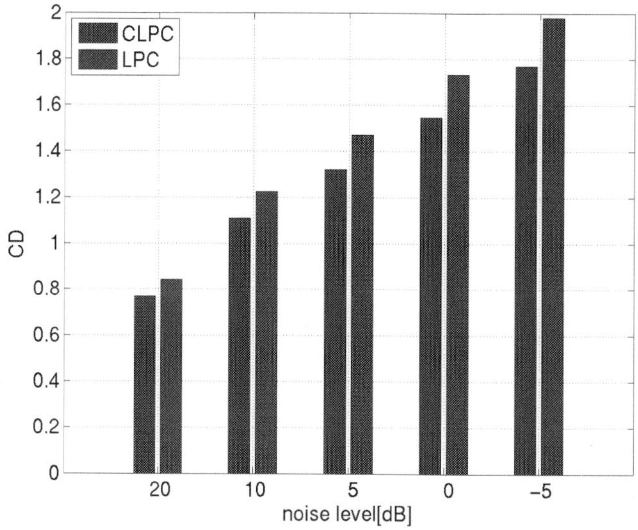

(3) CDs for additive Babble noise (8KHz)

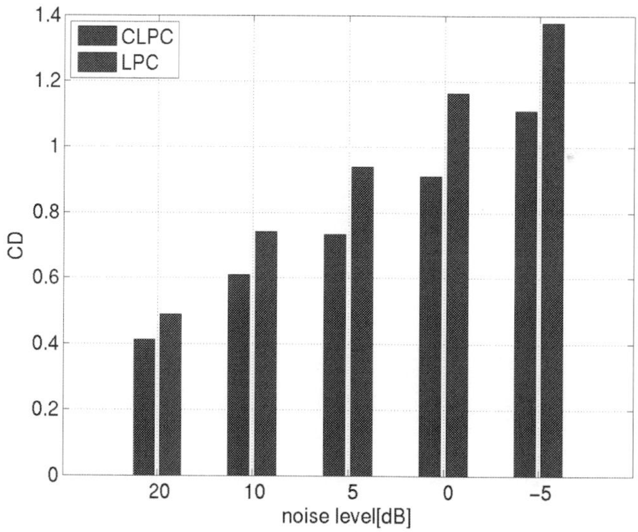

(4) CDs for additive Car Internal noise (8KHz)

Fig. 7. CDs for 8KHz speech

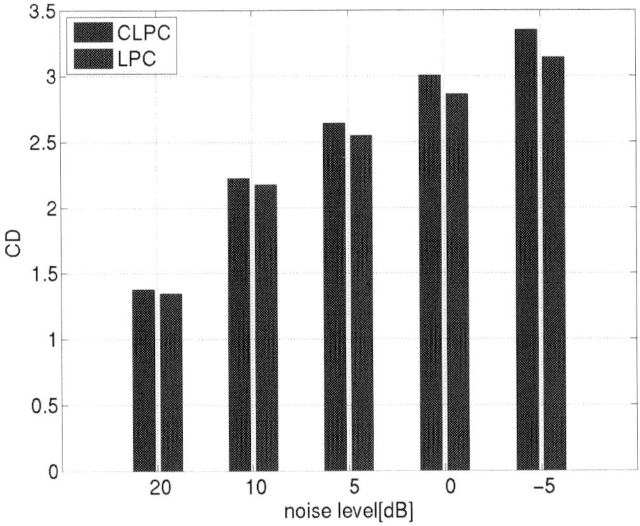

(1) CDs for additive white Gauss noise (16KHz)

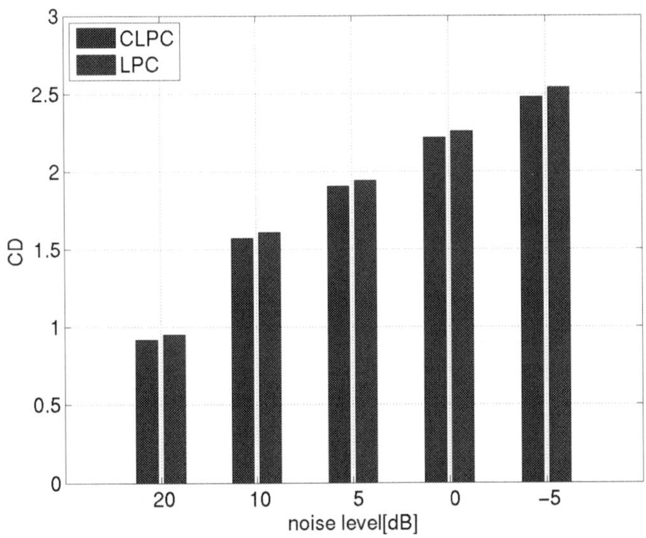

(2) CDs for additive Pink noise (16KHz)

Fig. 8. CDs for 16KHz speech

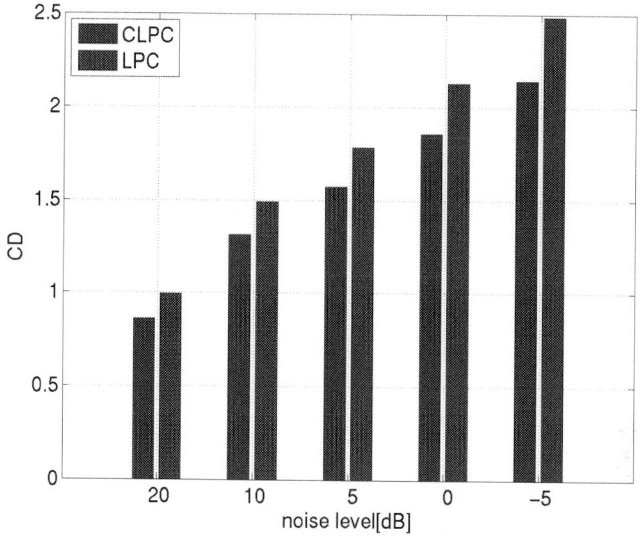

(3) CDs for additive Babble noise (16KHz)

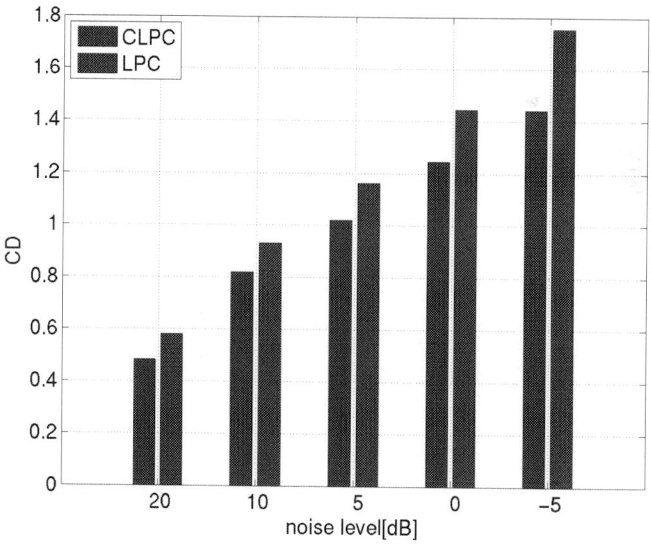

(4) CDs for additive Car Internal noise (16KHz)

Fig. 8. CDs for 16KHz speech

6. Conclusions

In this paper, we have proposed the improved iterative Wiener filter (IWF) algorithm based on the TV-CAR speech analysis in a single channel system. The performance has already been evaluated by means of LPC cepstral distance (CD) not only for 8KHz but also for 16KHz sampled speech signal corrupted by additive white Gauss, pink, babble or car internal noise. According to an informal listening test and objective evaluation of CD, the proposed method outperforms conventional IWF for additive pink, babble or car internal noise that contains much energy in low frequencies.
Future study is as follows.
(1)Improve the noise estimation
(2)Introduce robust TV-CAR speech analysis based on ELS method [14]
(3)Introduce the time-varying speech analysis (L=2).
(4)Introduce complex-valued Wiener filter.

7. References

[1] ``Minimum Performance Requirements for Noise Suppressor Application to the AMR Speech Encoder,'' 3GPP TS 06.77 V8.1.1,Apr.2001.
[2] M.Kato,et.al., ``Noise Suppression with High Speech Quality Based on Weighted Noise Estimation and MMSE STSA,'' IEICE Trans. Vol.E85-A. No.7, July 2002.
[3] ITU-T Recommendation G.722.2, ``Wideband coding of speech at around 16 kbit/s using Adaptive Multi-Rate Wideband (AMR-WB),'' Jul.,2003.
[4] S.F.Boll, ``Suppression of acoustic noise in speech using spectral subtraction,'' IEEE Trans., ASSP-27, pp.113-120,1979.
[5] Y.Ephraim and D.Malah, ``Speech enhancement using minimum mean-square error log-spectral amplitude estimator,'' IEEE Trans., ASSP-33, pp.443-445, 1985.
[6] J.S.Lim and A.V.Oppenheim, ``All-pole modeling of degraded speech,'' IEEE Trans., ASSP-26, pp.197-210, 1978.
[7] T.Lotter,et.al., "Speech enhancement by MAP spectral amplitude estimation using a super-gaussian speech model," EURASIP Journal on Applied Signal Processing, pp.1110-1126, Jul.2005.
[8] H.L.Hansen and M.A.Clements, ``Constrained iterative speech enhancement with application to speech recognition,'' IEEE Trans. Signal Processing, vol.39, pp.795-805, April 1991.
[9] P.C.Loizou,``Speech Enhancement, Theory and Practice,'' CRC Press, 2007.
[10] S.M.Kay, ``Maximum entropy spectral estimation using the analytic signal,'' IEEE Trans. ASSP-26, pp.467-469, 1980.
[11] T.Shimamura and S.Takahashi, ``Complex linear prediction method based on positive frequency domain,'' IEICE Trans., Vol.J72-A, pp.1755-1763, 1989. (in Japanese)
[12] K.Funaki, et.al., ``On a time-varying complex speech analysis,'' Proc. EUSIPCO-98, Rhodes, Greece, Sep. 1998.
[13] NOISE-X92, http://spib.rice.edu/spib/select_noise.html
[14] K.Funaki, ``A time-varying complex AR speech analysis based on GLS and ELS method,'' Proc. EUROSPEECH-2001, Alborg, Denmark, Sep. 2001.

16

Detection of echo generated in mobile phones

Tõnu Trump
Ericsson AB
Sweden

1. Introduction

Echo is a phenomenon where part of the sound energy transmitted to a receiver reflects back to the sender. In telephony it usually happens because of acoustic coupling between the receiver's loudspeaker and microphone or because of reflections of signals at the impedance mismatches in the analogue parts of the telephony system. In mobile phones one has to deal with acoustic echoes i.e. the signal played in the phones loudspeaker can be picked up by microphone of the same mobile phone.

People are used to the echoes that surround us in everyday life due to e.g. reflections of our speech from the walls of rooms where we are located. Those echoes arrive with a relatively short delay (in the order of milliseconds) and are, as a rule, attenuated. In a modern telephone system on the other hand the echoes may return with a delay that is not natural for human beings. The main reason for delay is in those systems signal processing like speech coding and interleaving. For example in a PSTN to GSM telephone call the one way transmission delay is around 100 ms making the echo to return after 200 ms. Echo that returns with this long delay is very unnatural to a human being and makes talking very difficult. Therefore the echo needs to be removed.

Ideally the mobile terminals should handle their own echoes in such a way that no echo is transmitted back to the telephony system. Even though many of the mobile phones currently in use are able to handle their echoes properly, there are still models that do not. ITU-T has recognized this problem and has recently consented the Recommendation G.160, "Voice Enhancement Devices" that addresses these issues (ITU-T G.160). Following this standard we concentrate on the scenario where the mobile echo control device is located in the telephone system.

It should be noted that differently from the conventional network- or acoustic echo problem (Sondhi & Berkley 1980; Signal Processing June 2006), where one normally assumes that the echo is present, it is not given that any echo is returned from the mobile phone at all. Therefore, the first step of a mobile echo removal algorithm should be detection of the presence of the echo, as argued in (Perry 2007). A simple level based echo detector is also proposed in (Perry 2007).

To design a mobile echo detector we first examine briefly the Adaptive Multi Rate (AMR) codec (3GPP TS 26.090) in Section 2. In Section 3 we present our derivation of the detector, which is followed by its performance analysis in Section 4. Some practicalities are explained in Section 5. Section 6 summarizes our simulation study.
Following the terminology common in mobile telephony, we use the term downlink to denote the transmission direction toward the mobile phone and the term uplink for the direction toward the telephony system.

2. Problem formulation

In order to detect the echo, which is a (modified) reflection of the original signal one needs a similarity measure between the downlink and the uplink signals. The echo path for the echo, generated by the mobile handsets is nonlinear and non-stationary due to the speech codecs and radio transmission in the echo path, which makes it difficult to use traditional linear methods like adaptive filters, applied directly to the waveform of the signals. As argued in (Perry 2007), the proper echo removal mechanism in this situation is a nonlinear processor, similar to the one that is used after the linear echo cancellation in ordinary network echo cancellers. In addition, as our measurements with various commercially available mobile telephones show, a large part of popular phone models are equipped with proper means of echo cancellation and do not produce any echo at all. Invoking a nonlinear processor based echo removal in such calls can only harm the voice quality and should therefore be avoided. That's why the first step of any mobile echo reduction system that is placed in the telephone system should be detection of the presence of echo. The nonlinear processor should then be applied only if the presence of echo has first been established.
Another important point is that speech traverses in the mobile system in coded form and that's why it is advantageous, if our detector were able to work directly with coded speech signals. Herein we therefore attempt to design a detector that uses the parameters present in coded speech to detect the presence of echo and estimate its delay. Exact value of the delay associated with the mobile echo is usually unknown and therefore needs to be estimated. The total echo delay builds up of the delays of speech codecs, interleaving in radio interface and other signal processing equipment that appear in the echo path together with unknown transport delays and is typically in the order of couple of hundreds of milliseconds.
The problem addressed herein is that the simple level based echo detector is not always reliable enough due to the impact of signals other than echo. The signals that are disturbing for echo detection originate from the microphone of the mobile phone and are actually the ones telephone system is supposed to carry to the other party of the telephone conversation. This is usually referred to as double talk problem in the echo cancellation literature. In this chapter we propose a detector that is not sensitive to double talk as shown in sequel of the chapter.
Let us now examine the structure of the AMR speech codec that is the codec used in GSM and UMTS mobile networks. The AMR codec switches between eight modes with different bit-rates ranging from 4.75 kbit/s to 12.2 kbit/s to code the speech signal. According to (3GPP TS 26.090), the AMR codec uses the following parameters to represent speech. The

Line Spectrum Pair (LSP) vectors, which are transformation of the linear prediction filter coefficients that have better quantization properties. The fractional pitch lags that represent the fundamental frequency of speech signal. The innovative codevectors that are used to code the excitation signal. And finally there are the pitch and innovative gains. In the detector, the LSP vectors are converted to the Linear Prediction (LP) filter coefficients and interpolated to obtain LP filters at each subframe. Then, at each 40-sample subframe the excitation is constructed by adding the adaptive and innovative codevectors scaled by their respective gains and the speech is reconstructed by filtering the excitation through the LP synthesis filter. Finally, the reconstructed speech signal is passed through an adaptive postfilter.

The basic structure of the decoder in a simplified form but sufficient for our purposes is shown in Figure 1 and described by the equation (1).

$$c \times g_c \times \frac{1}{1+g_p z^{-T}} \times \frac{1}{A(z)} \times \frac{A(z/\gamma_n)}{A(z/\gamma_d)} \tag{1}$$

In the above c denotes the innovative codevector, g_c denotes the innovative gain (fixed codebook gain), g_p is the pitch gain, γ_n and γ_d are the postfilter constants and $A(z)$ denotes the LP synthesis filter. T is the fractional pitch lag, commonly referred to as "pitch period" throughout this chapter.

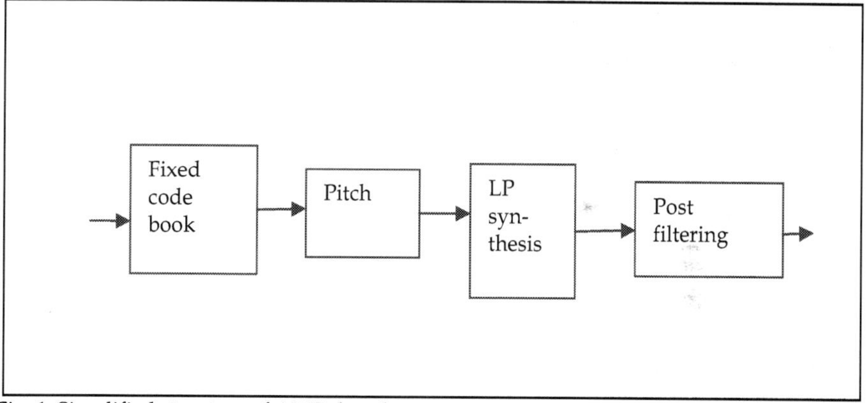

Fig. 1. Simplified structure of AMR decoder

Of the parameters present in AMR coded bit-stream, the pitch period or the fundamental frequency of the speech signal is believed to have the best chance to pass a nonlinear echo path unaltered or with a little modification. An intuitive reason for this is that a nonlinear system would likely generate harmonics but it would not alter the fundamental frequency of a sine wave passing it. We therefore select the pitch period as the parameter of interest.

3. Derivation

In this section we derive a structure for the echo detector based on comparison of uplink and downlink pitch periods. The derivation follows the principles of statistical hypothesis testing theory described e.g. in (Van Trees 1971; Kay 1998).

Denote the uplink pitch period for the frame t as $T_{ul}(t)$ and the downlink pitch period for the frame t - Δ as $T_{dl}(t-\Delta)$. The uplink pitch period will be treated as a random variable due to the presence of pitch estimation errors and the contributions from the true signal from mobile side.

Let us also denote the difference between uplink and downlink pitch periods as

$$w(t,\Delta) = T_{ul}(t) - T_{dl}(t-\Delta) \tag{2}$$

Then we have the following two hypotheses:

H_0: the echo is not present and the uplink pitch period is formed based only on the signals present at the mobile side

H_1: the uplink signal contains echo as indicated by the similarity of uplink and downlink pitch periods

Under hypothesis H_1, the process, w, models the errors of echo pitch estimation made by the speech codec residing in mobile phone but also the contribution from signal entering the microphone of the mobile phone. Our belief is that the distribution of the estimation errors can be well approximated by the Laplace distribution and that the contribution from the microphone signal gives a uniform floor to the distribution function. Some motivation for selecting this particular model can be found in Section 6.1.

We thus assume that under the hypothesis H_1 the distribution function of w is given by

$$p(w|H_1) = \begin{cases} \alpha \max\left(\dfrac{1}{2\sigma}\exp\left(-\dfrac{|T_{ul}(t) - T_{dl}(t-\Delta)|}{\sigma}\right), \dfrac{\beta}{b-a}\right), a < w < b \\ 0 \qquad \text{otherwise.} \end{cases} \tag{3}$$

The constant β, in the above equation, is a design parameter that can be used to weight the Laplace and uniform components and σ is the parameter of Laplace distribution. The variables a and b are determined by the limits in which the pitch period can be represented in the AMR codec. In the 12.2 kbit/s mode the pitch period ranges from 18 to 143 and in the other modes from 20 to 143. This gives us limits for the difference between uplink and downlink pitch periods a = -125 and b = 125 in 12.2 kbit/s mode and a = -123, b = 123 in all the other modes. α is a constant normalizing the probability density function so that it integrates to unity. Solving

$$\int_a^b p(w)dw = 1 \tag{4}$$

for α we obtain

$$\alpha = \frac{b-a}{2\sigma\beta\left(\ln\dfrac{2\sigma\beta}{b-a} - 1\right) + (1+\beta)(b-a)}. \tag{5}$$

Equation (3) can be rewritten in a more convenient form for further derivation

$$p(w|H_1) = \begin{cases} \dfrac{\alpha}{2\sigma} \exp\left(- \dfrac{\min\left(|T_{ul}(t) - T_{dl}(t-\Delta)|, -\sigma \ln \dfrac{2\delta\beta}{b-a} \right)}{\sigma} \right), a < w < b \\ 0, \qquad \text{otherwise.} \end{cases} \tag{6}$$

Under the hypothesis H_0, the distribution of w is assumed to be uniform within the interval [a, b],

$$p(w|H_0) = \begin{cases} \dfrac{1}{b-a}, a < w < b \\ 0, \quad \text{otherwise.} \end{cases} \tag{7}$$

We assume that the values taken by the random processes $w(t)$ at various time instances are statistically independent. Then the joint probability density is product of the individual densities

$$\begin{cases} p(\mathbf{w}|H_1) = \prod_{t=1}^{N} p(w(t)|H_1) \\ p(\mathbf{w}|H_0) = \prod_{t=1}^{N} p(w(t)|H_0). \end{cases} \tag{8}$$

Let us now design a likelihood ratio test (Van Trees 1971) for the hypotheses mentioned above. We assume that the cost for a correct decision is zero and the cost for any fault is one. We also assume that both hypotheses have equal a priori probabilities. Then the test is given by

$$\Lambda(T_{ul}) = \frac{\prod_{t=1}^{N} \dfrac{\alpha}{2\sigma} \exp\left(- \dfrac{\min\left(|T_{ul}(t) - T_{dl}(t-\Delta)|, -\sigma \ln \dfrac{2\delta\beta}{b-a} \right)}{\sigma} \right)}{\prod_{t=1}^{N} \dfrac{1}{b-a}} \mathop{\gtrless}_{H_0}^{H_1} 1, \tag{9}$$

Taking the logarithm and simplifying the above we obtain the following test

$$\sum_{t=1}^{N} - \min\left(|T_{ul}(t) - T_{dl}(t-\Delta)|, -\sigma \ln \frac{2\sigma\beta}{b-a} \right) \mathop{\gtrless}_{H_0}^{H_1} \sigma N \left(\ln \frac{2\sigma}{\alpha} - \ln(b-a) \right). \tag{10}$$

The decision device thus needs to compute the absolute distance between the uplink- and downlink pitch periods for all delays, Δ, of interest, saturate the absolute differences at $-\sigma \ln[2\sigma\beta / (b - a)]$, sum up the results and compare the sum with a threshold. The structure of the decision device is shown in Figure 2.

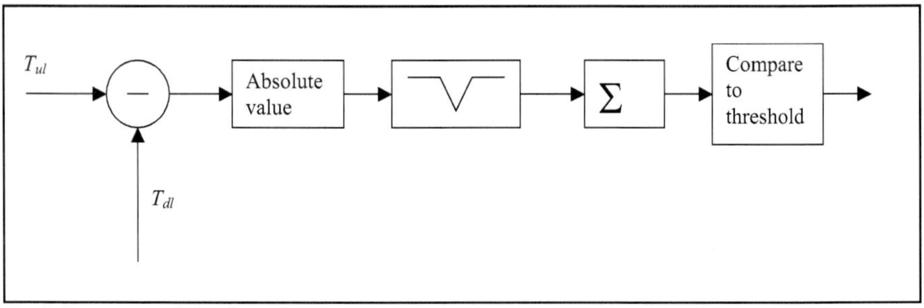

Fig. 2. Structure of the detector

4. Performance analysis

In this chapter we derive formulae for the probability of correct detection (we detect an echo when the echo is actually present) and the probability of false alarm (we detect an echo when there is none) of the detector. We start from reformulating the detector algorithm as

$$\frac{1}{N}\sum_{t=1}^{N} -\min\left(\left|w(t,\Delta)\right|,d\right) \underset{H_0}{\overset{H_1}{\gtrless}} -c, \tag{11}$$

where $c=\sigma\left[\ln(b-a)-\ln\frac{2\sigma}{\alpha}\right]$ and $d=-\sigma\ln\frac{2\sigma\beta}{b-a}$. The previous equation includes a nonlinearity that we denote as

$$y=h(w)=-\min\left(\left|w(t,\Delta)\right|,d\right). \tag{12}$$

$y=h(w)$ is a memoryless nonlinearity and hence the probability density function at the output of the nonlinearity is given by (Papoulis & Pillai 2002)

$$p_y(y)=\sum_{i=1}^{M}\frac{p_w(w)}{\left|{dy}/{dw}\right|}\Bigg|_{w=w_i=h_i^{-1}(y)}, \tag{13}$$

where $p_w(w)$ is the probability density function of the input. M is the number of real roots of $y=h(w)$. That is, the inverse of $y=h(w)$ gives $w_1,w_2,\ldots,w_M$ for a single value of y. Note that in the problem at hand M = 2 and y is a piecewise linear function which has piecewise constant derivatives.

Let us first consider the case where the echo is present and, hence, the input probability density function is given by (3). We can see from (3) that the Laplace component is replaced by the uniform component in the probability density function in the points where

$$|w|=-\sigma\ln\frac{2\sigma\beta}{b-a}=d. \tag{14}$$

In addition we know from (12) that the output of the nonlinearity is saturated precisely at d. The probability density function of the output is therefore

$$p_y(y|H_1) = \frac{\alpha}{\sigma}\exp\left(-\frac{y}{\sigma}\right)[u(0)-u(d)] + \alpha\beta\frac{b-a-2d}{b-a}\delta(y-d), \tag{15}$$

where $u(\cdot)$ denotes the unit step function and $\delta(\cdot)$ denotes the Dirac delta function. The mathematical expectation of the output signal from the nonlinearity, $y|H_1$, is $E(y|H_1) = \alpha\left[\sigma - (\sigma+d)\exp\left(-\frac{d}{\sigma}\right) + \beta d\frac{b-a-2d}{b-a}\right]$, the second moment equals $E(y^2|H_1) = \alpha\left[2\sigma^2 - (d^2+2d\sigma+2\sigma^2)\exp\left(-\frac{d}{\sigma}\right) - \beta d^2\frac{b-a-2d}{b-a}\right]$, and consequently the variance is $\sigma_{H_1}^2 = E(y^2|H_1) - E^2(y|H_1)$.

In the case the signal consist of contributions originating from the mobile side only (no echo) the input probability density is given by (7) and using this in (13) results in

$$p_y(y|H_0) = \frac{2}{b-a}[u(0-u(d))] + \frac{b-a-2d}{b-a}\delta(y-d). \tag{16}$$

The mean of this probability density function is $E(y|H_0) = 1 - \frac{d^2}{b-a}$, the second moment is given by $E(y^2|H_0) = \frac{2}{3}\frac{d^3}{b-a} + \frac{b-a-2d}{b-a}d^2$ and the variance equals $\sigma_{H_0}^2 = E(y^2|H_0) - E^2(y|H_0)$.

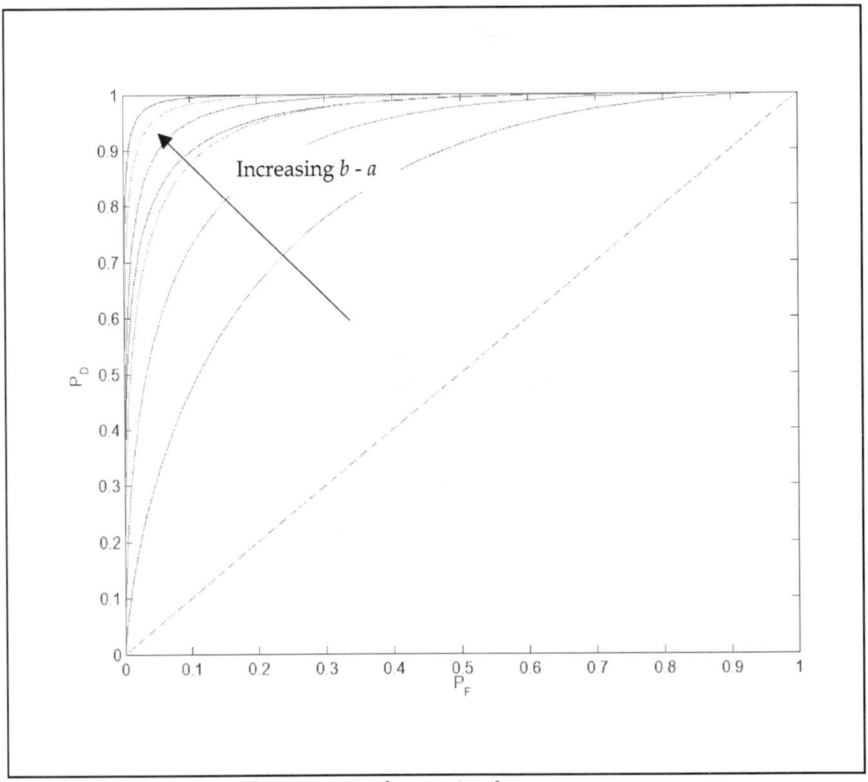

Fig. 3. Receiver operating characteristics for varying b - a.

Note that our test variable in (11) is $\frac{1}{N}\sum_{t=1}^{N} -\min(|w(t-\Delta)|,d) = \frac{1}{N}\sum_{t=1}^{N} y_i$, which is a sample average of N i.i.d. random variables that appear at the output of the nonlinearity $y=h(w)$. According to the central limit theorem (Papoulis & Pillai 2002) the probability distribution function of such a sum approaches with increasing N, rapidly the Gaussian distribution with mean $E[y|H_i]$ and variance $\sigma_{H_i}^2 / N$ irrespective of the shape of the original distribution.

We can now evaluate the probability of correct detection (Van Trees 1971) as

$$P_D = \int_{-\infty}^{Th} p_y(y|H_1)dy = \frac{N}{\sqrt{2\pi}\sigma_{H_1}} \int_{-\infty}^{Th} \exp\left(-\frac{[y-E(y|H_1)]N}{2\sigma_{H_1}^2}\right)dy = \frac{1}{2}\left(\operatorname{erf}\left(\frac{[Th-E(y|H_1)]\sqrt{N}}{\sqrt{2}\sigma_{H_1}}\right)+1\right), \tag{17}$$

where Th is the threshold used in the test and erf denotes the error function $\mathrm{erf}(x)=\frac{2}{\sqrt{\pi}}\int_0^x \exp(-t^2)dt$. Correspondingly the probability of fault detection is

$$P_F=\int_{-\infty}^{Th} p_y(y|H_0)dy=\frac{N}{\sqrt{2\pi}\sigma_{H_0}}\int_{-\infty}^{Th}\exp\left(-\frac{[y-E(y|H_0)]N}{2\sigma_{H_0}^2}\right)dy=\frac{1}{2}\left(\mathrm{erf}\left(\frac{[Th-E(y|H_0)]N}{\sqrt{2}\sigma_{H_0}}\right)+1\right). \tag{18}$$

The Receiver Operating Characteristic (ROC), which is the probability of correct detection P_D as a function of probability of fault alarm P_F, is plotted in Fig. 3. The parameters used to compute ROCs are N = 30, σ = 2 and β = 0.1. The distance between the endpoints of the uniform density, b - a, varies from 4 to 12. One can see that the ROC curves approach the upper left corner of the figure with increasing $b - a$.

It is also important to note that the detector derived in this chapter has a robust behavior. The decision algorithm is piecewise linear in signal samples and in addition each entry of the incoming signal is saturated at d, meaning that no single noise entry no matter how big it is can influence the decision more than by d. Hence, the detector constitutes a robust test in the terminology used in (Huber 2004).

5. Practical considerations

The detector, as given by equation (10) is not very convenient for implementation, as it needs computation of a sum over all subframes with each new incoming subframe. To give formula (10) a more convenient, recursive, form we define a set of distance metrics D, one for each echo delay Δ of interest

$$D(t,\Delta)=tc-\sum_{i=1}^{t}\min(|T_{ul}(i)-T_{dl}(i-\Delta)|,d). \tag{19}$$

The distance metrics are functions of time t or more precisely the subframe number. Computation of the distance metric can now easily be reformulated as a running sum i.e. at any time t we compute the following distance metric for each of the delays of interest and compare it with zero

$$D(t,\Delta)=D(t-1,\Delta)+c-\min(|T_{ul}(t)-T_{dl}(t-\Delta)|,d)\underset{H_0}{\overset{H_1}{\gtrless}}0. \tag{20}$$

Note that a large distance metric means that there is a similarity between the uplink and downlink signals and the other way around, a small distance metric indicates that no similarity has been found. Also note, that one can easily introduce a forgetting factor into the recursive detector structure in order to gradually forget old data as it is customary in e.g. adaptive algorithms (Haykin 2002). We are, however, not going to do this here. The echo is detected if any of the distance metrics exceeds a certain threshold level, which is zero in this case. The echo delay corresponds to Δ with largest associated distance metric, $D(t,\Delta)$.

There are several practicalities that need to be added to the basic detector structure derived in Section 3:

1. Speech signals are non-stationary and there is no point in running the detector if the downlink speech is missing or has too low power to generate any echo. As a practical limit, the distance metric is updated only if the down-link signal power is above -30 dBm0.
2. By a similar reason there is a threshold on the down-link pitch gain. The threshold is set to 10000.
3. The detection is only performed on "good" uplink frames i.e. SID frames and corrupted frames are excluded.
4. It has been found in practice that c = 7 and d = 9 is a reasonable choice.
5. To allow fast detection of a spurious echo burst, the distance metrics are saturated at -200 i.e. we always have $D(t,\Delta) \geq -200$.

Additionally one can notice that the most common error in pitch estimation occurs at double of the actual pitch period. This can be exploited to enhance the detector. In the particular implementation this has been taken into account by adding a parallel channel to the detector where the downlink pitch period is compared to half of the uplink pitch period

$$D(t,\Delta) = D(t-1,\Delta) + c_1 - \min\left(\left|\frac{T_{ul}(t)}{2} - T_{dl}(t-\Delta)\right|, d_1\right) \underset{H_0}{\overset{H_1}{\gtrless}} 0, \tag{21}$$

where the constants c_1 and d_1 are selected to be smaller than the corresponding constants c and d in (20) to give a lower weight to the error channel as compared to the main channel. Only one of the updates given by (20) and (21) is used each time t. The selected update is the one that results in a larger increase of the distance metric.

6. Simulation results

Our simulation study is carried out with the aim of investigating how well the derived detector works with speech signals. We first investigate if the distribution adopted in this work can be justified. This is followed by some experiments clarifying detection performance of the proposed algorithm using recordings made in an actual mobile network and finally we investigate the resistance of the detector to disturbances.

6.1 Distribution of pitch estimation errors

In this section we investigate the distribution function of the pitch estimation errors. The main question to answer is if the distribution function adopted in Section 3 is in accordance with what can be observed in the simulations.

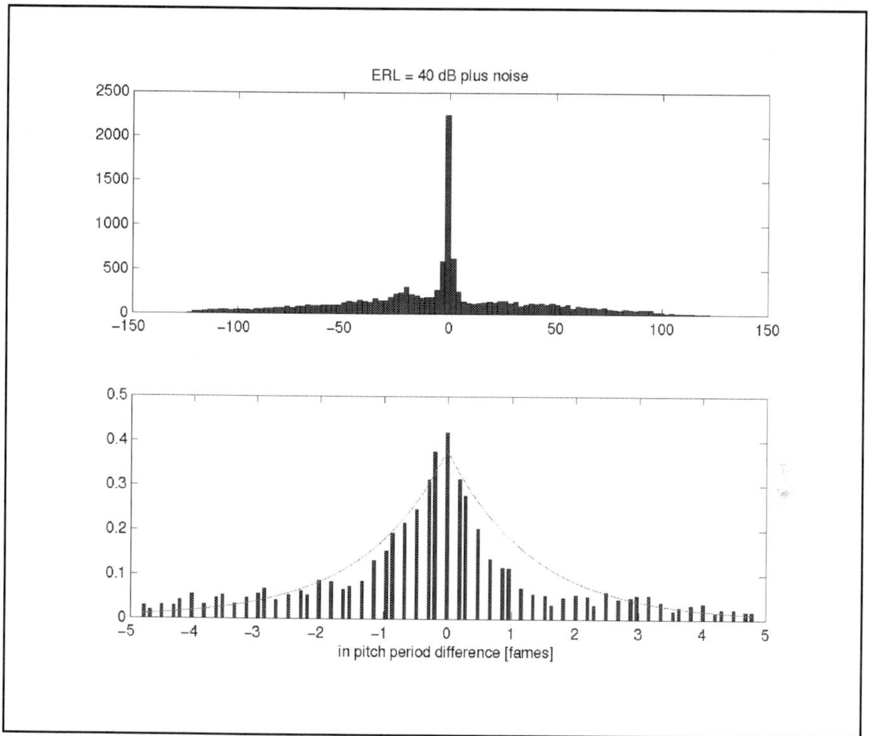

Fig.4. Histogram of pitch estimation errors. Echo path: single reflection and IRS filter, ERL = -40dB. Near end noise at -60 dBm0

To answer this question a two minute long speech file that includes both male and female voices at various levels was first coded with the AMR12.2 kbit/s mode codec and then decoded. Then a simple echo path model consisting either of a single reflection or the IRS filter (ITU-T G.191) was applied to the signal and the signal was coded again. Echo return loss was varied between 30 and 40 dB. The estimated pitch was registered from both codecs and compared. The pitch estimates were used only if the downlink power was above -40 dBm0 for the particular frame. A typical example is shown in Figure 4. The upper plot shows the histogram of pitch estimation errors. A narrow peak can be observed around zero and the histogram has long tails ranging from -125 to 125 (which are the limiting values for differences between two pitch periods). The lower plot shows the Laplace probability density function fitted to the middle part of the histograms. One can see that there is a reasonable fit.

6.2 Detection performance

Recordings made with various mobile phones were used to examine the detection performance. All the distance metrics in (20) were initialized to -50 and the echo was declared to be present if at least one of the distance metrics became larger than zero. Validity of the detection was verified by listening to the recorded file and comparing the listening and detection results. The two were found to be in a good agreement with each other.

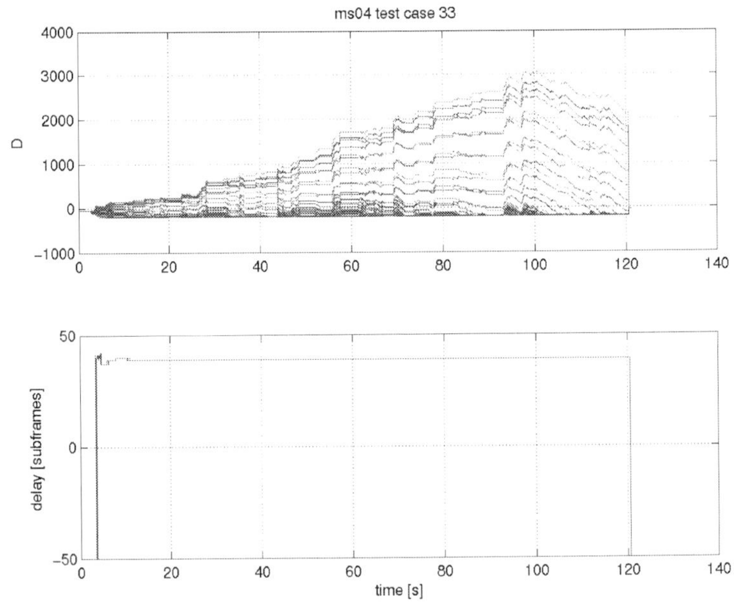

Fig. 5. Distance metrics (upper plot) and estimated delay (lower plot)

The delay was estimated as the one corresponding to the largest distance metric. As the experiments were done with signals recorded in real mobile systems, the author lacks knowledge of the true echo delays in the test cases. However, the estimates were proven in practice to provide good enough estimates for usage in a practical echo removal device.
Let us finally note that the resolution of the delay estimate is 5 ms due to the 5 ms subframe structure of the AMR speech codec.
A typical case with a mobile that produces echo is shown Figure 5. One can see that in this example echo is detected and the delay estimate stabilizes after a couple of seconds to 165 ms, which is a reasonable echo delay for a GSM system.

6.3 Resistance to disturbances

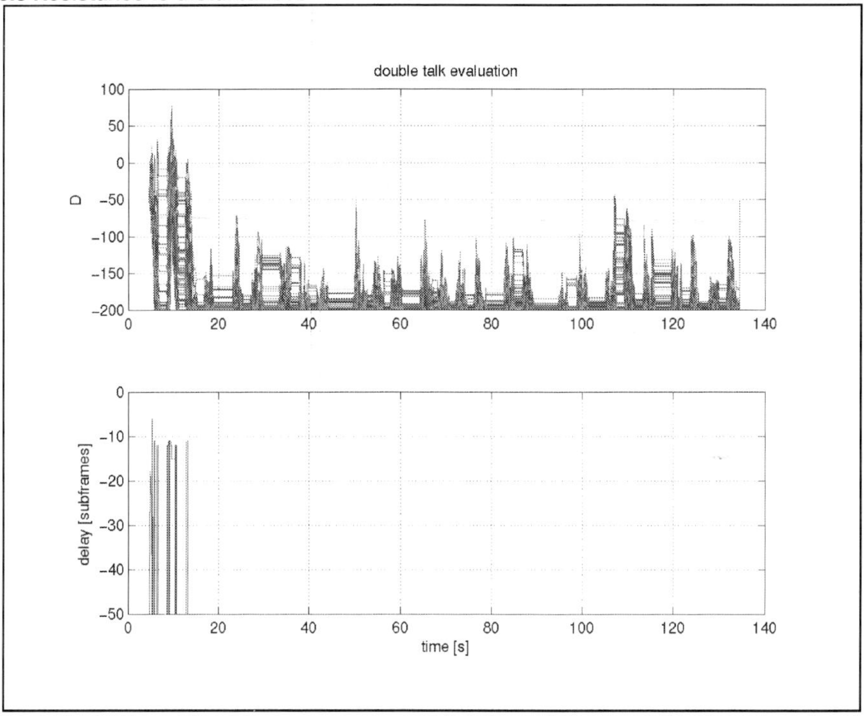

Fig. 6. Evaluation of the detector in severe double talk conditions, mobile side male, network side female.

Finally we check that the detector is not unnecessarily sensitive to disturbances. In echo context the most common disturbance is so called double talk i.e. the situation when both parties of the telephone conversation are talking at the same time. In this situation speech from the near end side forms a strong disturbance to any algorithm that needs to cope with echoes. The proposed detector algorithm was verified in a large number of simulations involving speech signals from both sides of the connection and its double talk performance was found to be good. This is expected as robustness against disturbances is built in the algorithm in form of limited distance measure update in equation (20).

As another and perhaps somewhat spectacular demonstration of double talk performance, we used two speech files with male and female voices speaking exactly the same sentences the same time. The result is shown in Figure 6 with female voice from network side and male voice from mobile side. In this case there are some fault echo detections initially, partly caused by initialization of the distance metrics to -50. Duration of the fault detection is, however, limited to the first two sentences (14 seconds) of the double talk. There was no echo detected in the opposite scenario i.e. male voice from the mobile side and female voice from the network side. Taking into account that it is very unlikely that in an actual telephone call both sides would talk the same sentences simultaneously we conclude that the detector is reasonably resistant to double talk.

7. Conclusion

This chapter deals with the problem of processing AMR coded speech signals without decoding them first. Importance of such algorithms arises from the fact that not all calls need enhancement and even if they need the quality loss from decoding and coding speech again may be higher than the potential improvement due to speech enhancement. Processing the signals directly in the coded domain avoids this problem.

The chapter proposes a detector that can be used to detect presence of echo generated by mobile phones and estimate its delay. The detector uses saturated absolute distance between uplink and downlink pitch periods as a similarity measure and is hence a robust algorithm. Performance of the detector was analysed and the equations for detection and error probabilities were derived. Finally a good performance of the detector with real life signals was demonstrated in our simulation study.

8. References

3GPP TS 26.090 V6.0.0 (2004-12) 3rd Generation Partnership Project; Technical Specification Group Services and System Aspects; Mandatory Speech Codec speech processing functions; *Adaptive Multi-Rate (AMR) speech codec; Transcoding functions (Release 6).*

Haykin, S. (2002) *Adaptive Filter Theory, fourth edition,* Prentice Hall

Huber, P. (2004) *Robust Statistics,* Wiley & Sons

ITU-T Recommendation G.160 (2008) *Voice Enhancement devices*

ITU-T Recommendation G.191, (2005) *Software Tools for Speech and Audio Coding Standardization*

Kay, S. (1998) *Fundamentals of Statistical Signal Processing, Volume II, Detection Theory,* Prentice Hall

Papoulis, A. and Pillai, S. U. (2002) *Probability, Random Variables and Stochastic Processes, Fourth edition,* McGraw Hill

Perry, A. (2007) *Fundamentals of Voice-Quality Engineering in Wireless Networks,* Cambridge University Press

Signal Processing, Volume 86, Issue 6, June 2006, Special issue on Applied Speech and Audio Processing.

Sondhi, M and Berkley, D. (1980) Silencing Echoes in Telephone Network, *Proc. IEEE,* Vol. 68, No. 8, Aug. 1980 pp. 948-963.

Van Trees, H. L. (1971) *Detection, Estimation, and Modulation Theory,* Wiley & Sons

Application of the Vector Quantization Methods and the Fused MFCC-IMFCC Features in the GMM based Speaker Recognition

Sheeraz Memon, Margaret Lech, Namunu Maddage and Ling He
School of Electrical and Computer Engineering, RMIT University, Melbourne, Australia

1. Introduction

Speaker recognition system which identifies or verifies a speaker based on a person's voice is employed as biometric of high confidence. Over three decades of research, voice prints have established very important security applications for the authentication and recognition from voice channels. Recent years, speaker recognition community is putting more efforts to further improve main factors such as robustness and the accuracy in the context independent speaker recognition systems. Signal segmentation where the temporal properties such as energy and pitch with in the speech signal frame is ideally considered stationary, is a major step in speaker recognition systems. Another important area where robustness can be acheived is identifying speaker characteristic sensitive feature extraction methods. However the segmentation and feature extraction stages are examined by modelling methods, thus speaker characteristic modelling is also an important state which should be carefully designed. Effective improvements in above key steps subsequently improve the robustness and accuracy of the speaker recognition system.

In this book chapter we evaluate the performances of the speaker recognition systems when different feature settings and modelling techniques are applied for above mentioned step 2 and step 3 respectively. In general content sensitive features play a vital role in achieving the globally optimized classification decisions. State of the art speaker recognition systems extract acoustic features which capture the characteristics of the speech production system such as pitch or energy contours, glottal waveforms, or formant amplitude and frequency modulation and model them with statistical learning techniques. However *Mel frequency cepstral coefficients* (MFCCs) have commonly being used to characterize the speaker characteristics. In this chapter we compare effectiveness of Inverted MFCC and fused MFCC-IMFCC features against solo MFCC feature for speaker recognition systems. It is commonly assumed that the speaker characteristic distribution is Gaussian. Thus Gaussian Mixture model is effectively used for speaker characteristics modelling in the literature. In this chapter we examine different learning techniques for the representation of the parameters in the GMM based speaker models. Vector Quantization (VQ) techniques effectively cluster the information distributions and reduce the effects of noise. Its found VQ techniques improve the robustness of speaker recognition systems which are deployed at different noisy environments. We propose several VQ methods to optimize GMM parameters (mean, covariance, and mixture weight). However expectation maximization (EM) algorithm is commonly used in the literature for the GMM parameter optimization. Thus we compare the performances of VQ based GMM -speaker modelling algorithms, K-means, LBG (Linde Buzo and Gray) and Information theoretic vector quantization (ITVQ) with EM-GMM setup in the speaker recognition.

The study includes speaker verification tests performed on the NIST2004 Speaker Recognition evaluation Corpus. NIST2004 SRE consists of conversational telephone speech. Thus performance evaluation of proposed methods using this corpus allows us to analyse and validate the results with high confidence. The results are presented using detection error trade-off (DET) plots showing the miss probability against the false alarm probability; a number of tables are also presented to compare the recognition rates based on different combination of these techniques.

2. Speaker Recognition

Speaker Recognition is a biometric based identity process where a person's identity is verified by the voice of a person. Biometrics based verification has received much attention in the recent times as such characteristics come natural to each individual and they are not required to be memorised, like passwords and personal identification numbers.

The speaker recogniton can be further classified in speaker identification and verification. Identification deals when a person is needed to verify from a group of people, however in verification task a person is accepted or rejected based on a claimant's identity.

In text-independent speaker verification the speaker is not bound to say a specific phrase to be identified but he/she is free to utter any sentence. However when we are dealing with text-dependent speaker recogntion the person is bound to utter a pre-defined phrase.

The speaker verification system comprises of three stages (see Fig. 1), in the first stage pre-processing and feature extraction is performed over a database of speakers. The second step addresses establishment of speaker models; where vectors representing speakers distinguishing characteristics are generated this corresponds to finding the distributions of feature vectors. The third step is of decision, which confirms or rejects the claimed identity of a speaker. In this stage the test set is also performed which includes the pre-processing and feature extraction of the test speaker and inputs to the classifier.

The introduction of the adapted Gaussian mixture models (Reynolds et al.,2000) with the introduction of UBM-GMM with MAP adaptation has established very good results on NIST evaluations. The use of expectation maximization (EM) optimization procedure is widely adapted to obtain the iterative updates for gaussian distributions. However EM encounters a number of problems, such as local convergence, mean adaptations etc. A number of EM variants are also proposed recently (Ueda, N. & R. Nakano, 1998), (Hedelin, P. Skoglund, J., 2000), (Ververidis, D. Kotropoulos, C.,2008) and (Ethem A.,1998).

3. Vector Quantization and EM based GMM

The study in (Hedelin, P. Skoglund, J., 2000) proposes how vector quantization based on GMM enhances the performance. A number of statistical tests are conducted in (Ververidis, D. Kotropoulos, C.,2008), it suggests around seven EM variants which under enhanced methods improve the GMM performance. The relation between number of vector quantization methods and EM is established in (Ethem A.,1998). To overcome the problem of local maxima caused by EM algorithm with an annealing approach is suggested in (Ueda, N. & R. Nakano, 1998).

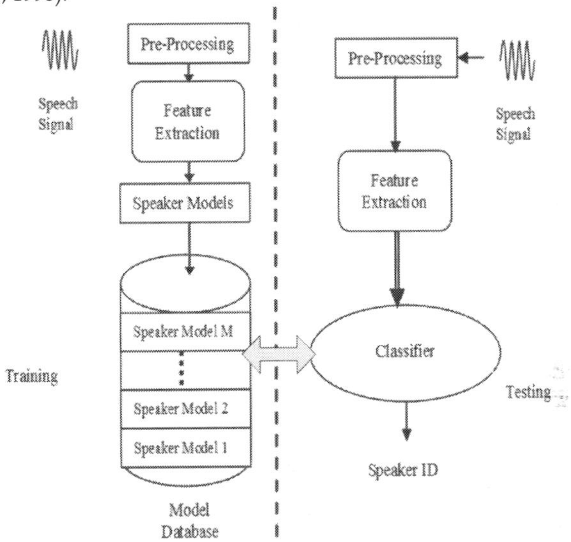

Fig. 1. overview of speaker verification systems

Vector Quantization (VQ) based speaker verification has been recognized as a successful method in the field of speaker recognition systems. A number of attempts have been made to use VQ methods with the GMM to optimize the performance of a speaker recognition system (Jialong et. Al, 1997) and (Singh et. al, 2003). The basic idea of VQ is to compress a large number of short term spectral vectors into a smaller set of code vectors. Until the development of GMM, vector quantization techniques were the most often applied methods in the field of speaker verification.
In this chapter we apply ITVQ algorithm (Tue et al.,2005), beside K-means and LBG VQ processes to estimate EM parameters. The ITVQ algorithm, which incorporates the Information Theoretic principles into the VQ process, was found to be the most efficient VQ algorithm (Sheeraz M. & Margaret L, 2008).

4. Feature Extraction Methods

Feature extraction is useful in speech (Davis, S. B. & P. Mermelstein,1980) and speaker recognition and the study of feature extraction has remained a core of research. A number of studies best support Mel-frequency cepstrum coefficients (MFCCs) (Reynolds, D. A. , 1994) and it does produce good results in most of the situations. In other studies, feature extraction based on pitch or energy contours (Peskin B. *et al.*,2003), glottal waveforms

(Plumpe, M. D. Et. al, 1999), or formant amplitude and frequency modulation (Jankowski C. R. jr. *et al.*,1996) are proposed, and good performance has been shown.
In their recent research (Sandipan, C. & Ghoutam, S.,2008) suggested, that the classification results can be significantly improved when the MFCC method is fused with the Inverse MFCC (IMFCC). This is because the IMFCC helps to capture the speaker specific information lying in the higher frequency range of the spectrum, which is largely ignored by the MFCC feature extraction method.

4.1 Mel-frequency cepstral coefficients (MFCC)

The primary concern of describing the MFCC algorithm here is to clearly map the working of Inverted MFCC and later in this chapter their fusion as a feature extraction set for GMM based on EM, K-means, LBG and ITVQ classifier. MFCC algorithm has been widely used for both the speech and speaker recognition in the recent years as it is designed keeping the human perception of listening as the core concern. According to psychophysical studies (Shaughnessy, D. O.,1987), human perception of the frequency content of sounds follows a subjectively defined nonlinear scale called the Mel scale (Gold, B. & Morgan, N.,2002) (Fig. 2). Mel scale is defined as a logarithmic scale of frequency based on human pitch perception. Equal intervals in Mel units correspond to equal pitch intervals. It is given by,

$$f_{mel} = 2595\log_{10}\left(1+\frac{f}{700}\right) \tag{1}$$

Where f_{mel} is the subjective pitch in Mels corresponding to f which is the actual frequency in Hz. This leads to the definition of MFCC, a baseline acoustic feature for Speech and Speaker Recognition applications, can be calculated by following steps.
Step.1: Let $\{x(n)\}_{n=1}^{M}$ represent a time-domain frame of pre-processed speech. The speech samples $x(n)$ are first transformed to the frequency domain by the M-point Discrete Fourier Transform (DFT) and then the signal energy is calculated as,

$$|X(k)|^2 = \left|\sum_{n=1}^{M} x(n).e^{\left(\frac{-j2\pi nx}{M}\right)}\right|^2 \tag{2}$$

Where, $k=1,2,\ldots,M$ and $X(k) = DFT(x(n))$.
Step.2: This is followed by the construction of a filter bank with triangular frequency responses centered at equally spaced points on the Mel scale. Fig. 2 shows the frequency response of the ith filter. The frequency response $\Phi_i(k)$ of this filter is calculated using Eq.(3).

$$\phi_i(k) = \begin{cases} 0 & for \quad k \le k_{b_{i-1}} \\ \dfrac{k-k_{b_{i-1}}}{k_{b_i}-k_{b_{i-1}}} & for \quad k_{b_{i-1}} \le k \le k_{b_i} \\ \dfrac{k_{b_{i+1}}-k}{k_{b_{i+1}}-k_{b_i}} & for \quad k_{b_i} \le k \le k_{b_{i+1}} \\ 0 & for \quad k \ge k_{b_{i+1}} \end{cases} \tag{3}$$

If N_F denotes the number of filters in the filter bank, then $\{k_{b_i}\}_{i=0}^{N_F+1}$ are the boundary points of the filters. The boundary points for each filter i $(i=1,.2,..., N_F)$ are calculated as equally spaced points in the Mel scale using the following formula,

$$k_{b_i} = \left(\frac{M}{f_s}\right) f_{mel}\left[f_{mel}(f_{low}) + \frac{i\{f_{mel}(f_{high}) - f_{mel}(f_{low})\}}{N_F + 1} \right] \tag{4}$$

Where, f_s is the sampling frequency in Hz and $f_{low}=f_s/M$ and $f_{high} = S_F/2$ are the low and high frequency boundaries of the filter bank, respectively.

Step.3: In the next step, the output energies $E(i)$ $(i=1,.2,..., N_F)$ of the Mel-scaled band-pass filters are calculated as a sum of the signal energies $|X(k)|^2$ falling into a given Mel frequency band weighted by the corresponding frequency response $\Phi_i(k)$. This is given as,

$$E(i) = \sum_{x=1}^{\frac{M_S}{2}} |X(k)|^2 \Phi_i(k) \tag{5}$$

Where M_s is the number of DFT bins falling into the ith filter.

Step.4: Finally, the Discrete Cosine Transform *(DCT)* of the log of the filter bank output energies $E(i)$ $(i=1,.2,..., N_F)$ is calculated yielding the final set of the MFCC coefficients C_m, given as

$$C_m = \sqrt{\frac{2}{N_F}} \sum_{l=0}^{N_F-1} \log[E(i+1)].\cos\left[m.\left(\frac{2l-1}{2}\right).\frac{\pi}{N_F} \right] \tag{6}$$

Where, $m=0,1,2,...,R-1$, and R is the desired number of the Mel Frequency Cepstral Coefficients.

4.2 Inverted Mel-frequency cepstral coefficients (MFCC)

The MFCC represent the information perceived by the human auditory system while the Inverse Mel Frequency Cepstral Coefficients capture the information which could have been missed by the MFCC (Yegnanarayana, B. et. al, 2005). The Inverted Mel Scale, which is shown as a dashed line in Fig.4, is defined by a filter bank structure that follows the opposite path to that of MFCC. The inverted filter bank structure can be generated by flipping the original filter bank around the mid frequency point f_c, of the filter bank frequency range (i.e. $f_c = (f_{high} - f_{low})/2$).

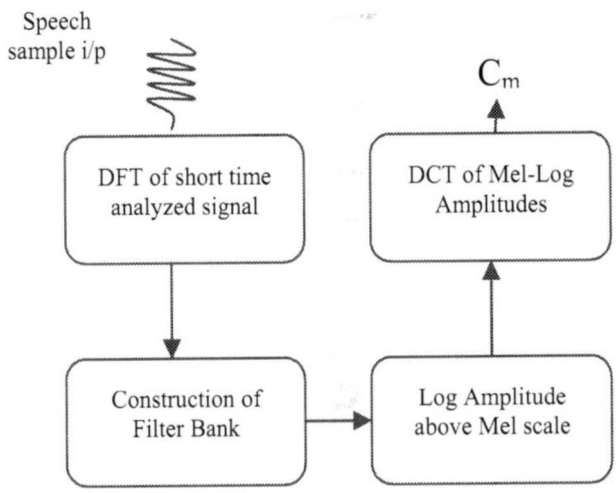

Fig. 2. Implementation structure of MFCC

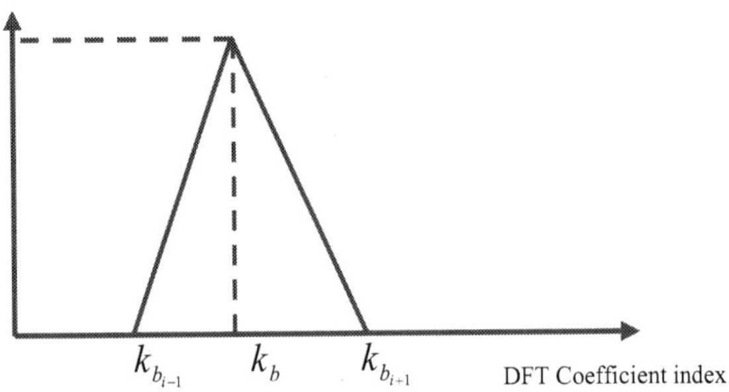

Fig.3. Response of a Mel scale Filter

The frequency responses $\hat{\Phi}_i(k)$ *(i=1,2,..., N_F)* for the inverted filter bank are given as,

$$\hat{\Phi}_i(k) = \Phi_{N_F+1-i}\left(\frac{M}{2}+1-k\right) \tag{7}$$

For a given frequency *f* in *Hz*, the corresponding inverted Mel-scale frequency $\hat{f}_{mel}(f)$ can be calculated as,

$$\hat{f}_{mel}(f) = 2195.2860 - 2595\log_{10}\left(1+\frac{4031.25-f}{700}\right) \tag{8}$$

The energies of the inverted filters outputs can be determined in the same way as for the non-inverted filters, i.e.,

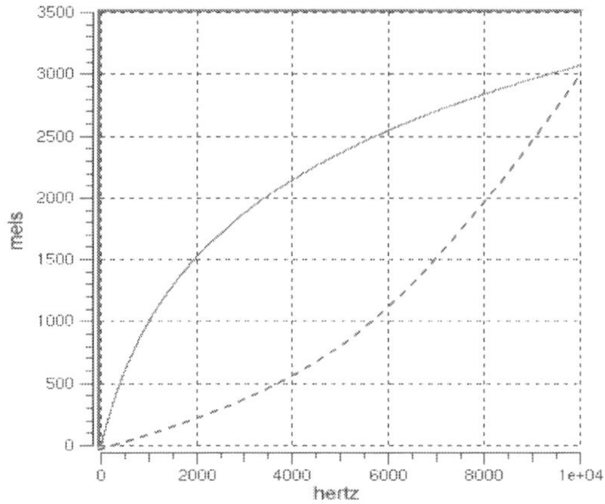

Fig. 4. Subjective pitch in Mels vs. frequency in Hz.

$$\hat{E}(i) = \sum_{x=1}^{\frac{M_S}{2}} |Y(k)|^2 \hat{\Phi}_i(k) \tag{9}$$

Finally, the *DCT* of the log filter bank energies is calculated, and the final Inverted Mel Frequency Cepstral Coefficients $\hat{C}_m$ are given as,

$$\hat{C}_m = \sqrt{\frac{2}{N_F}} \sum_{l=0}^{N_F-1} \log[\hat{E}(i+1)].\cos\left[m\left(\frac{2l-1}{2}\right)\frac{\pi}{N_F}\right] \tag{10}$$

Where, $m=0,1,2,...,R-1$, and R is the number of the Inverted Mel Frequency Cepstral Coefficients.

4.3 Fusion of MFCC and IMFCC

The idea of combining the classifiers to optimize the decision making process has been successfully applied in the fields of pattern recognition and classification (Mashao, DJ. & Skosan, M, 2006), (Murty, KSR. & Yegnanarayana, B.,2006). If the information supplied to the classifiers is complementary, such as the case of MFCC and IMFCC, the classification process could be largely improved (Sandipan, C. & Ghoutam, S.,2008) , (Chakroborty, S et. al, 2006).

The MFCC and the IMFCC feature vectors, containing complimentary information about the speakers, were supplied to a given classifier independently and the classification results for the MFCC features and for the IMFCC were fused in order to obtain optimal decisions in the process of speaker verification. A uniform weighted sum rule was adopted to fuse the scores from the two classifiers. If D_{MFCC} denotes the classification score based on the MFCC, and D_{IMFCC} denotes the classification score based on the IMFCC, then the combined score for the mth speaker was given as,

$$D_m = \omega D_{MFCC} + (1-\omega) D_{IMFCC} \tag{11}$$

The constant value of $\omega = 0.5$ was used in all cases. The speaker class was determined as,

$$m_{class} = \arg\left(\max_m D_m\right) \tag{12}$$

5. Vector Quantization (VQ) Methods

In this section of the chapter a number of VQ procedures are described, which have been used to optimize the EM parameters for GMM modelling.

5.1 K-means Method

It is an algorithm to classify or to group data based on attributes/features into K number of group. K is positive integer number. The grouping is done by minimizing the sum of squares of distances between data and the corresponding cluster centroid. Thus, the purpose of K-mean clustering is to classify the data. K-means algorithm (Furui, S., 1989) was developed for vector quantization codebook generation. It represents each cluster by the mean of the cluster. Assume a set of vectors $X=\{x_1,x_2,x_3,\ldots,x_T\}$ is to be divided into M clusters represented by their mean vectors $\{\mu_1, \mu_2, \mu_3,\ldots, \mu_M\}$ the objective of K-means algorithm is to minimize the total distortion given by,

$$total\_distortion = \sum_{i=1}^{M} \sum_{t=1}^{T} \left\| x_t - \mu_i \right\| \tag{13}$$

K-means is an iterative approach; in each successive iteration it redistributes the vectors in order to minimize the distortion. The procedure is outlined below:

(a) Initialize the randomized centroids as the means of M clusters.
(b) Data points are associated with the nearest centroid.
(c) The centroids are moved to the centre of their respective clusters.
(d) Steps b & c are repeated until a suitable level of convergence has been reached, i.e. the distortion is minimized.

When the distortion is minimized, redistribution does not result in any movement of vectors among the clusters. This could be used as an indicator to terminate the algorithm. The total distortion can also be used as an indicator of convergence of the algorithm. Upon convergence, the total distortion does not change as a result of redistribution. It **is** to be noted that in each iteration, K-means estimates the means of all the *M* clusters.

5.2 LBG Method

The LBG algorithm is a finite sequence of steps in which, at every step, a new quantizer, with a total distortion less or equal to the previous one, is produced. We can distinguish two phases, the initialization of the codebook and its optimization. The codebook optimization starts from an initial codebook and, after some iterations, generates a final codebook with a distortion corresponding to a local minimum. The following are the steps for LBG algorithm.

a. Initialization. The following values are fixed:
- N_C: number of codewords;
- $\varepsilon \geq 0$: precision of the optimization process;
- Y_0: initial codebook;
- $X = \{\mathbf{x}_j\ ; j = 1, \ldots, N_P\}$: input patterns;

Further, the following assignments are made:
- $m = 0$; where m is the iteration number.
- $D_{-1} = +\infty$; where D is the minimum quantization error calculated at every mth iteration.

b. Partition calculation. Given the codebook Y_m, the partition $P(Y_m)$ is calculated according to the *nearest neighbour condition*, given by

$$S_i = \{x \varepsilon X : d(x, y_i) \geq d(x, y_j), \quad i=1,2,\ldots,N_C. \\ j = 1,2,\ldots, N_C, j \neq i\} \tag{14}$$

c. Termination condition check. The quantizer distortion ($D_m = D(\{Y_m, P(Ym)\})$ is calculated according to following equation.

$$MQE \equiv D(\{Y, S\}) = \frac{1}{N_P}\sum_{p=1}^{N_P} d(x_p, q(x_p)) = \frac{1}{N_P}\sum_{i=1}^{N_C} D_i \tag{15}$$

Where D_i indicates the total distortion of ith cell.

If $|(D_{m-1} - D_m)| / D_m \leq \varepsilon$ then the optimization ends and Y_m is the final returned codebook.

d. New codebook calculation. Given the partition $P(Y_m)$, the new codebook is calculated according to the Centroid condition. In symbols:

$$Y_{m+1} = X\,(P(Y_m)) \tag{16}$$

After, the counter m is increased by one and the procedure follows from step b.

5.3 Information Theoretic VQ

The Vector Quantization methods are commonly used in the process of feature classification. The ITVQ (Tue, L. et. al, 2005) algorithm uses a new set of concepts from information theory and provides a computationally very efficient technique, which eliminates many disadvantages of classical vector quantization algorithms. Unlike LBG, this algorithm relies on minimization of a well defined cost function. The cost function used in LBG and K-means algorithms is defined as an average distortion (or distance), and as such, it is very complex and may contain discontinuities making the application of traditional optimization procedures very difficult (Erwin, E. et. al, 1991).

According to the information theory a distance minimization is equivalent to the minimization of the divergence between distribution of data and distribution of code vectors. Both distributions can be estimated using the Parzen density estimator method (Tue, L. et. al, 2005).

The ITVQ algorithm is based on the principle of minimizing the divergence between Parzen estimator of the code vectors density distributions and a Parzen estimator of the data distribution. The Parzen density estimator is given as,

$$p(x) = \frac{1}{N}\sum_{i=1}^{N} K(x - x_i) \tag{17}$$

Where $K(.)$ is the Gaussian Kernel, x is the independent variable for which we seek the estimate and x_i represents the data points. The Parzen estimate of the data has N kernels, where N is the number of data points, and the Parzen estimator of the code vectors has M kernels, where M is the number of code vectors and M<<N.

The density estimation is followed by minimization of the divergence between data points and centroids. In order to minimize the divergence between the data points distribution $a(x)$ and the centroids distribution $b(x)$, the following expression is minimized.

$$D_{C-S}(a(x), b(x)) = \\ \log \int a^2(x)dx - 2\log \int a(x)b(x)dx + \log \int b^2(x)dx \tag{18}$$

Where, $a(x)$ and $b(x)$ denote the Parzen density estimates for the data and centroids, respectively.
The cost function in Eq. (18) is minimized through a gradient descent search, which iteratively changes the positions of centroids until the decrease rate of the cost value becomes sufficiently small. The first term in Eq.(18), $\log \int a^2(x)dx$, represents the Renyi's quadratic entropy of data points, the third term, $\log \int b^2(x)dx$, represents the Renyi's quadratic entropy of centroids, and the second term, $-2\log \int a(x)b(x)dx$, is the *2log* of the cross information potential between the densities of the centroids and the data. Since the entropy of the data points remains constant during the iterations, the minimization of the cost function in Eq. (18) is equivalent to the maximization of the sum of the entropy of the centroids and the cross information potential between the densities of the centroids and the data.
As explained in more detail in (Tue, L. et. al, 2005), a typical ITVQ algorithm makes use of an annealing procedure, which allows the algorithm to escape from local minima.

6. Gaussian Mixture Models

In this section of the chapter we describe the modelling methods. GMM use EM procedure for the optimization however the use of VQ methods is proposed here.

6.1 GMM with EM

The Gaussian Mixture Model (GMM) (Douglas, A.R., 1995) with Expectation maximization is a feature modeling and classification algorithm widely used in the speech-based pattern recognition, since it can smoothly approximate a wide variety of density distributions.
The probability density function (pdf) drawn from the GMM is a weighted sum of M component densities given as,

$$p(x \mid \lambda) = \sum_{k=1}^{M} p_k b_k(x) \tag{19}$$

Where x is a D-dimensional random vector, $b_k(x)$, k =1… M are the component densities and p_k, k =1… M are the mixture weights. Each component density is a D-variate Gaussian function of the form

$$b_k(x) = \frac{1}{(2\pi)^{D/2}\left|\Sigma_k\right|^{1/2}} \exp\left\{-\frac{1}{2}(x-\mu_k)' \sum_i^{-1} (x-\mu_k)\right\} \tag{20}$$

Where μ_i is the mean vector and $\sum$ is the covariance matrix. The mixture weights satisfy the constraint that $\sum_{k=1}^{M} p_k = 1$ .The complete Gaussian mixture density is the collection of the mean vectors, covariance matrices and mixture weights from all components densities,

$$\lambda = \{p_k, \mu_k, \Sigma_k\}, k = 1, \ldots\ldots, M \tag{21}$$

Each class is represented by a mixture model and is referred by the class model λ.
The Expectation Maximization (EM) algorithm is most commonly used to iteratively derive class models. The EM algorithm initialized with a speaker model λ and estimates at each iteration a new model $\overline{\lambda}$ such that $p(X \mid \overline{\lambda}) \geq p(X \mid \lambda)$.

6.2 GMM with VQ

Although EM algorithm performs well but the literature has suggested that it suffers with some of the problems which can enhance its performance for pattern recognition applications such as speaker recognition (Ueda, N. & R. Nakano, 1998). The areas where the performance improvement can be achieved are listed below.

1. The number of mixtures is mostly set *a priori.*
2. The initialization procedure applied to set the parameters affects the final result.
3. EM converges to local optima instead of global optima.

Thus investigation of alternative training algorithms is unavoidable. However this may include either modifying the standard EM steps or by proposing enhanced optimization procedures. We in this paper propose the use of several VQ methods to replace the maximization step of EM algorithm. At each EM iteration expectation is set which is given by,

$$h_{kj} = \frac{g_j |\Sigma_j|^{-1/2} \exp\left[-(1/2)(x_k - \mu_j)^T \sum_j^{-1} (x_k - \mu_j)\right]}{\sum_l g_l |\Sigma_j|^{-1/2} \exp\left[-(1/2)(x_k - \mu_l)^T \sum_j^{-1} (x_k - \mu_l)\right]} \tag{22}$$

The above equation is the evaluation of a speaker model at each EM iteration. The numerator is the pdf of a target model and the denominator is the sum of all the pdf's.

However the next part of EM based GMM is to obtain the iterative updates where we propose to use the cost function of VQ methods. We apply the clustering techniques such as K-means, LBG and ITVQ to optimize the means. However the covariances are computed as evaluated in the initialization procedure, however based on the new clusters/distribution of the speaker data. The iterative weights are the updates from the new expectation h_{kj} as evaluated in the EM procedure (see equation 22).

$$g_j^{(n+1)} = \frac{1}{n} \sum_k h_{kj}^{(n)} \tag{23}$$

The K-means algorithm has been applied for finding a robust model approximation to the GMM in (Singh et. al, ,2003) and (Pelecanos et. al, 2000). Hence we are using a number of vector quantization algorithms including K-means, LBG and recently designed ITVQ to investigate its suitability to avoid local convergence when using EM algorithm. We also compare the performance of ITVQ over other vector quantization approaches.

How the cost minimization procedure is implemented for each clustering technique is described in section 2 and the distortion function for each the clustering techniques are listed in equations (1), (3) and (11) respectively.

A multi-dimensional Gaussian is calculated using the mean and variance statistics from the test vectors in each code vector region, with the training vectors already grouped into their code books. An approximation of the GMM is determined by estimating the mixture weights p_k, means μ_k, and covariances $\sum_k$. Each mean μ_k is assigned to its corresponding code vector, $\vec{c}_k$. The covariance matrix Σ_k for each GMM is calculated from the variances of the vector observations in each code vector region. To achieve the optimal approximation the feature vectors need to be well clustered and the VQ based GMM also need to have the features uncorrelated, for many applications including SV it is difficult to satisfy this condition, however by attempting to match these requirements, model estimation errors could be minimised. Normalization techniques (Mariethoz, J. & S. Bengio, 2005), (Barras, C. & J. Gauvain, 2003) are also applied for this purpose to reduce the mismatch of features.

7. Experiments

In this section of the chapter we describe the speaker verification tests. First we describe the speech corpora used for the experiments, secondly pre-processing and feature extraction settings are summarised. Finally the DET plots and EER scores are provided.

7.1 Speech Corpus

Recently the annual NIST speaker recognition evaluation (SRE) has become the state of the art corpora for evaluating the methods in the field of speaker recognition. GMM-based systems have been widely tested on NIST SRE. We evaluated our methods on NIST SRE 04. The 2004 evaluation uses conversational speech data collected in the Mixer Project using the Linguistic Data Consortium's new "Fishboard" platform. The data is not used by the previous evaluations. This data is mostly conversational telephone speech in English but it also includes some speech in languages other than English such as Spanish and Arabic. The evaluation includes twenty-eight different speaker detection tests defined by the duration and type of both the training and the test segments of the individual trials of which these tests are composed (NIST, 2004).

The performance of the system is based on the detection error tradeoffs DET function. This detection cost function is defined as a weighted sum of miss and false alarm error probabilities. The parameters of this cost function are the relative costs of detection errors, C_{Miss} and $C_{FalseAlarm}$ and the *a priori* probability of the specified target speaker, P_{Target}.

$$C_{Det} = C_{Miss} \times P_{Miss|Target} \times P_{Target} + C_{FalseAlarm} \times P_{FalseAlarm|NonTarget} \times (1 - P_{Target}) \tag{24}$$

7.2 Pre-processing and feature extraction

The performance of a modeling method depends intensively on how well the features are derived. The speaker speech is passed through a number of stages to avoid a number of drawbacks. First, the speech is segmented into frames by a 20ms sliding hamming window with a 15ms skip rate is used to obtain a sequence of frames for which speech feature vectors are estimated.

The frames are then passed through a speech activity detector (SAD) to remove the silence-noise frames. It is a self-normalizing and energy based detector that detects the noise floor of the speech signal frames. SAD can adapt to changing noise conditions (Erwin, E. et. al, 1991) and it removes 20–25% of the signal from conversational telephone recordings such as that in the fisher database from which the NIST SRE 04 corpus is derived.

After removing the silence-noise frames mel-scale cepstral feature vectors are derived from the speech frames. The mel-scale cepstrum is the discrete cosine transform of the log spectral energies of the speech segment. The spectral energies are calculated over logarithmically spaced filters with increasing bandwidths (mel-filters). The inverted MFCC are also computed, a detailed description of the feature extraction steps can be found in section 4. For band limited telephone speech, cepstral analysis is performed only over the Mel filters in the telephone pass band (300–3400 Hz). All cepstral coefficients except its zeroth value (the DC level of the log-spectral energies) are retained in the processing.

7.3 Experimental results

The experiments are designed to compare the performance of EM, K-means, LBG and ITVQ. All systems use the same test, train, GMM settings such as initialization procedure and number of mixtures and feature configurations. This point is important not only for direct comparisons of the modeling methods but also in assessing the fusion strategies. The GMM baseline is used; GMM models have *128* mixtures and features of various sizes individually and in fusion are used.

A standard GMM-UBM system was developed using NIST 04 SRE. The standard train and test conditions for NIST 04 were used to investigate the proposed protocols. We train the coefficient data by using the different vector quantization versions along with GMM to optimize the speaker models as described in section 5.1. Thre feature combinations are used to conduct the experiments. The feature sets include 13 MFCC, and 13 IMFCC.

Examination of the speaker verification results are based on equal error rate (EER) values which are listed in fig3 to fig 5. EER is the most commonly used criteria to compare the recognition rates. The results obtained can be summarized as follows:

1. In all cases the MFCC-IMFCC features give better results than the MFCC features.
2. The GMM-K-means and the GMM-LBG algorithms show very similar performance but both yield results that are clearly below the performance level of the GMM-EM method.
3. The results given by the GMM-ITVQ, on the other hand, are very close to the results given by the GMM-EM algorithm.

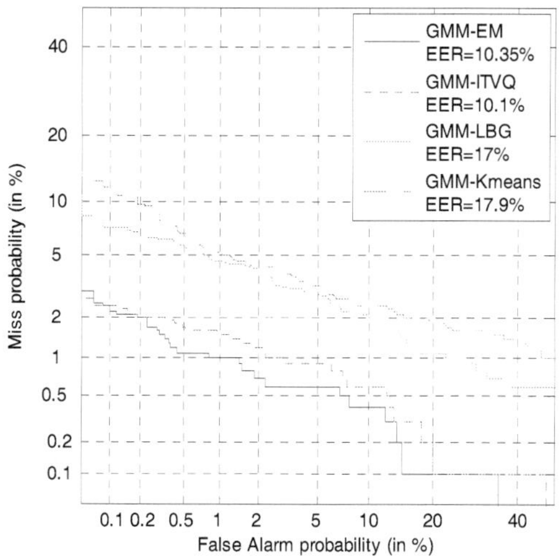

Fig. 3. DET plot for MFCC features

The experiments with different implementations of vector quantization were carried out such as K-means, LBG and ITVQ to make a comparative analysis and we observed that ITVQ behaves a better vector quantization approach than the other VQ implementations. The VQ methods were used as part of the standard GMM.

8. Conclusion

A number of tasks were focused in the experiments. One, to test the vector quantization algorithms for the speaker verification when used along with the GMM, Second to compare the performance of different VQ techniques, and third is to apply the recently established VQ technique called ITVQ for some experimental data.

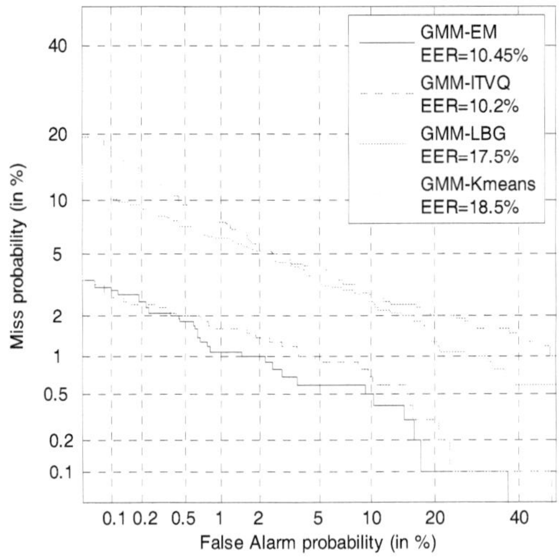

Fig. 4. DET plot for IMFCC features

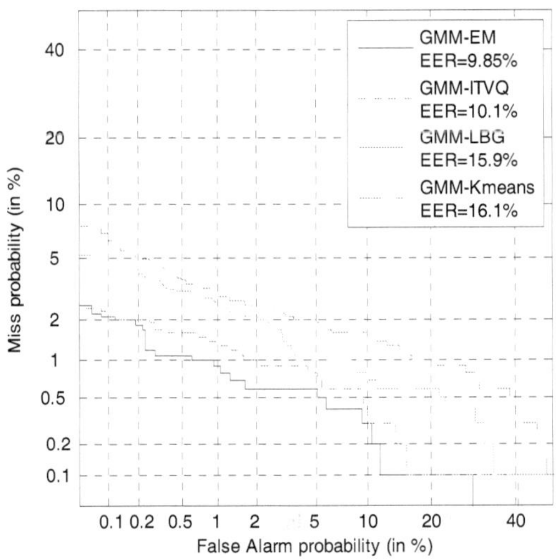

Fig. 5. DET plot for MFCC-IMFCC features

The GMM-EM speaker verification approach was compared with the GMM-Kmeans, GMM-LBG and GMM-ITVQ methods. The speaker verification tests were performed using combinations of the feature extraction methods such as MFCC, IMFCC and their fusion.
The ITVQ algorithm, which incorporates the Information Theoretic principles into the VQ process, was found to be the most efficient alternative for the EM algorithm. It gives correct classification rates at a similar level to that of EM.
In some applications the small degradation of performance in case of the GMM-ITVQ compare to the GMM-EM can be compensated by ITVQ advantages, such as the computational simplicity and ability to escape local minima, which provides a potential for better performance in case of irregular and complex potential functions.

9. References

Barras, C. & J. Gauvain, "Feature and score normalisation for speaker verification of cellular data", IEEE International conference on acoustics speech and signal processing, Vol.2, pp.49-52, 2003.

Chakroborty, S.; A. Roy, G. Saha "Fusion of a Complementary Feature Set with MFCC for Improved Closed Set Text-Independent Speaker Identification", IEEE International Conference on Industrial Technology, pp387- 390, Dec.2006.

Davis, S. B. & P. Mermelstein, "Comparison of parametric representations for monosyllabic word recognition in continuously spoken sentences," *IEEE Trans. Acoust., Speech, Signal Process.*, vol. 28, no. 4, pp. 357–366, 1980.

Douglas, A.R.; "Robust Text-Independent Speaker Identification Using Gaussian Mixture Speaker Models", IEEE Transactions on Speech and Audio Processing, vol. 3, No. 1, pp. 72-83, January 1995.

Erwin, E., Obermayer, K., Schulten, K.: Selg organizing maps, ordering, convergence properties and energy functions. In: Biological Cybernetics. vol. 67, No.1, pp. 47-55, 1991.

Ethem A."Soft vector quantization and EM algorithm", Neural networks, Vol 11, issue 3, , Pages 467-477, April 1998

Furui, S.: Digital Speech Processing, Synthesis and Recognition, Marcel Dekker Inc., New York, (1989).

Gold, B. & Morgan, N. " *Speech and Audio Signal Processing*", Part- IV, Chap.14, pp. 189-203, John Willy & Sons ,2002.

Hedelin, P. Skoglund, J. "Vector quantization based on Gaussian Mixture Models", IEEE transactions on **speech** and audio processing, Vol 8, issue 4, pp. 385-401, July 2000.

Jialong, H.; L. Liu, and P. Gunther, "A new codebook training algorithm For VQ-based speaker recognition", IEEE international conference on acoustics, speech and signal processing, Vol. 2, pp.1091-1094, 1997.

Jankowski C. R. jr. *et al.*, "Fine structure features for speaker identification," in *Proc. ICASSP*, 1996, pp. 689–692.

Mashao, DJ. & Skosan, M., "Combining Classifier Decisions for Robust Speaker Identification", *Pattern Recognition*, vol. 39, pp. 147-155, 2006.

Murty, KSR. & Yegnanarayana, B., "Combining evidence from residual phase and MFCC features for speaker recognition", *IEEE Signal Processing Letters*, vol 13, no. 1, pp. 52-55, Jan. 2006.

Mariethoz, J. & S. Bengio, "A unified framework for score normalisation techniques applied to Text independent Speaker verification", IEEE signal processing letters, Vol.12, No.7,July 2005.

NIST "The NIST 2004 Speaker Recognition Evaluation Plan" http://www.itl.nist.gov/iad/mig/tests/sre/2004/index.html

Peskin B. *et al.*, "Using prosodic and conversational features for high performance speaker recognition: Report from JHU WS02," in *Proc. ICASSP*, vol. 4, 2003, pp. 792–795.

Plumpe, M. D. ; T. F. Quatieri, and D. A. Reynolds, "Modeling of the glottal flow derivative waveform with application to speaker identification," *IEEE Trans. Speech Audio Process.*, vol. 7, no. 5, pp. 569–586, Sep. 1999.

Pelecanos, J.; S. Myers, S. Sridharan, and V. Chandran, "Vector Quantization Based Gaussian Modelling for Speaker Verification", In: International conference on pattern recognition", Vol. 3, pp. 294-297, 2000.

Reynolds, D. A. "Experimental evaluation of features for robust speaker identification," *IEEE Trans. Speech Audio Process.*, vol. 2, no. 4, pp. 639–643, Oct. 1994

Reynolds, D. ; Quatieri, T. & Dunn, R. "Speaker verification using adapted Gaussian mixture models", *Digital Signal Process.*, vol.10,pp. 19-41, 2000.

Singh, G.; A. Panda, S. Bhattacharyya, and T. Srikanthan, " Vector quantization techniques for GMM based speaker verification", IEEE international conference on acoustics, speech and signal processing, Vol. 2, pp. II65-II68, 2003.

Sheeraz M. & Margaret L, "Speaker Verification Based on Information Theoretic Vector Quantization", Wireless Networks, Information Processing and Systems, Springer Berlin Heidelberg, vol. 20, pp. 391-399, November 14, 2008.

Sandipan, C. & Ghoutam, S., "Improved Text-Independent Speaker Identification using Fused MFCC & IMFCC Feature Sets based on Gaussian Filter" IJSP, Vol. 5, No.1, 2008.

Shaughnessy, D. O., "*Speech Communication Human and Machine*", Addison-Wesley, New York, 1987.

Tue, L.; Anant, H.; Deniz, E. & Jose, C. "Vector Quantization using information theoretic concepts", *Natural Computing*, vol . 4, Issue. 1, pp. 39 - 51, January 2005.

Tue, L., Anant, H., Deniz, E., Jose, C., "Vector quantization using information theoretic concepts", In: Natural Computing: an international journal, vol. 4, Issue. 1, pp. 39 - 51. 2005.

Ueda, N. & R. Nakano, "Deterministic annealing EM algorithm," *Neural Netw.*, no. 11, pp. 271–282, 1998.

Ververidis, D. Kotropoulos, C. "Gaussian mixture modeling by exploiting the mahalanobis distance", IEEE transactions on signal processing, Vol 56, issue 7, pp. 2797-2811 , July 2008.

Yegnanarayana, B.; Prasanna S.R.M., Zachariah J.M. and Gupta C. S., "Combining evidence from source, suprasegmental and spectral features for a fixed-text speaker verification system", *IEEE Trans. Speech and Audio Processing*, Vol. 13, No. 4, pp. 575-582, July 2005.

18

Information Mining from Speech Signal

Milan Sigmund
Brno University of Technology
Czech Republic

1. Introduction

Language is the engine of civilization and speech is its most powerful and natural form that humans use to communicate or share thoughts, ideas, and emotions. Speech is talking, one way that a language can be expressed. Language may also be expressed through writing, signing, or even gestures. The representation of language as speech signals in digital form is, of course, of fundamental concern for all sub-fields of machinery speech processing. Speech data are characterized by a large variability. The production of connected speech is affected not only by the well-known coarticulation phenomena, but also by a large number of sources of variation such as regional, social, stylistic and individual ones. People speak differently according to their geographical provenance (accent or dialect) and according to factors such as the linguistic background of their parents, their social status and their educational background. Individual speech can vary because of different timing and amplitude of the movements of speech articulators. Moreover, the physical mechanism of speech undergoes changes, which can affect the nasal cavity resonance and the mode of vibration of the vocal cords. This is obvious, for instance, as a consequence of any laryngeal pathology, as when the speaker has a cold. Less obvious are changes in the fundamental frequency and phonation type, which are brought by factors such as fatigue and stress or in the long term by aging. A series of environmental variables like background noise, reverberation and recording conditions have also to be taken into account. In essence, every speech production is unique and this uniqueness makes the automatic speech processing quite difficult.

Information mining from speech signal as the ultimate goal of data mining is concerned with the science, technology, and engineering of discovering patterns and extracting potentially useful or interesting information automatically or semi-automatically from speech data. In general, data mining was introduced in the 1990s and has deep roots in the fields of statistics, artificial intelligence, and machine learning. With the advent of inexpensive storage space and faster processing over the past decade, data mining research has started to penetrate new grounds in areas of speech and audio processing.

This chapter deals with issues related to processing of some atypical speech and/or mining of specific speech information, issues that are commonly ignored by the mainstream speech processing research. Atypical speech can be broadly defined as speech with emotional content, speech affected by alcohol and drugs, speech from speakers with disabilities, and various kinds of pathological speech.

2. Speech Signal Characteristics

2.1 Information in speech

There are several ways of characterizing the communication potential of speech. According to information theory, speech can be represented in terms of its message content. An alternative way of characterizing speech is in terms of the signal carrying the message information, i.e. the acoustic waveform. A central concern of information theory is the rate at which information is conveyed. For speech, this rate is given by taking into consideration the fact that physical limitations on the rate of motion of the articulators require that humans produce speech at an average rate of about 10 phonemes (sounds) per second. The phonemes are language-specific units and thus each language needs a declaration of its own phonetic alphabet. The numbers of phonemes commonly in use in each literary language vary between 30 and 50. Assuming a six-bit numeric code to represent all the phonemes and neglecting any correlation between pairs of adjacent phonemes, we get an estimate of 60 bits/sec for the average information rate of speech. In other words, the written equivalent of speech contains information equivalent to 60 bits/sec at normal speaking rate. This is in a contrast to the minimal bit rate of 64 kb/sec measured in digital speech signal at lowest acceptable speech quality obtained with 8 bits/sample at sampling rate 8 kHz. The high information redundancy of a speech signal is associated with such factors as the loudness of the speech, environmental condition, and emotional, physical as well as psychological state of the speaker. Many of these characteristics are also subjectively audible, but much of the phonetically irrelevant information is few distinguishable by untrained humans. However, some specific information hidden in speech signal can be detected using advanced signal processing methods only.
Word duration from the information point of view was studied in different European languages. Figure 1 shows the average word length in number of syllables and corresponding information (Boner, 1992).

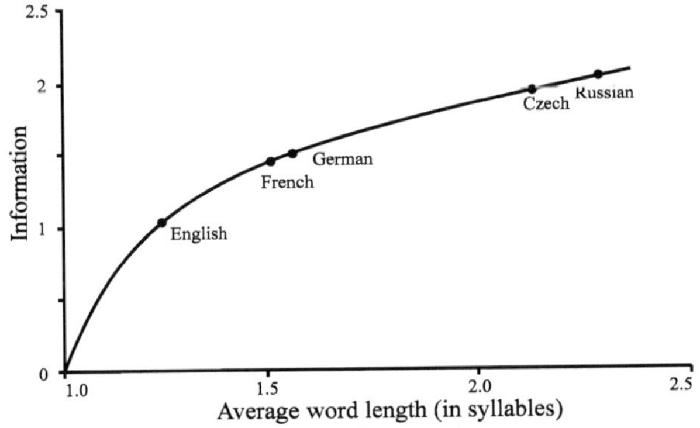

Fig. 1. Average word duration vs. information for some languages.

2.2 Phonemic notation of individual languages

With the growth of global interaction, the demands for communications across the boundaries of languages are increasing. In case of systems for speech recognition, before the machine can understand the meaning of an utterance, it must identify which language is being used. Theoretically, the differences between different spoken languages are manifold and large. Although these differences can be found at various levels (e.g. phoneme inventory, acoustic realization of phonemes, lexicon, etc.) how to reliably extract these features for is still an unsolved problem. A brief review of approaches for language identification can be found, for instance, in (Yan et al., 1996) and (Matějka, 2009). Navratil applied a particularly successful approach based on phonotactic-acoustic features and presented new system for language recognition as well as for unknown language rejection (Navratil, 2001).

Speech processing research focused on mining of specific information from speech signal aims to develop analyzers that are task-, speaker- and vocabulary-independent so as to be easily adapted to a variety of applications for different languages. When porting an analyzer to a new language, certain system parameters or components will have to be changed, i.e. those incorporating language-dependent knowledge sources such as the selection of the phoneme set, the recognition lexicon (alternate word pronunciations), and phonological rules. Many language dependent factors are related to the acoustic confusability of the words in the language (such as homophone, monophone and compound word rates) and the word coverage of a given size recognition vocabulary. There are other parameters which can be considered language independent, such as the language model weight and word or phoneme insertion penalties. The selection of these parameters can vary however depending on factors such as the expected out-of-vocabulary rate. In this section we discuss the important characteristics for the most widespread European languages (i.e. English, German, and French).

Comparing French and English we may observe that for lexicons, the number of words must be doubled for French in order to obtain the same word coverage as for English. The difference in lexical coverage for French and English mainly stems from the number and gender agreement in French for nouns, adjectives and past participles, and the high number of different verbal forms for a given verb (about 40 forms in French as opposed to at most 5 in English). German is also a highly inflected language, and one can observe the same phenomena as in French. In addition, German has case declension for articles, adjectives and nouns. The four cases: nominative, dative, genitive and accusative can generate different forms for each case which often are acoustically close. For example, while in English there is only one form for the definitive article *the*, in German number and gender are distinguished, giving the singular forms *der, die, das* (male, female, neuter) and the plural form *die*. Declension case distinction adds 3 additional forms *des, dem, den* to the nominative form *der*. In German most word can be substantivized, thus generating lexical variability and homophones in recognition. The major reason of the poor lexical coverage in German certainly arises from word compounding. Whereas compound words or concepts in English are typically formed by a sequence of words (e.g. *the speech recognition problem*) or in French by adding a preposition (e.g. *le probléme de la reconnaissance de la parole*), in German words are put together to form a new single word (e.g. *Spracherkennungsproblem*) which in turn include all number, gender and declension agreement variations.

Looking at language-dependent features in lexica and texts, we can observe that the number of homophones is higher for French and German that for English. In German homophones arise from case sensitivity and from compound words being recognized as sequences of component words. A major difficulty in French comes from the high number of monophone words. Most phonemes can correspond to one or more graphemic forms (e.g. the phoneme *ε* can stand for *ai, aie, aies, ait, aient, hais, hait, haie, haies, es, est*). The other languages have fewer monophones, and these monophones are considerably less frequent in the texts. Counting monophone words in newspaper texts, gave about 17% for French versus 3% for English (Lamel et al., 1995). In French, not only is there the frequent homophone problem where one phonemic form corresponds to different orthographic forms, there can also be a relatively large number of possible pronunciations for a given word. The alternate pronunciations arise mainly from optional word-final phonemes, due to liaison, mute *e* and optional word-final consonant cluster reduction. One particular feature of French is liaison. Liaison is where normally silent word final consonants are pronounced when immediately followed by a word initial vowel. This improves the fluency of articulation of natural French speech. Languages with a larger lexical variability require larger training text sets in order to achieve the same modeling accuracy.

For acoustic modeling we use the phoneme in context as basic unit. A word in the lexicon is then acoustically modeled by concatenating the phoneme models according to the phonemic transcription in the lexicon. The phonemes are language-specific units and thus each language needs a declaration of its own phonetic alphabet. The numbers of phonemes commonly in use in each literary language mentioned above are listed in Tab. 1.

Language	Phonemes
English	45
French	35
German	48

Table 1. Number of phonemes in some European languages.

The phoneme set definition for each language, as well as its consistent use for transcription is directly related to the acoustic modeling accuracy. The set of internationally recognized phonemic symbols is known as the International Phonetic Alphabet (IPA). This alphabet was first published in 1888 by the Association Phonétique Internationale. A comprehensive guide to the IPA is the handbook (IPA, 1999). In many EU countries, the SAMPA (Phonetic Alphabet, created within the Speech Assessment Methods) has been widely used recently. None of the above mentioned alphabets is directly applicable to Czech and other Slavic languages. It is because some sounds that are specific for Czech (not only the well-known *ř* but also some others, e.g. *ď, ť, ň*) are not included there. That is why it was necessary to define a Czech phonetic alphabet. The alphabet, denoted as PAC (Phonetic Alphabet for Czech) consists of 48 basic symbols that allows for distinguishing all major events occurring in spoken Czech language (Nouza et al., 1997). Typically, there are some tongue-twisting consonant clusters in Czech which are difficult to pronounce by non-Czechs, e.g. words such as *zmrznout* (English *to freeze*), *čtvrtek* (English *thursday*), *prst* (English *finger*), etc.

2.3 Basic model of speech production

Based on our knowledge of speech production, the appropriate model for speech corresponding to the electrical analogs of the vocal tract is shown in Figure 2. Such analog models are further developed into digital circuits suitable for simulation by computer.

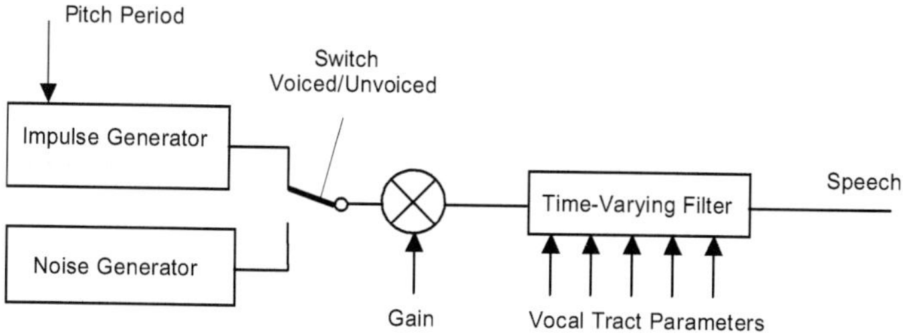

Fig. 2. Electrical model of speech production.

In modeling speech, the effects of the excitation source and the vocal tract are often considered independently. The actual excitation function for speech is essentially either a quasi-periodic pulse train (for voiced speech sounds) or a random noise source (for unvoiced speech sounds). In both cases, a speech signal $s(t)$ can be modeled as the convolution of an excitation signal $e(t)$ and an impulse response characterizing the vocal tract $v(t)$

$$s(t) = e(t) * v(t) \quad (1)$$

which also implies that the effect of lips radiation can be included in the source function (Quatieri, 2002). convolution of two signals corresponds to multiplication of their spectra, the output speech spectrum $S(f)$ is the product of the excitation spectrum $E(f)$ and the frequency response $V(f)$ the vocal tract.

$$S(f) = E(f)\, V(f) \quad (2)$$

The excitation source is chosen by a switch whose position is controlled by the voiced/unvoiced character of the speech. The appropriate gain G of the source is estimated from the speech signal and the scaled source is used as input to a filter, which is controlled by the vocal tract parameters characteristic of the speech being produced. The parameters of this model all vary with time.

Unvoiced excitation is usually modeled as random noise with an approximately Gaussian amplitude distribution and a flat spectrum over most frequencies of interest. More research has been done on voiced excitation because the naturalness of synthetic speech is crucially related to accurate modeling of voiced speech. It is very difficult to obtain precise measurements of glottal pressure or glottal airflow. The glottal airflow can be measured directly via electro-glottography, pneumotachography or photoglottography (Baken & Orlikoff, 2000). The mostly used electroglottography is a non-invasive method of measuring vocal fold contact during voicing without affecting speech production. The Electroglottograph (EGG) measures the variation in impedance to a very small electrical current between the electrodes pair placed across the neck as the area of vocal fold contact changes during voicing. Simultaneously with the glottal flow can be recorded also the speech pressure signal. The speech pressure signal includes information about glottal pulses waveform. Because of electroglottographs are quite expensive devices only the speech pressure signal is often recoded. The glottal airflow is then estimated from this signal. A typical glottal airflow $\Phi(t)$ of voiced speech in steady state is periodic and roughly resembles a half-rectified sine wave (see Fig. 3). From a value of zero when the glottis is closed, the airflow gradually increases as the vocal folds separate. The closing phase is more rapid than the opening phase due to the Bernoulli force, which adducts the vocal folds (O´Shaughnessy, 1987).

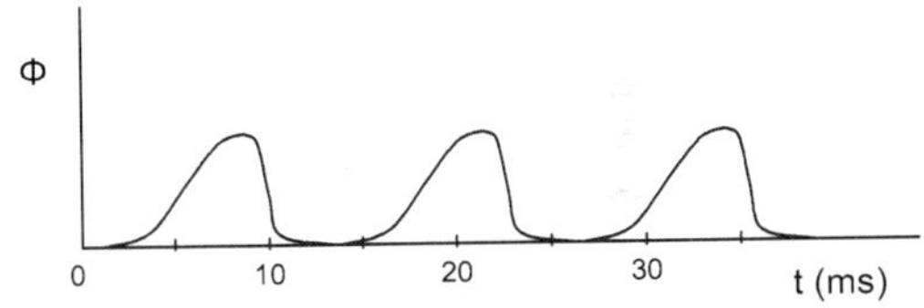

Fig. 3. Simplified glottal waveform during a voiced sound.

Figure 4 shows photography of the vocal folds during a voicing cycle when completely open and completely closed (Chytil, 2008). The vocal folds are typically 15 mm long in men and 13 mm in women. In general, the glottal source estimation has a great potential for use in identifying emotional states of speaker, non-invasive diagnosis of voice disorders, etc.

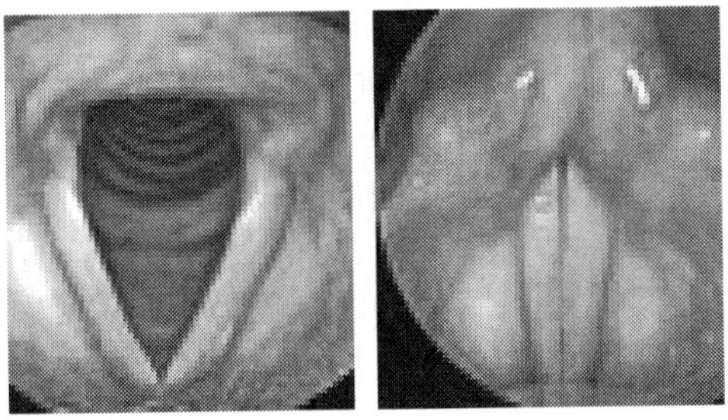

Fig. 4. Vocal folds in the open phase (left) and closed phase (right).

3. General Principles of Speech Signal Processing

The whole processing block chain common to all approaches to speech processing shows Fig. 5. The first step in the processing is the speech pre-processing, which provides signal operations such as digitalization, preemphasis, frame blocking, and windowing. Digitalization of an analog speech signal starts the whole processing. The microphone and the A/D converter usually introduce undesired side effects. Because of the limited frequency response of analog telecommunications channels and the widespread use of 8 kHz sampled speech in digital telephony, the most popular sample frequency for the speech signal in telecommunications is 8 kHz. In non-telecommunications applications, sample frequencies of 12 and 16 kHz are used. The second step, i.e. features extraction, represents the process of converting sequences of pre-processed speech samples $s(n)$ to observation vectors $\mathbf{x}$ representing characteristics of the time-varying speech signal. The properties of the feature measurement methods are discussed in great details in (Quatieri, 2002). The kind of features extracted from speech signal and put together into feature vector $\mathbf{x}$ corresponds to the final aim of the speech processing. For each application (e.g., speaker identification, gender selection, emotion recognition, etc.), the most efficient features, i.e. the features carrying best the mining information, should be used. The first two blocks represent straightforward problems in digital signal processing. The subsequent classification is then optimized to the final expected information. In contrary to the blocks of features extraction and classification, the block of pre-processing provides operations that are independent on the aim of speech processing.

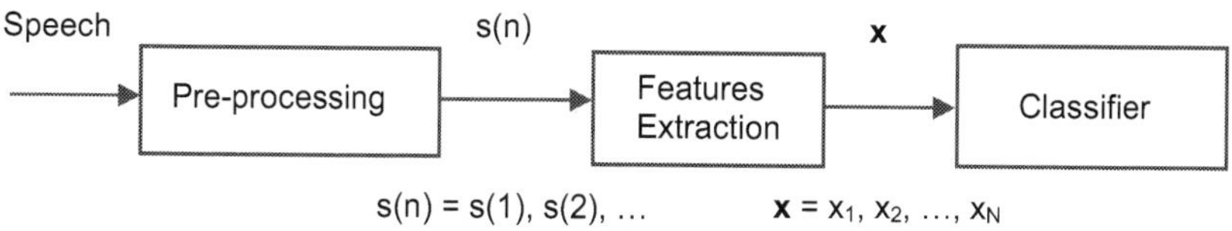

Fig. 5. Block diagram of the speech processing.

3.1 Preemphasis

The characteristics of the vocal tract define the current uttered phoneme. Such characteristics are evidenced in the frequency spectrum by the location of the formants, i.e. local peaks given by resonances of the vocal tract. Although possessing relevant information, high frequency formants have smaller amplitude with respect to low frequency formants. To spectrally flatten the speech signal, a filtering is required. Usually, a one coefficient FIR filter, known as a preemphasis filter, with transfer function in the z-domain

$$H(z) = 1-\lambda z^{-1} \tag{3}$$

is used. In the time domain, the preemphasized signal is related to the input signal by the difference equation

$$\tilde{s}(n) = s(n)-\lambda\, s(n-1) \tag{4}$$

A typical range of values for the preemphasis coefficient is $\lambda \in [0.9\text{-}1.0]$. One possibility is to choose an adaptive preemphasis, in which λ changes with time according to the relation between the first two values of autocorrelation coefficients

$$\lambda = R(1)\,/\,R(0) \tag{5}$$

The effect of preemphasis on magnitude spectrum of short phoneme can be seen in Fig. 6.

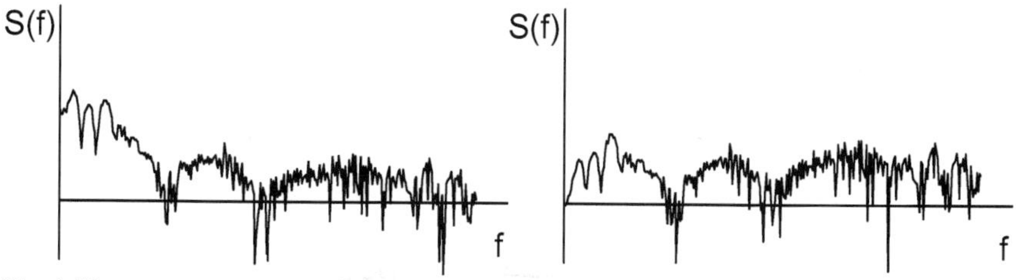

Fig. 6. Phoneme spectrum without preemphasis (left) and after preemphasis (right).

3.2 Frame blocking

The most common approaches in speech signal processing are based on short-time analysis. The preemphasized signal is blocked into frames of N samples. Frame duration typically ranges between 10-30 msec. Values in this range represent a trade-off between the rate of change of spectrum and system complexity. The proper frame duration is ultimately dependent on the velocity of the articulators in the speech production system. Figure 7 illustrates the blocking of a word into frames. The amount of overlap to some extent controls how quickly parameters can change from frame to frame.

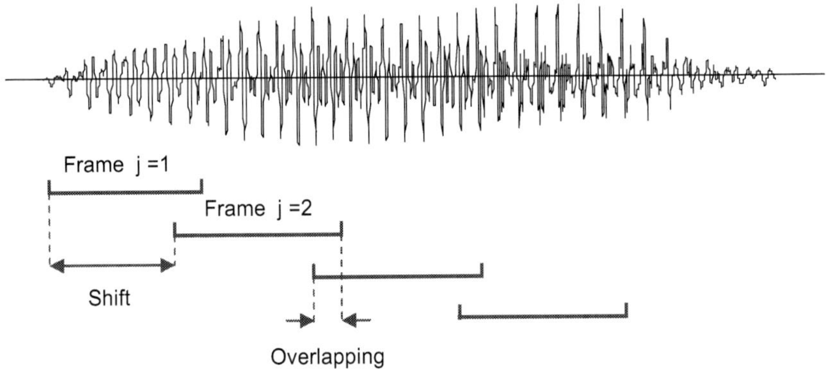

Fig. 7. Blocking of speech into overlapping frames.

3.3 Windowing

A signal observed for a finite interval of time may have distorted spectral information in the Fourier transform due to the ringing of the $\sin(f)/f$ spectral peaks of the rectangular window. To avoid or minimize this distortion, a signal is multiplied by a window-weighting function before parameter extraction is performed. Window choice is crucial for separation of spectral components which are near one another in frequency or where one component is much smaller than another. Window theory was once a very active topic of research in digital signal processing. The basic types of window function can be found in (Oppenheim et al., 1999). Today, in speech processing, the Hamming window is almost exclusively used. The Hamming window is a specific case of the Hanning window. A generalized Hanning window is defined as

$$w(n) = \frac{\alpha - (1-\alpha)\cos(2\pi n / N)}{\beta} \qquad \text{for} \quad n = 1,\ldots,N \tag{6}$$

and $w(n) = 0$ elsewhere. α is defined as a window constant in the range <0,1> and N is the window duration in samples. To implement a Hamming window, the window constant is set to $\alpha = 0.54$. β is defined as a normalization constant so that the root mean square value of the window is unity.

$$\beta = \sqrt{\frac{1}{N}\sum_{n=1}^{N} w^2(n)} \tag{7}$$

In practice, it is desirable to normalize the window so that the power in the signal after windowing is approximately equal to the power of the signal before windowing. Equation (7) describes such a normalization constant. This type of normalization is especially convenient for implementations using fixed-point arithmetic hardware.

Windowing involves multiplying a speech signal $s(n)$ by a finite-duration window $w(n)$, which yields a set of speech samples weighted by the shape of the window. Regarding the length N, widely used windows have duration of 10-25 msec. The window length is chosen as a compromise solution between the required time and frequency resolution. A comparison between the rectangular window and the Hamming window, their time waveforms and weighted speech frame, is shown in Fig. 8.

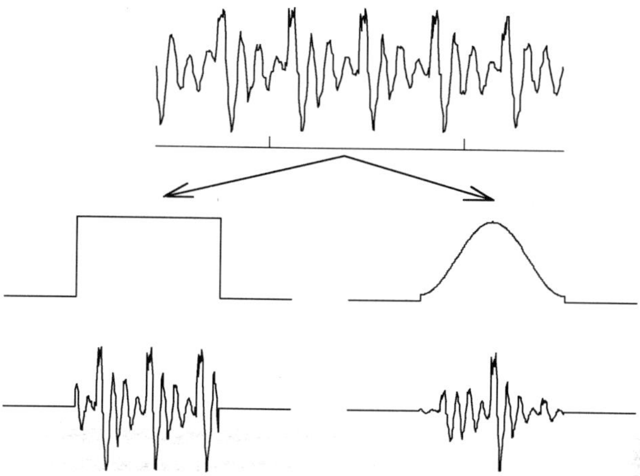

Fig. 8. Window weighting functions and the corresponding frames cut out from a speech signal by the rectangular window (left) and by the Hamming windows (right).

4. Effect of Stress on Speech Signal

The most emotional states of a speaker can be identified from the facial expression, speech, perhaps brainwaves, and other biological features of the speaker. In this section, the problem of speech signal under psychological stress is addressed. Stress is a psycho-physiological state characterized by subjective strain, dysfunctional physiological activity and deterioration of performance. Psychological stress has a broad sense and a narrow sense effect. The broad sense reflects the underlying long-term stress and the narrow sense refers to the short-term excitation of the mind that prompts people to act. In automatic recognition of stress, a machine would not distinguish whether the emotional state is due to long-term or short-term effect so well as it is reflected in facial expression. Stress is more or less present in all professions in today's hectic and fast-moving society. The negative influence of stress

on health, professional performance as well as interpersonal communication is well known. A comprehensive reference source on stressors, effects of activating the stress response mechanisms, and the disorders that may arise as a consequence of acute or chronic stress is provided, for example, in the Encyclopedia of Stress (Fink, 2007).
Stress may be induced by external factors (noise, vibration, etc.) and by internal factors (emotion, fatigue, etc.). Physiological consequences of stress are, among other things, changes in the heart rate, respiration, muscular tension, etc. The muscular tension of vocal cords and vocal tract may, directly or indirectly, have an adverse effect on the quality of speech. The entire process is extremely complex and is shown in a simplified model in Fig.9. The accepted term for the speech signal carrying information on the speaker's physiological stress is "stressed speech".

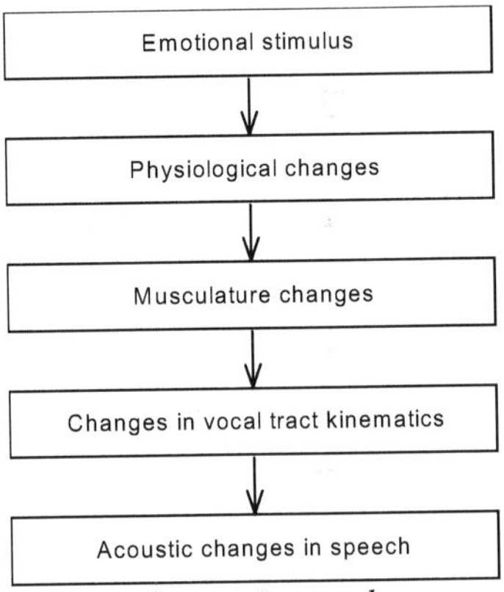

Fig. 9. Model of how emotion causes changes in speech.

Assessment of speaker stress has applications such as sorting of emergency telephone message, telephone banking, and hospitals. Stress is recognized as a factor in illness and is probably implicated in almost every type of human problem. It is estimated that over 50% of all physician visits involve complaints of stress-related illness.

4.1 Stressed speech databases

The evolution of algorithms for recognition of stressed speech is strictly related to the availability of large amount of speech whose characteristics cover all the variability of specific information required for the application target. However, it is really difficult to obtain realistic voice samples of speakers in various stressed states, recorded in real situations. "Normal people" (as well as professional actors) cannot simulate real case stress perfectly with their voices.
A typical corpus of extremely stressed speech from a real case is extracted from the cockpit voice recorder of a crashed aircraft. Such speech signals together with other corresponding biological factors are collected for example in the NATO corpus SUSC-0 (Haddad et al., 2002). The advantage of this database is that an objective measure of workload was obtained, and that physiological stress measures (heart rate, blood pressure, respiration, and transcutaneous pCO_2) were recorded simultaneously with the speech signal. However, such

extreme situations as crashed aircraft occur seldom in everyday life. The most frequently mentioned corpus in the literature is the SUSAS (Speech Under Simulated and Actual Stress) database of stressed American English described in (Hansen & Ghazale, 1997) and distributed by Linguistic Data Consortium at the University of Pennsylvania. For the French speech, the Geneva Emotion Research Group at the University of Geneva conducts research into many aspects of emotions including stress, and it also collected emotion databases. Their website provides access to a number of databases and research materials. The German database of emotional utterances including panic was recorded at the Technical University of Berlin. A complete description of the database called Berlin Database of Emotional Speech can be found in (Burkhardt et al., 2005). A list of existing emotional speech data collections including all available information about the databases such as the kinds of emotions, the language, etc. was provided in (Ververidis & Kotropoulos, 2006).

For our studies conducted within research into speech signals we created and used our own database. The most suitable event with realistic stress took place during the final state examinations at Brno University of Technology held in oral form in front of a board of examiners. The test persons were 31 male pre-graduate and post-graduate students, mostly Czech native speakers. The created database called ExamStress consists of two kinds of speech material: stressed speech collected during the state exams and neutral speech recorded a few days later, both spoken by the same speakers. The students were asked to give information about some factors, which can correlate with stress in influencing the voice, e.g. the number of hours of sleep during the previous night, the use of (legal) drugs or alcohol shortly before examination, etc. This information was added to the records in the database. The recording platform is set up to store the speech signals live in 16-bit coded samples at a sampling rate of 22 kHz. Thus, the acoustic quality of the records is determined by the speaking style of the students and the background noise in the room. A complete description of the ExamStress database can be found in (Sigmund, 2006). In some cases the heart rate *HR* of students was measured simultaneously with the speech recordings in both stressed and neutral state. A comparison of these measured data proves the influence of exam nerves on the speaker's emotional state. The oral examination seems to be a reliable stressor. On average, the *HR* values obtained for stressed state were almost doubled compared to the neutral state (such values usually occur if a person is under medium physical activity).

4.2 Changes in time and frequency domain

From various emotion analyses reported in the literature, it is known that emotion causes changes in three groups of speech parameters: a) voice quality; b) pitch contour; c) time characteristics. To get the quantitative changes of speech parameters, we applied in first study some simple features that had not been specifically designed for the detection of stressed speech, such as vowel duration, formants and fundamental frequency (Sigmund & Dostal, 2004).

Duration analysis conducted across individual vowel phonemes shows the main difference in the distribution of vowel "a". By contrast, the small differences in the distribution of vowels "e" and "i" seem to be irrelevant for the detection of emotional stress (Fig. 10).

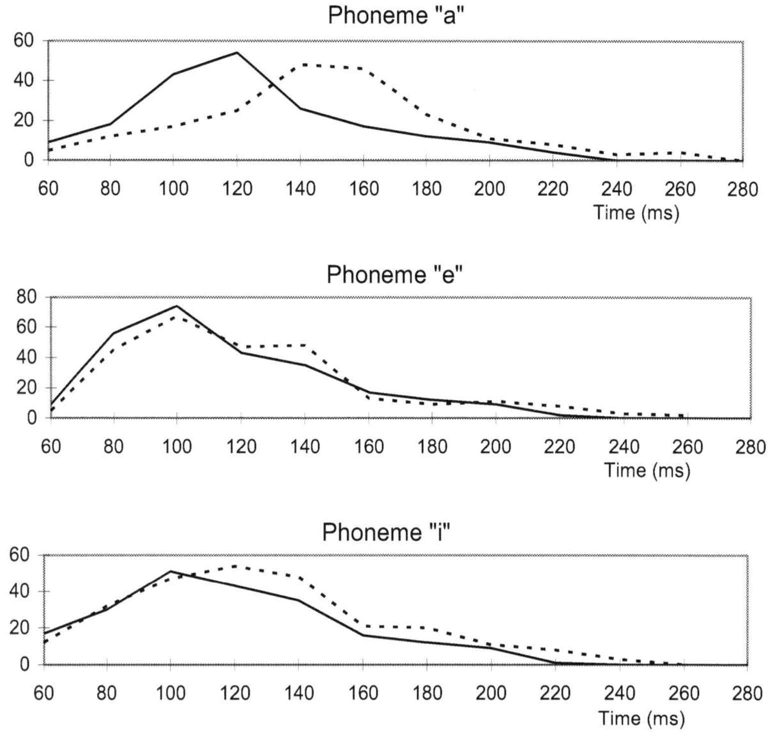

Fig. 10. Distribution of duration for the vowels "a", "e" and "i" (solid lines are for normal speech, dotted lines for speech under stress).

In general, more significant results are given by formants. Formant values were obtained via a formant-tracking algorithm based on peak-picking. The analysis of vocal tract spectrum focused on formant positions F_i and formant bandwidths B_i for selected vowel phonemes shows that only changes in the first and the second formants are significant. In stressed speech, both low formants F_1 and F_2 were shifted to higher frequencies as a rule. Table 2 shows the average formant values for phoneme "i".

	F_1	B_1	F_2	B_2	F_3	B_3	F_4	B_4
Normal	409	52	1981	218	2630	489	3356	371
Stressed	525	98	2068	142	2672	462	3347	383

Table 2. Formant changes in spectrum for phoneme "i" (all in Hz).

Further, the characteristics of pitch were estimated. The fundamental frequency F_0 contours were calculated on the frame-by-frame basis using the center-clipping autocorrelation method (Rabiner, 1993). From this information the distribution of F_0 values was obtained separately for the stressed and normal speech, and the mean F_0 values and standard deviations were calculated. In all cases, the average fundamental frequency increased and the range of fundamental frequency enlarged when the speaker was involved in a stressful situation. Table 4.11 shows the results obtained for three male speakers. Figure 11 illustrates the F_0 distribution obtained for speaker "Kl" in Tab. 3.

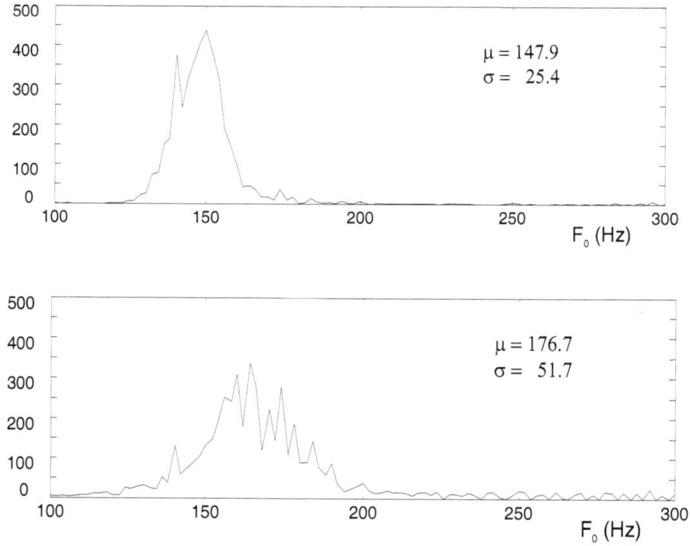

Fig. 11. Pitch distribution for speaker "Kl" (upper graph is for normal speech, lower graph is for speech under stress).

Normal speech has a single narrow high peak at around 148 Hz, alcoholic speech a somewhat broader peak while stressed speech is broader still. The area under each curve is related to the number of frames of speech observed, which is directly related to the speaking rate. The curves are comparable because they were obtained from speaking/reading the same text.

	Speaker "De"		Speaker "Fl"		Speaker "Kl"	
	Mean	Dev.	Mean	Dev.	Mean	Dev.
Normal Speech	127	16	142	13	148	25
Stressed Speech	162	25	243	61	177	52

Table 3. Mean values and standard deviation of F_0 distributions (all in Hz).

The current most commonly used short-term spectral measurements are cepstral coefficients and their frequency-warped alternative coefficients. To compute the cepstrum, we first compute the log spectral magnitudes and next the inverse Fourier transform (IFT) of the log spectrum. The output signal is a set of cepstral coefficients

$$cc(\tau) = \text{IFT}\{\log \mid \text{FT}[s(n)] \mid\} \tag{8}$$

called as the cepstrum of signal $s(n)$. The low-order terms of the cepstrum correspond to short-term correlation in the speech signal (vocal tract information). The local maxima in the higher order terms demonstrate long-term correlation or periodicity in the waveform (excitation information). Experiments in human perception have shown that frequencies of a complex sound within a certain bandwidth of some nominal frequency cannot be individually identified. When one of the components of this sound falls outside this bandwidth, it can be individually distinguished (Zwicker, 1999). The subjective nonlinear perception of frequency had led to an objective computational model that converts a physically measured spectrum into a psychological "subjective spectrum". Used mapping of acoustic frequency f to the so-called mel scale for subjective pitch is

$$pitch = 2595 \log\left(1 + \frac{f}{700}\right). \tag{9}$$

The mel scale attempts to map the perceived frequency of a tone onto a linear scale. This scale is often approximated as a linear scale from 0 to 1000 Hz and then a logarithmic scale beyond 1000 Hz. The algorithm for estimation of the mel-warped cepstral coefficients can be found, for instance, in (Rabiner & Juang, 1993).

In our experiments we focused the cepstral analysis on the data set within the vowel class. The first 12 mel-cepstral coefficients $mcc(1)$ to $mcc(12)$ were estimated for all individual basic Czech vowels cut out from a speech spoken normally and under stress. Finally, the same coefficients obtained from corresponded vowels were compared. The most effective indicator of stress seems to be the 9th mel-cepstral $mcc(9)$ coefficient computed from the vowel "u". Table 4 shows the mean values of $mcc(9)$ obtained for three various speakers. This indicator gives a higher value in case of stressed speech.

	Speaker "De"					
Test #	1		2		3	
Speech	N	S	N	S	N	S
mcc(9)	-0.191	-0.096	-0.206	-0.150	-0.121	0.056
	Speaker "Fl"					
Test #	1		2		3	
Speech	N	S	N	S	N	S
mcc(9)	-0.152	0.160	-0.101	-0.025	-0.024	0.002
	Speaker "Kl"					
Test #	1		2		3	
Speech	N	S	N	S	N	S
mcc(9)	-0.157	-0.094	-0.177	-0.107	0.110	0.187

Table 4. Mean values of the 9th mel-cepstral coefficient for the vowel "u" (N denotes normal speech and S is for stressed speech).

Figure 12 illustrates ten values of the coefficient *mcc*(9) obtained for speaker "De" in the Test # 3 mentioned in Tab. 4. The mean values in Tab. 4 were calculated from 10 speech frames (each of 40 msec).

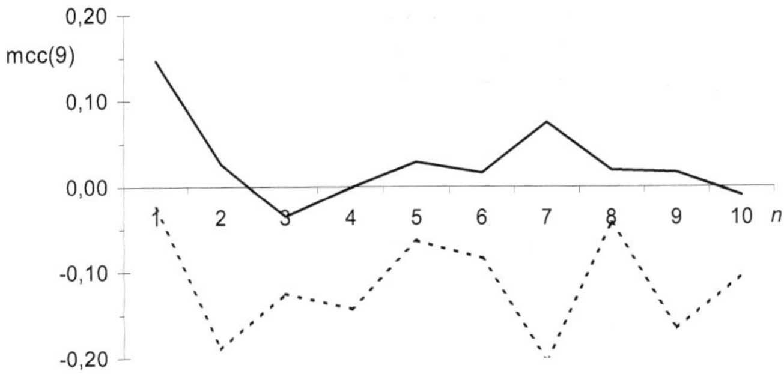

Fig. 12. Values of coefficient *mcc*(9) in ten corresponding speech frames for normal speech (dotted line) and stressed speech (solid line).

4.3 Changes in glottal pulse excitation

In our experiments, glottal pulses were obtained from speech by applying the IAIF (Iterative Adaptive Inverse Filtering) algorithm, which is one of the most effective techniques for extracting excitation from a speech signal (Alku, 1992). Other techniques for obtaining glottal pulses from speech signal can be found, for example, in (Bostik & Sigmund, 2003). The block diagram of the IAIF is shown in Fig. 13. This method operates in two repetitions, hence the word iterative in the name of the method. The first phase (blocks LPC 1st order, filter $H_1^{-1}(z)$, LPC 12th order, filter $H_2^{-1}(z)$) generates an estimate of glottal excitation, which is subsequently used as input of the second phase (blocks LPC 4th order, filter $H_3^{-1}(z)$, LPC 12th order, filter $H_4^{-1}(z)$) to achieve a more accurate estimate. The steps of the method are described in detail below. Firstly, the input speech signal is analyzed by first-order LPC predictor. This step gives an initial estimate of the effect of glottal flow on the speech spectrum. Using the obtained filter $H_1^{-1}(z)$ of 1st order, the input signal is inversely filtered. This step effectively removes the spectral tilt caused by the spectrum of the excitation signal. The output of the previous step is analyzed by the LPC predictor of 12th order to obtain a model of the vocal tract transfer function. The order of the LPC analysis is related to the number of formants to be modeled. The input signal is then inversely filtered by filter $H_2^{-1}(z)$ using the inverse of the 12th order model from the previous step. This yields the first estimate of the glottal pulse derivative and completes the first repetition. The second repetition runs analogously.

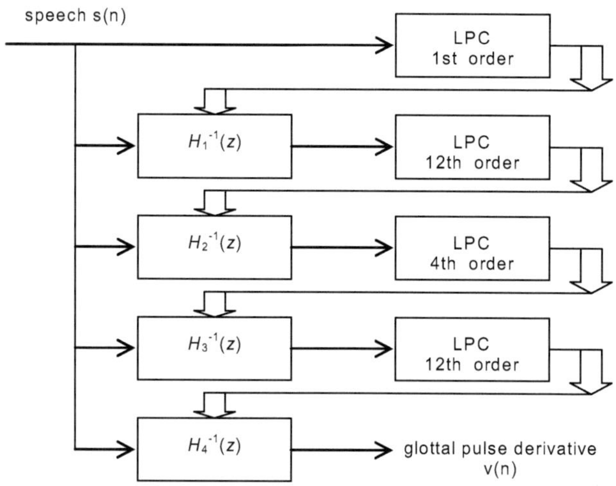

Fig. 13. Block diagram of the IAIF algorithm.

Figure 14 shows a typical waveform $s(n)$ of the vowel "a" and its corresponding glottal pulse derivative $v(n)$ estimated using IAIF. In order to minimize the influence of voice intensity (i.e. loud vs. soft voice), the amplitude normalization was used before applying the IAIF procedure. For the analysis, a pitch synchronous selection of segments from the obtained glottal pulse waveform was used. A position determining the special phase of the glottis (circles in Fig. 4) such as the maximum and the minimum of the glottal pulse derivative waveform was marked for every segment. The waveform was multiplied by rectangular window of one fundamental period in length. Selected segments were fixed in one of the two phases and overlaid.

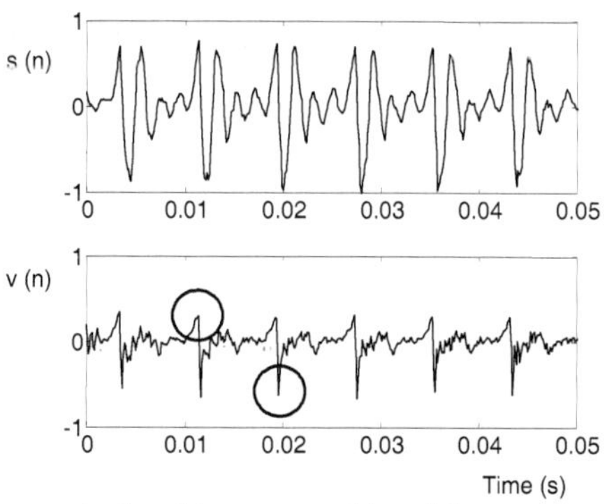

Fig. 14. Example of a speech signal (upper graph) and the corresponding glottal pulse derivative (lower graph).

Based on the graphical interpretation, a two-dimensional distribution matrix was generated. The amplitude-time space is divided into small elements via horizontal and vertical lines (180 intervals on the time axis, 100 intervals on the amplitude axis). The distribution matrix obtained was displayed as a gray scale image where the maximum and minimum values of the matrix are black and white. An example of such an image created from about 4000 segments can be seen in Fig. 15. In this case, the fixation point for all segments was in each period the maximum of the glottal pulse derivative waveform (upper circle in Fig. 14).

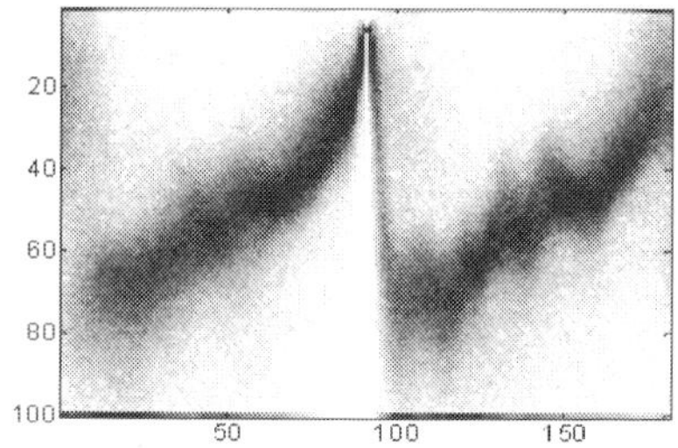

Fig. 15. Illustration of a distribution matrix of glottal pulses derivative waveform interpreted in gray scale.

The ultimate goal in our experiments was to find common speech characteristics of stressed speech based on distribution matrices of glottal pulses. In order to compare the distribution matrices automatically with each other, it is inevitable to find a useful description (a few significant features) of the matrices. An effective criterion seems to be straight cuts made at a reference position. Figure 16 shows the positions of applied cuts and the form of the intersection for two speakers in both neutral and stressed state. For the stressed state, the distribution matrix seems to be "blacker" than for the neutral state; it means that if the speaker is under stress, the derivative waveforms of the glottal pulses produced are more concentrated about the average waveform and the distribution form in the cuts is more asymmetric; in the cut the mass of the distribution is concentrated on the right of the figure. These effects are obvious in almost any speaker. Another type of cuts provides less useful information (Bostik, 2005).

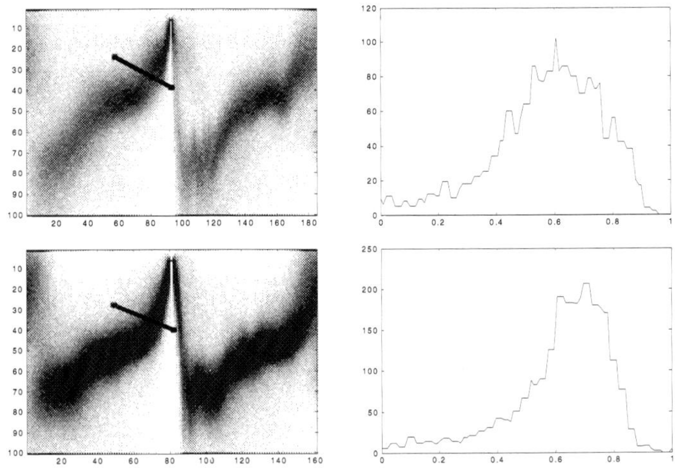

Fig. 16. Graphical samples of distribution matrices and their comparative cuts estimated for the vowel "a".

An experiment with mathematical description of applied cuts resulted in the use of two effective parameters: α and k. The first parameter, α, is defined by

$$\alpha = \frac{S_1}{S_2 + S_3}, \tag{10}$$

where S_1, S_2, and S_3 are the sub-areas of the cut located symmetrically to the maximum of the cut and bounded graphically by lines in 20%, 40%, 60%, and 80% of the total width of the cut, as illustrated in Fig. 17.

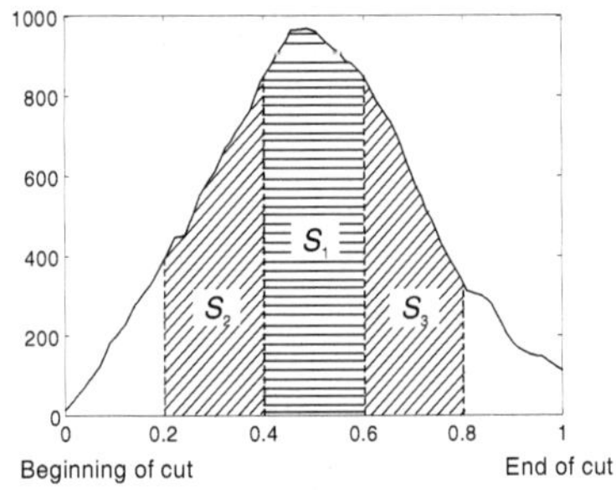

Fig. 17. Definitions of the sub-areas S_1, S_2, and S_3 in a distribution matrix cut.

The second parameter, k, is defined as

$$k = \frac{\mu_4}{\sigma^4} - 3, \tag{11}$$

where μ_4 is the fourth central moment and σ is the standard deviation. For our experiment, 31 male speakers from the ExamStress database were used. Approximately 2000 voiced segments of 5 vowels were extracted from the speech data of each speaker for each state. The IAIF algorithm was applied to those segments to estimate the glottal pulse waveforms. Two distribution matrices for both neutral and stressed state were calculated for each speaker and the speaker's state was estimated using the distribution parameters of cuts in a binomial classification (stress/no stress). The classification was performed by using the Mahalanobis distance measure. Table 5 (Sigmund et al., 2008) shows samples of parameters α and k computed from the speech signals of vowel phonemes for a group of ten male speakers in neutral state (denoted N) and stressed state (denoted S).

Speaker	Parameter a		Parameter k	
	N	S	N	S
M1	1.09	1.20	2.91	3.21
M2	0.85	1.92	2.66	3.50
M3	1.32	1.17	3.04	3.31
M4	0.93	1.18	2.88	2.96
M5	0.78	0.88	2.12	2.86
M6	0.76	1.40	2.45	3.30
M7	0.55	0.83	2.30	2.63
M8	1.03	1.40	2.68	3.19
M9	0.91	1.05	2.82	2.90
M10	0.87	1.32	2.71	3.25

Table 5. Values of applied parameters for neutral (N) and stressed (S) speech.

In the stressed state, slightly higher values of both applied parameters are indicated in most cases. The stress recognition rate in the speaker dependent recognition achieved 88%. In the speaker independent experiments without neutral reference speech data the recognition rate decreased to 72%.

5. Effect of Alcohol on Speech Signal

The term alcohol refers generically to compounds with a hydroxyl group [-OH]. In our work, alcohol refers only to ethanol also called ethyl alcohol. This is the specific compound found in alcoholic beverages. Research of alcohol detection from speech signal was started worldwide by accident of the tanker Exxon Valdez in March 1989. A suspicion arose the captain was influenced by alcohol during the accident, but it was impossible to prove it, because blood alcohol tests were executed too late. A tape with recordings of a dialogue between the captain and terrestrial radio communication station was the only material, which could clarify the situation. Therefore an intensive research of alcohol influence to speech signal followed and the suspicion was confirmed 2 years later (Brenner & Cash,

1991). Subsequently, insurance offices and security organizations began to support next research in this field.
There are two main ways of reporting alcohol concentration in the body, blood-alcohol concentration (BAC) and breath-alcohol concentration (BrAC). Of these two, BAC enjoys some primacy, and in fact, BrAC is very often converted to an expression of equivalent BAC. Alcoholic intoxication causes changes in emotional state and changes in psychomotorics in short-term point of view. It means that the recognition of alcohol influence from speech will be superimposed by the recognition of emotional state. It was proved that emotional information in a speech signal is mainly carried by excitation rather than by the vocal tract in linear modeling of speech. So if we want to separate the influence of alcohol from that of emotion, we must concentrate on vocal tract information. Vocal tract parameters and their changes can represent the quality of psychomotorics in fact. Psychomotorical changes are noticeable on levels of over 0.5 ‰ of blood-alcohol concentration (BAC). Exceeding the level of 1.5 ‰ BAC, changes in psychomotorics are so distinct that speech defects are audible by the human ear.
There are not many available corpora designed to allow the study of speech signal carrying information on the speaker's alcohol intoxication. The German database of alcoholic speech called Alcohol Language Corpus was recorded at the University of Munich (Schiel et al., 2008).). In our research, we used alcoholic voices from a small own database collected at the Brno University of Technology. This database was created by recording 25 speakers (13 males and 12 females) aged 18 to 50 years, who twice said a set of 5 utterances for each given phrase: one set at a level of 0.0 ‰ BAC (sober) and one set at a level of 0.5 ‰ to 1.0 ‰ BAC. The texts of recorded utterances were chosen by an empirical criterion, they are mostly words containing liquids ("r" and "l"), which are relatively difficult to pronounce. The values of BAC were measured by the Drivesafe breathalyzer. Thus, the alcoholic database contains records of sober speakers, records of speakers influenced by alcohol and the approximated BAC values of speakers.
We made several sets of measurements to detect alcohol intoxication in speech signal. Alcohol-induced changes in speech were observed in both the short-time and the long-time domains. First, an analysis of fundamental frequency F_0 was performed. Table 6 gives the mean F_0 values for speakers of both genders in sober state and after alcohol consumption. From the sober condition to a measurable alcohol level, the mean F_0 increased for 21 speakers, decreased for 3 speakers and for one male speaker it remained unchanged. The magnitude of change was greater for the increases in F_0 than for the decreases. The maximum increase in F_0 was 18 Hz for a female speaker.

	Male Speakers		Female Speakers	
	0.5 - 0.8 ‰	0.8 - 1.0 ‰	0.5 - 0.8 ‰	0.8 - 1.0 ‰
F_0 alcoholized	123.5	121.1	209.5	214.0
F_0 sober	121.4	116.2	205.8	207.4
Difference	2.1	4.9	3.7	6.6

Table 6. Changes in fundamental frequency F_0 for 25 speakers (all in Hz).

Because of the fact that an increase in the mean F_0 value can also be caused by other stimuli, fundamental frequency alone is not sufficient as an alcohol indicator. Further, a comparative observation of the significant speech features was performed to find among them the best candidate for alcohol identification. All records from the alcoholic database were parameterized in terms of linear predictive coefficients (LPC), cepstral coefficients (CC), PARCOR coefficients (PC), log area ratio coefficients (LAR), and delta parameters of each of the above features denoted by the prefix "Δ". More details to these speech features can be found e.g. in (Quatieri, 2002) and (Rabiner & Juang, 1993). The classification task was simplified using only two categories of speaker's state. The first state stands for sober speaker (0.0 ‰ BAC) and the second state for intoxicated speaker with an alcohol level of over 0.5 ‰ BAC. The utterance means were computed using dynamic time warping (Rabiner & Juang, 1993) averaging for each speaker, each state and each type of feature. We observed the dispersion inside each state and dispersion between both states. The ratio of inter-state to intra-state dispersion could represent a global ability of a feature to distinguish the two states.

	LPC	CC	PC	LAR	ΔLPC	ΔCC	ΔPC	ΔLAR
D_{inter}	107.40	20.34	17.61	58.75	49.00	6.74	6.96	22.78
D_{intra}	33.71	5.13	5.33	15.65	22.98	3.07	3.15	10.14
D_{inter}/D_{intra}	3.19	3.97	3.30	2.24	2.13	2.19	2.21	2.24

Table 7. Ratios of inter-state dispersion D_{inter} to intra-state dispersion D_{intra} for various speech features.

Table 7 shows word-dependent results for the key word "Laura", which seems to be very suitable word for this purpose. Although the best absolute ratio is given by cepstral coefficients, the log area ratio coefficients provide an approximately equal score in both direct and delta forms. The results for delta parameters are independent of timing in the pronunciation and thus more important. An objective function as a difference between the inter-state dispersion and intra-state dispersion was proposed in (Menšik, 1999). Using this criterion, the most effective phoneme to detection alcohol in speech seems to be consonant "r", especially on the boundaries between the trilled "r" and vowels. These results are particularly interesting from the point of view of acoustic theory, which sometimes cites "r" as an example of the many-to-one relationship between articulatory configuration and acoustic results.

At present, the two main spheres in which alcohol testing from voice becomes meaningful are vehicular traffic and workplaces. The increasing availability of digital speech processing techniques shifts the trend toward instrumental analysis in alcohol and speech research.

6. Conclusion

Human voice is the key tools that human use to communicate. In addition to the intended messages, a significant part of information contained in speech signal refers to the speaker. These phonologically and linguistically irrelevant speaker-specific information make speech recognition less effective but can be used for speaker recognition and analysis of the speaker's emotional and health state. Such a speech cue would allow an analysis without the physical presence of the speaker. While examining stress or alcohol we are only concerned with the physically measurable characteristics of the speech signal. Besides these changes in the spoken language the content of the language, e.g. repetition of selected words, structure of the sentence, etc. is also very important for speech analysis made by psychologists, psychiatrists and other experts.

Information mining from speech signal includes many ways of applying machine learning, speech processing, and language processing algorithms to benefit and serve commercial applications. It also raises and addresses several new and interesting fundamental research challenges in the areas of prediction, search, explanation, learning, and language understanding. Effective techniques for mining speech, audio, and dialog data can impact numerous business and government applications. The technology for monitoring conversational speech to discover patterns and generate alarms is essential for intelligence and law enforcement organizations as well as for enhancing call center operation.

7. References

Alku, P. (1992). An automatic method to estimate the time-based parameters of the glottal pulseform, *Proceedings of ICASSP'92*, pp. 29–32, ISBN 0-7803-0532-9, San Francisco, March 1992, IEEE Press, Piscataway, USA

Baken, R. J. & Orlikoff, R. F. (2000). *Clinical Measurement of Speech and Voice*, Singular Publishing Group, ISBN 1-56593-869-0, San Diego, CA, USA

Boner, A. (1992). *Spracherkennung mit Computer*, AT Verlag, ISBN 3-85502-435-9, Aarau, Switzerland

Bostik, M. & Sigmund, M. (2003). Methods for estimation of glottal pulses waveforms exciting voiced speech, *Proceedings of Eurospeech'03*, pp. 2389-2392, ISSN 1018-4074, Geneva, September 2003, International Speech Communication Association, Grenoble

Bostik, M. (2005). *Voice Analysis for Stress Recognition*, Ph.D. Thesis, Brno University of Technology

Brenner, M. & Cash, J. R. (1991). Speech analysis as an index of alcohol intoxication - the Exxon Valdez accident. *Aviation, Space, and Enviromental Medicine*, Vol. 62, No. 9, (September 1991), pp. 893-898, ISSN 0095-6562

Burkhardt, F.; Paeschke, A.; Rolfes, M; Sendlmeier, W. & Weiss, B. (2005). A database of German emotional speech, *Proceedings of Eurospeech'05*, pp. 1517-1520, ISSN 1018-4074, Lisbon, September 2005, International Speech Communication Association, Grenoble

Fink, G. (2007). *Encyclopedia of Stress*, Academic Press, ISBN 978-0-12-088503-9, London, New York

Haddad, D.; Walter, S.; Ratley, R. & Smith, M. (2002). *Investigation and Evaluation of Voice Stress Analysis Technology*. Project Report: Rome Laboratory, NY, USA

Hansen, J. H. & Ghazale, S. E. (1997). Getting started with SUSAS, *Proceedings of Eurospeech'97*, pp. 1743-1746, ISSN 1018-4074, Rhodes, Greece, September 1997, International Speech Communication Association, Grenoble

Chytil, P. (2008). *Voice Analysis for Detection of Diseases*, Ph.D. Thesis, Brno University of Technology

IPA-International Phonetic Association (1999). *A Guide to the Use of the International Phonetic Alphabet*, University Press, ISBN 0-521-63751-1, Camridge

Lamel, L.; Adda-Decker, M. & Gauvain, J. L. (1995). Issues in large vocabulary, multilingual speech recognition, *Proceedings of Eurospeech'95*, pp. 185-188, ISSN 1018-4074, Madrid, September 1995, International Speech Communication Association, Grenoble

Matějka, P. (2009). *Advancing Phonotactic and Acoustic Language Recognition*, Ph.D. Thesis, Brno University of Technology

Menšik, R. (1999). Recognition of Alcohol Influence on Speech, *Proceedings of Workshop on Text, Speech and Dialogue*, pp. 384-387, ISBN 978-3-540-66494-9, Plzeň, September 1999, Springer-Verlag, Heidelberg

Navratil, J. (2001). Spoken language recognition - a step toward multilinguality in speech processing. *IEEE Transactions on Speech and Audio Processing*, Vol. 9, No. 6, (September 2001), pp. 678-685, ISSN 1063-6676

Nouza, J.; Psutka, J. & Uhlíř, J. (1997). Phonetic alphabet for speech recognition of Czech. *Radioengineering*, Vol. 6, No. 4, (April 1997), pp. 16-20, ISSN 1210-2512

Oppenheim, A. V.; Schafer, R. W. & Buck, J. R. (1999). *Discrete-Time Signal Processing*, Prentice Hall, ISBN 0-13-7549202, Englewood Cliffs, NJ, USA

O´Shaughnessy, D. (1987). *Speech Communication - Human and Machine*, Addison-Wesley Publishing, ISBN 0-201-16520-1, New York, USA

Quatieri, T. F. (2002). *Discrete-Time Speech Signal Processing*, Prentice Hall, ISBN 0-13-242942-X, Englewood Cliffs, NJ, USA

Rabiner, L. R. & Juang, B. H. (1993). *Fundamentals of Speech Recognition*, Prentice Hall, ISBN 0-13-015157-2, Englewood Cliffs, NJ, USA

Schiel, F.; Heinrich, Ch.; Barfüßer, S. & Gilg, T. (2008). ACL - Alcohol Language Corpus, *Proceedings of LREC 2008*, pp. 1-5, ISBN 2-9517408-4-0, Marrakesh, Marocco, May 2008, European Language Resources Association, Paris

Sigmund, M. & Dostal, T. (2004). Analysis of emotional stress in speech, *Proceedings of IASTED Internat. Conf. on Artificial Intelligence and Applications*, pp. 317-322, ISBN 0-88986-404-7, Innsbruck, Austria, February 2004, ACTA Press, Calgary

Sigmund, M. (2006). Introducing the database ExamStress for speech under stress, *Proceedings of 7th IEEE Nordic Signal Processing Symposium*, pp. 290-293, ISBN 1-42244-0413-4, Reykjavik, Iceland, June 2006, IEEE Signal Processing Society, Piscataway

Sigmund, M.; Prokes A. & Brabec, Z. (2008). Statistical analysis of glottal pulses in speech under psychological stress, *Proceedings of EUSIPCO*, pp. 1-5, Lausanne, Switzerland, August 2008, EURASIP, Leuven

19

Estimation of the instantaneous harmonic parameters of speech

Elias Azarov and Alexander Petrovsky
Belarusian State University of Informatics and Radioelectronics
The Republic of Belarus

1. Introduction

Sinusoidal modelling was introduced in (McAulay and Quateri, 1986) and since then it has been used in many processing applications. The essential feature of the model is efficient representation of tonal quasistationary sounds that constitute significant part of speech and music. Because of that the model has been used in speech-coding systems such as multiband excitation vocoder (D. Griffin and J. Lim, 1988) and transform coder (McAulay and Quateri, 1992) as well as in wideband audio-coding (Levine and Smith, 1998). Sinusoidal representation considers the signal as a combination of sinusoids with slowly-varying amplitudes and frequencies, and therefore is not as efficient for transient and noise sounds. This fact gives rise to hybrid parameterization that implies signal separation into deterministic (quasistationary or periodic) and stochastic components (Serra, 1989). There are two and three-part models that are sines+noise (SN) or sines+transients+noise (STN) respectively. As long as sinusoidal modelling can be applied directly to the input in both cases the stochastic components is often referred to as residual.

Hybrid models give improved performance in high-quality coding using perceptual criteria (Painter and Spanias, 2003) and noise reduction systems. Such parametric representation is also used in audio effects processing (time-scale modifications, enhancement, pitch shifting) and text-to-speech (TTS) synthesis (Dutoit 1997). Speech representation by means of the hybrid approach is of great interest because speech segments of different nature (voiced and unvoiced) conform to different parts of the representation (deterministic and stochastic respectively). The model provides good parameterization of both parts and allows using different processing techniques for them. Voiced speech is often modelled by harmonically related sinusoids (harmonic model) that can significantly reduce number of parameters needed for storage, processing or transmission.

Signal separation into deterministic and stochastic components as well as estimation of sinusoidal parameters is still a fundamental problem of sinusoidal modelling. As a rule estimation accuracy drastically influences overall system performance that accounts for improving analysis techniques. Inaccurate periodic/noise decomposition can add some perceptible artefacts to the signal that cannot be taken away afterwards. The short-term Fourier transform (STFT) is usually used as the main tool for sinusoidal analysis. The signal in that case is assumed to be quasi-stationary that means retaining constant spectral parameters over a period of time. Although some very good results have been reported in speech synthesis (Dutoit 1997) and coding (Spanias 1994), the assumption of stationarity might be a considerable constraint for further development. First of all it is hard to make an adequate parametric representation of unsteady tonal sounds. Another problem is to analyze signals with rapidly changing pitch (for instance STFT is hardly applicable to higher-order harmonics of speech because of their large frequency variations). These issues require alternative methods that could give a more localized description of the signal and a suitable estimation of components with rapid frequency modulations.

As has been reported (Boashash, 1992) there are several alternatives to STFT-based techniques that can provide instantaneous parameters estimation. As long as instantaneous parameters of a monocomponent periodical signal can be easily estimated by discrete energy separation algorithm (DESA) (Maragos et al., 1993) or by Hilbert transform (Hahn, 1996), the general approach to analysis of multicomponent signals is to use narrow-band filtering (Gianfelici et. Al., 2007).

As well as sinusoidal modelling, linear predictive coding (LPC) is a very popular speech processing technique. The main reasons for it can be listed as follows:

- good approximation to the vocal tract spectral envelope (especially for voiced speech);
- source-vocal tract separation;
- simplicity and low computational load.

There are a lot of LPC-related papers that describe parameters estimation, transformation and spectrum analysis (Markel and Gray, 1976); (Rabiner and Juang, 1993). LPC can be very effective in coding applications due to its equivalent line spectral frequencies (LSF) representation that is robust against vector quantization. Additional powerful LPC feature is ability to extract vocal tract parameters that is used for formant tracking. According to the LPC model the source signal is presented as a set of prediction coefficients and an excitation sequence.

The prediction coefficients can be obtained either by the autocorrelation or covariance method (Huang et al., 2001). The main weak point of the methods is parameters averaging within the analysis frame that leads to poor performance for frequency-modulated signals.

As far as sinusoidal and linear prediction models are closely related it is possible to propose a direct conversion of sinusoidal parameters into prediction coefficients in order to get instantaneous LPC representation that might be useful in some speech and audio applications. Bringing all the benefits of instantaneous analysis into LPC model will result in more accurate vocal tract parameters estimation, particularly for segments with unsteady sinusoidal components.

The aim of the chapter is to introduce a method for accurate sinusoidal analysis and give some consideration to applications of the sinusoidal model. The analysis technique is based on the filter with a closed-form impulse response (Azarov et al., 2008). The filter produces an analytical signal at the output providing direct instantaneous parameters estimation. The impulse response of the filter can be adjusted in accordance with the instantaneous pitch contour ensuring appropriate processing of higher-order harmonics. The method of pitch estimation is given as well. In order to evaluate performance of the proposed methods, the technique is applied to speech and audio signals. Although the described techniques are focused mainly on speech processing they are also applicable to wideband audio signals.

Concatenative TTS system was chosen as the primary experimental application, since it demonstrates high flexibility of the sinusoidal modeling and provides insight into the analysis technique at the same time. The chapter also describes estimation of the LPC coefficients from sinusoidal parameters in order to improve prediction accuracy and spectral energy localization for signals with frequency modulations. An explicit parameters conversion technique is given and its performance is compared with well-known autocorrelation and covariance methods.

The chapter is organized as follows. Section 2 gives essentials of the sinusoidal and harmonic modelling. Section 3 describes synthesis of the analysis filter with modulated impulse response. In Section 4 some estimation techniques based on narrow band filtering are presented. The linear prediction model is briefly described and parameters conversion technique is presented in Sections 5 and 6 respectively. Section 7 gives some experimental results of using described harmonic analysis and conversion techniques in speech processing systems.

2. The sinusoidal and harmonic models

The sinusoidal model assumes that the signal $s(n)$ can be expressed as the sum of its periodic and stochastic parts:

$$s(n) = \sum_{k=1}^{K} \mathrm{MAG}_k(n)\cos\varphi_k(n) + r(n), \tag{1}$$

where $\mathrm{MAG}_k(n)$ - the instantaneous magnitude of the k-th sinusoidal component, K is the number of components, $\varphi_k(n)$ is the instantaneous phase of the k-th component and $r(n)$ is the stochastic part of the signal. Instantaneous phase $\varphi_k(n)$ and instantaneous frequency $f_k(n)$ are related as follows:

$$\varphi_k(n) = \sum_{i=0}^{n} \frac{2\pi f_k(i)}{F_s} + \varphi_k(0), \tag{2}$$

where F_s is the sampling frequency and $\varphi_k(0)$ is the initial phase of the k-th component. The harmonic model states that frequencies $f_k(n)$ are integer multiples of the fundamental frequency $f_0(n)$ and can be calculated as:

$$f_k(n) = k f_0(n). \tag{3}$$

The harmonic model is often used in speech coding since it represents voiced speech in a highly efficient way. The parameters $\mathrm{MAG}_k(n)$, $f_k(n)$ and $\varphi_k(0)$ are estimated by means of the sinusoidal (harmonic) analysis. The stochastic part obviously can be calculated as the difference between the source signal and estimated sinusoidal part

$$r(n) = s(n) - \sum_{k=1}^{K} \mathrm{MAG}_k(n)\cos\varphi_k(n). \tag{4}$$

Assuming that sinusoidal components are stationary (i.e. have constant amplitude and frequency) over a short period of time that correspond to the length of the analysis frame, they can be estimated using STFT

$$S(f) = \frac{1}{N}\sum_{n=0}^{N-1} s(n) e^{\frac{-j2\pi nf}{N}}. \tag{5}$$

The transformation gives spectral representation of the signal by sinusoidal components of multiple frequencies. The balance between frequency and time resolution is defined by the length of the analysis frame N. Because of the local stationarity assumption STFT can hardly give accurate estimate of frequency-modulated components, that gives rise to such approaches as harmonic transform (Zhang et al., 2004) and fan-chirp transform (Weruaga and Kepesi, 2007). The general idea of these approaches is using the Fourier transform of the warped-time signal. The signal warping can be carried out before transformation or directly embedded in the transform expression (Weruaga and Kepesi, 2007):

$$S(\omega,\alpha)=\sum_{n=-\infty}^{\infty} s(n)\sqrt{|1+\alpha n|}e^{-j\omega\left(1+\frac{1}{2}\alpha n\right)n}, \tag{6}$$

where ω is frequency and α is the chirp rate. The transform is able to identify components with linear frequency change, however their spectral amplitudes are assumed to be constant.

There are several methods for estimation instantaneous harmonic parameters. Some of them are connected with the notion of analytic signal based on the Hilbert transform (HT). A unique complex signal $z(t)$ from a real one $s(t)$ can be generated using the Fourier transform (Gabor, 1946). This also can be done as the following time-domain procedure:

$$z(t)=s(t)+jH[s(t)]=a(t)e^{j\varphi(t)}, \tag{7}$$

where H is the Hilbert transform, defined as

$$H[s(t)]=p.v.\int_{-\infty}^{+\infty}\frac{s(t-\tau)}{\pi\tau}d\tau, \tag{8}$$

where $p.v.$ denotes Cauchy principle value of the integral. $z(t)$ is referred to as Gabor's complex signal, $a(t)$ and $\varphi(t)$ can be considered as the instantaneous amplitude and instantaneous phase respectively. Signals $s(t)$ and $H[s(t)]$ are theoretically in quadrature. Being a complex signal $z(t)$ can be expressed in polar coordinates, and therefore $a(t)$ and $\varphi(t)$ can be calculated as follows:

$$a(t)=\sqrt{s^2(t)+H^2[s(t)]}, \tag{9}$$

$$\varphi(t)=\arctan\left(\frac{H[s(t)]}{s(t)}\right). \tag{10}$$

Recently the discrete energy separation algorithm (DESA) based on the Teager energy operator was presented (Maragos et al., 1993). The energy operator is defined as:

$$\Psi[s(n)]=s^2(n)-s(n-1)s(n+1), \tag{11}$$

where the derivative operation is approximated by the symmetric difference. The instantaneous amplitude $\mathrm{MAG}(n)$ and frequency $f(n)$ can be evaluated as:

$$\mathrm{MAG}(n)=\frac{2\Psi[s(n)]}{\sqrt{\Psi[s(n+1)-s(n-1)]}}, \tag{12}$$

$$f(n)=\arcsin\sqrt{\frac{\Psi[s(n+1)-s(n-1)]}{4\Psi[s(n)]}}. \tag{13}$$

The Hilbert transform and DESA can be applied only to monocomponent signals as long as for multicomponent signals the notion of a single-valued instantaneous frequency and amplitude becomes meaningless. Therefore the signal should be split into single components before using these techniques. It is possible to use narrow-band filtering for this purpose (Abe et al., 1995).

3. Analysis filter

In voiced speech harmonic components are spaced in frequency domain so that each component can be limited by a narrow frequency band. The harmonic components can be separated within the analysis frame by filters with non-overlapping bandwidths. Therefore proposed method for harmonic parameters estimation can be based on narrow band filtering. The analysis filter, used in this chapter has the following features (Azarov et al., 2008):

- filtering in an arbitrary bandwidth;
- the impulse response is described by a closed form expression (a continuous function of the bandwidth border frequencies);
- estimation of the instantaneous parameters directly from the output signal;
- impulse response adjustment according to frequency modulations of pitch (implicit time warping);
- continuous and smooth contours of estimated parameters $\mathrm{MAG}_k(n)$ and $f_k(n)$.

3.1 Filter synthesis

The filter can be synthesized using the N-point STFT that can be considered as a finite impulse response (FIR) filter for a specified normalized frequency f, producing the stationary sinusoid $\bar{s}(n)$ at the output

$$\bar{s}(n) = \mathrm{MAG}(S(f))\cos\left(\frac{2\pi nf}{N} + \varphi(S(f))\right). \qquad (14)$$

Constant amplitude $\mathrm{MAG}(S(f))$ and initial phase $\varphi(S(f))$ can be calculated as follows:

$$\mathrm{MAG}(S(f)) = \sqrt{\mathrm{Re}S(f)^2 + \mathrm{Im}S(f)^2}, \qquad (15)$$

$$\varphi(S(f)) = -\arctan\frac{\mathrm{Im}S(f)}{\mathrm{Re}S(f)}. \qquad (16)$$

where Re and Im denote real and imaginary parts respectively. The closed form impulse response $h(n)$ of this filter for frequency f in Hz is:

$$h(n) = \cos\left(\frac{2\pi}{F_s}nf\right). \qquad (17)$$

Generalizing this expression we can obtain the impulse response of a filter that produces a band-limited sinusoidal component:

$$h(n) = \frac{\int_{F_1}^{F_2}\cos\left(\frac{2\pi}{F_s}nf\right)df}{F_2 - F_1}, \qquad (18)$$

where F_1 and F_2 are limits of the frequency band ($F_1 < F_2$). Integrating of expression (18) leads to the impulse response in the following form:

$$h(n)=\begin{cases}1, & n=0\\ \dfrac{\frac{F_s}{n\pi}\cos\left(\frac{2\pi n}{F_s}F_c\right)\sin\left(\frac{2\pi n}{F_s}F_\Delta\right)}{2F_\Delta}, & n\neq 0\end{cases}\tag{19}$$

where $F_c=(F_1+F_2)/2$ and $F_\Delta=(F_2-F_1)/2$. Parameters F_c and F_Δ correspond to the center frequency of the filter band and the half of bandwidth respectively. The filter output $s_{F_c,F_\Delta}(n)$ can be calculated as the convolution of $s(n)$ and $h(n)$ and can be expressed as the following sum:

$$s_{F_c,F_\Delta}(n)=\sum_{i=0}^{N-1}\frac{s(i)F_s}{2\pi(n-i)F_\Delta}\cos\left(\frac{2\pi(n-i)}{F_s}F_c\right)\sin\left(\frac{2\pi(n-i)}{F_s}F_\Delta\right),\tag{20}$$

The expression can be rewritten as:

$$s_{F_c,F_\Delta}(n)=A(n)\cos(0n)+B(n)\sin(0n),\tag{21}$$

where

$$A(n)=\sum_{i=0}^{N-1}\frac{s(i)F_s}{2\pi(n-i)F_\Delta}\sin\left(\frac{2\pi(n-i)}{F_s}F_\Delta\right)\cos\left(\frac{2\pi(n-i)}{F_s}F_c\right),$$

$$B(n)=\sum_{i=0}^{N-1}\frac{-s(i)F_s}{2\pi(n-i)F_\Delta}\sin\left(\frac{2\pi(n-i)}{F_s}F_\Delta\right)\sin\left(\frac{2\pi(n-i)}{F_s}F_c\right).$$

Thus, considering (21), the expression (20) is a magnitude and frequency-modulated cosine function

$$s_{F_c,F_\Delta}(n)=\mathrm{MAG}(n)\cos(\varphi(n))\tag{22}$$

with instantaneous magnitude $\mathrm{MAG}(n)$, phase $\varphi(n)$ and frequency $f(n)$ that can be calculated as:

$$\mathrm{MAG}(n)=\sqrt{A^2(n)+B^2(n)},\tag{23}$$

$$\varphi(n)=\arctan\left(\frac{-B(n)}{A(n)}\right),\tag{24}$$

$$f(n)=\frac{\varphi(n+1)-\varphi(n)}{2\pi}F_s.\tag{25}$$

Instantaneous sinusoidal parameters of the filter output are available at every instant of time within analysis frame. The bandwidth specified by border frequencies F_1 and F_2 (or by parameters F_c and F_Δ) should cover the frequency of the periodic component that is being analyzed. The filter output $s_{F_c,F_\Delta}(n)$ can be converted into the analytical signal $s^a_{F_c,F_\Delta}(n)$ in the following way:

$$s^a_{F_c,F_\Delta}(n)=A(n)+jB(n).\tag{26}$$

3.2 Analysis filter with modulated impulse response

For accurate sinusoidal parameters estimation of periodical components with high frequency modulations a frequency-modulated filter can be used (Petrovsky et al., 1999). The closed form impulse response of the filter is modulated according to frequency contour of the analyzed component. This approach is quite applicable to analysis of voiced speech since rough harmonic frequency trajectories can be estimated from the pitch contour. Considering centre frequency of the filter bandwidth as a function of time $F_c(n)$ the equation (21) can be rewritten in the following form:

$$s_{F_c,F_\Delta}(n) = A(n)\cos(0n) + B(n)\sin(0n) \tag{27}$$

where

$$A(n) = \sum_{i=0}^{N-1} \frac{s(i)F_s}{2\pi(n-i)F_\Delta} \sin\left(\frac{2\pi(n-i)}{F_s}F_\Delta\right) \cos\left(\frac{2\pi}{F_s}\varphi_c(n,i)\right),$$

$$B(n) = \sum_{i=0}^{N-1} \frac{-s(i)F_s}{2\pi(n-i)F_\Delta} \sin\left(\frac{2\pi(n-i)}{F_s}F_\Delta\right) \sin\left(\frac{2\pi}{F_s}\varphi_c(n,i)\right),$$

$$\varphi_c(n,i) = \begin{cases} \sum_{j=n}^{i} F_c(j), & n < i \\ -\sum_{j=i}^{n} F_c(j), & n > i \\ 0, & n = i \end{cases}.$$

The required instantaneous parameters can be calculated using expressions (23)-(25). The frequency-modulated filter has a warped band-pass, aligned to the given frequency contour $F_c(n)$, that provides adequate analysis of periodic components with rapid frequency alterations. This approach is an alternative to time warping that is used in speech analysis (Weruaga and Kepesi, 2007). In Figure 1 an example of parameters estimation is shown. The frequency contour of the harmonic component can be covered by the filter band-pass specified by the centre frequency contour $F_c(n)$ and the bandwidth $2F_\Delta$.

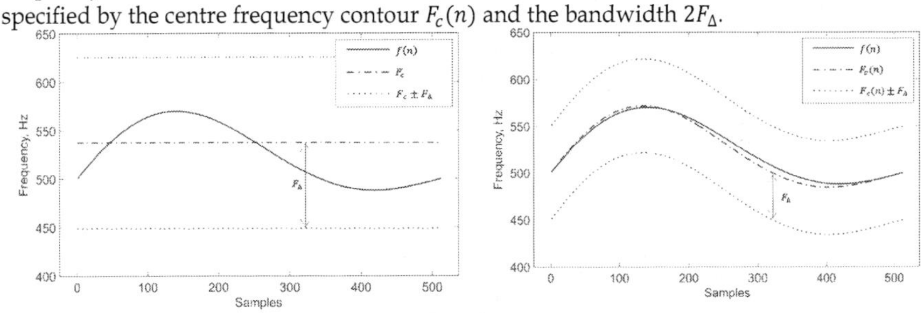

a) b)

Fig. 1. Short-time analysis using narrow-band filtering ($N = 512$): a) filter with simple impulse response; b) filter with modulated impulse response.

Centre frequency contour $F_c(n)$ is adjusted within the analysis frame providing narrow band filtering of the frequency-modulated component.

4. Estimation techniques

4.1 Sinusoidal analysis

In this subsection the general technique of sinusoidal parameters estimation is presented. The technique does not assume harmonic structure of the signal and therefore can be applied both to speech and audio signals.

In order to locate sinusoidal components in frequency domain the estimation procedure uses iterative adjustments of the filter bands with a predefined number of iterations. At every step the centre frequency of each filter is changed in accordance with the calculated frequency value in order to position energy peak at the centre of the band. At the initial stage the frequency range of the signal is covered by overlapping bands (where h is the number of bands) with constant central frequencies respectively.

At every step the respective instantaneous frequencies are estimated by formulas (21),(23)-(25) at the instant that corresponds to the centre of the frame . Then the central bandwidth frequencies are reset and the next estimation is carried out.

When all the energy peaks are located the final sinusoidal parameters (amplitude, frequency and phase) can be calculated using the expressions (21),(23)-(25) as well. During the peak location process some of the filter bands may locate the same component. Duplicated parameters are discarded by comparison of the centre band frequencies .

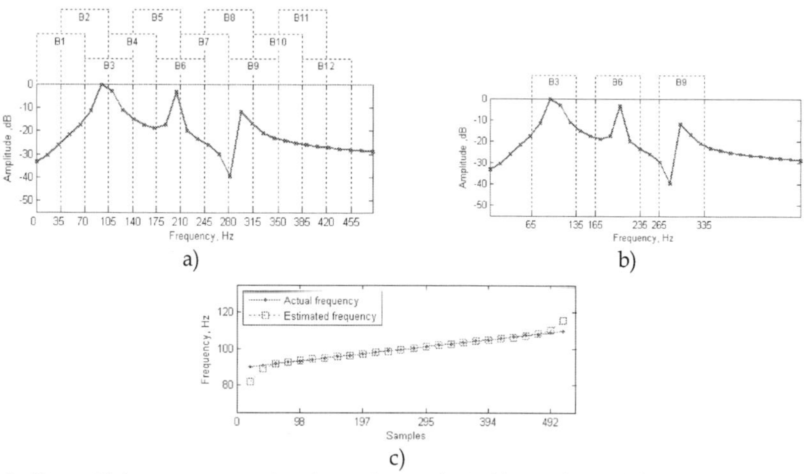

Fig. 2. Sinusoidal parameters estimation using analysis filters: a) initial frequency partition; b) frequency partition after second iteration; c) instantaneous frequency estimation by the analysis filter

In order to discard short-term components (that apparently are transients or noise and should be taken to the residual) sinusoidal parameters are tracked from frame to frame. The frequency and amplitude values of adjacent frames are compared, providing long-term component matching.

The technique has been used in the hybrid audio coder (Petrovsky et al., 2008), since it able to pick out the sinusoidal part and leave the original transients in the residual without any prior transient detection. In Figure 3 a result of the signal separation is presented. The source signal is a bell tune sampled at 44100 Hz (Figure 3(a)).

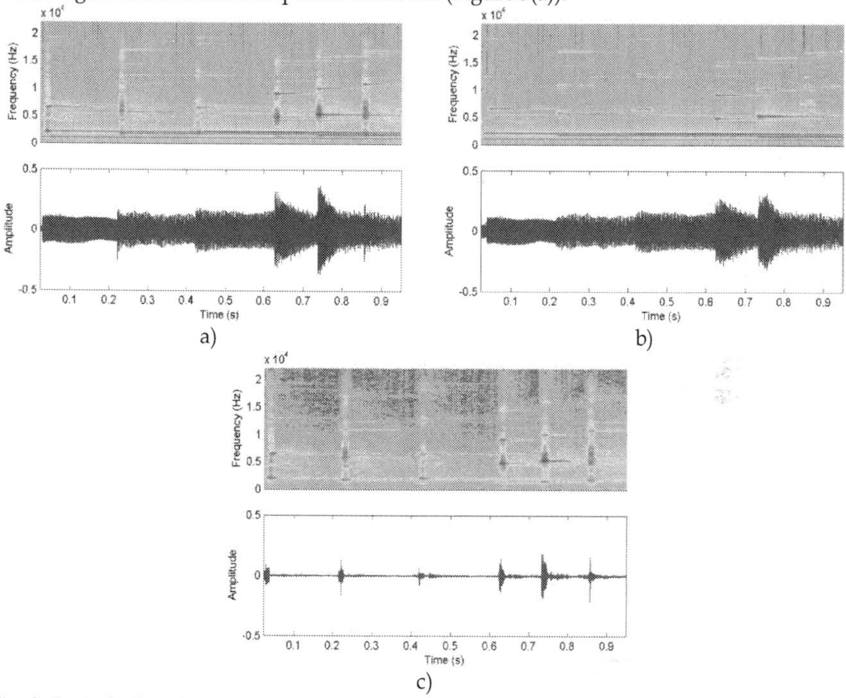

Fig. 3. Periodic/stochastic separation of an audio signal: a) source signal; b) periodic part; c) stochastic part

The analysis was carried out using the following settings: analysis frame length - 48 ms, analysis step - 14 ms, filter bandwidths - 70Hz, windowing function - the Hamming window. The synthesized periodic part is shown in Figure 3(b). As can be seen from the spectrogram, the periodic part contains only long sinusoidal components with high energy localization. The transients are left untouched in the residual signal that is presented in Figure 3(c). The periodic/residual ratio is rather high (14.77 dB) that indicates that the source signal is of a tonal nature.

4.2 Harmonic analysis

As was mentioned above it is possible to use frequency-modulated filters in speech applications in order to make accurate estimation of higher-order harmonics. The analysis process consists of the two following stages:

- fundamental frequency contour estimation and voiced/unvoiced classification;
- harmonic parameters estimation with fundamental frequency adjustment.

The fundamental frequency is estimated first in order to get rough frequency contours of the harmonic components needed for filter synthesis.
The problem of initial fundamental frequency estimation comes to finding a periodical component with the lowest possible frequency and sufficiently high energy at the same time. Within the fundamental frequency range ([60,420] Hz) all periodical components are extracted by means of the described sinusoidal analysis technique and then the suitable one is considered as the fundamental. In order to reduce computational complexity the source signal is filtered by a low-pass filter before the estimation. If it is not possible to track a long continuous sinusoid the corresponding frames are classified as unvoiced.
Having pitch contour estimated it is possible to use frequency-modulated filters that may enhance parameters estimation accuracy for harmonics with significant frequency modulations. Required centre frequency of the filter bands $F_c(n)$ are estimated as the instantaneous fundamental frequency $f_0(n)$ multiplied by the number k of the respective harmonic $F_C^k(n) = kf_0(n)$. The estimation procedure goes from the first harmonic to the last, adjusting fundamental frequency at every step. The fundamental frequency recalculation formula can be written as follows:

$$f_0(n) = \sum_{i=0}^{k} \frac{f_i(n)\mathrm{MAG}_i(n)}{(i+1)\sum_{j=0}^{k}\mathrm{MAG}_j(n)}. \tag{28}$$

The fundamental frequency values become more precise while moving up the frequency range. It allows making proper filter synthesis for increasing harmonic order k. The required harmonic parameters are estimated using expressions (27) and (23)-(25). The stochastic part of the signal is calculated by the formula (4).

5. Linear predictive coding

LPC model assumes that a given signal sample $s(n)$ can be approximated as a linear combination of the p past speech samples that leads to the following equality:

$$s(n) = \sum_{i=1}^{p} a_i\, s(n-i) + Gu(n), \tag{29}$$

where $a_1, a_2, \dots, a_p$ are prediction coefficients, $u(n)$ is a normalized excitation and G is the gain of the excitation (Rabiner and Juang, 1993). In z-domain the following transfer function can be written:

$$H(z) = \frac{G}{1 - \sum_{i=1}^{p} a_i z^{-i}} = \frac{G}{A(z)}. \tag{30}$$

The prediction error $e(n)$ is defined as the difference between the source and predicted samples:

$$e(n) = s(n) - \tilde{s}(n) = s(n) - \sum_{k=1}^{p} a_k s(n-k). \tag{31}$$

The basic problem of LPC is to find the set of predictor coefficients that minimize the mean-square prediction error. There are two primary solutions to this problem: the autocorrelation and covariance methods.

The autocorrelation method assumes that $s(n) = 0$ outside the interval $0 \le n < N$ and minimizes the prediction error within infinity. It comes to the system of linear equations (Markel and Gray, 1976):

$$\sum_{i=1}^{p} a_i r(|i-j|) = -r(j), \tag{32}$$

where $j = 1,2,\dots,p$ and $r(l)$ is the autocorrelation function $r(l) = \sum_{n=0}^{N-1-l} s(n)s(n+l), l \ge 0$.
The covariance method uses the interval where the signal is defined and can be expressed as the system:

$$\sum_{i=1}^{p} a_i c_{ij} = -c_{0j}, \tag{33}$$

where $j = 1,2,\dots,p$ and $c_{ij} = \sum_{n=p}^{N-1} s(n-i)s(n-j)$.
The autocorrelation method always produces a stable solution (i.e. all the roots of $A(z)$ are within the unit circle). Unlike it the covariance method does not and therefore it is less popular in speech processing though it may give more accurate results (Markel and Gray, 1976). The frequency domain behaviour of the $A(z)$ can be derived by evaluating

$$H(e^{i\omega}) = \frac{G}{1 - \sum_{k=1}^{p} a_k e^{-j\omega k}} = \frac{G}{A(e^{i\omega})}. \tag{34}$$

6. Conversion of sinusoidal parameters into prediction coefficients

6.1 System derivation

The conversion problem consists in finding the set of linear prediction coefficients $a_1(n), \dots, a_p(n)$ that provide the closest possible spectral envelope $A(e^{i\omega})$ to the one specified by parameters of the sinusoidal model $\text{MAG}_1(n), \dots, \text{MAG}_K(n)$ and $f_1(n), \dots, f_K(n)$. An obvious solution is to synthesize the periodic signal, specified by the parameters, and then apply a conventional LPC analysis technique in order to estimate the prediction coefficients. Although this approach seems very simple it is not the simplest regarding computation complexity and, moreover, is not the most accurate. If one uses the autocorrelation method it is necessary to analyze a long frame to provide good results. The covariance method theoretically can have better performance however it requires at least one period of the fundamental and is not used for spectral analysis because of specific spectrum interpretation (Markel and Gray, 1976).
Let us consider a sinusoid with a constant amplitude MAG, constant frequency f and zero initial phase:

$$s(n) = \text{MAG}\cdot\cos(fn). \tag{35}$$

The prediction error can be written in the following way:

$$\begin{aligned} e(n) &= s(n) - \tilde{s}(n) = \text{MAG}\cdot\cos(fn) - \sum_{i=1}^{p} \text{MAG}\cdot a_i \cos\big(f(n-i)\big) = \\ &= \text{MAG}\cdot\left[1 - \sum_{i=1}^{p} a_i \cos(fi)\right]\cos(fn) - \text{MAG}\cdot\left[\sum_{i=1}^{p} a_i \sin(fi)\right]\sin(fn). \end{aligned} \tag{36}$$

The prediction error is a sinusoid, which energy can be characterized by the squared amplitude:

$$E_a^2 = \mathrm{MAG}^2 \cdot \left(\left[1 - \sum_{i=1}^{p} a_i \cos(fi) \right]^2 + \left[\sum_{i=1}^{p} a_i \sin(fi) \right]^2 \right). \quad (37)$$

The residual of a harmonic signal is also a harmonic signal. It is possible to evaluate prediction coefficients that minimize the sum of squared amplitudes of the residual. Having an instantaneous vector of sinusoidal amplitudes $\mathrm{MAG}_1(n), \ldots, \mathrm{MAG}_K(n)$ and frequencies $f_1(n), \ldots, f_K(n)$ the relative residual energy can be evaluated as the following sum:

$$E_a^2 = \sum_{k=1}^{K} \mathrm{MAG}_k(n)^2 \left(\left[1 - \sum_{i=1}^{p} a_i \cos(f_k(n)i) \right]^2 + \left[\sum_{i=1}^{p} a_i \sin(f_k(n)i) \right]^2 \right). \quad (38)$$

In order to minimize E_a^2 it is possible to use the basic minimization approach by finding partial derivatives with respect to variables a_i and then solving the system of linear equations. Eventually the following system can be derived:

$$\sum_{i=1}^{p} a_i q(|i-j|) = -q(j), \quad (39)$$

where $j = 1,2, \ldots, p$ and $q(l) = \sum_{k=1}^{K} \mathrm{MAG}_k(n) \cos(f_k(n)l)$, $(l \geq 0)$.
The system is similar to the one in autocorrelation method and can be solved accordingly. There are several well-studied approaches that provide simple and effective solutions (Huang et al., 2001).
Rank of the matrix

$$Q = \begin{bmatrix} q(0) & \cdots & q(p-1) \\ \vdots & \ddots & \vdots \\ q(p-1) & \cdots & q(0) \end{bmatrix} \quad (40)$$

does not exceed $2K$ and therefore there is no need to choose $p > 2K$. However, if the prediction order p is to be more than $2K$ the system should be reduced to $2K$ order and then $p - 2K$ zeros should be added to the evaluated prediction coefficients.
In order to show how proposed conversion technique compares with other methods the spectrum analysis of a sinusoidal signal is illustrated in Figure 4. The signal consists of two sinusoids with equal constant amplitudes $\mathrm{MAG}_1(n) = 1$, $\mathrm{MAG}_2(n) = 1$ and harmonically related frequencies $f_1(n) = 200Hz$, $f_2(n) = 400Hz$. The sampling frequency is 8kHz. The results were obtained by different approaches with the same prediction order $p = 8$. In order to provide accurate results 400 samples of the signal weighted by the Hamming window were used for the autocorrelation method and one exact period of the f_1 (i.e. 40 samples) was used for the covariance method. The obtained prediction coefficients are listed in Table 1.

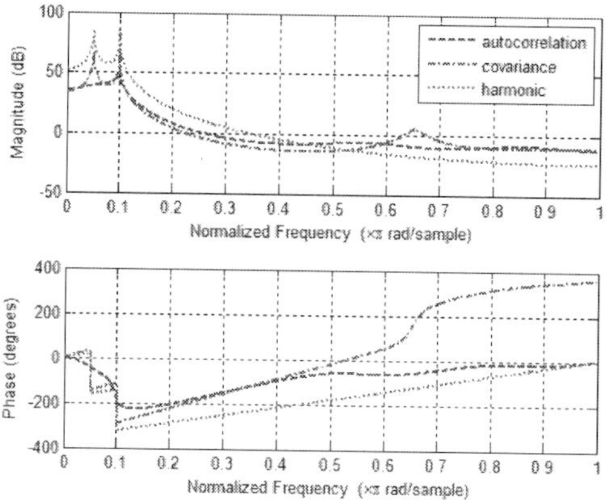

Fig. 4. LPC spectrum envelopes obtained through different methods

autocorrelation	covariance	harmonic
prediction coefficients		
-1.9816	-1.7037	-3.8775
0.6289	0	5.7574
0.4239	0	-3.8775
0.2187	1.7242	1.0000
0.0145	0	0
-0.1881	-1.4448	0
-0.3884	0	0
0.2889	0.4437	0
residual, dB		
-40.36	-278.99	-246.79

Table 1. LPC analysis result

As can be seen from the presented example the covariance method gives the smallest residual, however the conversion technique gives the most adequate spectral envelope. The autocorrelation method produces heavily smoothed spectrum and requires lengthening of the analysis frame in order to give more accurate results.

6.2 Stability problem

Almost all signal processing applications that use LPC require stability of the filter $1/A(z)$. The stability is guaranteed if all the roots of the polynomial $A(z)$ are inside the unit circle. The proposed technique may produce an unstable filter (when $p \geq 2K$) with roots on the circle. In this section a method of modifying prediction coefficients is proposed that provides a stable filter in such cases.

The method is based on the autocorrelation approach. Let us consider a signal $s(n) = t(n)$, $1 \leq n \leq 2p$, that satisfy the following conditions $\sum_{n=1}^{p}|t(n)| > 0$ and $\sum_{n=p+1}^{2p}|t(n)| = 0$.

Stability of the filter can be guaranteed if the coefficients minimize the prediction error for both $t(n)$ and (38).
Using (33) residual minimization of the signal $t(n)$ leads to the following system:

$$\sum_{i=1}^{p} a_i c_{ij} = 0 \tag{41}$$

where $j = 1,2,\dots,p$ and $c_{ij} = \sum_{n=p}^{N-1} s(n-i)s(n-j)$.
The following combination of (39) and (41) gives the required system:

$$\sum_{i=1}^{p} a_i\left[c_{ij} + q(|i-j|)\right] = -q(j). \tag{42}$$

Although choosing $t(n)$ may be arbitrary, it is possible to find a sequence that changes only one element $q(0)$ of the system (39). Let us consider $t(n)$ specified in the following way:

$$t(n) = \begin{cases} 0, & n \neq p \\ \Delta d, & n = p \end{cases}. \tag{43}$$

In this case the c_{ij} in (41) becomes

$$c_{ij} = \begin{cases} 0, & i \neq j \\ \Delta d, & i = j \end{cases}, \tag{44}$$

and (42) can be written in the following form:

$$\sum_{i=1}^{p} a_i q(|i-j|) = -q(j) \tag{45}$$

where $j = 1,2,\dots,p$ and $q(l) = \begin{cases} \sum_{k=1}^{K} \mathrm{MAG}_k(n)\cos(f_k(n)l) + \Delta d, & l = 0 \\ \sum_{k=1}^{K} \mathrm{MAG}_k(n)\cos(f_k(n)l), & l > 0 \end{cases}.$

The value of Δd specifies how close the roots $A(z)$ are to the unit circle. The closer Δd is to zero the closer filter is to instability. However large values of the parameter may degrade prediction accuracy.
Figure 5 shows a spectral analysis of a harmonic signal using different values of Δd. Increasing stabilizing parameter Δd makes the conversion envelope smoother and some large values can even make it very close to the autocorrelation one.

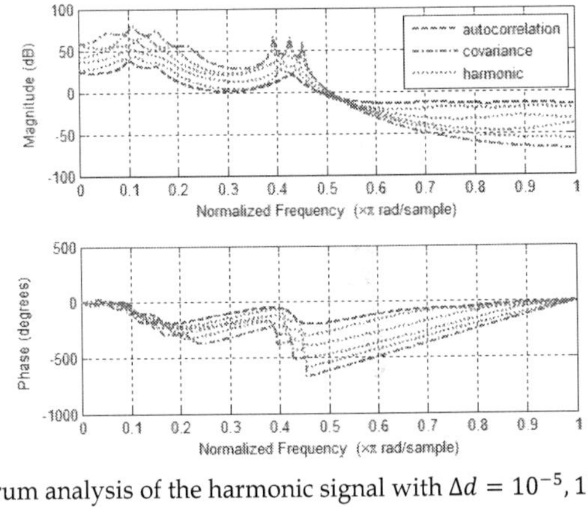

Fig. 5. LPC spectrum analysis of the harmonic signal with $\Delta d = 10^{-5}, 10^{-4}, 10^{-3}, 10^{-2}$

6.3 Instantaneous LPC analysis

In the present subsection the proposed conversion technique is applied to a synthetic frequency-modulated harmonic signal.

The signal frame consists of two harmonic components with frequency modulations (Figure 6). The frame length is 512 samples. The harmonic components have constant amplitudes (Figure 6(b)) and rapidly increasing frequencies (Figure 6(c)). The prediction coefficients for the frame were obtain via autocorrelation and harmonic conversion techniques (Figure 6 and Figure 7 respectively, prediction order is 14 in both cases).

The autocorrelation produces only one set of prediction coefficients for the entire frame (like in real speech/audio coding systems). The frame was weighted by the Hamming window before estimation. The obtained spectrum envelopes and residuals are presented in Figure 7(a)-(b). The spectrum reflects average values of instantaneous amplitudes and frequencies of the harmonic components. The energy of the residual signal is lower close to the centre of the frame; the total energy of the residual is -29.66 dB.

The analysis results obtained by direct sinusoidal parameters conversion are shown in Figure 7(c)-(d). The prediction coefficients were recalculated for every sample of the frame. The spectrum picture reflects instantaneous behaviour of the harmonic components. The energy of the residual signal is higher close to the centre of the frame with the total energy of -61.18 dB. Thus one can say that the energy of the source frequency-modulated signal was much more accurately localized both in time and frequency domain.

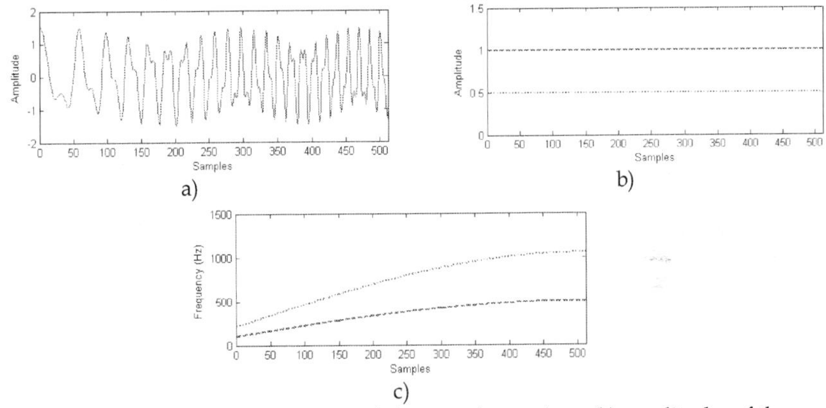

Fig. 6. Harmonic signal with frequency modulations: a) waveform; b) amplitudes of the harmonic components; c) frequencies of the harmonic components

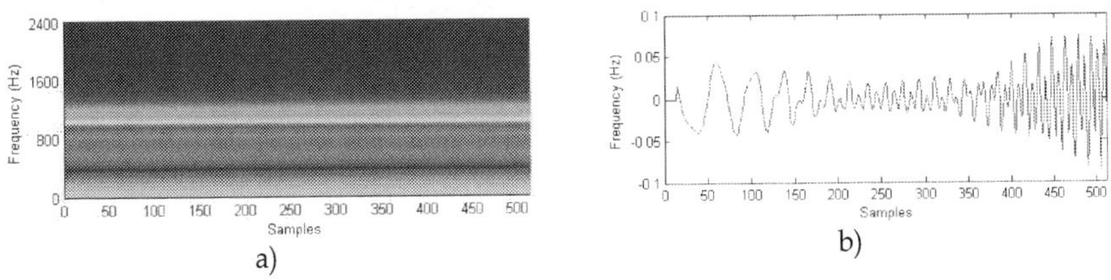

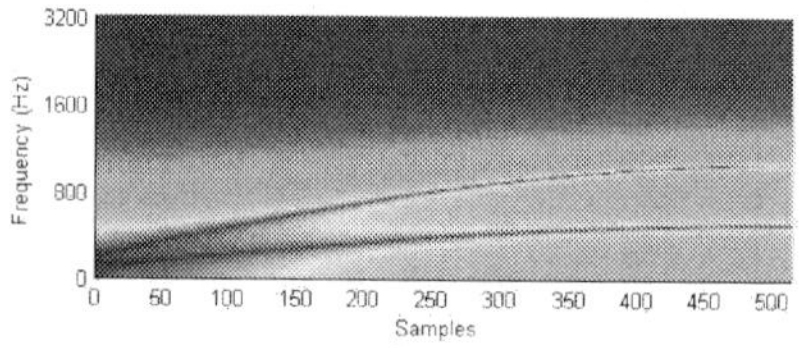

c)

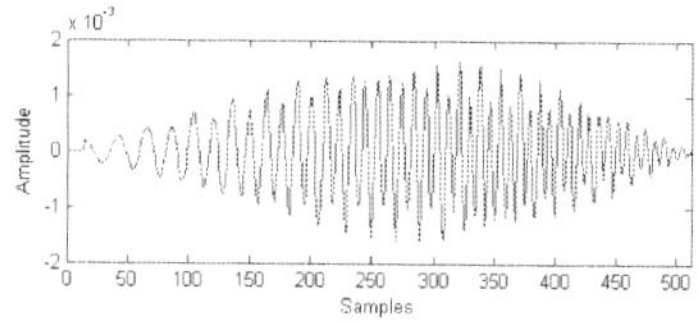

d)

Fig. 7. Frame analysis by autocorrelation and sinusoidal parameters conversion: a) autocorrelation spectrum estimation; b) autocorrelation residual; c) instantaneous LPC spectrum; d) instantaneous residual

7. Experimental applications

The described methods of sinusoidal and harmonic analysis can be used in several speech processing systems. This section presents some application results.

7.1 Application of harmonic analysis to parametric speech coding

Accurate estimation of sinusoidal parameters can significantly improve performance of coding systems. Well-known compressing algorithms that use sinusoidal representation may benefit from fine accurate harmonic/residual separation, providing higher quality of the decoded signal. The described analysis technique has been applied to hybrid speech and audio coding (Petrovsky et al., 2008).

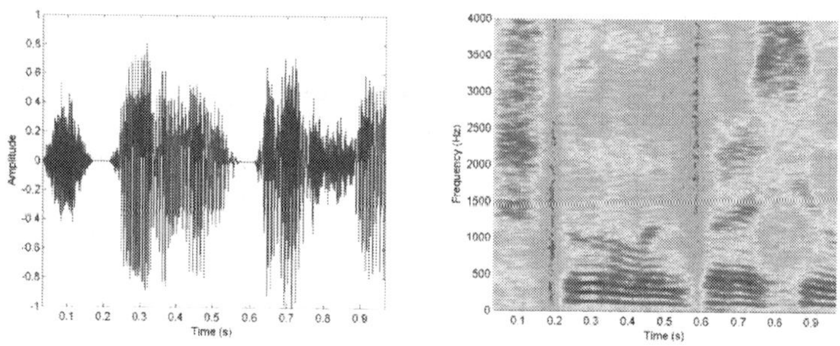

a)

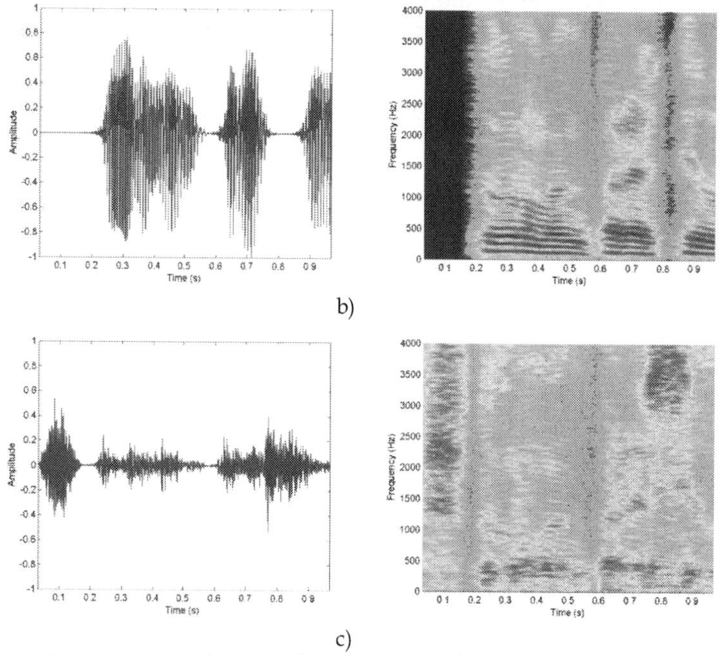

Fig. 8. Harmonic parameters estimation: a) source signal; b) estimated deterministic part; c) estimated stochastic part

An example of harmonic analysis is presented in Figure 8(a). The source signal is a phrase uttered by a male speaker ($F_S = 8$kHz). The deterministic part of the signal Figure 8(b) was synthesized using estimated harmonic parameters and subtracted from the source in order to get the stochastic part Figure 9(c). The spectrograms show that all steady harmonics of the source are modelled by sinusoidal representation when the residual part contains transient and noise components.

7.2 Harmonic analysis in TTS systems

This subsection presents an experimental application of sinusoidal modelling with proposed analysis techniques to a TTS system. Despite the fact that many different techniques have been proposed, segment concatenation is still the major approach to speech synthesis. The speech segments (allophones) are assembled into synthetic speech and this process involves time-scale and pitch-scale modifications in order to produce natural-like sounds. The concatenation can be carried out either in time or frequency domain. Most time domain techniques are similar to the Pitch-Synchronous Overlap and Add method (PSOLA) (Moulines and Charpentier, 1990). The speech waveform is separated into short-time signals by the analysis pitch-marks (that are defined by the source pitch contour) and then processed and joined by the synthesis pitch-marks (that are defined by the target pitch contour). The process requires accurate pitch estimation of the source waveform. Placing analysis pitch-marks is an important stage that significantly affects synthesis quality. Frequency domain (parametric) techniques deal with frequency representations of the segments instead of their waveforms what requires prior transformation of the acoustic database to frequency domain. Harmonic modelling can be especially useful in TTS systems for the following reasons:

- explicit control over pitch, tempo and timbre of the speech segments that insures proper prosody matching ;
- high-quality segment concatenation can be performed using simple linear smoothing laws;
- acoustic database can be highly compressed;
- synthesis can be implemented with low computational complexity.

In order to perform real-time synthesis in harmonic domain all waveform speech segments should be analysed and stored in new database, which contains estimated harmonic parameters and waveforms of stochastic signals. The analysis technique described in the chapter can be used for parameterization. In Figure 9 a result of such parameterization is presented. The analysed segment is sound [a:] of a female voice.

Speech concatenation with prosody matching can be efficiently implemented using sinusoidal modelling. In order to modify durations of the segments the harmonic parameters are recalculated at new instants, that are defined by some dynamic warping function, the noise part is parameterized by spectral envelopes and then time-scaled as described in (Levine and Smith, 1998).

Changing the pitch of a segment requires recalculation of harmonic amplitudes, maintaining the original spectral envelope. Noise part of the segment is not affected by pitch shifting and obviously should remain untouched. Let us consider the instantaneous frequency envelope as a function $E(n, f)$ of two parameters (sample number and frequency respectively). After harmonic parameterization the function is defined at frequencies of the harmonic components that were calculated at the respective instants of time: $E\big(n, f_k(n)\big) = \mathrm{MAG}_k(n)$. In order to get the completely defined function the piecewise-linear interpolation is used. Such interpolation has low computational complexity and, at the same time, gives sufficiently good approximation (Dutoit 1997).

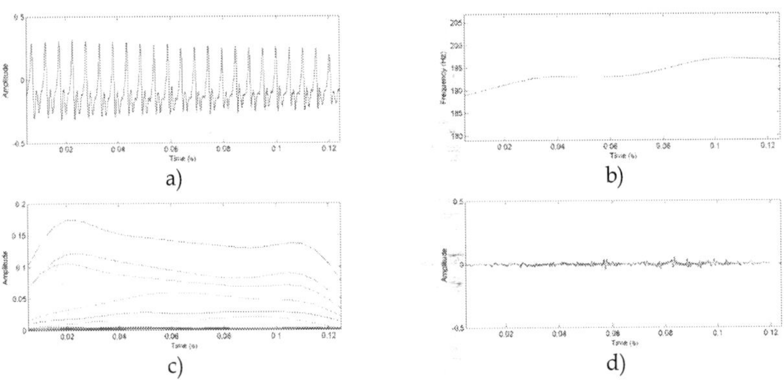

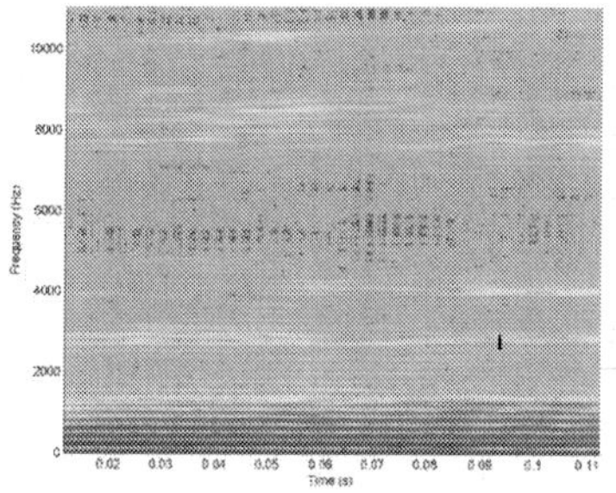

e)

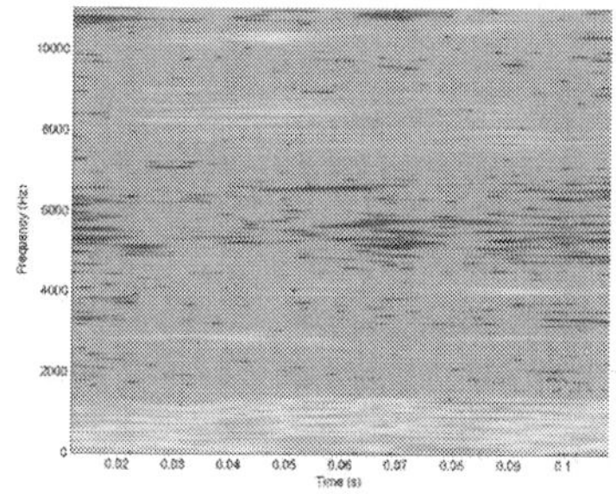

f)

Fig. 9. Segment analysis: a) source waveform segment; b) estimated fundamental frequency contour; c) estimated harmonic amplitudes; d) estimated stochastic part; e) spectrogram of the source segment; f) spectrogram of the stochastic part

The periodical signal $\bar{s}(n)$ with pitch shifting can be synthesized from its parametric representation as follows:

$$\bar{s}(n) = \sum_{k=1}^{K} E\left(n, \bar{f}_k(n)\right) \cos\bar{\varphi}_k(n). \tag{46}$$

Phases of harmonic components $\bar{\varphi}_k(n)$ are calculated according to the new fundamental frequency contour $\bar{f}_0(n)$:

$$\bar{\varphi}_k(n) = \sum_{i=0}^{n} \frac{2\pi \bar{f}_k(i)}{F_s} + \bar{\varphi}_k^{\Delta}(n). \tag{47}$$

Harmonic frequencies are calculated by the formula (3):

$$\bar{f}_k(n) = k\bar{f}_0(n). \tag{48}$$

Additional phase difference $\bar{\varphi}_k^{\Delta}(n)$ is used in order to maintain relative phases of harmonics and the fundamental:

$$\bar{\varphi}_k^{\Delta}(n) = \varphi_k(n) - (k+1)\varphi_0(n). \tag{49}$$

In synthesis process the phase differences $\bar{\varphi}_k^{\Delta}(n)$ are good substitutions of phase parameters $\varphi_k(n)$ since all the harmonics are kept coordinated regardless of the frequency contour and the initial phase of the fundamental.

Due to parametric representation spectral amplitude and phase mismatches at segments borders can be efficiently smoothed. Spectral amplitudes of acoustically related sounds can be matched by simultaneous fading out and in that is equivalent to linear spectral smoothing (Dutoit 1997). Phase discontinuities are also can be matched by linear laws taking into account that harmonic components are represented by their relative phases $\bar{\varphi}_k^{\Delta}(n)$. However, large discontinuities (when absolute difference exceeds π) should be eliminated by adding multiplies of $\pm 2\pi$ to the phase parameters of the next segment. Thus, phase parameters are smoothed in the same way as spectral amplitudes, providing imperceptible concatenation of the segments.

In Figure 10 the proposed approach is compared with PSOLA synthesis, implemented as described in (Moulines and Charpentier, 1990). A fragment of speech in Russian was synthesized through two different techniques using the same source acoustic database. The database segments were picked out from the speech of a female speaker. The sound sample in Figure 10(a) is the result of the PSOLA method.

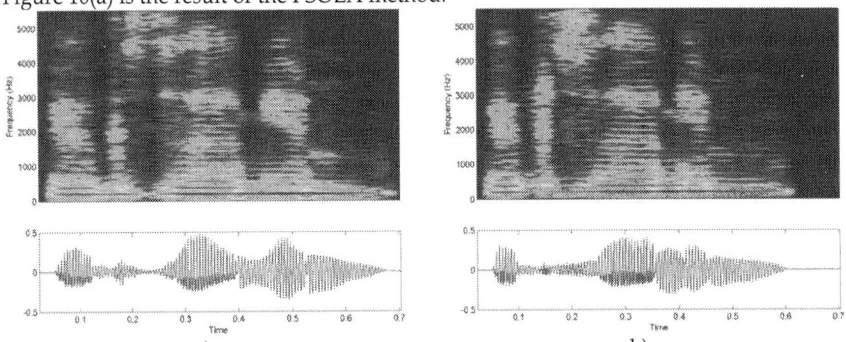

a) b)

Fig. 10. TTS synthesis comparison: a) PSOLA synthesis; b) harmonic domain concatenation

In Figure 10(b) the sound sample is shown, that is the result of the described analysis/synthesis approach. In order to get the parametric representation of the acoustic database each segment was classified either as voiced or unvoiced. The unvoiced segments were left untouched while the voiced were analyzed by the technique described in Section 4, then prosody modifications and segment concatenation were carried out. Both sound samples were synthesized at 22kHz, using the same predefined pitch contour.

As can be noticed from the presented samples the time domain concatenation approach produces audible artefacts at segment borders. They are caused by phase and pitch mismatching, that cannot be effectively avoided during synthesis. The described parametric approach provides almost inaudible phase and pitch smoothing, without distorting spectral and formant structure of the segments. The experiments have shown that this technique is good enough even for short and fricative segments, however, the short Russian 'r' required special adjustment of the filter parameters at the analysis stage in order to make proper analysis of the segment.

The main drawback of the described approach is noise amplification immediately at segment borders where the analysis filter gives less accurate results because of spectral leakage. In the current experiment the problem was solved by fading out the estimated noise part at segment borders. It is also possible to pick out longer segments at the database preparation stage and then shorten them after parameterization.

7.3 Instantaneous LPC analysis of speech

LPC-based techniques are widely used for formant tracking in speech applications. Making harmonic analysis first and then performing parameters conversion a higher accuracy of formant frequencies estimation can be achieved. In Figure 11 a result of voiced speech analysis is presented. The analysed signal (Figure 11(a)) is a vowel [a:] uttered by a male speaker. This sound was sampled at 8kHz and analyzed by the autocorrelation (Figure 11(b)) and the harmonic conversion (Figure 11(c)) techniques. In order to give expressive pictures prediction coefficients were updated for every sample of the signal in both cases.

The autocorrelation analysis was carried out with analysis frame 512 samples in length, weighted by the Hamming window. Prediction order was 20 in both cases.

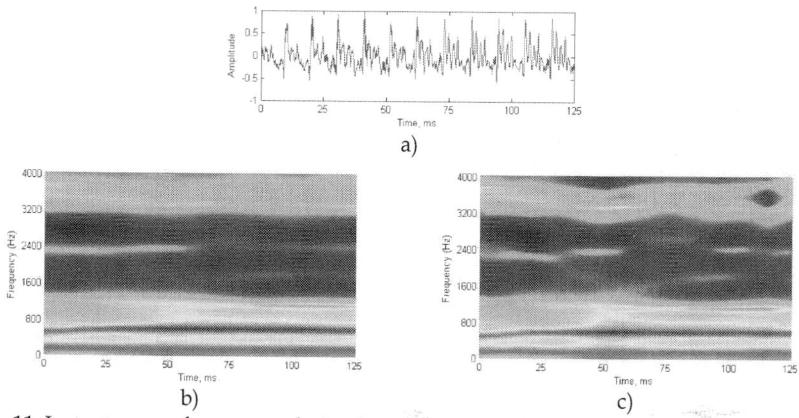

Fig. 11. Instantaneous formant analysis: a) source signal; b) autocorrelation analysis; c) instantaneous LPC analysis

As can be seen from the pictures harmonic analysis with subsequent conversion into prediction coefficients gives more localized formant trajectories. Some of them have more complex form, however overall formant structure of the signal remains the same.

8. Conclusions

An estimation technique of instantaneous sinusoidal parameters has been presented in the chapter. The technique is based on narrow-band filtering and can be applied to audio and speech sounds. Signals with harmonic structure (such as voiced speech) can be analysed using frequency-modulated filters with adjustable impulse response. The technique has a good performance considering that accurate estimation is possible even in case of rapid frequency modulations of pitch. A method of pitch detection and estimation has been described as well. The use of filters with modulated impulse response, however, requires precise estimation of instantaneous pitch that can be achieved through pitch values recalculation during the analysis process. The main disadvantage of the method is high computational cost in comparison with STFT.

Some experimental applications of the proposed approach have been illustrated. The sinusoidal modelling based on the presented technique has been applied to speech coding, and TTS synthesis with wholly satisfactory results.

The sinusoidal model can be used for estimation of LPC parameters that describe instantaneous behaviour of the periodical signal. The presented conversion technique of sinusoidal parameters into prediction coefficients provides high energy localization and smaller residual for frequency-modulated signals, however overall performance entirely depends on the quality of prior sinusoidal analysis. The instantaneous prediction

coefficients allow implementing fine formant tracking that can be useful in such applications as speaker identification and speech recognition.
Future work is aimed at further investigation of the analysis filters and their behaviour, finding optimized solutions for evaluation of sinusoidal parameters. It might be some potential in adapting described methods to other applications such as vibration analyzer of mechanical devices and diagnostics of throat diseases.

9. Acknowledgments

This work was supported by the Belarusian republican fund for fundamental research under the grant T08MC-040 and the Belarusian Ministry of Education under the grant 09-3102.

10. References

Abe, T.; Kobayashi, T. & Imai, S. (1995). Harmonics tracking and pitch extraction based on instantaneous frequency, *Proceedings of ICASSP 1995*. pp. 756–759. 1995.

Azarov, E.; Petrovsky, A. & Parfieniuk, M. (2008). Estimation of the instantaneous harmonic parameters of speech, *Proceedings of the 16th European Signal Process. Conf. (EUSIPCO-2008)*, CD-ROM, Lausanne, 2008.

Boashash, B. (1992). Estimating and interpreting the instantaneous frequency of a signal, *Proceedings of the IEEE*, Vol. 80, No. 4, (1992) 520-568.

Dutoit, T. (1997). *An Introduction to Text-to-speech Synthesis*, Kluwer Academic Publishers, the Netherlands.

Gabor, D. (1946). Theory of communication, *Proc. IEE*, Vol.93, No. 3, (1946) 429-457.

Gianfelici, F.; Biagetti, G.; Crippa, P. & Turchetti, C. (2007) Multicomponent AM–FM Representations: An Asymptotically Exact Approach, *IEEE Transactions on Audio, Speech, and Language Processing*, Vol. 15, No. 3, (March 2007) 823-837.

Griffin, D. & Lim, J. (1988). Multiband excitation vocoder, *IEEE Trans. On Acoustics, Speech and Signal Processing*, Vol. 36, No. 8, (1988) 1223-1235.

Hahn, S. L. (1996) *Hilbert Transforms in Signal Processing*, MA: Artech House, Boston.

Huang, X; Acero, A. & Hon H.W. (2001). *Spoken language processing*, Prentice Hall, New Jersey.

Levine, S. & Smith, J. (1998). A Sines+Transients+Noise Audio Representation for Data Compression and Time/Pitch Scale Modifications, *AES 105th Convention*, Preprint 4781, San Francisco, CA, USA.

Maragos, P.; Kaiser, J. F. & Quatieri, T. F. (1993). Energy Separation in Signal Modulations with Application to Speech Analysis", *IEEE Trans. On Signal Process.*, Vol. 41, No. 10, (1993) 3024-3051.

Markel J.D. & Gray A.H. (1976) *Linear prediction of speech*, Springer-Verlag Berlin Heidelberg, New York.

McAulay, R. J. & Quatieri, T. F. (1986). Speech analysis/synthesis based on a sinusoidal representation. *IEEE Trans. On Acoustics, Speech and Signal Process.*, Vol. 34, No. 4, (1986) 744-754.

McAulay, R. J. & Quateri T. F. (1992). The sinusoidal transform coder at 2400 b/s, *Proceedings of Military Communications Conference,* Calif, USA, October 1992, San Diego.

Moulines, E. & Charpentier, F. (1990). Pitch Synchronous Waveform Processing Techniques for Text-to-Speech Synthesis Using Diphones. *Speech Communication,* Vol.9, No. 5-6, (1990) 453-467.

Painter, T. & Spanias, A. (2003). Sinusoidal Analysis-Synthesis of Audio Using Perceptual Criteria. *EURASIP Journal on Applied Signal Processing,* No. l, (2003) 15-20.

Petrovsky, A.; Stankevich, A. & Balunowski, J. (1999). The order tracking front-end algorithms in the rotating machine monitoring systems based on the new digital low order tracking, *Proc. of the 6th Intern. Congress "On sound and vibration"*, pp.2985-2992, Denmark, 1999, Copenhagen.

Petrovsky, A.; Azarov, E. & Petrovsky, A. (2008). Harmonic representation and auditory model-based parametric matching and its application in speech/audio analysis, *AES 126th Convention*, Preprint 7705, Munich, Germany.

Rabiner, L. & Juang, B.H. (1993). *Fundamentals of speech recognition,* Prentice Hall, New Jersey.

Serra, X. (1989). A system for sound analysis/transformation/synthesis based on a deterministic plus stochastic decomposition, *Ph.D. thesis,* Stanford University, Stanford, Calif, USA.

Spanias, A.S. (1994). Speech coding: a tutorial review. *Proc. of the IEEE,* Vol. 82, No. 10, (1994) 1541-1582.

Weruaga, L. & Kepesi, M. (2007). The fan-chirp transform for non-stationary harmonic signals, *Signal Processing*, Vol. 87, issue 6, (June 2007) 1-18.

Zhang, F.; Bi, G. & Chen Y.Q. (2004). Harmonic transform, *IEEE Proc.-Vis. Image Signal Process.*, Vol. 151, No. 4, (August 2004) 257-264.

20

Music Structure Analysis Statistics for Popular Songs

Namunu C. Maddage, Li Haizhou[1] and Mohan S. Kankanhalli[2]
School of Electrical and Computer Engineering, Royal Melbourne Institute of Technology (RMIT) University, Swanston Street, Melbourne, 3000, Australia
[1]Dept of Human Language Technology, Institute for Infocomm Research, 1 Fusionopolis Way, Singapore 138632
[2]School of Computing, National University of Singapore, Singapore, 117417

Abstract

In this chapter, we have proposed a better procedure for manual annotation of music information. The proposed annotation procedure involves carrying out listening tests and then incorporating music knowledge to iteratively refine the detected music information. Using this annotation technique, we can effectively compute the durations of the music notes, time-stamp the music regions, i.e. pure instrumental, pure vocal, instrumental mixed vocals and silence, and annotate the semantic music clusters (components in a song structure), i.e. Verse -V, Chorus - C, Bridge -B, Intro, Outro and Middle-eighth.

From the annotated information, we have further derived the statistics of music structure information. We conducted experiments on 420 popular songs which were sung in English, Chinese, Indonesian and German languages. We assumed a constant tempo throughout the song and meter to be 4/4. Statistical analysis revealed that 62.46%, 35.48%, 1.87% and 0.17% of the contents in a song belong to instrumental mixed vocal, pure instrumental, silence and pure vocal music regions. We also found over 70% of English and Indonesian songs and 30% of Chinese songs used V-C-V-C and V-V-C-V-C song structures respectively, where V and C denote the verse and chorus respectively. It is also found that 51% of English songs, 37% of Chinese songs, and 35% of Indonesian songs used 8 bar duration in both chorus and verse.

1. Introduction

Music is a universal language people use for sharing their feelings and sensations. Thus there have been keen research interests not only to understand how music information stimulates our minds, but also to develop applications based on music information. For example, vocal and non-vocal music information are useful for sung language recognition systems (Tsai et at., 2004., Schwenninger et al., 2006), lyrics-text and music alignment systems (Wang et al., 2004), mood classification systems (Lu & Zhang, 2006) music genre classification (Nwe & Li, 2007., Tzanetakis & Cook, 2002) and music classification systems (Xu et al., 2005., Burred & Lerch, 2004). Also, information about rhythm, harmony, melody contours and song structures (such as repetitions of chorus verse semantic regions) are useful for developing systems for error concealment in music streaming (Wang et al., 2003), music protection (watermarking), music summarization (Xu et al., 2005), compression, and music search.

Computer music research community has been developing algorithms to accurately extract the information in music. Many of the proposed algorithms require ground truth data for both the parameter training process and performance evaluation. For example, the performance of a music classifier which classify the content in the music segment as vocal or non-vocal, can be improved when the parameters of the classifier are trained with accurate vocal and non-vocal music contents in the development dataset. Also the performance of the classifier can effectively be measured when the evaluation dataset is accurately annotated based on the exact music composition information. However it is difficult to create accurate development and evaluation datasets because it is difficult to find information about the music composition mainly due to copyright restrictions on sharing music information in the public domain. Therefore, the current development and evaluation datasets are created by annotating the information that is extracted using subjective listening tests. Tanghe et al., (2005) discussed an annotation method for drum sounds. In Goto (2006)'s method, music scenes such as beat structure, chorus, and melody line are annotated with the help of corresponding MIDI files. Li, et al., (2006) modified the general audio editing software so that it becomes more convenient for identifying music semantic regions such as chorus. The accuracy of subjective listening test hinges on subject's hearing competence, concentration and music knowledge. For example, it is often difficult to judge the start and end time of vocal phrases when they are presented with strong background music. If the listener's concentration is disturbed, then the listening continuity is lost and then it is difficult to accurately mark the phrase boundaries. However if we know the tempo and meter of the music, then we can apply that knowledge to correct the errors of the phrase boundaries which are detected in the listen tests.

Speed of music information flow is directly proportional to tempo of the music (Authors, 1949). Therefore the duration of music regions, semantic regions, inter-beat interval, and beat positions can be measured as multiples of music notes. The proposed music information annotation technique in this chapter, first locates the beats and onset positions by both listening and visualizing the music signal using a graphical waveform editor. Since the time duration of the detected beat or onset from the start of music is an integer multiple of the duration of a smallest note, we can estimate the duration of the smallest note. Then we carry out intensive listening exercise with the help of estimated durations of the smallest music note to detect the time stamps of music regions and different semantic regions. Using the annotated information, we detect the song structure and calculate the statistics of the music information distributions.

This chapter is organized as follows. Popular music structure is discussed in section 2 and effective information annotation procedures are explained in section 3. Section 4 details the statistics of music information. We conclude the chapter in section 5 with a discussion.

2. Music Structure

As shown in Fig. 1, the underlying music information can conceptually be represented as layers in a pyramid (Maddage, 2005). These information layers are:

1) First layer represents the time information (beats, tempo, and meter);
2) Second layer represents the harmony/melody which is formed by playing musical notes simultaneously;
3) Third layer describes the music regions, i.e. pure vocal (PV), pure instrumental (PI), instrumental mixed vocal (IMV) and silence (S);
4) Forth layer and above represent the semantics of the popular song.

The pyramid diagram represents music semantics which influence our imaginations. Jourdain (1997) also discussed how sound, tone, melody, harmony, composition, performance, listening, understanding and ecstasy lead to our imagination.

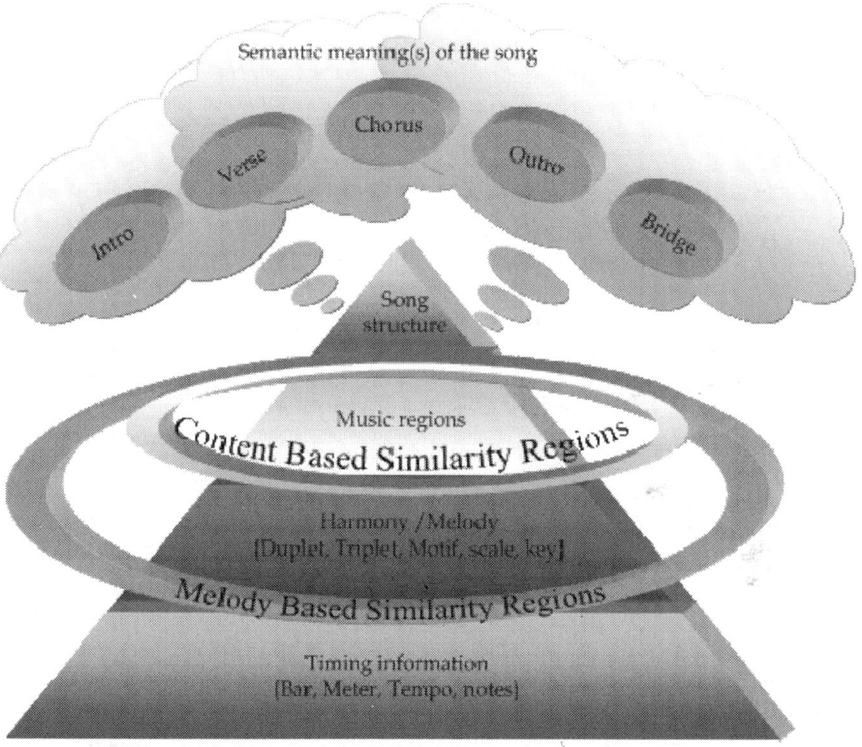

Fig. 1. Information grouping in the music structure pyramid

Time information describes the rate of information flow in music. Durations of Harmony / melody contours and phrases which create music regions are proportional to the tempo of music. *Melody* is created when a single note is played at a time. Playing multiple notes results in harmony sound. Psychological studies have suggested the human cognitive mechanism can effectively distinguish the tones of the diatonic scale (Burred & Lerch, 2004). Scale changes or modulation of the scale in a different section of the song can effectively be

noticed in the listening tests. Therefore, in our listening tests we detect the Middle-eighth regions (see next section) which have a different *Key* from the main *Key* of the song.
The rhythm of words can be tailored to fit into a music phrase (Authors, 1949). The vocal regions in music comprise of words and syllables, which are uttered according to a time signature. Fig. 2 shows how the words "Little Jack Horner sat in the Corner" are turn into a rhythm, and the music notation of those words. The important words or syllables in the sentence fall onto accents to form the rhythm of the music. Typically, these words are placed at the first beat of a bar. When TS is set to two Crotchet beats per bar, we see the duration of the word "Little" is equal to two Quaver notes and the duration of the word "Jack" is equal to a Crotchet note.

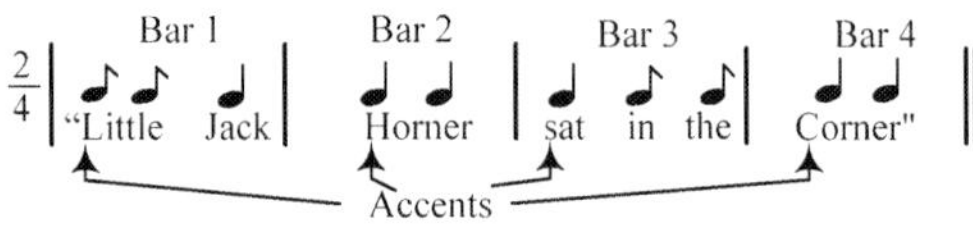

Fig. 2. Rhythmic flow of words

Popular song structure often contains Intro, Verse, Chorus, Bridge, Middle-eighth, instrumental sections (INST) and Outro (Authors, 2003). As shown in Fig. 1, these parts are built on melody-based similarity regions and content-based similarity regions. Melody-based similarity regions are defined as the regions which have similar pitch contours constructed from the chord patterns. Content-based similarity regions are defined as the regions which have both similar vocal content and melody. In terms of music structure, the Chorus sections and Verse sections in a song are considered the content-based similarity regions and melody-based similarity regions respectively. They can be grouped to form semantic clusters as in Fig. 3. For example, all the Chorus regions in a song form a Chorus cluster, while all the Verse regions form a Verse cluster and so on.

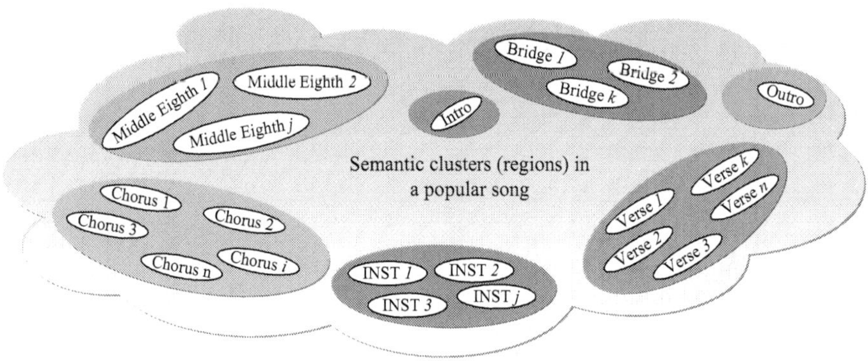

Fig. 3. Semantic similarity clusters which define the structure of the popular song

A song may have an Intro of 2, 4, 8 or 16 bars long, or do not have any at all. The Intro is usually comprised of instrumental music. Both Verse and Chorus are 8 or 16 bars long. Typically, the Verse is not melodically as strong as the Chorus. However, in some songs both verse and chorus are equally melodically strong. Most people can hum or sing both chorus and verse. A Bridge links the gap between the Verse and Chorus, and may have only two or four bars.

Song: 25 Minutes
Artist / Band: MLTR
Song structure: Intro (INST) Verse 1 Verse 2 Bridge Chorus 1 Verse 3 Bridge Chorus 2 Middle eight Chorus 3 Chorus 4 Outro (INST)

Intro: Instrumental (INST)

Verse 1
After some time
I've finally made up my mind
She is the girl
And I really want to make her mine

Verse 2
I'm searching everywhere
To find her again
To tell her I love her
And I'm sorry about the things I've done

Bridge
I find her standing
in front of the church
The only place in town where I didn't search
She looks so happy in her wedding dress
But she's crying while she's saying this

Chorus 1
Boy I've missed your kisses
All the time but this is
Twenty five minutes too late
Though you traveled so far
Boy I'm sorry you are
Twenty five minutes too late

Verse 3
Against the wind
I'm going home again
hummma (humming)
Wishing me back
To the time when we were more than friends

Bridge
But still I see her in front of the church
The only place in town where I didn't search
She looked so happy in her wedding dress
But she cried while she was saying this

Chorus 2
Boy I've missed your kisses
All the time but this is
Twenty five minutes too late
Though you traveled so far
Boy I'm sorry you are
Twenty five minutes too late

Middle Eight
Out in the streets
Places where hungry hearts have nothing to eat
Inside my head
Still I can
hear the words she said

Chorus 3
Boy I've missed your kisses
All the time but this is
Twenty five minutes too late
Though you traveled so far
Boy I'm sorry you are
Twenty five minutes too late

Chorus 4
Boy I've missed your kisses
All the time but this is
Twenty five minutes too late
its too late
Though you traveled so far
Boy I'm sorry you are
Twenty five minutes too late
I can still hear her say...

Outro - Instrumental (INST)

Song : Cant let go
Artist / Band: Mariah Carey
Song structure : Intro (INST) Verse 1 Chorus 1 Verse 2 Chorus 2 Bridge Chorus 3 Outro (INST)

Intro : Instrumental (INST)

Verse 1
There you are,
holding her hand
i am lost,
dying to understand
didnt i,
cherish u right
dont u know,
u were my life.

Chorus 1
even though i try, I cant
let go
something in your eyes
captures
my soul
and everynight i see you in my dreams
you're all i know
i cant let go

Verse 2
just cast aside,
u dont even know i'm alive
u just walk on by,
don't care to see me cry
and here i am
still holding on,
i cant accept
my world is gone
no no...

Chorus 2
even though i try,
i cant
let go.
something in your eyes captures my soul.
and everynight i see you in my dreams,
you're all i know,
i cant let go

Bridge
do you ever realise,
the sorrow i have inside,
everyday of my life.
do you know the way it feels
when all your love just dies,
i try and try to deny that i need you
but still you remain on my mind

Chorus 3
even though i try,
i cant let go
something in your eyes
captures my soul
and everynight i see you
in my dreams
you're all i know
i can't let go...

Outro - Instrumental (INST)

Fig. 4. Two examples for verse- chorus pattern repetitions.

Silence may also act as a Bridge between the Verse and Chorus of a song, but such cases are rare. Middle-eighth, which has 4, 8 or 16 bars in length, is an alternative version of a Verse with a new chord progression possibly modulated by a different key. Many people use the term "Middle-eighth" and "bridge" synonymously. However, the main difference is the middle-eighth is longer (usually 16 bars) than the bridge and usually appears after the third verse in the song. There are instrumental sections in the song and they can be instrumental versions of the Chorus, Verse, or entirely different tunes with a set of chords together. Typically INST regions have 8 or 16 bars. Outro, which is the ending of the song, is usually a fade–out of the last phrases of the chorus. We have described the parts of the song which are commonly arranged according to the simple verse-chorus and repeat pattern. Two variations on these themes are as follows:

(a) Intro, Verse 1, Verse 2, Chorus, Verse 3, Middle-eighth, Chorus, Chorus, Outro

(b) Intro, Verse 1, Chorus, Verse 2, Chorus, Chorus, Outro

Fig. 4 illustrates two examples of the above two patterns. Song, "25 minutes" by MLTR follows the pattern (a) and "Can't Let You Go" by Mariah Carey follows the pattern (b). For a better understanding of how artist have combined these parts to compose a song, we conducted a survey on popular Chinese and English songs. Details of the survey are discussed in the next section.

3. Music Structure Information Annotation

The fundamental step for audio content analysis is signal segmentation. Within a segment, the information can be considered quasi-stationary. Feature extraction and information modeling followed by music segmentation are the essential steps for music structure analysis. Determination of the segment size, which is suitable for extracting certain level of information, requires better understanding of the rate of information flow in the audio data. Over three decades of speech processing research has revealed that 20-40 ms of fixed length signal segmentation is appropriate for the speech content analysis (Rabiner & Juang, 2005). The composition of music piece reveals the rate of information such as notes, chords, key, vocal phrases, flow is proportional to inter-beat intervals.

Fig. 5 shows the quarter, eighth and sixteenth note boundaries in a song clip. It can be seen that the fluctuation of signal properties in both spectral and time domain are aligned with those note boundaries. Usually smaller notes, such as eighth, sixteenth and thirty-second notes or smaller are played in the bars to align the harmony contours with the rhythm flow of the lyrics and to fill the gap between lyrics (Authors, 1949). Therefore inter-beat proportional music segmentation instead of fixed length segmentation has recently been proposed for music content analysis (Maddage, 2004., Maddage, 2005., Wang, 2004).

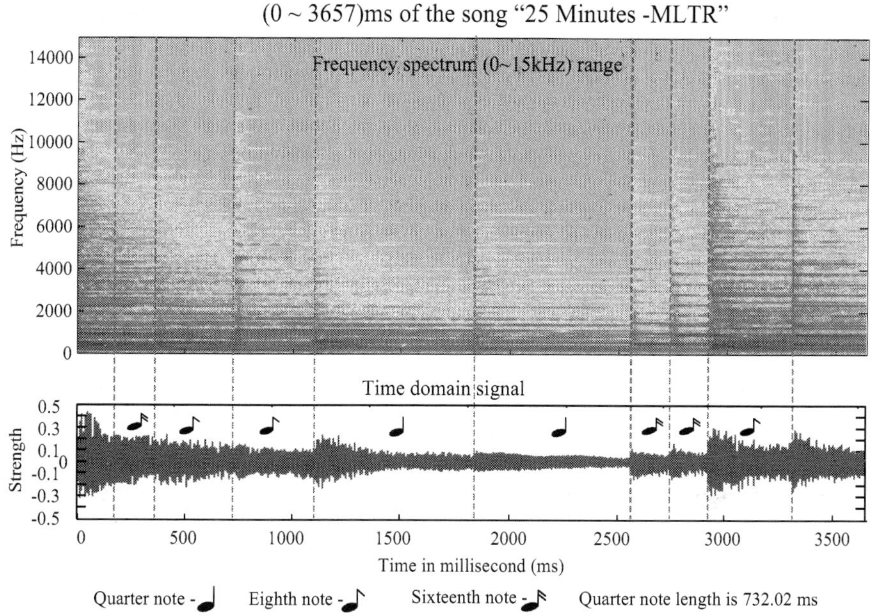

Fig. 5. Spectral and time domain visualization of (0~3657) ms long song clip from "25 Minutes" by MLTR. Quarter note length is 736.28 ms and note boundaries are highlighted using dotted lines.

3.1. Computation of Inter-beat interval

Once the staff of a song is available, from the value of tempo and time signature we can calculate the duration of the beat. However commercially available music albums (CDs) do not provide staff information of the songs. Therefore subjects with a good knowledge of theory and practice of music have to closely examine the songs to estimate the inter-beat intervals in the song. We assume all the songs have 4/4 time signature, which is the commonly used TS in popular songs (Goto, M. 2001, Authors, 2003). Following the results of music composition and structure, as discussed in section 2, we only allow the positions of beats to take place at integer multiple of smaller notes from the start point of the song. Estimation of both inter-beat interval and song tempo using an iterative listening is explained below, with Fig. 6 as an example.

- Play the song in audio editing software which has a GUI to visualize the time domain signal with high resolution. While listening to the music it is noticed that there is a steady throb to which one can clap. This duration of consecutive clapping is called inter-beat interval. As we assume 4/4 time signature which infers that the inter-beat interval is of quarter note length, hence four quarter notes form a bar.
- As shown in Fig. 6, the positions of both beats and note onsets can be effectively visualized on the GUI, and j^{th} position is indicated as P_j. By replaying the song and zooming into the areas of neighboring beats and onset positions, we can estimate the

inter-beat interval and therefore the duration of the note X_j. In Fig. 6, we can see the duration X_1 is the first estimated eighth note.

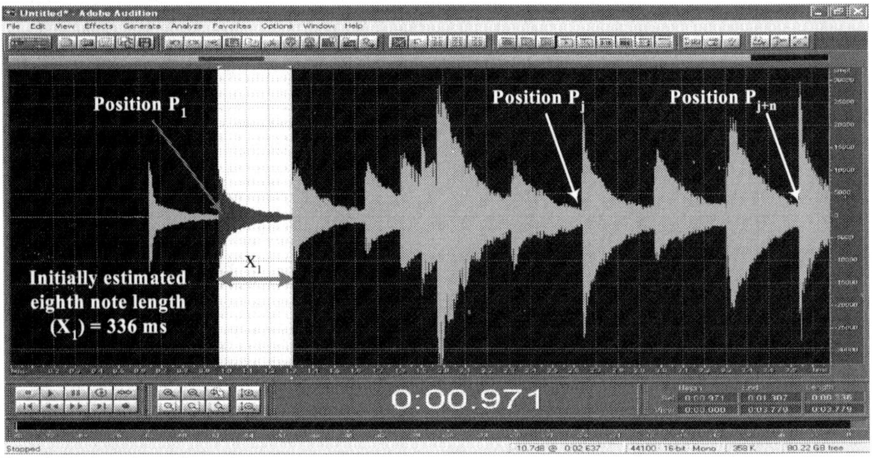

Fig. 6. Estimation of music note

- After the first estimation, we establish a 4-step iterative listening process discussed below to reduce the error between the estimates and the desired music note lengths. The constraint we apply is that beat position is equal to integer multiple of frames. To start with, first frame size is set to the estimated note, i.e. Frame size = X_1 in Fig. 6.

Step 1: Set the currently estimated note length as the frame size; calculate the number of frames NF_j at an identified beat or onset position. For the initialization, we set $j = 1$.

$$NF_j = \frac{P_j}{X_j} \tag{1}$$

Step 2: As the resulting NF_j is typically a floating point value, we measure the difference between round up NF_j and NF_j, referred to as DNF.

$$DNF = \left| NF_j - round\left(NF_j\right) \right| \tag{2}$$

IF $DNF > 0.35$,

This implies, the duration of current beat or onset position P_j is an integer multiple of the frames plus a half a frame. Therefore we set new note length to the half of X_j. For example the new frame size is equal to sixteenth note and if the previous frame was an eighth note. Then go to step 1

ELSE

$$NF_j = round\left(NF_j\right) \tag{3}$$

Step 3: At beat/ onset position P_j, we calculate the new note length X_{j+1} as below.

$$X_{j+1} = \frac{P_j}{NF_j} \tag{4}$$

Step 4: Iterate the step 1 to 3 at beat or onset positions towards the end of the songs. When these iterative steps are carried out over many of the beat and onset positions towards the end of the song, the errors of the estimated note length are minimized. Based on the final length estimate for the note, we can calculate the quarter note length.

Fig. 7 shows the variation of the estimated quarter note length for two songs. Beat/onset positions nearly divide the song into equal intervals. Beat/onset point zero ("0") represents the first estimation of quarter note length. The correct tempos of the songs "You are still one" and "The woman in me" are 67 BPM and 60 BPM respectively.

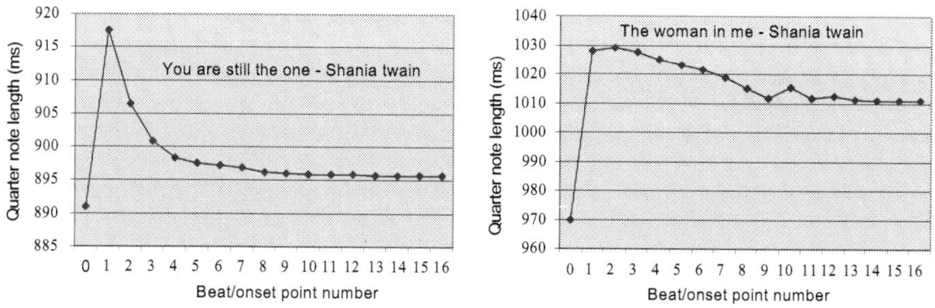

Fig. 7. Variation of estimated length of the quarter note at beat/onset points when the listening test was carried out till the end of the song.

It can be seen in the Fig. 7, that the deviation of the estimated quarter note is high at the beginning of the song. However estimated quarter note converges to the correct value at the second half of the song (end of the song). Reason for the fluctuation of the estimated note length is explained below.

As shown in Fig. 6, first estimation of the note length (X_1) is done using only audio-visual editing software. Thus first estimation (beat/ onset point P = 0 in Fig. 7) can have very high variation due to the prime difficulties of judging the correct boundaries of the notes. When the song proceeds, using Eq, (1), (2), (3) and (4), we iteratively estimate the duration of the note for the corresponding beat/onset points. Since beat/onset points near the start of the song have shorter duration (P_j), initial iterative estimations for the note length have higher variation. For example in Fig. 6, beat/onset point P_1 is closer to start of the song and from the Eq. (1) and first estimation of note length X_1, we compute NF_1. Eq. (2) and (3) are useful in limiting the errors in computed NF under one frame. When X_1 is inaccurate and also P_1 is short then the errors in computed number of frames NF_1 in Eq. (1) have higher effects in the next estimated note length in Eq. (4). However with distant beat/onset points, i.e Pj is longer and NF_j is high and more accurate, then the estimated note lengths tend to converge.

3.2. Annotation of music regions

Pure vocal (PV), pure instrumental (PI), instrumental mixed vocal (IMV) and silence (S) are the regions that can commonly be seen in a music signals (Third layer of the music structure pyramid in Fig. 1). PV regions in the music only have signals generated from the vocal tract. Note that the lyrics of songs would improve the music region annotation. We use lyrics text files and employ subjects who understand the singing language to accurately stamp the timing of the region boundaries. We obtain lyrics of the songs from the Web. Based on the found lyrics, which are often separated into different musical phrases, we attempt to reorganize these lyrics and further separate them into different lines based on their vocal region continuity. Subsequently, vocal humming, for example *hmm, aah,* which are usually not included in the published lyrics, is also aligned with the vocals. Common types of song structure tagging are then used to identify a block of lyrics (e.g. Intro, Verse, Chorus, Bridge, Middle-eighth, Outro, and Instrumental)

Based on the music knowledge explained in Fig. 2, the duration of musical phrases can be measured by the number of musical notes. Since we have already calculated the note length in section 3.2, we use this information to improve the listening test of time stamping of music regions. In our annotation we assume the tempo of the song doesn't change. Since music signals are digitized at non-linear sampling rate (usually 44.1 kHz for CD quality), it's usually difficult to find the exact boundaries of vocal-instrumental regions. And also due to the effects of subject's concentration, hearing sensitivity and music experiences, position markings may vary from the actual boundary positions of the region. We further propose a 4-step process to improve the time stamps of music regions.

Step 1: Subject within his/her listening capacity marks the boundary point (start or end) of the region. For example, let's assume P_j and P_{j+n} in Fig. 6 are the start and the end time assigned in the listening process for the kth pure vocal (PV) region. Let the note length be X. Then we estimate the number of frames for start and end time $\overline{NFvs(k)}$ and $\overline{NFve(k)}$ in Equation 5.

$$\overline{NFvs(k)} = \frac{P_j}{X} \quad and \quad \overline{NFve(k)} = \frac{P_{j+n}}{X} \tag{5}$$

It is empirically found that in popular songs, musical phrases are aligned with eighth or smaller note. Therefore at the beginning of the annotation we set the note length to eighth note.

Step 2: As the resulting $\overline{NFvs(k)}$ is usually an integer multiple of note length, we further measure the difference between $\overline{NFvs(k)}$ and round up $\overline{NFvs(k)}$ in order to refine the $\overline{NFvs(k)}$.

$$DFN = \left|\overline{NFvs(k)} - round\left(\overline{NFvs(k)}\right)\right| \tag{6}$$

IF (0.35 < DFN < 0.5)

IF (Note length > Thirty-second note)

Reduce the note length to next smaller one (e.g. Eighth to Sixteenth or Sixteenth to thirty-second note levels) and go to step

1 to update the previously calculated region boundaries based on new smaller note length frames.

ELSE

Minimum note resolution is considered as thirty-second note. Therefore there is no further note length adjustment. Go to step 3.

IF (DFN < 3.5)

Then do not alter the note length. Go to step3

Step 3: Re-estimate the number of frames $NFvs(k)$ and the time stamp for start position of kth PV region $Tvs(k)$ respectively,

$$NFvs(k) \quad = \text{round}\left(\overline{NFvs}(k)\right) \tag{7}$$

$$Tvs(k) = NFvs(k) \times X \tag{8}$$

Similar sequence of steps is followed for more accurate estimation of end time $Tve(k)$ and end frame $NFve(k)$ of kth PV region.

Step 4: Repeat Step 1-3 for annotating the next region boundaries.

Fig. 8 shows a section of an annotated song. Thirty-second note length resolution is used for the time stamp of music regions. Start-time and end-time of music regions found in the initial subjective listening tests are shown under STT and EDT columns respectively. Accurate start-frame and end-frame of the regions are shown under STF and EDF columns respectively. According to Equation 8 accurate end-time of the instrumental Intro region (PI-Intro) is 1263.06818182 ms (i.e. 135×93.56060606).

It can be seen in the Fig. 8 that end-time of PI has as high as 8 decimal points caused by multiplying frame numbers with the note length which has 8 decimal places. As explained earlier, music region boundaries can be measured as multiples of music notes. Thus it is necessary to have a better estimation for the note-length to reduce errors at boundaries when the number of frames for the boundary increases. Thus it becomes essential to have more decimal places in the estimated length for the note.

Artist: MLTR
Song: The Actor
Demisemiquaver Beat: 93.56060606 ms

STT Starting time
STF Starting frame
EDT Ending time
EDF Ending frame

Instrumental Mixed Vocal				Pure Vocal	Instrumental				Silence				Lyrics
STT	EDT	STF	EDF		STT	EDT	STF	EDF	STT	EDD	STF	EDF	
									0.000	0.250	1	3	
					0.250	12.598	4	135					<Intro>
12.598	16.715	136	179		16.715	18.586	180	199					<V1>He takes you out and he takes you up
18.586	21.580	200	231		21.580	24.573	232	263					'Cause he can show you so much
24.573	28.690	264	307		28.690	30.561	308	327					I go to bed and tomorrow again
30.561	32.807	328	351										There's a lot of
32.807	34.678	352	371		34.678	36.549	372	391					work to be done
36.549	40.291	392	431		40.291	42.537	432	455					He gives you gold and he'll promise you
42.537	45.531	456	487		45.531	48.525	488	519					The whole world will be yours
48.525	52.267	520	559		52.267	54.512	560	583					I just can tell you I love you so
54.512	55.636	584	595		55.636	56.384	596	603					Even though
56.384	57.474	604	614		57.474	57.833	615	618					my odds
57.833	59.004	619	631		59.004	60.500	632	647					are low
60.500	63.081	648	674		63.081	63.499	675	679					<C1>I'm not an actor I'm not
63.499	64.617	680	691		64.617	65.740	692	703					a star
65.740	67.981	704	727		67.981	68.364	728	731					And I don't even have
68.364	69.856	732	747		69.856	72.850	748	779					my own car
72.850	75.248	780	804		75.248	75.521	805	807					But I'm hoping so much
75.521	76.967	808	823		76.967	78.464	824	839					you'll stay
78.464	80.026	840	855		80.026	80.345	856	859					That you will love
80.345	81.832	860	875		81.832	84.452	876	903					me anyway
84.452	88.569	904	947		88.569	90.440	948	967					<V2>The dirty games and the neon shows
90.440	93.433	968	999		93.433	96.427	1000	1031					This is the world he knows

***STT and EDT are found in the listening test. STF and EDF are computed in the annotation process**

Fig. 8. Section of manually annotated vocal and instrumental boundaries of the first few phrases of the song "The Actor" by MLTR. The frame length is equal to the thirty-second note (93.56060606 ms).

3.3. Annotation of song structure

We follow these assumptions while annotating the semantic regions in a popular song.

- Verse and Choruses are usually 8 or 16 bars, but can be 4 bars.
- All the Verses only share similar melody but different vocals.
- All the Choruses have similar vocals and melody.
- The melody of the Verse and Chorus can be similar or different.
- The bridge is less than 8 bars and can be instrumental
- The Middle-eighth is usually 8 or 16 bars and has a different key from the original song. Middle-eighth regions are identified by detecting the region(s) which have a different key from the main key in the intensive listening test.
- INST is usually 8 or 16 bar long instrumental section which appears neither begin nor the end of the song.

Fig. 9 explains the general overview of the components of the song structure. Usually Verse, Chorus and Middle-eighth start with vocals and may end with either vocals or instrumental section. In Fig. 8, we have shown the annotation of the Intro, Verse 1, and Chorus 1, and the start of the Verse 2. We set the tolerance of ± 2 bars for judging the duration of Verse or Chorus.

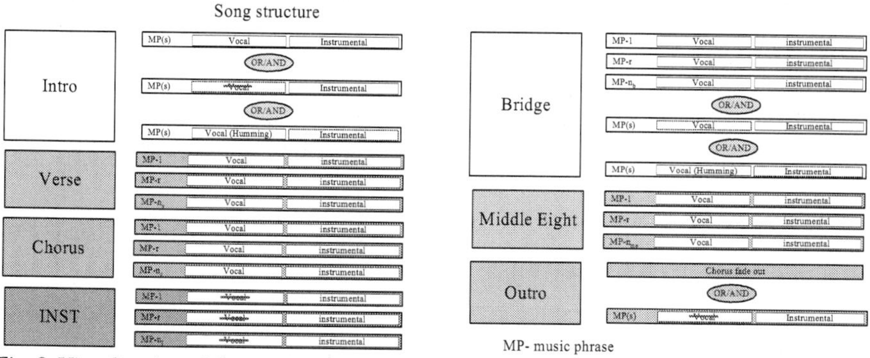

Fig. 9. Visualization of the components in a popular song.

4. Statistical Analysis of the Music Information

We conduct statistical analysis over a database of 420 songs, 120 English songs and 100 songs of each Chinese, Indonesian and German languages. Table 1 summarizes the database. We then carry out listening tests to extract the structural information. An average of 3 hours of intensive listening is required all the annotations per song. The following subsections pictorially discuss the statistics.

4.1. Time information statistics

Tempo describes the speed of the information flow in the music. Fig. 10-(a) discusses the average (Avg) and standard deviation (Std) of tempos based on gender male/ female and total for different languages. Avg and Std of all the songs (i.e. 420 songs) are shown in Fig. 10-(b). The standard deviation (Std) of tempos, in other words the fluctuation of the tempos tells us how dynamic the songs in that cluster are.

It can be seen in Fig. 10-(a) that for all the languages, Avg and Std of the tempos in the male song cluster are higher than they are in the female song cluster. In our song collection, Indonesian male songs have the highest Avg tempo with respect to other languages. As shown in Fig. 10-(b), Avg tempo of male songs is 15 BPM higher than the Avg tempo of female songs and Std of female songs is 5 BPM lower than that of male songs. Fig. 11 details the tempo statistics in histograms.

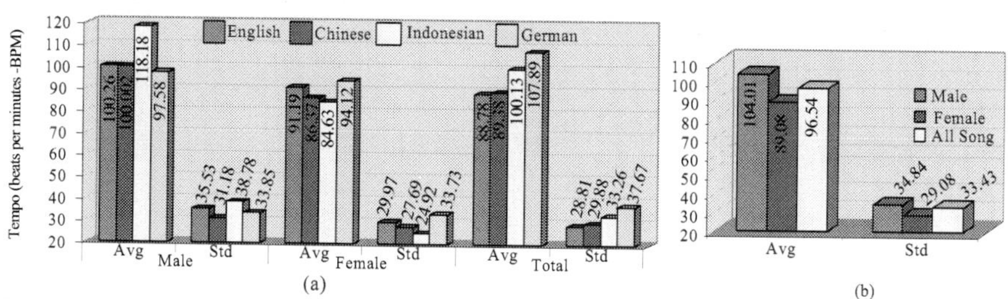

Fig. 10. Tempo statistics of the songs

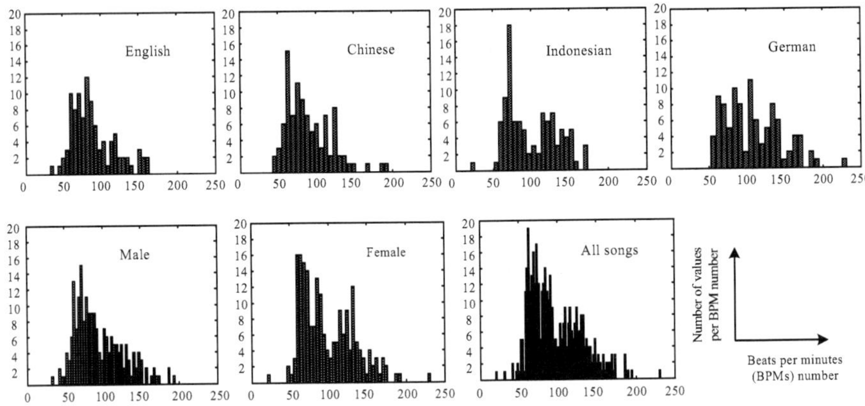

Fig. 11. Tempo statistic histograms

4.2. Music region statistics

Equation (9) describes the distribution of content with respect to region types for songs in the test database. We have $k = 1,2,3,4$ to represent PV, PI, IMV or S regions respectively. Let $NF(k)$ be the total number of frames belonging to region type k and NF_{all} be the total number of frames in a song or a collection of songs. We have

$$D_k = \frac{NF(k)}{NF_{all}} \tag{9}$$

Fig. 12 shows the average content distribution D_k in our database. According to Fig. 12-(a), pure vocal regions in popular music are rare. Silence regions mostly appear at the beginning and at the ending of a song, and constitute a small percentage in the distribution as well. Fig. 12-(b) explains the content distributions by genders and languages. The deviation of IMV and PV region contents is around 10% across the genders and languages. However the deviation is around 2% per song for silence regions. Fig. 13 explains the region content distributions in histograms.

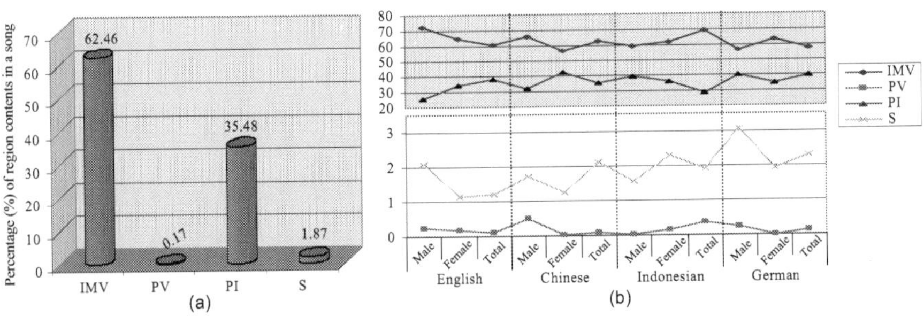

Fig. 12. Distribution of region contents over 420 songs

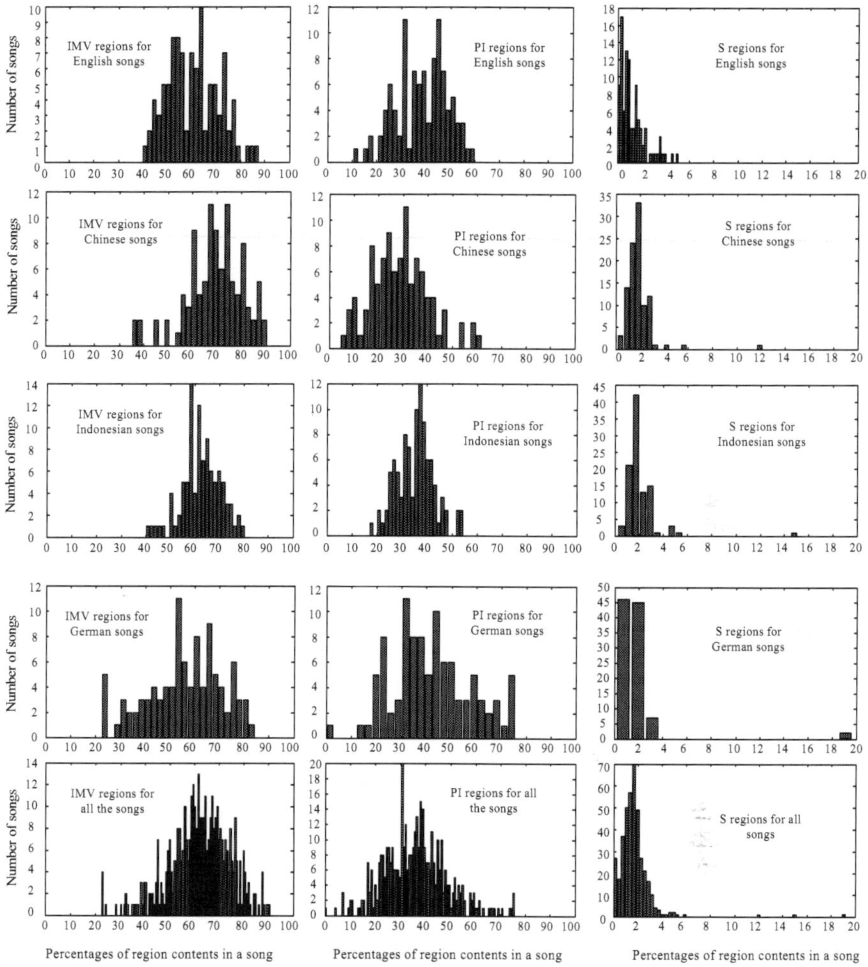

Fig. 13. Histograms of region content distributions

4.3. Song structure statistics

General knowledge about popular song structures is explained in section 2.4. In this section, important statistics about the components of the song structures are explained in point 1 to 9. Point 10 and 11 discuss the statistics of popular song structures. The song structure statistics are calculated using English, Chinese and Indonesian songs.

Total Songs	English 120	Chinese 100	Indonesians 100	All Songs 320
(1) How many songs have Intro?	95.83%	97.00%	99.00%	97.19%
(a) How many songs have instrumental Intros?	80.00%	74.00%	67.00%	74.06%
(b) How many songs have vocal mixed instrumental Intros?	15.83%	14.00%	32.00%	20.31%
(2) If no Intro,	4.17%	2.00%	1.00%	2.50%
(a)how many songs start with Verse?	4.17%	1.00%	1.00%	2.19%
(b) how many songs start with Chorus?	0.00%	1.00%	0.00%	0.31%
(3) How many songs have instrumental Outros?	13.33%	45.00%	39.00%	31.25%
(a) How many songs have chorus melody in the Outro?	0.83%	0.00%	0.00%	0.31%
(b) How many songs have verse melody in the Outro?	0.00%	0.00%	0.00%	0.00%
(4) How many songs have vocal mixed instrumental Outros?	86.67%	45.00%	59.00%	65.00%
(a) Howmany songs have fading choruse vocals and melody?	38.33%	8.00%	4.00%	18.13%
(b) Howmany songs have fading verses vocals and melody?	3.33%	0.00%	0.00%	1.25%
(5) How many songs have middle eighth?	53.33%	15.00%	2.00%	25.31%
(6) How many songs have INST regions?	51.67%	82.00%	65.00%	65.31%

	English	Chinese	Indonesian	All Songs
INST-0	**48.33%**	18.00%	35.00%	34.69%
INST-1	**42.50%**	**65.00%**	**51.00%**	**52.19%**
INST-2	9.17%	17.00%	12.00%	12.50%
INST-3			2.00%	0.63%

(7) Percentages of songs that have number of verses (n-V) and number of choruses (n-C)

No of regions	English		Chinese		Indonesian		All songs	
	Verse	Chorus	Verse	Chorus	Verse	Chorus	Verse	Chorus
0				1.00		1.00		0.63
1	2.50	3.33	10.00		2.00	1.00	4.06	1.56
2	64.17	20.00	41.00	30.00	32.00	23.00	37.50	24.06
3	22.50	50.00	33.00	48.00	50.00	45.00	28.75	47.81
4	9.17	23.33	11.00	13.00	14.00	23.00	22.50	20.00
5	0.83	2.50	4.00	5.00	2.00	3.00	5.94	3.44
6	0.83	0.83		1.00		3.00	0.94	1.56
7				1.00				0.31
8						1.00		0.31

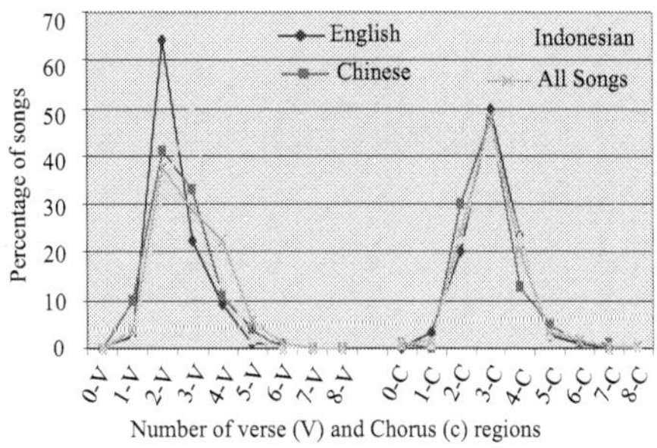

(8) Percentage of songs have verse - chorus combinations

English songs (Number of Verses × Number of choruses)

Number of Verses \ Number of choruses	1	2	3	4	5	6	7	8
1		2.50						
2	0.83	7.50	35.83	18.33	1.67			
3	1.67	6.67	9.17	4.17	0.83			
4	0.83	2.50	5.00	0.83				
5		0.83						
6						0.83		
7								
8								

Chinese songs (Number of Verses × Number of choruses)

Number of Verses \ Number of choruses	0	1	2	3	4	5	6	7	8
1			5.00	4.00		1.00			
2			13.00	18.00	8.00	2.00		1.00	
3			8.00	18.00	5.00	1.00	1.00		
4	1.00		4.00	5.00		1.00			
5			1.00	3.00					
6									
7									
8									

Indonesian Songs (Number of Verses × Number of choruses)

Number of Verses \ Number of choruses	0	1	2	3	4	5	6	7	8
1			1.00	1.00					
2	1.00	1.00	6.00	15.00	7.00	1.00			1.00
3			11.00	25.00	10.00	1.00	3.00		
4			3.00	4.00	6.00	1.00			
5			2.00						
6									
7									
8									

All the Songs (Number of Verses × Number of choruses)

Number of Verses \ Number of choruses	0	1	2	3	4	5	6	7	8
1			2.81	1.56		0.31			
2	0.31	0.63	8.75	23.75	11.56	1.56		0.31	0.31
3		0.63	8.44	16.88	6.25	0.94	1.25		
4	0.31	0.31	3.13	4.69	2.19	0.63			
5			1.25	0.94					
6							0.31		
7									
8									

(9) length of verse and chorus

For English Songs

Length of Verse in Bars \ Length of Chorus in Bars	4	8	16	Others
4	2%	5%	0%	0%
8	2%	51%	9%	5%
16	1%	6%	12%	2%
Others	0%	5%	1%	1%

For Chinese Songs

Length of Verse in Bars \ Length of Chorus in Bars	4	8	16	Others
4	4%	5%	2%	4%
8	1%	37%	18%	4%
16	0%	5%	9%	1%
Others	0%	4%	3%	3%

For Indonesian Songs

Length of Verse in Bars \ Length of Chorus in Bars	4	8	16	Others
4	1%	1%	2%	1%
8	3%	35%	24%	2%
16	0%	8%	13%	4%
Others	0%	3%	1%	2%

For All Songs

Length of Verse in Bars \ Length of Chorus in Bars	4	8	16	Others
4	2%	4%	1%	2%
8	2%	42%	17%	4%
16	0%	6%	11%	2%
Others	0%	4%	2%	2%

Song structures

	English	Chinese	Indonesians	All
(10) How many songs have V-C-V-C repetition?	58%	19%	27%	36%
a. how many songs have mid-eighth?	23%	3%	1%	10%
b. how many songs have inst?	26%	9%	17%	18%
(11) How many songs have V-V-C-V-C repetition?	10%	9%	50%	22%
a. how many songs have mid-eighth?	5%	3%	1%	3%
b. how many songs have inst?	3%	4%	33%	13%

4.4. Summary of song structure statistics

- It is found that over 95% of the English, Chinese and Indonesian songs have an introduction (i.e. Intro) and over 65% of them have instrumental Intros.
- Over 90% of songs have either instrumental mixed vocals or an instrumental Outro. Around 38% of English songs have fading Choruses (vocal + melody) as Outro.

- Middle-eighth is more commonly appear in English songs than Chinese and Indonesian songs.
- Over 50% of Chinese and Indonesian songs have an INST region and around half of the English songs may not have an INST region.
- Over 50% of the English songs have Middle-eighth regions but there these regions are rare in Chinese and Indonesian songs.
- Majority of the songs have 2~3 Verses and 2~4 Choruses.
- In many songs, the chorus and verse lengths are of 4, 8, or 16 bars. Most songs have the same chorus and verse length, i.e. 8 bars.
- Over 70% of the English and Indonesian songs have V-C-V-C and V-V-C-V-C song structures whereas it is around 30% for Chinese songs. (V and C are abbreviation of Verse and Chorus respectively.)

5. Discussion

This chapter reports a statistical analysis of the music information in popular English, Chinese, Indonesian and German songs. Intensive listening tests were carried out by subjects who have good knowledge of musicology and the language of the vocals, to determine the tempo, time indexing of music regions and song structures.
The reported statistics about the music information can be used as prior knowledge in formulating constraints for music information extraction systems. For example, for setting up the window size to detect onsets, beats in the rhythm extractor, to form heuristic rules to detect popular song structures. Sound of music is a combination of creative imaginations of the composer, singer and orchestra, which is diversified along many directions such as ethnicity, culture, and geographical locations. Therefore, song structures can differ from one composer to another. The current database that we used consists of 420 songs from four languages. Although the statistics may not be enough to draw general conclusions about song structures, they can be considered as an indication of common practice in popular song composition.

6. Acknowledgement

Authors thank students, Ng Ruijie, Lai Lihui, Zheng Haojie, Sugiarto Radjiman, Ridwan Natakusuma Malaka, Aming, Mohomad Erwin Bin Samawi, Lau Rong Jia and Daniel for their support in this project.

7. References

Authors (1949). *Rudiments and Theory of Music.* The associated board of the royal schools of music, 14 Bedford Square, London, WC1B 3JG, 1949.

Authors (1995). *The Best of Shania Twain – 14 Hit Songs, Piano, Vocal, Guitar.* Universal Music Publishing Group & Warner Bros. Publication, 1995.

Authors (2003). *Ten Minute Master No 18: Song Structure. MUSIC TECH magazine,* October, 2003, pp 62–63, www.musictechmag.co.uk

Burred, J. and Lerch, A. (2004). Hierarchical Automatic Audio Signal Classification, *Journal of the Audio Engineering Society*, July, 2004, Vol. 52, No. 7/8, pp. 724-739.

Goto, M. (2001). An Audio-based Real-time Beat Tracking System for Music With or Without Drum-sounds, *Journal of new Music Research,* June. 2001, Vol.30, 159-171.

Goto, M. (2006). AIST Annotation for the RWC Music Database, *International Conference on Music Information Retrieval*, 2006.

Jourdain, R. (1997). *Music, The Brain, and Ecstasy: How Music Captures Our Imagination,* HarperCollins Publishers, 1997.

Krumhansl, C. L. (1979). The Psychological Representation of Musical Pitch in a Tonal Context, *Journal of Cognitive Psychology*, 1979, Vol.11, No. 3, pp. 346-374.

Li, B., Burgoyne, J. A., and Fujinaga, I. (2006). Extending Audacity for Audio Annotation, *International Conference on Music Information Retrieval,* 2006.

Lu, Liu and Zhang. (2006). Automatic Mood Detection and Tracking of Music Audio Signals, *IEEE Transaction on Audio, Speech and Language Processing,* January 2006, Vol.14, No. 1.

Maddage, N. C., Xu, C., Kankanhalli, M.S., and Shao, X. (2004). Content-based Music Structure Analysis with the Applications to Music Semantic Understanding, *ACM Multimedia Conference,* 2004.

Maddage, N. C. (2005). *Content-Based Music Structure Analysis,* PhD Dissertation, School of Computing, National University of Singapore, 2005.

Nwe, T. L and Li, H. (2007). Exploring Vibrato-Motivated Acoustic Features for Singer Identification, In *IEEE Transaction on Audio, Speech and Language Processing,* February, 2007, Vol. 15, No. 2.

Rabiner, L.R. and Juang, B.H. (2005). *Fundamentals of Speech Recognition,* Prentice-Hall, 1993.

Schwenninger, J., Brueckner, R., Willett, D., and Hennecke, M. (2006). Language Identification in Vocal Music, *International Conference on Music Information Retrieval,* 2006.

Tanghe, K., Lesaffre, M. Degroeve, S., Leman, M., Baets, B.D., and Martens, J-P. (2005). Collecting Ground Truth Annotations for Drum Detection in Polyphonic Music, *International Conference on Music Information Retrieval,* 2005.

Tsai, W.-H and Wang, H. M. (2004). Towards Automatic Identification of Singing Language in Popular Music Recordings, *International Conference on Music Information Retrieval,* 2004.

Tzanetakis, G., and Cook, P. (2002). Music Genre Classification of Audio Signals, *IEEE Transaction on Audio, Speech and Language Processing,* July 2002, Vol. 10, No. 5, pp. 293-302.

Wang, Y., Ahmaniemi, A., Isherwood, D., and Huang, W. (2003). Content-Based UEP: A New Scheme for Packet Loss Recovery in Music Streaming, *ACM Multimedia Conference,* 2003.

Wang, Y., Kan, M. Y., Nwe, T. L., Shenoy, A. and Yin, J. (2004). LyricAlly: Automatic Synchronization of Acoustic Music Signals and Textual Lyrics, *ACM Multimedia Conference,* 2004.

Xu, C.S., Maddage, N.C., Shao, Xi., Cao, F., and Tian, Q. (2003). Musical Genre Classification Using Support Vector Machines, In Proc. *International Conference on Acoustics, Speech, and Signal Processing (ICASSP),* 2003.

Xu, C.S., Maddage, N.C., and Shao, Xi. (2005). Automatic Music Classification and Summarization, *IEEE Transaction on Audio, Speech and Language Processing,* May 2005, Vol. 13, pp 441-450.

	Album name	English songs (Female vocals)									
1	Celine Dion (Falling into you)	Falling Into You	Make You Happy	Seduces Me	All By Myself	Dreaming Of You	I Love You	If That's What It Takes	I Don't Know	14-Your Light	Call The Man
2	Dido (Life for rent)	White Flag	Stoned	Life For Rent	Mary's In Indian	See You When You Are 40	Don't Leave Home	Who Makes You Feel	Sand In My Shoes	Do You Have A Little Time	This Land Is Mine
3	Faith Hill (Love will always win)	This kiss	Me	Love Aren't Like That	Piece Of My Heart	The Secret Of Life	Better Days	I Love You	The Hard Way	Somebody Stand By Me	Let Me Let Go (Bonus Track)
4	Mariah Carey (Greatest Hits)	Vision of love	Love takes time	I don't wanna cry	Cant let go	Hero	Without you	Any time you need a friend	All I have ever wanted	I still believe	My all
5	Shania Twain (Come on Over)	From this Moment On	The woman in me	Honey I am Home	Don't be stupid (You know I love you)	Love Gets me every time	Still the one	Black eyes blue tears	When	Come on over	Im holdin on to love to save my life
	Album name	**English songs (Male vocals)**									
1	Ben Jelen (Give it all away)	Come On	Rocks	She'll Hear You	Give It Away	Every Step	Christine	Wicked Little Town	Falling Down	Stay	Criminal
2	Bryan Adams (On a Day Like Today)	How do u feel tonight	C'mon C'mon C'mon	On a day like today	Fearless	I am a Liar	When you are gone	Before the night is over	Where the angles fear to treads	Lie to me	Cloud No-9
3	Elton John (Greatest Hits 1970 - 2002)	Your Song	Daniel	Candle in the Wind	I Guess Thats Why They Call It the Blues	Nikita	Sacrifice	Can You Feel the Love Tonight	Circle of Life	Made in England	I Want Love
4	Michael Bolton (Vintage)	The Very Thought of You	All the Way	A Kiss to Build a Dream On	If I Could	At Last	When I Fall in Love	You Don't Know Me	mile	Daddys Little Girl	What Are You Doing the Rest of Your Life
5	Michael Learns to Rock - MLTR (Paint My Love)	25 Minutes	Breaking My Heart	Complicated Heart	How Many Hours	Paint My Love	Sleeping Child	Somday	That's Why (You Go Away)	The Actor	Wild Women
6	Richard Marx (Greatest Hits)	Slipping Away	Endless summer nights	Don't mean nothing	Children of the Night	Should have known better	Hazard	Angelia	Hold on to the nights	Take this heart	Right here waiting
7	West life (West life)	Change the World	Flying without wings	Fool Again	I Don't Wanna Fight	If I let you go	Miss You	My Love	Seasons in the Sun	Somebody needs you	Swear it Again
	Album name	**Chinese songs (Female vocals)**									
1	FIR□ Fly□ □ □ □ □ □ □	Fly Away	Lydia	Liu Lang Zhe Zhi Ge	Wo Men De Ai	Guang Mang	Ni De Wei Xiao	Ta Luo Pai	Hou Le Yuan	Revolution	You Make Me Want To Fall In Love
2	Liang jinru□ FISH-Lian ai de li liang□ □ □ □ □ □ □ □ □ □ □	Bu Xiang Shui	Ru Guo You Yi Tian	Cai Hong	Ai Ni Bu Shi Liang San Tian	Zui Xiang Huan You De Shi Jie	Dui Bu Qi Wo Ai Ni	Zhi Neng Bao Zhe Ni	Di San Zhe	Zuo Tian	Ming Tian De Wei Xiao
3	Rene Liu (Full Bloom) □ □ □	Bang Wan	Cheng Quan	Dian Liang Ju Zi Shu	Dui Mian Nan Sheng De Fang Jian	Mi Mi	Nian Hua	Wang Le	Wo Ceng Ai Guo	Yi Wang De Cheng Shi	Yong Gan
4	Pei Ni□ SoPenny-hao) □ □ □ □ □	Fang Kong Dong	Xin De Rui La	Bu Xiang	Xi Guan Zhe Yang	Tou Qi	Ri Qi	Zen Yang	Ni Yao De Ai	Hao Gan Jue	Ai Guo
5	Zhao Wei□ Vicky-Piao□ □ □ □ □ □	Bian Le	Zhe Yi Ke Wo Xiang Xin Ni Shuo Wi Ai Ni	Jian Jian	Wu Jin De Sha Shi Bi Ya	Yi Zhi Xia Yu De Xing Qi Tian	Biao Qing Dong Zuo Yan Yu	Zhuang Tai	Sheng Ming Li De Zhe Yi Tian	Shi Yi Yue	Tian Shi Zhi Ming

Table 1. List of songs, singers and their albums (ten songs from each album) used for the test

	Album name	Chinese songs (Male vocals)									
1	Zhou Jie Lun (Qi Li Xiang- JAY) ▯▯▯▯▯▯▯▯	Wo De Di Pan	Qi Li Xiang	Jie Kou	Wai Po	Jiang Jun	Ge Qian	Luan Wu Chun Qiu	Kun Shou Zhi Dou	Yuan You Hui	Zhi Zhan Zhi Shang
2	A du (Tianhei) ▯▯▯▯▯▯	Andy	Li bie	Ni heng hao	Right here waiting	Si ye	Ta yi ding	Tian Hei	TianTian	Wu fa zu dang	Yi ge ren zhu
3	Zhou Chuan Xiong (Transfer) ▯▯▯	Wang Ji	Chu Mai	Ji Mo Hong Zha	You Xi Ai Qing	Xin Jie	Ji Shi Ben	Pi Jiu Pao Pao	Xin Xue Lai Chao	Mo Ban Che	Shi Jian
4	Dao Lang▯▯	Ka Shi Ge Er Hu Yang	Guan Yu Er Dao Qiao	Wu Yi Ye Shi De Xiong Di	Zhi You Ai De Le Si Neng Kan Jian	Shou Zai Ling Chen Liang Dian De Shang Xin Show Bar	Da Yan Jing	Ya Ka Xi	Zai Jian Wu Lu Mu Qi	Da Qi Shou Gu Chang Qi Ge	Bing Shan Shang De Xue Lian
5	Ou De Yang▯▯▯ (Ocean)	Xing Fu Che Zhan	Xiu Xiu Xiu	Gu Dan Bei Ban Qiu	Lang Man Qun Dao	Li Qi	Ma Ya Jin Zi Ta	Yi Ren Yi Ban	Peng You Zui Jin Hao Ma	Liang Jian Shi	Shang Xuan Yue
	Album name	Indonesian songs (Female vocals)									
1	Rosa	Kembali	Aku Bukan Untukmu	Bicara Pada Bintang	Pudar	Cintai Aku	Akankah Bisa	Biar	Pujaan Hati	Wanita Yang Kau Pilih	Pudar Soundtrac k Version
2	Nina	Aku Bahagia	Kau Datang	Karena Ku Tak Bisa	Di Sore Nanti	Yang Terbaik	Baca Hatiku	Empat Musim	Kembali Padamu	Percuma	Tak Menjauh
3	Audy	Pertama Kali	Temui Aku	Kita Takkan Bersatu	Kutak Bisa Memberi	Silang Hati	Tiada Akhir	Lagu Sendu	Setelah Kau Pergi	Kisah Yang Sama	Lebih Baik Darimu
4	Andien	Denganmu Sahabatku	Milikmu Selalu	Ku Akan Menanti	Menyambut Kasihmu	Kucemburu	Menyanyi Menari	Satu Dua dan Tiga	Gemintang	Untukmu	Cerita Lama
5	Tere	Pencuri Hati	Dosa Termanis	Cukup Bagiku	Pasangan Sepadan	Pertanyaan Hati	Panggung Sandiwara	Kala Cinta Bicara	Begitu Berharga	Apa Adanya	Bukan Jalan Kita
	Album name	Indonesian songs (Male vocals)									
1	Naif (City of Joy)	Gula Gula	Benci Untuk Mencinta	Pujaan Hati	Takkan Pernah Melupakan mu	Nanar	Senyum Yang Hilang	Akulah Pasanganm u	Uang	Tak Mampu Mendua	Pagi
2	Mike	Semua Untuk Cinta	Kembali	Besar	Terbaik	Yang Hitam	Cinta Kan Membawa mu Kembali	Sempurnala h Mimpiku	Cinta Tak Bertuan	Persembah an	Arti Kesetiaan
3	Peterpan	Tak Bisakah	Jauh Mimpiku	Membebani ku	Menunggu Pagi	Kukatakan Dengan Indah	Sahabat	Aku & Bintang	Mungkin Nanti	Di Belakangk u	Langit Tak Mendenga r
4	Kerispatih	Maafkan Aku	Hanya Kamu Yang Bisa	Lagu Rindu	Berpisah	Memang Ini Jalanku	Cuma Manusia	Cinta Putih	Pertama dan Terakhir	Janji Kita	Lupakan Aku
5	Ello	Pergi Untuk Kembali	Mungkin Mereka Bilang	Terbaik	Dirimu	Kekasih Khayalan	Kau (feat. Glenn Fredly)	Sudahlah	Sampaikan Padanya	Kau Bukan Kekasihku	Kisah Kita T'lah Usai
	Album name	German songs (Female vocals)									
1	Wir Sind Helden	Wenn es passiert	Echolot	Von hier an blind	Ein Elefant fuer dich	Darf ich das behalten	Wuetend genug	Zieh dir was an	Nur ein Wort	Ich werde mein Leben lang	Bist du nicht muede
2	Silbermond	Machs dir selbst	Durch die Nacht	Du und ich	An dich	Passend gemacht	Symphonie	1000 Fragen	Letzte Bahn	Ohne dich	Wissen was wird
3	Nena	Willst du mit mir gehn	Lass mich	Und jetzt steh ich hier und warte	Liebe ist	Ich komm mit dir	Immer weiter	Ohne Liebe bin ich nichts	Vitamine	Wir fliegen	Neues Land
4	Juli	Warum	Sterne	Geile zeit	Tage wie dieser	Traenensch wer	Perfekte Welle	Regen und Meer	November	Anders	Ich Verschwin de
5	Annett Louisan	Das grosse Erwachsen	Thorsten Schmidt	Chancenlos	Gedacht ich sage nein	Eve	Laueft alles perfekt	Wo ist das Problem	Er gehoerte mal mir	Die Loesung	Der den ich will
	Album name	German songs (Male vocals)									
1	Ben	Herz aus Glas	Da fuer mich	Die Reise	Gesegnet seist Du	Irgendwo	Du bist mein Herz	Zurueck zu mir	Warum soll ich gehn	Sie bringt die Sonne mit	Es wird Zeit
2	Echt	Wie Geht Es Dir So	Meisterwer k	In Dieser Gegend	Wahrheit	Du Bist Nicht Echt	Haar	Wie Ein Maedchen	Nachbarsch aft	Kurz Nach Dem Aufstehen	An Deiner Seite
3	Mensch	Mensch	Neuland	Der Weg	Viertel Vor	Lache Wenn es nicht zum weinen reicht	Unbewohnt	Dort und hier	Blick zurueck	Kein Pokal	Zum Meer
4	Soehne Mannheims	Wenn Du Schlaefst	Vielleicht	Von Anfang An Dabei	Koenig Der Koenige	Traurige Lieder	Im Interesse Unserer Gemeinsch aft	Ich Geh Mit Dir	Dein Leben	Und Wenn Ein Lied	Vatter unser
5	Tocotronic	Freiburg	Du Bist Ganz Schoen Bedient	So Jung Kommen Wir Nicht Mehr Zusammen	Let There Be Rock	Jackpot	This Boy is Tocotronic	Aber Hier Leben Nein Danke	Gegen Den Strich	Pure vernunft darf niemals siegen	Pure vernunft darf niemals siegen

21

MIMO Channel Modeling and Simulation

R. Parra-Michel, A. Alcocer-Ochoa,
A. Sanchez-Hernandez and Valeri Kontorovich
CINVESTAV- IPN
Mexico

1. Introduction

New communications standards are continuously appearing as response to the increasing demands of users and telecommunication applications. Those demands reflect requirements regarding raising the data rates and user's mobility. During these years we shall witness an introduction of applications for indoor wireless networks at the 60GHz band, Vehicle to Vehicle wireless systems, mobile Internet and VoIP over WiMax based systems, etc. Those new applications will rely on Multiple Input and Multiple-Output (MIMO) systems for being able to handle concepts of radar, beamforming, and spatial multiplexing.

In such variety of applications where all of them uses radio waves to guarantee the mobility requirement, plenty of radio propagation channels will be undoubtedly utilized. It is then mandatory to count with channel models that adequately describe the propagation channel by means of some mathematical expressions. Thus, the communication researcher can devise algorithms to counteract the distortions introduced by the channel.

Once mathematical models for channels and algorithms for the communication blocks are conceived, the next step in communication systems design flow is to prove whether the proposed solution attains the desired functionality.

Notwithstanding, there are several factors intervening in these designs; e.g., the multiple choices for communication processing algorithms, the large variety of channel environments with their random nature, the inherent computational complexity of each communications algorithms, etc. These factors preclude obtaining closed form expressions for the entire system performance. One must thus rely on simulations. These simulations provide a system's performance at various design stages, while allowing design engineers to test several arrangements with different algorithms over several channel models, until the final architecture matches the requested performance.

The term *simulation* hereafter is referred to a performance analysis by means of computer programs. Another close related term is *emulation*, which refers to tests of the implemented system on digital circuits, such as Complex Programmable Logic Devices (CPLD) and Field Programmable Gate Arrays (FPGA). Emulation also avoids the final construction of a system under design; in fact, emulation has gotten to be a necessity for the newest communication systems, whose throughput is high enough to preclude simulation by computer programs. Even though simulation models are actually computer programs and

emulators are Hardware (HW) devices, we will refer to both of them hereafter by the single term of simulation.
But counting with simulations results still remains open the question whether the approved design will actually work as expected in the real implementation or not. The probability of success highly depends on how close the channel model resembles the real channel conditions, i.e. its ability to distort the signals in the same (statistically) manner than the real channel performs. The failing of good channel models will yield wrong results of system performance that can lead to system redesign, an incident that have happened in the development of initial standards (Woerner et al., 1994). Thus, strong efforts are devoted to obtain good channel models and its efficient implementations as channel simulators.
In this Chapter it will be discussed how to construct channel simulators for MIMO wireless systems. Considering that the channel is an artificial construction that can integrate the propagation media and several blocks of the communication system, we can obtain several definitions for channels. Here we consider the channel simulators that deal with the analogic channel; i.e. simulators for testing physical layer algorithms such as channel estimation.
The Chapter is organized as follows: The general problem of channel modeling is discussed in Section 2. Within this section, the main propagation phenomena of the radio channel and its deterministic mathematical expressions are devised. These descriptions are then analyzed in statistical terms to define the final radio channel expressions. The propagation media is then included in a MIMO System and the MIMO channel model is finally established. This Section ends with the delimitation of the channels to be discussed throughout this Chapter.
In Section 3 two main approaches that try to explain and/or replicate the propagation phenomena are presented. These models are the geometrical based approach and the method of artificial paths. Proposed simulators according to the commented modeling approaches are discussed in Section 4. This Section also provides a brief space of comments regarding the practical implementation issues. Section 5 defines a metric that permits the performance comparison of the proposed simulators along with simulation results. Section 6 is devoted to point out the open research areas and future trends in this topic. The Chapter ends with Section 7, where the conclusions of the manuscript are drawn. Finally, it is worth to mention here that this chapter does not try to enlist all the models and simulators for wireless channels, but to present the main ideas of the topic, connect all the details, and present the recent advances in this area of research.

2. The radio channel model

At the frequencies prescribed by communication standards, radio signals suffer the effects of attenuation, diffraction, refraction and reflection, with the last three causing multipath propagation. This means that several replicas of the transmitted signal will arrive at the receiver through different paths. Signals along each path will experience variations in amplitude and delay; consequently the composite signal at the receiver becomes distorted.
Due to the complexity involved in propagation analysis, all of the amplitude and delay variations are treated as random, as well as time variant features. A simplified example of multipath propagation is provided by Fig. 1, with small number of paths involved. It is considered in this figure that a signal departs from an array of N antennas at the

transmitter's side (Tx) and arrives to an antenna array of M elements at the receiver's side (Rx). For the figure N=M=3, and there are three main paths (dp1 to dp3) departing from Tx and four paths (ap1 to ap4) arriving at Rx.

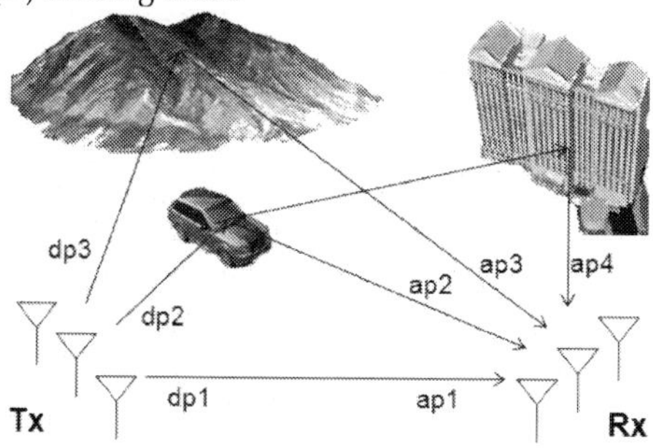

Fig. 1. Multipath propagation in a MIMO wireless link.

The following issues, concerning multipath propagation, become evident in Fig. 1:

1. Signals from each path can arrive at Rx with different azimuth and elevation angles.
2. From all the energy being transmitted, only a fraction of it will effectively reach the receiver. This can be interpreted as the transmitter scattering the energy over several paths, each one with a different angle of departure.
3. As some paths are longer than others (see path dp3-ap3), the different replicas will arrive with different time delays (τ) with respect to the first incoming signal (in this case, see dp1-ap1).
4. When scatters in the propagation media or the receiver are in movement, the signals will experience a Doppler frequency shift (ν) with respect to the carrier frequency. In the figure, the paths connected with dp2 will present this effect.

The above issues concerning multipath propagation are treated in detail in (Parsons, 2000).

2.1 Deterministic description of the MIMO Radio Channel

In what follows, adequate mathematical descriptions that comprise the main propagation phenomena are constructed. It has been, however, discarded the discussion concerning link budget and shadowing, but it will be centered on the effects of scattering.

Define a time dependent signal $x(t)$ transmitted nearby a point in the (three dimensional) space $\boldsymbol{\rho}^{\mathrm{Tx}}$, hereafter defined as the *transmitter reference point,* that modulates a carrier wave with central radian frequency ω_c, expressed as $\cos(\omega_c t)$. A received signal $y(t)$ can be measured in a point nearby a *receiver reference point* $\boldsymbol{\rho}^{\mathrm{Rx}}$. The received signal can be expressed as:

$$y(t)=\sum_{l=1}^{L_p(t)} A_l(t)x(t-d_l(t))\cos\left(\omega_c(t-d_l(t))-\theta_l^{\mathrm{Tx}}-\theta_l^{\mathrm{Rx}}\right). \qquad (1)$$

The last equation considers a single input and single output system (SISO), that according to the propagation phenomena, l=1,2,..., $L_p(t)$ paths with replicas of the transmitted signals will contribute with energy to the measurement point. Each path will arrive with a time dependent delay $d_l(t)$ with respect to the first incoming path, and with time varying amplitudes $A_l(t)$. Phases θ_l^{Tx} and θ_l^{Rx} correspond to the difference of phases between the l-path and a reference wave transmitted from $\boldsymbol{\rho}^{\mathrm{Tx}}$ and arriving at $\boldsymbol{\rho}^{\mathrm{Rx}}$, respectively.

Supposing that in a block of transmitted data, amplitudes $A_l(t)$ can be relaxed as constant parameter A_l, and that the number of paths remains constant (but relatively large) and is equal to L_p. Besides this, $d_l(t)$ is expressed as a linear function of t, it means, $d_l(t) = \tau_l + \varsigma_l t$, where τ_l is a fixed delay and ς_l is the rate of change of the delay of the l-path. With the commented assumptions, equation (1) can be written as:

$$y(t) = \sum_{l=1}^{L_p} A_l x(t - \tau_l - \varsigma_l t)\cos\left(\omega_c (t - \tau_l - \varsigma_l t) - \theta_l^{\mathrm{Tx}} - \theta_l^{\mathrm{Rx}}\right). \tag{2}$$

Considering now that the rate of change of the transmitted signal is much more bigger than every rate of change of the paths delays, $x(t - \tau_l - \varsigma_l t)$ can be fairly good approximated by $x(t - \tau_l)$; v_l is $\omega_c \varsigma_l$, the Doppler shift of the l-path and $\theta_l^c = \omega_c \tau_l$ is an unknown carrier phase. The former considerations are explained in detail in (Kennedy, 1969). Defining the points in the space $\boldsymbol{\rho}_1^{\mathrm{Tx}}$ and $\boldsymbol{\rho}_1^{\mathrm{Rx}}$ as the true positions of the transceivers, the received signal can be expressed as:

$$y(t) = \sum_{l=1}^{L_p} A_l x(t - \tau_l)\cos\left((\omega_c - v_l)t - \theta_l^c - \frac{2\pi}{\lambda}\mathbf{k}_l^{\mathrm{Tx}} \cdot \boldsymbol{\rho}_1^{\mathrm{Tx}} - \frac{2\pi}{\lambda}\mathbf{k}_l^{\mathrm{Rx}} \cdot \boldsymbol{\rho}_1^{\mathrm{Rx}}\right), \tag{3}$$

where $\mathbf{k}_l^{\mathrm{Tx}}$ and $\mathbf{k}_l^{\mathrm{Rx}}$ are unitary three dimensional vectors pointing at the angle of departure (AoD) and angle of arrival (AoA) of the l-path, respectively, and $(\cdot)$ is the dot product operator.

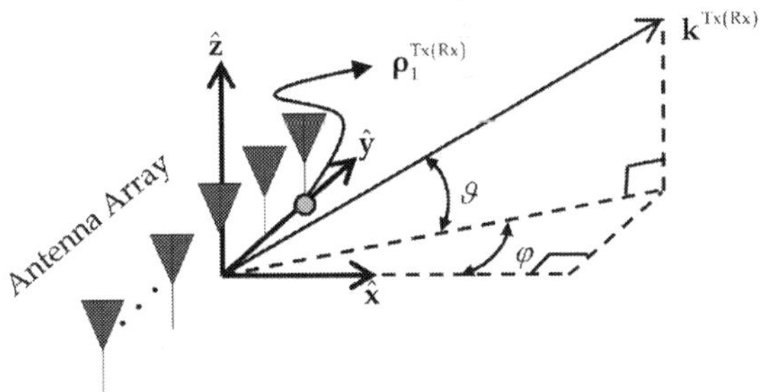

Fig. 2. Representation of wavefronts as vectors in the three-dimensional space.

Each vector $\mathbf{k}_l^{\mathrm{Tx}}$ and $\mathbf{k}_l^{\mathrm{Rx}}$ can be expressed with the aid of Fig. 2 in spherical coordinates as: $\left[\cos(\varphi)\cos(\vartheta)\hat{\mathbf{x}}, \sin(\varphi)\cos(\vartheta)\hat{\mathbf{y}}, \sin(\vartheta)\hat{\mathbf{z}}\right]$. Where angle φ is the azimuth angle, defined positive when going counter clock-wise; ϑ corresponds to the elevation angle. It has also been illustrated in the figure an antenna array located in the direction of $\hat{\mathbf{y}}$ for future

exemplifications. In the figure, it has been defined the reference point as the position of the first element of the antenna array.
It is worthwhile to mention that equation (3) has been considered that the change of phase depends only on the carrier frequency, when this parameter should be a phase function that depends on the signal (in passband) frequency. However, this approximation is justified for the large ratio between carrier frequency to signal bandwidth (Durgin, 2003).
Transmitting a delta function in order to measure the passband impulse response, and measuring the signal at the receiver point with a wideband quadrature receiver, the received signal is the well known complex baseband impulse response $h(.)$ (multiplying the quadrature component by the imaginary number j); this response is dependent of the exact positions of the transceivers, and then it can be defined as:

$$y(t)=h\left(t,\tau,\mathbf{\rho}_1^{\mathrm{Tx}},\mathbf{\rho}_1^{\mathrm{Rx}}\right)=\sum_{l=1}^{L_p}A_l\delta\left(\tau-\tau_l\right)e^{-j\nu_l t-j\theta_l^c}e^{-jk_0\mathbf{k}_l^{\mathrm{Tx}}\cdot\mathbf{\rho}_1^{\mathrm{Tx}}}e^{-jk_0\mathbf{k}_l^{\mathrm{Rx}}\cdot\mathbf{\rho}_1^{\mathrm{Rx}}}f_l^{\mathrm{Tx}}\left(\varphi,\vartheta\right)f_l^{\mathrm{Rx}}\left(\varphi,\vartheta\right). \quad (4)$$

Where instead of $2\pi/\lambda$ it has been utilized the wavenumber k_0. It has been also used the concepts of time-varying filters from (Bello, 1963), therefore, the time domain can be separated into the time and time delay variables to express $\delta\left(t-\tau_l\right)$ as $\delta\left(\tau-\tau_l\right)$.
Expressions $f_l^{\mathrm{Rx}}\left(\varphi,\vartheta\right)$ and $f_l^{\mathrm{Tx}}\left(\varphi,\vartheta\right)$ are, respectively, the response of the measuring system (or underlying antenna array) to the impinging wave, and the transmitter induced distortion to the transmitted signal in the AoD of the l-path. Both expressions correspond to the topology construction of the antenna system (Weichselberger, 2003). Hereafter it will be considered that those terms are both equal to unity and are not subsequently considered in the rest of the analysis for ease of explanation.
Equation (4) can be generalized for measuring the signal in a continuous three-dimensional space with the variable $\mathbf{r}^{\mathrm{Rx}}$, from sending signals in every point in the space $\mathbf{r}^{\mathrm{Tx}}$; in this case, the complex baseband channel is:

$$h\left(t,\tau,\mathbf{r}^{\mathrm{Tx}},\mathbf{r}^{\mathrm{Rx}}\right)=\sum_{l=1}^{L_p}A_l\delta\left(\tau-\tau_l\right)e^{-j\nu_l t-j\theta_l^c}e^{-jk_0\mathbf{k}_l^{\mathrm{Tx}}\cdot\mathbf{r}^{\mathrm{Tx}}}e^{-jk_0\mathbf{k}_l^{\mathrm{Rx}}\cdot\mathbf{r}^{\mathrm{Rx}}}. \quad (5)$$

This equation is the generalized form of a complex baseband space-time channel. It is not commonly encountered in literature, as the actual applications are mainly interested in the finite set of points $\left\{\mathbf{r}_n^{\mathrm{Tx}}\right\}$ and $\left\{\mathbf{r}_m^{\mathrm{Rx}}\right\}$, where the n = 1,2,...,N transmitters and the m = 1,2,...,M receivers are located, for the case of MIMO systems with M×N transceivers. Using (5) for a MIMO system, the previous expression becomes:

$$h\left(t,\tau,\mathbf{r}_n^{\mathrm{Tx}},\mathbf{r}_m^{\mathrm{Rx}}\right)=\sum_{l=1}^{L_p}A_l\delta\left(\tau-\tau_l\right)e^{-j\nu_l t-j\theta_l^c}e^{-jk_0\mathbf{k}_l^{\mathrm{Tx}}\cdot\mathbf{r}_n^{\mathrm{Tx}}}e^{-jk_0\mathbf{k}_l^{\mathrm{Rx}}\cdot\mathbf{r}_m^{\mathrm{Rx}}}. \quad (6)$$

Arranging the last expression for each of the M×N values in a matrix $\mathbf{H}\left(t,\tau\right)$ of M rows by N columns entries of two variables each, we have the MIMO channel model useful for system simulations:

$$\left\{\mathbf{H}\left(t,\tau\right)\right\}_{m,n}=h\left(t,\tau,\mathbf{r}_n^{\mathrm{Tx}},\mathbf{r}_m^{\mathrm{Rx}}\right);\quad m=1,2,\ldots,\mathrm{M};\quad n=1,2,\ldots,\mathrm{N}. \quad (7)$$

Equation (7) shows that general MIMO case can be seen as a set of SISO channels for each pair of transmitter and receiver antennas. Therefore a MIMO simulator needs to implement a set of M×N SISO channels in a structure as the one shown in Fig. 3, where $h_{m,n}\left(t,\tau\right)$ represents the SISO channel between antenna n at Tx and antenna m at Rx, while $x_1,\ldots,x_N$ and

$y_1,\ldots,y_M$, represent the respective input and output signals. All signals from the Tx antennas arriving at one Rx antenna must be added to generate the corresponding Rx output.

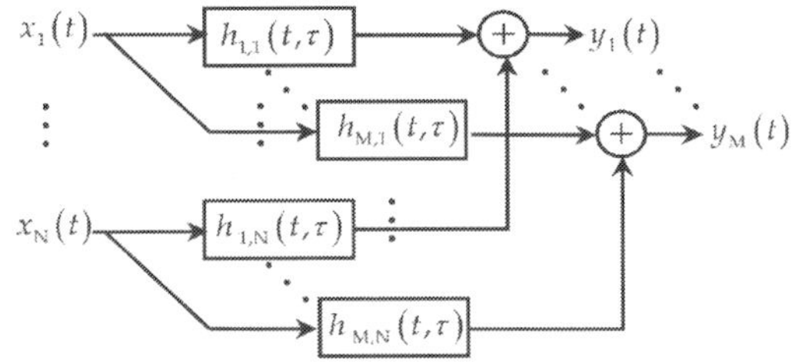

Fig. 3. Structure of a MIMO simulator.

Equation (6) can be simplified to gain insight, considering only linear arrays, located as shown in the Fig. 2 along $\hat{\mathbf{y}}$ direction. With this approach the channel impulse response of the system is measured in the positions r^{Rx} for signals transmitted along positions r^{Tx}:

$$h\left(t,\tau,r^{Tx},r^{Rx}\right)=\sum_{l=1}^{L_p}A_l\delta\left(\tau-\tau_l\right)e^{-j\nu_l t-j\theta_l^c}e^{-jk_0 sin(\varphi_l)r^{Tx}}e^{-jk_0 sin(\varphi_l)r^{Rx}}\ . \tag{8}$$

Or in its general form as:

$$h\left(t,\tau,r^{Tx},r^{Rx}\right)=\sum_{l=1}^{L_p}A_l\delta\left(\tau-\tau_l\right)e^{-j\nu_l t-j\theta_l^c}e^{-jk_l^{Tx}r^{Tx}}e^{-jk_l^{Rx}r^{Rx}}\ . \tag{9}$$

2.2 Simplified channel description by use of angle domains

Taking the Fourier transform of (9) with respect to r^{Tx} and r^{Rx}, we reach the spatial channel expressed in the wavenumber domain, as is explained in detail in (Durgin, 2003):

$$h\left(t,\tau,k^{Tx},k^{Rx}\right)=\sum_{l=1}^{L_p}A_l\delta\left(\tau-\tau_l\right)\delta\left(k^{Tx}-k_l^{Tx}\right)\delta\left(k^{Rx}-k_l^{Rx}\right)e^{-j\nu_l t-j\theta_l^c}\ . \tag{10}$$

In the last expression, it could be considered that all shifts in the wavenumbers should be positive, however, eq. (10) is utilized in accordance with expressions commonly found in literature. This can be used without lose of generality, as the final expression does not depend on this sign. Instead of using an expression that depends on the wavenumber, the most common expressions found are channel impulse responses (CIR) given in terms of the AoD and the AoA. By supposing that the entire propagation scenario lies in a plane with only the azimuth angle taken into consideration (a 2-dimensional propagation environment) we arrive to the following form of the angular dependant CIR,

$$h\left(t,\tau,\varphi^{Tx},\varphi^{Rx}\right)=\sum_{l=1}^{L_p}A_l\delta\left(\tau-\tau_l\right)\delta\left(\varphi^{Tx}-\varphi_l^{Tx}\right)\delta\left(\varphi^{Rx}-\varphi_l^{Rx}\right)e^{-j\nu_l t-j\theta_l^c}\ ; \tag{11}$$

where φ^{Tx} and φ^{Rx} are the azimuth angle variables as shown in Fig. 2, while φ_l^{Tx} and φ_l^{Rx} represents the azimuth AoD and AoA of the l-path, respectively. Equation (11) is rather simple, but can be made even simpler by taking its Fourier transform with respect to the t variable, to construct what have been called the double-direction channel model by (Steinbauer et al., 2001):

$$h\left(\nu,\tau,\varphi^{\mathrm{Tx}},\varphi^{\mathrm{Rx}}\right)=\sum_{l=1}^{L_p}A_l e^{-j\theta_l^c}\delta\left(\tau-\tau_l\right)\delta\left(\varphi^{\mathrm{Tx}}-\varphi_l^{\mathrm{Tx}}\right)\delta\left(\varphi^{\mathrm{Rx}}-\varphi_l^{\mathrm{Rx}}\right)\delta\left(\nu-\nu_l\right). \tag{12}$$

This expression is really easy to interpret: the radio channel is composed of paths that starts from φ_l^{Tx} degrees away the reference angle at the normal of the array, where during its traveling from Tx to Rx, suffer a delay τ_l with respect to the first incoming wave, and suffers a frequency shift ν_l from the carrier frequency, and arrives at Rx forming an angle φ_l^{Rx} with the normal of the array at the receiver side.

It is possible to pass from (12) to the MIMO channel defined in equation (7), via the transformation from the angle domains to the wavenumber domains and then to the space domain. This approach will be clarified in the subsection 2.4. In this paragraph a direct approach will be considered.

For linear arrays the variables r^{Tx} and r^{Rx} can be sampled in the values that define the location of the antennas. In this case, it can be considered the phase difference corresponding to the AoD and AoA of each path in the array, in a vector so-called the Array Manifold Vector (AMV) defined in (VanTrees, 2002). Using the AMV at each link end, the equation that connects realization in the angle domains with the MIMO channel is:

$$\mathbf{H}(t,\tau)=\sum_{l=1}^{L_p}A_l\delta\left(\tau-\tau_l\right)e^{-j\nu_l t-j\theta_l^c}V^{\mathrm{Tx}}\left(\varphi_l^{\mathrm{Tx}}\right)V^{\mathrm{Rx}}\left(\varphi_l^{\mathrm{Rx}}\right)^T; \tag{13}$$

where $V^{\mathrm{Tx(Rx)}}$ denotes the AMV at the transmitter Tx(Rx) side, respectively, and $(.)^T$ denotes the transposition operator. In the case of a linear antenna array and with the aid of (8), it becomes clear that the AMV takes the following form,

$$V^{\mathrm{Tx(Rx)}}\left(\varphi_l^{\mathrm{Tx(Rx)}}\right)=\left[1,\ e^{-\frac{2\pi j}{\lambda}d_1^{\mathrm{Tx(Rx)}}\sin\varphi_l^{\mathrm{Tx(Rx)}}}\ \cdots\ e^{-\frac{2\pi j}{\lambda}d_{\mathrm{N-1(M-1)}}^{\mathrm{Tx(Rx)}}\sin\varphi_l^{\mathrm{Tx(Rx)}}}\right]^T, \tag{14}$$

where $d_1^{\mathrm{Tx(Rx)}},\ldots,d_{\mathrm{N-1(M-1)}}^{\mathrm{Tx(Rx)}}$ denote the position of the antenna elements at the array at Tx and Rx, respectively. Each of these distances has been measured taking the first antenna of the array as the reference point.

An illustration of this approach will be presented to clarify the concepts: consider a 5x3 (N=3 antennas at Tx side and M=5 antennas at Rx side) MIMO system immersed in a propagation scenario which only has L_p = 3 paths, no one with Doppler shift, and its remaining parameters displayed in Table 1, where delays are expressed in μs, angles in degrees, and weights in volts. The Antennas are configured in a linear array spaced half wavelength.

l-path	Delay τ_l	Weight A_l	AoD φ_l^{Tx}	AoA φ_l^{Rx}
1	0	.5+.3j	-10	-20
2	3	1+0j	5	10
3	6	.8-.5j	20	50

Table 1. Parameters of an example to construct a MIMO channel realization

Using (13), the MIMO channel realization for all the time considered in a block of data consists of three matrices (assuming infinite bandwidth), each one for each of the delays considered. The result for the complex baseband channel for the delay at the second path is presented in the following table. Additionally, the channel realization for the SISO link established in $\mathbf{H}(\tau)_{3,2}$ is, considering infinite channel bandwidth and sampling each microsecond: [-0.5806 - 0.0543*j*, 0, 0, *0.2045 - 0.9789j*, 0, 0, 0.9309 - 0.1532*j*] for all *t*.

Tx\Rx Antenna	1	2	3	4	5
1	1.0000	0.8549 - 0.5189*j*	0.4615 - 0.8871*j*	-0.0658 - 0.9978*j*	-0.5740 - 0.8189*j*
2	0.9627 - 0.2704*j*	0.6827 - 0.7307*j*	0.2045 - 0.9789*j*	-0.3331 - 0.9429*j*	-0.7740 - 0.6332*j*
3	0.8538 - 0.5207*j*	0.4597 - 0.8881*j*	-0.0678 - 0.9977*j*	-0.5757 - 0.8177*j*	-0.9164 - 0.4003*j*

Table 2. Parameters of the channel realization $\mathbf{H}(t,\tau)^T$ for τ=3μs at any *t*

In Table 2, **H**(.) of size M×N have been presented transposed. It is important to stress here, that with the former discussion, given channel realizations in the angle domains, channel realization at the space domain can be carried out.

2.3 Statistical description of the MIMO Radio Channel

As $\theta_l^c = \omega_c \tau_l$ is the phase of the received carrier wave, and each delay is not commensurate with the carrier wave period, this quantity should be regarded as random and uniform between [-π,π), as discussed in detail in (Kennedy, 1969). It can be considered that several paths are clustering into a set of *L* principal paths, and then, the summation in (10) can be represented for the channel expressed in the wavenumber domains and the angular domains as (15) and (16), respectively:

$$h\left(t,\tau,k^{\text{Tx}},k^{\text{Rx}}\right)=\sum_{l=1}^{L}\alpha_l^k\delta\left(\tau-\tau_l\right)\delta\left(k^{\text{Tx}}-k_l^{\text{Tx}}\right)\delta\left(k^{\text{Rx}}-k_l^{\text{Rx}}\right)e^{-j\nu_l t}, \tag{15}$$

$$h\left(t,\tau,\varphi^{\text{Tx}},\varphi^{\text{Rx}}\right)=\sum_{l=1}^{L}\alpha_l\delta\left(\tau-\tau_l\right)\delta\left(\varphi^{\text{Tx}}-\varphi_l^{\text{Tx}}\right)\delta\left(\varphi^{\text{Rx}}-\varphi_l^{\text{Rx}}\right)e^{-j\nu_l t}. \tag{16}$$

Where α_l, α_l^k are complex Gaussian random variables with zero mean, and was obtained from the sum of several complex sinusoids within the same cluster (paths that departs mainly from the same angle, arrive at the same angle, suffers almost the same delay and Doppler shift, but traveled by separate ways). Those sums involves the sum of complex exponential with random phase, which rapidly tends to a Gaussian distribution, provided in practice that we deal with more than five waves (Pätzold, 2002). It is worthwhile to note that the main difference within α_l and α_l^k are their variances.

Transforming equation (15) in the sense of Fourier for the *t* variable, we arrive to the stochastic model in the wavenumber, delay and Doppler domains:

$$h\left(\nu,\tau,k^{\mathrm{Tx}},k^{\mathrm{Rx}}\right)=\sum_{l=1}^{L}\alpha_l^k\delta\left(\tau-\tau_l\right)\delta\left(\nu-\nu_l\right)\delta\left(k^{\mathrm{Tx}}-k_l^{\mathrm{Tx}}\right)\delta\left(k^{\mathrm{Rx}}-k_l^{\mathrm{Rx}}\right). \tag{17}$$

And applying the same transformation in (16) we arrive to the stochastic description of the bi-directional channel model:

$$h\left(\nu,\tau,\varphi^{\mathrm{Tx}},\varphi^{\mathrm{Rx}}\right)=\sum_{l=1}^{L}\alpha_l\delta\left(\tau-\tau_l\right)\delta\left(\nu-\nu_l\right)\delta\left(\varphi^{\mathrm{Tx}}-\varphi_l^{\mathrm{Tx}}\right)\delta\left(\varphi^{\mathrm{Rx}}-\varphi_l^{\mathrm{Rx}}\right). \tag{18}$$

For Gaussian processes, second order statistics completely describes the process. We hereafter consider only the double-directional channel model, but the same results directly apply to the model expressed by equation (17), that is dependent on wavenumber domains. The connection between correlation of the former expressions, i.e. the one that depends in angles and the one that depends on wavenumbers, will be explained in the following section.

Taking the autocorrelation function of last equation, we arrive to a multidimensional function than can be called the Multidimensional Power Density Spectrum of the double-directional (bi-directional) channel (MPDSB) $S_{Bh}(.)$:

$$S_{Bh}\left(\nu,\upsilon';\tau,\tau';\varphi^{\mathrm{Tx}},\varphi^{\mathrm{Tx}\,\prime};\varphi^{\mathrm{Rx}},\varphi^{\mathrm{Rx}\,\prime}\right)=E\left\{h\left(\nu,\tau,\varphi^{\mathrm{Tx}},\varphi^{\mathrm{Rx}}\right)h^{*}\left(\nu',\tau',\varphi^{\mathrm{Tx}\,\prime},\varphi^{\mathrm{Rx}\,\prime}\right)\right\}; \tag{19}$$

where $E\{.\}$ is the expected value operator and $(.)^*$ is the complex conjugate operator. The apostrophes are utilized to define auxiliary variables for each domain. This autocorrelation function is too complex to be treated, and its information is hard to count with. It is justified in (Durgin, 2003) that the channel can be regarded for several scenarios as uncorrelated in all domains, the last expression can then be expressed in terms of fewer variables, here called as the Multidimensional Scattering Function of the Bidirectional Channel (MSFB) $S_B(.)$ in the following way:

$$S_{Bh}\left(\nu,\upsilon';\tau,\tau';\varphi^{\mathrm{Tx}},\varphi^{\mathrm{Tx}\,\prime};\varphi^{\mathrm{Rx}},\varphi^{\mathrm{Rx}\,\prime}\right)=S_B\left(\nu,\tau,\varphi^{\mathrm{Tx}}\varphi^{\mathrm{Rx}}\right)\delta\left(\tau-\tau'\right)\delta\left(\nu-\nu'\right)\delta\left(\varphi^{\mathrm{Tx}}-\varphi^{\mathrm{Tx}\,\prime}\right)\delta\left(\varphi^{\mathrm{Rx}}-\varphi^{\mathrm{Rx}\,\prime}\right). \tag{20}$$

Which considering only the values where the last function is different from zero (the diagonals of each correlation in the domains of each variable and its auxiliary variable) collapses in the multipath description to:

$$S_B\left(\nu,\tau,\varphi^{\mathrm{Tx}},\varphi^{\mathrm{Rx}}\right)=\sum_{l=1}^{L}\sigma_l\delta\left(\tau-\tau_l\right)\delta\left(\nu-\nu_l\right)\delta\left(\varphi^{\mathrm{Tx}}-\varphi_l^{\mathrm{Tx}}\right)\delta\left(\varphi^{\mathrm{Rx}}-\varphi_l^{\mathrm{Rx}}\right). \tag{21}$$

In the last equation, $\sigma_l=E\left\{\alpha_l\alpha_l^{*}\right\}$ is the variance of the l-path. The taken simplification had assumed that all l-paths are uncorrelated between them, which in turn implies that in their dual domains are all stationary (Bello, 1963). These MSFB though is a simplification of the MPDSB is still complex to be measured and characterized; so, it is not strange to encounter partial description of it.

First of all, it will be taken into account only the temporal variables in the MSFB, which can be achieved via the integration of (21) for all AoA and AoD. This function can be also defined by taking the average intensity profile in the delay and Doppler variables for each SISO link in the MIMO channel. Using this delay and Doppler statistic information, it has been defined the well known Scattering Function (SF). This function provides a distribution of the signal-strength averages, for all incoming paths, in terms of delays and frequency shifts. An example of it is illustrated in Fig. (4a). The plotted SF has been taken from the COST-BU channel standard (COST 207, 1989) and the path energies have been normalized to the maximum energy. The delay axis (τ) is graded in μs, while the Doppler shift axis (ν) is in Hz. In the figure, the SF has been further simplified into a set of identifiable paths via paths integration for paths in the neighborhood of the chosen delay for the main path. The Doppler Spectrum of each path is shown in Fig. (4b), while its average power is plotted in Fig. (4c).

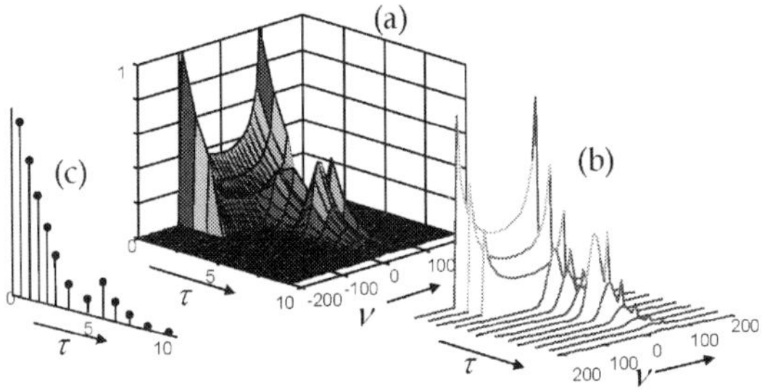

Fig. 4. The SF and its simplification by integration into finite set of paths.

Other simplification of the MSFB can provide only the information of the angular variables, which can be obtained through integration of the MSFB for all delays and Doppler shifts, as in:

$$\int_{\upsilon}\int_{\tau} S_B\left(\nu,\tau,\varphi^{\mathrm{Tx}},\varphi^{\mathrm{Rx}}\right) d\nu\, d\tau = S\left(\varphi^{\mathrm{Tx}},\varphi^{\mathrm{Rx}}\right); \tag{22}$$

the resulting functions can be called the Cross Power Azimuth Spectrum (xPAS). This function specifies what is the PAS at Rx for the transmitted signal at each angle at Tx. An example of a PAS is given in Fig. (5a). Integrating the MSFB for all angles at the transmitter side and all Doppler Shifts. The resulting function is called the Azimuth-Delay Power Spectrum (ADPS) function, and it provides the average profile for paths at each delay and azimuth AoA. See for instance Fig. (5b). On averaging the ADPS function for all delays, we obtain the PAS, while on averaging all the AoAs we obtain the Power Delay Profile (PDP). These two profiles are shown in Figs. (5a & c), respectively.

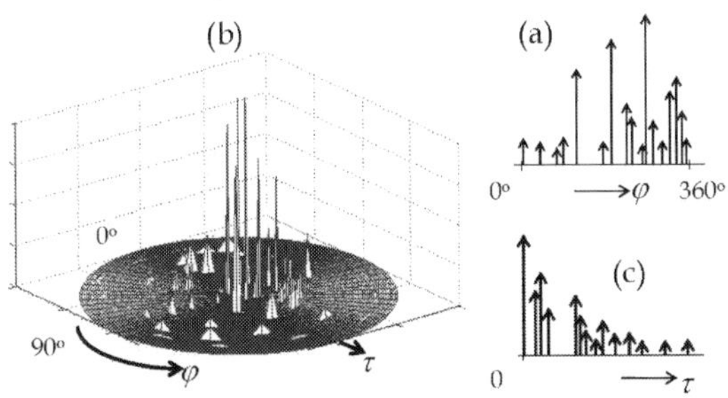

Fig. 5. Multipath intensity profile for angle and delay variables.

If in the explanation, it would have been utilized the channel function that depends on the wavenumbers, we had arrived to the Multidimensional Power Density Spectrum of the Spatial Channel (MPDSS). Using the uncorrelated assumption, its simplification in terms of the Multidimensional Scattering Function of the Spatial Channel (MSFS) $S_S(.)$ would be reached. From this expression, it is possible to integrate the MSFS for delay and Doppler variables, to obtain the cross Wavenumber Spectrum (xWNS), in the following way:

$$\int_{\upsilon}\int_{\tau} S_S\left(\nu,\tau,k^{\mathrm{Tx}},k^{\mathrm{Rx}}\right) d\nu d\tau = S\left(k^{\mathrm{Tx}},k^{\mathrm{Rx}}\right). \tag{23}$$

2.4 The Gans Mapping tool to pass from PAS functions to WNS

It has been already discussed how to pass from channel realization in the angular domain, to channel realizations in the spatial domain: through the use of the AMV. If the channel realizations are performed in the wavenumber or wavevector domains, the connection to the spatial domain is via a Fourier transform. In this subsection, it will be discussed how to connect PAS and WNS with autocorrelations in the space domain.

The Gans Mapping tool (GM), relate the expressions between angle and spatial domains. It was proposed in (Gans, 1972), but reintroduced in the modeling literature by Durgin; see (Durgin, 2003) and references there in. As it has been discussed, the PAS is one of the most important concepts in spatial channel modeling since it provides a simpler and more intuitive way to characterize the spatial channel than in terms of WNS. In its detriment, we can mention that the PAS is not the natural domain for relating spectral properties to spatial selectivity in a channel. Therefore, the PAS must be converted to a wavevector spectrum (or in this case WNS) whenever spatial correlations, spectral spreads or duality results are calculated. This means, having some PAS, the WNS can be obtained through GM and then the Spatial Correlation Function (SCF) is calculated via the Fourier transform of the WNS. It should be noticed that the information of spatial channels is not commonly provided in standards or sounding campaigns; instead of this, PAS functions are considered in the sounding measurement campaigns.

Given a (one dimensional) PAS $p(\varphi)$, it is possible to calculate the corresponding WNS by:

$$S(k) = 2\pi \frac{p\left(\varphi_{RG} + \cos^{-1}(k/k_0)\right) + p\left(\varphi_{RG} - \cos^{-1}(k/k_0)\right)}{\sqrt{k_0 - k^2}}. \tag{24}$$

where φ_{RG} is the azimuthal direction of movement, $S(k)$ is the WNS, and $|k| \le k_0$. These parameters are graphically shown with the aid of Fig. 6.

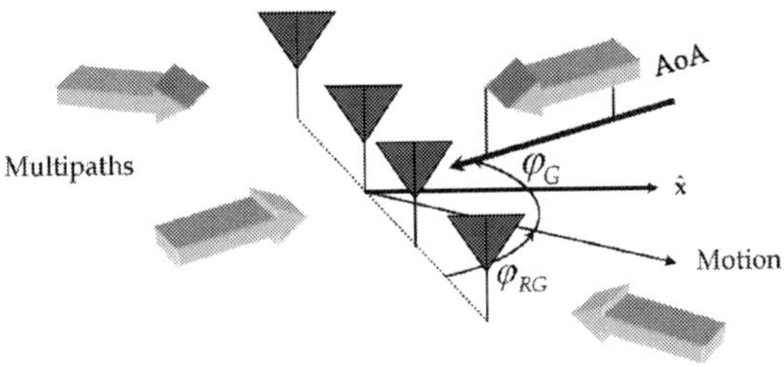

Fig. 6. The multipath components arriving at the antenna array.

The mapping given at equation (24) has a straight-forward physical interpretation from the propagation shown at Fig. 6. A multipath of plane wave arrives from the horizon at an angle φ_G and the direction of azimuthally motion that we wish to map is φ_{RG}. The phase progression of this multipath wave is the free space wavenumber $k_0 = 2\pi / \lambda$. However, to a receiver moving along the φ_{RG} direction, the actual wavenumber appears to be foreshortened by the factor $k_0 \cos(\varphi_G - \varphi_{RG})$ (Durgin, 2003). This mapping was utilized to analyze Doppler Spectra of a single Antenna considering some PAS and receiver movement. But it can be also utilized to analyze the WNS of an antenna array considering that the receiver array is located in the direction of the movement (or vice versa). Comparing this figure with Fig. 2, it becomes clear that φ_G in Fig. 6 is $\varphi + 90^{\circ}$ in Fig. 2.

Fig. 7 shows an example of the GM application. The particular form of the PAS is shown in Fig. (7a). The associated WNS in Fig. (7b) is obtained directly from the use of the GM over the PAS. The real and imaginary parts of the SCF (Fig. (7c) and Fig. (7d), respectively) are finally obtained through a Fourier transform on the WNS; a comparison to the result given in terms of closed form expression at (Salz & Winters, 1994) is also included in Fig. (7c) and (7d). In (Alcocer-Ochoa et al., 2008) the same SCF was presented with the use of the AMV.

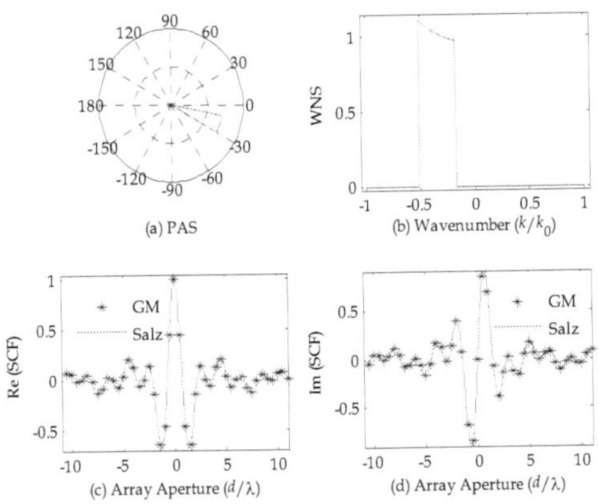

Fig. 7. The WNS and its SCF for a limited uniform distributed PAS.

Another approach to calculate the SCF is by departing from the PAS; it is performed by using the AMV. Consider that channel realizations only depends on the angular variables for ease of explanation:

$$h\left(\varphi^{\mathrm{Tx}},\varphi^{\mathrm{Rx}}\right)=\sum_{l=1}^{L}\alpha_l\delta\left(\varphi^{\mathrm{Tx}}-\varphi_l^{\mathrm{Tx}}\right)\delta\left(\varphi^{\mathrm{Rx}}-\varphi_l^{\mathrm{Rx}}\right). \tag{25}$$

The spatial values can be obtained with the use of the AMV. Consider the case of sampled points in the space for the construction of a MIMO channel, then:

$$\mathbf{H}=\sum_{l=1}^{L}\alpha_l V^{\mathrm{Tx}}\left(\varphi^{\mathrm{Tx}}{}_l\right)V^{\mathrm{Rx}}\left(\varphi^{\mathrm{Rx}}{}_l\right)^T. \tag{26}$$

The spatial autocorrelation tensor of the MIMO function R_H can be obtained through:

$$R_H=E\left\{H\times H^H\right\}=E\left\{\sum_{l=1}^{L}\alpha_l V^{\mathrm{Tx}}\left(\varphi^{\mathrm{Tx}}{}_l\right)V^{\mathrm{Rx}}\left(\varphi^{\mathrm{Rx}}{}_l\right)^T\times\left(\sum_{l'=1}^{L}\alpha_{l'}V^{\mathrm{Tx}'}\left(\varphi^{\mathrm{Tx}'}{}_{l'}\right)V^{\mathrm{Rx}'}\left(\varphi^{\mathrm{Rx}'}{}_{l'}\right)^T\right)^H\right\}. \tag{27}$$

Where $(.)^H$ denotes conjugate transpose (Hermitian), ($\times$) stands for the outer product, and the variables with the apostrophe are auxiliary variables. Invoking the uncorrelated assumption, we finally arrive to:

$$R_H=\sum_{l=1}^{L}\sigma_l V^{Tx}\left(\varphi^{Tx}{}_l\right)V^{Tx}\left(\varphi^{Tx}{}_l\right)^H\times V^{Rx}\left(\varphi^{Rx}{}_l\right)V^{Rx}\left(\varphi^{Rx}{}_l\right)^H. \tag{28}$$

In the last equation, we have used the fact that $V^{\mathrm{Tx}}\left(\varphi^{\mathrm{Tx}}{}_l\right)V^{\mathrm{Rx}}\left(\varphi^{\mathrm{Rx}}{}_l\right)^T$ are also external products. It is worthwhile to mention that the results of the sums on $V^{\mathrm{Tx}}\left(\varphi^{\mathrm{Tx}}{}_l\right)V^{\mathrm{Tx}}\left(\varphi^{\mathrm{Tx}}{}_l\right)^H$ become matrices of dimension N×N, and then R_H is a tensor of (M×N) ×(M×N) entries.

2.5 Determination of the channel modeling and simulation problem

From last expressions, it can now be state the problem that concerns channel modeling and simulation:

Channel Modeling: To conceive propagation models and mathematical expressions that justifies the shapes of the measured statistics in the MSFB. It means people focused on channel modeling area had tried to answer the following questions: Why in an urban environment the time correlation function tends to a Bessel Function? Which scattering model is underlying when the received PAS is Gaussian type?

Simulation: To conceive expressions based on the channel models which lead to mathematical expressions and algorithms suitable for its implementation as SW routines or HW implementations. People related to simulation of channels try to figure out how to produce channel realizations with prescribed statistics for all variables of interest; i.e. angles, time delay, etc.

It is worthwhile to note that in the previous discussion, it has been followed a channel representation consisting of a finite number of paths; this approach cannot be directly utilized when the channel behaves as a continuum in the variable of interest; i.e. when the PAS is a continuous function. Approaches to overcome this problem will be discussed.

Another subject of simulation is to perform the process in the best (economical) way. In HW implementation, it´s also a matter of research to settle what other trade-offs should be taken into account to guarantee the emulators will provide the same results than obtained in SW (which have infinite variable resolution).
In the remaining of this chapter, we will be concerned with only the spatial characteristics of the channel. We will also be restricted to linear arrays of finite dimension.

3. The channel modeling approaches in literature

The spatio-temporal models can be generally classified into two groups: deterministic and stochastic (Molisch, 2004).
Within the deterministic models, the CIR is obtained by tracing the reflected, diffracted and scattered rays, with the help of databases that provide information about the size and location of the physical structures in addition to the electromagnetic properties of their materials. Deterministic models have the advantage of providing the ability to generate accurate site specific and easily reproducible information; it is also helpful to propose some environment and to measure whatever it supplies.
Stochastic models, on the other hand, describe characteristics of the radio channel by means of the joint PDF and/or correlation functions. Statistical parameters employed in such models are usually estimated from extensive measurement campaigns or inferred from electromagnetic laws and geometrical assumptions. Stochastic models usually need less information than deterministic ones, and produce more general results, as many repetitions are considered.
There are many works related to this approaches, where classifications of the several approaches can be found, such as (Piechocki et al., 2001) and (Molisch et al., 2006). In what follows, we will discuss only one approach of determinist modeling, the geometrical modeling, and only one approach of stochastic modeling, which is the method of artificial paths. The rationale behind this is that geometrical models are useful to provide information that can be interpreted as MDSF, or ADPS, PAS, PDP, etc. In the other hand, the method of artificial paths provides the underlying approach to construct the best simulators, and they only depend on the commented profiles. With these two approaches, a MIMO simulator can be entirely constructed.

3.1 Geometrical modeling

The geometrical model tries to explain or construct functions that reflect the average behavior of the multipath phenomena in some environment, such as a PAS, by establishing a Tx and Rx in a scenario surrounded by scatterers. The spatial pattern of scatters is the principal actor in producing the statistics in the multipath, and thus, its specification and relation to real environments are of great interest.
A scatterer is an omni-directional reradiating element whereby the plane wave, on arrival, is assumed to be reflected directly to the mobile receiver antenna or to another scatterer without the influence from any other (Petrus, 2002).
Most of the existing geometric channel models take into account only the local scattering clusters as in (Ertel & Reed, 1999), which are always located around the mobile station (MS) with few available models defining the shape and distribution of far (or dominant) clusters. The geometrical channel models are well suited for simulations that require a complete

model of the wireless channel, due to its ray-tracing nature. However, the shape and size of the scatterers' PDF required to achieve a reliable simulation of the propagation phenomenon is still subject to debate.

If only one discrete scatterer is present (the Single Scattering Model in (Laurila et al., 1998)), a closed form expression can be easily found from the signal at the receiver by using fundamental wave propagation and scattering laws. However, if many objects are present, things become much more complicated, since the interaction between different objects must be accounted for. As an example, consider the scenario showed at Fig. 8; in there, the MS is surrounded by scatterers uniformly distributed. This scenario can be observed when the antenna at the base station at Tx is high enough, so there are no scatterers surrounding it, like in the cellular environment. In order to simplify the analysis, it will be assumed that the scatterers only change the direction of the impinging waves. The parameters of interest in this scenario are the Delay or Time of Arrival (ToA) and the AoA (φ_l^{Rx}, in Fig. 8) Probability Density Functions (PDF). Those PDFs will be calculated from the AoD (φ_l^{Tx}, in Fig. 8) and the position r of the scatterers. Finally, D in Fig. 8 correspond to distance from Tx to Rx. Note that the joint PDFs of the ToA and AoA can be directly interpreted as the ADPS, and then, from this function a SCF can be obtained.

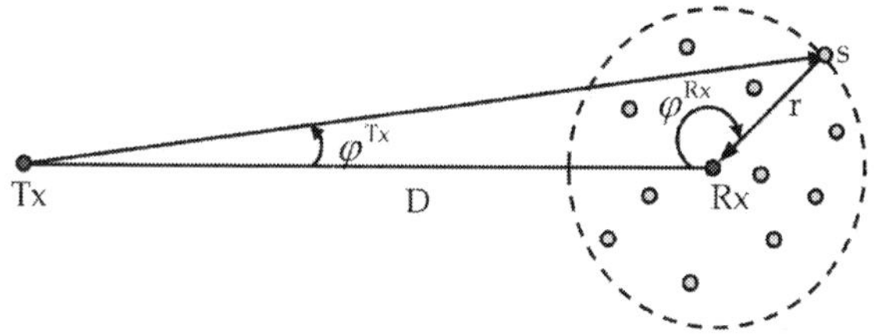

Fig. 8. Uniformly distributed scatterers around the Rx.

In order to obtain the joint ToA and AoA PDFs for this scenario, we consider the comments made in (Laurila et al., 1998) as well as the PDF transformation rules described in (Papoulis & Pillai, 2002). In such case, the joint Delay and AoA PDF is given by

$$p\left(c\tau,\varphi^{Rx}\right)=\frac{1}{\left(R^{Rx}\right)^2}\frac{\left[\left(c\tau\right)^2+D^2\right]p\left(\varphi^{Tx}\right)}{\left(c\tau\right)-D\cos\left(\varphi^{Rx}\right)}\left|J\left(c\tau,\varphi^{Rx}\right)\right|, \tag{29}$$

where the Jacobian of the transformation $J(c\tau,\varphi^{Rx})$ is defined below, and R^{Rx} denotes the radii where the scatterers lie in.

$$J\left(c\tau,\varphi^{Rx}\right)=\frac{\left(c\tau\right)^4-3\left(c\tau\right)^2D^2+2\left(c\tau\right)D\left[D^2-\left(c\tau\right)^2\right]\cos\left(\varphi^{Rx}\right)+D^2\left[\left(c\tau\right)^2+D^2\right]\cos\left(2\varphi^{Rx}\right)}{2\left[\left(c\tau\right)-D\cos\left(\varphi^{Rx}\right)\right]^2\left[D^2+\left(c\tau\right)^2-2\left(c\tau\right)D\cos\left(\varphi^{Rx}\right)\right]}. \tag{30}$$

Fig. 9 shows a plot of this joint PDF supposing a uniform AoD distribution, R = 30 m is the radio where the scatterers lie, and also D = 500 m, typical values for picocell scenarios.

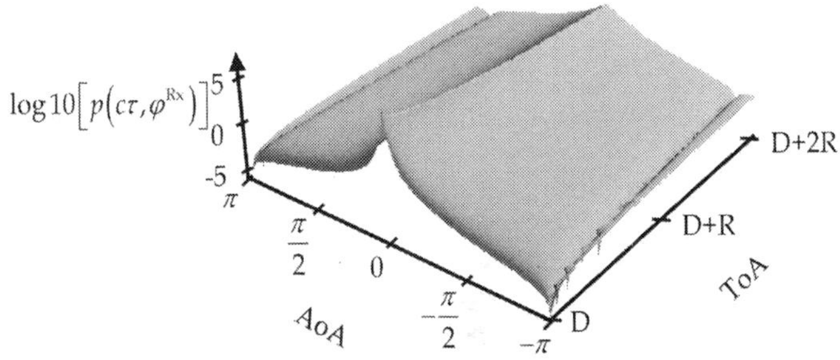

Fig. 9. The joint Delay and AoA for the scenario presented in Fig. 8.

From the previous figure, it seems that the most probable arrivals are those with a relatively low AoA. Observe also that integrating the function for all time delay, a PAS can be conceived. In this case, the PAS closely resemblance to a Gaussian type function, while the PDP can be well approximated by a decaying exponential functions, which is in agreement with common propagation standards, such as COST Typical Urban. Note also that the space and time delay domains are not separable.

Finally, the PDF analysis with the Jacobian method takes into account only those scatterers which are directly illuminated and neglects those which are not. A uniform spatial distribution of scatterers does not lead to a uniform distribution for the AoA. Actually, those distributions of scatterers that lead to this special case of the AoA are difficult to justify physically (Fuhl et al., 1998).

3.2 Method of artificial paths

It has been stated through this Chapter, that when the channel is composed of a finite number of paths, its statistics and calculation of the SCF are easy to obtain. However, when the number of physical paths is large, the direct approach cannot be longer used. This could happen, for example if the channel behaves as a continuum instead of identifiable paths. In such environments, we can model the channel as if it were composed by a finite number of paths, with no physical meaning, but reduced in number. In this case, the channel can be expressed as:

$$h\left(\varphi^{\mathrm{Tx}},\varphi^{\mathrm{Rx}}\right)=\sum_{c=1}^{C}\beta_c\psi_c\left(\varphi^{\mathrm{Tx}},\varphi^{\mathrm{Rx}}\right), \tag{31}$$

where β_c are the complex weights of the artificial paths, and are complex Gaussian random variables; c=1,2...,C is the indexing variable and C denotes the number of terms utilized in the approximation. Functions $\psi_c\left(\varphi^{\mathrm{Tx}},\varphi^{\mathrm{Rx}}\right)$ are the artificial paths. Note that with this model, the paths could not be deltas, it means, they could not point to a specific angle; besides this, there are not guarantee that these complex paths are uncorrelated. The main problem of this approach consists in defining the complex paths and the statistics of its weights in order to be capable to generate channel realizations with the same first and second order statistics that the targeted channel. The approach of these artificial paths was defined long ago in the time-delay domain, see for instance (Fechtel, 1993) and (Parra-Michel et al., 2003); although it has been proved to be a good modeling method for the variables of the space channels, as shown in (Kontorovich et al., 2008).

4. Simulation and Emulation construction of Channel models

In what follows, we will discuss how simulators can be constructed from the channel models discussed.

4.1 Statistical Paths generation

This is a rather simple approach to generate MIMO CIR realizations at the literature (Molisch, 2004). For the spatial domain this approach consist on the generation of ray paths with an Angle of Departure (AoD) and an Angle of Arrival (AoA) by random variable realizations following the suggested statistics at the standards. This statistics can be drawn from information provided by geometrical models, although the converse is also useful: generation of paths with some statistics in the AoD and upon defining some scatterers' distribution, new statistics at Rx can be devised with the aid of simulations. This approach is complementary to the analytical case illustrated in the geometrical models.

To generate realizations of a random variable with a predefined PDF $f(\varphi)$, we use the general method described in (Papoulis & Pillai, 2002), which works as follows: once the PDF is chosen, the Cumulative Distribution Function (CDF) $F(\varphi)$ must be calculated by a simple integration. A plot of a Gaussian CDF is presented in Fig. 10. The method says that once we have a uniformly distributed random variable realization, u ∈ [0, 1], the result from v=$F^{-1}(\text{u})$, will follow the predefined PDF.

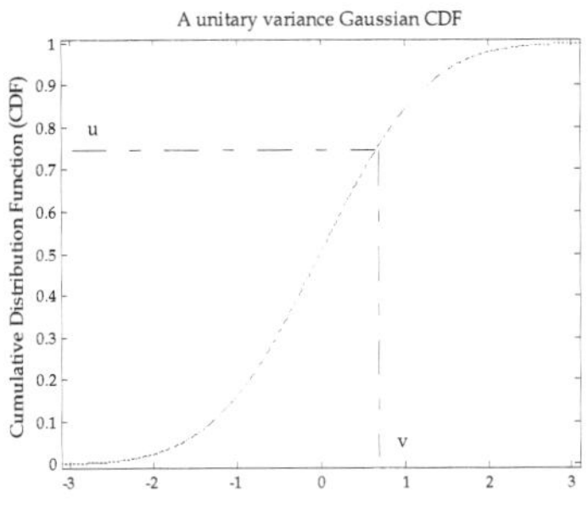

Fig. 10. A CDF calculated from a unitary variance Gaussian PDF.

As an example for the use of the general method, let us consider a 6 path ray tracing scenario which follows a Gaussian distribution. With the use of the Fig. 10, we toss 6 uniformly distributed random variable realizations: [0.9171; 0.7582; 0.8870; 0.0688; 0.1835; 0.7371], then the associated Gaussian distributed random variables are: [1.3802; 0.6989; 1.2068; -1.4799; -0.8999; 0.6329]. Multiplying this result with the desired variance will yield the desired values. The main advantage of the MIMO CIR realizations method described above, is its intuitive and easy way to generate CIR realizations with the desired statistics. In the literature there is a set of functions proposed for the AoA and ToA modeling, which mainly depend on the propagation scenario. The list of the most used forms AoA PDF in Table 3, where Erf(·) is the Error function and $I_0(\cdot)$ is the 0th order modified Bessel function.

Name	*Formula*	*Parameters*	
Uniform	$f(\varphi)=\dfrac{1}{\varphi_{mx}-\varphi_{mn}}, \quad \varphi_{mn}<\varphi\leq\varphi_{mx}$	Interval: $(\varphi_{mn},\varphi_{mx}]$	(f1)
Laplacian	$f(\varphi)=\dfrac{e^{-\frac{1}{\kappa}\lvert\varphi\rvert}}{2\kappa(1-e^{-\frac{\pi}{\kappa}})}, \quad -\pi<\varphi\leq\pi$	Decay Parameter: κ	(f2)
Gaussian	$f(\varphi)=\dfrac{e^{-\frac{1}{2\sigma^2}\varphi^2}}{\sqrt{2\pi\sigma^2}\,Erf\left(\frac{\pi}{\sqrt{2\pi\sigma^2}}\right)}, \quad -\pi<\varphi\leq\pi$	Variance: σ^2	(f3)
Von Mises	$f(\varphi)=\dfrac{e^{-\kappa\cos\varphi}}{2\pi I_0(\kappa)}, \quad -\pi<\varphi\leq\pi$	Parameter: κ	(f4)

Table 3. The most commonly used functional forms for the AoA

The 3GPP and 3GPP2 (3GPP, 2003), as an example, propose the use of the uniform distribution (f1) for the pedestrian and the truncated Laplacian distribution (f2) for the vehicular cases. For the urban and suburban macrocell environments, the standards recommend the use of a truncated Gaussian distribution (f3) and uniform distribution for the urban microcell environment. Many standards and recommendations suggest the use of these PDF for its use in several scenarios and operation frequencies. Clearly, the maximum angular spread depends on the particular scenario, and can be estimated from geometrical modeling of the radio propagation channel.
Even thought the von Mises PDF is not proposed at the standards, it has the advantage that approaches to a Gaussian distribution with variance $1/\kappa$ when κ is relatively large, approaches to a Laplacian distribution when κ is large; and when κ approaches to zero, a von Mises RV tends to be uniform distributed.

4.2 Paths integration

Within this approach, we can include those works intended to utilize the model of artificial paths, but using the delta functions for $\psi_c\left(\varphi^{\mathrm{Tx}},\varphi^{\mathrm{Rx}}\right)$. It means, the simulator still tries to reproduce the channel statistics but with an approximation as:

$$h\left(\varphi^{\mathrm{Tx}},\varphi^{\mathrm{Rx}}\right)=\sum_{c=1}^{C}\beta_c\delta\left(\varphi^{\mathrm{Tx}}-\varphi_c^{\mathrm{Tx}}\right)\delta_c\left(\varphi^{\mathrm{Rx}}-\varphi_c^{\mathrm{Rx}}\right), \tag{32}$$

where the problem now becomes the selection of weights and angles for the finite set of paths, for a given xPAS. Once given the sets of angles and weights, a channel realization is then composed via:

$$\mathbf{H}_{pl}=\sum_{c=1}^{C}\beta_C V_c^{\mathrm{Tx}}\left(\varphi_c^{\mathrm{Tx}}\right)V_c^{\mathrm{Rx}}\left(\varphi_c^{\mathrm{Rx}}\right)^T. \tag{33}$$

The general form of the approaches deal with separable functions in the angular domain, which means that xPAS can be represented via the outer product of two one-dimensional functions, in the way of:

$$S\left(\varphi^{\mathrm{Tx}},\varphi^{\mathrm{Rx}}\right)=S\left(\varphi^{\mathrm{Tx}}\right)S\left(\varphi^{\mathrm{Rx}}\right), \tag{34}$$

where each channel with a given PAS is then approximated via a set of reduced number of paths, for example, for the case of Tx it becomes:

$$h\left(\varphi^{\mathrm{Tx}}\right)=\sum_{c=1}^{C^{Tx}}\beta_c^{\mathrm{Tx}}\delta\left(\varphi^{\mathrm{Tx}}-\varphi_c^{\mathrm{Tx}}\right), \tag{35}$$

and each weight β_c^{Tx} is obtained by an integration of the physical paths, i.e.

$$\sigma_c^{\mathrm{Tx}}=E\left\{\beta_c^{\mathrm{Tx}}\left(\beta_c^{\mathrm{Tx}}\right)^*\right\}=\int_{\varphi_c}S\left(\varphi^{\mathrm{Tx}}\right). \tag{36}$$

Where the last equation means that the integration of paths assigns to the c-path some of the paths of the PAS. For example, we can select C_c^{Tx}, and the variance of each path equal to $1/C_c^{\mathrm{Tx}}$, and turn to find the set of values in the angle domain that delimitate the defined area. Finally, select the angle for the c-path that is at the middle of the integrated area. This method is known as Method of Equal Areas (MEA), and is discussed in detail in (Pätzold, 2002).

If we restrict the integration in such a way that the paths integrated for one of the artificial paths do not belong to any of the other artificial paths for all C_c^{Tx}, in this way, weights β_c^{Tx} are all uncorrelated and for the model we have presumed, Gaussian as well. Using this separable assumption, in the approximation of (32), each of the weights β_c have a variance equal to $\sigma_c^{\mathrm{Tx}}\sigma_c^{\mathrm{Rx}}$, where σ_c^{Rx} represents the variance of each path at the receiver side. Once we have selected the set of paths with variances and defined its angles, each MIMO channel realization is performed via a generation of independent random Gaussian variables, with variances defined by the integration method, and at the angle specified by the method. There are different approaches to paths integration; a comparison of the methods for delay and Doppler variables has been presented in (Parra et al., 2003); for the angular variables, we can cite the works of (Pätzold et al., 2008) for several integration methods, while (Pancaldi et al., 2006) explores the method of Gaussian Quadrature Rules (GQR).

An example of this approach is presented in the following figure, where the GQR method has been utilized for the paths integration. At Tx the PAS has uniform shape, while at Rx is Gaussian type. In the figure, it has been also depicted the angles of the paths. An example of this approach will be presented in detail in the following section.

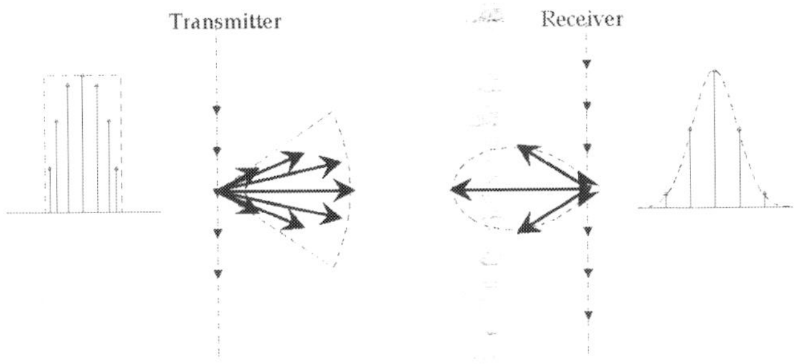

Fig. 11. An example of the method of paths integration.

As can be seen from Fig. 11, the continuous xPAS are approximatted by seven paths at the transmitter and five paths at the receiver, wich leads to an approximation of 35 paths for the entire xPAS.

4.3 Sum of complex functions

Under this approach, the approximations in the sense of eq. (31) no longer contain delta functions as paths, but they consist of complex functions. Among the main approaches found in literature, we can first say that all have considered approximations in the way:

$$h\left(\varphi^{\mathrm{Tx}},\varphi^{\mathrm{Rx}}\right)=\sum_{c=1}^{C}\beta_c\psi_c\left(\varphi^{\mathrm{Tx}}\right)\xi_c\left(\varphi^{\mathrm{Rx}}\right). \tag{37}$$

It means, functions composed via the outer product of artificial paths at the transmitters $\psi_c\left(\varphi^{\mathrm{Tx}}\right)$, and artificial paths at the receiver $\xi_c\left(\varphi^{\mathrm{Rx}}\right)$. These functions, however, are not defined in the angular domain in the available works, but they are used in the space domain. Then, a channel realization **H** can be performed with:

$$\mathbf{H}=\sum_{c=1}^{C}\beta_c\xi_c\psi^T{}_c, \tag{38}$$

where (columns) vectors ψ_c and ξ_c belong to the expansion of the spatial channel realizations at the transmitter and receiver sides, respectively. The matrix **H** can be stacked in a vector $\mathbf{H}_{vec}$ through the vec(.) operator, which arranges all columns of the vector in a tall vector. This can be carried out for the representation in (38), with the Kronecker product (⊗) of the complex functions, as in:

$$\mathbf{H}_{vec}=vec\{\mathbf{H}\}=\sum_{c=1}^{C}\beta_c\psi_c\otimes\xi_c. \tag{39}$$

The autocorrelation values of the MIMO channel can be represented as a tensor, as in (28), or as a matrix $\mathbf{R}_{\mathbf{H}_{vec}}$, as follows:

$$\mathbf{R}_{\mathbf{H}_{vec}}=E\left\{\mathbf{H}_{vec}\mathbf{H}_{vec}{}^{H}\right\}=\sum_{c=1}^{C}\sigma_{cc}\left(\psi_c\otimes\xi_c\right)\left(\psi_c\otimes\xi_c\right)^{H}, \tag{40}$$

where the variance σ_{cc} of the weights can be calculated by multiplying $\mathbf{R}_{\mathbf{H}_{vec}}$ with $(\psi_c \otimes \xi_c)^H$ at the left, and its complex transpose by the right, as in:

$$(\psi_c \otimes \xi_c)^H R_{H_{vec}} (\psi_c \otimes \xi_c) = \sigma_{cc} . \tag{41}$$

As the vector $(\psi_c \otimes \xi_c)^H$ is composed of the Kronecker product of two orthogonal functions, doing (41) with two different vectors, $(\psi_c \otimes \xi_c)$ and $(\psi_d \otimes \xi_d)$ will generate the coupling matrix $\mathbf{\Omega}$, formed by entries σ_{cd},

$$\mathbf{\Omega} \triangleq \begin{bmatrix} \sigma_{11} & \sigma_{12} & \cdots & \sigma_{1,C} \\ \sigma_{21} & \sigma_{22} & \cdots & \sigma_{2,C} \\ \vdots & \vdots & \ddots & \vdots \\ \sigma_{C,1} & \sigma_{C,2} & \cdots & \sigma_{C,C} \end{bmatrix} . \tag{42}$$

Defining $\boldsymbol{\psi}$, $\odot$, $\mathbf{G}$, and $\boldsymbol{\xi}$ as the matrix of vectors of the expansion at the transmitter side, the Walsh-Hadamard operator, a matrix of size M×N with i.i.d complex Gaussian variables and the vectors of the receiver side, respectively. Then, the state of the art channel simulators generate channel realizations with:

$$\mathbf{H} = \boldsymbol{\xi}\left(\tilde{\mathbf{\Omega}} \odot \mathbf{G}\right)\boldsymbol{\psi}^T . \tag{43}$$

Where $\tilde{\mathbf{\Omega}}$ is obtained by performing square root over each of the elements of $\mathbf{\Omega}$.
In (Weichselberguer, 2005) the matrices $\boldsymbol{\psi}$ and $\boldsymbol{\xi}$ are formed by the eigenvectors of $\mathbf{R}^{\mathrm{Tx}}$ and $\mathbf{R}^{\mathrm{Rx}}$, which are the one sided correlations at Tx and Rx, respectively; where those are calculated with:

$$\mathbf{R}^{\mathrm{Tx}} = E\left\{\mathbf{H}^H\mathbf{H}\right\}; \;\; \mathbf{R}^{\mathrm{Rx}} = E\left\{\mathbf{H}\mathbf{H}^H\right\} . \tag{44}$$

In (Sayeed, 2002), the matrices $\boldsymbol{\psi}$ and $\boldsymbol{\xi}$ are composed of AMVs, obtained from dividing the angles of interest in equally spaced paths. The number of vector in each matrix depends on the selected number of paths.
In (Kontorovich et al., 2008) and (Alcocer-Ochoa et al., 2008), matrices $\boldsymbol{\psi}$ and $\boldsymbol{\xi}$ are composed of the Discrete Prolate Sequences (DPS). These functions can be obtained through the eigen decomposition of a kernel proportional to:

$$\mathbf{R}^{\mathrm{Tx/Rx}} = \frac{\sin\left(2\pi k_m d(m-n)\right)}{(m-n)\pi}, \quad m,n = 0,1,\ldots,\mathrm{M}-1 , \tag{45}$$

where k_m is the maximum wavenumber spread and d is the distance between elements of the array. The choice of DPS is because they are a basis for channel expansion that depends only on the dimension of the antenna array and the maximum wavenumber, which is also directly related to the maximum AoA or AoD. The number of functions does not depend on the shape of the PAS. These functions are also the approximate Eigenfunctions for several profiles defined in standards. This can be understood considering that the kernel in (45) implies that in the WNS, the kernel Prolate should be a square function. This have been plotted in Fig. 12 along with the GM of truncated versions of Gaussian and Von Misses PAS;

due to their common shapes in the WNS, is not strange that Prolate be a good basis for approximation of channel realizations becoming from the mentioned PAS.

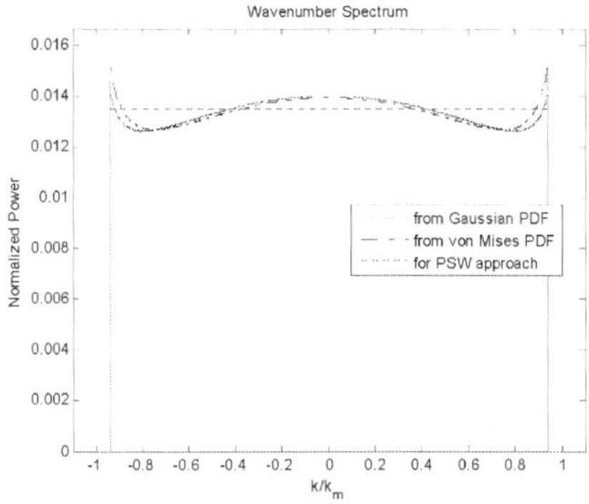

Fig. 12. WNS of the Prolate Kernel and most considered PAS in its truncated versions.

Finally, in Fig. 12 is presented the representation of the complex functions (actually Prolate) in a polar representation. Note that the artificial paths do not have physical sense, but provide an advantage in signal representation.

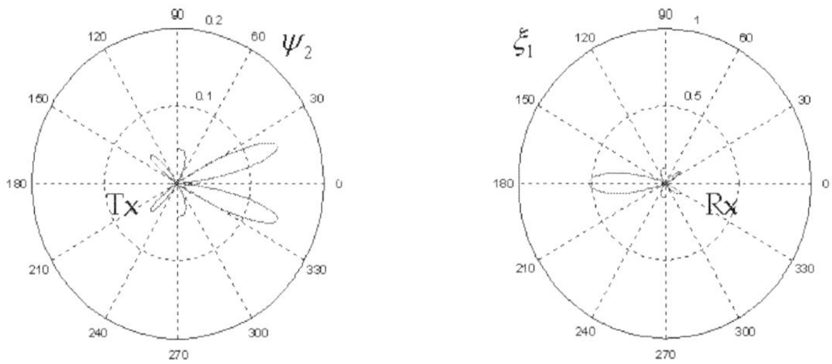

Fig. 13. Example of the complex funtions for the implementation of simulators.

4.4 A note on state of the art emulators

In this chapter has been reviewed the topic of channel simulator, but in reality, emulators construction is an important topic as well. When we consider the practical implementation issues of the simulators, several new problems become important that were left aside in simulators. Principally, modern simulators have to deal with different configurations at each side of the links, i.e. sometimes a configuration of a 3x3 MIMO will be necessary, and other times a 4x2. This imply that the emulator be flexible enough to count with the topologies needed in the newest standards. Emulators also have to be generic enough to provide capacities for different standards, as in the near future, communication systems comprising several standards in the same designs will be mandatory. In other hand, the necessity to increase data rates imposes a problem to real time channel emulators, which have to distort signals in real operation of systems; this is a big issue in coming standards where data

throughputs are in orders of GHz. It is interesting to note that there are also several technologies for channel emulators, since digital implementations, passing through RF passive and active circuits, up to optical technologies, and all with the same aim.
In (Kontorovich & Parra-Michel, 2008) can be reviewed some of the principal companies that work in constructing channel emulators, as well as a review of the latest patents in this area, while in (Loyola et al., 2008), an emulator with the idea of artificial paths is presented.

5. Performance analysis

One important thing in simulation is to guarantee that the employed method achieves some degree of similarity with the target model. In this context, some scenario defined in terms of certain xPAS will be utilized to provide some target SCF. From this channel, the proposed methods will be executed and its generated SCF will be stored. Comparisons between those two SCF will provide the similarity estimation.

5.1 A metric for performance comparison

The metric employed for the comparison is given by the direct distance between two matrices $\mathbf{A}$ and $\mathbf{B}$ specifying two SCF in the sense of the Frobenius norm: $\|\mathbf{A}-\mathbf{B}\|_F$, where Frobenius norm is defined as

$$\|\mathbf{A}\|_F = \sqrt{\sum_i \sum_j |\mathbf{A}_{ij}|^2}\,. \tag{46}$$

Translated to our specific case, we will get the existent difference of two SCF; let be $\mathbf{R}^A$ and $\mathbf{R}^B$ those matrices and they will be compared as follows:

$$\left\|\mathbf{R}_N^A - \mathbf{R}_N^B\right\|_F, \tag{47}$$

where for any correlation matrix $\mathbf{R}$, $\mathbf{R}_N$ is its normalized version, obtained with:

$$\mathbf{R}_N = \frac{\mathbf{R}}{\|\mathbf{R}\|_F}\,. \tag{48}$$

It is remarkable that this metric is equivalent to that defined by:

$$d_1(\mathbf{R}^A,\mathbf{R}^B) = \frac{\left\|\mathbf{R}_N^A - \mathbf{R}_N^B\right\|_F}{\left\|\mathbf{R}_N^A\right\|_F \left\|\mathbf{R}_N^B\right\|_F}, \tag{49}$$

where $d_1(.)$ is the distance between two matrices, considering that $\|\mathbf{R}_N\|_F = 1$. Another equivalent expression for (49) is:

$$d_1(\mathbf{R}^A,\mathbf{R}^B) = \frac{\left\|vec(\mathbf{R}_N^A) - vec(\mathbf{R}_N^B)\right\|}{\left\|vec(\mathbf{R}_N^A)\right\|\left\|vec(\mathbf{R}_N^B)\right\|}, \tag{50}$$

which can be interpreted as the normalized distance between correlation matrices, when those are seen as elements of a vector space.

5.2 Simulation results

Upon defined a xPAS composed of a uniform shape PAS at Tx and a Gaussian type PAS at Rx, and with the use of metric $d_1(.)$, the performance of main simulation methods were compared. The results are shown in Table 4, where the PAS at Tx was uniform from -20° to 20°, while PAS at Rx considered a standard deviation of 7°. The system is a 9x9 uniform linear array MIMO comunication system, the antenna intespace is of a half of the wavelength of the carrier transmitted signal (2GHz). In Table 2, VM stands for Weichselberguer method, MEA is the method of paths integration into equal areas, MGQR is the method of GQR.

Method	No. Fun. (error <0.1)	No. Fun. (error <0.01)
WM	26	42
MEA	110	1600
MGQR	169	900
Prolates	49	49

Table 4. Performance comparison of the simulation methods

As the complexity of the methods are related with the number of functions utilized in the approximation, it is clear that the best method is WM, which uses the optimal functions, with the trade off of being dependent on the specific SCF. The methods of paths integration do not behave very well. In the other hand, Prolate are not so far from WM, but they have the remarkable property that are invariant to the specific shape of the xPAS and only depends on the external parameters (maximum wavenumber dispersion and size of the antenna array). This property opens the possibility of Prolate to be a good basis for construction of a generic channel simulator.

6. Open research problems and Future Trends

From the concepts reviewed in this Chapter, and with the aid of (Kontorovich & Parra-Michel, 2008), we can state that the topic of channel simulation is far to be closed. This is due to the fact that the communication systems are continuously appearing, demanding new channel models and its efficient simulators. For example, the IEEE 802.15c standard would require the elevation angle for beamforming applications. Moreover, the new standards suggest the use of either OFDM or single carrier schemes, and some mixtures between them to improve the system performance. On the other hand, the use of planar antenna arrays both for Tx and Rx is also considered. This imply that the study of the propagation phenomena shall include the elevation angle as well as the azimuth one, but up to now, simulators do not consider this domain. Models that account with all degrees of freedom in the Space-Time channels are still to be done. As open research problems we can mention the conception of tractable models to deal with correlation between space and time variables. It is also a matter of research to understand how is connected the efforts of simulators with actual system performance, i.e. it suffices to guarantee approximations of second order statistics, or higher order are necessary to truly emulate the real channels? Additionally, works on channel simulators open the need for works in implementation issues for emulators. We can state that current work lines are principally devoted to a) Diminish the complexity of the simulator implementations, b) Integrate more statistical channel information or environment description and c) Provide flexible simulators to account for several configurations.

In future developments, we can expect that simulators will incorporate all statistical information for all domains (Doppler, AoA, etc.). Those simulators will show generic architectures and means to provide channel realizations in an efficient (not complex, yet accurate) way, and perhaps with reduced information, while being versatile enough to provide any channel configuration array.

7. Conclusions

Channel modeling and simulation topics have been presented in this Chapter. We intended to present the framework, the main problems, techniques, theories and results in this research area. Several examples were presented in order to clarify the concepts reviewed, with the aim of providing to the reader tools for understanding and manage the concepts of MIMO channel modeling. A comparison of the simulators performance was presented, and the generic properties of Prolate functions were highlighted. We close this Chapter with the mention that channel modeling and simulation is useful and worthy by itself, as it provides an insight to devise algorithms that mitigate the channel introduced distortions. In this sense, we can anticipate that works for channel compensation based on the ideas of artificial paths discussed here, shall be common in the near future.

8. Acknowledgment

This work was supported by research grant Intel CERMIMO-2008 and CONACYT research projects 84559-Y and 53769.

9. References

3GPP (2003). Spatial Channel Model for Multiple Input - Multiple Output (MIMO) Simulations *TR 25.996 v6.1.0 Technical Report.*

Alcocer-Ochoa, A; Kontorovitch, V. & Parra-Michel, R. (2008) A Wideband MIMO Channel Model based on Structured Vector Modes using Orthogonalization. *Proc. of IEEE WICOM 2008*, pp. 1-5. October 2008.

Bello, P. A. Characterization of randomly time-variant linear channels. *IEEE Trans. Commun. Syst.*, Vol. 11, pp. 360-393.

COST 207. (1989). *Digital land mobile radio communications.* Office for Official Pub. of the European Communities, Final Report. Luxembourg, 1989.

Durgin, G. D. (2003). Space-Time Wireless Channels, *Prentice Hall PTR*, ISBN: 0-13-065647-X, New Jersey, USA, 2003.

Ertel, R. B. & Reed, J. H. (1999). Angle and Time of Arrival Statistics for Circular and Elliptical Scattering Models, *IEEE Journal on Selected Areas in Communications.* Vol. 17, No. 11, pp. 1829-1840, November 1999.

Fechtel, S. A. (1993). A novel approach to modeling and efficient simulation of frequency selective radio channels. *IEEE J. Sel. Areas Commun.* Vol. 11, pp. 422-431, 1993.

Fuhl, J.; Molisch, A. F. & Bonek, E. (1998). Unified Channel Model for Mobile Radio Systems with Smart Antennas, *IEE Procedures on Radar and Sonar Navigation*, Vol. 145, No. 1, pp. 32-41. February 1998.

Gans, M. J. (1972). A Power-Spectral Theory of Propagation in the Mobile-Radio Environment. *IEEE Trans. on Vehic. Tech.*, Vol. 21, No. 1, pp. 27-38. February 1972.

Kennedy, R. S. (1969). *Fading Dispersive Communication Channels*, Wiley-Interscience, ISBN: 471-46903-3, USA.

Kontorovich, V. & Parra-Michel, R. (2008). Review of Patents in Simulation of Broadband Communication Channels. *Journal of Recent Patents on Electrical Engineering*, Vol. 1, pp. 188-200, 2008.

Kontorovich, V.; Primak, S.; Alcocer-Ochoa, A. & Parra-Michel, R. (2008). MIMO Channel Orthogonalisations applying Universal Eigenbasis. *IET Signal Processing*, Vol. 2, No. 2, pp. 87-96, 2008.

Laurila, J.; Molisch, A. F. & Bonek, E. (1998). Influence of the Scatters Distribution on the Power Delay Profile and the Power Azimuth Spectra of Mobile Radio Channels. *IEEE Intl. Symp. on Spread Spectrum Tech. and Applications*. Vol. 1, pp. 267-271, Sept. 1998.

Loyola. I. J.; Alcocer-Ochoa, A; Parra-Michel, R; Kontorovich, V. & Orozco-Lugo, A. (2008) An Efficient wideband channel emulator based on orthogonal functions expansion. *Proc. of IEEE WICOM 2008*, pp. 1-5, October 2008.

Molisch, A. F. (2004). A Generic Model for MIMO Wireless Propagation Channels in Macro- and Microcells. IEEE Trans. on Signal Processing, Vol. 52, No. 1, pp. 61-71, January 2004.

Molisch, A. F.; Asplund, H.; Heddergott, R.; Steinbauer, M. & Zwick, T. (2006). The COST259 Directional Channel Model-Part I: Overview and Methodology. *IEEE Transactions on Wireless Communications*, Vol. 5, No. 12, pp. 3421-3433. December 2006.

Pancaldi, F.; Greco, P. & Vitetta, G. M. (2006). GQR-Based models for directional wireless channels. *IEEE Trans. on Wireless Commun.*, Vol. 5, No. 3, pp. 642-651. March 2006.

Papoulis, A & Pillai, S. U. (2002). Probability, Random Variables, and Stochastic Processes. Mc Graw Hill. 4th Edition, New York, 2002

Parra-Michel, R.; Kontorovitch, V.; Orozco-Lugo, A. G.; Lara, M. (2003). Computational Complexity of Narrowband and Wideband Channel Simulators. *IEEE Vehicular Technology Conference, VTC 2003 -Fall*, October 2003.

Parsons, J. D. (2000). *The mobile radio propagation channel*, 2nd Edition, John Wiley & Sons, ISBN: 0-471-98857-X, England.

Pätzold, M. (2002). *Mobile fading channels*, John Wiley & Sons, 2002.

Pätzold, M.; Hogstad, B. O. & Youssef, N. (2008). Modeling, Analysis and Simulation of MIMO Mobile-to-Mobile Fading Channels. *IEEE Transactions on Wireless Communications*, Vol. 7, No. 2, pp. 510-520. February 2008.

Petrus, P; Reed, J. H. & Rappaport, T. S. (2002). Geometrical-Based Statistical Macrocell Channel Model for Mobile Environments, *IEEE Transactions on Communications*, Vol. 50, No. 3, pp. 495-502. March 2002.

Piechocki, R. J.; McGeehan, J. P. & Tsoulos, G. V. (2001). A New Stochastic Spatio-Temporal Propagation Model (SSTPM) for Mobile Communications with Antenna Arrays, *IEEE Transactions on Communications*, Vol. 49, No. 5, pp. 855-862, May 2001.

Salz, J. & Winters, J. H. (1994). Effect of Fading Correlation on Adaptive Arrays in Digital Mobile Radio. *IEEE Trans. on Vehic. Tech.*, Vol. 43, No. 4, pp. 1049-1057. November 1994.

Sayeed, A. M. (2002). Deconstructing Multiantenna Fading Channels. *IEEE Transactions on Signal Processing*. Vol. 50, No. 10, pp. 2563-2579, October 2002.

Steinbauer, M.; Molish, A. F. & Bonek, E. (2001). The double directional channel. *IEEE Antennas Propag. Mag.*, Vol. 43, pp. 52-63. Aug. 2001.

van Trees, H. L. (2002). *Detection, Estimation and Modulation Theory, Part IV. John Wiley & Sons*, 2002.

Weichselberger, W. (2003). Spatial *Structure of Multiple Antenna Radio Channels*, Ph. D. Thesis, December 2003, Wien.

Weichselberger, W.; Herdin, H.; Özcelik, H. & Bonek, E. (2006). A Stochastic MIMO Channel Model with Joint Correlation of Both Link Ends, *IEEE Transactions on Wireless Communications*, Vol. 5, No. 1, pp 90–100, January 2006.

Woerner B. D. ; Reed, J. H. & Rappaport, T. S. (1994). Simulation issues for future wireless modems. IEEE Commun. Mag., Vol. 32, No. 7, pp. 42-53.

22

On the role of receiving beamforming in transmitter cooperative communications

Santiago Zazo, Ivana Raos and Benjamín Béjar
Universidad Politécnica de Madrid
Spain

1. Introduction

Multiple Input - Multiple Output (MIMO) communications have challenged the research community with promising capacity increases with respect to the standard single-antenna systems (Telatar 1999; Foschini 1996). Most of the original work was motivated by the point-to-point link trying to provide structures achieving the theoretical capacity predicted by the logdet formula. Probably, the most well studied strategy is BLAST with many variants sharing in common the space-time layered structure.

More recently, there has been much interest in MIMO systems where a multi-antenna node transmits to multiple terminals, or where multiple nodes transmit to a single multi-antenna terminal. The former case is known as the broadcast channel (BC) while the latter is known as the multiple access channel (MAC).

Available literature shows many different approaches dealing with this topic. One of the most representative works are (Viswanath & Tse, 2003; Jindal et al, 2004) where theoretical analysis is provided through the duality principle between the downlink and the uplink case. The main point is that the achievable rate region of the BC is equivalent to the rate region of its dual MAC with a sum power constraint. This duality allows the characterization of the BC rate region to be performed in the dual MAC context where well-known optimization algorithms can be used. This achievable rate region will be considered as an upper bound for all the suboptimal approaches.

Our approach presented here is based on (Caire & Shamai, 2003) where a suboptimal precoder of a DPC structure is proposed using the QR decomposition of the channel matrix. However, this technique was discussed for the case of single-antenna terminals. We have extended this procedure where there could be several antennas at the receiver. Our contribution optimizes the receive beamforming strategy for any terminal assuming that its channel is known but that no other terminal's channel is known. On the other hand, the transmitter has full knowledge of every channel. We proposed a suboptimal precoder using a combination of DPC and zero-forcing criteria whose performance in terms of mutual information is close to the optimum case but with reduced complexity (Zazo & Huang 2006).

On the other hand, sensor networks and ad-hoc networks are receiving more and more attention from the research community in the recent years. There are several challenges from many points of view coming up from information theory limits, device efficiency (power

saving) and network issues (routing). In particular, cooperative diversity is a novel technique where several nodes work together to form a *virtual antenna array* (Scaglione et al, 2006; Stankovic et al, 2006). This point is quite important because it connects this new topic with the more mature field of MIMO communications using a *real antenna array*. Connecting with our previous points, Vector Gaussian, Broadcast, Multiple Access and Interference Channels (GC, BC, MAC, IC) are the standard models assumed for different degrees of cooperation in real MIMO links (Cover and Thomas, 1991) that can provide asymptotic performances in Wireless Sensor Networks (WSN) if cooperation is not penalized. However, although these results are very valuable it is also important to review critically these conclusions considering more realistic models. This is the fundamental goal of this second part.
The notion of cooperative communication has been formulated in several recent works (Jindal 2004 and references therein) and reviewed as an equivalent (degraded) BC or MAC channel. Basically, three following scenarios are considered depending on the available information: a) at the transmitter side a group of sensor are able to share the messages to be transmitted and also the set of channels, b) at the receiver side, nodes share their own received signals by a forwarding process (this is the relay principle, although other approaches may be considered) and also the channel themselves and c) the information is shared at both sides. Reference (Ng et al, 2006) presents a very suitable model for this link addressing penalizations in terms of required power and bandwidth to achieve the cooperation benefits establishing a trade off between them.
Our second contribution follows the idea in (Ng et al, 2006), although in our case a more general situation is considered including the effect of fading channels instead of just a phase shifting. Moreover we modelled the effect of interference coming from the adjacent clusters. In this case, where there is no intercluster coordination, performances degrades for whatever intracluster cooperation may be proposed. This effect may be modeled as an extra Gaussian noise following the Central Limit Theorem. Our reasoning is based on the idea of waking up an extra set of sensors in the cluster (N_b new degrees of freedom for each active node) that interchange the received signal within the group to create a beamforming pointing towards the transmitter (Ochiai et al, 2005; Mudumbai et al, 2007; Barton et al, 2007). Assuming that clusters are spatially separated, interference in minimized. Most of these ideas are presented in (Zazo et al, 2008). This second approach modifies the design of the first one because now instead of throughput maximization, the goal is interference minimization. Assuming that interference fading channels are known, beamformers maximize throughput constrained to belong to the null subspace of the interference. Performance compared to standard cases is clearly improved.

2. MIMO COMMUNICATIONS

2.1 System model

We consider a MIMO broadcast channel where a base station with N_t antennas transmits to N_u users, each with N_r receive antennas. We will further assume that we have the same number of transmit antennas as the number of users. Figure 1 shows the corresponding block diagram of the system, where $\mathbf{T}$ is the linear precoder (or transmit beamformer) (size N_txN_u), $\mathbf{H}_k$ represents the kth user's flat MIMO channel (size N_rxN_t), $\mathbf{r}_k$ represents the kth user's linear receiver (or receive beamformer) (size N_rx1), and $\mathbf{n}_k$ is the AWGN at receiver k.

The dirty paper coding block jointly encodes users so that the interference among users is reduced or eliminated at the output of their decoders.
All the schemes that we are going to describe in the paper are based on the following view: determine ($\mathbf{T}$, $\mathbf{r}_1$, $\mathbf{r}_2$, ..., $\mathbf{r}_{Nu}$) to optimize the performance, either in terms of maximizing the sum rate or maximizing a common SINR achievable by all users. In order to make a fair comparison, all schemes in the simulation results will be measured under a common figure of merit, the sum rate. The specific description of some of these contributions will be described in a forthcoming section, after describing our approach.

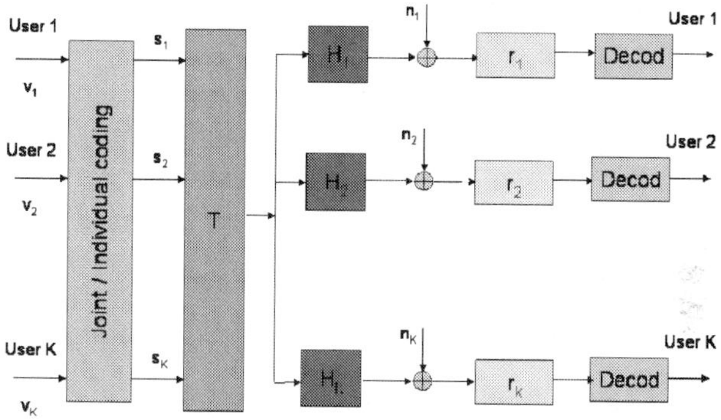

Fig. 1. Block diagram

2.2 Our proposal: ZF-DPC with receive beamforming

Our proposal intends to mix the concept of DPC with its simpler Zero Forcing (ZF) implementation with some beamforming design that provides an acceptable loss of performance. The received signal stacking all the users in a single column-vector becomes,

$$\mathbf{y} = \mathbf{R}^H \mathbf{H}\mathbf{T}\mathbf{s} + \mathbf{R}^H \mathbf{n} \tag{1}$$

where $\mathbf{R}$ is a diagonal block matrix collecting individual array processing at every receiver, and $\mathbf{0}$ vectors mean that the receivers do not cooperate

$$\mathbf{R} = diag\{\mathbf{r}_1 \quad \mathbf{r}_2 \quad \cdots \quad \mathbf{r}_{N_u}\} = \begin{bmatrix} \mathbf{r}_1 & \mathbf{0} & \mathbf{0} & \mathbf{0} \\ \mathbf{0} & \mathbf{r}_2 & \mathbf{0} & \mathbf{0} \\ \mathbf{0} & \mathbf{0} & \ddots & \mathbf{0} \\ \mathbf{0} & \mathbf{0} & \mathbf{0} & \mathbf{r}_{N_u} \end{bmatrix} \tag{2}$$

$\mathbf{H}$ is the channel matrix ($N_u N_r$ x N_t), that can be expressed as the stacking of the per user matrices $\mathbf{H}_i$ (N_r x N_t):

$$\mathbf{H} = \begin{bmatrix} \mathbf{H}_1 \\ \mathbf{H}_2 \\ \vdots \\ \mathbf{H}_{N_u} \end{bmatrix} \tag{3}$$

For the case of single-antenna receivers, the optimum precoding matrix **T** is obtained using the duality principle (Visvanath,& Tse, 2003). This strategy is also remarked in (Jindal, 2004) where a tight suboptimal design is proposed where **T** is the unitary matrix associated to the QR-decomposition of the channel matrix **H**. In this contribution we are going to follow this suboptimal design where the determination of **T** is straightforward for the transmitter if it knows all the channels and also the beamforming processing to be done at receivers,

$$\mathbf{H}_{eq} = \mathbf{R}^H \mathbf{H} = \mathbf{LQ} \tag{4}$$

where **L** is the upper triangular matrix and **Q** is the orthogonal matrix associated with the QR decomposition of matrix $\mathbf{H}_{eq}$. According to this idea, in our scenario we force $\mathbf{T} = \mathbf{Q}^H$. Therefore, the optimization procedure in this case is based on the design of the beamformers constrained to $\mathbf{r}_i = f(\mathbf{H}_i)$ remarking that its own channel is the only available information at each receiver. Applying these ideas to equation (1), we reach an equivalent model as follows,

$$\mathbf{y} = \mathbf{R}^H \mathbf{HTs} + \mathbf{R}^H \mathbf{n} = \mathbf{LQTs} + \mathbf{R}^H \mathbf{n} = \mathbf{LQQ}^H \mathbf{s} + \mathbf{R}^H \mathbf{n} = \mathbf{Ls} + \mathbf{R}^H \mathbf{n} \tag{5}$$

Assuming that DPC is working properly (recall that due to the triangular structure of **L**, DPC is able to cancel all the interference, this is thus labelled as ZF-DPC), the instantaneous sum rate R is given by

$$R = \sum_{k=1}^{N_u} \log_2\left(1 + snr\left|l_k\right|^2\right) \tag{6}$$

where l_k are the diagonal elements of the triangular **L** matrix and snr is the common Signal to Noise Ratio. Therefore, the optimization problem can be expressed as:

Optimization criteria

Find **R** constrained to be block diagonal with $\mathbf{R}^H\mathbf{R}=\mathbf{I}$ and $\mathbf{r}_i = f(\mathbf{H}_i)$, that maximizes

$$R = \sum_{k=1}^{N_u} \log_2\left(1 + snr\left|l_k\right|^2\right) \tag{7}$$

where l_k are the diagonal elements of the triangular **L** associated to the QR decomposition of $\mathbf{H}_{eq} = \mathbf{R}^H \mathbf{H} = \mathbf{LQ}$. Let us remark that the previous relationship $\mathbf{R}^H\mathbf{R}=\mathbf{I}$ transforms equation (6) into the standard problem with spatially uncorrelated noise:

$$\mathbf{y} = \mathbf{Ls} + \mathbf{R}^H \mathbf{n} = \mathbf{Ls} + \mathbf{n} \tag{8}$$

Solution

The set of beamformers $\mathbf{r}_i$ that maximizes the rate in (6) for high SNR are the eigenvectors related to the maximum eigenvalue of matrix $\mathbf{H}_i^H \mathbf{H}_i$:

$$\mathbf{H}_i \mathbf{H}_i^H \mathbf{r}_i = \lambda_{\max} \mathbf{r}_i \tag{9}$$

Proof
For high SNR, the sum rate can be expressed as

$$R = \sum_{k=1}^{N_u} \log_2\left(1 + snr\left|l_k\right|^2\right) \approx \sum_{k=1}^{N_u} \log_2\left(snr\left|l_k\right|^2\right) = N_u \log_2 snr + \log_2\left(\prod_{k=1}^{N_u} \left|l_k\right|^2\right) \quad (10)$$

Therefore, we just need to maximize the last term that can be expressed as a determinant

$$\log_2\left(\prod_{k=1}^{N_u} \left|l_k\right|^2\right) = \log_2\left(\det \mathbf{L}\mathbf{L}^H\right) = \log_2\left(\det \mathbf{L}\mathbf{Q}\mathbf{Q}^H\mathbf{L}^H\right) = \log_2\left(\det \mathbf{H}_{eq}\mathbf{H}_{eq}^H\right) \quad (11)$$

As the logarithm function is a monotonic increasing function, the optimization criteria may be expressed as follows

$$J(\mathbf{R}) = \max_{\mathbf{R}}\left(\det \mathbf{R}^H\mathbf{H}^H\mathbf{H}\mathbf{R}\right) \quad (12)$$

$$\text{Constrained to } \mathbf{R} \text{ block diagonal, } \mathbf{R}^H\mathbf{R} = \mathbf{I},\ \mathbf{r}_i = f\left(\mathbf{H}_i\right)$$

Recall that $\mathbf{R}$ is constrained to be block diagonal because users perform linear combining separately from one another. This constraint limits the determinant to the main diagonal of the desired matrix. This point is critical because if we consider the whole matrix, crossed terms depending on two different terminals' beamformers appear. The constraint $\mathbf{r}_i = f\left(\mathbf{H}_i\right)$ imposes that the optimization criteria depend only on the main diagonal elements.
Therefore, the original constrained optimization must be expressed as follows:

$$J(R) = \max_{\mathbf{R}}\left(\det\left(diag\left(\mathbf{R}^H\mathbf{H}^H\mathbf{H}\mathbf{R}\right)\right)\right) = \max_{\mathbf{r}_i} \prod_{i=1}^{N_u} \mathbf{r}_i^H\mathbf{H}_i\mathbf{H}_i^H\mathbf{r}_i \quad (13)$$

$$\text{Constrained to } \mathbf{r}_i^H\mathbf{r}_i = 1, \forall i \in \left(1, N_u\right)$$

The solution to this problem is very well known as the set of eigenvectors associated with the maximum eigenvalues of the corresponding matrices, as proposed in equation (9).
It is very important to remark that this approach is non-iterative and that receivers just need to estimate their own channels. The main disadvantage could be the implementation of DPC which is currently unknown and could be very complex. In this sense, we propose to substitute the DPC structure by a vectorized Tomlinson-Harashima precoder as described in (Peel et al, 2005; Hochwald et al, 2005). However, the performance of this structure is out of the scope of this contribution. The results that we are going to show will assume perfect DPC behaviour and must be considered as an upper bound of more realistic implementations.

2.3 Some representative existing approaches

In this section we will include a brief description of some of the most representative approaches dealing with our scenario in order to address their merits, show their limitations in terms or performance or complexity and make a fair comparison among them.
In (Wong et al, 2002) several suboptimal approaches for communicating on the BC are suggested. One of them is the design of the precoder according to the SVD decomposition, applying MMSE beamformers at receivers to cope with residual interference. The main advantage of this scheme is its simplicity, though we have to remark that received

covariance matrices must be estimated or fed back. Another proposal in (Wong et al, 2002), known as The Maximum Transmit SINR, maximizes an upper bound of the SINR.

JADE (Joint Approximated Diagonalization of Eigen-structures) refers to a well-known result coming from blind source separation (Cardoso and Soulumiac, 1996). This approach establishes that for a set of complex Hermitian matrices associated to the MIMO transmission, it is possible to find a unitary matrix that minimizes MAI. If the matrices do not have a common eigenstructure, the algorithm provides a kind of 'average eigenstructure'. Unfortunately, performance depends very much on the specific structure of the involved channels.

Reference (Pan et al, 2004) proposes another approach known as Orthogonal Space Division Multiplex (OSDM). This scheme is a zero-forcing strategy where optimization is performed iteratively through a recursive procedure between the transmitters and receivers. The main disadvantage of this scheme is that it requires multiple iterations of communication between both ends before reaching the desired solution. However, performance improves considerably in comparison to other suboptimal schemes.

SVD-MMSE

As we have already mentioned, the idea is quite straightforward: design the precoder according to the SVD decomposition (it is known to be optimal in the point to point link) and apply MMSE beamformers at receivers to cope with residual ISI. Assuming that

$$\mathbf{H}_k = \mathbf{U}_k \boldsymbol{\Sigma}_k \mathbf{V}_k^H \tag{14}$$

Precoder $\mathbf{t}_k$ for the k-user is chosen as $\mathbf{t}_k = \mathbf{V}_k(1)$ where $\mathbf{V}_k(1)$ refers to the column of $\mathbf{V}_k$ associated to the maximum singular value. The MMSE receiver for an arbitrary user k is therefore

$$\mathbf{r}_k = \left(\mathbf{H}_k \mathbf{T}\mathbf{T}^H \mathbf{H}_k^H + \sigma^2 \mathbf{I}\right)^{-1} \mathbf{H}_k \mathbf{t}_k \tag{15}$$

where σ^2 means the noise variance and obviously $\mathbf{T}\mathbf{T}^H \neq \mathbf{I}$ because different columns are related to independent SVDs. The main advantage of this scheme is its simplicity although we have to remark that received covariance matrices must be estimated or matrix $\mathbf{T}$ should be broadcasted.

JADE-MMSE

This approach establishes that for a set of N_u complex Hermitian matrices $\mathbf{H}_k^H \mathbf{H}_k$ it is possible to find a unitary matrix $\mathbf{U}$ that minimizes

$$\sum_{k=1}^{N_u} off\left(\mathbf{U}\mathbf{H}_k^H \mathbf{H}_k \mathbf{U}^H\right) \text{ where } off(\mathbf{A}) = \sum_{1 \le k \ne l \le N_t} |a_{kl}|^2 \tag{16}$$

If the matrices do not have a common eigenstructure, the algorithm provides a kind of 'average eigenstructure'. It is clear that the purpose of this strategy is to minimize the MAI although unfortunately, performance depends very much on the specific structure of involved channels.

According to our scenario, we select **T=U** for precoder and MMSE for receive beamformers,

$$\mathbf{r}_k = \left(\mathbf{H}_k \mathbf{H}_k^H + \sigma^2 \mathbf{I}\right)^{-1} \mathbf{H}_k \mathbf{t}_k \tag{17}$$

This approach is quite similar to the former one, but now the autocovariance matrices at the receivers do not need to be estimated, although the selected precoder $\mathbf{t}_k$'s still have to be transmitted to the corresponding users.

Maximum Transmit SINR (MTxSINR)

This algorithm has been proposed in (Pan et al, 2004) intending to maximize an upper bound of the SINR. Starting form the expression of SINR at user k,

$$SINR_k = \frac{E\left\{\left|\mathbf{r}_k^H \mathbf{H}_k \mathbf{t}_k\right|^2\right\}}{E\left\{\left|\mathbf{r}_k^H \mathbf{H}_k \mathbf{T}_k \mathbf{T}_k^H \mathbf{H}_k^H \mathbf{r}_k\right|^2\right\} + \sigma^2} \tag{18}$$

they found that assuming Gaussian entries, the channel capacity may be upper bounded by

$$C = \sum_{k=1}^{N_u} \log_2\left(1 + SINR_k\right) > \log_2\left(\prod_{k=1}^{N_u} SINR_k\right) \tag{19}$$

They found a quite interesting upper bound for

$$\prod_{k=1}^{N_u} SINR_k \geq \rho \prod_{k=1}^{N_u} \frac{\mathbf{t}_k^H \mathbf{H}_k^H \mathbf{H}_k \mathbf{t}_k}{\mathbf{t}_k^H \left(\sum_{m \neq k} \mathbf{H}_m^H \mathbf{H}_m + \sigma^2 \mathbf{I}\right) \mathbf{t}_k} \tag{20}$$

where ρ is a real constant.

Their procedure is based on the following steps to design the precoder. First find a set of matrices $\mathbf{W}_k$ such that

$$\mathbf{W}_k^H \left(\sum_{m \neq k} \mathbf{H}_m^H \mathbf{H}_m + \sigma^2 \mathbf{I}\right) \mathbf{W}_k = \mathbf{I} \tag{21}$$

The solution of this problem is simple taking into account the eigendecomposition of the involved matrices

$$eig\left(\sum_{m \neq k} \mathbf{H}_m^H \mathbf{H}_m + \sigma^2 \mathbf{I}\right) = \mathbf{U}\mathbf{S}\mathbf{U}^H \tag{22}$$

The desired matrix $\mathbf{W}_k$ is

$$\mathbf{W}_k = \mathbf{U}\mathbf{S}^{-1/2} \tag{23}$$

In a second step, they select

$$\mathbf{t}_k = \frac{\mathbf{W}_k \mathbf{v}_k}{\left(\mathbf{v}_k^H \mathbf{W}_k^H \mathbf{W}_k \mathbf{v}_k\right)^{1/2}} \tag{24}$$

where $\mathbf{v}_k$ is the eigenvector related to the maximum eigenvalue of $\mathbf{W}_k^H \mathbf{H}_k^H \mathbf{W}_k \mathbf{H}_k$. In fact, what they are doing is transforming the original problem into a standard Rayleigh quotient. At the receiver side, they apply an MMSE receiver with similar considerations regarding the estimation of the received autocovariance matrix or broadcasting the matrix $\mathbf{T}$.

OSDM (Orthogonal Space Division Multiplex)
This scheme is a zero forcing strategy where the optimization is performed iteratively through a recursive procedure between the transmitter and receiver. Their proposal can be understood in two steps. In a first step, they intend to force

$$\mathbf{r}_k^H \mathbf{H}_k \mathbf{T}_k = \mathbf{0} \quad \forall k \tag{25}$$

This can be guaranteed iff

$$\mathbf{t}_m \in Null\left(\begin{bmatrix} \mathbf{r}_1^H \mathbf{H}_1 \\ \vdots \\ \mathbf{r}_{k-1}^H \mathbf{H}_{k-1} \\ \mathbf{r}_{k+1}^H \mathbf{H}_{k+1} \\ \vdots \\ \mathbf{r}_{N_u}^H \mathbf{H}_{N_u} \end{bmatrix}\right) \tag{26}$$

as there is no MAI, at the receiver side they apply the MRC criteria $\mathbf{r}_k = \mathbf{H}_k \mathbf{t}_k$. In practice, iteration is started choosing $\mathbf{r}_k = 1 \ \forall k$ and after several iterations the scheme converges to the desired solution. The main disadvantage of this scheme is that it requires multiple iterative communications between both ends before reaching the desired solution. However, the performance improves considerably in comparison with previous suboptimal schemes.

2.4 Analytical results and simulations

We have calculated through simulations the sum rate for all the methods described in the previous section. Figure 2 shows the performance of these methods for three users (and three transmit antennas) and two antennas per terminal. It is important to remark that we have not included multiuser diversity in this analysis.
It can be observed that JADE and SVD perform quite badly because in fact they are not able to reduce the MAI effect. As they were defined for point to point communications, this performance is expected. Maximum transmit SINR (labelled as MTx SINR) performs a little bit better but the most interesting behaviour is provided by the OSDM. It is remarkable that our proposal labelled by ZF-DPC + BF has similar performance. It is important to have in mind that OSDM is iterative between the receiver and transmitter which makes this contribution quite impractical. Obviously, DPC and optimum beamforming show the best performance. Our method is shown to be as good as optimum beamforming for high SNR. Equation (27) presents the sum rate for DPC where $\mathbf{S}_n$ is the noise covariance matrix and $\mathbf{Q}_k$ are the optimized covariance matrices of different users.

$$R_{DPC} = \log_2 \det\left|\mathbf{S}_n + \sum_{k=1}^{N_u} \mathbf{H}_k^H \mathbf{Q}_k \mathbf{H}_k\right| \tag{27}$$

On the other hand, the sum rate for the beamforming structure is given by equation (28)

$$R_{BF} = \sum_{k=1}^{N_u} R_k = \sum_{k=1}^{N_u} \log_2 \frac{\det\left|\mathbf{S}_n + \sum_{j=1}^{N_u} \mathbf{H}_k^H \mathbf{Q}_j \mathbf{H}_k\right|}{\det\left|\mathbf{S}_n + \sum_{j=1, j\neq k}^{N_u} \mathbf{H}_k^H \mathbf{Q}_j \mathbf{H}_k\right|} \tag{28}$$

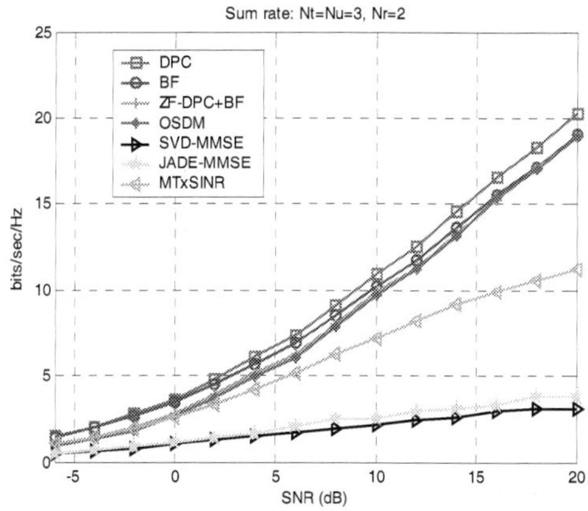

Fig. 2. Comparison of some existing algorithms for multiuser multiantennas schemes

Figure 3 shows for 6 transmit antennas, 6 users and a different number of receive antennas the ratio of our suboptimal proposal compared to the optimal DPC. The performance is similar for the different number of antennas and is close to the optimal for low and high signal to noise ratios (SNR). For high SNR, a saturated behaviour is observed stating that there will be a gap between both the approaches, as is seen in Figure 2. Unfortunately, for the most realistic interval of SNR between 0 and 10 dB, the ratio decreases, but it is always above 85 %. Clearly the loss of performance increases with the number of antennas, but in most mobile applications with 2 antennas at the terminals, the behaviour will reach more than 90%.

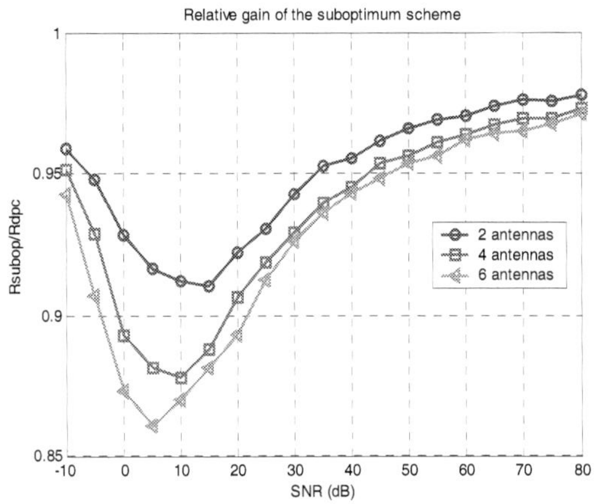

Fig.3. Relative gain of the suboptimal approach

3. Cooperative Communications in Wireless Sensor Networks

This section starts describing the new topic addressing two different scenarios, interference free and with interference to guide the reasoning to show how important is the role played by the beamforming in this second case.

3.1 Interference free scenario

The system model assumes that N simultaneously active (awake) sensors are split in N_c clusters, each one with $N_s = N/N_c$ sensors (assumed integer). P is the total assigned power to link N_s sensors between two clusters including the traffic link and also the transmitter and/or receiver cooperation. In the spirit of (Ng et al, 2006) but including fading effects, the 3 cooperative strategies already mentioned can be analysed. Schematically, the sensor configuration and situation are shown in figure 4.

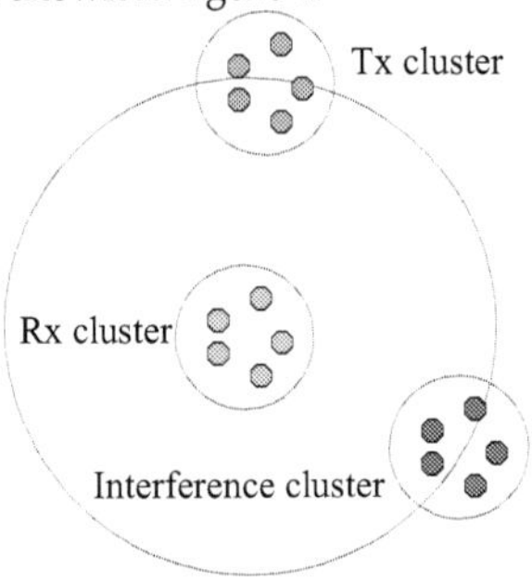

Fig. 4. Schematic scenario

In this contribution, the emphasis is put on the joint Tx /Rx cooperation strategy because it is the most general configuration, of which Tx or Rx cooperation are particular cases, and because it is the most suitable strategy for the analysed scenario. It will be showed that an important conclusion in (Ng et al, 2006) stating that Tx cooperation is the most feasible strategy where there is not intercluster interference is confirmed here. Nevertheless, assuming the existence of intercluster interference, some kind of Tx / Rx cooperation is recommended.

In order to simplify the notation, we assume that only the Tx and Rx clusters in Fig. 4 exist, where vectors $\mathbf{h}_k$ ($1xN_s$), $k \in (1, N_s)$ represents the Rayleigh fading between all the N_s transmitters and the k receiver. If we define P_t as the power consumed per sensor at the Tx part and similarly P_r at the Rx part to allow cooperation, clearly the available power for the intercluster link is $P_{MIMO}=P-N_sP_t-N_sP_r$. Denoting $\mathbf{x}$ ($1xN_s$) as the transmitted vector and y_k $k \in (1, N_s)$ the received signal at each sensor we have in the absence of interference:

$$y_k = \sqrt{P_{MIMO}}\,\mathbf{h}_k^H \mathbf{F}\mathbf{x} + n_k \tag{29}$$

where n_k is an AWGN noise signal with σ^2 power and $\mathbf{F}$ is a general precoder with normalized power. Following the spirit in (Ng et al, 2006) the cooperation link is assumed just a Gaussian channel with gain G representing that intracluster nodes are $\sqrt{G}$ times closer than intercluster distance normalized to 1. At the transmitter side, the achievable rate for cooperation is given by equation (30)

$$R_t = \log\left(1 + \frac{P_t G}{\sigma^2}\right) \tag{30}$$

If we allow the receivers to relay their own received signals in an equivalent channel also Gaussian with gain G, each sensor may create its own virtual MIMO. For instance, if we consider the receiving sensor 1, the virtual MIMO signal becomes after proper normalization:

$$\mathbf{y}_1 = \begin{bmatrix} y_1 \\ \sqrt{\dfrac{GP_r}{P_{MIMO}+\sigma^2}}\, y_2 + n_{12} \\ \vdots \\ \sqrt{\dfrac{GP_r}{P_{MIMO}+\sigma^2}}\, y_{N_s} + n_{1N_s} \end{bmatrix} \tag{31}$$

where new noise contributions appear due to the relaying process with powers defined in equation (32).

$$\begin{aligned} \sigma_{1k}^2 &= \frac{\sigma^2(1+GP_r)}{P_{MIMO}+\sigma^2} \qquad k \in (2, N_s) \\ \sigma_{11}^2 &= \sigma^2 \end{aligned} \tag{32}$$

If we want to normalize the noise contribution to 1 in all the entries of the virtual MIMO receiver, easily we get

$$\mathbf{y}_1 = \begin{bmatrix} \frac{1}{\sigma}\mathbf{h}_1^H\mathbf{F}\mathbf{x} + \tilde{n}_1 \\ \sqrt{\frac{P_{MIMO}GP_r}{\sigma^2(1+P_rG)}}\mathbf{h}_2^H\mathbf{F}\mathbf{x} + \tilde{n}_2 \\ \vdots \\ \sqrt{\frac{P_{MIMO}GP_r}{\sigma^2(1+P_rG)}}\mathbf{h}_{N_s}^H\mathbf{F}\mathbf{x} + \tilde{n}_{N_s} \end{bmatrix} = \mathbf{H}_1\mathbf{F}\mathbf{x} + \tilde{\mathbf{n}} \qquad (33)$$

Now $\mathbf{H}_1$ collects all the effects related to the virtual MIMO creation and $\tilde{\mathbf{n}}$ is the equivalent white normalized Gaussian noise. It is remarkable that this situation becomes a standard MIMO problem (as in equation (1)) but with non identical distributions of the matrix entries. Sum rate of this problem denoted as R_{Coop} using the dual BC-MAC decomposition is

$$R_{Coop} = \sum_{k=1}^{N_s} R_k \leq \log\det\left(\mathbf{I} + \sum_{k=1}^{N_s}\mathbf{H}_k^H\mathbf{Q}_k\mathbf{H}_k\right) \qquad (34)$$

$$\text{Constrained to} \sum_{k=1}^{N_s} tr\mathbf{Q}_k \leq P_{MIMO}$$

where matrices $\mathbf{Q}_k$ represent the autocorrelation matrices in the dual MAC problem. As this optimization problem in fact depends on the choice of P_t and P_r, the solution may be expressed as follows:

$$R_{Sum} = \max_{P_t, P_r}\left(R_{Coop} = N_s \log\left(1 + \frac{P_tG}{\sigma^2}\right)\right) \qquad (35)$$

that must be solved by exhaustive search in P_r and P_t. Fig. 5 shows the schematic equivalent view of the simplest case where 2 transmit sensors and 2 receiving sensors are allowed to cooperate. It is observed that the original interference channel is transformed into a BC channel with multiple receiving antennas. This is the reason of the performance improvement.

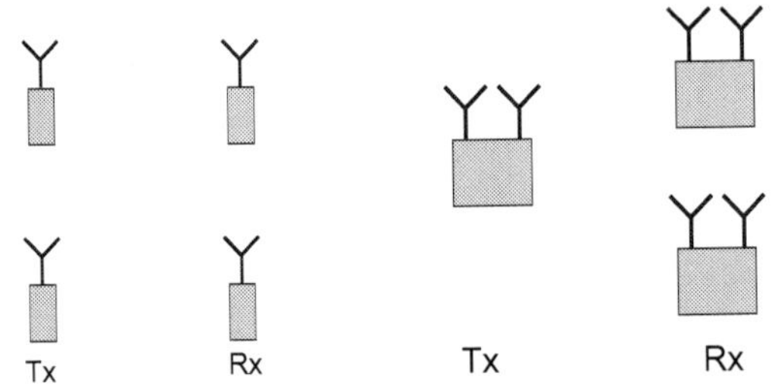

Fig. 5. Left hand side, original scenario. Right hand side, equivalent scenario with Tx /Rx cooperation

3.2 Scenario with intercluster interference

The model presented in this section permits us to quantify the new situation where another cluster is also transmitting and therefore causing interference to the aforementioned scenario in the previous section. Although only the case with one interfering cluster is modelled, the extension to several clusters is straightforward and will reinforce the Gaussian hypothesis for the interference that we will claim. The received signal i_1 at sensor 1 (our reference) in the original cluster coming from the interfering one is:

$$i_1 = \sqrt{\alpha P_{MIMO}}\,\mathbf{m}_1^H \mathbf{F}_{\text{int}} \mathbf{x}_{\text{int}} \tag{36}$$

Where $\mathbf{m}_1$ is the flat fading channel from interfering cluster to the reference sensor, $\mathbf{F}_{\text{int}}$ (also assumed power normalized) is the precoding performed at that cluster and $\mathbf{x}_{int}$ is the transmitted sequence. $\sqrt{\alpha} \in (0,1)$ means the extra loss compared to the desired link to represent the fact that the interfering cluster may be further away (according to Figure 1, α=1). The mean interference power clearly becomes:

$$P_{\text{int}} = P_{MIMO}\alpha \mathbf{m}_1^H \mathbf{F}_{\text{int}} \mathbf{F}_{\text{int}}^H \mathbf{m}_1 = P_{MIMO}\alpha \tag{37}$$

Central Limit Theorem confirms the Gaussian hypothesis as a linear combination of i.i.d. random variables. So, the equivalent effect of interference makes effective noise to be increased from:

$$\sigma_{eff}^2 = \sigma^2 + P_{MIMO}\alpha \tag{38}$$

Clearly, the SNR becomes negative if we consider the circular distributions of sensors in figure 4 and in any case, the throughput degrades very significantly. Fig. 6 shows this performance degradation compared to the no interference case, in a 4x4 system (4 transmit sensors, 4 receive sensors). Recalling that the interference is modelled as an additional AWGN contribution, the sum rate of the system is depicted for different Gains G already described and for different values of the noise variance, σ_{eff}^2.

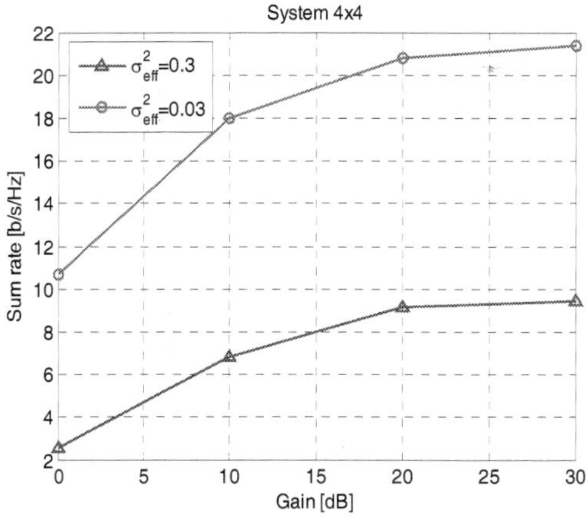

Fig. 6. Performance degradation due to interference

This previous result states that independently of the cooperation strategy, wireless ad hoc networks need some kind of coordination between neighbouring clusters in terms of multiple access strategy to avoid this large performance degradation.

In order to provide a feasible solution for this problem, we recall that in fact in a cluster are usually located many sensors additional to the already mentioned N_s that use to be sleeping until some event wakes them. The idea that we propose is to awake a set of sensors N_b -1 per every N_s sensors so involving N_bN_s sensors where in each group of N_b sensors, the N_b-1 sensors play the role of dumb antennas in an irregular bidimensional beamforming. This way, instead of Rx cooperation in terms of a throughput increase following the BC approach showed in Fig. 4, we exploit the SDMA (Space Division Multiple Access) principles. Although this is a well know topic in the literature, we have to claim that decentralized beamforming adds some new features that must be looked at carefully. In fact we are dealing with irregular spatially distributed beamformers (Ochiai et al, 2005;Mudumbai et al, 2007; Barton et al, 2007) where preliminary results point out a significant array gain. It is also important to remark that the main drawback of this approach is that synchronization must be quite accurate. In particular, (Ochiai et al, 2005) analysed this case from the point of view of spatially random sampling and it shows the significant average gain (now beamforming performance becomes a random variable) and an acceptable average side lobes level.
The use of dummy sensors and the equivalent MIMO system are shown in Fig. 7 and Fig. 8. The 2x2 system with 3 dummy sensors per each receive sensor is depicted. It can be seen that the equivalent system becomes a MIMO system with a single transmitter with N_t=2 antennas, and N_s=2 receivers with N_b (4) antennas. The equivalent MIMO fading channels are given by equation (33).

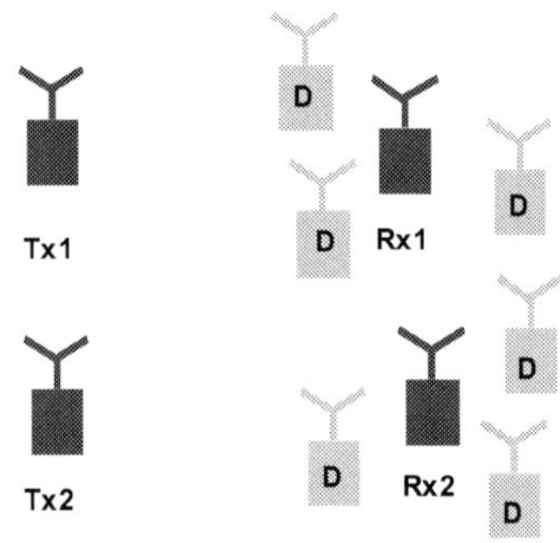

Fig. 7. 2x2 system with 3 dummy sensors per receive sensor

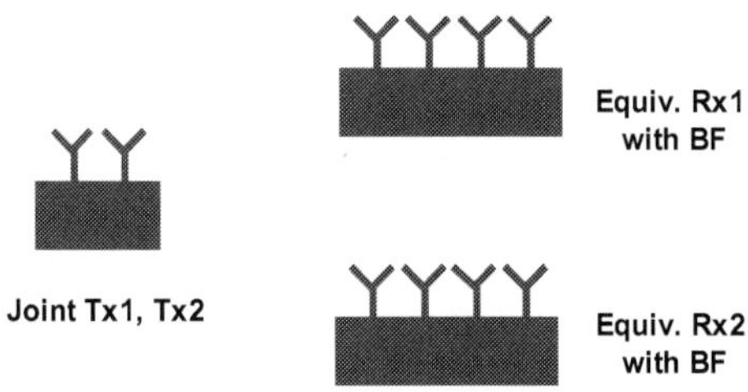

Fig. 8. Equivalent MIMO system of the 2x2 system with 3 dummy sensors per receive sensor

The key issue now is how to design the beamfoming to improve performance. Our proposal follows a double purpose: on the one hand, eliminate intercluster interference, and on the other maximize the intracluster throughput. In order to provide a reasonable model for this situation, we recall again the suboptimal approach described in section 1.

3.3 Proposed solution for the interference scenario

Fig.1 also shows the block diagram of the proposed scheme where $\mathbf{H}_k$ (N_b, N_s) represents the equivalent channel to the subcluster forming the beamforming. We will force N_b>N_s for rank reasons as we will describe later. $\mathbf{r}_k$ represents again the beamforming to be designed.

In the interference-free scenario, the beamforming design would be the same as that described in section 2. However, current criteria assume that the interference channels are known at the receiver beamformers location. The suboptimal procedure can be described in several key ideas:

First point: eliminate completely the intercluster interference. In order to guarantee this condition, every beamformer must fulfil $\mathbf{r}_k$:

$$\mathbf{r}_k^H \mathbf{M}_k \mathbf{F}_{\text{int}} \mathbf{x}_{\text{int}} = 0 \tag{39}$$

where $\mathbf{M}_k$ is the channel (Ns, N_b) between the interfering cluster and the beamformer k.

Equation (39) is quite simple under the rank condition already mentioned because $\mathbf{r}_k$ must belong to the null space of $\mathbf{M}_k$.

Second point: recalling (9) a suboptimal solution to this problem is proposed in the real multiantenna scenario without interference. We showed that the beamformers maximizing throughput must be found from the following eigenanalysis (we show this again for convenience).

$$\mathbf{H}_k \mathbf{H}_k^H \mathbf{r}_k = \lambda_{\max} \mathbf{r}_k \tag{40}$$

Third point: in order to fulfil both previous points, our solution is based on the decomposition of $\mathbf{H}_k$ into 2 orthogonal components, one of them expanding the null subspace of $\mathbf{M}_k$.

$$\mathbf{H}_k = \mathbf{H}_k^{\mathbf{M}_k} + \mathbf{H}_k^{\perp\mathbf{M}_k} \tag{41}$$

The final solution modifies the criteria given by (9) as

$$\mathbf{H}_k^{\perp\mathbf{M}_k} \left(\mathbf{H}_k^{\perp\mathbf{M}_k}\right)^H \mathbf{r}_k = \lambda_{\max} \mathbf{r}_k \tag{42}$$

3.4 Simulation Results

This section addresses some of the most remarkable results. The first scenario that is considered assumes a very closely spaced transmit sensor group, as well as the receive group, modelled with a high gain value (G=1000, that is, 30dB). The AWGN variance at the receive sensors is set to a very low value, in order to notice the degradation due to the intercluster interference and not to start with the scenario that is already close to saturation. Therefore, the noise variance is set to 0.03. A two transmit and two receive sensors (2x2) system is considered, with a variable number of dummy sensors - from 2 to 6 (that is, 3 to 7 cooperative sensors) and the simulation results are shown in Figure 9.

The sum rate capacity is depicted for the number of dummy sensors and for three configurations: a) system without intercluster interference and with beamforming according to equation (40), b) system with intercluster interference and beamforming according to equation (40) and finally, c) the proposed scheme, the system with intercluster interference and beamforming according to equation (42) that takes into account this interference and cancels it (Interference cancellation, IC). These schemes are denoted 'No interference', 'With Interference' and 'With Interference and IC', respectively.
These three scenarios enable the comparison of the proposed system in terms of the maximum sum rate when no intercluster interference is present and dummy sensors are used for throughput maximization. It is interesting in case a) to notice that incrementing the number of dummy sensors does not lead to a large capacity improvement. Moreover, the performance of this scheme is highly degraded when intercluster interference is included (case b)), and this is shown by the simulation results. It should be noted that above three or four dummy sensors, the sum rate improvement with increment of the number of dummy sensors is more pronounced in this case than in the former one. As the intercluster interference is modelled as an AWGN contribution, this shows that the throughput maximization with beamforming is more effective at lower SNR values. Finally, the third scheme (case c))is the ad hoc scheme for the analyzed configuration, with beamforming that takes into account the intercluster interference improving significantly the performance of the system, upper bounded by the sum rate of the system without intercluster interference. A smaller number of dummy sensors does not make sense for IC scheme as there are two transmitter sensors per interfering cluster, and at least two dummy sensors are needed to cancel the interference they cause.

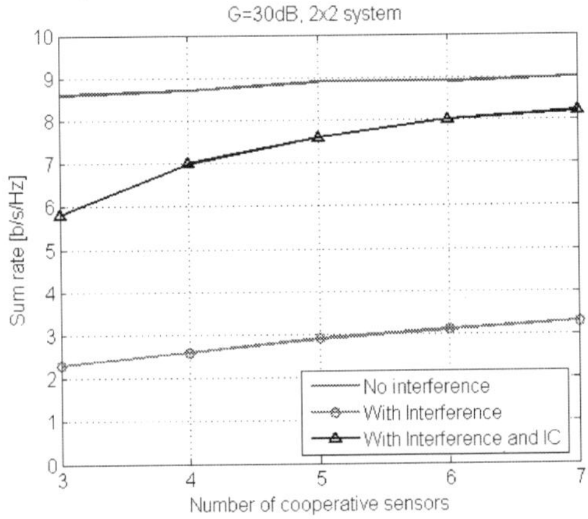

Fig. 9. Effect of the number of dummy sensors

Another aspect of the proposed scheme is its performance under a smaller gain between Tx and Rx groups. The same, 2x2 system is considered again, with four dummy sensors per each active Rx sensor (cooperative group of 5 sensors), and the same low noise variance (σ^2=0.03). The simulation results are depicted in Figure 10. This analysis is performed for gains greater than 100 (10dB), as cooperation is not recommendable at low gains (Ng et al,

2006). It can be observed that the performance loss of the system with intercluster interference and its cancellation with respect to the system without intercluster interference can be considered constant independent of the gain value.
Nevertheless, it is interesting to notice that the performance gain is less pronounced with the gain increment in the scenario with intercluster interference but without its cancellation, as the noise corresponding to the interference remains constant, independent of the gain.

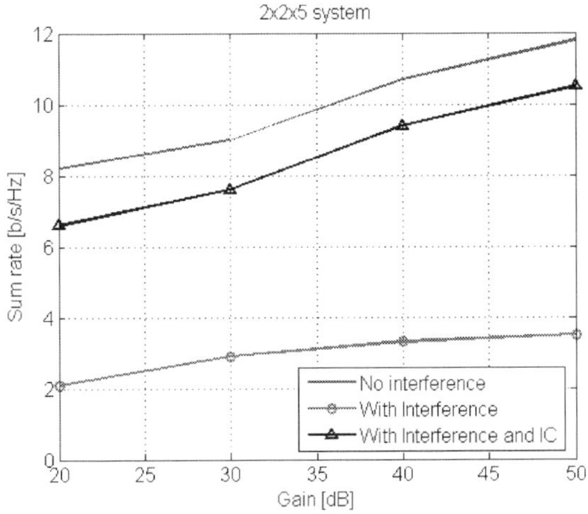

Fig. 10. Effect of the gain in Tx and Rx sectors

4. Conclusions

This chapter presents a new approach to the broadcast channel problem where the main motivation is to provide a suboptimal solution combining DPC with Zero Forcing precoder and optimal beamforming design. The receiver design just relies on the corresponding channel matrix (and not on the other users' channels) while the common precoder uses all the available information of all the involved users. No iterative process between the transmitter and receiver is needed in order to reach the solution of the optimization process. We have shown that this approach provides near-optimal performance in terms of the sum rate but with reduced complexity.
A second application deals with the cooperation design in wireless sensor networks with intra and intercluster interference. We have proposed a combination of DPC principles for the Tx design to eliminate the intracluster interference while at the receivers we have made use of dummy sensors to design a virtual beamformer that minimizes intercluster interference. The combination of both strategies outperforms existing approaches and reinforces the point that joint Tx /Rx cooperation is the most suitable strategy for realistic scenarios with intra and intercluster interference.

5. Acknowledgements

This work has been performed in the framework of the ICT project ICT-217033 WHERE, which is partly funded by the European Union and partly by the Spanish Education and Science Ministry under the Grant TEC2007-67520-C02-01/02/TCM. Furthermore, we thank partial support by the program CONSOLIDER-INGENIO 2010 CSD2008-00010 COMONSENS.

6. References

Barton, R.J., Chen, J., Huang, K, Wu, D., Wu, H-C.; Performance of Cooperative Time-Reversal Communication in a Mobile Wireless Environment. *International Journal of Distributed Sensor Networks,* Vol.3, Issue 1, pp. 59-68, January 2007.

Caire G., S. Shamai. On the Achievable Throughput of a Multiantenna Gaussian Broadcast Channel. *IEEE Transactions on Information Theory,* Vol.49, NO.7, July 2003.

Cardoso J.F., A. Souloumiac. Jacobi Angles for Simultaneous Diagonalization, *SIAM J. Matrix Anal. Applications.,* Vol. 17, NO1, Jan 1996.

Cover T.M., J.A. Thomas. *Elements of Information Theory, New York,* Wiley 1991.

Foschini G.J.. Layered space-time architectures for wireless communication in a fading environment when using multielement antennas. *Bell Labs Technical Journal,* Vol. 2, pag.41-59, Autumn 1996.

Hochwald B.M., C.B.Peel, A.L. Swindlehurst. A Vector Perturbation Technique for Near Capacity Multiantenna Multiuser Communication. Part II. *IEEE Transactions on Communications,* Vol.53, NO3, March 2005.

Jindal N., S. Vishwanath, A. Goldsmith. On the Duality of Gaussian Multiple Access and Broadcast Channels. *IEEE Transactions on Information Theory,* Vol.50, NO.5,May 2004.

Jindal N., Multiuser Communication Systems: Capacity, Duality and Cooperation. Ph.D. Thesis, Stanford University, July 2004.

Mudumbai, R., Barriac, G., Madhow, U.; On the Feasibility of Distributed Beamforming in Wireless Networks. *IEEE Transactions on Wireless Communications,* Vol.6, No.5, pp.1754-1763, May 2007.

Ng C., N. Jindal, A. Goldsmith, U. Mitra. Capacity of ad-hoc networks with transmitter and receiver cooperation. Submitted to *IEEE Journal on Selected Areas in Communications,* August 2006.

Ochiai, H., Mitran, P., Poor, H.V., Tarokh, V.; Collaborative Beamforming for Distributed Wireless Ad hoc Sensor Networks. *IEEE Transactions on Signal Processing,* Vol. 53, No11, November 2005.

Pan Z., K.-K. Wong, T.S Ng. Generalized Multiuser Orthogonal Space Division Multiplexing. *IEEE Transactions on Wireless Communications,* Vol.3, NO6, November 2004.

Peel C.B., B.M. Hochwald, A.L. Swindlehurst. A Vector Perturbation Technique for Near Capacity Multiantenna Multiuser Communication. Part I. *IEEE Transactions on Communications,* Vol.53, NO1, January 2005.

Scaglione A., D.L. Goeckel, J.N. Laneman. Cooperative communications in mobile ad-hoc networks, *Signal Processing Magazine*, IEEE Vol. 23 (5), September 2006.

Stankovic V., A. Host-Madsen, X. Zixiang. Cooperative diversity for wireless ad hoc networks. *Signal Processing Magazine,* IEEE Vol. 23 (5), September 2006.

Telatar I.E.. Capacity of multiantenna gaussian channels. *European Transactions on Telecommunications,* Vol. 10, November 1999.

Viswanath P., D. N. C. Tse. Sum capacity of the vector Gaussian broadcast channel and uplink - downlink duality. *IEEE Transactions on Information Theory,* Vol. 49, NO 8, August 2003.

Wong K.-K., R. D. Murch, K. Ben Letaief. Performance Enhancement of Multiuser MIMO Wireless Communication Systems. *IEEE Transactions on Communications,* Vol.50, NO12, December 2002.

Zazo S., H. Huang. Suboptimum Space Multiplexing Structure Combining Dirty Paper Coding and receive beamforming. *International Conference on Acoustics, Speech and Signal Processing,* ICASSP 2006, Toulouse, France, April 2006.

Zazo S., I.Raos, B. Béjar. Cooperation in Wireless Sensor Networks with intra and intercluster interference. *European Signal Processing Conference,* EUSIPCO 2008, Lausanne, Switzerland, August 2008.

23

Robust Designs of Chaos-Based Secure Communication Systems

Ashraf A. Zaher
Kuwait University - Science College - Physics Department
P. O. Box 5969 - Safat 13060 - Kuwait

1. Introduction

Chaos and its applications in the field of secure communication have attracted a lot of attention in various domains of science and engineering during the last two decades. This was partially motivated by the extensive work done in the synchronization of chaotic systems that was initiated by (Pecora & Carroll, 1990) and by the fact that power spectrums of chaotic systems resemble white noise; thus making them an ideal choice for carrying and hiding signals over the communication channel. Drive-response synchronization techniques found typical applications in designing secure communication systems, as they are typically similar to their transmitter-receiver structure. Starting in the early nineties and since the early work of many researchers, e.g. (Cuomo et al., 1993; Dedieu et al., 1993; Wu & Chua, 1993) chaos-based secure communication systems rapidly evolved in many different forms and can now be categorized into four different generations (Yang, 2004).

The major problem in designing chaos-based secure communication systems can be stated as how to send a secret message from the transmitter (drive system) to the receiver (response system) over a public channel while achieving security, maintaining privacy, and providing good noise rejection. These goals should be achieved, in practice, using either analog or digital hardware (Kocarev et al., 1992; Pehlivan & Uyaroğlu, 2007) in a robust form that can guarantee, to some degree, perfect reconstruction of the transmitted signal at the receiver end, while overcoming the problems of the possibility of parameters mismatch between the transmitter and the receiver, limited channel bandwidth, and intruders attacks to the public channel. Several attempts were made, by many researchers to robustify the design of chaos-based secure communication systems and many techniques were developed. In the following, a brief chronological history of the work done is presented; however, for a recent survey the reader is referred to (Yang, 2004) and the references herein.

One of the early methods, called additive masking, used in constructing chaos-based secure communication systems, was based on simply adding the secret message to one of the chaotic states of the transmitter provided that the strength of the former is much weaker than that of the later (Cuomo & Oppenheim, 1993). Although the secret message was perfectly hidden, this technique was impractical because of its sensitivity to channel noise and parameters mismatch between both the transmitter and the receiver. In addition, this method proved to have poor security (Short, 1994). Another method that was aimed at digital signals, called chaos shift keying, was developed in which the transmitter is made to alternate between two different chaotic attractors, implemented via changing the parameters of the chaotic system, based on whether the secret message corresponds to either its high or low value (Parlitz et al., 1992). This method proved to be easy to implement and, at the receiver side, the message can be efficiently reconstructed using a two-stage process consisting of low-pass filtering followed by thresholding. Once again, this method shares, with the additive masking method, the disadvantage of having poor security, especially if the two attractors at the transmitter side are widely separated (Yang, 1995). However, it proved to be more robust in terms of handling noise and parameters mismatch between the transmitter and the receiver, as it was only required to extract binary information.

Extending conventional modulation theory, in communication systems, to chaotic signals was then attempted such that the message signal is used to modulate one of the parameters of the chaotic transmitter (Yang & Chua, 1996). This method was called chaotic modulation and it employed some form of adaptive control at the receiver end to recover the original message via forcing the synchronization error to zero (Zhou & Lai, 1999). The recovered signal, using this technique, was shown to suffer from negligible time delays and minor noise distortion (d'Anjou et al., 2001). Another variant to this method that relied on changing the trajectory of the chaotic transmitter attractor, in the phase space, was also explored in (Wu & Chua, 1993). This method was distinguished by the fact that only one chaotic attractor in the transmitter side was used, in contrast to many attractors in the case of parameter modulation. Although these two techniques (second generation) had a relatively higher security, compared to the previously discussed methods, they still lack robustness against intruder attacks using frequency-based filtering techniques, as exemplified by (Zaher, 2009), especially in the case when the dominant frequency of the secret message is far away from that of the chaotic system.

Motivated by the generation of cipher keys for the use of pseudo-chaotic systems in cryptography (Dachselt & Schwarz, 2001; Stinson, 2005) and the poor security level of the second generation of chaos-based communication systems, a third generation emerged called chaotic cryptosystems. In these systems, various nonlinear encryption methods are used to scramble the secure message at the transmitter side, while using an inverse operation at the receiver side that can effectively recover the original message, provided that synchronization is achieved (Yang et al., 1997). Encryption functions depend on a combination of the chaotic transmitter state(s), excluding the synchronization signal, and one or more of the parameters so that the secret message is effectively hidden. The degree of complexity of the encryption function and the insertion of ciphers (secret keys) led to having more robust techniques with applications to both analog and digital communication (Sobhy & Shehata, 2000; Jiang, 2002; Solak, 2004).

Recently, new techniques, based on impulsive synchronization, were introduced (Yang & Chua, 1997). These systems have better utilization of channel bandwidth as they reduce the information redundancy in the transmitted signal via sending only synchronization impulses to the driven system. Other methods for enhancing security in chaos-based secure communication systems that are currently reported in the literature include employing pseudorandom numbers generators for encoding messages (Zang et al., 2005) and using high-dimension hyperchaotic systems that have multiple positive Lyapunov exponents (Yaowen et al., 2000).

The main purpose of this chapter is to provide a versatile combination of the parameter modulation technique, which belongs to the second generation of chaos-based secure com-

munication systems, and cryptography, which belongs to the third generation, such that the resulting system has the advantages of both of them and, in addition, exhibits more robustness in terms of improved security. The two main topics of chaos synchronization and parameter identification are covered in the next sections to provide the foundation of constructing chaos-based secure communication systems. This is being achieved via using the Lorenz system to build the transmitter/receiver mechanism. The reason for this choice is to provide simple means of comparison with the current research work reported in the literature; however, other chaotic or hyperchaotic systems could have been used as well. The examples illustrated in this chapter cover both analog and digital signals to provide a wider scope of applications. Moreover, most of the simulations were carried out using Simulink while stating all involved signals including initial conditions to provide a consistent reference when verifying the reported results and/or trying to extend the work done to other scenarios or applications. The mathematical analysis is done in a step-by-step method to facilitate understanding the effects of the individual parameters/variables and the results were illustrated in both the time domain and the frequency domain, whenever applicable. Some practical implementations using either analog or digital hardware are also explored.
The rest of this chapter is organized as follows. Section 2 gives a brief description of the famous Lorenz system and its chaotic behaviour that makes it a perfect candidate for implementing chaos-based secure communication systems. Section 3 discusses the topic of synchronizing chaotic systems with emphasis to complete synchronization of identical chaotic systems as an introductory step when constructing the communication systems discussed in this chapter. Section 4 addresses the problem of parameter identification of chaotic systems and focuses on partial identification as a tool for implementing both the encryption and decryption functions at the transmitter and the receiver respectively. Section 5 combines the results of the previous two sections and proposes a robust technique that is demonstrated to have superior security than most of the work currently reported in the literature. Section 6 concludes this chapter and discusses the advantages and limitations of the systems discussed along with proposing future extensions and suggestions that are thought to further improve the performance of chaos-based secure communication systems.

2. The Lorenz System

The Lorenz system is considered a benchmark model when referring to chaos and its synchronization-based applications. Although the Lorenz "strange attractor" was originally noticed in weather patterns (Lorenz, 1963), other practical applications exhibit such strange behaviour, e.g. single-mode lasers (Weiss & Vilaseca, 1991), thermal convection (Schuster & Wolfram, 2005), and permanent magnet synchronous machines (Zaher, 2007). Many researchers used the Lorenz model to exemplify different techniques in the field of chaos synchronization and both complete and partial identification of the unknown or uncertain parameters of chaotic systems. In addition, The Lorenz system is often used to exemplify the performance of newly proposed secure communication systems as illustrated in the references herein. The mathematical model of the Lorenz system takes the form

$$\begin{aligned}\dot{x}_1 &= -\sigma x_1 + \sigma x_2 \\ \dot{x}_2 &= \rho x_1 - x_2 - x_1 x_3 \\ \dot{x}_3 &= -\beta x_3 + x_1 x_2\end{aligned} \tag{1}$$

where $X = [x_1\ x_2\ x_3]^{\mathrm{T}}$ is the state vector and σ, ρ, and β are constant parameters. Notice that each differential equation contains only one parameter. The nominal values of the parameters are 10.0, 28.0, and 8/3 respectively. Using linear analysis techniques, it can be demonstrated that the free-running case corresponds to the following unstable equilibrium points

$$(0\,,0\,,0)\,\text{and}\left[\pm\sqrt{\beta(\rho-1)}\quad \pm\sqrt{\beta(\rho-1)}\quad (\rho-1)\right]^{T} \tag{2}$$

Starting from any initial conditions the Lorenz system will exhibit a chaotic behavior that is characterized by the typical response illustrated in Fig. (1), for which the initial conditions were assumed (1 , 0 , 0).

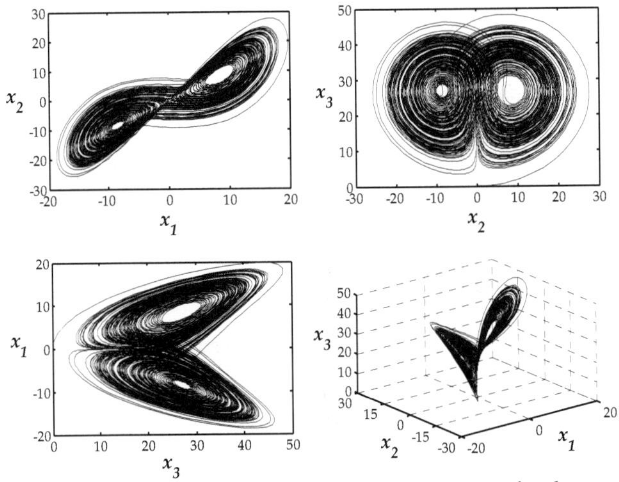

Fig. 1. Illustration of the chaotic performance of the Lorenz system for the nominal values of the parameters.

Throughout this chapter, it will be assumed that both ρ and β are kept constants and that only σ is allowed to change in the interval $8 \le \sigma \le 12$. For this specified interval of σ, it can be proven that the system will still exhibit a chaotic performance; however, the chaotic attractor will change.

3. Synchronization of Chaotic Systems

Synchronization of chaos refers to a process wherein two (or many) chaotic systems (either equivalent or nonequivalent) adjust a given property of their motion to a common behaviour due to a coupling or to a forcing (periodical or noisy) (Boccaletti, 2002). Because of sensitivity to initial conditions, two trajectories emerging from two different closely initial conditions separate exponentially in the course of the time. As a result, chaotic systems defy synchronization. There exist several types of synchronization including complete synchronization, lag synchronization, generalized synchronization, frequency synchronization, phase synchronization, Q-S synchronization, time scale synchronization, and impulsive synchronization. The reader is referred to (Zaher, 2008a) for a list of references that cover these different techniques

Synchronization for two identical, possibly chaotic, dynamical systems can be achieved such that the solution of one always converges to the solution of the other independently of the initial conditions (Balmforth, 1997). This type of synchronization is called drive-response (master-slave) coupling, where there is an interaction between one system and the other, but not vice versa, and synchronization can be achieved provided that all real parts of the Lyapunov exponents of the response system, under the influence of the driver, are negative (Pecora & Carroll, 1991). In the drive-response synchronization scheme it is usually assumed that the complete state vector of the drive system is not available and that only a single scalar output is used in unidirectional coupling between the drive and the response systems. This configuration found useful applications in both secure communication applications (Liao & Huang, 1999) and the construction of parameter identification algorithms (Carroll, 2004; Chen & Kurths, 2007).

This drive-response synchronization scheme is essentially a control problem as the drive signal is used as a feedback signal for the response system such that the synchronization error is continuously attenuated. Due to the nonlinear nature of the dynamics involved in chaos synchronization, Lyapunov functions proved to be successful for the purpose of achieving global stability for this type of synchronization via forcing the error dynamics to approach a zero steady state. In this section, a recursive algorithm, inspired from backstepping control, is proposed such that both fast and stable operation of the synchronization process is obtained. Backstepping is basically a recursive design procedure that can extend the applicability of Lyapunov-based designs to nonlinear systems via introducing virtual reference models to prescribe target behaviour for some or all of the original system states and then use some of them as virtual controls to the output (Krstic, 1995). This idea seems to be very appealing, especially when combined with Lyapunov-energy-like functions to design the control law. Using the Lorenz system, described by Eq. (1), and assuming identical dynamics for both the transmitter (drive system) and the receiver (response system), the following virtual (intermediate) functions are introduced

$$f_i = x_i - k_{i1}x_1 \ , i = 2,3 \tag{3}$$

where k_{21} and k_{32} are control parameters to be found later, x_1 is the drive signal, and both f_2 and f_3 are used implicitly to observe x_2 and x_3 of the transmitter.

Subsituting Eq. (1) in the derivative of Eq. (3) yields

$$\begin{aligned} \dot{f}_2 &= [\rho x_1 - (f_2 + k_{21}x_1) - x_1(f_3 + k_{31}x_1)] - k_{21}[-\sigma x_1 + \sigma(f_2 + k_{21}x_1)] \\ &= -f_2 - x_1 f_3 - \sigma k_{21} f_2 + \varphi_2(x_1) \end{aligned} \tag{4}$$

where

$$\varphi_2(x_1) = x_1\left[\rho - k_{21} + \sigma k_{21}(1-k_{21})\right] - k_{31}x_1^2 \tag{5}$$

and

$$\begin{aligned}\dot{f}_3 &= [-\beta(f_3 + k_{31}x_1 + x_1(f_2 + k_{21}x_1)] - k_{31}[-\sigma x_1 + \sigma(f_2 + k_{21}x_1)] \\ &= x_1 f_2 - \beta f_3 - \sigma k_{31} f_2 + \varphi_3(x_1)\end{aligned} \tag{6}$$

where

$$\varphi_3(x_1) = x_1\left[-\beta k_{31} + \sigma k_{31}(1-k_{21})\right] + k_{21}x_1^2 \tag{7}$$

Now, introducing the following synchronization errors

$$e_i = x_i - \hat{x}_i = f_i - \hat{f}_i \,, i = 2{,}3 \tag{8}$$

results in

$$\begin{aligned}\dot{e}_2 &= -(1+\sigma k_{21})e_2 - x_1 e_3 \\ \dot{e}_3 &= x_1 e_2 - \beta e_3 - \sigma k_{31} e_2\end{aligned} \tag{9}$$

The following simple Lyapunov function is now proposed

$$L = 0.5(e_2^2 + e_3^2) \tag{10}$$

leading to

$$\begin{aligned}\dot{L} &= e_2\dot{e}_2 + e_3\dot{e}_3 \\ &= -[(1+\sigma k_{21})e_2^2 + \sigma k_{31}e_2 e_3 + \beta e_3^2]\end{aligned} \tag{11}$$

which can be made negative definite via the following choice of the control parameters

$$k_{21} \geq \frac{\sigma k_{31}^2}{4\beta} - \frac{1}{\sigma} \tag{12}$$

From which global stability is assured as illustrated by Eq. (13)

$$\dot{L} = -(1 + \sigma k_{21} - \frac{\sigma^2 k_{31}^2}{4\beta})e_2^2 - (\frac{\sigma k_{31}}{2\sqrt{\beta}}e_2 + \sqrt{\beta}e_3)^2 \leq 0 \tag{13}$$

Figure (2) represents a graphical interpretation of the result obtained in Eq. (12), where it is shown that a wide range of values exist to implement the suggested technique. This offers flexibility, when implementing this synchronization method, in meeting any physical constraints imposed by the chosen analog or digital hardware. In addition, it should be emphasized that when both k_{21} and k_{31} are put equal to zero, the conventional method of synchronization, developed in (Pecora & Carroll, 1990), is obtained. This fact is taken an advantage of when comparing the speed of response of the suggested technique to other methods reported in the literature, as illustrated in Fig. (3).

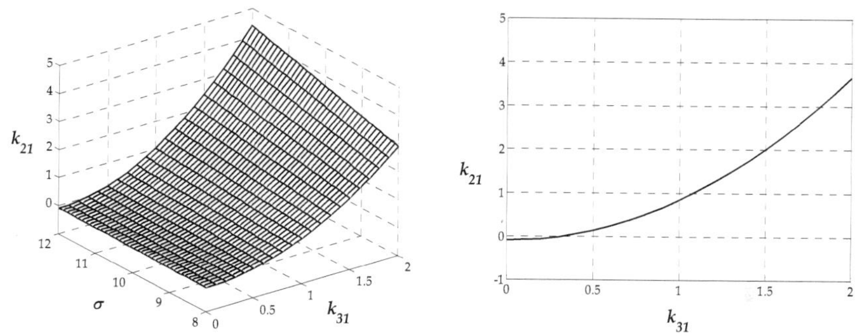

(a) (b)

Fig. 2. Stable range of the control parameters, showing k_{21} as a function of both σ and k_{31} corresponding to the ranges $8 \leq \sigma \leq 12$ and $0 \leq k_{31} \leq 2$ as illustrated in (a). The relationship between k_{21} and k_{31} for the nominal value of $\sigma = 10$ is shown in (b).

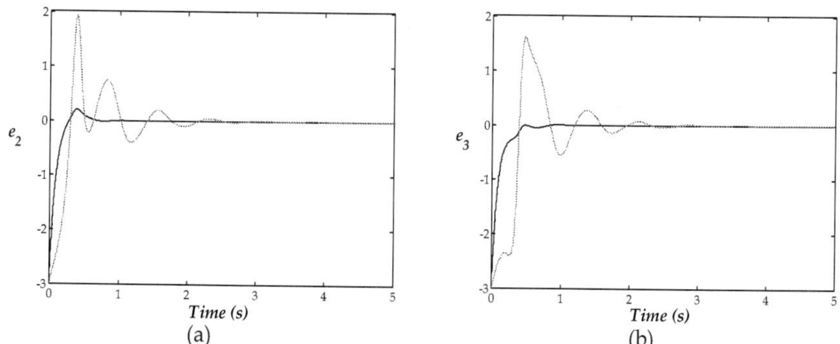

(a) (b)

Fig. 3. Comparison between the fast recursive synchronization method for the special case $k_{21} = k_{31} = 1$ (solid line) and the conventional synchronization when $k_{21} = k_{31} = 0$ (dotted line) for both e_2 and e_3 in (a) and (b) respectively.

3.1 A detailed example

The designed receiver acts as a state observer that uses one scalar time series (x_1) to estimate the remaining states of the transmitter (x_2 and x_3). Because of the nonlinear structure of the overall system comprising both the transmitter and the receiver, it will be difficult to draw general conclusions about the best values of the control parameters that result in the fastest response while avoiding too much control effort that might lead to saturation and consequently adding more nonlinearities into the system. To investigate the practicality of the design, a simple version of the design is now implemented in analog hardware using $k_{21} = 1$ and $k_{31} = 0$. The resulting system is governed by Eq. (14) and is illustrated by the Simulink block diagram, shown in Fig. (4).

$$\begin{aligned}
\dot{x}_1 &= -\sigma x_1 + \sigma x_2 \\
\dot{x}_2 &= \rho x_1 - x_2 - x_1 x_3 \\
\dot{x}_3 &= -\beta x_3 + x_1 x_2 \\
\dot{\hat{f}}_2 &= -(\sigma + 1)\hat{f}_2 - x_1 \hat{f}_3 + (\rho - 1)x_1 \\
\dot{\hat{f}}_3 &= x_1 \hat{f}_2 - \beta \hat{f}_3 + x_1^2 \\
\hat{x}_2 &= \hat{f}_2 + x_1 \\
\hat{x}_3 &= \hat{f}_3
\end{aligned} \tag{14}$$

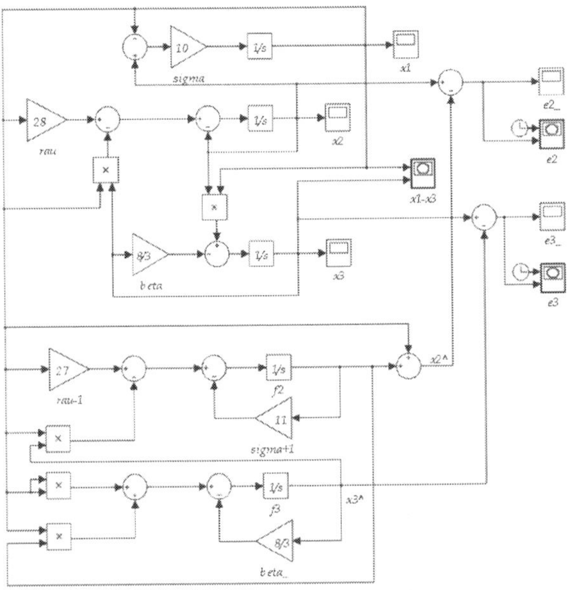

Fig. 4. A Simulink model for the simulation and implementation of Eq. (14) for the special case when $k_{21} = 1$ and $k_{31} = 0$.

3.2 Practical considerations in the implementation phase

To meet practical considerations when implementing the drive-response system using analog hardware, it will be required to adjust the peak values of the signals to fall within the saturation levels imposed by the power supply and, in addition, to change the frequency band of the system to conform to that of the signals involved, e.g. the transmitted secret message in the case of secure communication systems. This can be achieved by using the linear transformation in Eq. (15) that results in the modified system depicted by Eq. (16) for which saturation nonlinearity is avoided.

$$\begin{aligned} & t \leftarrow t/\tau \\ & u = 0.2x_1 \,, v = 0.2x_2 \,, w = 0.1x_3 \,, \\ & \hat{g}_2 = 0.2\hat{f}_2 \,, \text{and } \hat{g}_3 = 0.1\hat{f}_3 \end{aligned} \tag{15}$$

$$\begin{aligned} & \tau\dot{u} = -\sigma u + \sigma v \\ & \tau\dot{v} = \rho u - v - 10uw \\ & \tau\dot{w} = -\beta w + 2.5uv \\ & \tau\dot{\hat{g}}_2 = -(\sigma+1)\hat{g}_2 - 10u\hat{g}_3 + (\rho-1)u \\ & \tau\dot{\hat{g}}_3 = -\beta\hat{g}_3 + 2.5u\hat{g}_2 + 2.5u^2 \\ & \hat{v} = \hat{g}_2 + u \\ & \hat{w} = \hat{g}_3 \end{aligned} \tag{16}$$

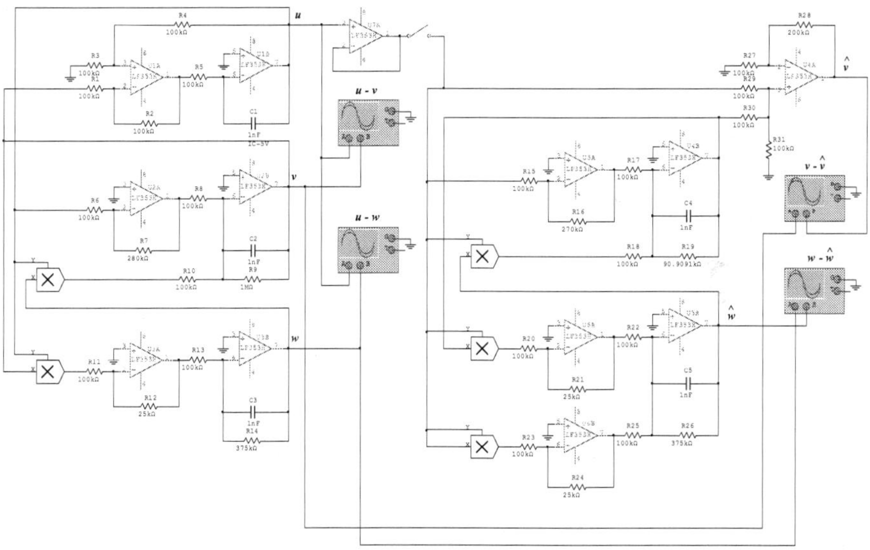

Fig. 5. An analog implementation using the proposed fast recursive drive-response mechanism of the Lorenz system for the special case when using $k_{21} = 1$ and $k_{31} = 0$.

The experimental results for the synchronization process are illustrated in Fig. (6), where it evident that the response system is capable of generating faithful estimates of the states of the transmitter with the help of one driving signal.

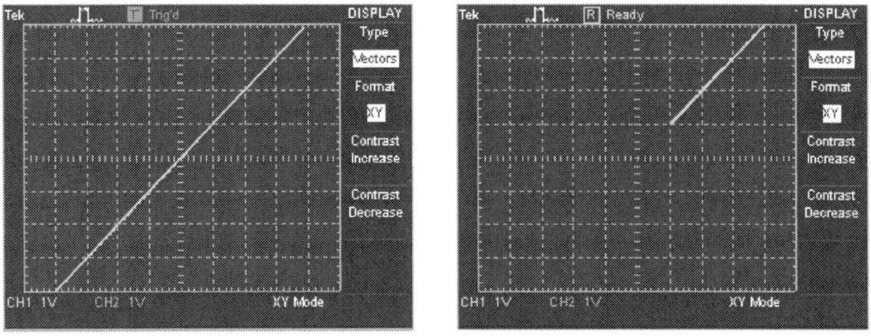

(a) (b)

Fig. 6. The steady state results of the synchronization, illustrating perfect matching between the states of both the drive and response systems for x_2 and x_3 in (a) and (b) respectively.

3.3 Case study I

Constructing a secure communication system is now investigated where the fast recursive synchronization mechanism is now combined with a nonlinear encryption function, *E*, at the transmitter in order to hide the secret message $s(t)$. At The receiver side, a decryption function, *D*, reverses the scrambling process to reconstruct the original message. Figure (7) illustrates this idea where the frequency band of both the transmitter and the receiver are adjusted using the time scaling factor, τ, and the public channel is used to transmit both x_1 (the driving signal necessary for synchronization), and *E*, the encrypted secret message, which is similar to the work done in (Jiang, 2002; Solak, 2004; Zaher, 2009). Figure (8) illustrate the power spectrum analysis for both the secret message and the chaotic transmitter.

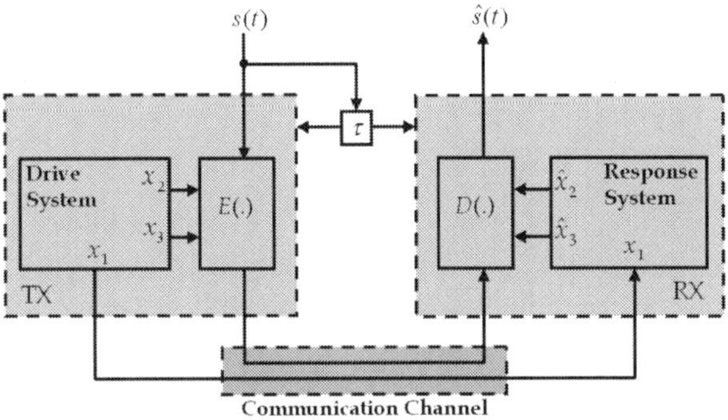

Fig. 7. A block diagram representation of the chaos-based secure communication system.

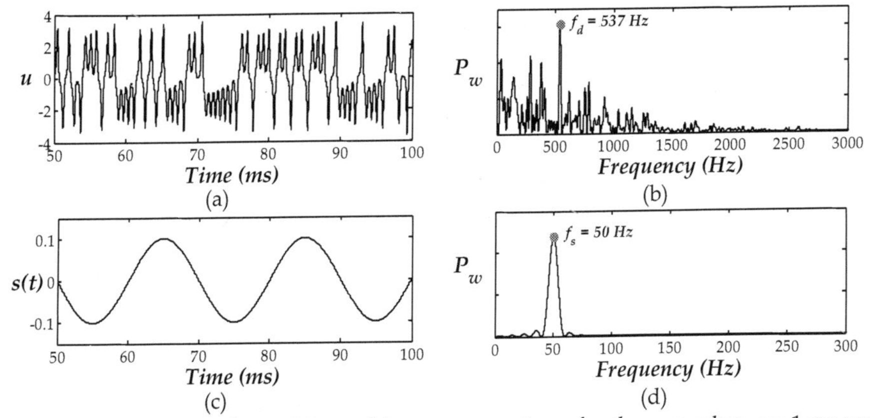

Fig. 8. The driving signal, $u = 0.2x_1$ and its power spectrum for the case when $\tau = 1$ ms are shown in (a) and (b) respectively. The sample transmitted secret message and its power spectrum are illustrated in (c) and (d) respectively.

Both the encryption and decryption functions are given in Eq. (17), where only x_2 was used to construct the nonlinear scrambling. The decryption function should settle very fast to the inverse of the encryption function, once synchronization is achieved.

$$\begin{aligned} E(X,s,t) &= x_2^2 + (1 + x_2^2)s(t) \\ \hat{s}(t) = D(\hat{X},s,t) &= (E(X,s,t) - \hat{x}_2^2)/(1 + \hat{x}_2^2) \end{aligned} \tag{17}$$

For improved security, the amplitude of the secret message should be much smaller than that of x_2. For simplicity and without loss of generality, a sinusoidal signal is chosen for illustration purposes with the form $s(t) = A_s \sin(2\pi f_s t)$, $f_s << f_d$, for which the frequency, f_s, is chosen to be much less than the dominant frequency of the chaotic attractor of the transmitter, f_d, to ensure minimum effects of transients. Figure (9) illustrate the improvements in the decryption error, $e(t) = D(t) - s(t)$, when using the conventional and the fast recursive methods for synchronization, where the absolute value of $e(t)$ over five periods of the transmitted signal was found to reduce from 4.2% to 1.7% respectively.

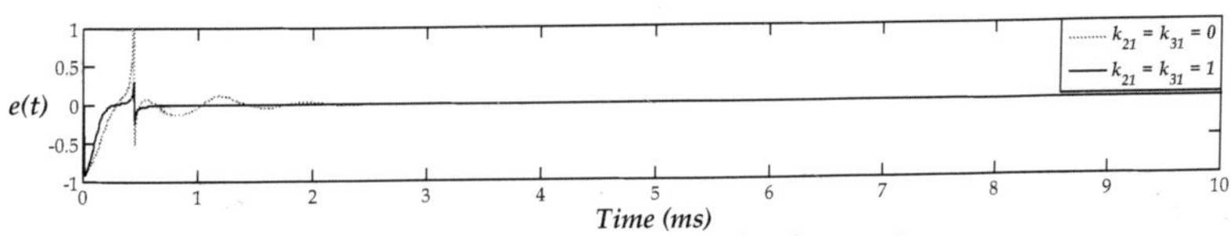

Fig. 9. A comparative study of the transient effects on the decryption error.

Figure (10) illustrate the complete response of the communication system, demonstrating the satisfactory performance of the proposed technique.

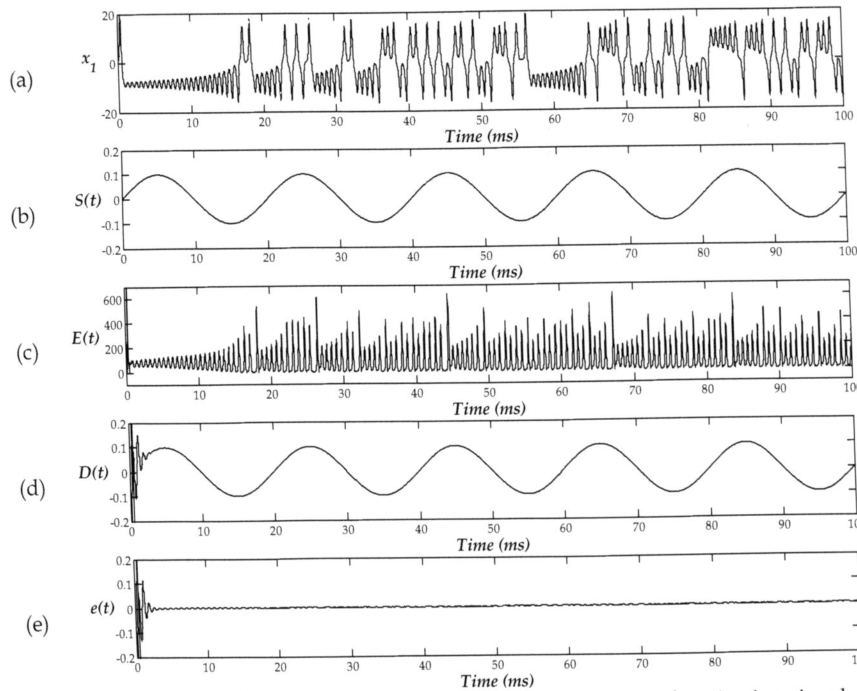

Fig. 10. Signals profile of the secure communication system. The synchronization signal, x_1, is shown in (a), the secret message, $s(t)$, in (b), the encrypted signal, $E(t)$, in (c), the decrypted signal, $D(t)$, in (d), and finally the decryption error, $e(t)$, in (e).

3.4 Sensitivity and security analysis for case study I

The encryption function considered in the previous section depends only on x_2 and consequently the decryption error is sensitive to synchronization errors. To investigate this problem, two cases will be considered that include both multiplicative and additive errors. These errors can result from channel noise, modelling errors, or both. The mathematical representation of this problem is described in Eq. (18).

$$\begin{aligned} &\text{Multiplicative error}: \hat{x}_2 = x_2(1+\Delta) \\ &\text{Additive error}: \hat{x}_2 = x_2 + \delta \end{aligned} \tag{18}$$

Figure (11) shows the synchronization error problem for the case when the transmitted message is an analog sinusoidal signal for different values of Δ and δ, illustrating the strong dependence of the decryption error on the synchronization errors. Figures (12) and (13) confirm the same result when the frequency of the transmitted message is comparable to and much greater than the dominant frequency of the chaotic attractor of the transmitter, corresponding to 500 Hz and 5 kHz respectively.

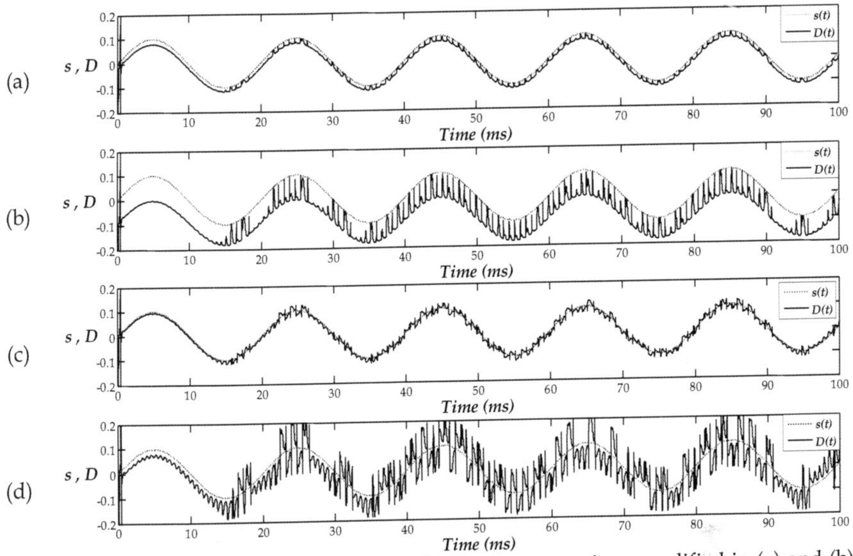

Fig. 11. The sensitivity to synchronization multiplicative errors is exemplified in (a) and (b), corresponding to $\Delta = 0.01$ and 0.05 respectively and to synchronization additive errors in (c) and (d), corresponding to $\delta = 0.02$ and 0.1 respectively ($f_s = 50$ Hz).

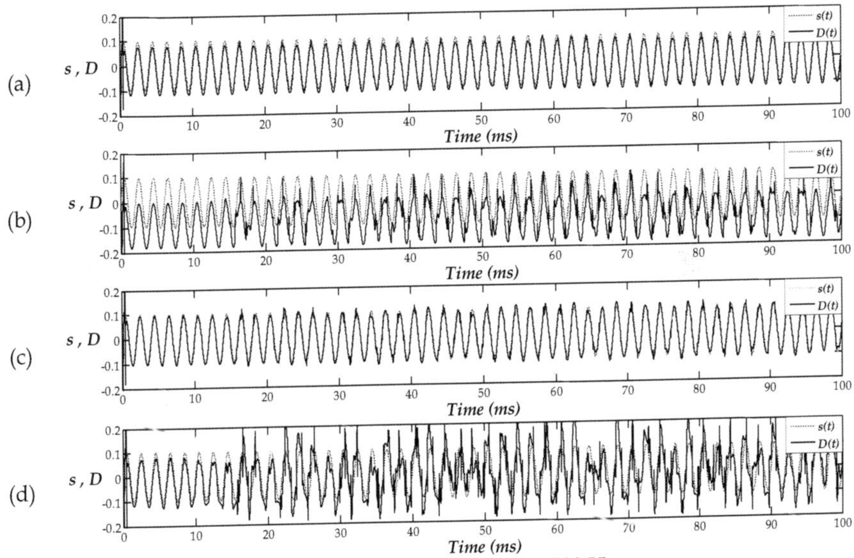

Fig. 12. The sensitivity to synchronization errors, when $f_s = 500$ Hz.

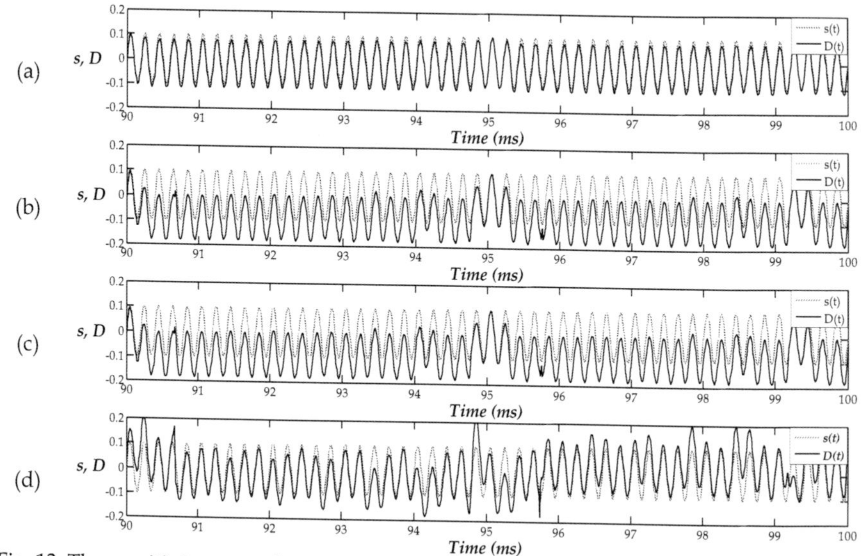

Fig. 13. The sensitivity to synchronization errors, when f_s = 5 kHz.

Figures (11-13) show that the effect of additive error is more critical than multiplicative error. In addition, as the frequency of the transmitted signal increases the decrypted signal deteriorates, as transient effects will persist. Although the envelope of the transmitted signal can be clearly seen from the distorted decrypted signal, for the transmission of digital signals this is not the case. To complete the analysis of the communication system, its security is investigated by assuming that an intruder picks up the encrypted message from the communication channel and then tries to isolate the digital secret message by employing a two-stage process consisting of low-pass filtering and thresholding. This is illustrated in Fig. (14).

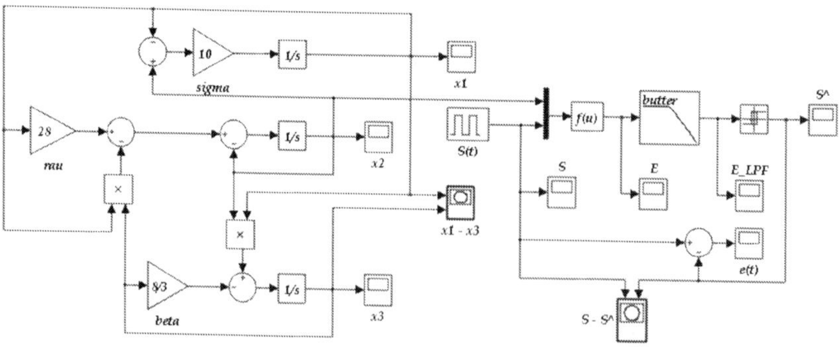

Fig. 14. A Simulink model illustrating the possibility of breaking the security of the communication system via utilizing simple filtering techniques.

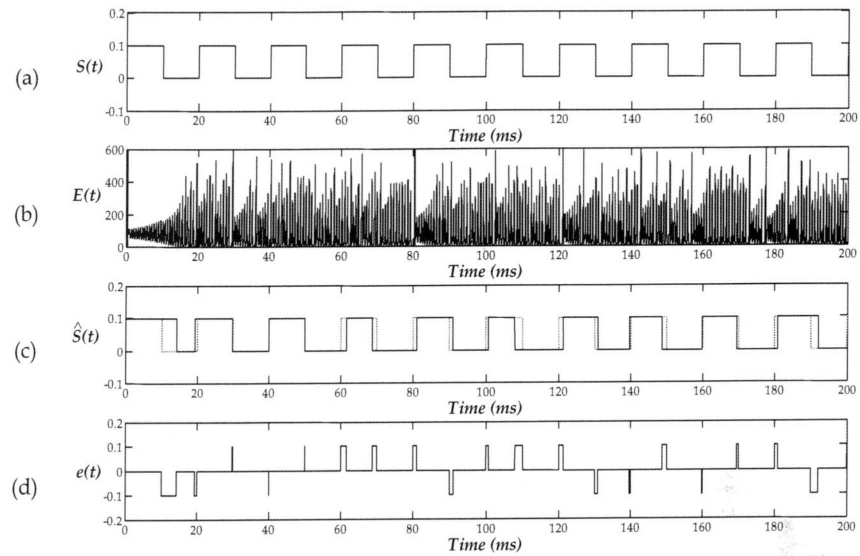

Fig. 15. The response of the intruder system showing the original secret message; $s(t)$, its encryption using only x_2; $E(t)$, the decrypted signal; $D(t)$ superimposed on $s(t)$, and the decryption error; $e(t)$, in (a), (b), (c), and (d) respectively.

Figure (15) shows a successful attack of an intruder for the case when the frequency of the digital secret message, f_s, was much less than that of the chaotic transmitter, f_d. The same argument applies when f_s is much higher than f_d as using a high-pass filter can isolate the digital message; however, the effect of time delays and channel noise will be more obvious. When f_s and f_d occupy the same frequency interval, it will not be possible to use filtering techniques to separate them from each other. This fact will be used later in this chapter to robustify the design of the secure communication system. It can be also demonstrated that it is easier to break into the system and recover digital message rather than analog messages because of the sensitivity of the later to noise.

3.5 Case study II

The aforementioned discussion requires modifying the encryption function at the transmitter, depicted by Fig. (7) and Eq. (17), to make it more difficult for the intruder to break the security of the communication system. This will be the topic of the next section; but first the parameter modulation technique is now investigated as a possible replacement to encryption. Figure (16) shows a Simulink model for such purpose, where the secret message is used directly to modulate the value of σ. The analysis carried out in (Álvarez, 2004; Zaher, 2009) is now used to prove that it is easy to recover the original digital signal using low-pass filtering followed by thresholding, without having to know the structure of the transmitter or to synchronizer a receiver model with that of the transmitter. Figure (17) illustrate the results of such system.

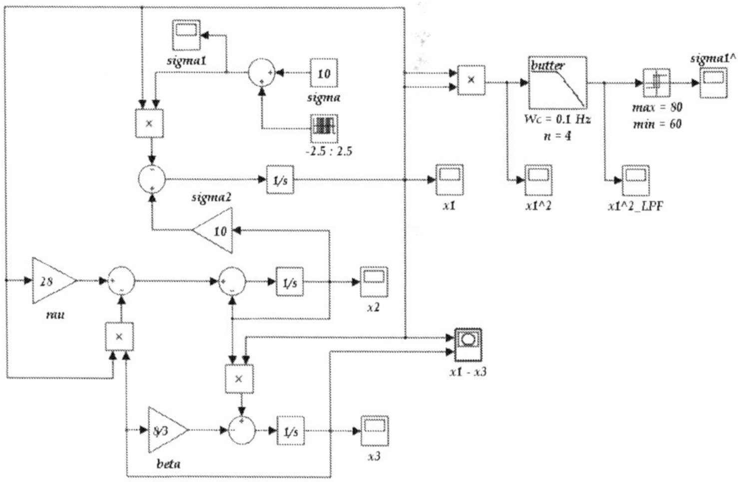

Fig. 16. A Simulink block diagram illustration of using simple filtering techniques to break into a chaos-based communication system that relies on parameter modulation.

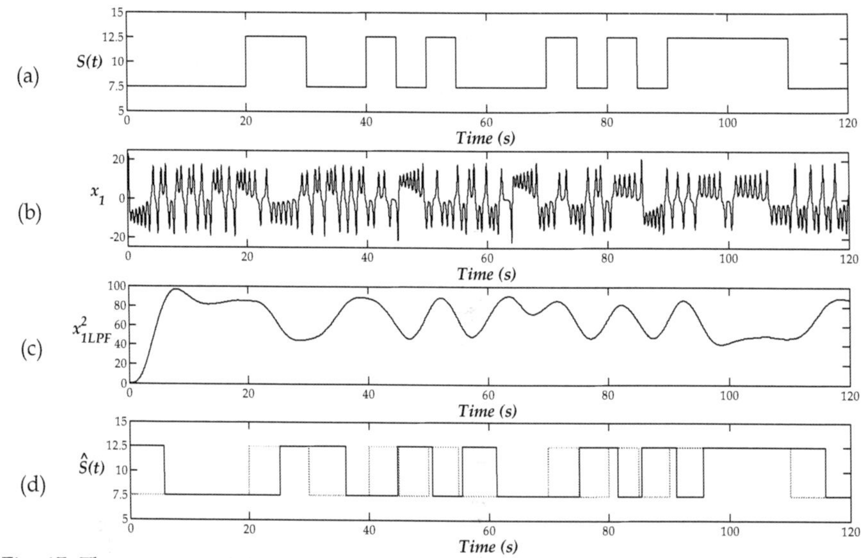

Fig. 17. The response of the intruder system showing the original secret message; $s(t)$, its encryption; $E(t)$, the output of the low-pass filter, and the reconstructed message, superimposed on $s(t)$, in (a), (b), (c), and (d) respectively.

4. Identifying the Parameters of Chaotic Systems

A feasible improvement to chaos-based cryptosystems can be made via making the encryption process a function of one or more of the parameters of the chaotic transmitter and not only the states. A possible candidate is given in Eq. (19) and is illustrated in Fig. (18).

$$E(X,\sigma,s,t) = x_2^2 + (\sigma^2 + x_2^2)s(t)$$
$$\hat{s}(t) = D(\hat{X},\sigma,s,t) = (E(X,\sigma,s,t) - \hat{x}_2^2)/(\sigma^2 + \hat{x}_2^2) \tag{19}$$

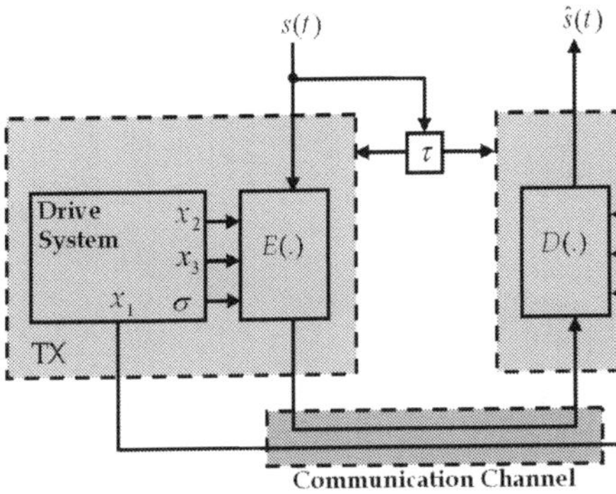

Fig. 18. A block diagram representation of the modified chaos-based secure communication system for which the encryption function depends on σ.

Although the scrambling of the message is improved, this has the effect of increasing the message strength; thus making it more vulnerable to be digged out of the encrypted signal using simple filtering techniques. This is illustrated in Fig. (19) using the same filtering technique discussed in Sec. (3.5). Figure (20) shows a Simulink model for implementing Eq. (19), while Figs. (21) and (22) show the effect of guessing σ by the intruder, assuming that only the model of the transmitter and the structure of the encryption function are known.

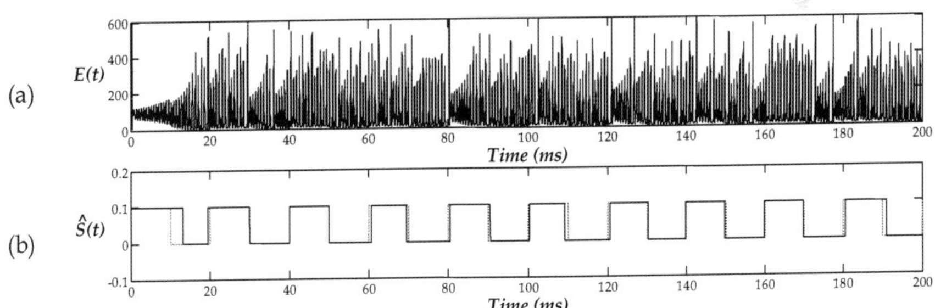

Fig. 19. The response of the modified intruder system showing $E(t)$ that depends on both x_2 and σ, and the decrypted signal, $D(t)$, superimposed on $s(t)$, in (a), (b) respectively.

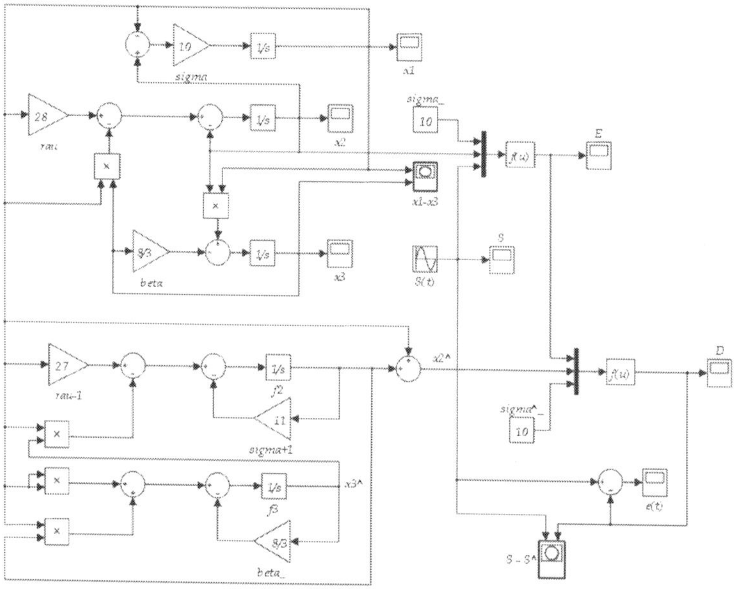

Fig. 20. A Simulink block diagram illustration of using the modified encryption function in Eq. (19) assuming a constant value of σ.

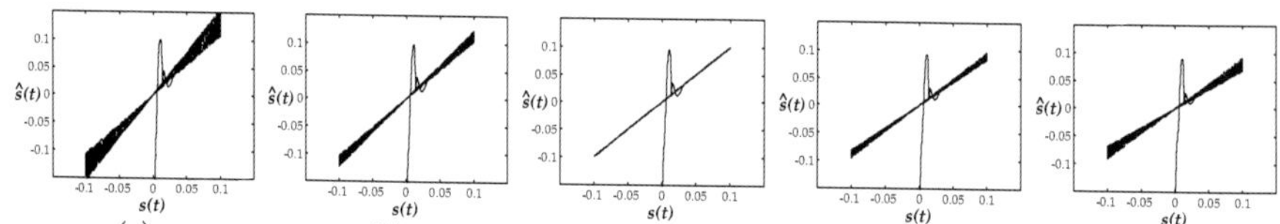

(a) (b) (c) (d) (e)

Fig. 21. The response of the receiver (or intruder) system assuming complete knowledge of the encryption function and guessing different values for σ corresponding to 8, 9, 10, 11, and 12 in (a), (b), (c), (d), and (e) respectively (analog case).

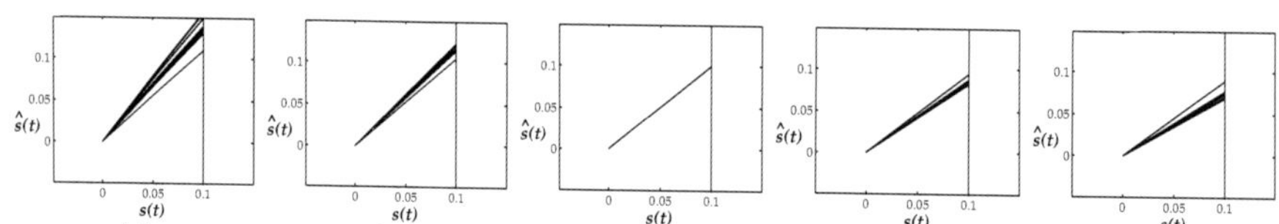

(a) (b) (c) (d) (e)

Fig. 22. The response of the receiver (or intruder) system assuming complete knowledge of the encryption function and guessing different values for σ corresponding to 8, 9, 10, 11, and 12 in (a), (b), (c), (d), and (e) respectively (digital case).

4.1 Partial identification of the transmitter parameters

Many chaos-based applications require the estimation of some or all of the chaotic system parameters. The degree of complexity of the estimation process depends crucially on many factors; among them the structure and type of nonlinearity of the system at hand, complete or partial availability of the states for direct measurement, and the nature of the application, e.g., whether it is required to control the chaos, or to synchronize two identical or different chaotic systems (Zaher, 2008b). Meanwhile, it is interesting to notice that most, if not all, parameter identification algorithms come together with some form of synchronization, i.e. it is required to identify the unknown parameters in order to achieve synchronization, or synchronization is used as an intermediate step to identify the unknown parameters.

The design procedure for both synchronization and parameter identification usually achieves the desired objectives by constructing a suitable Lyapunov function and forcing its derivative to be negative definite. However, the construction of Lyapunov functions remains to be a difficult task, and is usually considered a bottleneck in the design. Achieving the stability and convergence of the parameter identification algorithms is usually difficult to prove analytically, especially when using synchronization due to the increased order of the overall system (Kocarev & Parlitz, 1995).

Utilizing a single scalar time series for the purpose of parameter identification, synchronization, or both usually puts some constraints on the ability to identify all the parameters of the chaotic system. Many techniques were reported in the literature that only deal with partial identification with application to the Lorenz system (d'Anjou, 2001; Sakaguchi, 2002; Solak, 2004; Zaher, 2007). Motivated by the requirement to improve the security of the encryption function, the parameter σ can be considered as a secret key (cipher). Choosing the interval for σ should ensure the persistence of chaos; otherwise, the encryption process will fail. For the Lorenz system and considering the nominal values for both ρ and β it was found that the chosen range of $8 \le \sigma \le 12$ is satisfactory. In the next section we derive the mathematical foundation for estimating σ at the receiver side using only the knowledge of x_1 under the assumption that both ρ and β are kept constants.

4.2 Design of the parameter update law

Under the assumptions in the previous section, the modified receiver dynamics are now described by

$$\begin{aligned} \dot{\hat{x}}_1 &= -\hat{\sigma}\hat{x}_1 + \hat{\sigma}\hat{x}_2 \\ \dot{\hat{x}}_2 &= \rho x_1 - \hat{x}_2 - x_1\hat{x}_3 \\ \dot{\hat{x}}_3 &= -\beta\hat{x}_3 + x_1\hat{x}_2 \end{aligned} \tag{20}$$

where the "^" symbol stands for the estimated value of the unknown state or parameter. Thus, the synchronization and identification errors, respectively, are given by

$$\begin{aligned} e_i &= \hat{x}_i - x_i \, , i = 1,2,3 \\ e_\sigma &= \hat{\sigma} - \sigma \end{aligned} \tag{21}$$

resulting in

$$\begin{aligned}\dot{e}_1 &= \dot{\hat{x}}_1 - \dot{x}_1 \\ &= (-\hat{\sigma}\hat{x}_1 + \hat{\sigma}\hat{x}_2) + (\sigma x_1 - \sigma x_2) \\ &= (-\hat{\sigma}\hat{x}_1 + \hat{\sigma}\hat{x}_2 + \hat{\sigma}x_1 - \hat{\sigma}x_2) + (\sigma x_1 - \sigma x_2 - \hat{\sigma}x_1 + \hat{\sigma}x_2) \\ &= \hat{\sigma}[(\hat{x}_2 - x_2) - (\hat{x}_1 - x_1)] + (\hat{\sigma} - \sigma)(x_2 - x_1) \\ &= \hat{\sigma}(e_2 - e_1) + e_\sigma(x_2 - x_1)\end{aligned} \tag{22}$$

and

$$\begin{aligned}\dot{e}_2 &= \dot{\hat{x}}_2 - \dot{x}_2 \\ &= (\rho x_1 - \hat{x}_2 - x_1\hat{x}_3) - (\rho x_1 - x_2 - x_1 x_3) \\ &= -(\hat{x}_2 - x_2) - x_1(\hat{x}_3 - x_3) \\ &= -e_2 - x_1 e_3\end{aligned} \tag{23}$$

and

$$\begin{aligned}\dot{e}_3 &= \dot{\hat{x}}_3 - \dot{x}_3 \\ &= (-\beta\hat{x}_3 + x_1\hat{x}_2) - (-\beta x_3 + x_1 x_2) \\ &= -\beta(\hat{x}_3 - x_3) - x_1(\hat{x}_2 - x_2) \\ &= -\beta e_3 - x_1 e_2\end{aligned} \tag{24}$$

The goal now is to force the synchronization errors to zero, and, at the same time, to design a parameter update law for σ such that the overall system is asymptotically stable. Notice that the receiver has an order of four, compared to the previous one, given by Eqs. (3-9), which has an order of only two. Introducing the following Lyapunov function

$$L = 0.5[e_1^2 + \mu_{23}(e_2^2 + e_3^2) + \mu_\sigma e_\sigma^2] \tag{25}$$

where μ_{23} and μ_σ are positive constants, leads to

$$\begin{aligned}\dot{L} &= e_1\dot{e}_1 + \mu_{23}e_2\dot{e}_2 + \mu_{23}e_3\dot{e}_3 + \mu_\sigma e_\sigma^2 \\ &= (\hat{\sigma}e_1e_2 - \hat{\sigma}e_1^2 + x_2e_1e_\sigma - x_1e_1e_\sigma) - (\mu_{23}e_2^2 + \mu_{23}x_1e_2e_3) + (\mu_{23}x_1e_2e_3 - \mu_{23}\beta e_3^2) + \mu_\sigma e_\sigma\dot{\hat{\sigma}} \\ &= -(\hat{\sigma}e_1^2 - \hat{\sigma}e_1e_2 + \mu_{23}e_2^2) - \mu_{23}\beta e_3^2 + e_\sigma[e_1(x_2 - x_1) + \mu_\sigma\dot{\hat{\sigma}}]\end{aligned} \tag{26}$$

Proving negative definiteness of Eq. (26) can be greatly simplified by using the assumptions given in Eqs. (27) and (28)

$$\mu_{23} = \frac{\hat{\sigma}}{4}, 0 \le \hat{\sigma} \le \sigma_{\max} \tag{27}$$

$$\dot{\hat{\sigma}} = -\frac{1}{\mu_{23}}(x_2 - x_1)e_1 = -\frac{1}{\sigma\mu_{23}}e_1\dot{x}_1 = k\dot{x}_1(x_1 - \hat{x}_1) \tag{28}$$

where $k = 1/(\sigma\mu_{23})$, as this results in

$$\begin{aligned}\dot{L} &= -[(\sqrt{\hat{\sigma}}e_1)^2 - 2\sqrt{\hat{\sigma}}\frac{\sqrt{\hat{\sigma}}}{2}e_1e_2 + (\frac{\sqrt{\hat{\sigma}}}{2}e_2)^2] - \frac{\hat{\sigma}}{4}\beta e_3^2 \\ &= -(\sqrt{\hat{\sigma}}e_1\frac{\sqrt{\hat{\sigma}}}{2}e_2)^2 - \frac{\hat{\sigma}}{4}\beta e_3^2 \leq 0\end{aligned} \tag{29}$$

The parameter update law, given in Eq. (28), and the result, outlined in Eq. (29) completes the design of the modified secure communication system. Thus, at the receiver side, the message can be decrypted provided that the time delay required for synchronization and identification errors is negligible. This can be guaranteed via choosing a large value for k. Based on the previous results, using a constant value for σ results in poor security, as the intruder can still guess its value. Moreover, if the bandwidths of the transmitted signal and the chaotic transmitter are widely separated, simple filtering techniques can still recover the original message, despite the improved encryption done at the transmitter side. To overcome these problems, another technique will be attempted, in the next section, to achieve improved encryption in both time and frequency domains.

5. A Proposal for a Robust Communication System

A better scrambling of the secret message can be obtained if the encryption function is made to depend on a continuously changing parameter along with the chaotic states of the transmitter. This parameter can correspond to one of the chaotic transmitter parameters and consequently it can accomplish two tasks:

i. to act as a cipher key that makes the scrambling process of the transmitted message more robust,
ii. to continuously change the chaotic attractor of the transmitter; thus making it harder for an intruder to break into the communication channel

At the receiver, it will be required to accomplish both synchronization with the transmitter and identification of the unknown parameter. Careful examination of Eq. (20) reveals a very important property of the proposed system, which is the decoupling between the states to be synchronized and the parameter to be identified; i.e. the parameter update law has no effect of the synchronization mechanism. In addition, the transmitted signal and the secret key can be made to occupy the same frequency band, thus, retrieving the original message using filtering techniques is impossible. Thus, a new proposal for the robust secure communication system, choosing x_1 as the synchronizing signal, and both x_2 and σ for implementing the encryption function, can take the form

$$\begin{aligned}E(X,\sigma,s,t) &= x_2^2 + (\sigma^2 + x_2^2)s(t) \\ \hat{s}(t) = D(\hat{X},\hat{\sigma},s,t) &= (E(X,\sigma,s,t) - \hat{x}_2^2)/(\hat{\sigma}^2 + \hat{x}_2^2)\end{aligned} \tag{30}$$

With reference to Figs. (7) and (18), Fig. (23) shows a block diagram representation of the robust system, while Fig. (24) illustrates a Simulink model. For both simulation and comparison purposes, $s(t)$ was chosen to correspond to the digital signal considered in (Álvarez,

2004), and a piecewise linear profile for σ was chosen such that both $s(t)$ and σ occupy the same frequency band. No time scaling was necessary in this case and consequently τ was set to one, while all other parameters are shown in Fig. (24) that is seen to consist of five parts, the transmitter, the encrypter, the synchronization mechanism, the parameter update law, and the dycrypter followed by low pass filtering and thresholding (Zaher, 2009).

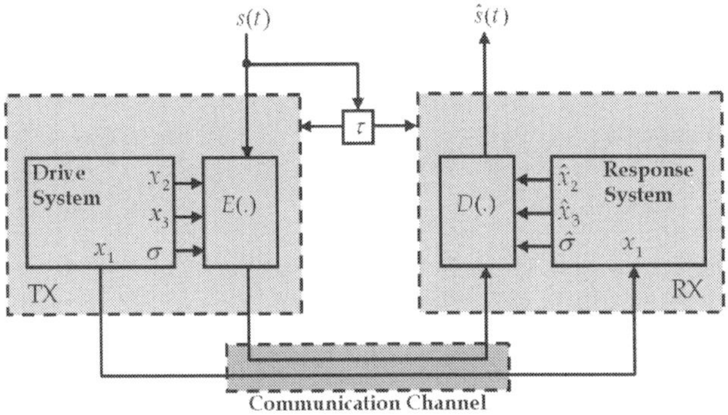

Fig. 23. Block diagram of the robust secure communication system for which both the encryption function and the chaotic transmitter use a piecewise linear profile for σ.

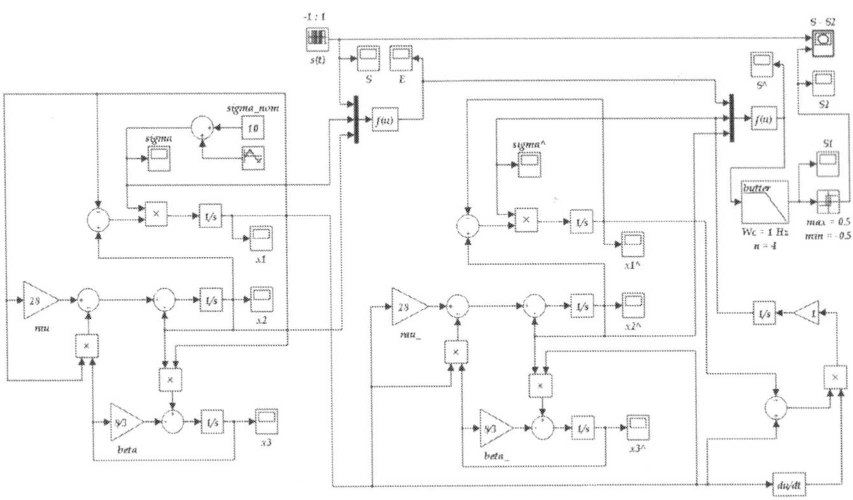

Fig. 24. A Simulink block diagram illustration of the system depicted in Fig. (23).

5.1 case study III

Figure (25) shows the simulation results when using the Simulink model, in Fig. (24), after attenuating $s(t)$ by a factor of 100 so that its envelope will be perfectly hidden in the transmitted encrypted signal, $E(t)$, which looks almost like a whit noise. As illustrated in Fig.

(25d), the recovered message is a time-delayed replica of the original message.

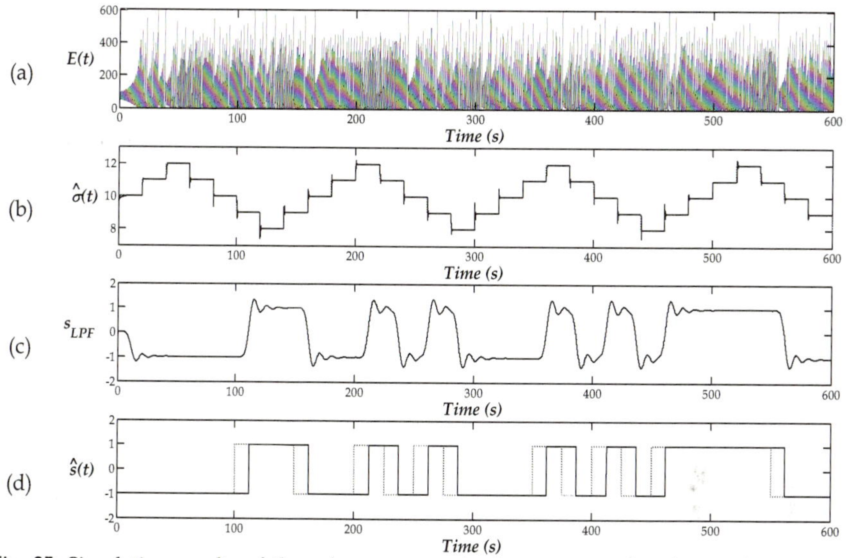

Fig. 25. Simulation results of the robust communication system, when k = 1, showing the encrypted signal, E, the estimated value of σ superimposed on its original profile, the output after the low-pass filter stage, and the thresholding stages in (a) - (d) respectively.

5.2 Security analysis of case study III

Using filtering techniques to break the security of this system is not possible as both $s(t)$ and σ are shown to occupy almost the same bandwidth with overlapping frequencies. The time-based decrypter can effectively extract $s(t)$ from the scrambled message provided that σ is identified fast enough. This can be achieved by increasing the gain of the parameter update low, k, along with attenuating the magnitude of $s(t)$ before using it in the encrypter. To demonstrate this, the Simulink model, shown in Fig. (26), was used to attempt breaking the system security via intercepting the signals available in the public communication channel, namely $E(t)$ and $x_1(t)$, and the results, shown in Fig. (27), verify the robustness of the system. It is also possible to cope with transmitting different messages having different bandwidths via adjusting the time scaling factor, τ, which has the effect of controlling the dominant frequency of the chosen chaotic attractor as well as the time profile for σ. Other linear and/or nonlinear forms of the encryption functions can be used to promote the security of the system, e.g. using both x_2 and x_3 in the encryption process. Finally, it can be demonstrated that this system is capable of transmitting both analog and digital signals.

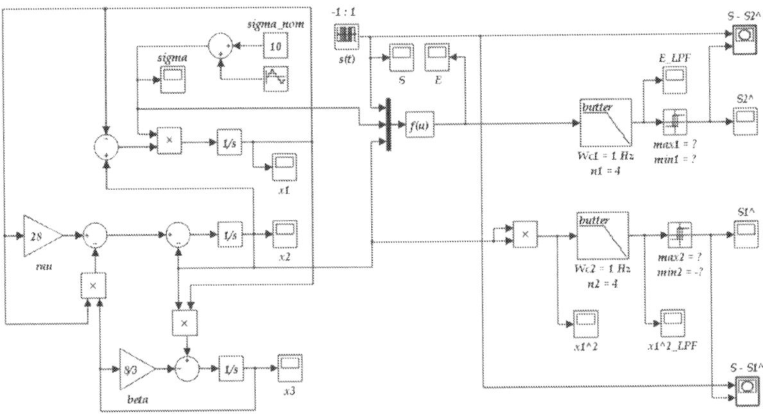

Fig. 26. A Simulink block diagram illustration of the two-filter intruder system.

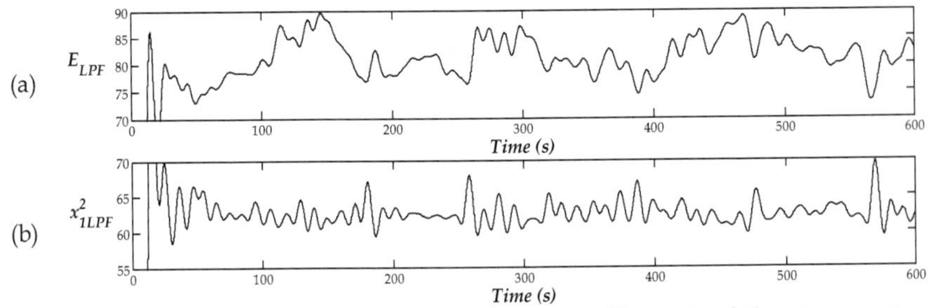

Fig. 27. Results of low-pass filtering of the intruder system, illustrating failure to reconstruct the original message using the encrypted or the driving signals in (a) and (b) respectively.

6. Summary and Conclusion

The topic of chaos-based secure communication systems was investigated. The main two processes of chaos synchronization and parameter identification were explored as they represent the corner stone in designing chaos-based cryptosystems. A fast synchronization mechanism was designed using a recursive technique that allows the control of the convergence rate of the synchronization errors. This technique proved to be easy to implement and tune at the same time, compared to other complete synchronization methods reported in the literature. Three case studies were considered that deal with different scenarios involving both analog and digital signals having different bandwidths. Using encryption functions with different forms was attempted, and it was found that some of these forms provide poor security when the frequencies of the transmitted signal and the chaotic attractor are far away in the frequency domain. By augmenting parameter modulation with cryptography, robustness can be improved and the communication system can have a better chance to survive intruder attacks. Although, the Lorenz system was used in this chapter, extensions to other chaotic systems, satisfying the same design characteristics, is straightforward.

7. References

Álvarez, G.; Montoya, F.; Romera, M. & Pastor, G. (2004). Breaking parameter modulated chaotic secure communication system. *Chaos Solitons Fractals*, Vol. 21, No. 4, pp. 783-787

Balmforth, N.; Tresser, C.; Worfolk, P. & Wu, C. (1997). Master-slave synchronization and the Lorenz equations. *Chaos*, Vol. 7, No. 3, pp. 392-394

Boccaletti, S.; Kurths, J.; Osipov, G.; Valladares, D. & Zhou, C. (2002). The synchronization of chaotic systems. *Phys Rep*, Vol. 366, No. 1-2, pp. 1-101

Carroll, T. (2004). Chaotic control and synchronization for system identification. *Phys Rev E*, Vol. 69, No. 4, pp. 046202:1-7

Chen, M. & Kurths, J. (2007). Chaos synchronization and parameter estimation from a scalar output signal. *Phys Rev E*, Vol. 76, No. 2, pp. 027203:1-4

Cuomo, K. & Oppenheim, A. (1993). Circuit implementation of synchronized chaos with applications to communications. *Phys Rev Lett*, Vol. 71, No. 1, pp. 65-68

Cuomo, K.; Oppenheim, A. & Strogatz, S. (1993). Synchronization of Lorenz-based chaotic circuits with applications to communications. *IEEE Trans Circ Syst II*, Vol. 40, No. 10, pp. 626-633

d'Anjou, A.; Sarasola, C.; Torrealdea, F.; Orduña, R. & Grana, M. (2001). Parameter-adaptive identical synchronization disclosing Lorenz chaotic masking. *Phys Rev E*, Vol. 63, No. 4, pp. 046213:1-5

Dachselt, F. & Schwarz, W. (2001). Chaos and Cryptography. *IEEE Trans Circ Syst I*, Vol. 48, No. 12, pp. 1498-1508

Dedieu, H.; Kennedy M. & Hasler, M. (1993). Chaos shift keying - modulation and demodulation of a chaotic carrier using self-synchronizing Chua's circuits. *IEEE Trans Circ Syst II*, Vol. 40, No. 10, pp. 634-642

Jiang, Z. (2002). A note on chaotic secure communication systems. *IEEE Trans Circ Syst I*, Vol. 49, No. 1, pp. 92-96

Kocarev, L. & Parlitz, U. (1995). General approach for chaotic synchronization with application to communication. *Phys Rev Lett*, Vol. 74, No. 25, pp. 5027-5031

Kocarev, L.; Halle, K.; Eckert, K.; Parlitz, U. & Chua, L. (1992). Experimental demonstration of secure communications via chaotic synchronization. *Int J Bifur Chaos*, Vol. 2, No. 3, pp. 709-713

Krstic, M.; Kanellakopoulus, I. & Kokotovic, P. (1995). *Nonlinear and Adaptive Control Design*. John Wiley & sons Inc., ISBN: 978-0471127321

Liao, T. & Huang, N. (1999). An observer-based approach for chaotic synchronization with applications to secure communications. *IEEE Trans Circ Syst I*, Vol. 46, No. 9, pp. 1144-1150

Lorenz, E. (1963). Deterministic nonperiodic flow. *J Atmos Sci*, Vol. 20, No. 2, pp. 130-141

Parlitz, U.; Chua, L.; Kocarev, L.; Halle, K. & Shang, A. (1992). Transmission of digital signals by chaotic synchronization. *Int J Bifurc Chaos*, Vol. 2, No. 4, pp. 973-977

Pecora, L. & Carroll, T. (1990). Synchronization in chaotic systems. *Phys Rev Lett*, Vol. 64, No. 8, pp. 821-825

Pecora, L. & Carroll, T. (1991). Driving systems with chaotic signals. *Phys Rev A*, Vol. 44, No. 4, pp. 2374-2284

Pehlivan, I. & Uyaroğlu, Y. (2007). Rikitake attractor and its synchronization application for secure communication systems. *J Appl Sci*, Vol. 7, No. 2, pp. 232-236

Sakaguchi, H. (2002). Parameter evaluation from time sequences using chaos synchronization, *Phys Rev E*, Vol. 65, No. 2, pp. 027201:1-4

Schuster, H. & Wolfram, J. (2005). *Deterministic Chaos: An Introduction.* Wiley-VCH, ISBN: 978-3527404155

Short, K. (1994). Steps toward unmasking secure communications. *Int J Bifurc Chaos*, Vol. 4, No. 4, pp. 959-977.

Sobhy, M. & Shehata, A. (2000). Secure computer communication using chaotic algorithms. *Int J Bifurc Chaos*, Vol. 10, No. 12, pp. 2831-2839

Solak, E. (2004). Partial identification of Lorenz system & its application to key space reduction of chaotic cryptosystems. *IEEE Trans Circ Syst II*, Vol. 51, No. 10, pp. 557-560

Stinson, D. (2005). *Cryptography: theory and practice, 3rd ed.* CRC Press, ISBN: 978-1584885085

Weiss, C. & Vilaseca, R. (1991). *Dynamics of Lasers.* VCH, Weinheim, ISBN: 978-0895739667

Wu, C. & Chua, L. (1993). A simple way to synchronize chaotic systems with applications to secure communication systems. *Int J Bifurc Chaos*, Vol. 3, No. 6, pp. 1619-1627

Yang, T. & Chua, L. (1996). Secure communication via chaotic parameter modulation. *IEEE Trans Circ Syst I*, Vol. 43, No. 9, pp. 817-819

Yang, T. & Chua, L. (1997). Impulsive stabilization for control and synchronization of chaotic systems - theory and application to secure communication. *IEEE Trans Circ Syst I*, Vol. 44, No. 10, pp. 976-988

Yang, T. (1995). Recovery of digital signals from chaotic switching. *Int J Circ Theory App*, Vol. 23, No. 6, pp. 611-615

Yang, T. (2004). A survey of chaotic secure communication systems. *Int J Comput Cogn*, Vol. 2, No. 2, pp. 81-130

Yang, T.; Wu, C. & Chua, L. (1997). Cryptography based on chaotic systems. *IEEE Trans Circ Syst I*, Vol. 44, No. 5, pp. 469-472

Yaowen, L.; Guangming, G.; Hong, Z; & Yinghai, W. (2000). Synchronization of hyperchaotic harmonics in time-delay systems and its application to secure communication. *Phys Rev E*, Vol. 62, No. 6, pp. 7898-7904.

Zaher, A. (2007). A nonlinear controller design for permanent magnet motors using a synchronization-based technique inspired from the Lorenz system. *Chaos*, Vol. 18, No. 1, pp. 013111:1-12

Zaher, A. (2008a). Design of fast state observers using a backstepping-like approach with application to synchronization of chaotic systems. *Chaos*, Vol. 18, No. 2, pp. 023114:1-10

Zaher, A. (2008b). Parameter identification technique for uncertain chaotic systems using state feedback and steady-state analysis. *Phys Rev E*, Vol. 77, No. 3, pp. 036212:1-12

Zaher, A. (2009). An improved chaos-based secure communication technique using a novel encryption function with an embedded cipher key. *Chaos Solitons Fractals*, (in press)

Zhang, Y.; Tao, C.; Du, G. & Jiang, J. (2005). Synchronized pseudorandom systems and their application to speech communication. *Phys Rev E*, Vol. 71, No. 1, pp. 16217290:1-5

Zhou, C. & Lai, C. (1999). Decoding information by following parameter modulation with parameter adaptive control. *Phys Rev E*, Vol. 59, No. 6, pp. 6629-6636

24

Simultaneous EEG-fMRI Analysis with Application to Detection of Seizure Signal Sources

Min Jing[1] and Saeid Sanei[2]
[1]*Intelligent Systems Research Centre*
University of Ulster
[2]*Centre of Digital Signal Processing*
Cardiff University
United Kingdom

1. Introduction

1.1 Brain Function Monitoring Modalities

Introduced by Hans Berger in 1929, Electroencephalography (EEG) is a recording of the electrical current potentials spontaneously generated by cortical nerve cell inhibitory and excitatory postsynaptic potentials. These postsynaptic potentials summate in the cortex and extend to the scalp surface where they are recorded as the EEG signals (EEGs). EEG provides a noninvasive means of monitoring brain activity and investigating brain function disorders. Generally, the EEG reflects the changes of cerebral function directly and reliably, especially if the structural lesions are localized near the surface of the hemispheres. EEG plays a very important role in the diagnosis of specific neurological diseases such as epilepsy and it is a very useful tool in clinical applications.

Functional Magnetic Resonance Imaging (fMRI) is an advanced imaging technique which delineates the brain activated areas responding to the designed stimuli such as sound, light or finger's movement. The principles of MRI are based on nuclear magnetic resonance (NMR). The NMR signal originates from the hydrogen nucleus which has a single proton. When the proton is placed in an external magnetic field, transitions of energy occur as the proton absorbs or emits a photon. The NMR signals generated by this energy transition can be detected and presented in an anatomical image. fMRI is able to show the blood flow within the brain activated areas in the image as the blood oxygen level-dependence (BOLD) response, which provides valuable spatial information on the brain. However, because it relies on blood flow response rather than electrical activity, it has a relatively slow response to temporal changes.

Many unanswered questions about the relationship between the cerebral haemodynamic changes (measured by fMRI) and the underlying neural electrical activity (revealed by EEG) are of interest to many researchers. Although the spatiotemporal relationship between fMRI and EEG is still far from straightforward, there are promising perspectives presented in the literature. Logothetis et al. compared local field potentials (LFPs) with the fMRI responses from the visual cortex of monkeys (Logothetis et al, 2001). The largest magnitude changes observed in LFPs at recording sites characterized by transient responses were the signals that highly correlated with the haemodynamic response. The relationship between fMRI and event-related potential (ERP) was also examined during an auditory odd-ball paradigm (Horovitz et al, 2002). The results have shown for the first time that for auditory stimuli, the amplitude of the hemodynamic response in the region of interest (ROI) follows the amplitude of the ERP changes, and BOLD signals from the source location of P300 have high correlation with the amplitude of the P300. In a more recent simultaneous EEG-fMRI study of painful electric stimulation (Christman et al, 2007), it has been shown that the BOLD changes in ROI were correlated with the dipole strength of the EEG source. The results revealed a close relationship of BOLD signal and possible underlying neural electrical activity in ROI. The results provided evidence that there were underlying connections between fMRI and EEG.

1.2 Aspects of Application in Fusion of EEG and fMRI

It is obvious that each modality has its own advantages. For example, EEG reflects the brain changes on a timescale of milliseconds (1kHz or more), which is capable of capturing the dynamic changes of the brain very well. However, it has poor spatial resolution due to being recorded from a limited number of electrodes on the scalp, and the problem of source localization from the EEG still remains a research challenge. On the other hand, fMRI is extremely powerful in investigating the brain function, but it is slow to follow the brain activities because it relies on the brain blood flow response rather than electrical activities. How to integrate these two modalities technically and maximize their advantages in real applications has started to attract more attention in recent years.

Numerous efforts have been directed towards combining high spatial information provided by fMRI, with the high quality temporal data generated by EEG or MEG. These approaches mainly focus on three aspects (Horwitz & Poeppel, 2002). The first aspect is referred to as direct data fusion, which is normally applied in EEG source localization. The geometrical information on the source activation region obtained from fMRI can be used as the constraint for localizing the EEG dipole sources (Ahlfors et al, 1999; Phillips et al, 2002; Babiloni et al, 2003; Christman et al, 2007), because there is no unique solution for the ill-posed inverse problem for EEG source localization in the absence of constraints. For example, in (Babiloni et al, 2003), the geometrical information from fMRI provided the realistic head model as a volume conductor medium to help reduce the EEG localisation solution space. In (Ahlfors et al, 1999), fMRI was not used as a rigid constraint but helped in selecting more likely inverse solution among the possible solutions. The second aspect is based on the use of computational neural models, in which the relation of EEG and fMRI is modelled on the basis of some hypotheses of certain neural activities (Schilling et al, 2001; Babajani & Soltanian-Zadeh, 2006). In these approaches, the EEG and fMRI data are not linked directly, but are compared inside a simulated neural model. The main challenge for this approach is to construct a recurrent neural model for simulation of the complex neural physiological activities, which is still questionable from the physiological aspect because the simulated neural model simplifies the complexity of neural activities (Horwitz & Poeppel, 2002). The third type of these fusion approaches is more commonly used in the clinical or neurological field in which temporal information from the EEG helps to time-lock the events in the fMRI. In some studies (Lemieux et al, 2001; Diehl et al, 2003), the epileptic EEG and fMRI data were simultaneously recorded during seizure onset, and the spikes within the seizure EEG were modelled as the stimuli which can be used in the statistical parametric mapping in fMRI. The provided brain map of seizure can be used for help in surgical planning. In this study, the work is related to the third aspect, which aims at incorporating information from EEG into fMRI analysis for the detection of the "epileptogenic zone".

1.3 Analysis for Epileptic Seizure fMRI

Epilepsy covers a group of related disorders characterized by a tendency for recurrent seizures. The seizures are due to a sudden development of synchronous neuronal firing in the cerebral cortex. The cause of epilepsy still remains unknown and different types of epilepsy have been discovered. For example, based on whether the whole brain or just part of it is involved, the seizure can be classified as generalized, focal or partial. Generalized type means that the seizure involves the whole brain at once. Focal or partial seizure means that the seizure originates from one area of the brain. In the present study, the work is related to focal seizure, and the "epileptogenic zone" is known as priori.

Analysis of epileptic seizure fMRI remains a challenging problem in the related research field. In comparison with the common fMRI analysis, for which the functional data are acquired from the designed experiments, the fMRI data of epileptic seizures are very different. As the spontaneous brain activity caused by brain functional disorders, the response of epileptic seizure is very difficult to be modelled as the normal hemadynamic response, which means the commonly used method as General Linear Model (GLM) for fMRI analysis faces the challenge for epileptic seizure fMRI. There has been limited literature (Lemieux et al, 2001; Salek-Haddadi et al, 2003; Diehl et al, 2003) that investigated the statistical parametric mapping of epileptic seizure spikes. Those results were limited by carefully choosing functional data that have distinguishable periodic seizure spikes, in which the spikes were used as the stimulus to construct the design matrix in GLM. Although these approaches partly solved the problem of model specification in GLM, the clinical expertise is required to time-lock the spikes, which makes those methods practically difficult to be applied to the unpredictable brain events, such as seizures. However, the seizure active area can be detected without concerning the model specification by using a data-based method such as Independent Component Analysis (ICA). If the information available in EEG and fMRI can be incorporated in the separation process of ICA, then the performance of ICA can be improved, which is the main objective of the present work.

This chapter is arranged as follows. First, the most commonly used fMRI analysis method GLM is introduced. Second, the spatial ICA model is described in detail and a comparison between the spatial and temporal ICA models is discussed, with the development of the constrained spatial ICA algorithm given afterwards. In the final section, the experimental results are given and discussed.

2. Methods of fMRI Analysis

2.1 Model Based Method

The most commonly used model-based approach is the general linear model (GLM) (Friston et al. 1995). According to GLM, fMRI data from each voxel is considered as a linear combination of the hemodynamic responses of stimuli and their corresponding weighted parameters. The stimuli are modelled as delta functions and the response is the convolution of the stimulus and the predefined hemodynamic response functions (HRF). The response is referred to as design matrix in GLM, and the HRF can be chosen from some well defined functions such as the Gamma function and Fourier set (windowed sines and cosines). Therefore, based on GLM, in order to specify the model, prior knowledge or specific assumptions about the time courses contributing to the signal changes are required. After the model specification, the weight parameters can be estimated by using estimation techniques such as maximum likelihood estimation (MLE) or Bayesian estimation. The active areas are then detected by evaluating the statistical significance of the whole brain voxels (Friston et al, 1995). Several software toolboxes for fMRI analysis have been developed based on GLM, which can be used for fMRI data preprocessing, model specification, statistical parameter estimation and parameter mapping, such as statistical parametric mapping (SPM) and FMRIB Software Library (FSL). The general linear model is a linear model which can be presented as,

$$\mathbf{Y} = \mathbf{XB} + \mathbf{E} \tag{1}$$

where **Y** is an N × V matrix representing the fMRI time series in each voxel, N is the number of scans, and V is the number of voxels involved in the analysis. **X** is an N × F matrix referred to as the design matrix, which is the predicted event response by convolving the stimulus with the predefined hemadynamic response function, and F is the number of stimuli (events). B is an F × V matrix of unknown parameters which are to be estimated, and **E** represents the errors which are assumed to be independently and identically distributed normal random variables (Friston et al, 1995), For the fMRI data from the jth voxel, the elements of the above matrix equation can be represented as:

$$\begin{pmatrix} y_{1j} \\ \vdots \\ y_{ij} \\ \vdots \\ y_{Nj} \end{pmatrix} = \begin{pmatrix} x_{11} & \cdots & x_{1j} & \cdots & x_{1F} \\ \vdots & \ddots & \vdots & \ddots & \vdots \\ x_{i1} & \cdots & x_{ij} & \cdots & x_{iF} \\ \vdots & \ddots & \vdots & \ddots & \vdots \\ x_{N1} & \cdots & x_{Nj} & \cdots & x_{NF} \end{pmatrix} \begin{pmatrix} b_{1j} \\ \vdots \\ b_{ij} \\ \vdots \\ b_{Fj} \end{pmatrix} + \begin{pmatrix} \epsilon_{1j} \\ \vdots \\ \epsilon_{ij} \\ \vdots \\ \epsilon_{Nj} \end{pmatrix} \tag{2}$$

From the above equation, one can see that the column vector $\mathbf{b}_j = [b_{1j},\ldots,b_{Fj}]^T$ is actually the weight factor of each event response at the *jth* voxel. An estimation of the parameter **B** which represents the weight for all voxels, denoted as $\hat{\mathbf{B}}$, can be obtained as,

$$\hat{\mathbf{B}} = (\mathbf{X}^T\mathbf{X})^{-1}\mathbf{X}^T\mathbf{Y} \tag{3}$$

The conventional approach for fMRI analysis is based on evaluation of the statistical significance in each voxel, for example by means of the t-statistic (Friston et al, 1995). The activated areas are detected by selecting the voxels in which the statistical significance is higher than a certain threshold value.

2.2 Data Based Method

In contrast to the model-based GLM, the data-based model relies on the data instead of prior information on stimuli or predefined brain function. One of the data-based approaches, proposed by McKeown et al as the first application of ICA to fMRI data analysis (McKeown et al, 1998), has attracted more attention (McKeown et al, 1998; Biswal & Ulmer, 1999; Suzuki et al, 2002; Duann et al, 2002; Beckmann & Smith, 2004; Calhoun et al, 2006; Reidl et al, 2007). In the ICA model, the fMRI data are considered as a linear combination of a number of temporally or spatially independent components. Comparing with GLM, the data-driven model is more suitable for analysis of brain signals because no assumptions regarding the stimulus response are required. The brain function and its hemadynamic response are so complicated that it is still questionable to simply choose certain predefined HRF and to assume that the shape of the HRF remains constant during the events for each brain voxel. In the following section, the details of the ICA model are discussed. The experimental results show that the ICA approach can be used to analyze the fMRI data in those cases that the GLM is difficult to work.

Apart from ICA, some other model-free approaches have been applied to fMRI analysis, such as support vector machine (SVM) (LaConte et al, 2005; Fan et al, 2006; Wang et al, 2006). The core concept of using SVM or any other pattern classification method is based on the fact that the voxels within the active areas certainly contain some special patterns which can distinguish the active part from the rest of the brain. These features can be image features such as image intensity, probability density, statistical information from each voxel, or the shape of the temporal sequence of the designed event. By means of feature extraction, the region of activation can be detected.

Information theory has also been applied to fMRI analysis. The main idea is to estimate the information across the whole brain voxels under the designed experiments and then to decide the active areas based on the mutual information (MI) criterion. As in (Galit et al, 2007), Galit et al. proposed a model-free method based on measuring the entropy and MI, which detected the location of the event-related activity by evaluation of the temporal information across different brain regions. The stimulus was used as a reference, the MI between the fMRI signals in each voxel and the stimulus was measured. The active areas were then detected by selecting those voxels which had higher MI according to the task conditions.

2.2.1 Spatial ICA

The first application of the spatial ICA model for fMRI analysis was proposed by McKeown et al. According to the authors, the physiological foundation for the ICA model is based on the two complementary principles of brain function, namely localization and connectionism. Localization implies that each psychomotor function is performed in a small region of the brain area; the principle of connectionism reveals that the active brain area involved in certain functions may be widely distributed in the multiple distinct brain systems (McKeown et al, 1998). The spatial ICA model was introduced based on these two principles. In this model, the brain areas executing different tasks are assumed to be spatially independent. Each of these areas can be considered as an independent component associated with a time course. According to the statistical definition of independency, the spatial independence can be defined as:

$$p(\boldsymbol{c}_1, \boldsymbol{c}_2, \dots, \boldsymbol{c}_n) = \prod_{i=1}^{n} p_i(\boldsymbol{c}_i) \tag{4}$$

where $\mathbf{c}_i$ is the ith independent spatial component, and the joint pdf $p(.)$ is the multiplication of the marginal pdfs of the components. As for the conventional ICA model, the spatial ICA model is formed as:

$$\mathbf{X} = \mathbf{MC} \tag{5}$$

where **X** is a T × V matrix of the mixtures, T is the length of the fMRI scan, V is the number of brain voxels involved in the analysis. **C** is an N × V matrix of unknown sources. **M** is a T × N mixing matrix, and N is the number of unknown spatially independent sources. Each column of **M** represents the time course of the corresponding independent component. Based on this model, fMRI signals can be decomposed into a number of spatially independent components **C** and their associated time course of activation **M**. The spatial components can be estimated from:

$$\mathbf{C} = \mathbf{WX} \tag{6}$$

where **W** is an N × T unmixing matrix to be estimated, and **W** is the pseudoinverse of **M**, i.e. $W = M^{\dagger}$.

In contrast to conventional ICA, which is based on temporal independence, the spatial ICA is based on the assumption of spatial independence. Although some research has exploited both the spatial and temporal independence (Stone et al, 2002), most approaches are still based on the assumption of spatial independence due to lack of good understanding of the unknown brain activities for the temporal dynamics of fMRI. Another reason that spatial ICA is more favourable for decomposing fMRI data is that it is computationally less expensive. Temporal and spatial ICA analysis of fMRI data has been compared in the previous work (Calhoun et al, 2001). Figure 1 illustrates the difference between the two models. It is noticed that, for the mixture, **X** (fMRI data matrix) in the spatial model is the transpose of **X** in the temporal model, and the spatial dimension is much higher than the temporal one because the number of brain voxels is larger than the number of time points of the scans. For estimation of the unmixing matrix in temporal ICA, a covariance matrix on the order of V^2 must be calculated, which is more computationally expensive than that for spatial ICA. For these reasons, spatial ICA is selected in this work and is denoted as SICA in the following section.

2.2.2 Constrained ICA for fMRI Analysis

The constrained ICA has been applied to fMRI signal analysis in order to incorporate prior information since the SICA model does not take the fMRI time course into account. Although very limited, recent work has shown that the performance of the application of ICA to fMRI analysis is improved if some prior information is incorporated into the estimation process (Calhoun et al, 2006; Lu & Rajapakse, 2005). Lu et al applied a predefined stimulus as the reference signal in the temporal ICA model. By minimizing the distance between the output and reference signal, the source component closest to the reference can be obtained. Calhoun et al. developed a semi-blind spatial ICA (Calhoun et al, 2005), in which a constraint is introduced by incorporating the GLM design matrix which contains information on the fMRI time course. The column vectors of the mixing matrix are constrained according to their closeness to the time course estimated from the design matrix.

In each iteration, apart from updating **W** based on the Infomax algorithm, an additional updating rule is set by measuring the correlation between the columns of the mixing matrix $[\mathbf{W}]^{-1}$ and the time course estimated from the design matrix. The additional updating rule is only performed if the correlation is lower than a certain threshold.

Although the semi-blind spatial ICA developed by Calhoun provides some promising results, their constraint still relies on GLM, therefore it is only suitable for the case that the stimuli of the fMRI data are pre-specified. For an epileptic fMRI, this approach cannot work because it is very difficult to model the epileptic seizures. In this work, the idea is to incorporate the information from the simultaneously recorded EEG as the constraint into the spatial ICA. As one can see from the spatial ICA model (shown in Figure 1), the fMRI data can be decomposed into spatially independent components and the associated time courses, for which each column of the mixing matrix represents the time course of one component activation. Therefore, the temporal constraint can be introduced by linking the EEG with the columns of $[\mathbf{W}]^{-1}$ in the separation process. In the following section, constrained spatial ICA is denoted CSICA.

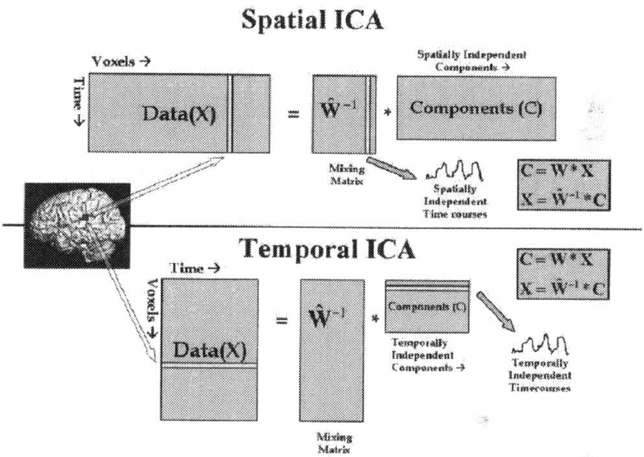

Fig. 1. Comparison of the key stages of processing within spatial ICA and temporal ICA (Calhoun et al, 2001).

2.3 Development of Algorithm

The performance of different ICA algorithms for fMRI data separation has been studied (Calhoun et al, 2004; Correa et al, 2005). Basically, selection of the separation algorithm depends on the assumption about the distribution of the sources. For example, fMRI data are commonly assumed to have super-Gaussian distribution (Calhoun et al, 2006), from which one can expect that the algorithm which is more suitable for super-Gaussian signals will achieve a better performance. As shown in (Correa et al, 2005), Infomax consistently yields reliable results for separation of fMRI followed by JADE and FastICA. Therefore, Infomax was selected in this work. In the following sections, the principle of Infomax is explained. Then the constraint is introduced to the Infomax learning rule and the development of the constrained algorithm is given.

2.3.1 Infomax

Infomax (Bell & Sejnowski, 1995) is based on information theory by maximizing the output entropy or information flow of a neural network with nonlinear outputs, hence the name Infomax. Assume that the neural network with output y and input x is of the form:

$$\mathbf{y}_i = \varphi_i\left(\mathbf{w}_i^T\mathbf{x}\right) + \mathbf{e} \tag{7}$$

where $\varphi_i(\cdot)$ are some nonlinear scalar functions, the $\mathbf{w}_i$ are the weight vectors of the neurons, and $\boldsymbol{e}$ is the additive Gaussian white noise. The entropy of the output is:

$$\mathrm{H}(\mathbf{y}) = \mathrm{H}\left(\varphi_1\left(\mathbf{w}_1^T\mathbf{x}\right), \dots \varphi_n\left(\mathbf{w}_n^T\mathbf{x}\right)\right) \tag{8}$$

For an invertible transformation of the random vector $\mathbf{x}$, $\mathbf{y} = f(\mathbf{x})$, the relation between the entropies of $\mathbf{y}$ and $\mathbf{x}$ can be expressed as (Hyvarinen et al, 2001),

$$\mathrm{H}(\mathbf{y}) = \mathrm{H}(\mathbf{x}) + \mathrm{E}\{\log|\det \mathrm{J}f(\mathbf{x})|\} \tag{9}$$

where $Jf(\cdot)$ is the Jacobian matrix of function $f(\cdot)$, and $\mathrm{E}\{\cdot\}$ denotes the expectation operation. According to Eq. (9), the transformation of the entropy in Eq. (8) can be obtained as

$$\mathrm{H}(\mathbf{y}) = \mathrm{H}(\mathbf{x}) + \mathrm{E}\left\{\log\left|\det\frac{\partial \mathrm{F}}{\partial \mathbf{W}}(\mathbf{x})\right|\right\} \tag{10}$$

where $\mathrm{F}(\mathbf{x}) = \varphi_1\left(\mathbf{w}_1^T\mathbf{x}\right), \dots \varphi_n\left(\mathbf{w}_n^T\mathbf{x}\right)$ denotes the nonlinear function defined by the neural network. As $H(\mathbf{x})$ is independent of $\mathbf{W}$, the entropy of output can be expressed as

$$\mathrm{H}(\mathbf{y}) = \sum_i \mathrm{E}\{\log\varphi_i'(\mathbf{w}_i^T\mathbf{x})\} + \log|\det\mathbf{W}| \tag{11}$$

It is noticed that maximization of the output entropy is very closely related to the maximum likelihood (ML) estimation. The ML estimation yields (Bell & Sejnowski, 1995),

$$\Delta\mathbf{W} \propto [(\mathbf{W}^\mathrm{T})^{-1}\,\mathrm{g}(\mathbf{y})\mathbf{x}^\mathrm{T}] \tag{12}$$

where the nonlinear function $\mathrm{g}(\mathbf{y})$ is the column vector whose i-th component is

$$\mathrm{g}_i(\mathrm{y}_i) = -\frac{\frac{\partial \mathrm{p}(\mathrm{y}_i)}{\partial \mathrm{y}_i}}{\mathrm{p}(\mathrm{y}_i)} \tag{13}$$

where $\mathrm{p}(\mathrm{y}_i)$ is an approximate model of the pdf of the i-th source signal. In practice, $\mathrm{g}_i(\mathrm{y}_i) = 2\tanh(\mathrm{y}_i)$ is selected as it is suitable for super-Gaussian signals (Hyvarinen et al, 2001). By defining $\mathrm{g}(\cdot)$ in a different way, the Infomax can also work for sub-Gaussian signals, which is referred to as extended-Infomax (Lee et al, 1999). An efficient way to maximize the log-likelihood is to follow the natural gradient learning method

$$\Delta \mathbf{W} \propto \frac{\partial H(\mathbf{y}, \mathbf{W})}{\partial \mathbf{W}} \mathbf{W}^T \mathbf{W} = [\mathbf{I} - \varphi(\mathbf{y})\mathbf{y}^T]\mathbf{W} \tag{14}$$

Then, the updating rule can be written as

$$\mathbf{W}(k+1) = \mathbf{W}(k) - \eta(k)[\mathbf{I} - \varphi(\mathbf{y}(k))\mathbf{y}(k)^T]\mathbf{W}(k) \tag{15}$$

where k is the iteration number, **I** is the identity matrix and $\eta(k)$ is the learning rate. The optimal solution for **W** is obtained when the estimated sources y_i and y_j are independent. As shown in (Cichochi & Amari 2002), the stability condition of the learning rule in Eq. (14) converges to an equilibrium point corresponding to the optimal solution which can be expressed as $\mathbf{E}\{g_i(y_i)y_i\} = 1$. This is not only the condition for local stability of the algorithm, but also determines the scaling of the estimated sources. This condition is invariant with respect to the sign of y_i as $g_i(y_i)$ is selected as an invertible (monotonic) function $\tanh(y_i)$. As Infomax is very similar as ML estimation as shown in Eq. (11), the unmixing matrix must be constrained to be orthogonal such that the determinant of **W** is one and the second term in Eq. (11) can be ignored.

2.3.2 Constrained Algorithm

In this work, the objective is to incorporate the EEG signal as the constraint into the fMRI data separation process since EEG contains valuable temporal information about the brain activity. As the columns of the mixing matrix represent the time courses of the estimated components, intuitively the temporal constraint can be added to the columns of the mixing matrix such that the EEG information can be taken into account. However, incorporating this information into the separation process is a problem to be resolved.

The relationship between fMRI and EEG is far from straightforward due to the complexity of the brain mechanism and very limited understanding of it at present. Although neural networks have been exploited to model the relationship between fMRI and EEG (Schilling et al, 2001; Babajani & Soltanian-Zadeh, 2006), it is still hard to be established in the neuro-physiological and clinical fields, because theoretically the complexity between the hemadynamic changes and neural activities cannot be fully represented by a simple mathematical model (Horwitz & Poeppel, 2002). Practically, correlation measurement has been widely used in the existing studies for investigating the relationship between fMRI and EEG (Logothetis et al, 2001; Horovitz et al, 2002; Mathalon et al, 2003; Calhoun et al, 2006; Christman et al, 2007). Therefore, in this work, correlation is used to connect the time course of fMRI components and the corresponding EEG signals.

The constrained term reflects the closeness between the *i*-th column vector of the inverse of unmixing matrix $[\mathbf{W}]^{-1}$ and the processed EEG time series **u**. The seizure signal **u** has to be selected carefully either by applying temporal ICA to EEG data to obtain the seizure component, or based on prior clinical information about the seizure. In this work, **u** is formed on the basis of prior clinical information, since the epileptogenic zone is known as a *priori*.

The constraint is imposed in the Infomax update rule in Eq. (15). A similar method to add a constraint in the natural gradient rule can be found in the nonholonomic learning rules (Cichochi & Amari 2002; Amari et al, 2002). The basic natural gradient learning equation is then extended as:

$$\mathbf{W}(\mathrm{k}+1) = \mathbf{W}(\mathbf{k}) - \eta(\mathrm{k})\left[\mathbf{I} - \varphi(\mathbf{y}(\mathrm{k}))\mathbf{y}(\mathrm{k})^{\mathrm{T}} - \alpha\boldsymbol{\Lambda}(\mathrm{k})\right]\mathbf{W}(\mathrm{k}) \tag{16}$$

where α is the factor adjusted based on the stability of the algorithm. Λ= diag{ Λ_{ii}}, i=1,..,N is a diagonal weight matrix containing the information from the EEG, which is updated as

$$\boldsymbol{\Lambda}(k) = diag\left(cor([\mathbf{W}]_i^{-1}(k), \mathbf{u})\right) \tag{17}$$

where $cor(\cdot)$ denotes correlation. (Here, correlation is defined as a normalised version of covariance, i.e., $cor(y_i, y_j) = E\{y_i y_j\}$). According to the adaptive learning rule in Eq. (16), **W** is updated based on the Infomax principle, also the column vectors of its inverse are forced to be close to the corresponding processed EEG signal **u**. As shown in Eq. (17), Λ is updated iteratively according to the closeness between and **u**. Here, the entries of Λ are bounded since the absolute value of correlation coefficient is less than 1. Due to the additional constraint, the new algorithm can converge to the lower minimum of the cost function than the one before imposing a constraint, whereby the performance of algorithm can be improved.

3 Implementation of the Algorithm

The experiments comprise two parts. In the first part, the format of fMRI data and the basic preprocess procedure are introduced. In the second experiment, SICA and CSICA are applied to the epileptic fMRI data. GLM cannot work in this case because it is very difficult to model the epileptic seizure signals. The simultaneously recorded EEG was introduced as the constraint in CSICA and the process of constructing the constraint is described in detail. The performances of SICA and CSICA are compared in terms of algorithm convergence, the detected seizure area, and the closeness between the seizure component and EEG signal.

3.1 Preprocessing of fMRI Data

3.1.1 fMRI Data Format

The primary functional image data format used in this work is Analyze 7.5. An Analyze 7.5 data format consists of two files, an image file and a header file, with extensions ".img" and ".hdr" respectively. The .img file contains the image data information. The .hdr file contains the volume information of the .img file, such as voxel size, and the number of pixels in the x, y and z directions (dimensions). Also, a MATLAB file .mat is added to the .hdr and .img pair. The .mat file includes some information on the orientation of the image, which are generated by the realignment and coregistration processes. In the coordinate system for Analyze data format, the x-direction is from left to right, the y-direction is from back to front, and the z-direction is from bottom to top. The image obtained from one scan is referred to as one volume. Each volume consists of a number of slices through the brain, and each slice has a certain thickness and is composed of a number of 3D unit elements called voxels. The volume of a voxel is approximately 3 mm^3. In general, the analysis of fMRI is executed based on each voxel.

3.1.2 Preprocessing

In order to apply ICA to the functional data, certain preprocessing must be performed before the data are ready for further analysis. The preprocessing includes not only the basic temporal and spatial preprocessing as needed in GLM, but also the data dimension reduction and data structure conversion which are required before applying ICA.

The first basic step is temporal and spatial preprocessing for the raw fMRI data by means of slice timing and realignment in order to remove the motion artifacts. In the experiments, this preprocessing is carried out by using the established tool in the SPM. The second step is data dimension reduction. The analysis of fMRI is always computationally expensive due to a large number of brain voxels involved. Therefore, a very important step of preprocessing before performing any fMRI analysis is to reduce the number of voxels involved in the analysis, and thereby to reduce the data dimension for further analysis. This can be executed by either removing the off-brain voxels (i.e. the voxels which fall outside the brain boundary), or extracting the voxels within the area of interest. Both processes can be carried out by applying various techniques.

For example, in SPM, the standard images of grey and white matter of the brain are provided to be used as mask images, so that the user can extract the voxels of interest. In another medical image viewing and processing toolbox MRIcro (Rorden, C. & Brett, M., 2000), the user can choose some masking images as in SPM. Also, in MRIcro, extraction of the region of interest (ROI) can be performed directly by drawing the ROI on the original images manually. Then the ROI can be converted to the Analyze 7.5 format which is readable in SPM. In the Matlab based software FMRLAB (http://sccn.ucsd.edu/fmrlab), the off-brain voxels are excluded by manually setting a threshold value. The user can visually check the changes in brain images during the process of removing off-brain voxels in the graphic interface, and decide on the threshold value. In the following experiment, the toolbox in FMRLAB was used to extract the brain voxels.

In the case of applying GLM to fMRI analysis, the above two steps of preprocessing are required. But for applying ICA to fMRI, one also needs to construct the input (data mixture) in order to perform the ICA. As seen from the ICA model (Eq. 5), the input data mixture has dimensions of $T \times V$, where T is the number of scans and V is the number of brain voxels involved in the analysis, which are the voxels after excluding the off-brain voxels. For each scan (one time point of fMRI data), which is referred to as one volume, the data are in 3D form (i.e., with x, y and z directions). In order to construct the 2D mixture with size $T \times V$, it is necessary to first compress all scans into a 4D dataset, then reshape it into the 2D mixture with dimension $T \times V$.

In the following experiment, the data were first centred to have zero mean. Then preliminary whitening was performed to make the data have unit variance before further separation processing. The estimation of number of spatial components in fMRI has been attempted recently (Li et al, 2007), in which the information-theoretic criteria was applied on the simulated data based on the minimization of the Kullback-Leibler divergence between the true model and the fitted model. However, it is still a relatively new research topic and many questions remain. In this study, the number of source was selected as the same as the number of input channels, which is the time points of fMRI data.

3.2 Experiment: Analysis of Epileptic EEG-fMRI

3.2.1 Data Details

The simultaneously recorded EEG and fMRI data were provided by the National Society for Epilepsy, University College London (UCL). The functional data were acquired on a modified 3T GE Horizon system and EEG data were recorded by the Brain Product system. The length of EEG-fMRI data is approximately 5 minutes before and during the seizure onset. The functional data were acquired from the 16*th* scan. In this experiment, the functional data were truncated from acquisition 20 to acquisition 107, which is the scan just before seizure onset. The first four scans were discarded in order to remove the initial magnetic gradient effect in the fMRI recording. Each acquisition comprised 47 contiguous slices, with image dimension of 64 × 64 × 47, and the volume size was 3.75*mm* × 3.75*mm* × 2.5*mm*. The interval between each scan was 3 sec. The simultaneous 64 channel EEGs were sampled at 250 Hz. Before applying the proposed algorithm over the simultaneous EEG-fMRI data, the scanner artifacts were removed from EEGs by the data provider. The epileptic seizure area was known as the right temporal area.

3.2.2 Experiment Setup

In this experiment, SICA and CSICA were applied to the epileptic EEG-fMRI data and the performances of these two algorithms were compared. After realignment to remove the motion artifacts, the raw functional data were first compressed into 4D format, then the off-brain voxels were removed and the 2D data were constructed for ICA.

As described in the above section, the constraint was formulated as the closeness between the EEG information and the column vectors of the mixing matrix, in which the closeness was measured by correlation. The special electrodes F8 and P8, which contain the most significant seizure information, were selected as the reference signal as suggested by the clinical consultant.

For measuring the correlation, the difference in resolution between the EEG and fMRI must be resolved first, because the temporal resolution of EEG is much higher than that of fMRI time series. In order to solve this problem, the following process was performed: (1) selecting electrode P8 or F8 as the EEG reference signal; (2) filtering the reference signal by lowpass filter with cut-off frequency 15 Hz, thus ensuring that the important seizure information is kept because the dominant frequency of seizure is in the range of 2.5 Hz to 15 Hz (Lantz et al, 1999; Blanke et al, 2000); (3) down-sampling the reference EEG and up-sampling each column of the mixing matrix to ensure that they have the same data length.

3.2.3 Results and Discussion

SICA and the proposed CSICA were applied to the processed fMRI data. In each iteration of CSICA, the correlation between the column vectors of $[\mathbf{W}]^{-1}$ and the EEG reference vector was measured. Then, the unmixing matrix $\mathbf{W}$ was updated according to Eq. (16). The performances of the two algorithms were compared in terms of algorithm convergence, the correlation between the seizure EEG and the corresponding columns of the mixing matrix, and the mapping of the selected component. The selection of component was based on the prior information about the seizure area, which was the right temporal area. The epileptic seizure area was known as the right temporal area.

Figure 2 gives the algorithm convergence curve. It clearly shows that the proposed CSICA algorithm converges to the minimum of the cost function, which is less than that for unconstrained SICA. It means that CSICA attained less estimation error than SICA. Figure 3 illustrates the region of activation obtained from both algorithms. The level of activity is represented by the standard deviation (z-value). The activated area is the brain area in which the voxels have a higher z-value than the threshold level (1.5 in this experimental result). The mapping of the component (activated area) is then displayed by overlaying the area on top of the high resolution structural images. Based on the clinical expertise, the highlighted part in the left frontal area is introduced as the MRI scan noise, and the right temporal area is verified to be within the epileptic seizure area. This means that the detected BOLD is in line with the clinical findings. Also based on clinical investigations, the small patch at the right temporal region is more focused in the result obtained from CSICA.

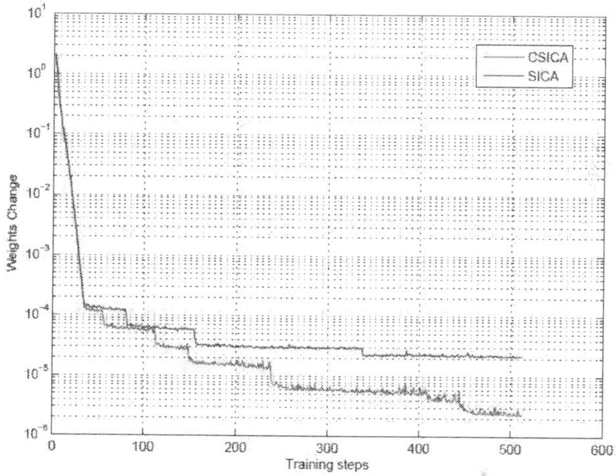

Fig. 2. Comparison of algorithm estimation error for SICA and CSICA.

The maximum correlation coefficient between the column vectors of the mixing matrix and the EEG reference vector **u** were obtained by averaging five trials for SICA and CSICA, which are 0.181 and 0.195 respectively. It shows that the results from CSICA provide a higher correlation between the seizure signal and the corresponding column vectors of $[\mathbf{W}]^{-1}$ than that from SICA.

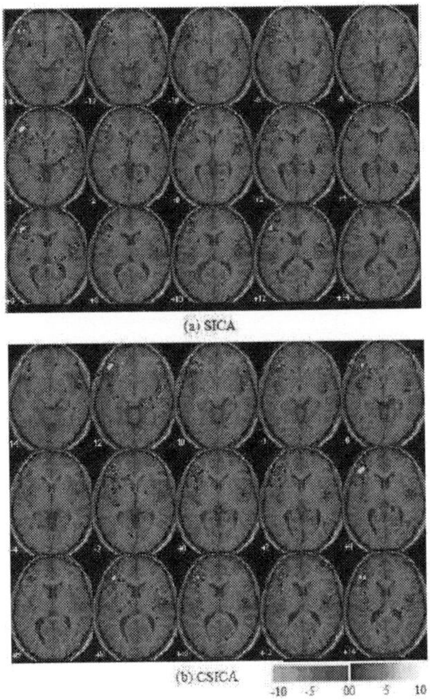

Fig. 3. The BOLD obtained from separation of fMRI data by using (a) SICA and (b) the proposed CSICA, which incorporates the EEG signals as the constraint into the update equation.

4 Concluding Remarks

In this chapter, various techniques for fMRI analysis have been reviewed and the established techniques such as GLM and SICA have been discussed in terms of their mathematical frameworks. More importantly, a novel constrained spatial ICA algorithm has been proposed which incorporates the simultaneously recorded seizure EEG into the fMRI separation process. The experimental results have shown that the BOLD region, as the result of seizure onset, has been detected using the proposed constrained SICA. This algorithm outperforms the existing unconstrained ICA algorithm in terms of estimation error and closeness between the component time course and the seizure EEG signals.

The relationship between fMRI and EEG has indeed been a challenging problem to date, therefore in this study, this relationship was simply chosen by closeness between time course of fMRI component and processed EEG signal. Further improvements to the proposed method can be achieved if a better mathematical modelling of the relationship between EEG and fMRI can be developed. Another limitation of the proposed method is that the EEG signal used in this work was the scalp EEG, which is the signal that is mixed with noise and artifacts, and is therefore not a perfect choice for seizure reference. This may be the reason why the results for the correlation measurement are not sufficiently significant. Further investigations can be carried out by applying a proper ICA algorithm to extract the EEG seizure component. These can be an agenda for future research in this area. Nevertheless, the results presented here are still very promising, and have shown a new direction for fusion of fMRI and EEG. The idea can be further exploited in both separation and localization of seizure signals in joint EEG-fMRI signal processing.

5. Acknowledgement

The authors would like to thank Dr. Khalid Hamandi in University Hospital of Wales for his valuable advices and providing data.

6. References

Ahlfors, S. P.; Simpson, G. V.; Dale, A. M.; Belliveau, J. W.; Liu, A. K.; Korvenoja, A.; Virtanen, J.; Huotilainen, M.; Tootell, R.; Aronen, H. J. & Iimoniemi, R. J. (1999). Spatiotemporal activity of a cortical network for processing visual motion revealed by MEG and fMRI. *J. Neurophysiol.* Vol. 82, pp. 2545-2555.

Amari, S.; Chen, T. P. & Cichocki, A. (2002). Nonholonomic Orthogonal Learning Algorithms for Blind Source Separation. *Neural Computation.* Vol. 12, pp. 1463-1484.

Babajani, A. & Soltanian-Zadeh, H. (2006). Integrated MEG/EEG and fMRI Model Based on Neural Masses. *IEEE Tran on Biomedical Eng.* Vol. 53, No. 7, pp. 1794-1801.

Babiloni, F.; Babiloni, C.; Carducci, F.; Romani, G. L.; Rossini,P. M.; Angelone, L. M. & Cincottia, F. (2003). Multimodal integration of high-resolution EEG and functional magnetic resonance imaging data: a simulation study. *NeuroImage.* Vol. 19, pp. 1-5.

Beckmann, C. and Smith, S. M. (2004). Probabilistic independent component analysis for functional magnetic resonance imaging. *IEEE Trans. Med. Imaging.* Vol. 23, pp. 137-142.

Bell, A. J. and Sejnowski, T. J. (1995). An information-maximization approach to blind separation and blind deconvolution. *Neural Computation.* Vol. 7, pp. 1129 - 1159.

Blanke, O.; Lantz, G.; Seeck, M.; Spinelli, L.; Peralta, R. G. D.; Thut, G.; Landis, T. & Michel, C. M. (2000). Temporal and Spatial Determination of EEG-Seizure Onset in the Frequency Domain. *Clin. Neurophysiol.* Vol. 111, pp. 763-772.

Biswal, B. B. & Ulmer, J. L. (1999). Blind source separation of multiple signal sources of fMRI data sets using independent component analysis. *J. Comput. Assist. Tomogr.* Vol. 23, No. 2, pp. 265-271.

Calhoun, V. D.; Adali, T.; Pearlson, G. D. & Pekar, J. J. (2001). Spatial and temporal independent component analysis of functional MRI data containing a pair of task-related waveforms. *Human Brain Mapping.* Vol.13, pp. 43-53.

Calhoun, V. D.; Adali, T. & Pearlson, G. D. (2004). Independent component analysis applied to fMRI data: A generative model for validating results. *J. VLSI Signal Process. Syst.* Vol. 37, pp. 281 - 291.

Calhoun, V. D.; Stevens, M.; Pearlson, G. D. & Kiehl, K. A. (2004). FMRI analysis with the general linear model: removal of latency-induced amplitude bias by incorporation of hemodynamic derivative terms. *NeuroImage.* Vol. 22, pp. 252 - 257.

Calhoun, V. D.; Adali, T.; Stevens, M.; Kiehl, K. A. and Pekar, J. (2005). Semi-blind ICA of fMRI: A method for utilizing hypothesis-derived time courses in a spatial ICA analysis. *NeuroImage.* Vol. 25, No. 2, pp. 527-538.

Calhoun, V. D. and Adali, T. (2006). Unmixing fMRI with independent component analysis. *IEEE Eng. in Medicine and Biology Magazine*, pp. 79-90, March/April, 2006.

Calhoun, V. and Adali, T. (2006). Fusion of Multisubject Hemodynamic and Event-Related Potential Data Using Independent Component Analysis. *IEEE International Conference on Acoustics, Speech and Signal Processing (ICASSP) Proceedings,* Vol. 5, pp. 14-19, May, 2006.

Christman, C.; Koeppe, C.; Braus, D. F. & Flora, H. (2007). A simultaneous EEG and fMRI study of painful electric stimulation. *NeuroImage.* Vol. 34, pp. 1428-1437.

Cichochi, A. & Amari, S. (2002). *Adaptive blind signal and image processing, learning algorithm and application.* John Wiley and Sons.

Correa, N.; Adali, T.; Li, Y. & Calhoun, V. D. (2005). Comparison of blind source separation algorithms for fMRI using a new matlab toolbox: GIFT. *Proc. IEEE Int. Conf. Acoustics, Speech, Signal Processing (ICASSP)*, pp. 401 - 404, Philadelphia, PA, 2005.

Diehl, B.; Salek-Haddadi, A.; Fish, D. R. & Lemieux, L. (2003). Mapping of spikes, slow waves, and motor tasks in a patient with malformation of cortical development using simultaneous EEG and fMRI. *Magn. Reson. Imaging*, Vol. 21, No. 10, pp. 1167-1173.

Duann, J. R.; Jung, T. P.; Kuo, W. J.; Makeig, S.; Hsieh, J. C. & Sejnowski, T. J. (2002). Single-trial variability in event-related bold signals. *NeuroImage,* Vol. 15, No. 4, pp. 823-835.

Fan, Y.; Shen, D. & Davatzikos, C. (2006). Detecting Cognitive States from fMRI Images by Machine Learning and Multivariate Classiffication. *Computer Vision and Pattern Recognition Workshop*, pp. 89 - 89, June 2006.

Friston, K.; Holmes, A.; Worsley, K.; Poline, J. B.; Frith, C. & Frackowiak, R. (1995). Statistical parametric maps in functional imaging: a general linear approach. *Human Brain Mapping*. Vol. 2, pp.189 - 210.

Galit, F. A.; Sun, F. T.; Daniel, H. Desposito, M. & Knight, R. T. (2007). Spatio-temporal information analysis of event-related BOLD responses. *NeuroImage.* Vol. 34, pp. 1545 - 1561.

Horovitz, G.; Skudlarski, P. & Gore, J. C. (2002). Correlations and Dissociations Between BOLD Signal and P300 Amplitude in an Auditory Oddball Task: a Parametric Approach to Combining FMRI and ERP. *Magn. Reson. Imaging,* Vol. 20, pp. 319-325.

Horwitz, B. & Poeppel, D. (2002). How can EEG/MEG and fMRI/PET data be combined? *Hum. Brain Mapp.,* vol. 17, pp. 1-3.

Hu, D.; Yan, L.; Liu, Y.; Zhou, Z.; Friston, K. J.; Tan, C. & Wu, D. (2005). Unified SPM-ICA for fMRI analysis. *NeuroImage.* Vol. 25, No. 3, pp. 746 - 755.

Hyvarinen, A.; Karhunen, J. & Oja, E. (2001). *Independent Component Analysis.* Wiley-Interscince Publication.

Ji, Y.; Liu, H. B.; Wang, X. K. & Tang, Y. Y.(2004). Cognitive states classification from fMRI data using support vector machines. *Proc. Machine Learning and Cybernetics,* Vol 5, pp. 2919 - 2926, Aug., 2004.

Josephs, O.; Turner, R. & Friston, K. J. (1997) Event-related fMRI. *Hum. Brain Mapp.,* Vol. 5, pp. 243-248.

LaConte, S.; Strother, S.; Cherkassky, V.; Anderson, J. & Hu, X. (2005). Support vector machines for temporal classification of block design fMRI data. *NeuroImage.* Vol. 26, pp. 317 - 329.

Lantz, G.; Michel, C. M.; Seeck, M.; Blanke, O., Landis, T. & Rose, I. (1999). Frequency domain EEG source localization of ictal epileptiform activity in patients with partial complex epilepsy of temporal lobe origin. *Clin. Neurophysiol.* Vol. 110, pp. 176 - 184.

Lee, T. W.; Girolami, M. and Sejnowski, T. J. (1999). Independent Component Analysis Using an Extended Infomax Algorithm for Mixed Subgaussian and Supergaussian Sources. *Neural Computation.* Vol. 11, pp. 417-441.

Lemieux, L.; Salek-Haddadi, A.; Josephs, O.; Allen, P.; Toms, N. and Scott, C. (2001). Event-related fMRI with simultaneous and continuous EEG: description of the method and initial case report. *Neuroimage,* Vol. 14, No. 3, pp. 780-787.

Li, Y.; Adal, T. and Calhoun, V. D. (2007). Estimating the number of independent components for functional magnetic resonance imaging data. *Human Brain Mapping.* Vol. 28, Issue 11, pp. 1251-1266.

Logothetis, K.; Pauls, J.; Augath, M.; Trinath, T. & Oeltermann, A. (2001). Neuro-physiological Investigation of the Basis of the FMRI Signal. *Nature,* Vol. 412, pp. 150-157.

Lu, W. & Rajapakse, J. C. (2005). Approach and Applications of Constrained ICA. *IEEE Tran. on Neural Network.* Vol. 16, No. 1, pp. 203 - 212.

Mathalon, D. H.; Whitfield, S. L. & Ford, J. M. (2003). Anatomy of an Error: ERP and FMRI. *Biol. Psychol.,* Vol. 64, pp. 119-141.

McKeown, M. J.; Makeig, S.; Brown, G. G.; Jung, T. P.; Kindermann, S. S.; Bell, A. J. & Sejnowski, T. J. (1998). Analysis of fMRI data by blind separation into independent spatial components. *Hum. Brain Map.* Vol. 6, No. 3, pp. 160 - 188.

McKeown, M. J. & Sejnowski, T. J. (1998). Independent component analysis of fMRI data: Examining the assumptions. *Hum. Brain Map.* Vol. 6, No. 5, pp. 368 - 372.

McKeown, M. J.; Hansen, L. K. & Sejnowsk, T. J. (2003). Independent component analysis of functional MRI: What is signal and what is noise? *Curr. Opin. Neurobiol.,* Vol. 13, No. 5, pp. 620-629.

Phillips, C.; Rugg, M. D. & Friston, K. J.(2002). Anatomically Informed Basis Functions for EEG Source Localization: Combining Functional and Anatomical Constraints. *NeuroImage,* Vol. 16, pp. 678-695.

Price, C. J. & Friston, K. J. (1997). Cognitive conjunction: a new approach to brain activation experiment. *NeuroImage.* Vol. 5, pp. 261-270.

Reidl, J.; Starke, J.; Omer, D. B.; Grinvald, A. & Sporsa, H.(2007). Independent component analysis of high-resolution imaging data identifies distinct functional domains. *NeuroImage.* Vol. 34, pp. 94 - 108.

Rorden, C. & Brett, M. (2000). Stereotaxic display of brain lesions. *Behavioural Neurology,* Vol. 12, pp. 191-200.

Salek-Haddadi, A.; Merschhemke, M.; Lemieux, L. & Fish, D. (2002). Simultaneous EEG-Correlated Ictal fMRI. *Neuroimage,* Vol. 16(1), pp. 32-40.

Salek-Haddadi, A.; Friston, K. J.; Lemieux, L. & Fish, D. R. (2003). Studying spontaneous EEG activity with fMRI. *Brain Research Reviews.* Vol. 43, pp. 111-133.

Schilling, R. J.; Carroll, J. J. & Al-Ajlouni, A. F.(2001). Approximation of nonlinear systems with radial basis function neural networks" *IEEE Tran. Neural Network,* Vol. 12, pp. 1-15.

Stone, J. V.; Porrill, J.; Porter, N. R. & Wilkinson, I. D. (2002). Spatiotemporal independent component analysis of event-related FMRI data using skewed probability density functions. *NeuroImage.* Vol. 15, No. 2, pp. 407- 421.

Suzuki, K.; Kiryu, T. & Nakada, T. (2002). Fast and precise independent component analysis for high field fMRI time series tailored using prior information on spatiotemporal structure. *Hum. Brain Map.* Vol. 15, No. 2, pp. 407-421.

Wang, Z.; Childress, A. R. and Detre, J. A. (2006). Boost up the detection sensitivity of ASL perfusion fMRI through support vector machine. *The 28th IEEE Engineering in Medicine and Biology Society (EMBS)*, pp. 1006-1009, Aug., 2006.

25

Real-Time Signal Acquisition, High Speed Processing and Frequency Analysis in Modern Air Data Measurement Instruments

Theodoros Katsibas[1], Theodoros Semertzidis[1], Xavier Lacondemine[2] and Nikos Grammalidis[1]
[1]*Centre for Research and Technology Hellas, Informatics and Telematics Institute Greece*
[2]*THALES Aerospace Division France*

1. Introduction

There is no doubt that the signal processing task is a very critical issue in the majority of new technological inventions and challenges in the area of electrical engineering. Despite the fact that during the last thirty years numerous algorithms and techniques have been developed in the field and classical methods of DSP technology were established, it is still an extremely skilled work to properly design, build and implement an effective signal processing unit able to meet the requirements of the increasingly demanding and sophisticated modern applications. This is especially true when it is necessary to deal with real-time applications of huge data rates and computational loads.

It is the objective of this book chapter to present all the successive steps of such a processs in the framework of an ambitious plan to develop a functional and reliable lidar-based air data measurement instrument, launched by the FP6 Aeronautics and Space NESLIE project. Designed to perform in real-time (onboard the plane) and to provide vital flight parameters to the cockpit of the aircraft, this remote sensing equipment dictates the implementation of a robust, flexible and very fast signal processing unit.

This chapter starts by introducing the characteristics of the expected signal as well as the overall requirements of the system. Taking into account the very low signal-to-noise ratio (SNR) of a signal resulting from aerosol particles light backscattering and the different flight levels in a non-uniform and unstable environment, at which the measurement unit has to operate, we specify the appropriate algorithms and develop the necessary techniques for an effective signal processing scheme. The high speeds of modern aircrafts imply the use of a correspondingly impressive sampling rate which inevitably necessitates the use of parallelism of the computations and the optimum usage of all available resources. Very powerful FPGA boards have been selected for that purpose, making the fast processing implementation feasible. A "slow signal processing" module, performed in the CPUs and using input from these fast FPGA boards, produce the final measurements at a slower data

rate. This software integrates the entire system by estimating the air data parameters, presenting them to a suitable MMI and synchronizing all the modules of the signal processing unit.
Many simulations and real flight test results are also shown in order to prove the ability of the developed unit to perform real-time measurements of the vital flight parameters in a very effective and reliable way.

2. The Doppler lidar measurement mechanism

The well known Doppler effect is widely used in many radar, sonar and ultrasonic applications providing accurate velocity measurements of various remote objects or flows. Using much higher frequency waves and lasers instead of the radio and acoustic waves of the technologies above, it comes to the relative new technique of the LIght Detection And Ranging or LIDAR. This technique has already found great application in many fields of science such as geology, seismology, geography, atmospheric chemistry and physics as well as meteorology. Calculating the frequency shift that moving targets may cause to the backscattered optical signal and estimating the corresponding radial component of their velocity, numerous important parameters can be measured performing advanced surveying and mapping tasks.
More specifically, Doppler lidars illuminate the aerosol particles or molecules in the atmosphere (depending on the target we have IF or UV emission respectively) and have already been proven to be an important tool for remote measurement of atmospheric wind fields and detailed observation of weather phenomena (Bilbro et all., 1984, Bilbro et all., 1986, Post & Cupp, 1990).
Starting from ground-based lidar systems, ongoing advances in optics and laser industry have led to the development of efficient airborne and space-based lidar units (Browell et all., 1998). Coherent CO_2 Doppler lidar, operating in NASA Marshall Space Flight Center at a wavelength of 10.6-μm (Bilbro et all., 1984, Bilbro et all., 1986), has been followed by the introduction of solid-state Doppler lidar, (Kavaya et all., 1989, Henderson et all., 1993, Frehlich et all., 1994), and

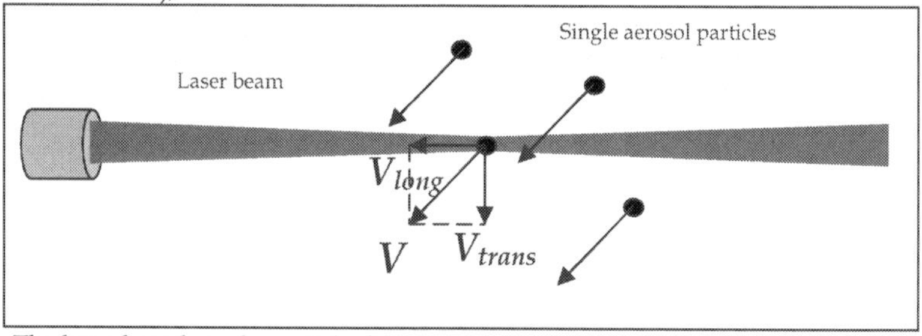

Fig. 1. The laser-based single particle detection and velocimetry

demonstrated the capability of the continuous wave system to perform single-particle detection. In addition, the fact that the Doppler frequency shift for optical wavelengths is high enough enables us to estimate the radial velocity for each backscattered pulse (Levin, 1965, Mahapatra & Zrnic, 1983, Frehlich & Yadlowsky, 1994). Furthermore, the advent of the

eye-safe 1.5-μm infrared laser technology that proved of great performance (Korb et all., 1997) allowed the implementation of low cost compact optical systems.
These last technological achievements showed the road to the development of reliable, airborne, lidar measurement instruments for commercial use in civil and military aircrafts. The demonstration of the fact that such an evolution may be realizable nowadays constitutes the aim of the EU funded NESLIE research project in the framework of which a laser-based, air data standby channel has been built. This system has been designed to perform real-time measurements of vital flight parameters such as the true air speed (TAS), the angle of attack (AOA) and the slide slip angle (SSA) to the cockpit of the aircraft. The unit is going to be used complementary to the existing, traditional, pneumatic, measurement systems (Pitot tubes) significantly increasing the safety of the flights.

2.1 Signal characteristics

It is pointed out that the ultimate goal of the signal processing task of such a sophisticated, real-time application is to constantly guarantee clear signal particle detection, accurate Doppler frequency shift estimation and finally the necessary vector velocity calculation. That is to provide the speed of the aircraft relative to the air mass in which it flies (aerosol scatterers). The longitudinal component of this 3-D air speed vector (projection to the laser axis) is given by the following equation

$$V_{long} = \frac{f_D \cdot \lambda}{2} \tag{1}$$

where, V_{long} is the longitudinal velocity component, f_D the Doppler frequency shift due to the relative motion between the aircraft and the air mass and λ the wavelength of the laser.
During the time a particle crosses the beam in the small focal volume of the laser it is illuminated with an optical power of very high density and scatters back a significant amount of energy. The principal of the single particle laser-based velocimetry is schematically depicted in Fig. 1. Resulting from such a process, the received signal is a sequence of random bursts at random time instants plus noise. Fig. 2 shows two such modeled sinusoidal carriers with Gaussian envelope in a noisy environment. Of course, this is an idealized representation of the signal to be processed in order to show the randomness of the shape and the time duration of the expected, typical signal bursts as well as of the time instants they occur. In reality, on the other hand, a signal burst cannot be clearly distinct in the time-domain received signal since it has a very low SNR and it is deeply buried in noise.

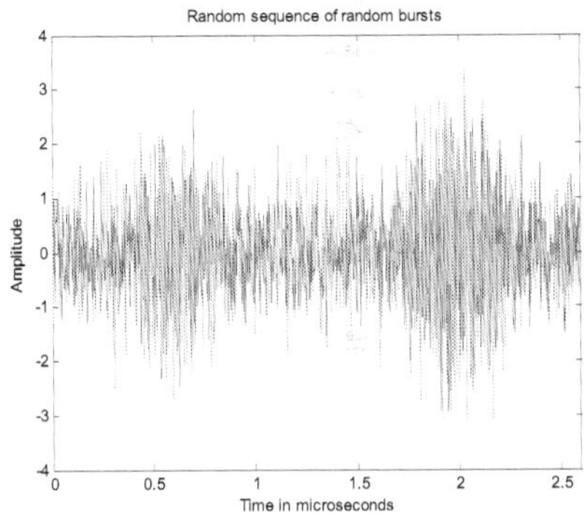

Fig. 2. Two successive model signal bursts buried in noise

However, the frequency of such a burst corresponds to the value of the Doppler frequency shift and depends on the longitudinal velocity component as already written in Eq. (1). The time duration of each burst is a function of the transversal velocity component and the laser's beam diameter whereas the amplitude a function of the particle's cross-section and its characteristic trajectory crossing the laser beam. Of course, we mostly expect to receive only noise, especially at higher flight levels where low concentration of aerosol scatterers occurs.

2.2 Lidar system description

The developed lidar measurement unit follows the general principal of the coherent single particle Laser Doppler Anemometry (LDA) and it is concisely described in the block diagram form of Fig. 3. A continuous wave optical signal is being produced by the laser source and emitted in the atmosphere via the beam splitter and the separator. The received backscattering signal, which comes from a single, every time, aerosol particle and has been shifted in frequency according to the Doppler effect, is finally driven to the interferometer for comparison with the local oscillator reference beam (an identical copy of the emitted signal) coming from the beam splitter. The two beams are superimposed and feed the photo-detector which converts the incoming optical power into a practical electrical HF signal analogous to the frequency difference that these input waves present each other. That is the Doppler frequency shift information we are seeking for and can be effectively derived, in real-time, after the proper signal processing procedure we have developed and present in the following paragraphs.

Since we aim to deliver at a constant rate the three-dimensional vector of the true air-speed, at least three identical such laser units are needed to be installed on board the plane. However, one additional unit is going to be used for better precision and control as well as to secure continuing measurements in case of failure of one of the laser modules. All laser beams are focalized at the same measurement volume and at a properly chosen distance close to the fuselage, since we are interested in single particle detection and thus the focal volume should be relatively small. Fig. 4 illustrates the onboard set up of the lidar measurement equipment.

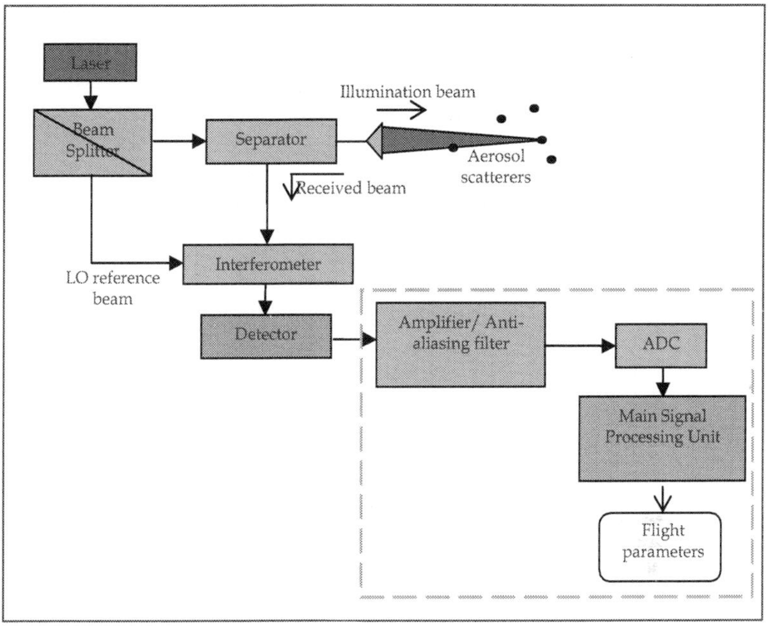

Fig. 3. Schematic diagram of the airborne lidar measurement unit

3. The signal processing unit implementation

The NESLIE signal processing task has been developed for the real-time acquisition and processing of the HF signals received from the detectors, in order to extract the aircraft velocity information and the other useful flight parameters. It is a composition of a fast signal processing firmware and a host software which both work in close association each other. The fast signal processing firmware is coming first to perform the signal burst detection and the Doppler frequency shift information. These operations have been implemented in properly selected powerful FPGA boards since such a real-time application dictates the processing of a data sequence that comes at an extremely high rate. Then, the slow processing software, executed in the host CPU, is responsible for the collection and processing of the produced data in the FPGA boards. Finally, the 3D air-speed and the other flight parameters are computed, recorded and sent to a suitable MMI for presentation.

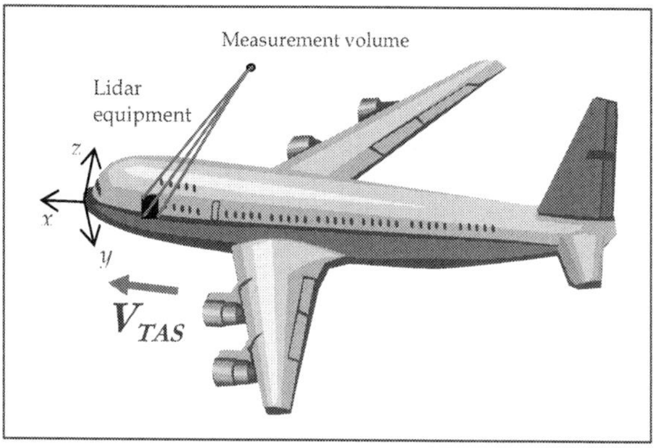

Fig. 4. Onboard installation of the lidar equipment

3.1 Signal preprocessing

Just before proceeding to the main signal processing functions it is necessary to perform some basic preprocessing steps of the acquired signals. Thus, the amplification and the low-pass filtering (actually band-pass filtering since we are not interested in very low frequencies) of the continuous, time-domain signals, aim to eliminate the aliasing effect. That is the input signal at or above half the sampling frequency must be severely attenuated at a level below the dynamic range of the analog-to-digital (ADC) converter. The signal is then digitized in the ADC with m bits resolution, i.e. 2^m quantization levels are used to cover the full amplitude range of the received signal. It is noted that there is a limitation on the selected resolution since it is strongly related with the SNR of the signal in question. A relative high level of noise restricts the possibility for accurate resolution up to a certain number of bits. Any effort for increasing the quantization levels in order to perform further analysis does not add anything more than just measuring noise. The sampling frequency according to the Shannon-Nyquist sampling theorem should be higher than twice the highest frequency of interest. This is the maximum Doppler frequency shift that is expected to be caused to the received signal and it is determined from the corresponding maximum aircraft speed we wish to measure every time. As a consequence, the data samples have to be obtained at an extremely high rate.

3.2 The fast signal processing module

The constitutive tasks of the firmware implemented in the FPGA for the fast signal processing of the raw data stream, coming from the ADC, are presented in this paragraph. A simplified block diagram of the main FPGA firmware tasks are shown in Fig. 5.

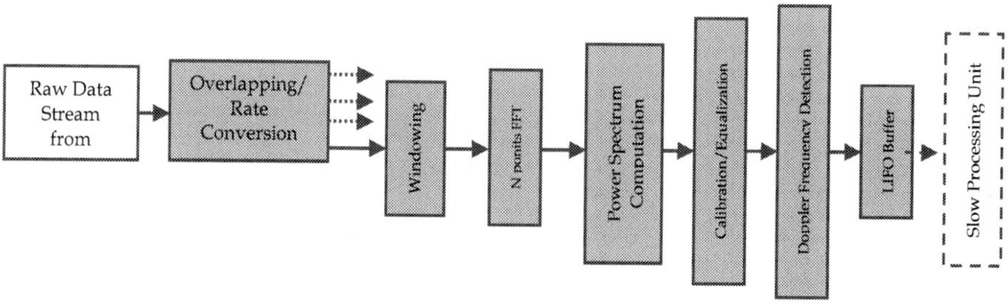

Fig. 5. The FPGA firmware schematic diagram

FFT-based signal analysis

Since the whole concept relies on the exact calculation of the frequency shift caused in the received signal due to the Doppler effect, the Fast Fourier Transform (FFT) and the power spectrum computation and analysis constitute powerful tools for effectively treating and processing the acquired data sequence (Proakis & Manolakis, 2006, Oppenheim & Schafer, 1999).

In order to achieve an accurate Doppler frequency estimation the frequency range and resolution at the horizontal axis of the spectrum plot must be carefully examined and determined. These parameters depend on the defined sampling rate as well as the number of points of the acquired signal time-window (*N* points, the FFT size). The proper selection of these parameters is a very important issue since they are closely connected to the final accuracy of the whole set of measurements.

The number of frequency points or lines or FFT bins in the single-sided power spectrum is given from the equation:

$$FFT_{bins} = \frac{N}{2} \tag{2}$$

The start frequency is at 0 Hz (the DC term) whereas the last frequency bin corresponds to the value:

$$f = \frac{f_s}{2} - \Delta f \tag{3}$$

where Δf is the interval between two successive frequency bins or else the frequency resolution. This parameter is computed by the following equation:

$$\Delta f = \frac{f_s}{N} = \frac{1}{N \cdot \Delta t} \tag{4}$$

Δt is the sampling period and thus the product $N \cdot \Delta t$ is the length of the time-window record we process every time. Consequently, it is pointed out that the sampling frequency determines the obtained frequency range or else the bandwidth of the spectrum and that for a given sampling frequency we can determine the desired frequency resolution by choosing, in the time domain, the appropriate length of the signal record to be processed.

As a conclusion, the signal data are properly time-windowed in frames of N samples and driven to the FFT block for the frequency content calculation.

Windowing and spectral leakage

Processing, every time, a specific finite interval of the continuous signal data sequence is equal to applying the FFT to the product of the sampled signal and a rectangular window function (convolution of the corresponding spectra in the frequency domain).

The assumption in the FFT algorithm that the finite, in time, record is exactly repeated throughout all time and thus being a periodic signal may cause spectral leakage. This is the effect that the Fourier transform of a windowed, single frequency, signal has non-zero values at the neighbouring frequencies (side lobs). Fig. 6 shows the Fourier transform of a 100 MHz cosine windowed by a rectangular (a) and a Gauss (b) window function. It can be observed in both cases that the power spectrum does not contain only the single frequency of 100 MHz, as it would be expected, but shows some power content at the neighbouring frequencies as well. This is an effect of windowing the signal sequence in the time-domain and should be taken under serious consideration in this signal processing task.

The rectangular window is characterised as low-dynamic-range window and presents excellent resolution characteristics since the width of the main lobe is extremely narrow. The Gauss window, on the other hand, has a lower sensitivity but is of much higher dynamic range than the first. Since we are searching for a single frequency signal (i.e. the Doppler frequency) in a very noisy environment (narrowband application) and despite the fact that the generated bursts are expected to be Gaussian shaped by nature it is preferred the data frames be properly weighted by a Gaussian function and not just using the rectangular window. This is because the Gauss weighting window substantially improves the obtained SNR due to the high dynamic range it presents and at the same time it also reaches the excellent resolution characteristics of the rectangular window. Thus, it constitutes a good choice among other moderate window functions in an effort to reach the best trade-off between a satisfying SNR and an increased frequency resolution.

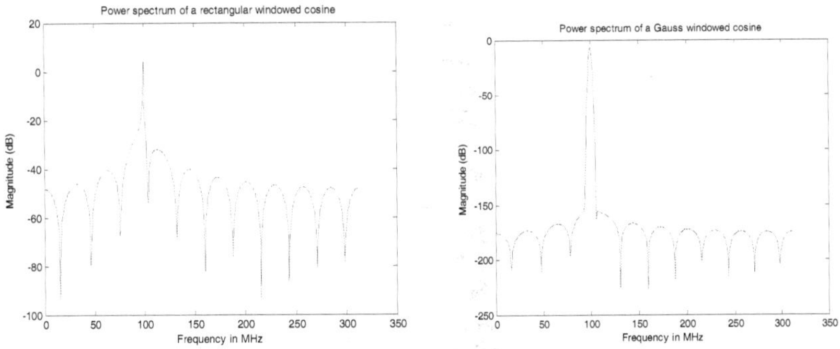

(a) (b)

Fig. 6. Power spectrum of a 100 MHz rectangular (a) and Gauss (b) signal window

Window adjustment to the exact signal burst

It has already been mentioned that the signal bursts are not going to be of the same length. The obtained SNR can thus be further improved by fitting the time-window to the exact length of the shortest expected burst in an effort to easy the detection process. Fig. 7(a) depicts a relatively long signal time-window containing a backscattering burst, the length of which is marked by a rectangular frame, as well as the respective power spectrum. On the other hand, Fig. 7(b) shows the same burst in a time-window that almost fits its length and the corresponding power spectrum presenting a clearly improved SNR. This happens because it is just the bursts that contain all the useful information of the signal. The other parts contain pure noise and when they are subtracted from the data window the SNR is notably raised. This is, of course, at the cost of the obtained frequency resolution due to the fewer data samples used (FFT points).

The zero-padding technique may be employed to overcome that drawback by adding zeros and increasing the length of the data time-window to the desired magnitude. In this case, the detection is slightly improved due to the scalloping loss reduction and at the same time the frequency estimation is better enough, without the need for post processing.

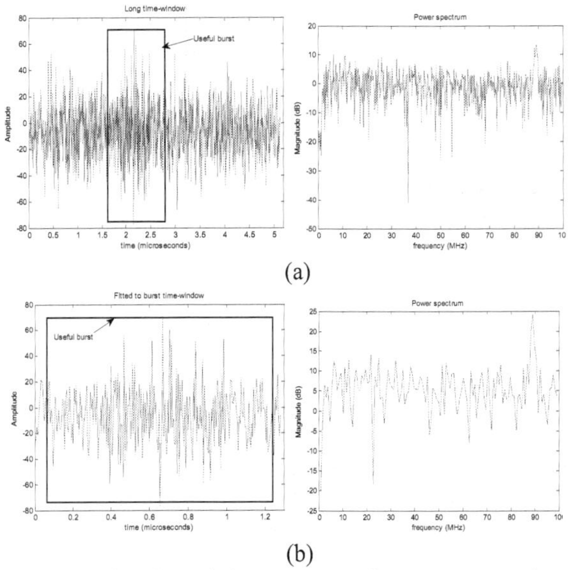

Fig. 7. Spectral analysis of a relatively long time-window containing a burst (a) and a time-window almost fitting the burst (b)

Overlapping

Since we acquire and process successive time windows of the signal sequence and we do not know the exact time a burst may occur, it is possible to loose the desired adjustment of the window to the full length of the burst if, for example, the latter happens between to successive data acquisitions. The SNR in such a case dramatically deteriorates making the detection doubtful. In order to tackle with the problem above the overlap processing is taking place. That means we can calculate every time the spectrum of a data sequence that

contains part of the samples from the old time-window and part of the samples from the new time-window. Fig. 8(a) illustrates the successive data windows for the 50% overlapping procedure.
Conducting overlapping in signal processing, however, has the result that the amount of the data to be processed be dramatically increased. In the 50% case, particularly, the computational cost is doubled. A serial-to-parallel conversion with adequate overlapping can fully secure the effective processing of the data sequence. In that way, a number of parallel data streams are generated and processed in blocks of N samples using all the available computational resources of the FPGA boards.

Calibration
Before detection, it is also necessary to calibrate the power spectrum for the bias removal and the equalization reasons. In order to calculate the calibration coefficients, spectrums are regularly acquired with the laser power set to off.

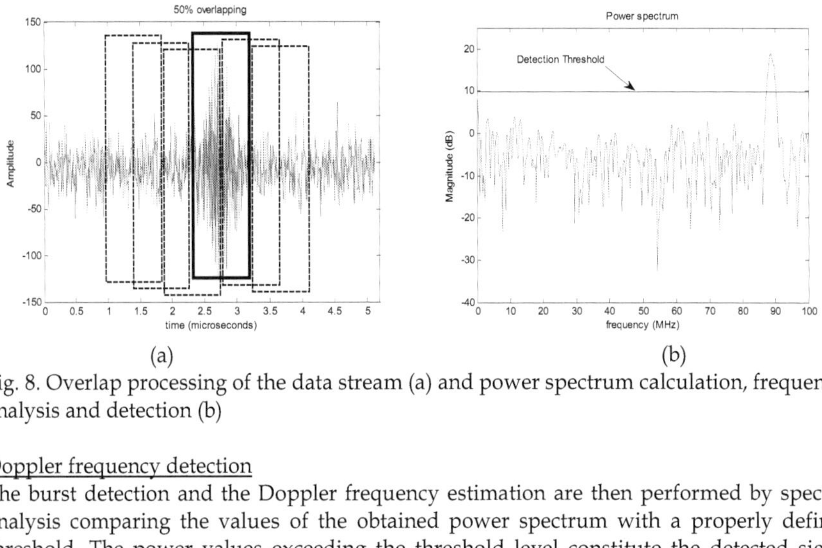

(a) (b)

Fig. 8. Overlap processing of the data stream (a) and power spectrum calculation, frequency analysis and detection (b)

Doppler frequency detection
The burst detection and the Doppler frequency estimation are then performed by spectral analysis comparing the values of the obtained power spectrum with a properly defined threshold. The power values exceeding the threshold level constitute the detected signal whereas the FFT bin of the peak value determines the corresponding Doppler frequency. Fig. 8(b) shows the spectrum of the powerful burst depicted in Fig. 8(a) that can provide a strong signal and an easy detection.
Finally, the detected frequencies are registered in a FIFO buffer, from where they are read in the slow processing unit for the aircraft velocity calculation.

3.3 The real-time processing

Aiming to provide the real-time processing of the NESLIE signal data we had to study and define the highest frequency at which we can calculate a spectrum and the other necessary parameters without missing any data. That is we have to give careful consideration to the data collection time as well as to the processing speed of our FPGA processor or else to the time it takes to perform the FFT spectrum analysis and all the needed additional computations and tasks described above.

There are three possible cases regarding the relation between the data acquisition time and the processing time as Fig. 9 shows. If the signal time-windows come with a rate higher than that at which the FPGA processor can perform the corresponding calculations, certainly there will be gaps in the acquired data (Fig. 9(a)). That results in the inevitable loss of an amount of data which may enclose useful information (i.e. the Doppler frequency shift of a burst). In such a case the whole procedure fails and the signal cannot be effectively analysed. On the other hand, if the processing speed is higher or equal to the speed that the signal windows are being collected we can really speak about a real-time application (Fig. 9(b) and Fig. 9(c) respectively).

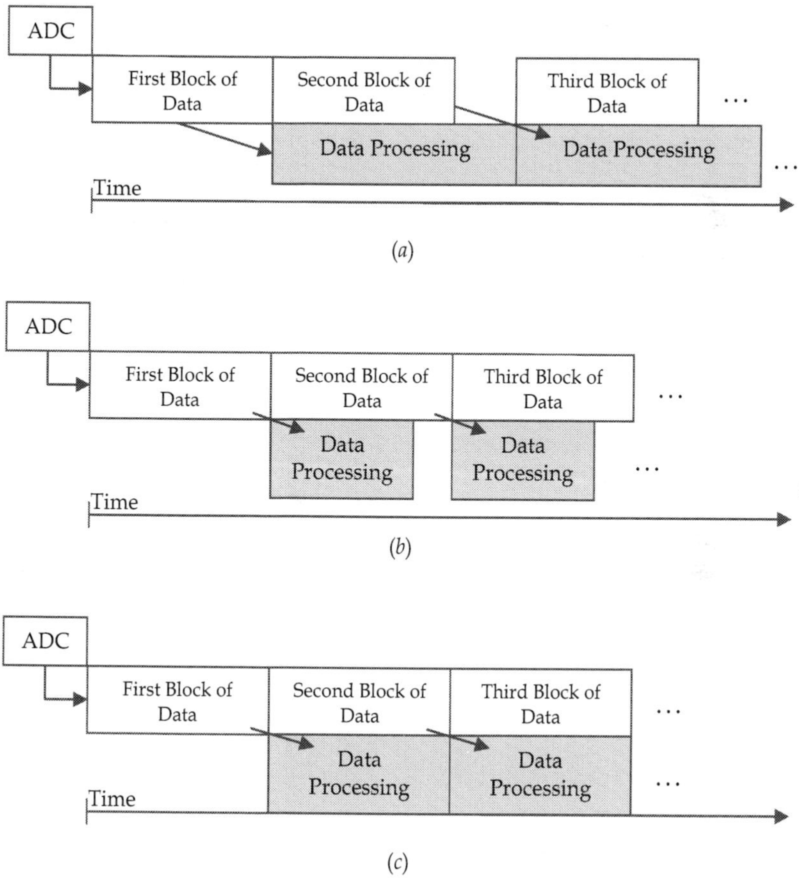

Fig. 9. The three possibilities regarding the relation of the data acquisition time and the processing time.

3.4 Hardware selection and development tools

The Fast Signal Processing module was implemented on a special-purpose FPGA development board for programming a Xilinx Virtex 5-SX95T FPGA with more than 46,000 logic cells. This board, making optimum use of the inherent parallelism of the logic resources in the FPGA, can meet the application's advanced requirements, satisfy the strict timing constraints and effectively manage the huge computational throughput at a considerably high clock rate. The hardware platform is complemented with an ADC board and a PCI 64 bit carrier card.

The FPGA firmware was developed using the 3L's Diamond FPGA tool in association with the Xilinx ISE Foundation 9.2. 3L Diamond FPGA is a software development tool that shortens the development cycle by defining self-contained blocks of code or tasks that communicate each other. A task can be built for a DSP or an FPGA board and consists a simple but efficient abstraction from the actual hardware, hiding many of the low-level details and adding flexibility in the firmware design.

Diamond 3L tasks can be created with a wide range of FPGA tools, including Matlab Simulink, Celoxica DK suite, Impulse-C, Xilinx System Generator. It can build individual tasks into bitstreams that are finally incorporated into the complete application. Tasks are a good mechanism for sharing and exchanging ideas and technology.

Xilinx ISE® Foundation™ software integrates everything we need in a complete logic design environment for all leading Xilinx FPGA and CPLD products. The build-in tools and wizards make I/O assignment, power analysis, timing-driven design closure and HDL simulation. The Xilinx ISE tool is Xilinx's solution in compiling the design, targeting their hardware.

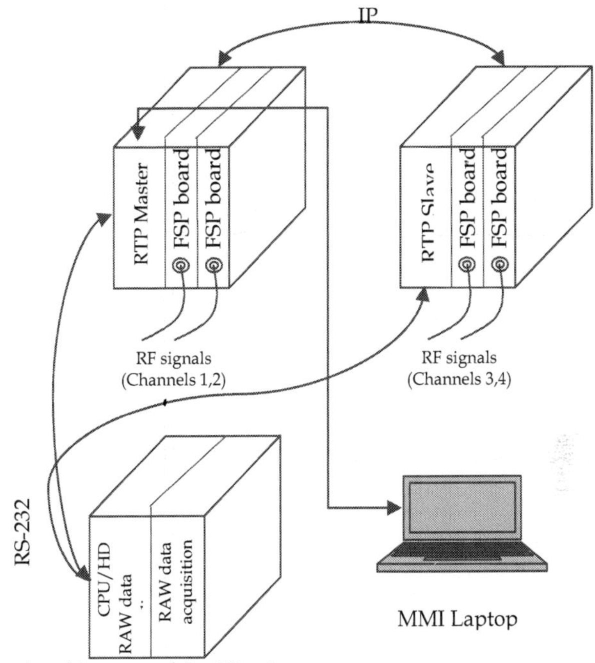

Fig. 10. The general architecture of the SP unit.

3.5 The architecture of the signal processing unit

Since there are four independent signal inputs, corresponding to the four identical laser measurement units installed on board the plane, the system has to perform the processing of these inputs in parallel so that the real-time estimation of the 3D air-speed vector becomes possible. The selected architecture uses two almost identical PC units, each using a dedicated FSP board to perform signal acquisition and processing of one channel. These two PCs, referred as the Real Time Processing (RTP) unit, exchange data between them via TCP/IP (Ethernet). This dual PC setup was selected in order to cope with the computational requirements and secure enough PCI bandwidth by splitting the data in the both PCI buses. Furthermore, it allows the system to function (reduced performance) even if only one PC board (two signal channels) is available.

An auxiliary PC board, referred as the Raw Data Recorder (RDR), is responsible for the control of the lasers as well as for raw data (digitized signal) recording for validation and post processing purposes.

One of the RTP PCs, referred as the RTP Master, can transmit information through to the RDR using RS-232 connection. However, both RTP PCs are able to receive information from RDR, using a simple T shaped cable connection. This approach was seen to reduce significantly the communication overhead required to achieve synchronization between the 3 PCs and makes the setup less vulnerable to Ethernet delays and/or communication errors.

A laptop is used as an MMI to display results of the system in a Web browser, as well as to allow the modification of an RTP configuration file containing all necessary system parameters. The entire system architecture is illustrated in Fig.10.

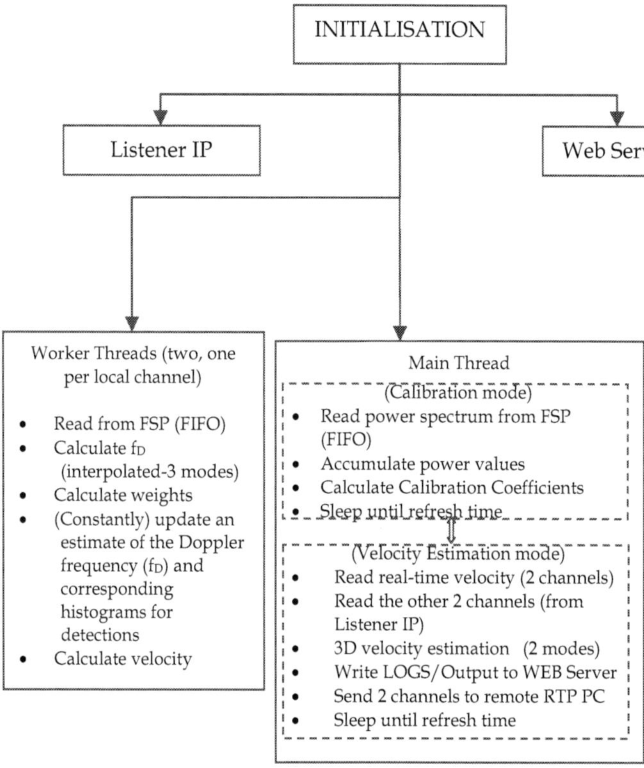

Fig. 11. Concise diagram of the SSP software.

3.6 The slow signal processing module

An efficient C++ software module was developed for the last stage of processing as well as the data storage and display. It is a multi-threaded application that ensures the necessary interconnection between the two independent units, the RDR and the MMI, the accurate computation of the 3D air-speed vector and finally the adequate output presentation at the User Interface (MMI). Fig. 11 depicts the threads that were defined as well as the main functions performed, which are almost the same for both RTP CPUs.

Immediately after its initialization, the procedure initiates four auxiliary threads responsible for:

- receiving and processing of information from the other SP unit and the RDR
- presentation of the final results (Web server)

- receiving and processing data from the FSP board (two "worker threads", one for each local channel)

Two modes of operation are defined, i.e. the "real-time velocity estimation" and update (calculation of TAS components at the corresponding laser axes) mode, performed in a constantly repeated loop as well as the calculation mode, which is periodically used to update the calibration coefficients.

While the "Worker threads" perform their tasks as fast as possible, the main thread uses a fixed time cycle (defined by output (measurement) rate requirements. Within this time cycle, communication with the Worker threads and the remote RTP PC is used to obtain the four samples required to estimate the 3D velocity vector as well as the associated flight parameters, such as the True Air Speed (TAS), the Angle of Attack(AOA) and the Side-Slip Angle (SSA) and various error statistics. Finally, within the same data cycle, the results are being recorded into disk logs and are provided to the Web server thread, so that they can be displayed in the MMI.

The real-time velocity estimation function

In this function a set of seven values is being repeatedly read from the FIFO buffer in the FSP board. The first is a timestamp corresponding to the detection and the next is the index **x** of the maximum (FFT bin) which corresponds to the estimated Doppler frequency. Finally, five values **y[i]**, **i=1,...,5** correspond to the useful power spectrum values of the detected burst (Fig. 12). More specifically, **y[3]** is the maximum value of the power spectrum while its four neighboring values (two on each side) are **y[1]**, **y[2]** and **y[4]**, **y[5]** respectively.

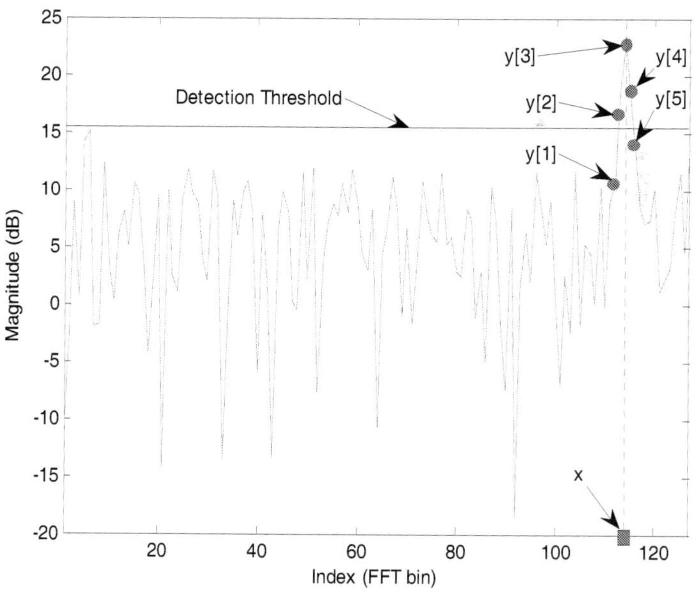

Fig. 12. The power spectrum of a detected burst and the six values read in the CPU from the FIFO buffer for the SSP.

In order to improve the resolution for the estimated Doppler frequency, an interpolation method can optionally be applied to the acquired data. Two interpolation techniques with low computational cost are parabolic interpolation using either 3 or all 5 available spectrum samples:

Three point parabolic interpolation

With that mode three values of the useful power spectrum are being used to form the interpolating parabola and calculate the interpolated frequency from:

$$x_{\text{int}} = x + \frac{1}{2} \cdot \frac{y[4] - y[2]}{2y[3] - y[4] - y[2]} \tag{5}$$

Five point parabolic interpolation

All five data points are being used to calculate the Least Squares parabola:

$$y = f(x) = \alpha_2 x^2 + \alpha_1 x + \alpha_0 \tag{6}$$

Fig. 13 depicts the useful spectrum (five data values) and the interpolated frequency value which is being computed from:

$$x_{\text{int}} = -\frac{\alpha_1}{2\alpha_2} \tag{7}$$

After every new detection and estimation of the corresponding Doppler frequency $\mathbf{x_{int}}$, a weight coefficient is calculated and associated to that value in an effort to rate the reliability of the measurement. Two criteria can be used for the calculation of the weight **w** that is assigned to the estimated frequency value:

a) The power of the useful spectrum, in each signal detection, with respect to the detection threshold. The mean value of the five recorded spectrum magnitudes is being computed for that purpose:

$$\mu = \frac{\sum_{i=1}^{5} y[i]}{5} \tag{8}$$

If that value is higher than the detection threshold (μ **>th**) the weight **w** is set to: **w=**μ**/th,** while otherwise it is set to zero.

b) The maximum frequency index of the detected burst has to lie within a periodically updated frequency window. The expected frequency widow depends on the previous velocity estimations.

The next step is to calculate an estimate of the Doppler frequency f_D from all detections (valid frequencies estimates) obtained for the specific channel, within each cycle of the slow processing unit. For this calculation, three possible options are being supported:

a) A weighted mean f_D of the estimated Doppler frequency values using their corresponding weights:

$$f_D = \frac{\sum_{i=1}^{n} x_{\text{int}}(i) w(i)}{\sum_{i=1}^{n} w(i)} \tag{9}$$

The weighted variance is used as a reliability estimate in this case.

b) An estimate of the pdf of f_D is generated by estimating a histogram (or weighted histogram) of its values within each cycle. If the underlying function is known or can be assumed (e.g. Gaussian), then this function can be fit on the estimated pdf. The mean and the variance of the estimated distribution yield the estimated Doppler frequency and its reliability, respectively.

c) Robust estimate: This technique is similar to (b), however instead a robust estimate (e.g. the median) of the values is being used. This method is computationally efficient, avoids outliers, and has satisfactory resolution. The reliability of the estimate in this case can be defined based on the desired percentage of detections (percentage of samples within the window versus the total number of samples).

Finally, the component of the 3D air-speed vector at the corresponding laser axis is given by the equation:

$$v = \frac{f_D \cdot \lambda}{2} \quad (V_{axis}) \tag{10}$$

where λ is the wavelength of the emitted signal. The value of this parameter is very important, so it is constantly measured by the RDR and is provided to the RTP in a regular basis. All the parameters of the estimation accumulators and histograms are reset to zero at the start of each cycle of the slow processing unit.

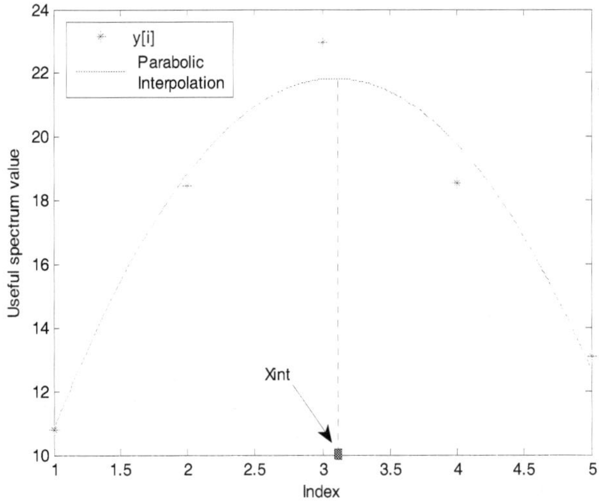

Fig. 13. The parabolic interpolation of the five spectrum values and the estimated index of the maximum.

Calculation of calibration coefficients

Since the lower frequencies in the pure noise power spectrum show the tendency to be stronger than higher frequencies it is necessary to calibrate the data after the FFT computation in order to remove the bias and easy the detection process. The calibration coefficients used for that purpose in the fast signal processing module (FSP) are calculated in a separate mode of the slow processing module (SSP).

During this mode, the laser power is set to 'OFF' and RTP accumulates successive noise spectrums. Fig. 14 shows the existing noise bias after accumulating 1000 noise spectrum frames. These values constitute the coefficients with which the corresponding data of the signal spectrum have to be divided (within the FSP) before each detection in order to eliminate the inherent inclination and equalise the noise level.

Another alternative to is interpolate the accumulated spectrum and divide the data with the new coefficients coming from liner, quadratic or polynomial interpolation (Fig. 14).

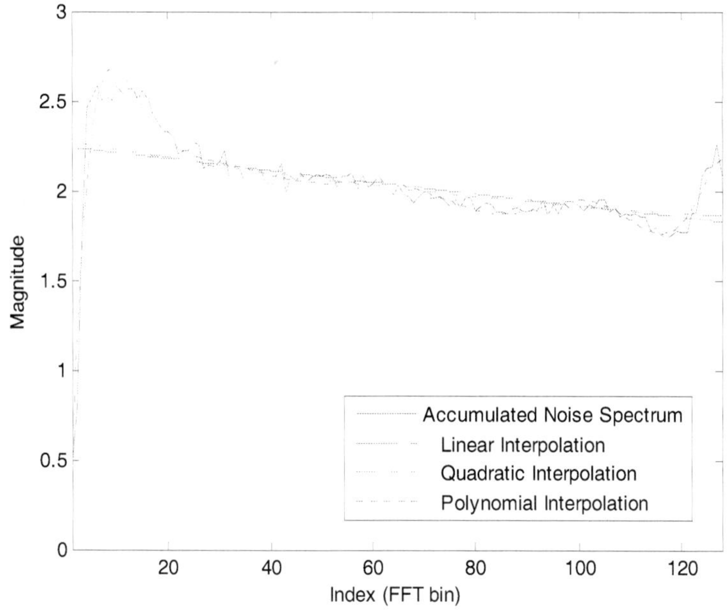

Fig. 14. Accumulation of 1000 noise spectrums and interpolation of the data.

3-D Velocity estimation at the main thread

As already described, the main thread reads velocity estimates for its two local channels, as well as for the two remote laser channels from the remote RTP PC via Etherent. If all four channel estimates are available, we form a system of four equations with three unknowns (V_x, V_y, and V_z), which is solved by standard least squares:

$$\begin{bmatrix} \alpha_{1x} & \alpha_{1y} & \alpha_{1z} \\ \alpha_{2x} & \alpha_{2y} & \alpha_{2z} \\ \alpha_{3x} & \alpha_{3y} & \alpha_{3z} \\ \alpha_{4x} & \alpha_{4y} & \alpha_{4z} \end{bmatrix} \begin{bmatrix} V_x \\ V_y \\ V_z \end{bmatrix} = \begin{bmatrix} V_{axis1} \\ V_{axis2} \\ V_{axis3} \\ V_{axis4} \end{bmatrix} \tag{11}$$

where α_{ik} are the x, y, z coordinates of the unit vectors at the four laser axis (i=1,2,3,4 and k=x,y,z). A solution can also be found even if only three channels are available.

4. Flight results

A number of flight tests have been planned and performed in order to test the operation of the developed unit as well as to prove its effectiveness for on board real-time air-data measurements.

During the flights, the calculated parameters as well as all the other useful system's data are being recorded, constantly updated and properly displayed in a functional Man Machine Interface (MMI). The Doppler frequency histogram as well as the power spectrum (SNR) histogram corresponding to the two local channels are also presented.

Fig. 15 shows the MMI at such a state during one of the flights.

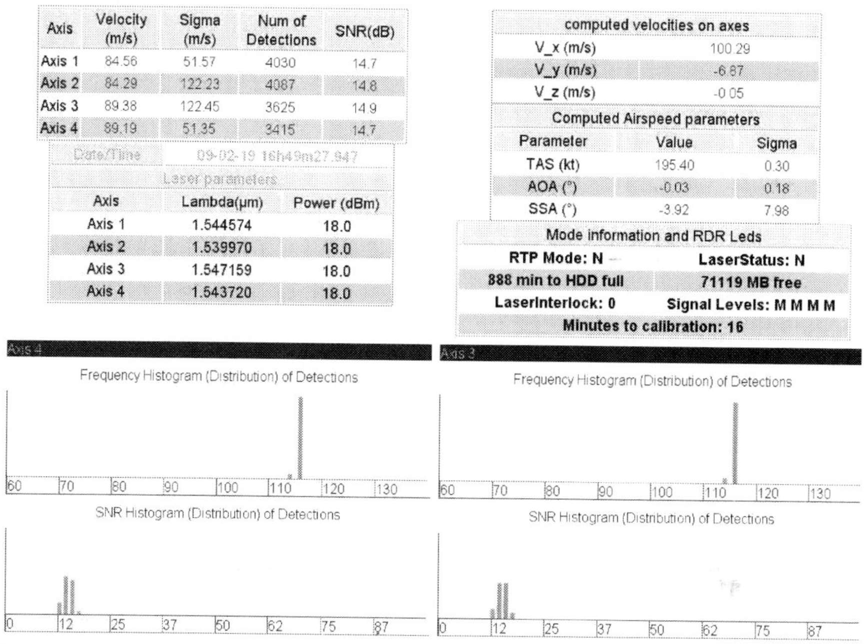

Fig. 15. The MMI of the NESLIE measurement unit at a specific time instant, presenting the computed flight parameters and other useful data

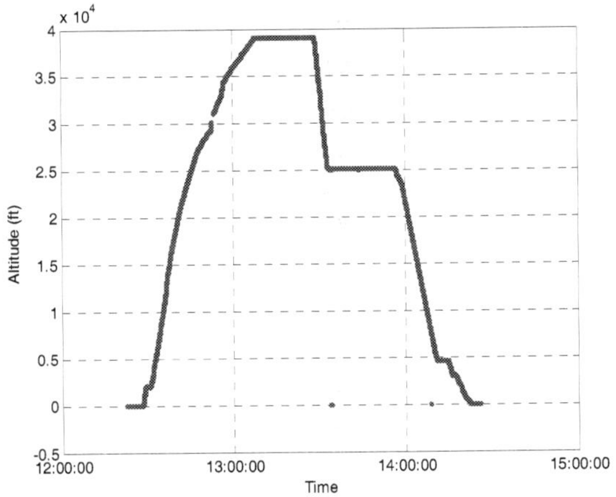

Fig. 16. The flight altitude as a function of time during one of the tests

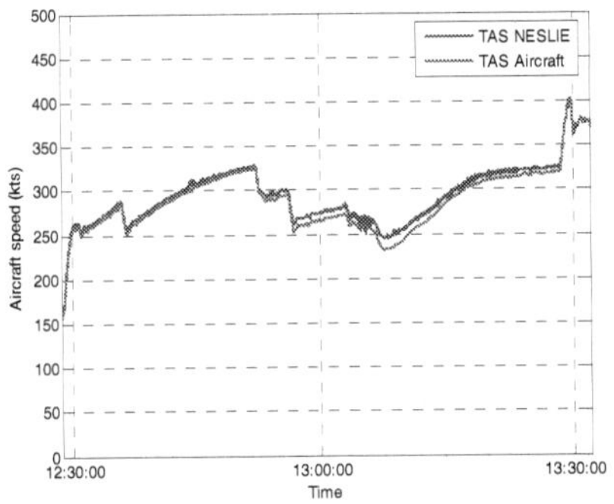

(a)

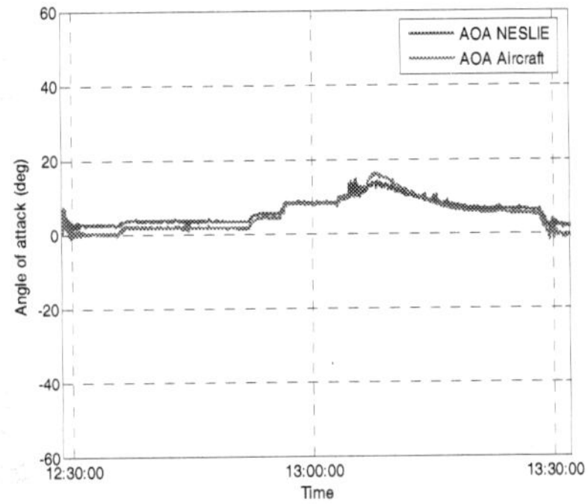

(b)

Fig. 17. Comparison of NESLIE measurements of True Air-Speed (a) and Angle of Attack (b) during a flight with the reference data recorded by the aircraft

The testing flights covered a wide range of altitudes (up to 39.000 feet) as well as different weather conditions in order to better evaluate and validate the performance of the system. Fig. 16 depicts the flight level during such a test according to the time.

The NESLIE measurements were also recorded in order to compare them with the corresponding data from the aircraft's standard measurement channels (Pitot tubes). The obtained results show a significant agreement between these two completely different modes of air-speed measurements as it can be clearly seen in Fig. 17(a) for the true air-speed (TAS) of the aircraft during the flight and in Fig. 17(b) for the angle of attack (AOA). However, a more thorough analysis of the test results is required and is already being conducted by the NESLIE consortium.

5. Summary

The methodology and the consecutive steps of an efficient signal processing scheme, developed to provide real-time measurements of the true air-speed and other useful flight parameters in the framework of the EU funded NESLIE research project, were analytically presented.

The NESLIE signal processing unit consists of a distributed system that uses two embedded PCs and four FPGA signal processing boards, corresponding to each of the laser axis. The fast signal processing module performs the analog-to-digital conversion, the frequency analysis (FFT) and the burst detection from the adequate spectrum values. These operations are implemented in powerful FPGA boards that finally provide the detected Doppler frequency as well as the useful power spectrum. Using the data above, the slow signal processing module calculates the vector velocity of the aircraft and the other parameters necessary for the safety of the flight. It is the software for disk logging and also responsible for the MMI and communication tasks with the other real-time processing PC and the RDR server.

The whole unit was set on board for flight testing showing more than satisfactory results. That encourages us to proceed to further optimization of the modules demonstrating that such an instrument can really work as a reliable air-data standby measurement channel.

6. Acknowledgements

This work was supported by the European Community (EC) under the FP6 Aeronautics and Space "NESLIE - NEw Standy Lidar InstrumEnt" project (Contract no.: 30721).

7. References

Bilbro, J.; Fichtl, G.; Fitzjarrald, G. & Krause, M. (1984). Airborne Doppler lidar wind field measurements. *Bull. Am. Meteorol. Soc.*, 65, pp. 348-359.

Bilbro, J. W.; DiMarzio, C.; Fitzjarrald, D.; Johnson, S. & Jones, W. (1986). Airborne Doppler lidar measurements. *Appl. Opt.*, 25, pp. 3952-3960.

Browell, E. V.; Ismail, S. & Grant, W. B. (1998). Differential absorption lidar (DIAL) measurements from air and space. *Appl. Phys.*, B 67, pp. 399-410.

Frehlich, R.; Hannon S. M. & Henderson, S. W. (1994). Performance of a 2 μm coherent Doppler lidar for wind measurements. *Journal Atm. Oc. Tech.*, vol.11, pp. 1517-1528.

Frehlich R. G. & Yadlowsky, M. J. (1994). Performance of mean-frequency estimators for Doppler radar and lidar. *Journal Atm. Oc. Tech.*, vol.11, pp. 1217-1229.

Henderson, S. W.; Suni, P. J. M.; Hale, C. P.; Hannon, S. M.; Magee, J. R.; Bruns D. L. & Yuen, E. H. (1993). Coherent laser radar at 2 μm using solid state lasers. *IEEE Trans. Geosci. Remote Sens.*, 31, pp. 4-15.

Kavaya, M. J.; Magee, J. R.; Hale, C. P. & Huffaker, R. M. (1989). Remote wind profiling with a solid-state Nd:YAG coherent lidar system. *Opt. Lett.*, 14, pp. 776-778.

Korb, C. L.; Gentry, B. M. and Xingfu Li, S. (1997). Edge technique Doppler lidar wind measurements with high vertical resolution. *Applied Optics*. Vol. 36, No. 24, pp. 5976-5983.

Levin, M. J. (1965). Power spectrum parameter estimation. *IEEE Trans. Inform. Theory,* vol. 1, pp. 100-107.

Mahapatra, P. R. & Zrnic, D. S. (1983). Practical algorithms for mean velocity estimation in pulse Doppler weather radars using a small number of samples. *IEEE Trans. Geosci. Remote Sens.*, vol. GE-21, No 4, pp. 491-501.

Oppenheim A. V. & Schafer, R. W. (1999). *Discrete-Time Signal Processing.* Prentice Hall, 1999. Post, M. J. & Cupp, R. E. (1990). Optimizing a pulsed Doppler lidar. *Appl. Opt.*, 29, pp. 4145-4158.

Proakis J. G. & Manolakis, D. K. (2006). *Digital Signal Processing.* Prentice Hall (forth edition).

Performance analysis of port-starboard discrimination for towed multi-line array

Biao Jiang
Hangzhou Applied Acoustics Research Institute
China

1. Introduction

Towed receiving line array has been successfully utilized in military underwater surveillance and seismic exploring. The developments and applications of towed line array sonar can be traced back to 1910s (Lemon, 2004). And the signal processing algorithms for the towed array has been studied extensively in recent a few decades (Nielsen, 1991, Schurman, 1996). Since beampattern of a single-line array is symmetric around the array axis, it cannot tell us whether the target signal is coming from port (left) or from starboard (right), the port-starboard ambiguity is the main shortcoming of a single-line towed array with omni-directional hydrophones. Multi-line array is a simple and convenient way to resolve the problem of port-starboard ambiguity. Considering the system complexity, the twin-line array is the most feasible (Feuillet et al., 1995, Li, 2007) method, triple-line or even larger multi-line array can further improve the detection and localization performance. By now, only twin-line array sonar has been equipped to the surface ships or submarines, there are no reports that triple-line array sonar has been equipped. Triplet array, which uses three closely separated hydrophones acting as a directional sensor, is another solution to the port starboard ambiguity (Groen et al., 2005). The triplet array is easy to be towed and deployed since there is only one tow cable, in spite of its relatively larger diameter. However, because the diameter of triplet array cannot be large enough, it is best applicable to active mode with operational frequency being around 1kHz or higher, not quite satisfactory for low frequency long range passive surveillance. Vector-sensor array is a new method still being studied to achieve port-starboard discrimination (PSD) due to its two-dimensional beampattern in azimuth and elevation (Nehorai & Paldi, 1994, Theriault et. al, 2006). However, the vector-sensor array is very sensitive to the array shape and the installation conditions, so the techniques of vector-sensor have not been so perfect that can be used to fully replace the conventional pressure sensor. Consequently, multi-line array with significantly larger transversal aperture, i.e., the maximum array separation, is promising, especially in littoral environment in which long horizontal single-line array is not appropriate to be used. Multi-line array can also provide vertical aperture to perform range and depth estimation using matched-field processing (MFP). MFP using multi-line array is in research now.

Besides the improved detection capability, port-starboard discrimination is the most important feature of multi-line array. How to evaluate the performance of port-starboard discrimination is the key to design the multi-line array spatial structure. Left/right suppressed ratio by twin-line array directivity function was commonly used to analyze the left/right ambiguity resolution performance (Li, 2007). Groen used the array gain and port-starboard rejection to analyze the theoretical and experimental performance of three triplet array beamformers: Optimum triplet beamformer, Cardioid beamformer and adaptive triplet beamformer (Groen, 2005). However, these performance analyses are only applicable to the narrowband signal case. For passive sonar, it is desirable to localize the ship radiated wideband noise, so it is important for us to analyze the performance of wideband port starboard discrimination.

In this chapter, we'll discuss the performance of the PSD for the target detected by a towed multi-line array. First, the narrowband port-starboard rejection ratios (PSRR's) are defined and mathematically derived, for both the twin-line array and the triple-line array. Then, the optimum array separation for which the PSRR achieves the maximum is analyzed.

By integrating the narrowband PSRR expression in the processing frequency bandwidth, we obtain the wideband PSRR. Setting the transversal array apertures be equal, the wideband PSRR's of a twin-line array and a triple-line array are compared, and some analytical and simulation results are demonstrated.

Furthermore, two special aspects are studied in this chapter. First, the probability of target the PSD, both narrowband and wideband, for a twin-line array is derived based on the signal detection theory. In a similar way, the probability of PSD for a triple-line array can be obtained. Secondly, the expressions are developed which describe the adaptive port-starboard discrimination for a twin-line array when a correlated interfering signal is present. Conventional beamforming is applied to each line array, followed by a beam-space two-element adaptive beamforming. Then the PSRR is derived in terms of a few parameters, including array separation, signal-to-noise-ratio (SNR), signal-to-interference-ratio (SIR), angular separation and correlation coefficient between the desired signal and the interference. Simulation results are given to demonstrate the results.

2. Signal model

Consider a parallel N-hydrophone multi-line array with the number of lines L, and each of the lines comprises M sensors with inter-element spacing d, so that $N=LM$. The transversal array aperture is D. Fig. 1 depicts a diagram of a twin-line array. The jth sensor on the line i is denoted as A_{ij}, and the signal of arrival (DOA) θ is relative to the front end fire. For convenience, we let θ be positive in the starboard direction, whereas negative in the port direction.

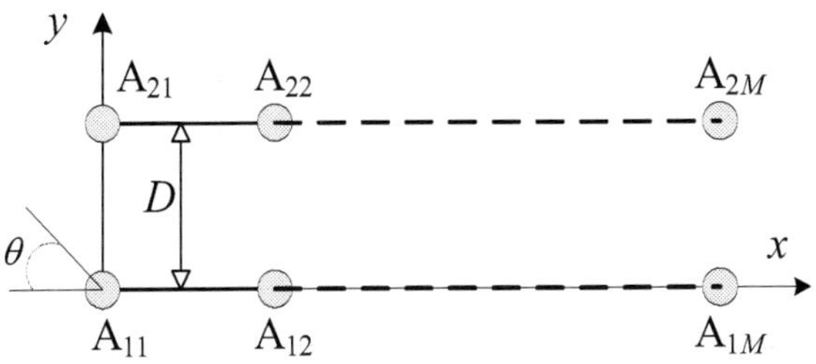

Fig. 1. Diagram of a twin-line array

Assume one narrowband signal with central frequency f impinging on the array, the wavefront propagating speed is c, and the array output signal vector can be written as:

$$\boldsymbol{x}(t) = \boldsymbol{a}(\theta)s(t) + \boldsymbol{n}(t) \tag{1}$$

where $s(t)$ denotes the source signal, and $\boldsymbol{n}(t)$ the additive noise vector. $\boldsymbol{a}(\theta)$ is the multi-line array steering vector:

$$\boldsymbol{a}(\theta) = \boldsymbol{a}_T(\theta) \otimes \boldsymbol{a}_L(\theta) \tag{2}$$

where $\otimes$ denotes the Kronecker product. $\boldsymbol{a}_L(\theta)$ is the steering vector of the leftmost line array, and $\boldsymbol{a}_T(\theta)$ is the transversal steering vector, given by:

$$\boldsymbol{a}_L(\theta) = \left[1, e^{-j2\pi fd\cos\theta/c}, \cdots, e^{-j2\pi f(M-1)d\cos\theta/c}\right]^T \tag{3}$$

$$\boldsymbol{a}_T(\theta) = [1, e^{j2\pi fD\sin\theta/[c(L-1)]}, \cdots, e^{j2\pi fD\sin\theta/c}]^T \tag{4}$$

2.1 Multi-line array directivity

In this section, we'll discuss the directivity functions of two types of multi-line array: twin-line array and triple-line array. When the desired signal direction is θ_0, the normalized multi-line directivity function can be written as (Li, 2007, Nielsen, 1991):

$$\begin{aligned} B(f,\theta;\theta_0) &= \frac{1}{LM}\left|\boldsymbol{a}^H(\theta)\boldsymbol{a}(\theta_0)\right| \\ &= \frac{1}{LM}\left|[\boldsymbol{a}_T(\theta)\otimes\boldsymbol{a}_L(\theta)]^H[\boldsymbol{a}_T(\theta_0)\otimes\boldsymbol{a}_L(\theta_0)]\right| \\ &= \frac{1}{LM}\left|\boldsymbol{a}_T^H(\theta)\boldsymbol{a}_T(\theta_0)\boldsymbol{a}_L^H(\theta)\boldsymbol{a}_L(\theta_0)\right| \end{aligned} \tag{5}$$

After substituting (3) and (4) to (5) and performing some algebraic manipulation, we get the twin-line and triple-line array directivity functions, as follows

$$B_{\text{twin}}(f,\theta;\theta_0) = \left|\frac{\sin(\pi fMd(\cos\theta-\cos\theta_0)/c)}{M\sin(\pi fd(\cos\theta-\cos\theta_0)/c)}\right| \times \left|\cos[\pi fD(\sin\theta-\sin\theta_0)/c\right| \tag{6}$$

$$B_{\text{triple}}(f,\theta;\theta_0)=\frac{1}{3}\left|\frac{\sin(\pi fMd(\cos\theta-\cos\theta_0)/c)}{M\sin(\pi fd(\cos\theta-\cos\theta_0)/c)}\right|\times\left|1+2\cos[kD(\sin\theta-\sin\theta_0)/2]\right| \tag{7}$$

2.2 Port-starboard rejection ratio (PSRR)

We use port-starboard rejection ratio to evaluate the performance of port-starboard discrimination. The PSRR is defined as the ratio of the output power in the desired signal direction to that in the mirror direction. Using (6) and (7), we have

$$\text{PSRR}_{\text{twin}}=\frac{\left|B_{\text{twin}}(f,\theta_0;\theta_0)\right|^2}{\left|B_{\text{twin}}(f,-\theta_0;\theta_0)\right|^2}=\frac{1}{\cos^2(2\pi fD\sin\theta_0/c)} \tag{8}$$

$$\text{PSRR}_{\text{triple}}=\frac{\left|B_{\text{triple}}(f,\theta_0;\theta_0)\right|^2}{\left|B_{\text{triple}}(f,-\theta_0;\theta_0)\right|^2}=\frac{9}{\left|1+2\cos\left(2\pi fD\sin\theta_0/c\right)\right|^2} \tag{9}$$

Consequently, from (8), we can see that, for a desired narrowband signal, when the array spacing is $D=(n\pm1/4)\lambda/\sin\theta_0, n\in\mathbb{Z}$, where λ is the signal wavelength, the twin-line array achieves the maximum PSD performance. Similarly, from (9), the PSRR is optimal for the triple-line array when the transversal aperture satisfies $D=(n\pm1/3)\lambda/\sin\theta_0, n\in\mathbb{Z}$.

2.3 Wideband PSRR

Consider a scenario of one wideband source and noise, the signal is modeled by a white stationary process with power σ_s^2 with central frequency f_0 and bandwidth B, and the noise by a spatially white complex process, with power σ_n^2. Thus, the wideband port-starboard rejection ratios of twin-line and triple-line arrays can be written as

$$\text{PSRR}_{\text{twin}}^{\text{wb}}=\frac{2\int_{f_0-B/2}^{f_0+B/2}\frac{\sigma_s^2}{B}df}{2\int_{f_0-B/2}^{f_0+B/2}\frac{\sigma_s^2}{B}\cos^2\left(2\pi fD\sin\theta_0/c\right)df+\sigma_n^2}=\frac{2\text{SNR}+1}{\text{SNR}\left[1+\text{sinc}(\psi B/f_0)\cos(2\psi)\right]+1} \tag{10}$$

$$\text{PSRR}_{\text{triple}}^{\text{wb}}=\frac{3\int_{f_0-B/2}^{f_0+B/2}\frac{\sigma_s^2}{B}df+\sigma_n^2}{\int_{f_0-B/2}^{f_0+B/2}\frac{\sigma_s^2}{B}[1+2\cos(2\pi fD\sin\theta_0/c)]^2/3df+\sigma_n^2}$$

$$= \frac{3\mathrm{SNR}+1}{\mathrm{SNR}\left\{1+4/3\cos(\psi)\mathrm{sinc}(\psi B/2f_0)+2/3\cos(2\psi)\mathrm{sinc}(\psi B/f_0)\right\}+1} \tag{11}$$

where $\psi = 2\pi D f_0 \sin\theta_0 / c$, $\mathrm{SNR} = \sigma_s^2/\sigma_n^2$ is the signal-to-noise ratio (SNR). It can be seen from (10), (11) that, the wideband PSRR is mainly determined by the SNR, the transversal aperture, the spectral distribution, and the signal arriving angle. Interestingly, the value of PSRR is independent of the number of sensors of each single-line array.

2.4 Simulation results

2.4.1 Narrowband beampatterns

In this section, the beampattens of the twin-line array and the triple-line array are presented. The number of elements of each line is M=16, Fig. 2 shows the beampatterns of twin-line array and triple-line array by the optimal array separations, for which the PSRR's are maximum for the broadside signals. Fig. 3 is the transversal cardioid beampatterns, which are the second terms in (6) and (7), of the two multi-line arrays for broadside signals. It's because there is a null in the mirror direction on the cardioid beampattern that the multi-line array can resolve the port-starboard ambiguity.
In Fig.2, the red line is a dash-dot line as in the word file, in case not to be confused with the blue line.

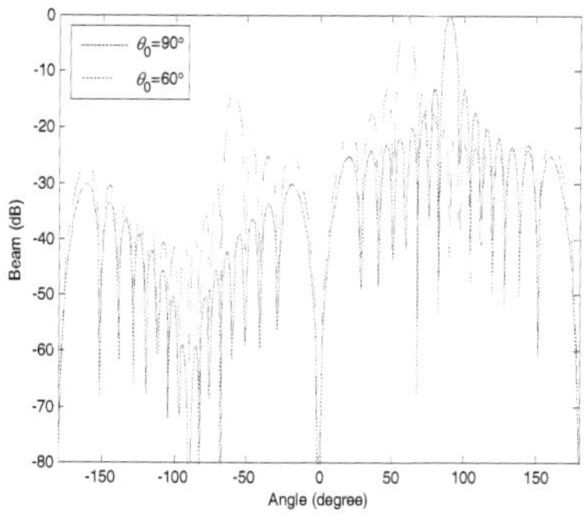

(a) Twin-line array (D=λ/4)

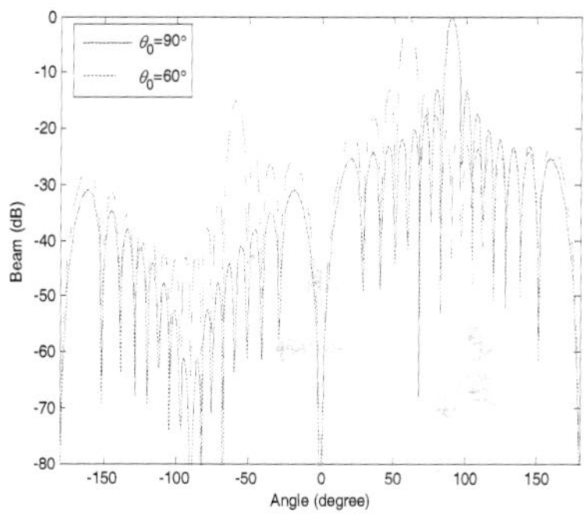

(b) Triple-line array (D=λ/3)

Fig. 2. Beampatterns of the twin-line array and the triple-line array for M=16

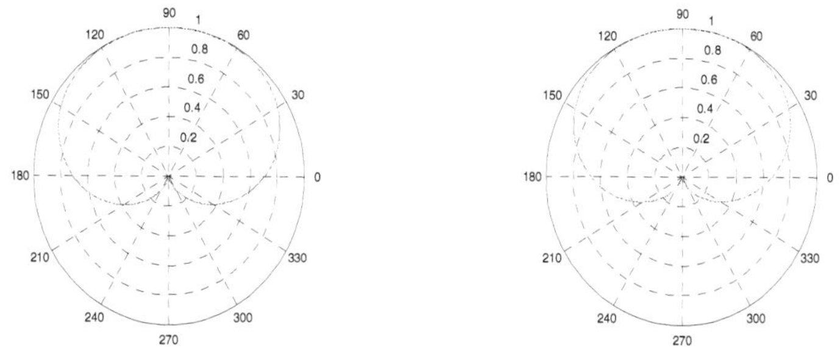

(a) Twin-line array (D=λ/4) (b) Triple-line array (D=λ/3)

Fig. 3. Cardioid beampatterns of the twin-line array and the triple-line array for θ_0=90°

2.4.2 Wideband PSRR

In this section, the wideband PSRR performance of the twin-line array and the triple-line array is compared. The simulation parameters are B/f_0=2/3, D=2.5f_0/c=2.5λ_0. Fig. 4 shows the influence of the signal incident angle on the port-starboard discrimination performance. Considering the angular symmetry in (10), (11), only the range of signal arriving angle from 0° to 90° is plotted. From Fig. 4, we observe that, under the condition of equal transversal aperture, the performance of port-starboard discrimination for triple-line array is superior to that of the twin-line array, and the value of PSRR is increasing with the SNR is increasing.
Fig.4 , the three lines are in "solid", "dashed" and "dotted" styles, just as in the word file, when transformed to the pdf file, please assure that they must not be changed to "solid lines" entirely.

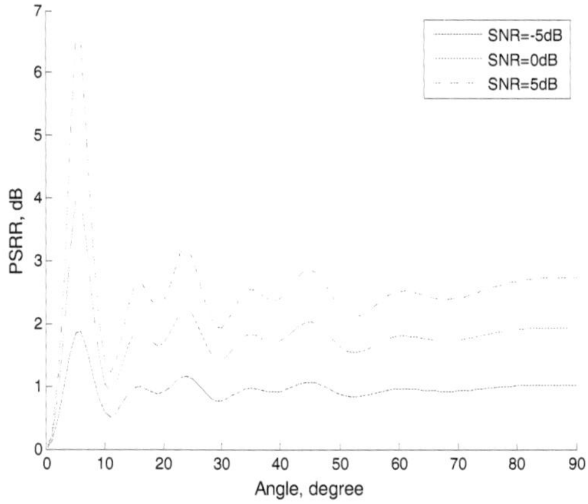

(a) Twin-line array

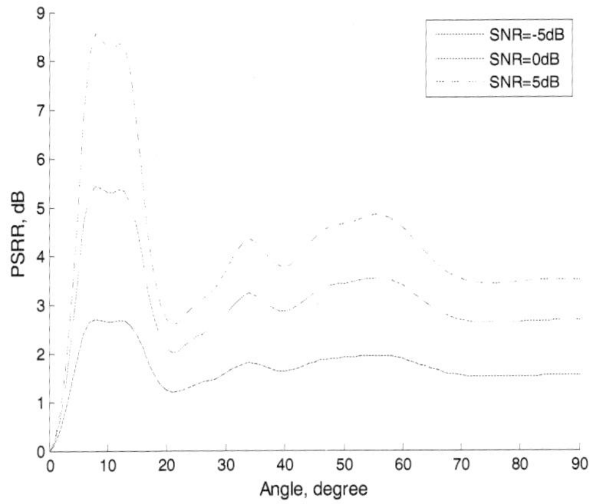

(b) Triple-line array

Fig. 4. Wideband PSRR versus the signal arriving angle

Fig. 5 depicts the wideband PSRR versus the input SNR for different signal arriving angles. It can be seen that, in low SNRs, the PSRR is increasing with the SNR monotonously, and it will level up when the SNR is high enough. Fig. 5 also demonstrates the superiority of the triple-line array in port-starboard discrimination performance than the twin-line array.

The same matter as in Fig.4 is happened in Fig.5, that the four different line styles are all changed to "solid lines" , please check them and revised.

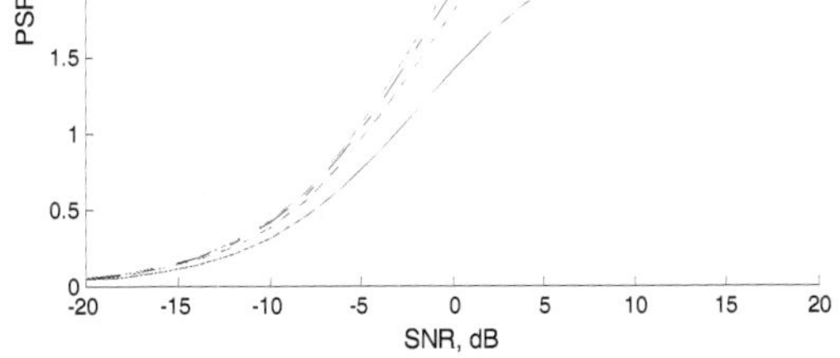

(a) Twin-line array

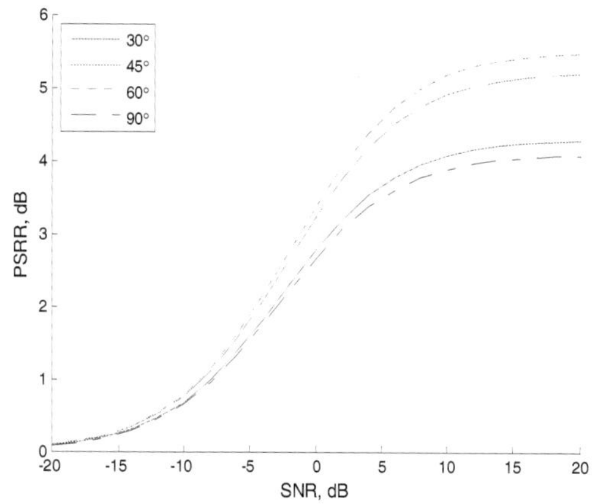

(b) Triple-line array

Fig. 5. Wideband PSRR versus the SNR

3. Probability analysis of PSD

Sometimes, it is often be attentioned that how well the PSD is performed over a duration of the observation time. Thus, it is necessary to know the correct probability of source PSD. In this section, the probability of source PSD for underwater towed twin-line array will be derived based on the signal detection theory. The PSD probability of other multi-line can be obtained in the similar way.

3.1 Narrowband PSD probability

We use the hypothesis testing theory to decide whether the target signal is coming from port side or starboard side based on the observed data. Using the nomenclature of detection theory, we have to choose between two hypotheses:

$$\text{H}_1\text{: } \boldsymbol{x}_1(t) = \boldsymbol{a}_1 s(t) + \boldsymbol{n}(t) \text{, port} \tag{12.1}$$

$$\text{H}_2\text{: } \boldsymbol{x}_2(t) = \boldsymbol{a}_2 s(t) + \boldsymbol{n}(t) \text{, starboard} \tag{12.2}$$

where $\boldsymbol{a}_1 = \boldsymbol{a}_T(-\theta) \otimes \boldsymbol{a}_L(\theta)$, $\boldsymbol{a}_2 = \boldsymbol{a}_T(\theta) \otimes \boldsymbol{a}_L(\theta)$ are the array response vector steering to the port side and the starboard side, respectively. The signal and noise are assumed to be mutually uncorrelated zero-mean Gaussian processes. The signal power is $E\{s(t)s^*(t)\} = \sigma_s^2$, and the noise covariance matrix is $E\{\boldsymbol{n}(t)\boldsymbol{n}^H(t)\} = \sigma_n^2 \boldsymbol{I}$.

Let $\boldsymbol{R}_1/\boldsymbol{R}_2$ be the $N \times N$ spatial covariance matrix when H_1/H_2 is true. We have

$$\boldsymbol{R}_i = \sigma_s^2 \boldsymbol{a}_i \boldsymbol{a}_i^H + \sigma_n^2 \boldsymbol{I} \quad i = 1, 2 \tag{13}$$

The probability density function (pdf) of K independent data snapshots is given by (Gavish, 1996, Whalen, 1983):

$$\text{H}_1\text{: } f(\{\boldsymbol{x}(k)\} \mid \boldsymbol{R}_1) = [\det(\pi \boldsymbol{R}_1)]^{-K} \exp[-K \text{tr}(\boldsymbol{R}_1^{-1} \hat{\boldsymbol{R}})] \tag{14.1}$$

$$\mathrm{H}_2\text{:}\ f(\{\boldsymbol{x}(k)\} \mid \boldsymbol{R}_2) = [\det(\pi \boldsymbol{R}_2)]^{-K} \exp[-K\mathrm{tr}(\boldsymbol{R}_2^{-1}\hat{\boldsymbol{R}})] \tag{14.2}$$

where $\hat{\boldsymbol{R}}$ is the data sample covariance matrix (SCM):

$$\hat{\boldsymbol{R}} = \frac{1}{K}\sum_{k=1}^{K} \boldsymbol{x}(k)\boldsymbol{x}^H(k) \tag{15}$$

To decide between the hypotheses H_1 and H_2, we form the likelihood ratio:

$$\frac{f(\{\boldsymbol{x}(k)\} \mid \boldsymbol{R}_2)}{f(\{\boldsymbol{x}(k)\} \mid \boldsymbol{R}_1)} \underset{\mathrm{H}_1}{\overset{\mathrm{H}_2}{\gtrless}} 1 \tag{16}$$

Substituting (14.1) and (14.2) in (16), we obtain the test statistic:

$$\Lambda = \frac{1}{K}\sum_{k=1}^{K} \boldsymbol{x}^H(k)(\boldsymbol{R}_1^{-1} - \boldsymbol{R}_2^{-1})\boldsymbol{x}(k) \underset{H_1}{\overset{H_2}{\gtrless}} \ln\left(\frac{\det(\pi \boldsymbol{R}_2)}{\det(\pi \boldsymbol{R}_1)}\right) = 0 \tag{17}$$

The probability of port-starboard discrimination is defined as the probability of choosing $\mathrm{H}_1/\mathrm{H}_2$ when $\mathrm{H}_1/\mathrm{H}_2$ is true, and it can be written as

$$P_{\mathrm{PSD}} = \mathrm{Prob}\{\Lambda < 0|H_1\} = \mathrm{Prob}\{\Lambda > 0|H_2\} = \mathrm{erf}(\mu_2 / \delta_2) \tag{18}$$

where erf($\cdot$) is the standard error function defined by

$$\mathrm{erf}(x) = \frac{1}{\sqrt{2\pi}}\int_{-\infty}^{x} e^{-t^2/2} dt \tag{19}$$

and μ_2 and δ_2^2 denote the statistical mean and variance of Λ in the case of when H_2 is true. When K is large enough, the distribution of Λ is approximately normal, and by some algebraic manipulations using (13) and (17), we have

$$\mu_2 = \rho[1-|\beta|^2] \tag{20}$$

where

$$\rho = \frac{(\|\boldsymbol{a}_2\|^2 \sigma_s^2 / \sigma_n^2)^2}{1+\|\boldsymbol{a}_2\|^2 \sigma_s^2 / \sigma_n^2} = \frac{(N\sigma_s^2 / \sigma_n^2)^2}{1+N\sigma_s^2 / \sigma_n^2} \tag{21}$$

$$\beta = \boldsymbol{a}_1^H \boldsymbol{a}_2 / N = (1+e^{j4\pi D\sin\theta/\lambda})/2 \tag{22}$$

$$\delta_2^2 = \frac{1}{K}\{[\rho(1-|\beta|^2)+1]^2 - 1\} \tag{23}$$

Inserting (20)-(23) to (18), we get the probability of PSD:

$$P_{\mathrm{PSD}} = \mathrm{erf}\left[\sqrt{\frac{K}{1+2/[\rho(1-|\beta|^2)]}}\right] \tag{24}$$

From (22) and (24), we can see that for narrowband the signal, the probability of PSD is dependent on the array spacing D. For example, when the signal direction is 90°, then the value of P_{PSD} achieves the maximum when $D=\lambda/4$, and has a minima when $D=\lambda/2$ in which case the array cannot discriminate port from starboard.

3.2 Wideband PSD probability

For wideband signal, we assume the signal bandwidth is $[f_l, f_h]$, and there are N_f frequency bins. The probability of PSD in the kth frequency bin is denoted by $P_{PSD}(k)$, then two wideband probability of PSD are defined, i.e., the frequency weighting averaged least square (LS) probability estimate and the beam weighting averaged one, which can be written as follows:

$$\hat{P}_{\mathrm{PSD}}^{(1)} = \sum_{k=1}^{N_f} f_k^2 P_{\mathrm{PSD}}(k) \Big/ \sum_{k=1}^{N_f} f_k^2 \tag{25}$$

$$\hat{P}_{\mathrm{PSD}}^{(2)} = \sum_{k=1}^{N_f} B_L^{\,2}(\theta, f_k) P_{\mathrm{PSD}}(k) \Big/ \sum_{k=1}^{N_f} B_L^{\,2}(\theta, f_k) \tag{26}$$

where $B_L(\theta, f_k)$ is the left array beam power at the steering direction θ, in the kth frequency bin. It can be seen from (25) and (26) that, through wideband smoothing, to discriminate port from starboard for wideband signal is less influenced by the array spacing.

3.3 Simulation results of PSD probability

Consider an N=32 elements twin-line array. The element spacing d is 1m, corresponding to half-wavelength of 750Hz narrowband signal, the number of data snapshots is K=100, and 200 independent Monte-Carlo experiments are performed. Fig. 6 shows the probabilities of narrowband port-starboard discrimination versus the signal-to-noise-ratio (SNR). The results are in nice agreement with the theoretical analyses above. If $D=\lambda/4$, the probability of PSD for signal near broadside is greater than from other directions, and the SNR threshold of PSD is lower as well. But when $D=\lambda/2$, the signal from 30° will attain the best port-starboard discrimination performance, and the broadside signal has the port-starboard ambiguity, as can be seen from (24).

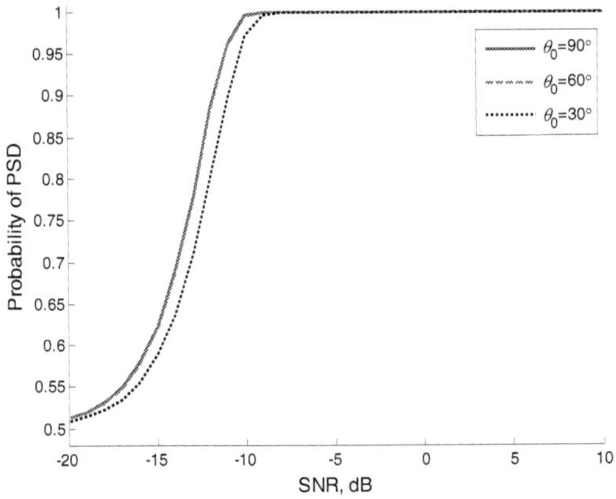

(a) D=0.5m (a quarter of the signal wavelength)

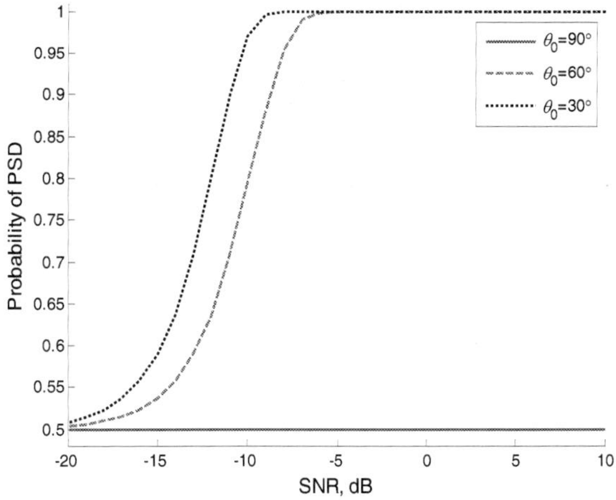

(b) D=1m (half of the signal wavelength)

Fig. 6. Probabilities of narrowband port-starboard discrimination versus the SNR

Fig. 7 depicts the probability of PSD for wideband signal. The source signal is assumed to be band-limited Gaussian process with flat spectra from 400Hz to 750Hz. The signal frequency band is divided into N_f=31 subbands. The twin-array spacing is set to be 6m. Fig. 7 demonstrates the robustness of wideband port-starboard discrimination to the array spacing.

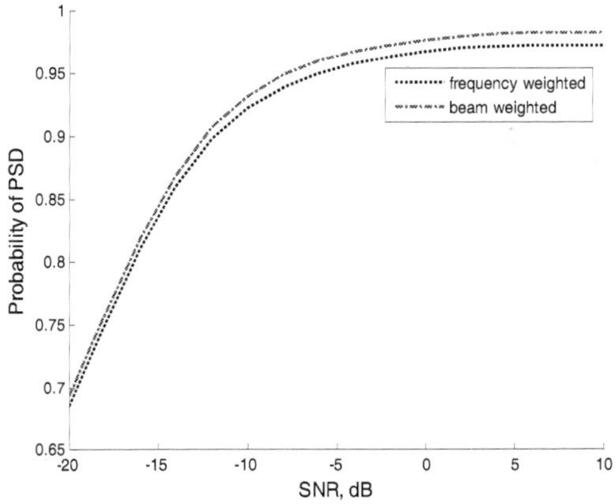

Fig. 7. Probabilities of wideband port-starboard discrimination versus the SNR

4. General PSRR analysis for twin-line array

In section 2, the narrowband PSRR is analyzed in noise-free scenarios, which exhibits an optimal PSD performance. The SNR is considered in wideband PSRR performance analysis, and it was shown that the PSRR performance is improved with the SNR.

In fact, the PSRR is determined by a lot of parameters. Besides the array separation, other parameters including the SNR, the interference-to-noise-ratio (INR), the signal-to-interference-ratio (SIR), the angular separation and correlation between the desired signal and the interference, the array size and the finite sample size.

In this section, we will present a complete analysis of the PSRR as a function of a few important parameters which may affect the PSD performance. With no loss of generality, the twin-line array is considered here.

4.1 General signal model in the presence of interferences

Consider a totally N-hydrophone (N=2M) twin-line array towed in the horizontal x-y plane in the direction of decreasing x, and D denotes the array separation, and other parameters defined as in section 2. The array received $N\times1$ signal vector $x(t)$ can be written as

$$\boldsymbol{x}(t) = \boldsymbol{a}(\theta_1)s_1(t) + \boldsymbol{v}(t) \tag{27}$$

where $v(t)$ denotes the interference-plus-noise vector, and it can be written as (Wax and Anu, 1996)

$$\boldsymbol{v}(t) = \sum_{k=2}^{q} \boldsymbol{a}(\theta_k)s_k(t) + \boldsymbol{n}(t) \tag{28}$$

where $s_k(t)$ denotes the signal of the kth source, and $\boldsymbol{n}(t)$ is the additive Gaussian noise vector, and $\boldsymbol{a}$ is as (2).

The output of the conventional plane-wave beamforming is given by

$$y(t) = \boldsymbol{w}^H \boldsymbol{x}(t) \tag{29}$$

where w is the weight vector, for conventional delay-and-sum beamforming, w is the same as the steering vector toward the desired signal.

From (27), we can express the sample covariance matrix (SCM) as (Wax and Anu, 1996, Raghunath & Reddy, 1992):

$$\hat{\boldsymbol{R}} = \frac{1}{K}\sum_{t=1}^{K} \boldsymbol{x}(t)\boldsymbol{x}^H(t) = \hat{\sigma}_{s_1}^2 \boldsymbol{a}_1\boldsymbol{a}_1^H + \boldsymbol{a}_1\hat{\boldsymbol{r}}^H + \hat{\boldsymbol{r}}\boldsymbol{a}_1^H + \hat{\boldsymbol{Q}} \tag{30}$$

where K is the number of samples, $\boldsymbol{a}_1$ is the abbreviation for $\boldsymbol{a}(\theta_1)$, and $\hat{\sigma}_{s_1}^2$ denotes the sample-mean of the desired signal power:

$$\hat{\sigma}_{s_1}^2 = \frac{1}{K}\sum_{t=1}^{K} |s_1(t)|^2 \tag{31}$$

where $\hat{\boldsymbol{r}}$ denotes the sample-mean of the correlation between the desired signal and the interference-plus-noise:

$$\hat{\boldsymbol{r}} = \frac{1}{K}\sum_{t=1}^{K} s_1^*(t)\boldsymbol{v}(t) \tag{32}$$

and $\hat{\boldsymbol{Q}}$ is the sample covariance matrix of the interference-plus-noise

$$\hat{\boldsymbol{Q}} = \frac{1}{K}\sum_{t=1}^{K} \boldsymbol{v}(t)\boldsymbol{v}^H(t) \tag{33}$$

Now we redefine the PSRR as the ratio between the practical output power toward the desired signal arriving direction and that in the back-beam direction, as follows

$$\widehat{\text{PSRR}} = \frac{\boldsymbol{w}_+^H \hat{\boldsymbol{R}} \boldsymbol{w}_+}{\boldsymbol{w}_-^H \hat{\boldsymbol{R}} \boldsymbol{w}_-} \tag{34}$$

where w_+ and w_- denote the weight vector steered to the desired signal direction and to the mirror signal direction, respectively. For conventional beamforming, $w_+ = \boldsymbol{a}_1$, and $w_- = \boldsymbol{a}_{1-}$, here $\boldsymbol{a}_{1-}$ stands for $\boldsymbol{a}(-\theta_1)$, then (33) can be rewritten as

$$\begin{aligned}\widehat{\text{PSRR}} &= \frac{\boldsymbol{a}_1^H \hat{\boldsymbol{R}} \boldsymbol{a}_1}{\boldsymbol{a}_{1-}^H \hat{\boldsymbol{R}} \boldsymbol{a}_{1-}} = \frac{\boldsymbol{a}_1^H [\hat{\sigma}_{s_1}^2 \boldsymbol{a}_1 \boldsymbol{a}_1^H + \boldsymbol{a}_1 \hat{\boldsymbol{r}}^H + \hat{\boldsymbol{r}} \boldsymbol{a}_1^H + \hat{\boldsymbol{Q}}] \boldsymbol{a}_1}{\boldsymbol{a}_{1-}^H [\hat{\sigma}_{s_1}^2 \boldsymbol{a}_1 \boldsymbol{a}_1^H + \boldsymbol{a}_1 \hat{\boldsymbol{r}}^H + \hat{\boldsymbol{r}} \boldsymbol{a}_1^H + \hat{\boldsymbol{Q}}] \boldsymbol{a}_{1-}} \\ &= \frac{\hat{\sigma}_{s_1}^2 N^2 + 2N \operatorname{Re}(\boldsymbol{a}_1^H \hat{\boldsymbol{r}}) + \boldsymbol{a}_1^H \hat{\boldsymbol{Q}} \boldsymbol{a}_1}{\hat{\sigma}_{s_1}^2 \,|\boldsymbol{a}_{1-}^H \boldsymbol{a}_1|^2 + 2\operatorname{Re}(\boldsymbol{a}_{1-}^H \hat{\boldsymbol{r}} \boldsymbol{a}_1^H \boldsymbol{a}_{1-}) + \boldsymbol{a}_{1-}^H \hat{\boldsymbol{Q}} \boldsymbol{a}_{1-}}\end{aligned} \tag{35}$$

where Re($\cdot$) means the real part, and

$$|\boldsymbol{a}_{1-}^H \boldsymbol{a}_1| = N\cos(2\pi fD\sin\theta_1 / c) \tag{36}$$

Substituting (28) into (32), we have

$$\begin{aligned}\hat{\boldsymbol{r}} &= \sum_{k=2}^{q} \boldsymbol{a}(\theta_k)\left(\frac{1}{K}\sum_{t=1}^{K} s_1^*(t) s_k(t)\right) + \frac{1}{K}\sum_{t=1}^{K} s_1^*(t)\boldsymbol{n}(t) \\ &= \sum_{k=2}^{q} \boldsymbol{a}(\theta_k)\hat{\sigma}_{s_1}\hat{\sigma}_{s_k}\hat{\rho}_{1k} + \hat{\sigma}_{s_1}\hat{\boldsymbol{\sigma}}_n \odot \hat{\boldsymbol{\rho}}_{1n}\end{aligned} \tag{37}$$

where $\hat{\rho}_{1k}$ is the sample-mean of the correlation coefficient between $s_1(t)$ and $s_k(t)$, $\hat{\boldsymbol{\sigma}}_n$ is the noise standard deviation vector, and $\hat{\boldsymbol{\rho}}_{1n}$ is the sample-mean of the correlation coefficient vector between $s_1(t)$ and $\boldsymbol{n}(t)$, $\odot$ denotes the element-wise vector or matrix product. When the desired signal and the noise is uncorrelated, then the second term in (37) can be omitted. From (35) and (37), we can see that the performance of port-starboard discrimination is determined by a few parameters, such as the power of the desired signal, the interference and noise, the correlation between the desired signal and the interference, the array separation, and so on.

4.2 Theoretical PSRR in some special cases

In section 4.1, we obtain the sample-based expression for PSRR, see (35). Now, replacing the sample covariance matrix $\hat{\boldsymbol{R}}$ with the exact covariance matrix $\boldsymbol{R}$, we obtain the theoretical PSRR expression for large sample condition. The expectation of (35) can be written as

$$\text{PSRR}=\frac{\boldsymbol{w}_+^H \boldsymbol{R}\boldsymbol{w}_+}{\boldsymbol{w}_-^H \boldsymbol{R}\boldsymbol{w}_-}=\frac{\sigma_{s_1}^2 N^2+2N\,\text{Re}(\boldsymbol{a}_1^H\boldsymbol{r})+\boldsymbol{a}_1^H\boldsymbol{Q}\boldsymbol{a}_1}{\sigma_{s_1}^2\,|\boldsymbol{a}_{1-}^H\boldsymbol{a}_1|^2+2\,\text{Re}(\boldsymbol{a}_{1-}^H\boldsymbol{r}\boldsymbol{a}_1{}^H\boldsymbol{a}_{1-})+\boldsymbol{a}_{1-}^H\boldsymbol{Q}\boldsymbol{a}_{1-}} \tag{38}$$

4.2.1 Desired signal only

In the case that only the desired signal is present, we have

$$\boldsymbol{v}(t)=\boldsymbol{n}(t) \tag{39}$$

Assume $\boldsymbol{n}(t)$ is independent of $s_1(t)$, and has zero mean and covariance matrix $\sigma_n^2\boldsymbol{I}$, it gives

$$\boldsymbol{r}=E\{s_1^*(t)\boldsymbol{v}(t)\}=E\{s_1^*(t)\boldsymbol{n}(t)\}=\boldsymbol{0} \tag{40}$$

where $\boldsymbol{0}$ is a all-zero vector, and

$$\boldsymbol{Q}=E\{\boldsymbol{n}(t)\boldsymbol{n}^H(t)\}=\sigma_n^2\boldsymbol{I} \tag{41}$$

Substituting (39)-(40) into (38), and after some algebraic manipulation, we readily get

$$\text{PSRR}=\frac{N\sigma_{s_1}^2+\sigma_n^2}{N\sigma_{s_1}^2\cos^2(2\pi fD\sin\theta_1/c)+\sigma_n^2} \tag{42}$$

Denoting by SNR as the signal-to-noise ratio of the desired signal at a single omnidirectional sensor

$$\text{SNR}=\frac{\sigma_{s_1}^2}{\sigma_n^2} \tag{43}$$

we can rewrite (42) as

$$\text{PSRR}=\frac{N\text{SNR}+1}{N\text{SNR}\cos^2(2\pi fD\sin\theta_1/c)+1}. \tag{44}$$

Thus, for the SNR is fixed, we have

$$1\le\text{PSRR}\le N\text{SNR}+1 \tag{45}$$

and for fixed D, f and θ_1, when

$$\text{SNR}\gg 1/[N\cos^2(2\pi fD\sin\theta_1/c)],$$

we have

$$\text{PSRR}\simeq\frac{1}{\cos^2(2\pi fD\sin\theta_1/c)} \tag{46}$$

that is, (44) is reduced to (8), while for

$$\text{SNR}\ll 1/[N\cos^2(2\pi fD\sin\theta_1/c)],$$

we have

$$\text{PSRR}\simeq N\text{SNR}+1 \tag{47}$$

From (46) and (47), we can conclude that, the PSRR is linearly increasing with SNR up to (46) where it levels up and fixed.

4.2.2 Desired signal and a single interference

In the case of a single interference, we have

$$\boldsymbol{v}(t) = \boldsymbol{a}_2 s_2(t) + \boldsymbol{n}(t) \tag{48}$$

and also, $\boldsymbol{n}(t)$ is independent of $s_2(t)$ and has zero mean and covariance matrix $\sigma_n^2 \boldsymbol{I}$, then

$$\boldsymbol{r} = E\{s_1^*(t)\boldsymbol{v}(t)\} = \boldsymbol{a}_2 E\{s_1^*(t)s_2(t)\} = \boldsymbol{a}_2 \sigma_{s_1}\sigma_{s_2}\rho_{12} \tag{49}$$

where ρ_{12} is the correlation coefficient between $s_1(t)$ and $s_2(t)$

$$\rho_{12} = \frac{E\{s_1^*(t)s_2(t)\}}{\sigma_{s_1}\sigma_{s_2}} \tag{50}$$

And

$$\boldsymbol{Q} = \sigma_{s_2}^2 \boldsymbol{a}_2 \boldsymbol{a}_2^H + \sigma_n^2 \boldsymbol{I}. \tag{51}$$

Using (2) and (49), we can get

$$\mathrm{Re}(\boldsymbol{a}_1^H \boldsymbol{r}) = \sigma_{s_1}\sigma_{s_2}\,\mathrm{Re}(\boldsymbol{a}_1^H \boldsymbol{a}_2 \rho_{12}) = N\sigma_{s_1}\sigma_{s_2}\,\mathrm{Re}(\alpha\rho_{12}) \tag{52}$$

$$\boldsymbol{a}_1^H \boldsymbol{Q} \boldsymbol{a}_1 = \sigma_{s_2}^2 N^2 |\alpha|^2 + N\sigma_n^2 \tag{53}$$

$$\boldsymbol{a}_{1-}^H \boldsymbol{Q} \boldsymbol{a}_{1-} = \sigma_{s_2}^2 |\boldsymbol{a}_{1-}^H \boldsymbol{a}_2|^2 + N\sigma_n^2 \tag{54}$$

where

$$\alpha = \boldsymbol{a}_1^H \boldsymbol{a}_2 / |\boldsymbol{a}_1||\boldsymbol{a}_2| = \boldsymbol{a}_1^H \boldsymbol{a}_2 / N \tag{55}$$

is a complex scalar characterizes the *spatial correlation coefficient* between the steering vectors of the desired signal and the interference. And using (2)-(4), we readily have

$$\begin{aligned}
\boldsymbol{a}_{1-}^H \boldsymbol{a}_2 / N &= \boldsymbol{a}_T^H(-\theta_1)\boldsymbol{a}_T(\theta_2)\boldsymbol{a}_L^H(-\theta_1)\boldsymbol{a}_L(\theta_2)/N \\
&= \boldsymbol{a}_T^H(-\theta_1)\boldsymbol{a}_T(\theta_2)\boldsymbol{a}_L^H(\theta_1)\boldsymbol{a}_L(\theta_2)/N \\
&= e^{jk(M-1)d(\cos\theta_1-\cos\theta_2)/2}\frac{\sin(kMd(\cos\theta_1-\cos\theta_2)/2)}{M\sin(kd(\cos\theta_1-\cos\theta_2)/2)} \\
&\times e^{jkD(\sin\theta_1+\sin\theta_2)/2}\cos[kD(\sin\theta_1+\sin\theta_2)/2] = B(f,-\theta_1;\theta_2)
\end{aligned} \tag{56}$$

So, we get

$$|\boldsymbol{a}_{1-}^H \boldsymbol{a}_1|^2 / N^2 = \cos^2(kD\sin\theta_1) \tag{57}$$

$$\frac{\mathrm{Re}(\boldsymbol{a}_{1-}^H \boldsymbol{r} \boldsymbol{a}_1^H \boldsymbol{a}_{1-})}{N^2} = \sigma_{s_1}\sigma_{s_2}\beta \tag{58}$$

and β is derived as

$$\beta = \cos(kD\sin\theta_1)\cos[kD(\sin\theta_1+\sin\theta_2)/2]\frac{\sin(kMd(\cos\theta_1-\cos\theta_2)/2)}{M\sin(kd(\cos\theta_1-\cos\theta_2)/2)}$$

$$\times \mathrm{Re}\left\{ \rho_{12} e^{jk[(M-1)d(\cos\theta_1 - \cos\theta_2) - D(\sin\theta_1 - \sin\theta_2)]/2} \right\} \tag{59}$$

Substituting the results (52)-(59) into (38), and let both the nominator and denominator be divided by N^2, we get

$$\mathrm{PSRR} = \frac{P_+}{P_-} \tag{60}$$

where

$$P_+ = \sigma_{s_1}^2 + 2\sigma_{s_1}\sigma_{s_2}\mathrm{Re}(\alpha\rho_{12}) + \sigma_{s_2}^2 |\alpha|^2 + \sigma_n^2 / N \tag{61}$$

$$P_- = \sigma_{s_1}^2 \cos^2(kD\sin\theta_1) + 2\sigma_{s_1}\sigma_{s_2}\beta + \sigma_{s_2}^2 |B(f, -\theta_1; \theta_2)|^2 + \sigma_n^2 / N \tag{62}$$

Let $\mathrm{INR} = \sigma_{s_1}^2 / \sigma_n^2$ denote the interference-to-noise ratio, and then dividing (61) and (62) by σ_n^2, we get

$$P_+ = \mathrm{SNR} + 2\sqrt{\mathrm{SNR}\cdot\mathrm{INR}}\,\mathrm{Re}(\alpha\rho_{12}) + \mathrm{INR}|\alpha|^2 + 1/N \tag{63}$$

$$P_- = \mathrm{SNR}\cos^2(kD\sin\theta_1) + 2\sqrt{\mathrm{SNR}\cdot\mathrm{INR}}\,\beta + \mathrm{INR}|B(f, -\theta_1; \theta_2)|^2 + 1/N \tag{64}$$

That is, the PSRR is affected by a few parameters in practice, such as the SNR, the INR, or signal-to-interference ratio (SIR, SIR=SNR/INR), the correlation coefficient between the desired signal and the interference, the spatial correlation coefficient related to the angular separation between the desired signal and the interference, array separation and the array size, *etc.*

From (63)–(64), when the INR is much smaller than the SNR, or when the spatial correlation coefficient α approaches zero, then (60) will reduce to (44).

4.3 Simulation results

In our simulations, we consider an N=32 twin-line array with half-wavelength inter-element spacing, and the array separation is a quarter of wavelength. The experimental results were computed using (35) by 100 Monte-Carlo runs, and the analytical results were computed by (60), (63)-(64), the number of samples is 100.

In the first experiment, we consider that there is a correlated interference near the front endfire with direction 20°, and the desired signal is in the broadside, i.e. θ_1=90°.

Fig. 8 shows the analytical PSRR and simulated experimental PSRR versus the input SNR, for SIR=20dB and SIR=–20dB, respectively. For high SIR, the analytical curve coincides with the practical result precisely, and we can obtain the satisfactory port-starboard discrimination performance. However, when there are strong interferences, the PSRR can not increase with SNR, and it will level up when the SNR is large enough.

In the second experiment, we consider the effect of the correlation between the desired signal and the interference, to the value of the PSRR. Fig. 9 depicts the resulting PSRR versus the SNR. For low SIR, the PSRR will decrease when the interference is correlated with the desired signal, while the correlation has little effect to the PSRR for high SIR.

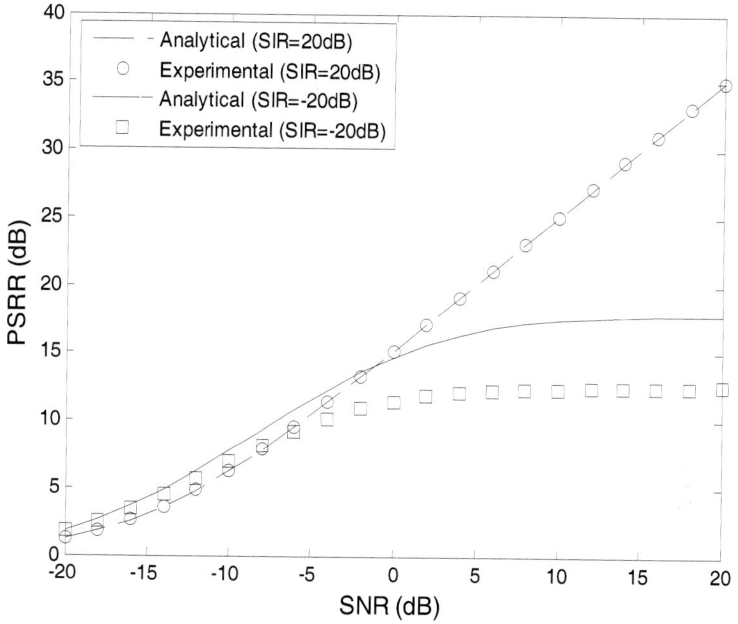

Fig. 8. The PSRR of the desired signal versus the SNR ($D=\lambda/4$, $\theta_1=90°$, $\theta_2=20°$, $|\rho 12|=0.4$)

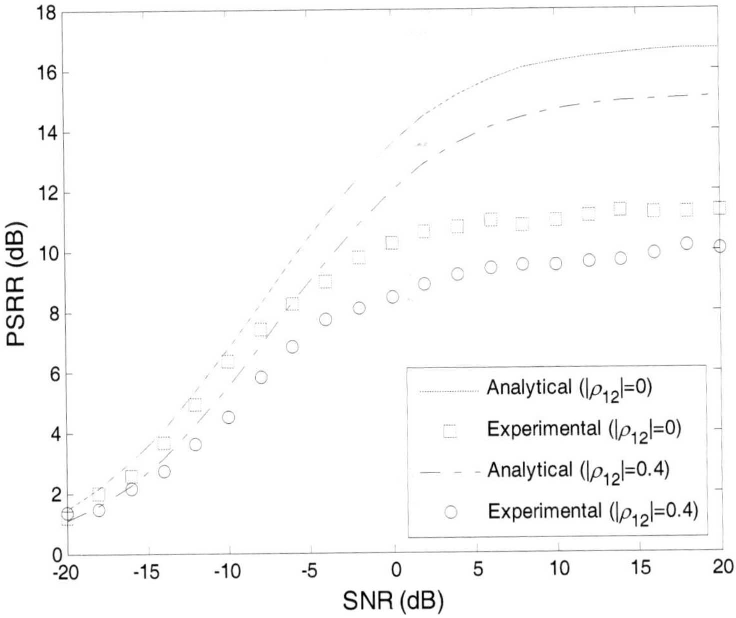

18
16
14
12
10
8
6
4
2
0
PSRR (dB)
-20
-15
-10
-5
0
5
10
15
20
SNR (dB)
Analytical (|ρ12|=0)
Experimental (|ρ12|=0)
Analytical (|ρ12|=0.4)
Experimental (|ρ12|=0.4)

(a) SIR=-20dB

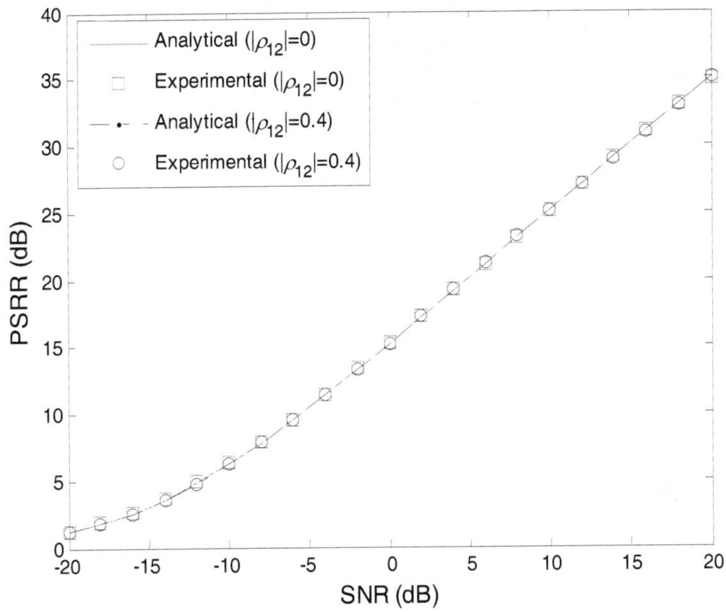

(b) SIR=20dB

Fig. 9. The PSRR of the desired signal versus the SNR ($D=\lambda/4$, θ_1=90°, θ_2=20°)

Numerical results demonstrate that the PSRR performance was mainly affected by the array separation, the signal-to-interference ratio, the correlation between the desired signal and the interference, and the SNR.

5. Conclusion

In this chapter, we have discussed the issue of the target signal port-starboard discrimination (PSD) for underwater towed multi-line array. The port-starboard rejection ratios (PSRR's) are defined to evaluate the PSD performance, for both narrowband and wideband signals. The optimum array separations with perfect PSD performance are proposed. And the closed forms of the wideband PSRR's are derived in this chapter, it was pointed out that the wideband PSRR of the triple-line array is greater than that of the twin-line array under the condition of equal transversal aperture.

The narrowband and wideband PSD probability for the twin-line array are derived based on the signal detection theory. The analytical and simulation results show that the wideband PSD probability is robust to the array separation. Furthermore, the general PSRR expressions are developed in the presence of a correlated interfering signal. The results show that a lot of parameters together determine the PSD performance, such as the array separation, the SNR, the SIR, the angular separation and the correlation coefficient between the desired signal and the interference.

In a word, the theoretical and numerical analyses of the multi-line array PSD performance are in detail. However, more lake trial or sea trial data are needed to validate the practical PSD performance, and to compare with the theoretical performance. We have been researching and developing the multi-line array, and the experimental results will be provided later.

6. References

Cox, H. et al (2003). Hybrid adaptive beamforming for multi-line arrays. *Proc. 37th Asilomar Conf. on Signals, Systems and Computers*. pp. 1858-1862, Vol. 2, Nov

Doisy, Y. (1995). Port-starboard discrimination performances on active towed array systems, *Proc. Underwater Defense Technology (UDT)*, pp. 125-129, Cannes, France

Feuillet, J. P.; Allensworth, W. S.; & Newhall, B. K. (1995). Nonambiguous beamforming for a high resolution twin-line array. *J. Acoust. Soc. Amer.*, Vol. 97, No. 5, p. 3292

Gavish, M. & Weiss, A. J. (1996). Array Geometry for ambiguity resolution in direction finding. *IEEE Trans. Antennas Propag.*, Vol. 44, No. 6, pp. 889–895

Groen, J.; Beerens, S. P.; & Doisy, Y. (2005). Adaptive port-starboard beamforming of triplet sonar arrays. *IEEE J. of Oceanic Eng.*, Vol. 30, No. 2, pp. 348–359

Lemon, S. G. (2004). Towed-array History, 1917–2003. *IEEE J. of Oceanic Eng.*, Vol. 29, No. 2, pp. 365–373

Li, Q. H. (2007). Preliminary analysis of left-right ambiguity resolution performance for twin-line array. *Chinese Journal of Acoustics*, Vol. 26, No. 1, pp. 1–6

Nehorai, A. & Paldi E. (1994). Acoustic vector-sensor array processing. *IEEE Trans. Signal Process.*, Vol. 42, No. 9, pp. 2481–2491

Nielsen, R. O. (1991). *Sonar Signal Processing*. Norwood, MA: Artech House, Boston

Raghunath, K. J. & Reddy, V. U. (1992). Finite data performance analysis of MVDR beamformer with and without spatial smoothing. *IEEE Trans. Signal Process.*, Vol. 40, No. 11, pp. 2726–2736

Schurman, I. W. (1996). Reverberation rejection with a dual-line towed array. *IEEE J. of Oceanic Eng.*, Vol. 21, No. 2, pp. 193–204

Theriault, J. A. et al. (2006). Performance comparison of arrays of directional versus omnidirectional sensors using base '04 data. *Proc. 8th European Conference on Underwater Acoustics (8th ECUA)*, 12-15, June, Carvoeiro, Portugal

Wax, M. & Anu, Y. (1996). Performance analysis of the minimum variance beamformer. *IEEE Trans. Signal Process.*, Vol. 44, pp. 928–937, Apr. 1996

Whalen, A. D. (1983). *Detection of signals in noise*. Academic Press, New York

27

Audio and Image Processing Easy Learning for Engineering Students using EasyPAS Tool

Javier Vicente, Begoña García, Amaia Méndez and Ibon Ruiz
University of Deusto
Spain

1. Digital signal processing teaching in the new European scenario

Nowadays European universities are involved in the European convergence process, which implies important changes as regards the Bologna agreement (1999).

Universities are making changes in their programs favouring the student mobility and obtaining equivalence in academic credentials. Moreover, all these changes involve a new teaching pedagogy.

To facilitate this process, a common framework for comparing the same studies within the EU has been defined: the European Credit Transfer System (ECTS).

Each subject has assigned the equivalent ECTS to student dedication hours. According to this system, student dedication hours include class time and the hours dedicated to study, exercises, assignments or exams.

The authors have added the ECTS measurement to the signal processing subject program studied in Telecommunication and Electronics engineering. The new system has entailed several changes: on the one hand, the number of hours dedicated to each activity, and on the other hand, pedagogic innovation elements have been inserted to replace the classic method of masterly class.

The authors, as lecturers in the University of Deusto, have added the ECTS measurement in signal processing subject program studied in Telecommunication and Electronics engineering degrees.

For example, the subject on digital signal processing, in the 4th year of Telecommunications Engineering has 7.5 ECTS and this involves 175 hours. These hours are distributed according to estimated working time:

1) Class Work. 78 class hours plus 4 exam hours. The classes will have the lecturer's exposition, practical sessions, student exposition, problems solving and exams.
2) Autonomous work out of the classroom. 93 hours. These will be dedicated to the reading and study of the material, to do theoretical-practical exercises and the development of a final project using the EasyPAS tool.

To do that, the authors have developed the application named EasyPAS which main objective is to improve the learning process of signal processing subject respecting Bologna requirements and including pedagogical innovation.

The EasyPAS tool is a user environment developed in Java which includes in plug-ins some examples related to the contents of digital signal processing subject. This would be basic operations about signals and systems, convolution, correlation, filtering, modulations, image and audio signals processing, etc. These plugins have been developed in Octave (free version of Matlab). The students learn to work with previously mentioned software, specialized in mathematical operations. Some advantages that the authors see in this change of teaching methodology are:

- Motivating students to develop projects using digital signal processing techniques by avoiding programming difficulties.
- Enhancing the integration of an algorithm's results in a graphic environment of simple programming.
- Favouring students' creativity when carrying out the projects and dissertations necessary for their university degree.
- Reducing the cost of licences for mathematical programs through the use of free software, such as Octave (specialised in digital signal processing).

This methodology follows the teaching-learning model based on competencies as "the group of behaviours arranged at the heart of a structure that is mental, relatively stable and movable when necessary".
This means that the studies focus on providing students with the ability to deal with complex and real contexts well. Therefore, the student should boast knowledge, abilities, attitudes, and values. As regards the teaching of digital signal processing subjects, the professional profile of each degree has been taken as a starting point, according with the Spanish Ministry of Science and Innovation and professional colleges.
Taking this situation into consideration, the following sections are centred on the EasyPAS application as a new tool for teaching signal processing.

2. State-of-the-art Tools for Signal Processing Learning

During the last ten years, the universities and research groups have shown their interest in the development of new tools to learn digital signal processing. In the literature, it can be found multiple approaches in this area. The authors have chosen some of them that are described below and the main characteristics of each one are compared with EasyPAS. The main characteristics of each approach can be seen in Table 1.

	J-DSP	Simulink	SciLab	EasyPas
GUI quality	☑	☑	☑	☑
Open Source	☑	☒	☑	☑
Easy to use	☒	☑	☒	☑
Web interface	☑	☒	☒	☒
Plug-in platform	☒	☒	☒	☑
Example development language	Graphical	Graphical	Graphical	XML

Aplication developed with	Java	C++	C++	Java

Table 1. Different approaches comparison

2.1 J_DSP

J-DSP is written as a platform-independent Java applet that resides either on a server or on a local hard-drive. It is accessible through the use of a web browser. J-DSP has a rich suite of signal processing functions that facilitate interactive on-line simulations of modern statistical signal and spectral analysis algorithms filter design tools, QMF banks, and state-of-the-art vocoders.

2.2 Simulink

Simulink is an environment for multidomain simulation and Model-Based Design for dynamic and embedded systems. It provides an interactive graphical environment and a customizable set of block libraries that let you design, simulate, implement, and test a variety of time-varying systems, including communications, controls, signal processing, video processing, and image processing.

2.3 Scilab

Scilab has been developed for system control and signal processing applications. It is freely distributed in source code format.
The general philosophy of Scilab is to provide the following sort of computing environment: To have data types which are varied and flexible with syntax which is natural and easy to use.

2.4 applet resources

Many universities provide Java Applications to execute them from a web browser. With them, different signal processing applications and demonstrations can be analyzed.

3. General Description of the Tool

EasyPAS is an application that facilitates the provision of GUI Octave functions with a predefined structure. This can be done by defining a simple XML file in which the elements needed by the user interface are specified. Therefore, demonstrations of signal processing algorithms can be generated simply and rapidly, without needing knowledge of another language except Octave, in straightforward cases.
As can be seen in Fig. **1**, the tool's user interface is very simple and intuitive: one only has to open the XML plug-in menu where all categories of signal processing demos are listed and choose the required plug-in within each category.
The application can be used by two different user profiles:

- The basic user, who employs the plug-in installed in the tool
- A user developing new plug-ins

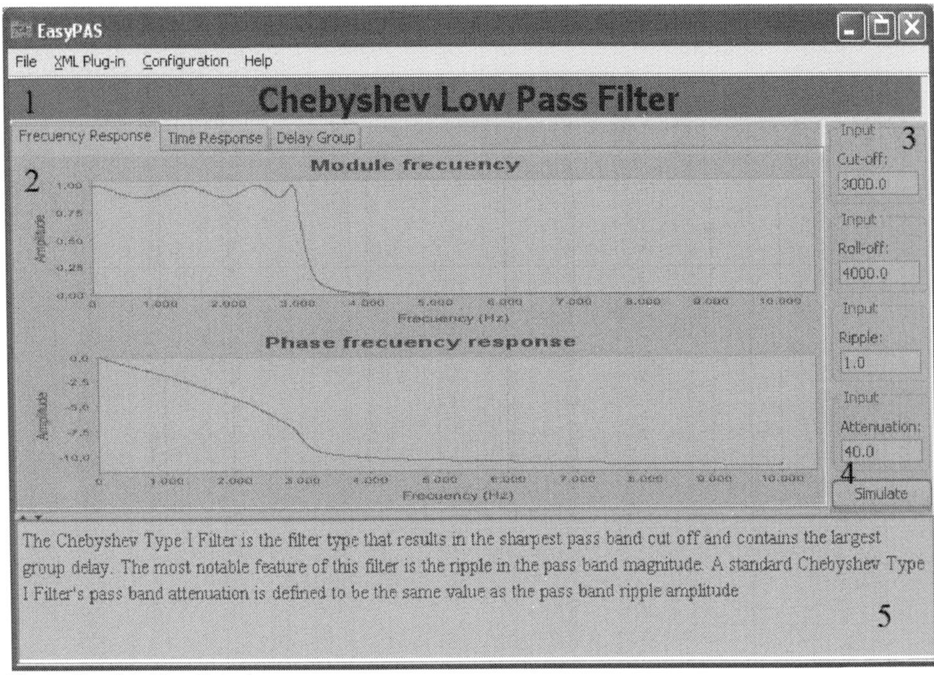

Fig. 1. Graphic User Interface

3.1 EasyPAS plug-ins structure

The examples containing the easyPAS application take the form of plug-ins and can be added by the user. They are programmed by means of an XML file in which both the graphic user interface and the simulation algorithm are defined.

The easyPAS plug-in language specifies a group of XML labels which can be used in order to generate the graphic interface and to run the simulation algorithm.

The plug-in graphic interface is divided into five areas, each of which has a specific function and may contain specific types of control. These five areas can be observed in Fig. **1**:

1	Plug-in name.	In this area the plug-in's name will be displayed.
2	Graphic representation area.	The charts specified in the XML file are drawn in this area. These are grouped inside tabs; as many charts as wanted can be added to each tab, yet a maximum of 3 is recommended. At the same time, the tabs are added to the area of graphic representations. The user can surf between the various charts by clicking on the tabs.
3	Area of input and output parameters.	The input and output controls are inserted in this area. The application allows the introduction of scalar values, data files, and audio and image files. Such output data as scalar values, data files, and audio and image files are permitted.
4	Buttons for	This application enables the user to define more than one

	processing execution.	button launching the simulations, thus making it possible for each button to treat the input and output parameters differently.
5	Area for text giving theoretical explanation of algorithm.	The bottom area contains a practical explanation of the plug-in being used. This area can be concealed or re-dimensioned to the desired size by the user. This area allows the introduction of plain text, of codes formatted in HTML, as well as the possibility of including images.

Table 2. Areas of the Graphical User Interface

So as to describe the graphic interface, a specific XML language has been defined. The labels defined serve to indicate which elements will appear in each area and also to specify the algorithm to be run. The main labels defined in this language are at Table 4.

Category	Label indicating the category in which the processing will be listed. Thanks to this element, the application will organise all the *plug-ins* added into categories.
Title	Label containing the name of the window generated by the application.
Description	Label defining the theoretical explanation of the processing(s) implemented in the plug-in.
Input	Label defining the scalar input value, allowing the definition of the input value by default, the name of the variable in Octave and the name of the input parameter.
InputFile	Label defining an input signal, enabling the user to specify a file with an input signal, the name of the variable in Octave and the name of the input signal.
InputImage	Label defining an input image, which allows the user to specify a file with an input image, the name of the variable in Octave and the name of the input signal.
Output	Label defining a scalar output value, providing the value resulting from a simulation.
OutputFile	For the storage of a signal resulting from a simulation in a specified file.
OutputImage	This allows the storage of a signal resulting from a simulation in a specified file.
Button	Labels defining the tabs containing the charts that can be seen.
Function	Label defining the call to the function, or command, in/from Octave that implements the signal processing.

Table 3. Labels defined

These top-level labels can contain second-level attributes and labels, which are described below.

Category

The category label (see Fig. 2) denotes the name of the category and contains no attribute. The Category label should contain at least one Lang label specifying the name of the category in the default language. Lang labels can be included as the desired number of languages specified for the plug-in (in this case English and Spanish).

```
<Category>
        <Lang value="default">Image processing</Lang>
        <Lang value="es">Procesado de imagen</Lang>
</Category>
```

Fig. 2. Category Label example

Title

This label denotes the title of the plug-in and contains no attribute either (Fig. 3). It should contain at least one Lang label in which the category name is specified in the default language. Lang labels can be included as the desired number of languages specified for the plug-in.

```
<Title>
        <Lang value="default">Edge detection</Lang>
        <Lang value="es">Detección de bordes</Lang>
</Title>
```

Fig. 3. Title label example

Description

The Description label provides a description of the plug-in, contains no attribute and should contain at least one Lang label in which the category name is specified in the default language (Fig. 4). Lang labels can be included as the desired number of languages specified for the plug-in. As opposed to the previous cases, the description can contain HTML labels at the same time; these can be used to include images, to highlight text in bold, etc.

```
<Description>
        <Lang value="default">
                The <b>FM</b> modulator is:
                        <IMG src="file:./plugins/XML/fm.jpg"
        </Lang>
        <Lang value="es">
                El modulador <b>FM</b> es:
                        <IMG src="file:./plugins/XML/fm.jpg"
        </Lang>
</Description>
```

Fig. 4. Description Label example

Input

The input label specifies an input parameter (Table 4). It has parameters that must be specified by the user. The label content must include at least one Lang label indicating the text to be displayed in the application (Fig. 5).

Attribute name	Description	Type
Value	The default value of the input parameter is specified here. This value can be changed by the user in the simulation.	Obligatory

Octave Name	Name of the Octave variable created with the value it holds in the parameter when launching a simulation.	Obligatory
Max	Maximum value that can be assigned to the input parameter.	Optional
Min	Minimum value that can be assigned to the input parameter.	Optional

Table 4. Description of the input label attributes

```
<Input value="1" max="2" min="-2" OctaveName="st1">
        <Lang value="default">Modulator amplitude (Volts) </Lang>
        <Lang value="es">Amplitud de moduladora (Voltios)</Lang>
</Input>
```

Fig. 5. Input Label example

Input File

The Input File label denotes an input signal and it has parameters that the user needs to identify (Table 1Table 5). The content of this label must include at least one Lang label indicating the text to be displayed in the application. The user will specify the name of the file containing the simulation signal (Fig. 6).

Attribute name	Description	Type
OctaveName	Name of the Octave variable created with the file signal specified by the user.	Obligatory

Table 5. Description of the inputFile label attributes

```
<InputFile OctaveName="signal1">
    <Lang value="default">Signal A</Lang>
    <Lang value="es">Señal A</Lang>
</InputFile>
```

Fig. 6. InputFile Label example

InputImage

This label specifies an input image and its parameters should be selected by the user (Table 6). The label must include at least one Lang label indicating the text to be seen in the application. The user specifies the name of the file containing the simulation image (Fig. 7).

Attribute name	Description	Type
OctaveName	Name of the Octave created with the image specified by the user.	Obligatory

Table 6. Description of the inputImage label attributes

```
<InputImage OctaveName="ImageA">
    <Lang value="default">Input Image</Lang>
    <Lang value="es">Imagen de entrada</Lang>
</InputImage>
```

Fig. 7. InputImage Label example

Output

This label specifies output data one wishes to be displayed after a simulation and its parameters should be selected by the user (Table 7). The label must include at least one Lang label indicating the text to be seen in the application (Fig. 8).

Attribute name	Description	Type
OctaveName	Name of the Octave variable displayed after the simulation.	Obligatory

Table 7. Description of the output label attributes

```
<Output OctaveName="result">
    <Lang value="default">Filter order</Lang>
    <Lang value="es">Orden del filtro</Lang>
</Output>
```

Fig. 8. Output Label example

OutputFile

The OutputFile label denotes a signal one wishes to store after a simulation and its parameters should be selected by the user (Table 8). The label must include at least one Lang label indicating the text to be displayed in the application. The user specifies the name of the file in which the signal is to be stored (Fig. 9).

Attribute name	Description	Type
OctaveName	Name of the Octave variable containing the signal saved in the file.	Obligatory

Table 8. Description of the outputFile label attributes

```
<OutputFile OctaveName="signal1">
    <Lang value="default">Signal A</Lang>
    <Lang value="es">Señal A</Lang>
</OutputFile>
```

Fig. 9. OutputFile Label example

OutImage

The OutImage label specifies an image that will be saved in a file after a simulation (Table 9). It has parameters that the user should select. The label must include at least one Lang label indicating the text to be displayed in the application. The user specifies the name of the file in which the image is saved (Fig. 10).

Attribute name	Description	Type
OctaveName	Name of the Octave variable containing the image to be saved to a file.	Obligatory

Table 9. Description of the outputImage label attributes

```
<OutputImage OctaveName="ImageA">
    <Lang value="default">Input Image</Lang>
    <Lang value="es">Imagen de entrada</Lang>
</OutputImage>
```

Fig. 10. OutputImage Label example

Graph

This label specifies a graph the user wishes to see after a simulation (Table 10). Its parameters should be selected by the user. The label must include at least one Lang label indicating the text to be displayed in the application (Fig. 11).

Attribute name	Description	Type
varY	Name of Octave variable for Y axis	Obligatory
varX	Name of Octave variable for X axis	Optional
Type	Type of graph: plot, stem or image	Optional

Table 10. Description of the graph label attributes

```
<Graph varX="F" varY="absH" type="Polt">
        <Lang value="default" Title="Frecuency response" xTitle=" Frecuency (Hz) "
              yTitle=" Amplitude" />
        <Lang value="es" Title="Respuesta frecuencial" xTitle=" Frecuencia (Hz)"
              yTitle=" Amplitud" />
</Graph>
```

Fig. 11. Graph Label example

Button

This label specifies a tab for the inclusion of graphs and it does not have parameters that need to be selected. The label has to contain at least one Name label and one Graph label. The former indicates the name of the thumb index and the latter specifies the graphs to be included in the tab (Fig. 12).

```
<Button>
      <Name>
            <Lang value="default">Respuesta frecuencial</Lang>
            <Lang value="en">Frecuency Response</Lang>
   </Name>
      <Graph varX="t" varY="in" type="Stem">
         <Lang value="default" Title="Impulse Respone" xTitle="Time (s)" yTitle="
         Amplitude " />
         <Lang value="es" Title="Respuesta al impulso" xTitle="Tiempo (s)"
         yTitle="Amplitud" />
   </Graph>
      <Graph varX="F" varY="absH" type="Polt">
         <Lang value="default" Title="Frecuency response" xTitle=" Frecuency (Hz) "
               yTitle=" Amplitude" />
         <Lang value="es" Title="Respuesta frecuencial" xTitle=" Frecuencia (Hz)"
               yTitle=" Amplitud" />
   </Graph>
</Button>
```

Fig. 12. Button Label example

Function

The Function label specifies a button for launching a simulation. The label should contain at least one Name label and one Callback label. The former indicates the tab name and the latter specifies an Octave command that will be run during the simulation (Fig. 13).

```
<Function>
        <Name>
            <Lang value="default">Simular</Lang>
            <Lang value="en">Simulate</Lang>
    </Name>
    <Callback>Fs=20000</Callback>
    <Callback>[n,w]=buttord(fs/(Fs/2),fc/(Fs/2),R,A)</Callback>
    <RunOnStartUp>true</RunOnStartUp>
</Function>
```

Fig. 13. Function Label example

4. Audio and Image Application Examples

In this section the examples are divided in two groups. Firstly, examples of signal processing basics: addition, convolution, filtering... Secondly, examples of audio and image processing specific applications.

4.1. Basic Examples

Basic addition plugin

This example simply contains two output parameters and displays them in an input parameter (Fig. 14). Two INPUT-type components are defined in the XML file; the user introduces the input values into these components and also defines an OUTPUT component which displays the result of the simulation: the total of the two input parameters. After clicking on the simulation button, the application converts the previously introduced values into Octave values and the instructions specified in the FUNCTION tab are run.

```
<?xml version="1.0" encoding="UTF-8" ?>
    <Plugin version="2.0">
        <Category>
                <Lang value="default">Basico</Lang>
                <Lang value="en">Basic</Lang>
        </Category>
        <Title>
                    <Lang value="default">Primer ejemplo</Lang>
                    <Lang value="en">First example</Lang>
        </Title>
        <Description>
                    <Lang value="default">Suma los dos parametros de entrada</Lang>
                    <Lang value="en">It's add the two input parameters</Lang>
        </Description>
        <Input value="1" OctaveName="A">
                <Lang value="default">Primer dato</Lang>
        <Lang value="en">First input</Lang>
```

```
        </Input>
        <Input value="4" OctaveName="B">
                <Lang value="default">Segundo dato</Lang>
                <Lang value="en">Second input</Lang>
        </Input>
        <Output OctaveName="C">
                <Lang value="default">Dato de salida</Lang>
                <Lang value="en">Output value</Lang>
        </Output>
        <Function>
                <Name>
                    <Lang value="default">Simular</Lang>
                <Lang value="en">Simulate</Lang>
                </Name>
                <Callback>C=A+B;</Callback>
                <RunOnStartUp>true</RunOnStartUp>
        </Function>
</Plugin>
```

Fig. 14. Basic Example of Plugin Structure code (addition)

The result can be seen in the graph below (Fig. 15).

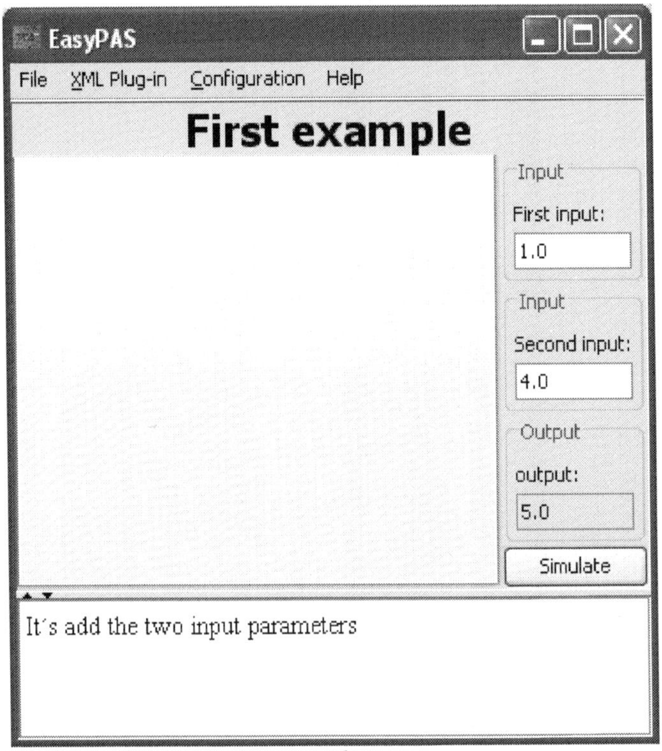

Fig. 15. Basic Example of Plug-in Structure result

Radom data plugin

This plug-in displays a chart with random data. The XML file defines an INPUT component in which the user indicates the number of random data contained in the chart. Moreover, two output components are specified; in the former, the maximum value of the series of random data will be displayed and the minimum value in the latter (Fig. 16). On pressing the simulation button that executes the XML file Octave instructions, a vector with random data is created in these instructions, and the minimum and maximum values of the vector are calculated. After the simulation, the easyPAS application -following the GRAPH label instructions from the XML file- displays a STEM chart on the screen.

```
<?xml version="1.0" encoding="UTF-8" ?>
    <Plugin version="2.0">
        <Category>
            <Lang value="default">Basico</Lang>
            <Lang value="en">Basic</Lang>
        </Category>
        <Title>
            <Lang value="default">Segundo ejemplo</Lang>
            <Lang value="en">Second example</Lang>
```

```
        </Title>
        <Description>
                <Lang value="default">Datos aleatorios</Lang>
                <Lang value="en">Ramdon data</Lang>
        </Description>
        <Input value="10" OctaveName="N">
                <Lang value="default">Numero de muestras</Lang>
         <Lang value="en">Number of samples</Lang>
        </Input>
        <Output OctaveName="vMax">
                <Lang value="default">Valor maximo</Lang>
                <Lang value="en">Max value</Lang>
        </Output>
        <Output OctaveName="vMin">
                <Lang value="default">Valor minimo</Lang>
                <Lang value="en">Min value</Lang>
        </Output>
        <Button>
                <Name>
                    <Lang value="default">Primera Pestaña</Lang>
                    <Lang value="en">First Graph </Lang>
                </Name>
                <Graph varY="R" type="Stem">
                        <Lang value="default" Title="Datos aleatrorios" xTitle="muestras (s)"
                        yTitle="Amplitud"/>
                        <Lang value="en" Title="Randon Data" xTitle="sample (s)"
                        yTitle="Amplitude"/>
                </Graph>
        </Button>

        <Function>
                <Name>
                    <Lang value="default">Simular</Lang>
                    <Lang value="en">Simulate</Lang>
                </Name>
                <Callback>R=rand(1,N)</Callback>
                <Callback>vMax=max(R)</Callback>
                <Callback>vMin=Min(R)</Callback>
                <RunOnStartUp>true</RunOnStartUp>
        </Function>
</Plugin>
```

Fig. 16. Random plugin code

The result can be seen in the graph below (Fig. 17).

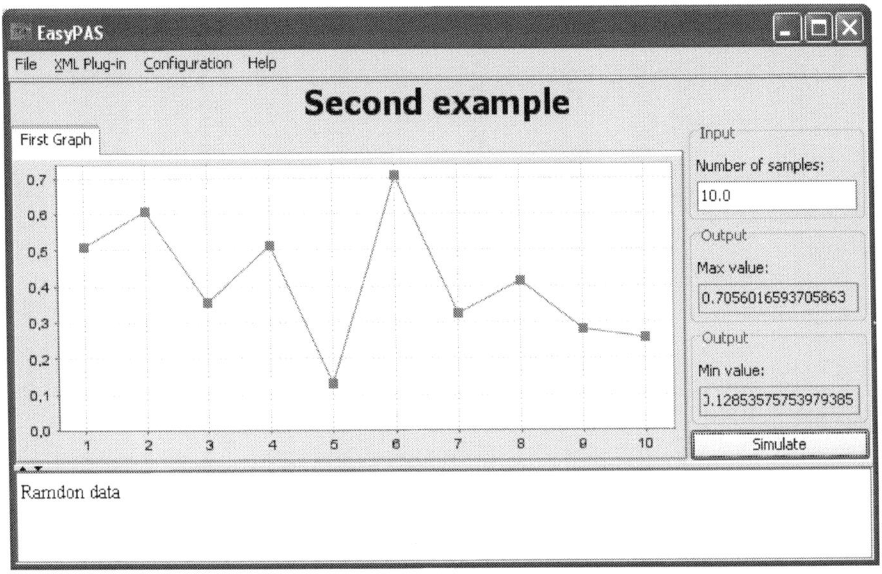

Fig. 17. Second plug-in result

Signals Addition Plugin

This plug-in loads two signals from a file and adds them together, saving the result in a third file. The XML file defines two INPUTFILE and one OUTPUTFILE component. The user chooses two signal-type files and on pressing the simulation button, the two signals specified by the user are converted into Octave variables (Fig. 18). The Octave instructions specified in the XML file add up the two signals and finally, the total of the two signals is saved in the file indicated by the user.

```
<?xml version="1.0" encoding="UTF-8" ?>
<Plugin version="2.0">
        <Category>
                <Lang value="default">Funciones</Lang>
                <Lang value="en">Functions</Lang>
        </Category>
        <Title>
                <Lang value="default">Suma</Lang>
                <Lang value="en">Add</Lang>
        </Title>
        <Description>
                <Lang value="default">Suma dos señales</Lang>
                <Lang value="en">Add two signals</Lang>
        </Description>
        <InputFile OctaveName="x1">
```

```
        <Lang value="default">Señal 1</Lang>
        <Lang value="en">First signal</Lang>
    </InputFile>
    <InputFile OctaveName="x2">
        <Lang value="default">Señal 2</Lang>
        <Lang value="en">Second signal</Lang>
    </InputFile>
    <OutputFile OctaveName="y">
        <Lang value="default">Salida</Lang>
        <Lang value="en">Output</Lang>
    </OutputFile>
    <Button>
        <Name>
            <Lang value="default">Señal suma</Lang>
            <Lang value="en">Added signal</Lang>
        </Name>
        <Graph varX="t" varY="y" type="stem">
            <Lang value="default" Title="Suma" xTitle="Numero Muestras"
                yTitle="Amplitude" />
            <Lang value="en" Title="Add" xTitle="Samples" yTitle="Amplitude"
                />
        </Graph>
        <Graph varX="t" varY="x1" type="stem">
            <Lang value="default" Title="Entrada 1" xTitle="Muestras"
                yTitle="Amplitude" />
            <Lang value="en" Title="First Input" xTitle="Samples"
                yTitle="Amplitude" />
        </Graph>
        <Graph varX="t" varY="x2" type="stem">
            <Lang value="default" Title="Entrada 2" xTitle="Muestras"
                yTitle="Amplitud" />
            <Lang value="en" Title="Second Input" xTitle="Samples"
                yTitle="Amplitude" />
        </Graph>
    </Button>
    <Function>
        <Name>
            <Lang value="default">Simular</Lang>
            <Lang value="en">Simulate</Lang>
        </Name>
        <Callback>a=comparar(x1,x2);</Callback>
        <Callback>x1=x1(1:length(a));</Callback>
        <Callback>x2=x2(1:length(a));</Callback>
        <Callback>t=[0:0.1:length(x1)];</Callback>
        <Callback>y=x1+x2</Callback>
        <RunOnStartUp>false</RunOnStartUp>
```

```
        </Function>
</Plugin>
```

Fig. 18. Signals Addition Plugin code

The result can be seen in the graph below (Fig. 19Fig. 15).

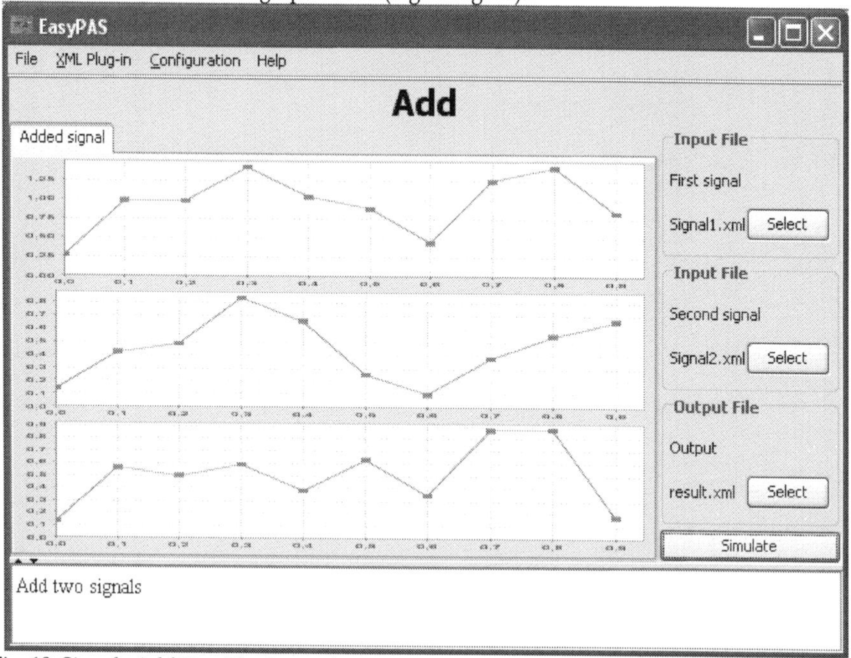

Fig. 19. Signals Addition Plugin result

Convolution Plugin

Two INPUTFILE-type and one OUTPUTFILE-type components are defined in this plug-in. By means of the inputfile components, the user specifies two files with the signals he wishes to convolute (Fig. 20). On pressing the simulation button, the application converts the indicated signals into Octave variables and the Octave instructions are run. One of the instructions run is conv, which carries out the convolution of the two signals, following the equation below:

$$y(n) = x1(n) * x2(n) = \sum_k x1(k)x2(n-k) \qquad (2)$$

Students can analyse the performance of one of the most basic digital signal processing tools with this plug-in: discrete convolution, which is used in numerous signal processing algorithms, the clearest case being a signal filtering by means of an impulsive response from an FIR.

```
<?xml version="1.0" encoding="UTF-8" ?>
<Plugin version="2.0">
        <Category>
            <Lang value="default">Funciones</Lang>
            <Lang value="en">Functions</Lang>
        </Category>
        <Title>
            <Lang value="default">Convolución</Lang>
            <Lang value="en">Convolution</Lang>
        </Title>
        <Description>
            <Lang value="default">Convolución</Lang>
            <Lang value="en">Convolution</Lang>
        </Description>
        <InputFile OctaveName="x1">
            <Lang value="default">Entrada 1</Lang>
            <Lang value="en">First Input</Lang>
        </InputFile>
        <InputFile OctaveName="x2">
            <Lang value="default">Entrada 2</Lang>
            <Lang value="en">Second Input</Lang>
        </InputFile>
        <OutputFile OctaveName="y">
            <Lang value="default">Salida</Lang>
            <Lang value="en">Output</Lang>
        </OutputFile>
        <Button>
            <Name>
                <Lang value="default">Señal Convolucionada</Lang>
                <Lang value="en">Convolutionated Signal</Lang>
            </Name>
            <Graph varX="ty" varY="y" type="stem">
                <Lang value="default" Title="Convolucion" xTitle="Tiempo (s)"
                    yTitle="Amplitud" />
                <Lang value="en" Title="Convolution" xTitle="Time (s)"
                    yTitle="Amplitude" />
            </Graph>
            <Graph varX="t1" varY="x1" type="stem">
                <Lang value="default" Title="Entrada 1" xTitle="Tiempo (s)"
                    yTitle="Amplitud" />
                <Lang value="en" Title="First Input" xTitle="Time (s)"
                    yTitle="Amplitude" />
            </Graph>
            <Graph varX="t2" varY="x2" type="stem">
                <Lang value="default" Title="Entrada 2" xTitle="Tiempo (s)"
                    yTitle="Amplitud" />
```

```
        <Lang value="en" Title="Second Input" xTitle="Time (s)"
            yTitle="Amplitude" />
      </Graph>
    </Button>
    <Function>
      <Name>
        <Lang value="default">Simular</Lang>
        <Lang value="en">Simulate</Lang>
      </Name>
      <Callback>x1=real(x1);</Callback>
      <Callback>x2=real(x2);</Callback>
      <Callback>t1=[0:length(x1)-1];</Callback>
      <Callback>t2=[0:length(x2)-1];</Callback>
      <Callback>y=conv(x1, x2)</Callback>
      <Callback>ty=[0:length(y)-1];</Callback>
      <RunOnStartUp>false</RunOnStartUp>
    </Function>
</Plugin>
```

Fig. 20. Convolution Plugin code

The result can be seen in the graph below (Fig. 21).

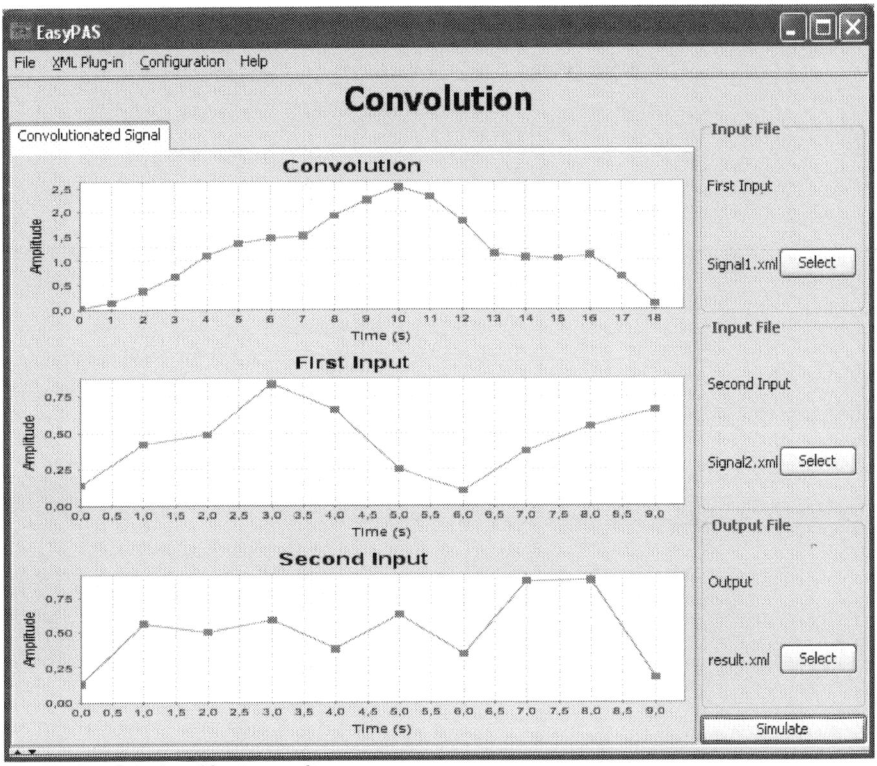

Fig. 21. Convolution Plugin result

Butterworth Filter Plugin

This plugin designs a Butterworth filter from the parameters specified by the user. Four Input-type components are specified in the XML file: cut frequency, reject frequency, pass-band attenuation and attenuation in the reject band (Fig. 22). On pressing the simulation button, the easyPAS application converts the values provided by the user into Octave values and the Octave instructions are run. The Octave instructions contained in the function tab design the optimum Butterworth filter for the indicated parameters, following the equations below:

$$N \geq \frac{log\left(\left(1/_G\right)^2 - 1\right)}{log(w_p)} \tag{3}$$

Students can analyse the frequential performance of Butterworth filters and the link between the transition band and the filter command, enabling him to easily develop new plug-ins for other sorts of filters, such as elliptic or Chebyshev filters. Another exercise recommendable for students is adding the necessary controls to the XML file so that the user may specify an input file, as well as a second simulation button that applies the designed filter to the signal specified by the user.

```xml
<?xml version="1.0" encoding="UTF-8" ?>
<Plugin version="2.0">
    <Category>
        <Lang value="default">Diseño de filtros</Lang>
        <Lang value="en">Filter Design</Lang>
    </Category>
    <Title>
        <Lang value="default">Filtro Paso Bajo Butterworth</Lang>
        <Lang value="en">Butterworth Low Pass Filter</Lang>
    </Title>
    <Description>
        <Lang value="default"> El filtro de Butterworth es uno de los filtros
            electrónicos más básicos, diseñado para producir la respuesta más plana
            que sea posible hasta la frecuencia de corte. En otras palabras, la salida
            se mantiene constante casi hasta la frecuencia de corte, luego disminuye
            a razón de 20n dB por década (ó 6 dB por octava), donde n es el número
            de polos del filtro.</Lang>
        <Lang value="en"> The Butterworth filter is one type of electronic filter
            design. It is designed to have a frequency response which is as flat as
            mathematically possible in the passband. Another name for it is
            maximally flat magnitude filter. The Butterworth type filter was first
            described by the British engineer Stephen Butterworth in his paper "On
            the Theory of Filter Amplifiers", Wireless Engineer (also called
            Experimental Wireless and the Wireless Engineer), vol. 7, 1930, pp. 536-
            541.</Lang>
    </Description>
    <Input value="3000" OctaveName="fs">
        <Lang value="default">Frecuencia de corte</Lang>
        <Lang value="en">Cut-off</Lang>
    </Input>
    <Input value="4000" OctaveName="fc">
        <Lang value="default">Frecuencia de rechazo</Lang>
        <Lang value="en">Roll-off</Lang>
    </Input>
    <Input value="1" OctaveName="R">
        <Lang value="default">Rizado</Lang>
        <Lang value="en">Ripple</Lang>
    </Input>
    <Input value="40" OctaveName="A">
        <Lang value="default">Atenuaci n</Lang>
        <Lang value="en">Attenuation</Lang>
    </Input>
    <Button>
        <Name>
            </Name><Lang value="default">Respuesta frecuencial</Lang>
            <Lang value="en">Frecuency Response</Lang>
```

```
        <Graph varX="F" varY="m">
            <Lang value="default" Title="M dulo frecuencial" xTitle="Frecuencia
                (Hz)" yTitle="Amplitud" />
            <Lang value="en" Title="Module frecuency" xTitle="Frecuency (Hz)"
                yTitle="Amplitude" />
        </Graph>
        <Graph varX="F" varY="p">
            <Lang value="default" Title="Fase de la respuesta frecuencial"
                xTitle="Frecuencia (Hz)" yTitle="Amplitud" />
            <Lang value="en" Title="Phase frecuency response" xTitle="Frecuency
                (Hz)" yTitle="Amplitude" />
        </Graph>
    </Button>
    <Button>
        <Name>
            <Lang value="default">Respuesta en el tiempo</Lang>
            <Lang value="en">Time Response</Lang>
        </Name>
        <Graph varX="t" varY="i" type="stem">
            <Lang value="default" Title="Respuesta impulsional" xTitle="Tiempo
            (s)" yTitle="Amplitud" />
            <Lang value="en" Title="Impulse Response" xTitle="Time (s)"
                type="stem" yTitle="Amplitude" />
        </Graph>
        <Graph varX="t" varY="s">
            <Lang value="default" Title="Respuesta al escal n" xTitle="Tiempo (s)"
                type="escal n" yTitle="Amplitud" />
            <Lang value="en" Title="Step Response" xTitle="Time (s)" type="stem"
                yTitle="Amplitude" />
        </Graph>
    </Button>
    <Button>
        <Name>
            <Lang value="default">Retardo de grupo</Lang>
            <Lang value="en">Delay Group</Lang>
        </Name>
        <Graph varX="F" varY="g">
            <Lang value="default" Title="Retardo de grupo" xTitle="Frecuencia (Hz)"
                yTitle="Retardo (s)" />
            <Lang value="en" Title="Delay Group" xTitle="Frecuency (Hz)"
                yTitle="Delay (s)" />
        </Graph>
    </Button>
    <Function>
        <Name>
            <Lang value="default">Simular</Lang>
```

```
            <Lang value="en">Simulate</Lang>
        </Name>
        <Callback>Fs=20000</Callback>
        <Callback>[n,w]=buttord(fs/(Fs/2),fc/(Fs/2),R,A)</Callback>
        <Callback>[b,a]=butter(n,w)</Callback>
        <Callback>[H,F]=freqz(b,a,1024,Fs)</Callback>
        <Callback>m=abs(H)</Callback>
        <Callback>mdB=20*log10(m+eps)</Callback>
        <Callback>p=unwrap(angle(H))</Callback>
        <Callback>[i,t]=impz(b,a,[],Fs)</Callback>
        <Callback>s=filter(b,a,ones(1,length(t)))</Callback>
        <Callback>g = grpdelay(b,a,1024)</Callback>
        <RunOnStartUp>true</RunOnStartUp>
    </Function>
</Plugin>
```

Fig. 22. Butterworth Filter Plug-in code

The result can be seen in the graph below (Fig. 23).

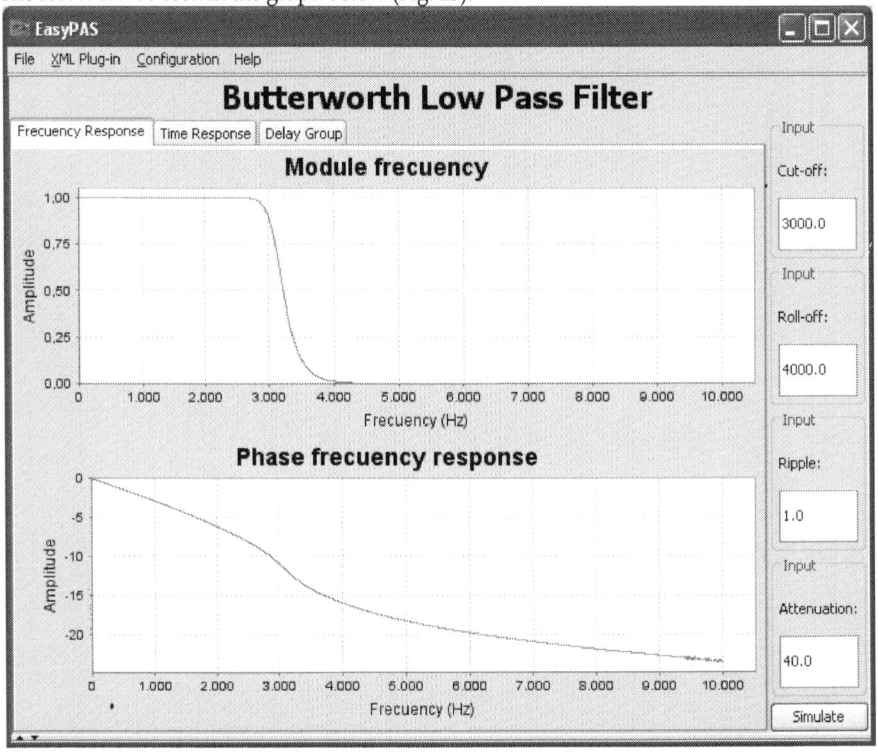

Fig. 23. Butterworth Filter Plug-in result

4.2. Audio and image examples

Contour detection Plug-in

An InputImage-type control and an OutputImage-type one are specified in this plug-in. On pressing the simulation button, the application loads the input image specified by the user, it applies a Sobel-type edge detection filter and saves the result in the file selected by the user (Fig. 24).

The original image and the Sobel filter result can be seen on the screen. Sobel filters are suitable for the detection of contours. Technically speaking, it is a differential operator that calculates an approximation to the gradient of the intensity function of an image. For each point of the image to be processed, the result of the Sobal operator is both the corresponding gradient vector and the square of this.

$$G_x = \begin{bmatrix} +1 & 0 & -1 \\ +2 & 0 & -2 \\ +1 & 0 & -1 \end{bmatrix} * A \quad and \quad G_x = \begin{bmatrix} +1 & +2 & +1 \\ 0 & 0 & 0 \\ -1 & -2 & -1 \end{bmatrix} * A \qquad (4)$$

Having analysed the result of this plug-in, students are asked to create the plug-ins that carry out the same operation, but using different operators, such as Canny, Prewitt, Roberts…

```
<?xml version="1.0" encoding="UTF-8" ?>
<Plugin version="2.0">
    <Category>
        <Lang value="default">Imagen</Lang>
        <Lang value="en">Image</Lang>
    </Category>
    <Title>
        <Lang value="default">Contorno</Lang>
        <Lang value="en">Edge</Lang>
    </Title>
    <Description>
        <Lang value="default">Este plugin permite obtener el contorno de la imagen
            de entrada seleccionada.</Lang>
        <Lang value="en">This plugin allows to get the edge of the selected input
            image.</Lang>
    </Description>
    <InputImage OctaveName="original">
        <Lang value="default">Imagen de entrada</Lang>
        <Lang value="en">Input image</Lang>
    </InputImage>
    <OutputImage OctaveName="salida">
        <Lang value="default">Imagen de Salida (JPG)</Lang>
        <Lang value="en">Output image (JPG)</Lang>
    </OutputImage>
    <Button>
        <Name>
            <Lang value="default">Original / Salida</Lang>
```

```
        <Lang value="en">Original / Output</Lang>
    </Name>
    <Graph varX="original" type="image">
        <Lang value="default" Title="Imagen Original" xTitle="Frecuencia (Hz)"
            />
        <Lang value="en" Title="Original image" xTitle="Frequency (Hz)" />
    </Graph>
    <Graph type="image" varX="salida">
        <Lang value="default" Title="Contornos con sobel" xTitle="Frecuencia
            (Hz)" />
        <Lang value="en" Title="Edges with sobel" xTitle="Frequency (Hz)" />
    </Graph>
</Button>
<Button>
    <Name>
        <Lang value="default">Original</Lang>
        <Lang value="en">Original</Lang>
    </Name>
    <Graph type="image" varX="original">
        <Lang value="default" Title="Imagen Original" xTitle="Frecuencia (Hz)"
            />
        <Lang value="en" Title="Original Image" xTitle="Frequency (Hz)" />
    </Graph>
</Button>
<Button>
    <Name>
        <Lang value="default">Salida</Lang>
        <Lang value="en">Output</Lang>
    </Name>
    <Graph type="image" varX="salida">
        <Lang value="default" Title="Contornos con sobel" xTitle="Frecuencia
            (Hz)" />
        <Lang value="en" Title="Edges with sobel" xTitle="Frequency (Hz)" />
    </Graph>
</Button>
<Function>
    <Name>
        <Lang value="default">Simular</Lang>
        <Lang value="en">Simulate</Lang>
    </Name>
    <Callback>[x,map]=rgb2ind(original_R,original_G,original_B)</Callback>
    <Callback>x=ind2gray(x,map)</Callback>
    <Callback>[x,t]=edge(x,'sobel')</Callback>
    <Callback>salida_R=x*255;</Callback>
    <Callback>salida_G=x*255;</Callback>
    <Callback>salida_B=x*255;</Callback>
```

```
            <RunOnStartUp>false</RunOnStartUp>
        </Function>
</Plugin>
```

Fig. 24. Contour detection Plug-in code

The result can be seen in the graph below (Fig. 25).

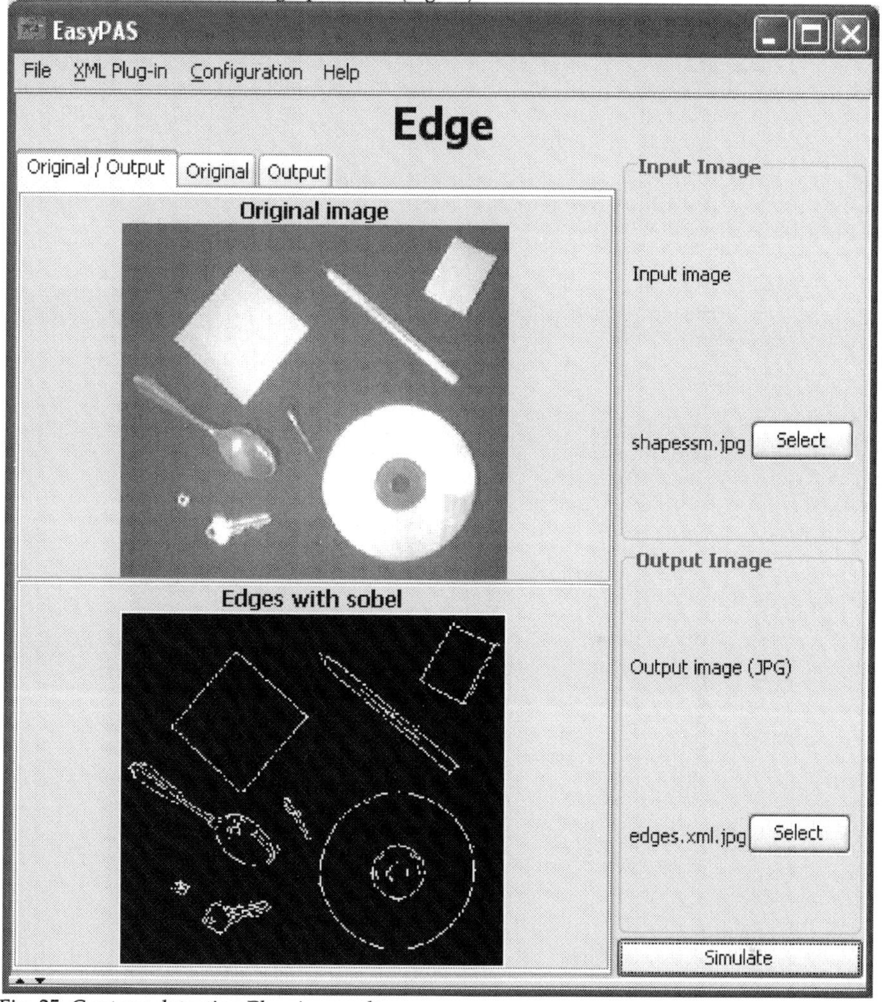

Fig. 25. Contour detection Plug-in result

Flanger Effect

This plug-in implements the flanger guitar effect in the audio file that the user specifies in the application. An InputAudio control is specified in the plug-in's XML file, in which the input file to be processed is indicated, as well as an OutputAudio control indicating the file where the simulation result is to be saved (Fig. 26). On pressing the simulation button, the plug-in loads the indicated signal file in an Octave variable and runs the Octave instructions that process the signal. When the instructions are fulfilled, the result is saved to a file and charts displaying the original and resulting signal appear.

Flanger is a sound effect that produces an oscillating metallic sound in medium and high frequencies above all. The flanger effect is obtained by duplicating the original sound wave. One of the waves is not affected by the processing, while the other phases itself out by increasing and decreasing its delay in a modulated way with a pre-determined oscillation.

Common controls in flanger processing modules are as follows:

- Delay: This is the maximum threshold gap between the duplicated and original wave, it is usually expressed in milliseconds.
- Frequency: The frequency of the duplicated wave's delay oscillation.
- Depth: The proportion of the original wave blended with the duplicated wave.

$$y(n) = x(n) + x\big(n - (D - Acos(2\pi f_0 n))\big) \tag{4}$$

```xml
<?xml version="1.0" encoding="UTF-8" ?>
<Plugin version="2.0">
        <Category>
            <Lang value="default">Efectos Musicales</Lang>
            <Lang value="en">Musical Effects</Lang>
        </Category>
        <Title>
            <Lang value="default">FLanger</Lang>
            <Lang value="en">FLanger</Lang>
        </Title>
        <Description>
            <Lang value="default">
                    <IMG src="file:./plugins/XML/FLanger.gif" />
                    <IMG src="file:./plugins/XML/FLanger.jpg" />
            </Lang>
            <Lang value="en">
                    <IMG src="file:./plugins/XML/FLanger.gif" />
                    <IMG src="file:./plugins/XML/FLanger.jpg" />
            </Lang>
        </Description>
        <InputAudio OctaveName="input">
            <Lang value="default">Audio de entrada (Mono, 44100 Hz, 16 bit)</Lang>
            <Lang value="en">Input audio (Mono, 44100 Hz, 16 bit)</Lang>
        </InputAudio>
        <OutputAudio OctaveName="output">
            <Lang value="default">Audio de Salida (WAV)</Lang>
            <Lang value="en">Output Audio (WAV)</Lang>
        </OutputAudio>
        <Input value="0.1" OctaveName="v">
            <Lang value="default">Variacion</Lang>
            <Lang value="en">Variation</Lang>
        </Input>
        <Input value="2" OctaveName="r">
            <Lang value="default">Ratio</Lang>
            <Lang value="en">Rate</Lang>
        </Input>
        <Button>
            <Name>
                    <Lang value="default">Señales en tiempo</Lang>
                    <Lang value="en">Time domain signals</Lang>
            </Name>
            <Graph varX="w" varY="q">
                    <Lang value="default" Title="Señal Original" xTitle="Tiempo (muestras)"
                          yTitle="Amplitud" />
                    <Lang value="en" Title="Original Signal" xTitle="Time (samples)"
                          yTitle="Amplitude" />
```

```
        </Graph>
        <Graph varX="w" varY="p">
            <Lang value="default" Title="Señal Procesada" xTitle="Tiempo
                (muestras)" yTitle="Amplitud" />
            <Lang value="en" Title="Processed Signal" xTitle="Time (samples)"
                yTitle="Amplitude" />
        </Graph>
    </Button>
    <Function>
        <Name>
            <Lang value="default">Simular</Lang>
            <Lang value="en">Simulate</Lang>
        </Name>
        <Callback>fs=44100;</Callback>
        <Callback>y=auload(input);</Callback>
        <Callback>x=y;</Callback>
        <Callback>md= ceil(v*fs);</Callback>
        <Callback>n=1:length(y)+md;</Callback>
        <Callback>v=round(v*fs);</Callback>
        <Callback>z=zeros(md,1);</Callback>
        <Callback>m=max(abs(y));</Callback>
        <Callback>y=[z;y;z];</Callback>
        <Callback>rr=2*pi/round(fs*r);</Callback>
        <Callback>b=round((v/2)*(1-cos(rr.*n)));</Callback>
        <Callback>y=y(n+md)+y(n+md-b);</Callback>
        <Callback>m=m/max(abs(y));</Callback>
        <Callback>y=m*y;</Callback>
        <Callback>q1=rot90(x);</Callback>
        <Callback>q=q1(1:5:5000);</Callback>
        <Callback>w=(1:5:5000);</Callback>
        <Callback>p1=rot90(y);</Callback>
        <Callback>p=p1(1:5:5000);</Callback>
        <Callback>ausave(output,y,44100);</Callback>
        <RunOnStartUp>false</RunOnStartUp>
    </Function>
</Plugin>
```

Fig. 26. Flanger Effect plug-in code

The result can be seen in the graph below (Fig. 27).

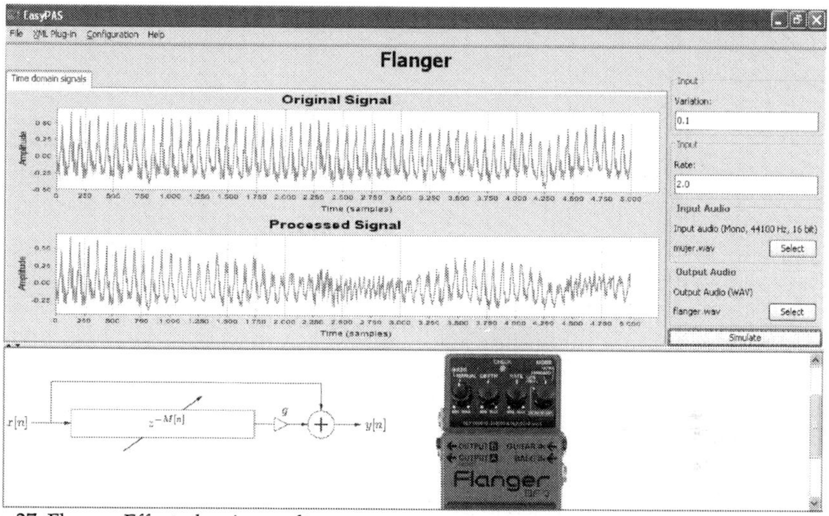

Fig. 27. Flanger Effect plug-in result

Pitch Scaling plug-in

This plug-in implements the pitch scaling in the audio file the user specifies in the application. An InputAudio control is specified in the plug-in's XML file, where the input file to be processed is indicated, as well as an OutputAudio control, in which the file the simulation result will be saved in is indicated (Fig. 28). On pressing the simulation button, the plug-in loads the indicated file signal in an Octave variable and runs the Octave instructions that process the signal. When finished, the result is saved to a file and charts displaying the original and resulting signal are displayed.

Pitch scaling is accomplished when each one of the frequency components in a given signal individually are scaled by a factor α, where α =2 represents one octave up and α =0.5 one octave down. This is to be done without changing the duration of the signal. For example, one can easily raise the pitch of the music on a vinyl record by simply increasing the rpm above normal. However, the duration of the music will then be shorter.

```
 <?xml version="1.0" encoding="UTF-8" ?>
<Plugin version="2.0">
    <Category>
        <Lang value="default">Efectos Musicales</Lang>
        <Lang value="en">Musical Effects</Lang>
    </Category>
    <Title>
        <Lang value="default">Pitch Shifter</Lang>
        <Lang value="en">Pitch Shifter</Lang>
    </Title>
    <Description>
        <Lang value="default">
            <IMG src="file:./plugins/XML/Shifter.gif" />
```

```
            <IMG src="file:./plugins/XML/Shifter.jpg" />
        </Lang>
        <Lang value="en">
            <IMG src="file:./plugins/XML/Shifter.gif" />
            <IMG src="file:./plugins/XML/Shifter.jpg" />
        </Lang>
    </Description>
    <InputAudio OctaveName="input_file">
        <Lang value="default">Audio de entrada (Mono, 44100 Hz, 16 bit)</Lang>
        <Lang value="en">Input audio (Mono, 44100 Hz, 16 bit)</Lang>
    </InputAudio>
    <OutputAudio OctaveName="output">
        <Lang value="default">Audio de Salida (WAV)</Lang>
        <Lang value="en">Output Audio (WAV)</Lang>
    </OutputAudio>
    <Input value="0.5" OctaveName="alpha">
        <Lang value="default">Shifting</Lang>
        <Lang value="en">Shifting</Lang>
    </Input>
    <Button>
        <Name>
            <Lang value="default">Señales en tiempo</Lang>
            <Lang value="en">Time domain signals</Lang>
        </Name>
        <Graph varX="w" varY="q">
            <Lang value="default" Title="Señal Original" xTitle="Tiempo
                (muestras)" yTitle="Amplitud" />
            <Lang value="en" Title="Original Signal" xTitle="Time (samples)"
                yTitle="Amplitude" />
        </Graph>
        <Graph varX="w" varY="p">
            <Lang value="default" Title="Señal Procesada" xTitle="Tiempo
                (muestras)" yTitle="Amplitud" />
            <Lang value="en" Title="Processed Signal" xTitle="Time (samples)"
                yTitle="Amplitude" />
        </Graph>
    </Button>
    <Function>
        <Name>
            <Lang value="default">Simular</Lang>
            <Lang value="en">Simulate</Lang>
        </Name>
        <Callback>[w,q,p,ffx,ffy,fx,fy]=shifter(alpha,input_file,'salida.wAV');</Callb
        ack>
        <RunOnStartUp>false</RunOnStartUp>
    </Function>
```

```
</Plugin>
```

Fig. 28. Plugin Pitch Scaling plug-in code

```
function [w,q,p,ffx,ffy,fx,fy]=shifter(alpha,x,output)
    [inp,fs]=auload(x);
        N = 2048;
        overlap = .75;
        window = hanning(N)';
        inp_length = length(inp);
        frame_count = floor((inp_length-2*N)/(N*(1-overlap)));
        Ra = floor(N*(1-overlap));
        Rs = floor(alpha*Ra);
        Wk = (0:(N-1))*2*pi/N;
        out = zeros(1, round(inp_length*alpha));
        inp=rot90(inp);
        xx=window.*inp(1:N);
        Xu_current = fft(xx,2048);
        PhiY_current = angle(Xu_current);
        for u=1:frame_count
                Xu_prev = Xu_current;
                PhiY_prev = PhiY_current;
                Xu_current = fft(window.*inp(u*Ra:u*Ra+N-1),2048);
                DPhi = angle(Xu_current) - angle(Xu_prev) - Ra*Wk;
                DPhip = mod(DPhi+pi, 2*pi) - pi;
                w_hatk = Wk + (1/Ra)*DPhip;
                PhiY_current = PhiY_prev + Rs*w_hatk;
                Yu = abs(Xu_current).*exp(j*PhiY_current);
                out(u*Rs:u*Rs+N-1) = out(u*Rs:u*Rs+N-1) + real(ifft(Yu,2048));
        end
        out = out./max(abs(out));
        [t,d]=rat(alpha);
        shifted = resample(out,d,t);
        q1=(inp);
        q=q1(1:10000);
        w=(1:10000);
        p1=(shifted);
        p=p1(1:5000);
        fX=fftshift(abs(fft(inp,2048*20)));
        fY=fftshift(abs(fft(shifted,2048*20)));
        fx=rot90(fX);
        fy=fY;
        tamanoX=length(fX);
        tamanoY=length(fY);
        ffx=((0:(tamanoX-1))/tamanoX*fs)-fs/2;
        ffy=((0:(tamanoY-1))/tamanoY*fs)-fs/2;
```

```
endfunction
```

Fig. 29. Pitch Scaling plug-in function code

The result can be seen in the graph below (Fig. 30Fig. 15).

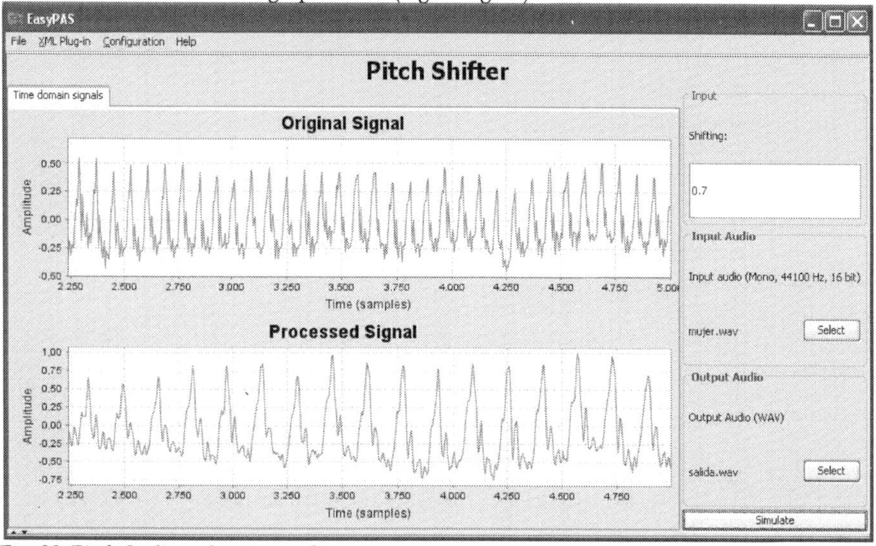

Fig. 30. Pitch Scaling plug-in result

AM Modulation Plug-in

In this plug-in an AM modulation can be analysed in both time and frequency. The user can introduce the modulating frequency, the carrier frequency, the carrier amplitude and the modulation index (Fig. 31). On pressing the simulation button, the application converts the parameters introduced by the user into Octave variables and runs the Octave instructions, presenting the resulting charts on screen.

The student can analyse variations not only in time but also frequency by varying the input parameters, so as to attain a greater understanding of the modulation.

```xml
<?xml version="1.0" encoding="UTF-8" ?>
<Plugin version="2.0">
    <Category>
        <Lang value="default">Modulación</Lang>
        <Lang value="en">Modulation</Lang>
    </Category>
    <Title>
        <Lang value="default">Ejemplo de modulación AM</Lang>
        <Lang value="en">AM modulation example</Lang>
    </Title>
    <Description>
        <Lang value="default">La modulación AM es...</Lang>
        <Lang value="en">AM modulation is...</Lang>
    </Description>
    <Input value="1" OctaveName="st1">
        <Lang value="default">Amplitud de moduladora (Voltios)</Lang>
        <Lang value="en">Modulator amplitude (Volts)</Lang>
    </Input>
    <Input value="100" OctaveName="st2">
        <Lang value="default">Frecuencia de moduladora</Lang>
        <Lang value="en">Modulator frequency</Lang>
    </Input>
    <Input value="3" OctaveName="st3">
        <Lang value="default">Amplitud de portadora (Voltios)</Lang>
        <Lang value="en">Carrier amplitude (Volts)</Lang>
    </Input>
    <Input value="1000" OctaveName="st4">
        <Lang value="default">Frecuencia de portadora (Hz)</Lang>
        <Lang value="en">Carrier frequency (Hz)</Lang>
        </Input>
    <Input value="1" OctaveName="Im">
        <Lang value="default">Indice de modulación</Lang>
        <Lang value="en">Index modulation</Lang>
    </Input>
    <Button>
        <Name>
                <Lang value="default">Señal temporal</Lang>
                <Lang value="en">Time domain signal</Lang>
        </Name>
        <Graph varX="tt" varY="m">
                <Lang value="default" Title="Oscilograma de la modulación"
                        xTitle="Tiempo (s)" yTitle="Amplitud" />
                <Lang value="en" Title="Modulation oscilogram" xTitle="Time (s)"
                        yTitle="Amplitude" />
        </Graph>
    </Button>
```

```
        <Button>
          <Name>
                <Lang value="default">Señal en frecuencia</Lang>
                <Lang value="en">Frequency domain signal</Lang>
          </Name>
          <Graph varX="f" varY="M">
                <Lang value="default" Title="Espectro de la Señal" xTitle="Frecuencia
                      (Hz)" yTitle="Amplitud" />
                <Lang value="en" Title="Spectrum representation" xTitle="Frequency
                      (Hz)" yTitle="Amplitude" />
          </Graph>
        </Button>
        <Function>
          <Name>
                <Lang value="default">Simular</Lang>
                <Lang value="en">Simulate</Lang>
          </Name>
          <Callback>Fs=3*(st2+st4)</Callback>
          <Callback>Tf=(1/st2)*10</Callback>
          <Callback>tt=0:1/(Fs*2):Tf</Callback>
          <Callback>tf=0:1/Fs:(Tf*10)</Callback>
          <Callback>p=st3*cos(2*pi*tt*st4)</Callback>
          <Callback>f=((0:length(tt)-1)/(length(tt)-1)*Fs*2)-(Fs)</Callback>
          <Callback>x=st1*cos(2*pi*tt*st2)</Callback>
          <Callback>m=(1+Im*x).*p</Callback>
          <Callback>M=fftshift(abs(fft(m)))</Callback>
          <RunOnStartUp>true</RunOnStartUp>
        </Function>
</Plugin>
```

Fig. 31. AM Modulation code.

The result can be seen in the graph below (Fig. 32).

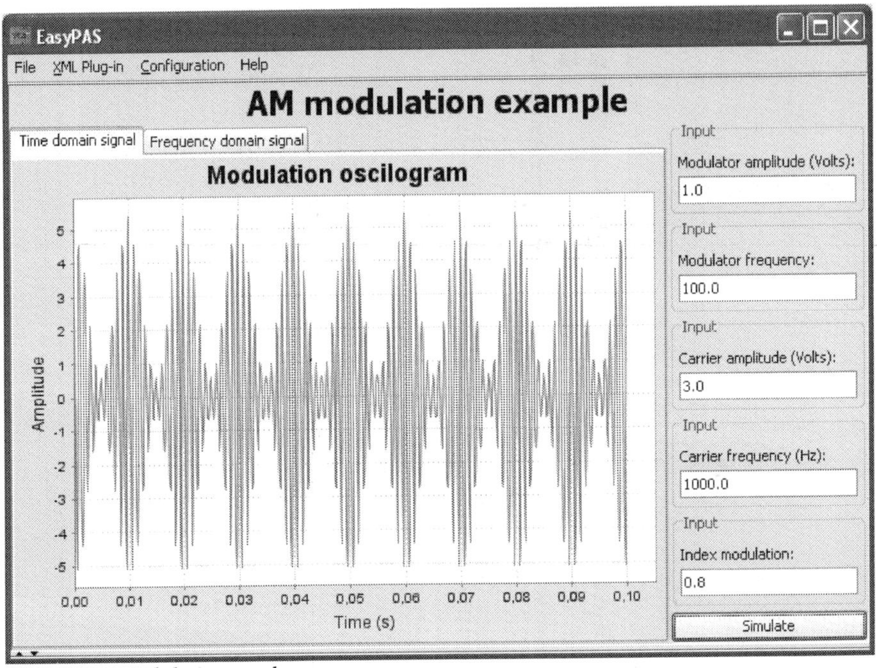

Fig. 32. AM Modulation result

FM Modulación Plug-in

An FM modulation in both time and frequency can be analysed. The user can introduce the modulating frequency, carrier frequency, carrier amplitude and frequency deviation as input parameters (Fig. 33). On pressing the simulation button, the application converts the parameters introduced by the user into Octave variables and runs the Octave instructions, presenting the resulting charts on screen.

The student can analyse variations not only in time but also frequency by varying the input parameters, so as to attain a greater understanding of the modulation.

```
<?xml version="1.0" encoding="UTF-8" ?>
<Plugin version="2.0">
    <Category>
        <Lang value="default">Modulación</Lang>
        <Lang value="en">Modulation</Lang>
    </Category>
    <Title>
        <Lang value="default">Ejemplo de modulación FM</Lang>
        <Lang value="en">FM modulation example</Lang>
    </Title>
    <Description>
        <Lang value="default">Ejemplo de modulación FM</Lang>
        <Lang value="en">FM modulation example</Lang>
    </Description>
    <Input value="1" max="2" min="-2" OctaveName="st1">
        <Lang value="default">Amplitud de moduladora (Voltios)</Lang>
        <Lang value="en">Modulator amplitude (Volts)</Lang>
    </Input>
    <Input value="100" max="100" min="80" OctaveName="st2">
        <Lang value="default">Frecuencia de moduladora (Hz)</Lang>
        <Lang value="en">Modulator frequency (Hz)</Lang>
    </Input>
    <Input value="3" min="2" OctaveName="st3">
        <Lang value="default">Amplitud de portadora (Voltios)</Lang>
        <Lang value="en">Carrier amplitude (Volts)</Lang>
    </Input>
    <Input value="750" max="6000" min="-500" OctaveName="st4">
        <Lang value="default">Frecuencia de portadora (Hz)</Lang>
        <Lang value="en">Carrier frequency (Hz)</Lang>
    </Input>
    <Input value="800" OctaveName="Fd">
        <Lang value="default">Desvío de frecuencia</Lang>
        <Lang value="en">Frequency deviated</Lang>
    </Input>
    <Button>
        <Name>
            <Lang value="default">Señal temporal</Lang>
            <Lang value="en">Time domain signal</Lang>
        </Name>
        <Graph varX="tt" varY="mt">
            <Lang value="default" Title="Oscilograma de la modulación"
                xTitle="Tiempo (s)" yTitle="Amplitud" />
            <Lang value="en" Title="Modulation oscilogram" xTitle="Time (s)"
                yTitle="Amplitude" />
        </Graph>
        <Graph varX="f" varY="M">
```

```
            <Lang value="default" Title="Espectro de la Señal" xTitle="Frecuencia
                (Hz)" yTitle="Amplitud" />
            <Lang value="en" Title="Spectrum representation" xTitle="Frequency
                (Hz)" yTitle="Amplitude" />
        </Graph>
    </Button>
    <Button>
        <Name>
            <Lang value="default">Señal en frecuencia</Lang>
            <Lang value="en">Frequency domain signal</Lang>
        </Name>
        <Graph varX="f" varY="M">
            <Lang value="default" Title="Espectro de la Señal" xTitle="Frecuencia
                (Hz)" yTitle="Amplitud" />
            <Lang value="en" Title="Spectrum representation" xTitle="Frequency
                (Hz)" yTitle="Amplitude" />
        </Graph>
    </Button>
    <Function>
        <Name>
            <Lang value="default">Simular</Lang>
            <Lang value="en">Simulate</Lang>
        </Name>
        <Callback>Fs=(((3*(Fd/st2)+1)*st2/2)+st4)*3</Callback>
        <Callback>x=st1*sin(2*pi*t*st2)</Callback>
        <Callback>p=st3*cos(2*pi*t*st4)</Callback>
        <Callback>Tf=(1/st2)*10</Callback>
        <Callback>tt=0:1/(Fs*2):Tf</Callback>
        <Callback>tf=0:1/Fs:(Tf*10)</Callback>
        <Callback>f=((0:length(tf)-1)/length(tf)*(Fs))-((Fs)/2)</Callback>
        <Callback>xt=st1*sin(2*pi*tt*st2)</Callback>
        <Callback>xf=st1*sin(2*pi*tf*st2)</Callback>
        <Callback>mt=(cos((2*pi*tt*st4)+((Fd/st2)*xt))).*st3</Callback>
        <Callback>mf=(cos((2*pi*tf*st4)+((Fd/st2)*xf))).*st3</Callback>
        <Callback>M=(fftshift(abs(fft(mf))))</Callback>
        <RunOnStartUp>true</RunOnStartUp>
    </Function>
</Plugin>
```

Fig. 33. FM Modulación Plug-in code

The result can be seen in the graph below (Fig. 34).

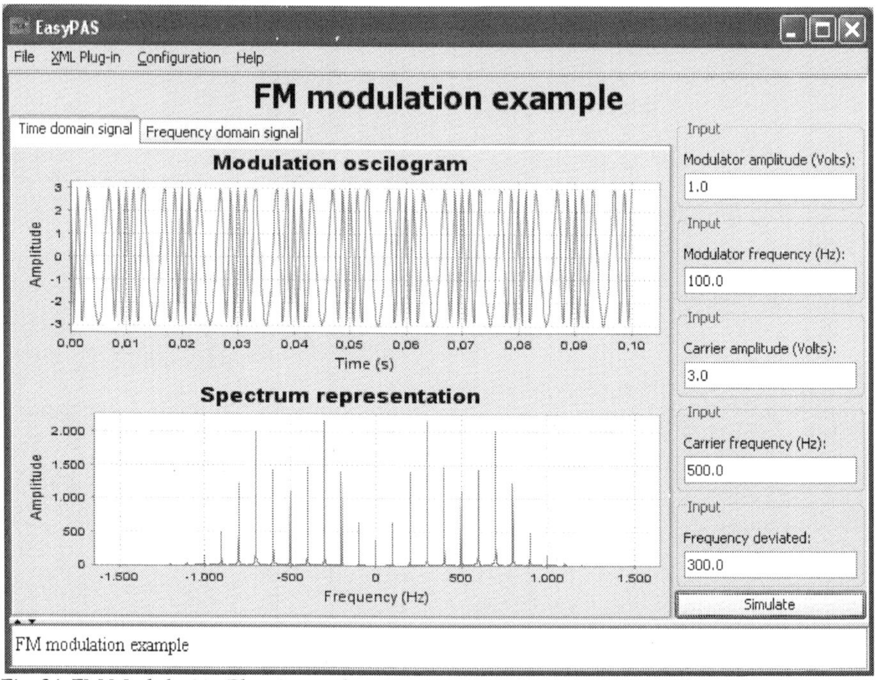

Fig. 34. FM Modulación Plug-in result

5. New Proposals Using EasyPAS

The students use easyPAS software in the subjects of engineering degree in order to learn digital signal processing area. Usually, during the last years of engineering, the teaching-learning methodology is "Project Based Learning" (PBL). Using this methodology the students are able to carry out very complex projects.
This section describes three real applications developed by engineering students using this methodology:

1. To simulate of the system using EasyPAS tool.
2. To create plug-ins with EasyPAS format.
3. To program the final application in high level language integrating the plug-ins developed.

The applications chosen, as examples for this section are from the Biomedical Engineering. These applications work on voice and image which is the issue of this chapter.

Objective analysis of vocal fold images

This project consists of a medical software application which includes digital image processing. It is specially designed for othorhinolaryngologist. They can make a diagnosis of any voice pathology. It can be carried out the whole consultation process easily. It permits to process all the patient information digitally and automated.

This software consists of these main areas:

- Patient's enquiry.
- Voice and video recording.
- Voice and video processing.
- Results

The assessment is carried out taking to account different kind of information, such as: subjective assessment, perceptual assessment, stroboscopy images and acoustic-aerodynamics analysis. You can see the results tab in Fig. 35:

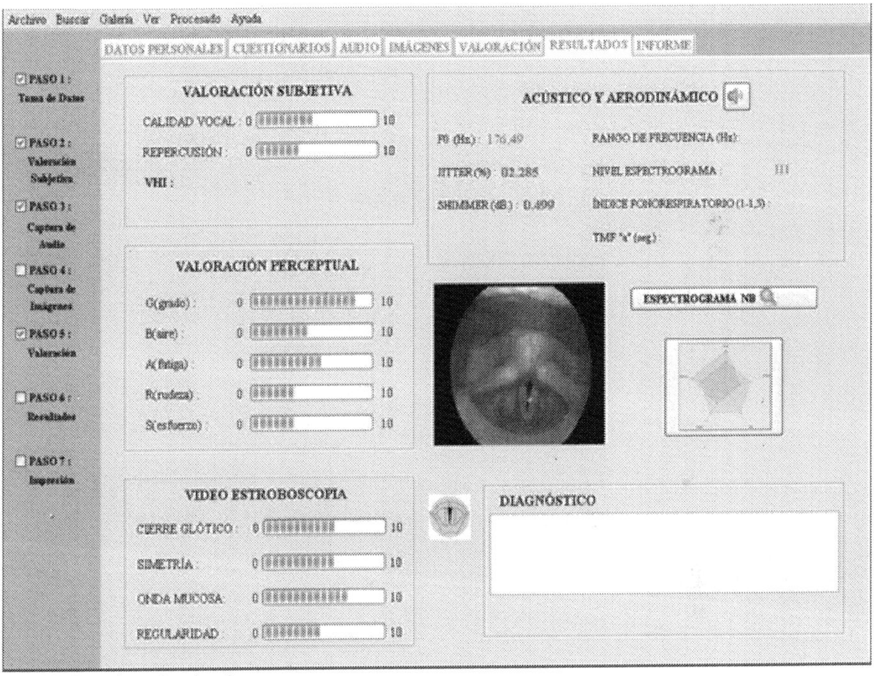

Fig. 35. Results tab of software

Laryngeal and oesophageal voice analysis and processing

This project consists of software specially designed for othorhinolaryngologist, speech therapist and so on. The most relevant of this software is the algorithms to detect pitch period marks of any kind of voice: healthy or pathological. Among the pathological voices, oesophageal ones have the lowest quality and intelligibility.

This program consists of some sections in the results part as you can see in the next figures:

- Acoustic signals with pitch period marks (oscillogram[1]).
- Detection of pitch frames.

---

[1] The oscillogram is a graphical representation of the sound wave which has been recorded by the microphone

- Pitch, Jitter and Shimmer measurement
- Wide-band and narrow-band spectrogram
- Vocaligram

The program user can obtain many graphic representation of voice signal measurement. The Fig. 36 represents the oscillogram of voice signal including pitch periods marks. This representation includes the measurement of acoustic parameters: Pitch, Jitter and Shimmer. The wide-band and narrow-band spectrogram[2] are shown in the bottom part.

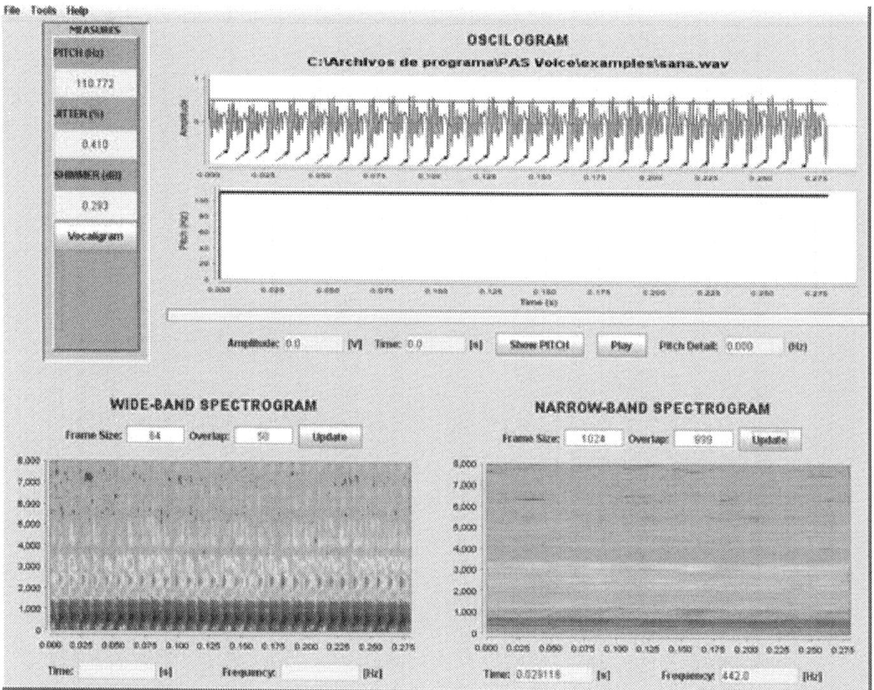

Fig. 36. Results of software

The Fig. 37 shows the vocaligram of the signal. This figure shows the set of objective parameters. This representation is used for showing graphically if the signal voice is inside of normality ranges.

[2] A spectrogram is an image that shows how the spectral density of a signal varies with time

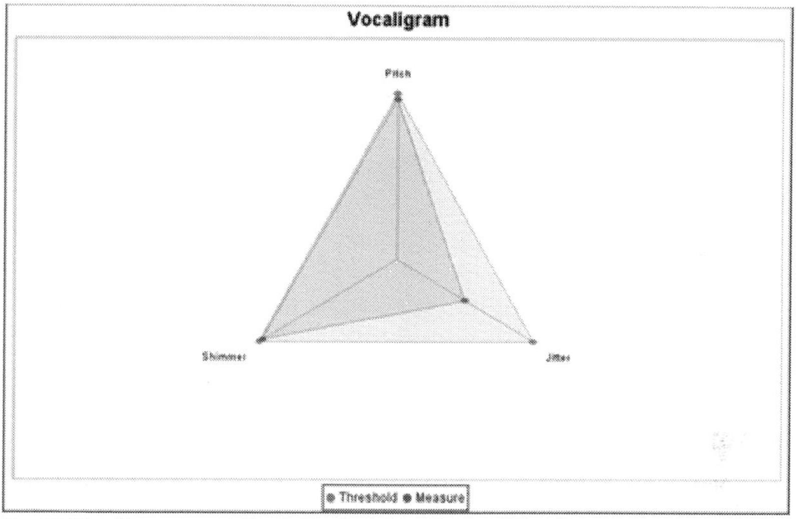

Fig. 37. Vocaligram specially design for normal ranges

Application of analysis cutaneous mole images

Taking to account the Biomedical Engineering area, this project is focused on dermatology. The students use the skin mole database. In order to make an objective analysis and processing, segmentation and image processing algorithms are applied. That permits to analyze the injury's texture, colour, form, etc. to be able to determine if the tumour is malignant or not. Both the objective parameters which imply the diagnosis done by the presented system and the images will be stored in a database so that in any subsequent evaluation it will be possible to compare the evolution of the injury. By means of this program, we will help dermatologists detect cancer in its first phases of formation and therefore increase the probabilities of preventing it.

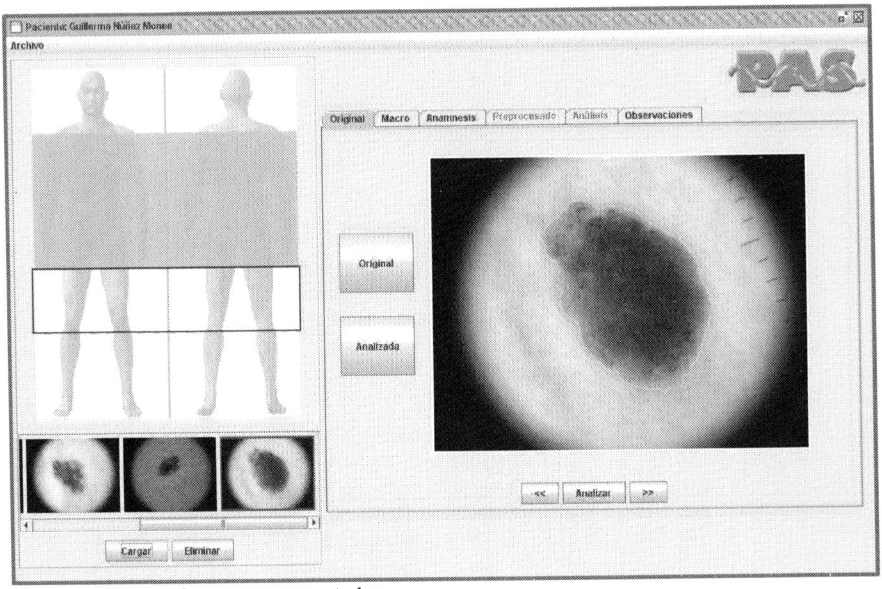

Fig. 38. GUI to analyze cutaneous moles

As can be seen in the Fig. 38, one of the processed images corresponds to a patient with skin cancer. The result of analysis of these images will be displayed in a table including a set of objective parameters: asymmetry, edge, colour and diameter, as you can see in Fig. 39.

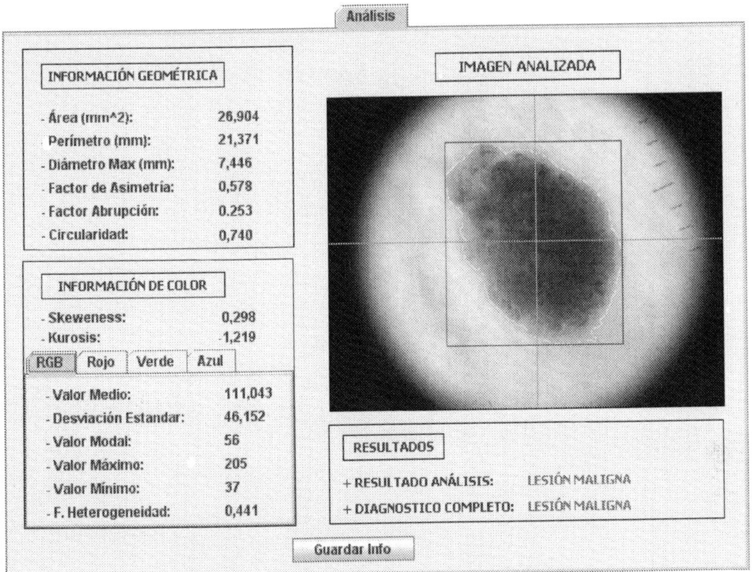

Fig. 39. Objective results of moles analysis

6. References

A. Spanias and F. Bizuneh, (2001). Development of new functions and scripting capabilities in Java-DSP for easy creation and seamless integration of animated DSP simulations in web courses. *IEEE ICASSP-2001*, Salt Lake city, Utah, May 2001.

J. Campbell, F Murtagh, M. Köküer, (2001) DataLab-J: A Signal and Image Processing Laboratory for Teaching and Research. *IEEE Transactions on Education.*

WS Gan, (2002). Teaching and Learning the Hows and Whys of Real-Time Digital Signal Processing. *IEEE Transactions on Education.*

M Murphy (1997), Octave: A Free, High-Level Language for Mathematics. *Linux Journal.*

Vinay K. Ingle & John G. Proakis, (2000). Digital Signal Processing Using MATLAB. Brooks/Cole Publishing Company,.

John G. Proakis. (1995). Digital Communications. Ed. McGraw-Hill, 3ª edición,.

K. Hornik, F. Leisch, A. Zeileis, (2004). Ten Years of Octave Recent Developments and Plans for the Future. *Proc. DSC 2003*, Vienna, Austria,.

JW Eaton, (2001). Octave: Past, Present, and Future. *DSC 2001*, Vienna, Austria,.

A. Spanias and V. Atti, (2005). Interactive on-line undergraduate laboratories using J-DSP. *IEEE Trans. on Education Special Issue on Web-based Instruction.*

Communications And Multimedia Technologies To High School. *FIE 2003*, Boulder, Colorado.

A. Spanias and V. Atti, (2005). WORKSHOP - Designing Laboratories, Exercises, and Demos using the Java-DSP Laboratory Software in Signals and Systems Courses. *IEEE Proceedings of Frontiers in Education (FIE-2005)*, Oct. 19-22, Indianapolis.

C. Bunks, J.P. Chancelier, F. Delebecque, C. Gomez, M. Goursat, R. Nikoukhah, S. Steer. (1999). Engineering and Scientific Computing with Scilab. *Birkhäuse.*

V. Atti, A. Spanias, (2003). On-Line Simulation Modules For Teaching Speech And Audio Compression Techniques. *FIE 2003,* Boulder, Colorado.

M. Yasin, J. Karam, A. Spanias, (2003). On-line laboratories for image and two-dimensional signal processing. *FIE 2003,* Boulder, Colorado.